JON R. BOND | KEVIN B. SMITH | RICHARD A. WATSON

THE PROMISE
AND PERFORMANCE
OF AMERICAN DEMOCRACY

SEVENTH EDITION

www.wadsworth.com

www.wadsworth.com is the World Wide Web site for Thomson Wadsworth and is your direct source to dozens of online resources.

At *www.wadsworth.com* you can find out about supplements, demonstration software, and student resources. You can also send email to many of our authors and preview new publications and exciting new technologies.

www.wadsworth.com
Changing the way the world learns®

The Promise and Performance of American Democracy

Seventh Edition

Jon R. Bond
Texas A&M University

Kevin B. Smith
University of Nebraska

Richard A. Watson
Late of University of Missouri

THOMSON

WADSWORTH

Australia • Canada • Mexico • Singapore • Spain • United Kingdom • United States

THOMSON
™
WADSWORTH

The Promise and Performance of American Democracy, Seventh Edition

Jon R. Bond/Kevin B. Smith/Richard A. Watson

Executive Editor, Political Science: David Tatom
Senior Development Editor: Stacey Sims
Assistant Editor: Rebecca Green
Editorial Assistant: Cheryl Lee
Technology Project Manager: Michelle Vardeman
Senior Marketing Manager: Janise Fry
Marketing Assistant: Tara Pierson
Marketing Communications Manager: Kelley McAllister
Project Manager, Editorial Production: Jennie Redwitz
Art Director: Maria Epes
Print Buyer: Doreen Suruki

Permissions Editor: Sarah Harkrader
Production Service: Robin C. Hood
Text Designer: Jeanne Calabrese
Photo Researcher: Billie Porter
Copy Editor: Jennifer Gordon
Illustrator: Carol Zuber-Mallison
Cover Designer: Brian Salisbury
Cover Image: © Joel Sartore/Getty Images
Cover Printer: Phoenix Color Corp
Compositor: Progressive Information Technologies
Printer: Courier Corporation/Kendallville

Printed in the United States of America
3 4 5 6 7 09 08 07 06

For more information about our products, contact us at:
Thomson Learning Academic Resource Center
1-800-423-0563
For permission to use material from this text or product, submit a request online at
http://www.thomsonrights.com.
Any additional questions about permissions can be submitted by email to **thomsonrights@thomson.com.**

Library of Congress Control Number: 2004113380

Student Edition: ISBN 0-534-64315-9

Instructor's Edition: ISBN 0-534-61053-6

Thomson Higher Education
10 Davis Drive
Belmont, CA 94002-3098
USA

Asia (including India)
Thomson Learning
5 Shenton Way
#01-01 UIC Building
Singapore 068808

Australia/New Zealand
Thomson Learning Australia
102 Dodds Street
Southbank, Victoria 3006
Australia

Canada
Thomson Nelson
1120 Birchmount Road
Toronto, Ontario M1K 5G4
Canada

UK/Europe/Middle East/Africa
Thomson Learning
High Holborn House
50–51 Bedford Road
London WC1R 4LR
United Kingdom

Brief Contents

Contents

CHAPTER 8   The Mass Media and Politics   230

CHAPTER 13   **The Presidency**   400

PART FOUR   CONCLUSION

List of Boxes

Preface

If undergraduates read only one textbook on American politics during their college career, it should meet a number of demanding standards: It must be comprehensive; it must be accessible; it must go beyond popular culture's perceptions (and misperceptions) about politics and convey the knowledge of scholarly research; and most importantly, it must provide students with the intellectual tools necessary to promote independent analytic thought about the often confusing world of American politics. The seventh edition of *The Promise and Performance of American Democracy* is a deliberate attempt to meet these goals.

The seventh edition continues the core vision of previous versions of the text while adding a number of significant revisions. As in previous editions, the book is pedagogically structured around the promise and performance framework. Beginning in Chapter 1 we establish a benchmark for judging the performance of a representative democracy. This benchmark is based on four core democratic values: popular sovereignty, political freedom, political equality, and majority rule. Together these values represent the theoretical promise of democracy: The process of collective decision making, as well as the outcomes of that process, will reflect those four core values.

Each of the subsequent chapters deals with the particular institutions and processes of the American political system viewed through the prism of these core values. This theme provides a systematic framework for navigating content and making coherent sense of the American political system without burdening undergraduates with overly abstract academic theory or forcing subject matter into a theme ill suited to an organizing thesis.

The seventh edition enhances the promise and performance framework in several ways. At the beginning of each chapter is a "promise" section that links the institution or process under consideration to the goal of upholding core democratic values. Each chapter ends with a "performance assessment" that offers an analysis of how well the institution or process is playing that role. Chapter boxes are fully integrated into the promise and performance theme. The content of all chapters has been fully revised to include the latest changes in the political system and advances in political science scholarship.

Other key changes to the seventh edition include:

- A completely new chapter on the media. This addition provides an overview of the changing role of the media in the political system and its impact on the promise of democracy.
- A completely new chapter on policy. This addition, the last chapter in the book, ties together all the institutions and processes considered separately in previous chapters and examines their role in democratic decision making. The idea of this

chapter is to show how institutions and processes from previous chapters combine to make policy, and how the promise and performance framework can help make systematic sense of why the political system does what it does.

- A significant reorganization of the table of contents. The seventh edition is now organized into five distinct sections. The first section consists of an introductory chapter that lays out the basic framework for studying representative democracy in the United States. The second section covers the constitutional framework of the political system, with separate chapters on the Constitution, federalism, civil liberties, and civil rights. The third section focuses on the institutions and processes that connect the will of the people to the actions of government, and includes separate chapters on interest groups, political parties, the media, political attitudes and socialization, elections, and voting behavior and political participation. The fourth section focuses on the four key institutions of the federal government, with separate chapters on Congress, the presidency, the bureaucracy, and the judiciary. The final section is the policy chapter that ties together the individual elements discussed in previous chapters into a coherent picture of how the American political system operates, and how the operation of that system upholds the promise of democracy.
- All chapters have undergone significant updates and revisions to reflect the latest developments in the political system and in political science scholarship. This edition is current through the 2004 presidential elections.

Though much has changed for the seventh edition, we have continued (with appropriate revisions) popular elements from previous versions of the text. Every chapter ends with a summary of main points, a list of key terms, and a brief annotated list of contemporary readings. Key terms are also defined in a glossary at the end of the book for easy reference, and an appendix includes the major documents of American democracy. Because we believe that the text used in political science courses should show students how political scientists report the results of their research, we use the American Political Science Association (APSA) style of in-text citations with a comprehensive of list of references.

With comprehensive coverage of the institutions and processes of the American political system, expansion of the pedagogical framework, the addition of new chapters, and a significant reorganization and revision, the seventh edition of *The Promise and Performance of American Democracy* is designed to report what political science has learned about American government, to challenge students, and to provide them with the intellectual tools they need to understand politics and evaluate the functioning of democracy. The ultimate aim of this book is not just to help students grasp the facts of the American political system, but to develop their capacity to make informed and independent decisions as citizens.

ACKNOWLEDGMENTS

The seventh edition of *The Promise and Performance of American Democracy* is a product of the talents of many people. The authors would like to extend special recognition to Richard Watson, the originator of the concept that drives this book, the sole author of its first five editions, and co-author of the sixth. This recognition, alas, is posthumous: Richard Watson succumbed to illness before publication. Dick Watson's legacy, however, is on every page of this book, and he deserves a full measure of credit for those who value what follows.

Recognition is also due to the Wadsworth editorial team who backed the seventh edition with their faith, patience, and lots of hard work. These include David Tatom, Stacey Sims, Michelle Vardeman, Rebecca Green, Cheryl Lee, Jennie Redwitz, and Robin C. Hood. When the good folks at Wadsworth commit to a project, they do so 100 percent. Behind every good book is a superb editorial and support team with wisdom, talent, and a skillful hand at the whip.

Thanks are also due to the distinguished team of teacher-scholars who reviewed the chapters. Their feedback and input was invaluable in what turned out to be an extensive set of revisions. They include Danny Adkinson, Oklahoma State University; Robert Alexander, Northern Ohio University; Lydia Andrade, The University of the Incarnate Word; Robert Cook; Rick Farmer, University of Akron; Richard Fleisher, Fordham University; Audrey Haynes, University of Georgia; Jane Rainey, Eastern Kentucky University; William Salka, Eastern Connecticut State University; Patrick Schmidt, Southern Methodist University; James T. Smith, Rollins College; Raymond Tatalovich, Loyola University of Chicago; and Jonathan R. Tompkins, University of Montana.

We would also like to recognize Ken Meier, who made the original phone call that brought the two authors together on this project. Every time we think of all the hard work we've put in since you made that call Ken, well, we'd like to beat you with a baseball bat.

Jon Bond is grateful to numerous friends and colleagues. Rich Fleisher at Fordham University deserves special recognition. I have learned a great deal from Rich over the years of discussion and collaboration on numerous other projects. Colleagues at Texas A&M University who shared their expertise on various topics include Jim Anderson, George Edwards, Roy Flemming, Bob Harmel, Kim Hill, Pat Hurley, Jan Leighley, Paul Kellstedt, Norm Luttbeg, and Jim Rogers. Several of my current and former graduate students helped with background research, provided technical support, and contributed in many other ways (yes, students, "many" is the appropriate adjective here). I am grateful to Lydia Andrade, Emily Bonneau, Kristi Campbell, Michelle Chin, Jim Cottrill, Brandy Durham, Nathan Ilderton, Todd Kent, Glen Krutz, Sarah Kessler, and Jose Villalobos. I also appreciate help and advice from Frank Baumgartner of Pennsylvania University, Beth Leech of Rutgers University, and John Bibby of the University of Wisconsin, Milwaukee. Finally, I appreciate the love and support of my wife, Karon, and my daughters, Lynn, Mika, and Monika.

Kevin Smith would like to thank students and colleagues at the University of Nebraska–Lincoln, especially Christopher Larimer, Rebecca Hannagan, Dan Bratten, Tyler White, Eric Whitaker, and Joel Wiegert. These grad students had the misfortune to serve as my research and teaching assistants during the revision process. They are still speaking to me, though I'm not sure why. Thanks also to my long-suffering wife, Kelly, who continues to put up with me, though I'm not sure why. And finally, to the Dallas Cowboys, who every fall provided me with a distraction from work, even though they never won another Super Bowl. And after spending countless hours watching them, I know why.

The Promise and Performance of American Democracy

1 | The Promise of Democracy

John Adams, second president of the United States and one of the dominant figures of the nation's founding, worried that Americans would misinterpret, misunderstand, perhaps miss completely the point of the democratic experiment he worked so hard to set in motion. "The history of our Revolution," he wrote to his friend Benjamin Rush in 1790, "will be one continued lie from one end to the other" (Brands 2003). He thought the Founders' notion of a democracy would be romanticized rather than appreciated by future generations of Americans: its purpose only vaguely understood and its products often viewed with distaste.

Adams was right.

Today, an overwhelming majority of Americans believe their form of government is "best." Yet similar majorities mistrust their government, and give it poor marks for job performance (Hibbing and Theiss-Morse 2003, 103). What explains this contradiction? In the abstract Americans express strong support for democracy. They equate democracy with freedom, liberty, and self-determination. What they do not like in practice is a government that produces "uncertainty, conflicting options, long debate, competing interests, confusion, bargaining, and compromised imperfect solutions." They want government to "do its job quietly and efficiently, sans conflict and sans fuss" (Hibbing and Theiss-Morse 1995, 147). In short, Americans do not seem to like democratic politics in practice (Slater 1991, 10).

The fundamental reason Americans hold government and politics in such disdain—and the premise of this book—is that they do not really understand the promise of democracy. As Adams feared, Americans' judgments of politics and government are not based on a hard-nosed assessment of the realities of democracy. Much of the frustration Americans express about their government is anchored in a misunderstanding of what democracy is supposed to do, an unrealistic expectation of what it can do, and a failure to comprehend the dangers of pursuing undemocratic alternatives to solving problems.

This book is about how democracy is designed to work in the United States. Here we will examine what a democracy is, what it is supposed to do, and how the institutions and processes of the American political system are designed to deliver on the democratic promise. The goal is to give you the tools to make your own informed and realistic assessment about whether the reality of democracy in America is living up to its promise.

To begin this process, it is first necessary to understand what the promise of democracy really means. What is a democracy and what is it supposed to do? The first chapter is designed to answer this all-important question—to give you an intellectual baseline for making your own judgments on what, in democratic terms, constitutes a success or failure in American politics and government. Achieving this goal requires a firm conceptual understanding of politics, government, and democracy and what their combination means in the American context.

John Adams, second president of the United States, was a native of Massachusetts. A graduate of Harvard University, where he studied law, he was a delegate to the first Continental Congress in 1774, where he contributed heavily to the debates on the Declaration of Independence. After serving two vice presidencies under Washington, he became president in 1796.

The Promise of Democracy

For many people, the word *politics* has a negative connotation. To call others "political" is to accuse them of being manipulative and self-serving. Scholars, however, tend to view politics in more neutral terms. Two famous definitions of **politics** are:

1. Harold D. Lasswell's (1938): Politics is "who gets what, when and how."
2. David Easton's (1953): Politics is the "authoritative allocation of values."

Both definitions say the same thing: All groups must have some way to make collective decisions, and politics is the process of making those decisions. It is the process of coming to some definitive understanding of who is going to get what or whose values everyone is going to live by. Because individuals often disagree about who should get what or whose values should be binding on everyone, politics is a process of conflict management and resolution: It is a natural outcome of human interaction, not just something in which politicians and governments engage. Three people in a video store arguing over what DVD to rent are engaging in politics; they are trying to figure out whose values (in this case, taste in movies) will be binding on the group.

While disagreements among friends over what movie to watch can usually be resolved without resorting to formal decision-making institutions and processes, this is not the case for large groups such as nations. How can we decide what to do as a society? Who or what gets to decide which values are binding on everyone? The institution that has the authority to make decisions that are binding upon everyone is generally referred to as **government.**

Government is not the only institution that seeks to manage conflict and make authoritative decisions about who gets what. Churches, for example, make decisions about what behaviors are right and wrong and admonish their followers to follow church teachings. What separates government from other decision-making institutions is coercion. Churches can coerce members of their congregation through threats of excommunication and the like, but they cannot extend that power over nonmembers and other organizations. Governments can. A church that decides that abortion or consumption of alcohol is wrong can attempt to make these values binding on its congregation. A government can make these values binding on everyone. Act in defiance of government decisions—that is, break the law—and the government can take your property, your liberty, even your life. Government is the only institution in society that can legitimately use such coercion on all individuals and organizations, and as such it is the ultimate decider of who gets what (Downs 1957, 22).

Governments take three basic forms. The power to authoritatively allocate values can be vested in a single person—a form of government called an **autocracy.** Absolute monarchs and dictators have the ultimate power, and they delegate it as they see fit. Nazi Germany under Adolf Hitler and the Soviet Union under Joseph Stalin are examples of autocracies. Power vested in a small group of people is called an **oligarchy.** A military junta (a group of generals) is an example of an oligarchy. The third option is a **democracy,** a form of government where power is shared by all citizens. The word itself is derived from two Greek roots: *demos,* which means "people" and *kratia,* which means "rule." Literally, democracy means "rule by the people." In a democracy, all citizens have the opportunity to participate in the process of making binding decisions about who gets what.

Process and Substance

Politics occurs in all forms of government. An audience with a king is an opportunity to influence the decisions he makes. A small group of rulers may use their power to broker compromises among opposing interests in society. What separates politics in a democracy from politics in an autocracy or an oligarchy is both *how* decisions are made and *what* those decisions are.

Democracy as Process   How decisions are made in a democracy is at least as important as what those decisions are. Indeed, some scholars view democracy as much more about means than ends (Schumpeter 1942). The means of democracy—the institutions and rules that organize and operate the political system—create a decision-making process that is often slow and inefficient. Democratic decision making requires patience, demands tolerance of opposing viewpoints, and rewards compromise. The inevitable result of a democratic process is what Americans find most objectionable about their political system: inefficiency, gridlock, and lots and lots of conflict (Hibbing and Theiss-Morse 1995, 147).

Why put up with this? Why opt for a form of government that uses a decision-making process all but guaranteed to be slow, inefficient, and constantly embroiled in conflict? As one astute observer put it, "Democracy is the worst form of government. It is the most inefficient, the most clumsy, the most unpractical. . . . Yet democracy is the only form of social order admissible, because it is the only one consistent with justice" (Briffault 1930, quoted in Thomsett and Thomsett 1994, 37). The promise of a democratic process is not efficiency, agreement, clarity, or speed. The promise is simply that *all* citizens have the right to participate in the decision-making process. The right to vote, publicly voice viewpoints, petition an elected representative, sue, form an organization with policy goals, engage in a political campaign, belong to or support a political party—all these are characteristics of a democratic process. Together they provide a wide variety of ways for citizens and interest groups to participate in decision making. These characteristics help bring disagreements out into the open where they can be debated, where minority views can be aired, and where dissenters have a wide range of options to express their opinions.

Democratic Substance   A democratic process means ordinary citizens can participate in Easton's "authoritative allocation of values," but widespread participation is insufficient in itself to guarantee a democratic result. For example, in the United States broad majorities have historically supported systematic discrimination against racial and ethnic minorities, and legislatures have responded to these preferences with laws that denied individuals their civil rights and liberties. Though the process of making these decisions could be considered democratic—opposing viewpoints were aired and the majority preference became law—the substance of the resulting decision was not.

To be truly democratic, a government must follow a set of procedures *and* produce policies that, at a minimum, are consistent with four fundamental democratic values: popular sovereignty, political freedom, political equality, and majority rule. The crucial thing to understand is that for a system to be democratic, both the process of making decisions and the outcomes of those decisions must be compatible with these core values. These values represent both the promise of democracy and a yardstick by which to assess democratic performance.

Core Democratic Values

Popular Sovereignty   The concept of sovereignty refers to the highest political authority in a state or society. **Popular sovereignty** means that in a democracy, the highest political authority is the will of the people. A democracy is supposed to be responsive to the needs and demands of ordinary people. If the government does not respond to the expressed preferences of the people, democracy provides a mechanism for citizens to exercise their sovereignty and hold government accountable for its actions. The people may hold government accountable by either altering or abolishing it.

Popular sovereignty does not guarantee specific outcomes; this value is oriented more toward process than substance. Popular sovereignty means people have the right to participate in the process of deciding what ought to be done. There is no guarantee that any individual's preferences will become public policy. Everyone has exactly the same rights, and values, interests, and preferences may differ. Ultimately what popular sovereignty guarantees is that an individual's values will be included in the discussion, not that those values will prevail.

The notion that the will of the people should represent the highest political authority rests on a belief in the basic integrity of the individual. In other words, democracies support the belief that the state exists for the individual rather than the other way around. Democratic governments are not seen as creating the rights that individuals hold. Rather, the government itself is a creation by individuals to protect rights that are derived from a higher power than the government. The government has no legitimate basis to take away individual rights, even if a majority supports such action. As free individuals who create government and possess rights that the government has no legitimate power to take away, citizens in democracies are viewed as the ultimate source of political authority, and popular sovereignty is thus adopted as the basis of government and politics.

Political Freedom   Government cannot respond to the will of the people if people are not free to express their wants and demands. In a democracy, minorities—even if they consist only of one or two people with views repellent to everyone else—have the right to participate and express their views about what government should do. The necessary ingredients for political freedom are the right to criticize current governmental leaders and policies, the right to propose new courses of action for government to follow, the right to form and join interest groups, the right to discuss political issues free from government censorship, and the right of all citizens to seek and hold public office.

Note that the objects of free expression are plural; if *the people* all have the right to express *their* wants, demands, and preferences, the people are only rarely going to express the same wants, demands, and preferences. Certainly in the United States, political freedom means a cacophony of conflicting preferences that makes it difficult for government to respond to the people. A primary reason why democratic governments often seem to have difficulties responding to the will of the people is not because they fail to listen. To the contrary, it is because they are listening all too well to a set of vague, conflicting, and contradictory preferences.

Political freedom also means a basic guarantee of individual liberty. Individual citizens are free to make their own choices, to select their own goals and the means to achieve them. However, there are limits on individual liberty. Society, for example, will not sanction an individual's desire to become a skillful thief. Yet the limits on individual freedom are kept to a minimum in democracies. Political freedom bestows upon the individual the right to choose, advocate, or follow different political, social, and economic ideas, paths, and plans.

Political Equality   Because it can take many forms, equality is one of the most misunderstood of democratic values. The **political equality** at the core of the democratic creed simply means that individual preferences are given equal weight. For example, when citizens vote, each vote counts the same. Wealth, partisanship, or ideology cannot make one's vote count more than anyone else's. This notion of equality refers not only to participation in influencing governmental decisions; it also involves being subject to those decisions. Everyone is entitled to **equality under the law.** The law is applied impartially without regard to the identity or status of the individual involved. In a democracy, wealth, fame, and power are not supposed to exempt anyone from the sanction of law.

While few quarrel with the notion of political and legal equality, **social equality**—the idea that people should be free of class or social barriers and discrimination—is more controversial. Many view social equality as a desirable ideal but disagree on what, if anything, the government should do to achieve it. The long battle over racial equality in the United States reflects different attitudes on the basic question and the difficulties faced in attempting to answer it.

The most controversial form of equality is **economic equality,** and this is also the most troublesome to the democratic concept. Under a strict interpretation, economic equality means each individual would receive the same amount of material goods regardless of his or her contribution to society. Equal distribution of wealth, especially as a coercive government policy, is unlikely to be considered compatible with the core values of American democracy. Redistributing power and wealth from the well-off to the less well-off is always controversial, and for good reason: It limits the freedom individuals have to decide how to use their economic and social resources.

Still, social and economic resources have implications for political equality. People with wealth and status can participate in politics more easily and more effectively than others. Since democratic government responds to the preferences of those who participate—those who actually exercise the right to express their preferences—government policy will tend to benefit those with wealth and status. This upper-class bias, in turn, gives them even greater ability to influence government in the future. When economic and social resources are unevenly distributed, merely giving all citizens the freedom to participate to the best of their ability may have the disturbing result of producing less political equality.

How to handle the conundrum connecting political equality with economic equality is largely unresolved. At a minimum, democracies must preserve political equality in the sense that everyone has an equal right to express their preferences. Yet inequitable distribution of wealth also undoubtedly allows certain individuals more effective and forceful ways to express their preferences than others. A wealthy campaign contributor is much more likely to get the attention of a legislator than a harried single parent who can hardly find the time to vote. If accused of a crime, a rich individual can hire a top-notch attorney, a private investigator, and an independent set of experts for the defense. A poor person accused of the same crime may have to rely on an overworked and inexperienced public defender.

Instead of equal distribution of wealth, democratic societies try to reconcile political and economic equality by favoring **equality of opportunity,** meaning the right of every individual to develop to the fullest extent of his or her abilities. In other words, all individuals should have the opportunity to go as far in life as their desires, talents, and efforts allow. The advantage of embracing equality of opportunity is that it permits a reconciliation of the values of liberty and equality. If individuals differ in ability, then to give every person the liberty to develop to the fullest extent of his or her ability will result in some acquiring more goods than others. Democracy aims to give individuals the paradoxical right of an *equal opportunity to become unequal.* Although everyone has the same opportunities, some will have more talent, put in more effort, and make better choices, and as a result end up with more wealth.

Does everyone really have the same opportunity "to become unequal"? Those who are born to wealth, who live in neighborhoods with good schools, who have nurturing parents—they have a set of advantages providing a greater set of opportunities than those born to poverty, trapped in sub-par schools, and suffering from abusive or neglectful parents. This disparity raises the question of whether government is required to level the playing field by guaranteeing a set of services (such as adequate nutrition, housing, education, and health care) considered essential to individual development. Equal opportunity to become unequal suggests that although democratic society does not have to guarantee equality at the end of the individual's developmental process, it should ensure equality at the beginning. What constitutes equality at the beginning—what level of educational, health, and social services provides a roughly equal set of opportunities for all to develop to the fullest extent of their abilities—is a matter of constant controversy and debate.

Majority Rule   The final core value of democracy is majority rule. **Majority rule** simply means that government follows the course of action preferred by most people. The preferred alternative does not necessarily have to be an **absolute majority,** defined as 50 percent plus 1 of all eligible citizens, or even a **simple majority,** defined as 50 percent plus 1 of those who vote. If voters' preferences are divided among three or more courses of action so that none have more than 50 percent support, the choice with the greatest support is called a **plurality.** In the 1992 presidential election, for example, Bill Clinton won with a plurality rather than a majority of the popular vote cast. He received 43 percent of the votes cast, while his closest rival, George H. Bush, received 37 percent.

Though majority rule governs political decision making in democracies, it must also be balanced with **minority rights.** A minority is any group numerically inferior to the majority, and they retain the full rights of democratic citizenship. In democracies, minority viewpoints are permitted to be heard and to criticize the majority's views and actions. Only by guaranteeing minority rights can minority viewpoints develop into majority viewpoints. At least in theory, the rights of minorities—their political freedom—cannot be taken away by majorities.

Conflicting Values: A Delicate Balancing Act

Generally speaking, then, democracy is a form of government characterized by popular sovereignty, political freedom, political equality, and majority rule. Although these values have been discussed separately, no one of these values is by itself enough to make a government democratic. All four values must be reflected in both the process and the outcomes of government decisions. Achieving all four core values is often a difficult balancing act because these values come into conflict. Maximizing freedom may lead to less equality; achieving more equality may require limitations of someone's freedom; the majority may use the power of government to limit individual freedom.

In a democracy, one of the core values does not trump or outrank another. If a large majority of citizens take away the political freedoms of certain minorities and consign them to political, social, and economic second-class status, the promise of democracy has been broken. The historical treatment of African Americans and other minorities shows that the American political system is capable of producing just such undemocratic outcomes. The key point is that all four core values must be reflected in how decisions are made and in the substance of those decisions. When evaluating the performance of American democracy in the chapters that follow, keep in mind the extent to which it achieves all four of the basic democratic values.

Two Basic Forms of Democracy

While there is agreement on the general features and beliefs of democracy, democracy itself can take different forms. This diversity springs from differences in how the core values are translated into specifics. For example, how much control do ordinary citizens exercise over government decisions? Is it sufficient that they choose the decision makers, or should they make the decisions themselves? How should this influence be exercised? How is equality defined—as political equality, legal equality, economic equality, all three, or something else? How rational does the average person need to be? Do citizens need to be capable of determining for themselves what kind of policy is needed to preserve and advance liberty and equality in society, or is it sufficient to judge among policies suggested by others?

There are no definitive answers to these questions; reasonable people equally committed to democratic values may disagree on them. Thus, while there is a general theory of democracy that rests on a core set of values, there are different theories about the specific procedures, ideals, and assumptions associated with a democratic society. These differences can be divided into two broad categories: direct democracy and representative democracy.

Direct Democracy

In a **direct democracy,** the citizens themselves are principal participants in making government decisions. The original form of direct democracy was practiced in certain city-states of ancient Greece, notably Athens. About 2,500 years ago, Athens was ruled by the Assembly, a town-meeting type of gathering that included all male citizens (in Athens, women and slaves were not considered citizens). The Assembly met ten times a year to make major policy decisions and to select the members of the Council, a committee of 500 that had the day-to-day responsibilities of running the government.

In a number of ways, direct democracy survives today in the United States. For instance, the New England town meeting, where all citizens in the community are eligible to participate in making local government policy decisions, is much like the Assembly in ancient Athens. As well, direct democracy is evident in ballot initiatives and **referendums,** elections where citizens vote on policy decisions. About half of the states have the initiatives, which in the past thirty years have been increasingly used to make major policy decisions on everything from setting tax rates to eliminating affirmative action to decriminalizing marijuana.

Historically, however, systems that rely on direct democratic processes are rare. Successful direct democratic systems are even scarcer because they have a number of inherent problems that lead to instability and poor policy decisions. Part of the difficulty is due to the unwieldy decision-making processes that often accompany direct democracy (imagine setting tuition rates by inviting all taxpayers in the state to a series of meetings to decide what your college education should cost). More serious are the demands direct democracy places on the citizen. Sound decision making in a direct democracy requires a huge commitment to public life on the part of average citizens. At a minimum it requires citizens to have a solid understanding of government and politics, to be fully informed of the issues on which they vote, and to be very engaged in public life. If citizens have only a shallow understanding of the issues and do not fully grasp the consequences of these decisions for the government or for society generally, they can be easily misled or manipulated. The net result is a direct democracy prone to producing bad policy decisions. Critics argue this is exactly the problem with modern forms of direct democracy such as the ballot initiative (see the Living the Promise feature "Direct Democracy in the Modern Era").

Even with well-informed and fully engaged citizens, direct democracies are vulnerable to tyranny of the majority or mob rule. Whatever passions incite a majority of the citizens at a given moment can be translated into policy very quickly. Those who advocate unpopular minority viewpoints in a direct democracy and incur the displeasure of the majority may face some unpleasant consequences. These risks are especially acute in a large and diverse society with obvious social fault lines—such as race, religion, and ideology—separating the majority from the minority. Abiding by the core values of democracy is wholly the responsibility of the majority in direct democracy; the majority must consist of individuals who understand and are deeply committed to those values. A constant temptation for the majority is to abandon those values and benefit themselves by using democratic processes to make decisions that are undemocratic in substance because they discriminate or persecute a minority. For these reasons, the history of direct democracies is often one of instability and failure (Broder 2000).

Representative Democracy

Because direct democracy was not a practical basis for government in large, diverse societies, an alternate form of democracy developed in Western nations during the past three centuries. The form of democracy practiced in nations such as Great Britain and the United States is known by a number of different terms. Two common names are *liberal democracy,* for its concern with the liberty of the individual, and *Western democracy* for the geographical location of the countries where it developed. The generic term we adopt is **Western representative democracy,** defined as a system of government where ordinary

LIVING THE PROMISE
Direct Democracy in the Modern Era

Cockfights, pig pens, marijuana, class size, and cash bonuses for college students. These days, elections mean a lot more than choosing representatives. Increasingly citizens are cutting the legislature out of the decision-making process altogether and making policy directly.

Just in the past few years, voters have considered outlawing cock fights in Oklahoma, setting maximum class sizes in public schools, banning pig gestation crates in Florida, legalizing marijuana in Nevada, and awarding cash bonuses to college graduates who stay in state in North Dakota. Even when it comes to electing people, things can get a little unusual. In 2003 California voters pondered "unelecting" Governor Gray Davis less than a year after electing him and were offered a list of 135 potential replacements. These included a porn star, a self-described smut merchant, a child actor, and action movie star Arnold Schwarzenegger. The vote to **recall** Governor Davis passed with 55.4 percent voting yes, and Mr. Schwarzenegger was elected to replace him with 48.7 percent of the vote. All this goes to show that direct democracy is not only alive and well in America, it is thriving. And, argue many of its critics, it is creating enormous problems for the political system.

The form of direct democracy that had voters considering everything from gestation crates for pigs to recalling the governor of California is the ballot **initiative**—a process begun a century ago by progressive reformers seeking to curb the abuses of legislatures. The initiative allows citizens to bypass legislatures and make laws directly by putting proposals to a popular vote. About half the states have the ballot initiative.

In those states, the initiative is broadly popular. Supporters say it is no secret why initiatives are popular. "Initiatives are fundamental to freedom," says M. Dane Waters, president of the Initiative and Referendum Institute. Opponents of initiatives say they are better at making mischief than promoting freedom and have a damning legacy of undermining good government.

The modern popularity of the initiative is traced to 1978, when California voters triggered a nationwide tax revolt by passing Proposition 13. Proposition 13 rolled back tax assessments to their 1975 levels, mandated that property could be assessed at no more than 1 percent of its value, capped assessment increases at a maximum of 2 percent a year, and allowed reassessments only when property is sold.

To its supporters, Proposition 13 is the best-known example of the benefits of direct democracy—it let the people deal directly with an issue the legislature could not or would not satisfactorily address. To its detractors, Proposition 13 represents everything that is bad about direct democracy. While cutting property taxes was popular, Proposition 13 clamped down on the primary revenue source of local governments, leaving them increasingly dependent on the state. Local governments (especially schools) never fully recovered from this blow, and many remain chronically underfunded. Upset with the impact on services, California voters compensated with a raft of new initiatives (such as mandating state levels of education spending). The end result, critics point out, is what you would expect from making major policy decisions without thinking through the consequences: a mess. Property taxes are now wildly uneven—some would say wildly unfair—and California government is increasingly boxed in. Its hands are tied by a complicated tangle of laws passed by initiative, limiting its ability to effectively respond to problems. This, of course, upsets people even more and leads to yet more initiative proposals—a vicious cycle that undermines effective government.

Part of the problem is that ballot initiatives may be a policymaking vehicle for well-heeled special interest groups. It is expensive to qualify a proposal for the ballot, and as a result, most ballot initiatives come from individuals or groups with very narrow agendas that are painted over with a populist ad campaign. Even genuine populism, though, is sometimes no substitute for deliberation. Voters in initiative states typically fail the basic requisites of a successful direct democracy, that is, to be very involved in public life and highly knowledgeable about the voting issues and informed about their potential consequences. Voters are often presented with propositions that are couched in lengthy legalese or have multibillion-dollar consequences, and they may be confused about what the initiatives mean. Rather than a vehicle to exercise individual liberty, critics of the initiative process see it as doing little more than breeding bad policy, frustration, and resentment.

The Founders explicitly rejected direct democracy as a basis of government for just such reasons. As James Madison put it in *Federalist* Number 10, direct democracies "have ever been spectacles of turbulence and contention; have ever been found incompatible with personal security or the rights of property; and have in general been as short in their lives as they have been violent in their deaths."

Critics suggest supporters of the ballot initiative should pay a little less attention to populist PR and a little more to the arguments of the Founders. The solution to unrespon-

sive and ineffective government lies in the hands of the voters every election day. If you do not like what government is doing, vote the rascals out. The problem with direct democracy is that rather than a government of laws, it produces laws *without* government (Broder 2000, 243).

Sources: Broder, David S. 2000. *Democracy Derailed*. New York: Harcourt; Quinn, Andrew. 2002. "From Cockfights to Pig Pens, Vote Sets Agenda." Reuters News Service. *http://story.news.yahoo.com/news?tmpl=story2&ncid=584&e=4&u=/nm/20021103/pl_nm_/election_initiatives_dc.* Accessed November 3, 2002.

citizens do not make governmental decisions themselves but choose public officials—representatives of the people—to make decisions for them. Western democracies embody the four basic values of democracy, but they use different institutions and slightly different ideals to accomplish these goals. In contrast to Athens and other direct democracies, only a tiny fraction of citizens actually hold policymaking positions in Western representative democracies, especially at the national level. For example, each

A clear example of direct democracy at work was the recall of a state governor by the people of California. On February 5, 2003, former State Assemblyman Howard Kaloogian announced he would lead an effort to recall Governor Gray Davis (D-CA) from office. The announcement included notice of a Web site created to monitor the process and serve as a hub for collecting funds, recruiting volunteers, and gathering signatures. Following several months of active campaigning on both sides, the recall was decided when voters went to the polls on October 7 and elected Arnold Schwarzenegger to take over the governorship of the state.

© Reuters/Gary Hershorn/Landov

member of the U.S. House of Representatives has a constituency of over 600,000 people; that is, a single individual represents the interests of more than a half million.

The form of representative democracy we know today first developed in three Western nations: Great Britain, Switzerland, and the United States. In the late 18th and early 19th centuries, a large number of people in these countries first began to select their political leaders. From this narrow base, democracy spread to other nations of western Europe and the British Commonwealth. Western representative democracy, then, is a relatively new form of government, originally practiced by just a handful of nations. In fact, if genuine democracy requires that a majority of the population have the right to affect governmental decisions by choosing its leaders, then this type of government is a modern phenomenon. In the United States, male citizens did not gain universal voting rights until the latter part of the 19th century, and women had to wait until the 1920s. Ethnic minorities were systematically excluded from political participation even longer, at least up until the early 1960s. Thus, one can reasonably argue that the core values of democracy were not securely embedded in representative democratic systems until very recently indeed.

How Representative Systems Achieve Democracy

Because citizens do not govern directly in a representative democracy, ensuring that basic democratic values are protected and advanced rests on a set of different political techniques and institutions than those used in a direct democracy. Representative democracy may be described as the many watching the few, but it requires more than mere watching. Key in such a democratic system is not just the few who rule but the many who select and hold those rulers accountable. The many must be able to implement their observations through political action, and there must be an incentive for representatives to be responsive to the wishes of the people. The promise of democracy in such a system—that is, its potential to reflect the core democratic values in both the process and the outcomes of decision making—is heavily dependent upon the institutions used to organize the political system and the values that underpin its operation. A number of democratic institutions are common in representative democracies. Some of the most familiar ones are elections, political parties, and interest groups.

Elections

The most obvious mechanism that representative democracies employ to incorporate democratic values into the political system is elections. Representative democracies deliberately create insecurity of tenure for major officeholders. Those who hold office are periodically required to go before the people to have their terms of office renewed. If the citizens in a democracy are displeased with the performance of those in public office, the remedy is to replace them. In this fashion, the rulers have an incentive to be responsive to the needs and demands of the ruled, and rulers can be held accountable if they fail to be responsive. Elections are the central mechanism for achieving popular sovereignty in representative democracies.

In a representative democracy, voting is a right every citizen can exercise and, in so doing, can have a direct voice in the choice of elected officials. By creating insecurity of tenure for major officeholders, elections create incentive for the elected to respond to the needs of the electors and also provide recourse for the electors if the elected are not being responsive.

Political Parties

For elections to be a mechanism of accountability, a democratic system must offer citizens choices among alternative leaders. All democratic societies develop some means to propose alternative political leaders for the consideration of the populace. The institution that typically fills this need is the political party, defined as an organization that puts forward candidates for public office. To provide an element of choice, there must be at least two competing parties that propose candidates. With competition, voters can choose the party that best represents their preferences. Political parties must accept one another's existence as a necessity to a functioning representative democracy. Accordingly, the party (or parties) that control the government must allow the opposition party (or parties) to criticize what current government leaders are doing and to propose alternative courses of action for the consideration of voters. That is, the party in control of government must recognize the political freedom of those out of power.

Interest Groups

Beyond holding periodic elections, a representative democracy must provide for continuous communication between the leaders in government and ordinary citizens. This communication is critical to ensure that citizens' views on public issues are transmitted to those who make major political decisions and thus fosters popular sovereignty. Political parties fulfill this function to some extent; decisive election results can send a very clear message to government. But elections occur only once every few years, and citizens need ways to communicate their changing needs between elections. Although citizens have the freedom to express their opinions individually, communication is more effective if diverse individual views are aggregated and transmitted in a coherent way. Citizens in a democracy also have the freedom to organize around common interests and communicate those interests to government.

An institution that has emerged to promote such communication is the interest group. Interest groups aggregate the interests of like-minded individuals and organize to press their common views on government decision makers. Interest groups are likely to contain only a small proportion of the total population, but they enable elected officials to gain some understanding of how a number of people in a common situation—say, students, businesspeople, or farmers—feel about matters such as student loan programs, taxes, or farm price supports. Moreover, because communication is a two-way process, interest groups not only press demands on decision makers, they also transmit proposals by political leaders back to their memberships. Just as parties compete to place their candidates in public office, so interest groups vie to influence public policy. If the system is operating properly, these groups check and balance one another's efforts so that no one group or small number of groups dominates the political process.

Representative Democracy in the United States

Although these institutions and values characterize representative democracies in general, there is considerable variation in the way democratic government is implemented in different nations. We turn now to a discussion of American representative democracy.

The Promise of American Democracy

Representative democracy as practiced in the United States seeks to embody the basic values of democracy. At its core is a belief that people are, for the most part, rational and capable of deciding what is good for them personally. Even if the average person is not always correct, there is an assumption that no elite group is wise enough or unselfish enough to rule in the interests of all members of society. The only way to ensure that the interests of everyone will be taken into account is to give the bulk of the population the right to influence the basic decisions that affect their lives through mechanisms such as elections and by protecting individuals' rights to liberty and free expression.

It is this *process*—the universal prerogative to participate in collective decision making while simultaneously holding a set of fundamental rights inviolate—that forms the commitment to democratic values. As such, it also provides a basis for judging the performance of American democracy. If this process, and the institutions that organize it, reflect core democratic values and produce outcomes compatible with those values, the system can be considered democratic. To figure out whether democracy in America is living up to its promise, the question to ask is: Is this decision or action consistent with all four core values of democracy? If the answer is yes, then democracy in America is living up to its promise. If the answer is no, because the action infringes to a substantial degree on one or more of the core democratic values, the promise is being broken. Most people succumb to temptation to ask other questions to judge the performance of the American political system: Is the government doing what I want? Does this fit with my partisan and ideological beliefs? Is this policy efficient? Do I like the people who are making the decisions? Is that policy really working? While these are important questions to ask—and if the system lives up to its democratic promise, you certainly have the right to pose them—the questions do not cut to the core of the democratic promise: that is, whether the political system is following and upholding the core values of democracy.

No political system produced by human beings ever completely lives up to its ideals; there is always a gap between the ideals and the political institutions designed to embody them. To understand more clearly the theoretical promise of democracy—and thus be better equipped to judge its performance—we must not only understand what that promise is in the American context but also what it is not.

Fallacies Associated with Democracy in America

A promise based largely on process contrasts sharply with a number of popularly held fallacies, or incorrect beliefs, about democracy. One fallacy is that democracy promises the "best" policy decisions. It does not. Representative democracy handles disagreements about what we ought to do by allowing everyone to get involved in the conflict. The result is often untidy, confusing decisions with which few are wholly satisfied. The outcomes, in other words, are frequently less than optimal. What we end up with is usually not what we want, just what we can live with. Such outcomes do not represent the failure of democracy; it is the whole point of the democratic promise: to broker compromises among competing points of view and arrive at a decision that the majority supports and that the minority can tolerate.

A second such fallacy is a belief that majority rule means that the majority should always get what it wants. The Founders of the American form of democracy placed no particular trust in the majority, and in the United States, the majority has never been given the freedom to decide all matters that affect people's lives. If people have fundamental rights, as the Founders believed, then the majority must be kept from depriving the minority of those rights. Western representative democracy is founded on the notion that while government should respond to the wishes of the majority, the majority is limited. There are certain fundamental rights that cannot be taken away by majority vote. For example, in the United States and Great Britain, majorities of the population are Protestant. But they are not allowed to tell people of Catholic, Jewish, or other faiths how to worship. Likewise in Western democratic nations, the individual's right to private property is respected, and personal goods cannot be taken for public use without just compensation. It is precisely these sorts of limitations on the scope of government that distinguish democratic societies from totalitarian ones.

A third fallacy is that it is the institutions of representative democracy and the people who occupy them that produce social conflict. Representative institutions are reflections rather than the sources of existing social conflict. Indeed, if the diverse views and conflicting interests that exist in society as a whole did not show up in our representative institutions, then they would not be "representative." Political scientist Benjamin Barber

(1996, 20) argues that it is important to realize that, "in democracies, representative institutions do not steal our liberties from us, they are the precious medium through which we secure those liberties." In other words, representative institutions help ensure that the people's often conflicting views are expressed and dealt with. They are not designed to make these conflicts disappear but to provide an arena and a set of ground rules where they can clash.

Exposing the fallacies of democracy is not intended to paint a cynical portrait of the promise of American democracy but rather a more realistic one. To begin a fruitful exploration of the performance of American democracy, it is critical to grasp that the promise of democracy lies first in process. The system of representative democracy seeks to embody the core democratic values by instilling them in the institutions and mechanisms that organize the political system and by embedding a set of beliefs about individual liberty in the values that operate it. For the whole system to be judged democratic, it is also important that the outcomes, not just the process, reflect core democratic values. A messy, less than optimal policy in which all views and rights are taken into account is not a failure of democracy. A failure is a fast, efficient policy where the dissent is ignored or, worse, quashed. (For a view of what could be considered a failure of democracy, see the Living the Promise feature "College Students: Voting or Volunteering?")

The Challenge of American Democracy

The enormous challenge of the American political system is to live up to the promise of democracy. There are a number of reasons for this.

Diversity and Difference

The United States is one of the most populous countries on the planet and geographically one of the largest. Its people are highly mobile and come from diverse religious, cultural, demographic, geographic, racial, ethnic, and socioeconomic backgrounds. The astonishing diversity in these characteristics produces a wide range of different political interests and preferences. Blacks and whites may hold broadly different views about the merits of affirmative action. Latinos and blacks may have different ideas about what rights, if any, should be granted to illegal immigrants. An urban city dweller in New York, Chicago, or Los Angeles likely has little interest in farm subsidies; those same subsidies may be the central topic of conversation in the coffee shop of a rural agricultural community in Nebraska, Kansas, or Iowa. Conservative Christians may view the posting of the Ten Commandments in public buildings and on public monuments with pride and approval; Muslims and agnostics may view such actions with trepidation or even fear. A wealthy individual may view the capital gains tax as fundamentally unjust; a poor individual may not know what the capital gains tax is and care even less. For a college student at a public university, there may be no more important issue than government support for higher education (at least as it affects tuition); for a senior citizen, Social Security may be thought much more important than subsidizing the studies of teenagers at the local state college.

The vast diversity in the backgrounds of American citizens leads to very different ideas of what we should do and who should get what. The challenge for American democracy is to manage all these differences within a democratic framework, to make decisions in a way that ensures the rights of all are upheld in both the process and substance of government decision making. Given that many of the differences

LIVING THE PROMISE
College Students: Voting or Volunteering?

It takes a lot to get college students interested in politics. Not even terrorism, war, and a recession—events that make politics more relevant for most people—seem to motivate the average undergraduate to meaningfully engage in the political system.

Consider this: In the academic year 2002–2003 only a third of college students were registered to vote. Only a third kept up with politics on a regular basis. Only a tenth had participated in a political campaign, and just a little more than a tenth had participated in a government, political, or issues-related organization. Majorities viewed politics as largely irrelevant to their lives. These attitudes were expressed while the nation was fighting messy guerrilla wars in Iraq and Afghanistan, worrying about terrorism at home, and suffering through a severe job market contraction.

Why are college students not interested in politics? The polls suggest college students see politics as producing more noise than action, more conflict than resolution, and not likely to produce the outcomes and solutions they want.

Yet while college students are for the most part disengaged from politics, they are certainly involved in other ways. Voting might be out on the nation's college campuses, but volunteering is definitely in. Two-thirds of students report volunteering time in their community, and majorities view volunteering as a more important way to bring about social change than voting.

So, overall, college students have little interest or faith in politics and government but are involved in their communities and give generously of their time to service-based organizations. What does this mean? Do college students understand and live the promise of democracy?

No.

That may seem an overly harsh assessment to draw from reading the statistical tea leaves in a handful of opinion polls. Yet what those polls consistently indicate is this: College students view politics as too divisive, too removed from their day-to-day lives, and a poor way to find solutions to problems. In contrast, volunteering with a community service organization—helping out at a food bank, volunteering in a school, and so on—brings with it a concrete feeling of contributing to a communally desired goal. Fair enough. Volunteer organizations do important work and do make an important and very real difference to people's lives. College students make a real civic contribution when they volunteer.

Yet volunteering is not a particularly good civics lesson. Here's why. Most voluntary service organizations tend to have noncontroversial goals and attract people with similar attitudes toward those goals. What they tend to lack are the very things that characterize democratic politics. Adversarial goals, organized opposition, dissenting views, divisive issues—that's democratic politics. That is not why people typically are attracted to volunteering. Who

wants to volunteer to do good deeds only to find most of their time engaged in knock-down arguments about what should be done or who should get what?

Despite the many undeniable good deeds and worthy goals achieved by volunteering, it tends to promote a misunderstanding about democratic politics. Achieving non-controversial, service-based goals prompts those who volunteer toward unrealistic attitudes: "Look what we did! Why can't those bozos in Washington do the same thing?" (Hibbing and Theiss-Morse 2003, 186–187).

Those "bozos in Washington" are dealing with the harsh realities of making decisions in a democracy. That means working without a consensus, dealing with sharp disagreement, and striving for what you can live with, not necessarily what you feel good about. College students are absolutely correct if they see politics as messy and combative; they are also correct to believe their participation in politics will not bring about the changes they really want. The obstacle to those changes, though, is not the political system: It is other people and other groups who oppose those changes and have just as much right to participate as anyone else.

How do you deal with dissenting views? How do you constructively engage with people with whom you disagree? How do you accept that what you support—a policy, a candidate, a campaign—may well lose? These are the tough issues of living the democratic promise. Given what the polls say about their attitudes toward politics and government, college students are not striving particularly hard to find answers. Indeed, they do not seem to be particularly interested in asking the questions.

continued

continued

Sources: The Panetta Institute. 2002. "Volunteerism, Education, and the Shadow of September Eleventh: A Survey of American College Students." *http://www.panettainstitute.org/lib/02/hart_05.html.*

Accessed September 16, 2003; Sax, L. J., J. A. Lindholm, A. W. Astin, W. S. Korn, and K. M. Horn. 2003. *The American Freshman: National Norms for Fall 2002.* Los Angeles: UCLA Higher Education Research

Institute; "Students Engaged, but Skeptical, Survey Says." 2002. *Harvard Gazette. http://www.news.harvard.edu/gazette/2002/12.12/22-survey.html.* Accessed September 16, 2003.

produced by the nation's huge diversity are seemingly unbridgeable—for example, on abortion, gun control, the role of prayer in schools, budget deficits, gays in the military, and the government's role in the economy—this is an enormously ambitious undertaking for a democratic system.

Dynamics

An additional element of Americans' diversity is its dynamism. As aspects of each dimension shift, so does the context of American politics. Old conflicts lessen in importance as new ones take their place. Getting a firm handle on American politics may

A prominent characteristic of American citizens is their extensive diversity. Responding to the variety of perspectives and goals resulting from such a diverse population presents a challenge for elected officials. Although it is not possible for government to satisfy all the various demands, representative democracy holds the promise that the rights of all are upheld in both the process and substance of government decision making.

© Chuck Savage/Corbis

be difficult because the conflicts processed by democracy are shaped by a constantly changing backdrop. This changing context shapes and reshapes questions of "what we ought to do."

Consider that the first census of the United States, taken in 1790, indicated that the 13 original colonies accounted for 900,000 square miles forming a relatively narrow corridor along the eastern seaboard. Within this narrow corridor were fewer than 4 million people. Both of these basic characteristics have changed almost beyond recognition. Geographically the United States grew west, steadily pushing its boundaries to the Pacific and beyond. Today the 50 states include roughly 3.6 million square miles and a population of about 280 million. Population and geographic growth have a profound effect on politics. States do not grow at the same rate (see Figure 1.1), and because the number of representatives a state sends to Congress is based on population, as population shifts so can the size of a state's congressional delegation. Presently, power in the Congress is following population

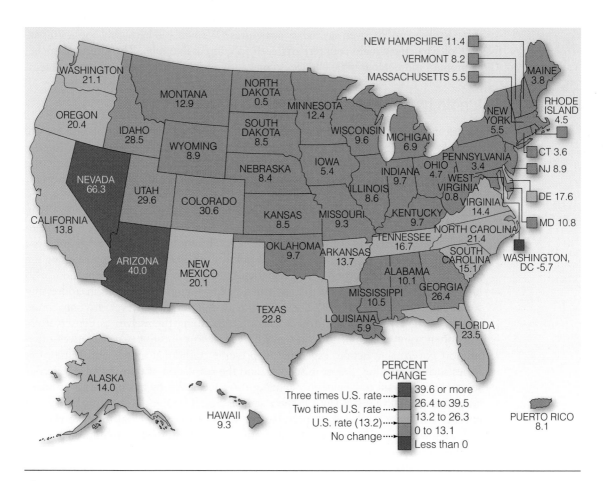

Figure 1.1
Population Growth for the 50 States, the District of Columbia, and Puerto Rico, 1990–2000
Source: U.S. Census Bureau. 2003.

trends and shifting south and west. What New Yorkers and Wisconsinites want the government to do is becoming less important compared to what Californians and Texans want.

It is not just overall growth that presents a challenge. The population is becoming more diverse ethnically and economically. In the past few years, Latinos eclipsed blacks as the largest minority group. In 1980 the wealthiest 5 percent of Americans received a little less than 15 percent of all the income generated in the country, while the poorest 20 percent of Americans received about 5 percent of the income. Today, the wealthiest 5 percent of Americans receive more than 20 percent of the income, while the poorest 5 percent receive about 4 percent of the income (U.S. Census Bureau 2003). As America becomes more urban, more racially and ethnically diverse, and the gap grows between the poorest and wealthiest citizens, political interests and ideas about "what we should do" shift. America is no longer a nation of farmers, so agriculture policy is less important to most people. America is much less white, so the concerns of ethnic minorities occupy a larger space in the political spectrum. Or consider that women are increasingly better represented in jobs traditionally held by men in law, business, and politics. Might not the shift in the gender makeup of the workforce lead to conflict over, say, salary structures? Women still earn only about 70 percent of what their male counterparts earn in comparable jobs. The churn of social, economic, and demographic change is constantly reshaping the political environment.

Ideology and Partisanship

Americans have very different ideas about what government should and should not do, and they have decidedly different preferences about who should or should not run the government. An **ideology** is a consistent set of values, attitudes, and beliefs about the appropriate role of government in society (Campbell et al. 1960). Ideology is important to democratic politics because it helps people figure out what they do or do not support, even on issues of minor interest and of which they know very little (Bawn 1999). Broadly speaking, in America the range of ideological beliefs runs across a spectrum from liberals (the left) to conservatives (the right). Traditionally, *conservatives* are those who favor keeping the status quo, which in political terms means they oppose using the government to initiate economic or social change. In contrast, *liberals* are those who favor change and believe government should play a more active role in addressing social and economic problems. These traditional definitions, however, are only rough guides. In American politics, it is the people describing themselves as conservatives who often want government action and liberals who oppose it. Conservatives often support government action, especially to preserve traditional morals and values. On issues such as abortion, prayer in schools, and the regulation of pornography, it is conservatives who want to change the status quo—specifically, by having the government adopt their moral values as law. On these same issues, it is typically liberals who oppose government action and seek to preserve the right of the individual to make choices without government interference. Conservatives are thus more likely to oppose regulating individual economic choices and more likely to support the government regulating individual moral choices. Liberals do the opposite.

For most people, ideology acts as a useful political gyroscope; they use their enduring system of beliefs about government as way to orient themselves to the proposals, issues, and questions churning through the public arena. Even if you are very vague on the specifics and implications of a given issue or policy proposal, your ideology can still give you a position. Most Americans do not have strong ideological beliefs—over the last several decades an average of about 50 percent of Americans identified themselves as moderate or reported that they did not know what these terms mean (Figure 1.2). Of those that did report having ideological beliefs, about 31 percent identified themselves as conservatives and about 19 percent self-identified as liberal (National Election Survey 2003). The difference in ideological beliefs (or the absence of them) produce very different opinions about what government should or should not do.

Many Americans wed their ideological beliefs to their support for a political party. Traditionally, **partisanship** is viewed as a psychological attachment to a political party (Campbell et al. 1960). In simple terms, this means that most people view one of the parties as standing for their brand of politics. Broadly speaking, Republicans are seen as representing the conservative brand and Democrats the liberal brand of politics. Roughly 24 percent of Americans identify themselves as Republicans, and 34 percent as Democrats. The remaining 42 percent are spread between these two—some of them independents leaning toward the Republicans, some leaning toward the Democrats, some who claim to have not the slightest preference for either party (National Election Survey 2003). Political parties (as we will discuss in Chapter 7) are the dominant organizing force of American politics: They organize the government, provide coherence to elections, and mobilize voters. Because neither party has the

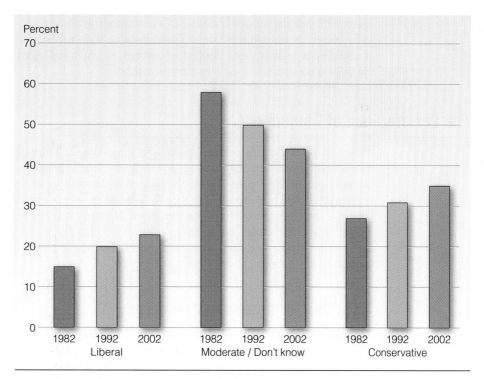

Figure 1.2
Ideological Self-Identification
Source: National Election Survey. *www.umich.edu/~nes/nesguide/toptable/tab3_1/htm.*

support of a commanding majority, and because many citizens either have weak party ties or shuttle their support between the parties, parties are more likely to reflect the differences of Americans rather a bridge between them.

False Consensus

Despite the huge variation in everything from ideology to ethnicity, from religion to geography, from wealth to partisanship, Americans by and large believe that most people agree on most issues. Indeed, many studies confirm that most citizens tend to believe their views are shared by a majority of others (Hibbing and Theiss-Morse 2003, 132, fn 3). This astonishingly unrealistic view of politics is known as the **false consensus,** or the tendency of people to believe their views are "normal" or "common sense" and therefore shared by most people. This false consensus creates a challenge and even a danger to democratic decision making. If most people believe their views represent the majority position, and the government fails to adopt that position, people are likely to believe that the political system is not working. The core value of majority rule is being broken by something or someone. (In the popular mind, that something or someone is often viewed as "special interests.") In reality, the false consensus rests on an unrealistic and uninformed view of politics. While huge majorities support democratic values and the American political system in the abstract, there is more disagreement than agreement on specific proposals or issues. Many see the disagreements as evidence that something has gone wrong. In reality the noisy clash of interests is just the natural outcome of a democracy as diverse, dynamic, and ideologically mixed as the United States. Democracy in such a place is always going to be marked by at least as much conflict as consensus, which may not be fully appreciated by those who attribute their own views to others.

The Performance of Democracy

How well does the U.S. political system live up to the challenges of democracy? Does its organization and operation account for diversity and change in a way that upholds the core democratic values in both the process and substance of resolving questions of who gets what? The purpose of this book is not to answer this question for you, but to give you the tools to make up your own mind. If your answer, either in a general sense or on a specific issue, is different from your classmates, do not be surprised. Reasonable people have long disagreed about whether the performance of democracy lives up to the promise of democracy in America.

The Case for American Democracy

The case for American democracy rests on the assessment that our political techniques and institutions operate, for the most part, according to democratic principles. The American political system in this view is a highly **pluralistic** one in which power is fragmented and distributed widely among diverse groups and interests. Businesspeople, laborers, farmers, African Americans, Latinos, students, the elderly, gays—virtually every conceivable group and interest has access to the political process. Although some may have more political assets—money, numbers, and campaign and propaganda skills—all have at least some political resources. At a minimum, all have the vote.

The American political system is thus open to people and groups from diverse backgrounds and with diverse views. Although some citizens may be more active in the political process than others—so-called political elites, activists, or influentials—they ultimately represent a wide-ranging set of interests from the entire polity. The political moves and countermoves of this broad variety of political elites produce the energy for the American political system to work. They compete vigorously with one another but abide by the democratic rules of the game. They remain committed to the major values of a democratic society—individual liberty, freedom of expression, the right of privacy, and the like. Indeed, these political activists are counted upon to defend these values when other less politically aware and educated individuals oppose them. In this fashion, the bulk of the population's views do indeed play a role in shaping decisions on who gets what, and fundamental rights are protected. American democracy, in other words, performs reasonably well. It largely passes the democratic acid test by maintaining a process of decision making that upholds the core democratic values and producing outcomes that reflect those same values.

In the final analysis, supporters of the pluralistic view feel the American democracy serves well the interests of a wide variety of individuals and groups. Although competing elites may take the initiative in public affairs, they must also take into account the interests of ordinary citizens. The elites require the latter to provide support for public policy and to win elections. The entire process takes place within the prescribed democratic procedures, moderates differences among diverse people, and provides for social peace and progress.

Major Criticisms of American Democracy

Although most students of American democracy have tended to support the system, it also has had its share of critics. Such dissatisfaction has numerous sources and is often based on disappointments with the outcomes of the political process. Despite decades of effort, for example, we are still far from any solution for numbers of major social problems ranging from racial tensions to the decline in credibility of public officials. These failures provide a basis to question the operation, ideals, and assumptions about the political system.

One of the major criticisms of American democracy is that it simply does not operate as its supporters claim. For example, many Americans believe that candidates and officeholders are more interested in manipulating public attitudes than in understanding and acting on them. Republicans and Democrats are charged with standing for little more than the acquisition of power and of robbing the voters of meaningful choices rather than providing alternatives. Some critics argue that significant minorities—African Americans, Latinos, Native Americans, the poor, the young, women[1]—are poorly served by the American political process. It is certainly the case that these groups are proportionally underrepresented in major political institutions such as

[1]Women are not technically a minority. They constitute more than half of both eligible voters and the population as a whole. But they may be considered a social minority in the sense that they have historically been both economically and politically disadvantaged compared to men.

Congress, the executive department, and the Supreme Court. None of these minorities is as effectively organized as the more dominant affluent groups, casting an unflattering shadow across the sunny pluralist portrait. Moreover, the groups that are organized do not check and balance one another as pluralist orthodoxy claims. Instead, each concentrates on getting what it wants from government: business interests are served by the Department of Commerce, farmers by the Department of Agriculture, unions by the Department of Labor, and so on. Instead of regulating these groups in the public interest, government is organized to dole out favors to those with political muscle at the expense of the general taxpayer.

For such critics, the American system is not pluralistic, but **elitist** in the sense that organized, influential minorities — checked neither by one another nor by the general populace — dominate the political process. These critics offer a very different picture of the American political system. The privileged status of elites and their overrepresentation in government enables them to set the public agenda, determining which issues government considers of legitimate concern and which it does not. The result is a biased system that favors the status quo and that provides an advantage to established groups over unorganized ones. If they have merit, these sorts of charges raise questions about the American system's commitment to core democratic ideals and provide ample justification for pursuing reforms.

The contrasting overviews of American democracy represented by the positive pluralistic portrait and the negative elitist critique are not absolutes. Leading advocates of both lines of thought recognize elements of the other in the reality of American political life. Pluralists have acknowledged that some groups have greater control over the outcomes of political decision making than others; elitists have observed that while a handful of organized interests control many major political decisions, they do not control all of them. There clearly is a difference between the promise of theoretical democratic ideals and the pluralist and elitist assessments of its performance. Whose assessment is more accurate remains a matter of intense debate.

 ## Performance Assessment

"Democracy," as one observer succinctly put it, "is a complicated concept" (Hudson 1995, 1). The bulk of this book is designed to provide you with a clearer picture of the promise behind the complexity. Democracy is a system of governance founded on a series of core values aimed at shaping the process of how people go about making communal decisions. It makes few guarantees about outcomes, beyond a commitment that the outcomes should also reflect core democratic values. Democracy comes in two basic forms (direct and representative democracy), and each basic form may include differing sets of institutions and varying attitudes reflecting the underlying core values. In the American context, governance is classified as a Western representative democracy. Such systems are characterized by a clearly identifiable set of institutions and values, all predicated on dispersing political power among ordinary citizens and protecting their right to exercise that power. How well the American democracy works is a matter of some dispute. Even a cursory examination of the context of the political system in the United States reveals enormous diversity and constant change, putting a good deal of pressure on the procedures and institutions of the democratic process.

A basic understanding of these issues provides a solid platform for understanding a more detailed analysis of the American political system, both in the chapters that follow and in the everyday world outside the classroom.

General Approach and Organization of the Book

With these concepts and a little historical perspective in mind, the remainder of the book provides the factual information needed to make an informed judgment on how the performance of American democracy is living up to its promise. At the end of each chapter is our personal assessment of the particular institution or process under study. Readers are not necessarily expected to agree with this assessment. Our primary goal is not to proselytize but rather to stimulate independent thinking. Each individual should ultimately make an informed, rational, and analytical judgment about the performance of the American political system. Our assessments are examples of what such judgments look like, but they are not the only ones.

The book is divided into four parts. Part One consists of four chapters analyzing the constitutional framework. Chapter 2 looks at the political forces that led to the drafting and ratification of the Constitution and analyzes the values and assumptions underlying that framework. Chapter 3 focuses on one major element of this framework and a dominant feature of American politics—federalism, a system that divides power between state and national governments. Chapters 4 and 5 examine the liberties and rights guaranteed by the Constitution and how they have (or have not) been extended to various groups.

Part Two addresses the general subject of connecting citizens to government, that is, how citizens encourage those in power to be responsive to their needs and hold them accountable for their actions. Chapter 6 focuses on the major institutional mechanism for connecting citizens to government between elections—the interest group. Chapter 7 examines the role that political parties play in organizing politics and translating public preferences into coherent policy agendas. Chapter 8 looks at the mass media's role in shaping opinions and structuring the public agenda. Chapter 9 explores the general nature of Americans' political views, how those views are acquired, and the various outlets for expressing those views in the political process. Chapters 10 and 11 examine elections by reviewing the processes of nominating and electing candidates and analyzing the voting behavior of the American electorate.

Part Three focuses on the institutions involved in official decision making in government. These institutions are the Congress (Chapter 12), the presidency (Chapter 13), the bureaucracy (Chapter 14), and the courts (Chapter 15). We examine these institutions in terms of the kinds of people who serve in them, their general structure, and the procedures that each utilizes to carry on its activities. In addition, we analyze the relationships and interactions among the officials who serve in these separate institutions.

Part Four concludes the book with an assessment of the performance of American democracy. In Chapter 16 we will examine how the processes and institutions of the American political system combine to make public policy in terms of living up to the democratic promise.

The appendices contain important supplemental information and documents. We include a glossary of all terms used in the book, the Constitution of the United States, the Declaration of Independence, and two frequently used *Federalist Papers* (Numbers 10 and 51).

Summary

- Democracy is a system of governance in which all citizens have the opportunity to participate in the process of making decisions about who gets what.
- Democracy is based on four core values: popular sovereignty, political freedom, political equality, and majority rule.
- The promise of democracy is that both the method of making collective decisions and the substance of those decisions will uphold these core values.
- There are two basic forms of democracy. In direct democracy, citizens are the principal participants in making government decisions. In representative democracy, citizens choose public officials to make decisions on their behalf. The United States is a representative democracy.
- Representative democracies try to uphold the core democratic values through such institutions as elections, political parties, and interest groups.
- There are a number of popular fallacies about democracy, including beliefs that democracy promotes the best solutions to problems and that the majority should always get what it wants. Neither is necessarily true.
- There is disagreement about the extent to which the United States fulfills the promise of democracy. Some argue that core democratic values are widely reflected both in the process of making public policy and in the substance of the policies themselves. Others argue that the American political system tends to favor elites who dominate public decision making for their own benefit.
- Disagreements about how well the American political system fulfills the promise of democracy are at least partially explained by the context of American democracy. The United States is a diverse and populous country that is constantly changing. All these differences promote political conflict and disagreement.
- The purpose of this book is to provide sufficient information about the American political system to allow the reader to come to an independent, informed judgment about how well the performance of democracy matches its promise in the United States.

Key Terms

absolute majority   9
autocracy   5
democracy   5
direct democracy   10
economic equality   8
elitist   26
equality of opportunity   8
equality under the law   8
false consensus   24
government   5
ideology   22
initiative   12
majority rule   9

minority rights   9
oligarchy   5
partisanship   23
pluralistic   24
plurality   9
political equality   8
politics   4
popular sovereignty   6
recall   12
referendum   11
simple majority   9
social equality   8
Western representative democracy   13

Selected Readings

Dahl, Robert. 1998. *On Democracy.* New Haven: Yale University Press. A brief but comprehensive overview of what a democracy is and how a democracy works. Written to be easily accessible to undergraduates.

Dionne, E. J. 1991. *Why Americans Hate Politics.* New York: Simon & Schuster. A good analysis of why Americans are turned off by politics and the political system.

Hibbing, John R., and Elizabeth Theiss-Morse. 2003. *Stealth Democracy.* New York: Cambridge University Press. Argues that Americans are not particularly democratic and that the government they want, and the politics they approve of, are a considerable distance from the classic vision of democracy.

Minogue, Kenneth. 1994. *Politics: A Very Short Introduction.* New York: Oxford University Press. A short and accessible introduction to the theory and practice of politics, including analyses of citizenship, justice, and democracy.

2 | The American Constitution

Given its purpose, the U.S. Constitution is a remarkably succinct document. It is a complete instruction manual that has required relatively few revisions to guide the operation of one of the world's major representative democracies for more than two centuries. It sets up the framework of a democratic process; specifies the powers, obligations, and limits of the major institutional actors; and, with the Bill of Rights included, articulates fundamental liberties of individuals that must not be violated by government. In short, the operating guidelines for a nation of 280 million are contained in about 5,000 words,[1] a text that can easily be stuffed into a back pocket. As humorist P. J. O'Rourke observed, the owner's manual of a mid-sized sedan is five times as long, twice as confusing, and seats only four (1991, 11). No wonder the Constitution is revered as a remarkable achievement and an embodiment of successful democratic ideals.

The Constitution is also surprisingly misunderstood. Although the vast majority of Americans express abiding faith in and support for the Constitution, large numbers have never read it, and few know the politics that produced it. It seems to be viewed almost as the product of divine guidance, a sage bequest of universally agreed-on democratic wisdom brought down from the Revolutionary mount by the Founders.

Historical reality is in sharp contrast to this idealized portrait, and more than one scholar has suggested that the motives of some of the Constitution's framers were considerably less than pure. A closer look at the personali-

ties who gathered in Philadelphia during the sweltering summer of 1787 to hammer out the Constitution strips away some of the sober semi-divinity that is often used to characterize them. For example, Luther Martin, a fierce advocate of states rights, was not even sober. He was a heavy drinker who managed to severely damage the cause of states rights by giving a 6-hour, rambling, apparently alcohol-soaked speech to a room full of uncomfortably hot and irritated delegates (Collier and Collier 1986, 158–161).

This example is not meant to suggest that the Constitution was a happenstance product of bumblers. The convention that drew up the document included dazzling intellectual and political talents like James Madison, Alexander Hamilton, Roger Sherman, Gouverneur Morris, and Charles Pinckney. But the Founders also had deep disagreements and the full complement of human foibles and flaws that Martin serves to exemplify.

The point is that the Constitution is a supremely political document. It is the product of a lengthy battle over the big question of "what we ought to do" that has governed all similar questions in the polity since its adoption. Embedded in this text is the clearest articulation of the democratic promise of America. Understanding what the Constitution says and why it says it is fundamental to understanding that promise. To that end, this chapter examines the circumstances that led to the calling of the Constitutional Convention and the politics that shaped the document itself.

---

[1]The total does not include the seventeen amendments subsequent to the Bill of Rights.

The Promise of the Constitution

The basic promise of a constitution is simple: A **constitution** provides the basic principles that define the conduct of its political affairs. These principles can be categorized into three fundamental aspects:

1. The *functions* of government: the powers and responsibilities that rest in the public rather than the private sphere
2. The *procedures:* the manner in which government carries out the powers and responsibilities entrusted to it
3. The *structure:* the institutions and mechanisms that constitute the framework of government

Together these provide the basic rules and guidelines for exercising political authority. Note that this is a definition of constitutions in general. The particular functions, procedures, and structure specified by a constitution determine whether the government will be an autocracy, oligarchy, or democracy.

Thus, a constitution in a democracy will spell out how the core values of democracy are to be upheld. Consider, for example, the powerful role of public officials and institutions in a representative democracy. They have the authority and power to make binding decisions regulating individual and group behavior. A constitution performs a similarly powerful role in relation to the public officials themselves; it determines what they can and cannot do and the nature of their relationship with other officeholders and the general populace. **Reciprocity,** a state of mutual dependence and influence, thus characterizes a constitutional form of government. The people grant public officials the power to enact laws and decrees, but ordinary citizens ultimately control how that power is exercised. A democratic constitution thus spells out that popular sovereignty is the basis of political authority and constrains those who exercise that power from limiting the political freedom of others.

A constitution, then, establishes a set of legal relationships between leaders and the led. It is the heart of a nation's political process, and it shapes the process by determining the rules for accessing and exercising political power. The content and form of a constitution is in turn shaped by a political process as groups struggle to write the rules to favor their own interests.

To understand the creation of the U.S. Constitution and how it upholds the four core values of democracy, we need to appreciate two sets of contemporary circumstances that shaped it. The first is the historical antecedents—the Declaration of Independence, the Articles of Confederation, and the various state constitutions—that provided a basic philosophy of governance. The second is the economic and social conditions that created dissatisfaction with the forms of governance established by these earlier frameworks.

Historical Antecedents of the Constitution

The Declaration of Independence   The Declaration of Independence lays the foundation of American constitutional theory. Penned with little input from other members of the committee established by the Second Continental Congress,[2] Thomas Jefferson

---

[2]The committee included John Adams, Benjamin Franklin, Roger Sherman, and Robert Livingston.

© Bettman/Corbis

Thomas Jefferson wrote the Declaration of Independence, and John Hancock was the first to sign it in July 1776. In the document, Jefferson presents a comprehensive idea of popular sovereignty, one that laid the foundations for the Constitution's major principles.

justified the struggle for independence with a republican theory of government based on the concept of natural rights. Borrowing from the ideas of John Locke, Jefferson's elegant prose asserts that "All men are created equal," and they enjoy "unalienable Rights" that include "Life, Liberty and the pursuit of happiness." These statements reject arguments of Thomas Hobbes that people surrender certain natural rights when they leave the state of nature. In response to such arguments, the Declaration provides the basis of republican government by saying that governments are created by men to secure these rights, and governments derive their "just Powers from the Consent of the Governed." If a government fails to protect these rights, "it is the Right of the People to alter or to abolish it, and to institute new Government." Together, these ideas can be viewed as a comprehensive conception of popular sovereignty (Becker 1922; Wiecek 1992).

The legal status of the Declaration of Independence is somewhat ambiguous. Although Congress placed it in the U.S. Code under the heading "Organic Laws of the United States of America," the Supreme Court has rarely interpreted it to have binding legal force. Some legal authorities deny that there is a constitutional right of revolution. Nonetheless, the Declaration of Independence is a basic statement of constitutional principles and lays the foundation for American constitutional order (Wiecek 1992). (To read a version of the Declaration in more accessible, if less elegant, language, see the Living the Promise feature "Declaring the Promise . . . in English.")

LIVING THE PROMISE
Declaring the Promise . . . in English

College students (and others) often find it difficult to read documents such as the Declaration of Independence, the Federalist Papers, and even the Constitution itself. This is because the formal language of the late 1700s does not always translate well for those accustomed only to modern English. Recognizing this, many have attempted over the past century or so to translate the founding documents of U.S. governance into language for the average citizen. H. L. Mencken, a famous satirist and newspaper columnist of the early 20th century, penned one of the better known of these efforts. What follows is a condensed version of his translation of the Declaration of Independence:

WHEN things get so balled up that the people of a country got to cut loose from some other country, and go it on their own hook, without asking no permission from nobody, excepting maybe God Almighty, then they ought to let everybody know why they done it, so that everybody can see they are not trying to put nothing over on nobody.

All we got to say on this proposition is this: first, me and you is as good as anybody else, and maybe a damn sight better; second, nobody ain't got no right to take away none of our rights; third, every man has got a right to live, to come and go as he pleases, and to have a good time whichever way he likes, so long as he don't interfere with nobody else. That any government that don't give a man them

rights ain't worth a damn; also, people ought to choose the kind of government they want themselves, and nobody else ought to have no say in the matter. That whenever any government don't do this, then the people have got a right to give it the bum's rush and put in one that will take care of their interests. . . . The administration of the present King, George III, has been rotten from the start, and when anybody kicked about it he always tried to get away with it by strong-arm work. Here is some of the rough stuff he has pulled:

He vetoed bills in the Legislature that everybody was in favor of, and hardly nobody was against. . . .

When people went to work and gone to him and asked him to put through a law about this or that, he give them their choice: either they had to shut down the Legislature and let him pass it all by himself, or they couldn't have it at all.

He made the Legislature meet at one-horse tank-towns, so that hardly nobody could get there and most of the leaders would stay home and let him go to work and do things like he wanted.

He give the Legislature the air, and sent the members home every time they stood up to him and give him a call-down or bawled him out.

When a Legislature was busted up he wouldn't allow no new one to be elected, so that there wasn't nobody left to run things, but

anybody could walk in and do whatever they pleased. . . .

He got the judges under his thumb by turning them out when they done anything he didn't like, or by holding up their salaries, so that they had to knuckle down or not get no money. . . .

Without no war going on, he kept an army loafing around the country, no matter how much people kicked about it. . . .

He let grafters run loose, from God knows where, and give them the say in everything. . . .

He has burned down towns, shot down people like dogs, and raised hell against us out on the ocean.

He hired whole regiments of Dutch, etc., to fight us, and told them they could have anything they wanted if they could take it away from us, and sicked these Dutch, etc., on us. . . .

Every time he has went to work and pulled any of these things, we have went to work and put in a kick, but every time we have went to work and put in a kick he has went to work and did it again. When a man keeps on handing out such rough stuff all the time, all you can say is that he ain't got no class and ain't fitten to have no authority over people who have got any rights, and he ought to be kicked out.

When we complained to the English we didn't get no more satisfaction. . . . We asked them to get us a square deal, and told them that if this thing kept on we'd have to do something about it and maybe they wouldn't like it. But the more we talked, the more they didn't pay no attention to us. Therefore, if they ain't for us they must be agin us, and we are ready to give them the fight of their lives, or to shake hands when it is over.

Therefore be it resolved, That we, the representatives of the people of the United States of America, in Congress assembled, hereby declare as follows: That the United States, which was the United Colonies in former times, is now a free country, and ought to be; that we have throwed out the English King and don't want to have nothing to do with him no more . . .

Source: *http://www.io.com/gibbonsb/mencken/declaration.html*. Accessed October 25, 2003.

The Articles of Confederation   The **Articles of Confederation** served as the first constitution of the United States. A committee of the Continental Congress began drafting this constitution in June 1776—even before independence had been declared—though bickering and political divisions in Congress meant the document was not submitted for approval by the states until November 1777.

The Articles of Confederation established a national government consisting of a unicameral (one-house) legislature; there was no independent executive or judiciary. Under the Articles, the national government's powers were limited primarily to raising an army and navy, entering into treaties and alliances, and sending and receiving diplomatic representatives—matters of war and peace that wartime experience indicated should be vested in the nation. The national government had no authority to regulate interstate and foreign commerce, which the Confederation's framers associated with the Acts of Trade and Navigation, passed by Parliament, which helped spark the Revolution.

The national government also lacked the power to levy taxes, so it had no control over its revenues. Although it was authorized to requisition funds from the states for expenses, the taxes to pay these requisitions had to be levied by the states themselves, and the states often refused to do so. National troops also had to be furnished by the states. Lacking the authority to make the states meet their obligations, and bereft of the power to tax or conscript individuals, the national government essentially did not have the means to fulfill the basic governmental responsibilities entrusted to it. Moreover, there was little chance of changing these arrangements, because all the states had to consent to any alteration of the document.

State Constitutions as Models of Government   While the national government was off to a fragile start, the states were busy asserting their independence not only from Great Britain but also from one another and from any national government that might be formed.

State constitutions often reflected the institutional arrangements of the Articles of Confederation, with dominant legislatures and weak (or nonexistent) executives and judiciaries. In most states, for example, the governor was chosen by the legislature; only four states had a popularly elected executive. There were some notable exceptions to this general pattern: New York, for example, had a strong governor system. State judiciaries were also weak and largely subservient to legislatures, which frequently appointed judicial officials and gave them only limited powers.

Terms of legislators were short—only one year in most of the states. Rhode Islanders were even more wary, allowing their representatives only six months. For the popular legislator, there was an additional limitation in the form of forced rotation. Most state constitutions (and the Articles of Confederation) put term limits on legislators and allowed citizens to recall an unpopular elected official at any time.

State constitutions and the Articles of Confederation clearly went to some lengths to uphold at least some of the core values of democracy. Recall provisions and the dominance of legislatures, for example, reinforced popular sovereignty. Yet whatever their advantages in this regard, state constitutions and the Articles of Confederation shared a common weakness: They produced weak and ineffective governments. The central concern reflected in these constitutions was a distrust of centralized power. The colonists' experience with the British led them to see a strong, centralized government as too vulnerable to the temptation to ignore the core values of democracy for its own interests. The revolution, after all, was fought in no small part because of the colonists' resentment of taxes imposed by a legislature to which they sent no delegates and in which they had no voice. This certainly seemed to violate the core values of popular sovereignty and political equality.

Yet, in overthrowing British rule state constitutions (and the Articles of Confederation) perhaps went too far in emphasizing these values in setting up new governments. Rather than being too powerful and too willing to trample the freedom and liberty of their citizens, the state and national governments of the early United States were often too weak to effectively do much at all. This weakness carried enormous risks—including the very real potential that the United States would fail as a political system.

Hard-won experience at the state level, however, led to some constitutional innovations that minimized the risk of failure, and later served as examples for the framers of the U.S. Constitution to follow. For example, British occupation of New York required that state to develop a strong governorship free of legislative dominance in order to handle military and civilian affairs. This experience showed the worth of an independent executive and demonstrated that such an executive was not necessarily a threat to political freedom. Encouraged by John Adams, voters in Massachusetts adopted a constitution that included a popularly elected house of representatives and an "aristocratic" senate apportioned on the basis of taxable wealth. It also included a popularly elected governor vested with considerable powers, such as a veto, who was eligible for reelection and an independent judiciary. Both the New York and Massachusetts constitutions would help shape the deliberations at the Constitutional Convention.

Economic Conditions

Like other emerging nations in the modern world, the United States in the 1780s faced a period of major adjustment following the successful revolt against Great Britain. Within a few years of the end of the Revolutionary War in 1781, America was plunged into a depression. Accounts differ as to how serious it was. Some claim the critical period was brief and the corner turned by the time the Constitutional Convention met in mid-1787. Others claim it was serious enough to threaten the existence of the new nation. There is general agreement that the economic downturn affected groups differently. Small farmers and the few hired laborers of the day experienced little of the effect. People in commerce and finance were hit hard.

Domestic rivalries worsened the economic problems. Fierce economic protectionism developed as states levied duties to raise revenue and to protect local interests against out-of-state competitors. Lacking the authority to regulate interstate commerce, the national government was powerless to remove the obstacles to free trade within the nation.

Adding to the economic woes were the worsening fortunes of creditors who financed both public and private ventures in the young nation. Debtors often used the political process at the state level to lighten their financial obligations. For example, some states enacted "stay" laws that postponed the due dates of promissory notes. Another type of law allowed a debtor to declare bankruptcy, pay off his obligation at less than face value, and begin his financial life anew with a clean slate. Another advantage for debtors was the issuance of cheap paper money by state legislatures. This practice fueled inflation, meaning that the face value of debt was worth far less in purchasing power than the money originally borrowed.

Even more financially frustrated were those who had lent the nation money to fight the Revolution. They had no way to collect on public securities issued by a government that lacked the financial ability to pay its debts. Similarly affected were veterans of the war, who had volunteered their services on the promise of compensation of proceeds from government bonds. Given the precarious financial situation facing the new nation, there was a risk that the government would default on its debts.

Although the United States had theoretically achieved an independent status in the family of nations, its sovereignty was vulnerable even after the guns had fallen silent. The structure of government lent itself to internal divisions and united the states in little more than name. Economic strife pitted one group against another. And the world's major powers remained active on the North American continent. Spain closed the mouth of the Mississippi to all shipping. The supposedly vanquished British troops refused to withdraw from some northwestern forts until the claims of British creditors were honored. The new nation tottered on the uncertain economic and political legs of its newfound independence. George Washington, the Revolutionary War's great hero, observed that something had to change in order "to avert the humiliating and contemptible figure we are about to make on the annals of mankind" (Collier and Collier 1986, 3).

Group Rivalries and the Movement for a Convention

The groups particularly aggrieved in the postwar period were manufacturers, merchants, shipowners, and creditors. The professional classes—lawyers, doctors, newspaper editors—sympathized with their clients, as did former soldiers who felt cheated out of their rightful claims for services rendered in the cause of nationhood. Combined, they comprised a potent group of people who wanted change. After the Constitution had been drafted, they were to come together to support its adoption under the name of **Federalists.**

Although Federalist interests were for the most part concentrated in the cities, some rural Americans also found their interests jeopardized by postwar conditions. These were the commercial farmers who produced a surplus of crops that they wanted to sell in interstate and foreign markets. Most were large landholders who ran agricultural operations dependent on slave labor; they found common cause with merchants whose futures were also linked to commerce.

Patrick Henry, a lawyer from Virginia and a controversial member of the Continental Congress, made the first speech when it convened. Despite being a well-known representative for the Anti-Federalists, who did not support the idea of a strong central government, Henry did not attend the Constitutional Convention.

Arrayed against the emergent Federalists were people who were not dependent on trade for their livelihoods. Forming the core of this opposition were small subsistence farmers satisfied with scratching out a living on poor soil remote from river valleys, producing crops for their own families or marketing small surpluses in nearby localities. Also included were small businessmen, artisans, mechanics (the small laboring class of that time), and debtors who welcomed government assistance in their perennial struggle to keep one step ahead of creditors. It was this coalition of interests, labeled **anti-Federalists,** that led efforts to defeat ratification of the Constitution.

As a group, the Federalists were wealthier and better educated and worked in higher-status occupations. Anti-Federalists tended to be lower-class, obscure individuals of modest means. Although the leadership of the anti-Federalists did include a number of prominent Revolutionary-era luminaries—such as Richard Henry Lee, Patrick Henry, and George Clinton—the anti-Federalists could not match either in numbers or fame those who—like George Washington, Alexander Hamilton, and James Madison—lent their skill and prestige to the Federalist cause.

Two events in the fall of 1786 enabled the Federalists to act on their desires for a stronger national government. One was a meeting at Annapolis, Maryland, convened to discuss problems of interstate trade and the possibility of adopting a uniform system of commercial regulations. Delegates from only a few states showed up, and most of them had Federalist sympathies. The Federalist majority, notably Hamilton and Madison, seized the opportunity to issue a report to the Continental Congress suggesting that a commission be assembled the following May to revise the Articles of Confederation.

The second event was the outbreak of an armed revolt by farmers in western Massachusetts who were resisting state efforts to seize their property for failure to pay taxes and debts. Shays' Rebellion—named for its leader, Daniel Shays—was put down, but some Americans regarded it as a threat to the very existence of the United States. Among them was George Washington, the most popular American of all. Appalled by the news that a former officer in his army had brought the state of Massachusetts to the brink of civil war, Washington lent his great prestige to the movement for a convention.

The Constitutional Convention

Pushed by these two events, in February 1787 Congress called on the states to send delegates to a convention in Philadelphia to revise the Articles of Confederation. All except Rhode Island, which was dominated by debtor interests, eventually responded. Yet, some states responded more quickly than others. Although the convention was supposed to open on May 14, 1787, a quorum was not achieved until May 25. The New Hampshire delegation did not arrive until July 1787, some two months after the deliberations began.

The Founders

The most important feature of the Constitutional Convention was that an overwhelming proportion of the delegates were would-be Federalists. As soon as the convention assembled, it made two important decisions: naming George Washington the presiding officer and binding the delegates to secrecy. Naming Washington as presiding officer gave the convention immediate credibility, and the Federalist majority could exercise a larger degree of influence behind closed doors than in open public debate.

The anti-Federalists matched and perhaps exceeded their opponents as a proportion of the general populace. Given their numbers, it is somewhat puzzling that more anti-Federalists were not represented at the convention, especially since the state legislatures that selected delegates had strong anti-Federalist sentiments. There are two possible explanations. One is that some anti-Federalists did not want to dignify the convention with their presence. The best-known instance was Patrick Henry, whose oft-quoted reason for staying away was that he "smelt a rat." The second possible explanation is that anti-Federalists thought attendance was unnecessary because the convention's legal mandate was limited to revising the Articles of Confederation. The anti-Federalists believed they could block anything contrary to their interests because such changes had to be approved by all states. As it turned out, the convention quickly abandoned its assignment of reworking the Articles of Confederation and secretly began drafting a blueprint for a new government.

Anti-Federalists were represented in this enterprise (Luther Martin was one example), but they were outnumbered. And most anti-Federalists who were in attendance belonged to the social, political, and economic elite. The nation's subsistence farmers, who constituted the rank-and-file of the anti-Federalist cause and were the most numerous economic group in the nation, were hardly represented at all. In fact, the fifty-five delegates were decidedly unrepresentative of American life and interests. Most were lawyers, most were college educated, and most had political experience. Three-quarters had served in the Continental Congress, eight had signed the Declaration of Independence, and most were dominant figures in the political lives of their states. Although unrepresentative, they were a gathering of political talent of the highest order, a collection with few historical comparisons.

Most delegates took an active role in the proceedings, but a few are remembered as its dominant figures. By far the most influential was James Madison of Virginia. Madison was hardly a dashing Revolutionary hero, as were some of his contemporaries. Short, frail, and uncomfortable with public speaking, he possessed a towering intellect. He spent months preparing for the convention, poring over treatises on government and historical accounts of the ancient Greek city-states, and he arrived at the convention with

Often called the father of the Constitution because of his huge contribution to its writing and ratification, Madison also collaborated in the writing of *The Federalist Papers,* which described the justifications for the political institutions and processes the Constitution established. He was elected to the first national Congress, and after serving as secretary of state under Jefferson, he served two terms as the fourth president of the United States.

a well-defined plan for a new government. Called the **Virginia plan,** it was the first major proposal presented to the convention, and it formed the basis of the Constitution. Madison's contributions went far beyond his labors at the convention. He was a key figure both before and after the convention, and his diary constitutes the main historical record of the four-month proceedings. Because of these efforts, Madison is remembered as the father of the Constitution.

Ranking only slightly below Madison in importance were the two delegates from Pennsylvania: James Wilson and Gouverneur Morris. Wilson was a Scotsman in his mid-40s, a lawyer known for his penetrating logical mind, who placed great faith in the common people. Morris, eleven years Wilson's junior, was a swashbuckling figure. Tall, handsome, and known for his biting wit, Morris viewed the common people with aristocratic mistrust. Despite their differences, both advocated a strong federal government with a powerful executive; and through their service on influential committees at the convention, they shaped both the content and the phraseology of the document that ultimately emerged.

Two of the most famous figures present were George Washington and Benjamin Franklin, both of whom made significant contributions to the convention. Washington did not play an active role in shaping the Constitution, but his enormous national prestige and the assumption that he would be the nation's first chief executive provided the convention and the document it produced with a crucial air of legitimacy. Franklin was long past his peak of political creativity in 1787, but his justly famed wit served to cool tempers. These two renowned and revered figures played key roles in the fight for ratification simply by lending the Constitution their approval.

Agreement and Disagreement at the Convention

There was a good deal of common ground among the delegates at the convention. Key among these agreements was the expressed need for a stronger national government with the power to fulfill the responsibilities entrusted to it. The dilemma faced by the Founders was how to achieve this goal. How can a government be powerful enough to protect and serve the common good without tempting tyranny by placing power into too few hands? This conundrum was complicated by the delicate question of relations between state and national governments. The states would have to approve the Constitution, and it was universally recognized that the states had a legitimate interest in defending their sovereignty. Differences over such specifics often divided the convention into shifting and competing groups: large state versus small state, North versus South, and, of course, Federalist versus anti-Federalist.

Thus, the proposed structure of the new government percolated through several proposals. For example, Madison's Virginia plan called for a **bicameral** or two-house legislature with a popularly elected lower house and an upper house nominated by state legislatures. Representation in each was to be based on the financial contributions or population of the state. This plan was supported by large states, whose representatives would dominate the national legislature, and opposed by small states. A rival proposal was the **New Jersey plan,** which proposed a one-house legislature with equal state representation, similar to that established by the Articles of Confederation. This approach favored small states, which would wield equal power with their more populous neighbors. The conflict was resolved by the **Connecticut Compromise** or Great Compromise, so-called because delegates from Connecticut worked hard for its acceptance. It proposed a two-house legislature, with a House of Representatives apportioned on the basis of population and a Senate representing the states on an equal basis. Similar battles were fought over the composition and selection of the executive branch (these are detailed in Chapter 13).

Such political compromises are a notable feature of the document produced by the convention. Some of these compromises seem unsavory today, and some left fundamental issues unresolved. For example, northern and southern states were split over the question of slavery. The South wanted slaves counted for purposes of representation, even though there was no thought of allowing slaves to vote, but not for purposes of taxation. Northern states favored the reverse. The bargain struck was to count each slave as three-fifths of a person for both representation and taxation. As for the very controversial question of ending the slave trade, the convention simply put it off for the future with a provision that barred Congress from outlawing it until 1808. The unresolved question of slavery perpetuated a problem that neither a bloody Civil War in the 19th century nor an extended battle for civil rights in the 20th has fully resolved.

A number of factors contributed to the willingness of delegates to accommodate their sometimes sharp differences. Many believed that the nation was on the brink of dissolution and that this was the last chance to secure a government that united the states into a single country. Since most of the delegates were Federalists, they agreed on the essential structure of government, even if they differed on the details. This underlying consensus permitted the delegates to find ways to agree on how to apply these principles. The secrecy of the proceedings also fostered compromise. Free of public scrutiny and pressures, the delegates could change their minds and modify their stands as they groped for answers to the nation's most difficult problems.

Ironically, the conditions that promoted agreement at the convention made the subsequent ratification process difficult. Anti-Federalists did not see national disintegration as imminent, and they believed that the difficulties attributed to the Articles of

Confederation were manageable or temporary. Although they were a minority of convention delegates, anti-Federalists were well represented in state legislatures and the general populace. The secrecy that promoted cooperation at the convention invited suspicion and resentment among those denied information about the proceedings. Thus, when the delegates met on September 17 and thirty-nine of the fifty-five signed the Constitution, their work had not ended. In a very real sense, it had only begun. They now faced the task of persuading their fellow citizens to approve what they had done.

The Ratification Campaign

Before the convention dissolved, the delegates made some decisions designed to facilitate the adoption of the proposed Constitution. They ignored the unanimous consent required by the Articles of Confederation and specified that ratification could be secured with the approval of nine states. This provision meant that a single state such as Rhode Island, which had no representatives at the convention, would not be able to block the entire enterprise. Aware of the anti-Federalist sentiments in state legislatures, the delegates also specified that elected state conventions were to be the ratifying bodies. The Federalists could influence the selection of representatives to these conventions as well as shape the broader course of deliberations. Ratification was also given a boost by the Continental Congress. This body, which the new Constitution proposed to put out of business, somewhat surprisingly forwarded the convention's instructions to the states.

Having slanted the rules of ratification to favor adoption, the Federalists set out to transform their opportunity into reality. They labored to get themselves and their sympathizers elected as state convention delegates, and twenty-five of the Constitution's thirty-nine signatories were so chosen. They developed strategies for convention proceedings. They began a campaign to win public support for the new Constitution.

The Federalists had some notable political advantages, including the endorsements of Washington and Franklin, worth thousands of votes in and of themselves. Trading on the important contacts of such luminaries also provided an important communications network for the various state and local campaigns. And the Federalists had a vital asset that their opponents lacked—a positive program to sell. The anti-Federalists had been neatly maneuvered into the position of favoring some changes in the Articles of Confederation but having no concrete plan to substitute for it. Lacking a viable alternative, anti-Federalists were forced to adopt a negative, defensive stance in the ratification battle, while the Federalists argued that rejection of the Constitution would lead to a return of the chaos promoted under the Articles.

Still, even with such advantages, ratification was no sure thing. There was genuine and fierce opposition to the Constitution. Some states, such as Delaware and New Jersey, were burdened with heavy taxes and debts, and squeezed by high interstate duties. The Constitution held obvious appeal to such states, which could be counted on for support. Others, like Rhode Island, offered little hope to the Federalists. Four states were crucial because of their size and political strength: Massachusetts, New York, Pennsylvania, and Virginia. If one of these major states failed to ratify, even a legally constituted union of nine or more states would be shaky.

Federalist activities in some of the key states reveal the efforts they were willing to expend to get support for the Constitution. The Pennsylvania state legislature had been in session in the upstairs chamber of the Philadelphia State House even as the convention was finishing its work on the Constitution downstairs. The day after the convention adjourned, the state assembly obtained an unofficial copy of the document. The day after that, it was printed in the newspapers; and within a week, a rising tide of public opposition threatened to engulf the chances of ratification in the state. The Pennsylvania legislature threatened to swing to the anti-Federalists in upcoming elections, even before the assembly had summoned a state ratifying convention. Realizing the danger of allowing a legislature dominated by anti-Federalists to set up the procedures for electing the ratifying convention, the Federalists pushed a motion calling for a ratification convention even though the Continental Congress had yet to officially present the Constitution to the states for approval. Sensing their opportunity, nineteen anti-Federalists bolted the chamber during a noon recess on September 29, denying the legislature a quorum and the legal ability to pass the motion. In response, the sergeant at arms of the Philadelphia legislature assembled a Federalist mob that physically carried two of the recalcitrant representatives back to the chamber, forced them into their seats, and barred the doors! The two captives were enough to muster a quorum, and the Federalists passed the necessary motions to secure a ratifying convention (Morgan 1992, 150–151).

Even in relatively open and free debate, the Federalists often faced tough opposition. In Virginia, Madison, with the able assistance of future Supreme Court Justice John Marshall, had to take on the formidable opposition of Patrick Henry and future president James Monroe. Although he was not a participant at the state convention, Washington's influence was clearly felt in Virginia's 89 to 79 vote for approval. The vote in New York was 30 to 27 in favor of ratification.

With the major states in the fold, the Federalists had their victory, and the other states eventually fell in line to make approval unanimous. Prompted by concerns about the secession of its major city, Providence, reluctant Rhode Island finally approved the new Constitution in May 1790. The pangs of the formation and adoption struggle were over.

Constitutional Principles

What had the Federalists created? What were the underlying objectives of the Constitution, and what democratic ideals and purposes did it embody? Embedded in the document approved by the states are a set of values and goals shared by the delegates to the Constitutional Convention. These were most clearly articulated by Madison, who—along with Hamilton and John Jay—wrote the best-known explanation and defense of the Constitution. The **Federalist Papers** were originally published as a series of political essays under the pseudonym Publius with the express purpose of persuading New Yorkers to ratify the proposed Constitution. They were subsequently published together as *The Federalist,* and they remain the single best source for understanding the justifications for the political institutions and processes the Constitution established.

Madison wrote thirty of the eighty-five essays, and his contributions make clear that the democratic value he cherished most was liberty: the individual's right to choose reasonable goals and the means to reach those goals. Madison also recognized that unchecked liberty could cause problems. Freedom to pursue individual goals and the means to achieve them meant there would be an uneven distribution of wealth; some people would be better at acquiring worldly goods than others.

Madison was very much attached to the notion of private property rights, which he saw as the cornerstone of his notion of political freedom. Yet he also reasoned that the unequal distribution of property could cause problems. In *Federalist Number 10* (all essays in *The Federalist* are titled by the order of their original publication), he observed that societies naturally divide into various factions. He defined **faction** as "a number of citizens, whether amounting to a majority or a minority of the whole, who are united and actuated by some common impulse of passion, or of interests, adverse to the right of other citizens, or to the permanent and aggregate interests of the community." The causes of factions are numerous and can include religious and political differences. But Madison argued that "the most common and durable source of factions has been the . . . unequal distribution of property. Those who hold and those who are without property have ever formed distinct interests in society. Those who are creditors and those who are debtors, fall under a like discrimination." Yet, Madison did not divide the world into two simple classes, the rich and the poor. He viewed property as a distinguishing characteristic of a variety of groups, all willing to act in their own self-interest to the detriment of the interests of others.

The existence of factions sets up a difficult problem that is sometimes called the **Madisonian dilemma:** How can self-interested individuals administering stronger governmental powers be prevented from using those powers to destroy the freedoms that government is supposed to protect? Madison and his contemporaries were under no illusions about the civic altruism of their fellow citizens. They thought the rich would use political power to exploit the poor, and the poor would plunder the rich; those attached to one religious belief or partisan agenda would similarly use power to force their beliefs on others with little regard for their individual liberties.

To avoid these ugly consequences, Madison saw two options: either remove the cause of factions or control the effects. He rejected the first option as not only impossible but also repellent. The only way to remove the cause of factions is to eliminate individual differences and give everyone the same "common impulse of passion, or of interests." Individual differences are rooted in human nature and nothing, least of all government, will make them disappear. So Madison turned to the other option — controlling the effect of factions. He believed minority factions posed little difficulty, because the majority could always protect its interest by voting them down. The more serious threats are factions that constitute a majority. Madison realized that a majority of his fellow citizens were capable of quashing or persecuting a minority to serve their own interests. As Madison put it, the grand objective of the constitutional undertaking was "To secure the public good and private rights against the danger of such a faction, and at the same time to preserve the spirit and form of popular government."

To achieve this goal, Madison rejected morals or religion as an effective check on the self-interested appetites of humans. Since "men are not angels," society itself would have to take on the job of blunting and controlling the opinions and wishes of a majority that threaten private rights and the public good.

He argued that this restraint could be best accomplished through a **republican form of government,** which is defined primarily as representative government.[3]

---

[3]This discussion describes the Founders' view of republican government and does not necessarily describe the platforms and principles of any contemporary political party that may use the name.

The two primary goals of republican government are to create a government that governs with the consent of the governed while at the same time limiting a tyrannical majority from using the power of government to infringe on liberty. Thus, a republic can be distinguished from a monarchy in that representatives who exercise power are responsible to the people either directly through election or indirectly through appointment by representatives who are elected. Yet, it differs from pure or direct democracy in that representatives make decisions on behalf of the people rather than allowing the people to make binding decisions directly by majority rule.

In essence, Madison was making an argument for how the U.S. Constitution would uphold the core values of democracy. Political freedom and political equality were tied to the notion of individual property rights and the right of like-minded people to pursue their own interests as they saw fit. Popular sovereignty was tied to the notion of a representative form of government and the limits of those who hold power. Majority rule was accepted, but Madison placed special emphasis on the rights of the minority.

The Constitution includes a number of features designed to incorporate and uphold these basic principles:

Written Constitution

The first feature to notice about the U.S. Constitution is that it is a written document. Recall that a constitution defines rules and powers under which government operates. It also establishes the "rule of law" so that no one, not even the lawmakers, is above the law.

Note that constitutions may be written or unwritten. Governmental powers can be established and limited in ways other than in a written document. Great Britain, for example, has an unwritten constitution. Nonetheless, writing down the basic rules and processes of government for everyone to see is one way to establish limits on governmental power: If it is written down on parchment what government can and cannot do, then it will be more apparent if government exceeds its legitimate authority. Yet words on parchment alone cannot prevent abuse of power. Traffic lights, for example, are generally effective in regulating the safe flow of traffic through a busy intersection. But just as a traffic light cannot prevent someone from running the light and crashing into crossing traffic, writing down powers and limitations on government cannot prevent self-interested individuals from using those powers to infringe on liberty. Thus, although the Founders provided a written constitution to create a stronger government that would remain limited, they relied on a number of other features to protect liberty.

Representative Government

One of the most important republican principles incorporated into the American Constitution is representative government. This system operates with the consent of the governed without establishing a direct democracy. A representative system allows deliberation and refinement of public views by passing the views through a body of citizens whose knowledge of the public good is superior to that of the general populace. In addition, representative government permits effective popular rule over a much larger area than direct democracy, bringing under its control a greater variety of people and interests than direct democracy. As well, representative democracy makes it difficult for groups with diverse interests to band together into a majority that could threaten the basic rights of minorities or the general public.

Fragmentation of Power

Another way to protect liberty is to divide power among a number of different institutions and offices so that no single individual has absolute power (as under a monarchy), and no single class or faction is able to control government. The Constitution fragments power in different ways.

Separation of Powers   A major feature of the Constitution aimed at pitting leaders against one another is the principle of **separation of powers.** The concept is borrowed from the French political philosopher Charles Montesquieu, who had argued that liberty is associated with the dispersal of power and tyranny with its concentration. As framed by the Constitution, separation of powers might more accurately be termed a *separation of processes.* Each of the three branches of government is authorized to carry out a separate portion of the political process: The legislature makes the laws, the executive implements them, and the judiciary interprets them.

Such ideas have been around at least since the ancient Greeks. In the American context, however, the processes are not made wholly independent of one another. Although each of the branches is assigned the major responsibility for one of these processes, each to some degree also participates in the principal activities of the others. For example, Congress has the primary responsibility for enacting legislation, but the president is authorized to recommend measures to Congress and to veto laws passed by that body. Similarly, Congress can decline to appropriate money to fund the operation of executive branch departments, and the Senate can affect the president's execution of the laws by failing to approve his nominees for major positions in the executive branch. Congress can influence the courts' interpretations of the laws through its power to define their jurisdiction, that is, the kinds of cases they are entitled to hear.

By participating in one another's major areas of responsibilities, the three branches can **check and balance** one another's influence and political power. One branch can assert and protect its own rights by withholding its support for the essential activities of another. But because the three branches are also dependent on one another, the system of shared processes also requires them to cooperate. In this fashion, separation of processes and checks and balances complement each other to achieve the desired effect in the political system. The first prevents one branch from usurping the responsibilities of another; the second allows each branch to counteract the influence of the others. The result is a fragmentation of political power. Figure 2.1 illustrates the separation and overlap of processes among the branches of government.

The separation of powers calls for more than just separation of process; it also requires separation of personnel. People who serve in one branch of government are not allowed to concurrently serve in another branch. For example, an individual may not hold a congressional office and a position in the executive branch at the same time. To allow such a practice would obviously permit power to concentrate.

Another aspect of the separation of powers doctrine reflected in the American system is the separation of **constituency.** That is, different groups choose the personnel of the three branches. As originally envisaged in the Constitution, the president would be selected by the electoral college, an independent group of electors chosen by means

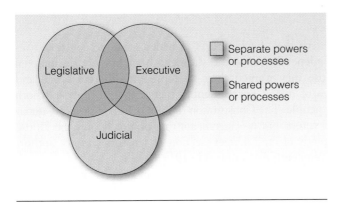

Separate powers or processes

Shared powers or processes

Figure 2.1
Separation and Overlap of Government Powers

specified by each state legislature, none of whom could be a member of Congress. Senators also were chosen by state legislatures, while members of the House of Representatives were popularly elected from smaller political districts. Members of the national courts were to be nominated by the president and confirmed by the Senate, so that a single branch of government did not choose them. Once appointed and confirmed, judges serve for a term of good behavior, which amounts to life tenure. Thus, the personnel of the three branches had largely separate and independent bases of political support and power.

Federalism   Madison conceived of another check on the majority, which we examine in detail in the next chapter. **Federalism** is the division of powers between the national government and the states. Madison's major concern is reflected in *Federalist* Number 10: "The influence of factious leaders may kindle a flame within the particular states, but they will be unable to spread a conflagration through the other states."

Thus, Madison's system for checking the evils of factionalism was to create a series of dikes to interfere with the free flow of majority will. First, majority interests are filtered by the actions of their elected representatives, who have more refined views of the public good than the voters themselves. Second, the wishes of the majority are diluted because republicanism allows the expansion of the sphere of government to take in a wide variety of interests. Moreover, the distribution of power between the national government and the state governments under federalism contains, or at least segregates, the problems of factionalism. And finally, the majority will is directed into many channels by the joint effects of federalism and the separation of powers. As Madison put it in *Federalist* Number 51:

> In the compound republic of America, the power surrendered by the people is first divided between two distinct governments, and then the portion allotted to each subdivided among distinct and separate governments. Hence a double security arises to the rights of the people. The different governments will control each other, at the same time each will be controlled by itself.

The importance of grasping this idea is fundamental to understanding the American political system. The system was designed to make it difficult for any faction, even a majority, to wield broad political power. The Constitution essentially divides the various elements of sovereignty, divides them again, and then parcels off the pieces to different institutional actors governed by different processes and characterized by different constraints. It is enormously difficult to get a government designed in such a fashion to do anything that a portion of the population opposes. The reason American government is often slow, conflict-riddled, and able to produce only brokered compromises is that it was designed to be exactly that way. The idea is to make it so difficult to bring together all those pieces the Constitution carefully distributes that it is likely to be done only in those rare circumstances when the public will and the public good are so unified as to be indistinguishable.

Mixed Government

There is good reason to believe that the Founders provided separate constituencies not only to preserve the independence of the different branches of the national government, but also because they wanted them to represent different social and economic interests. The idea of **mixed government** is that it should represent both property and the number of people. The Constitution did not mandate property qualifications for officeholders or voters, but it is significant that originally only the House of Representatives was popularly elected. Direct election of senators was not authorized until adoption of the Seventeenth Amendment in 1913.

The other offices were to some extent insulated from popular influence. As Figure 2.2 illustrates, members of the Senate were two, the president three, and the Supreme Court four steps removed from the direct control of the people. Furthermore, the longer terms of senators (six years), the president (four years), and Supreme Court members (life) would make them less subject to public pressures than members of the House of Representatives. Since fewer people were chosen for these three political bodies, they would be more prestigious than the lower house of the national legislature. This greater prestige in turn would attract more-qualified people to these bodies, and since property ownership was considered a reflection of natural ability, the individuals chosen would be those of economic substance from the upper social classes. Thus, in all

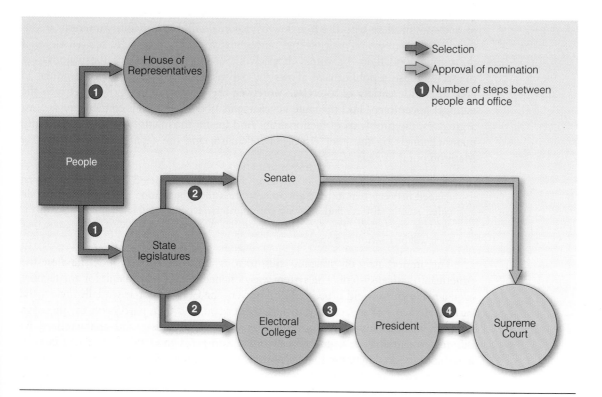

Figure 2.2
Relationship between the People and the Selection of Officeholders under the Original Constitution

probability the Founders expected the House of Representatives to represent the interests of the common people who owned no private property of consequence. The Senate—with its smaller, more prestigious membership, insulated from popular control by its longer terms of office and (then) indirect method of selection—would constitute the more aristocratic division of the legislature.

Changing the American Constitution

A constitution necessarily reflects the interests and values of the groups responsible for its original formulation. In time, new groups arise that are dissatisfied with the existing distribution of values, and they often seek to rewrite the rules of democratic governance to change this distribution. Recognizing the political motivations of such changes, humorist Will Rogers (1974, 14) once observed:

> See where there is a bill up in Congress now to change the Constitution all around. . . . It seems the men who drew up this thing years ago didn't know much and we are just now getting a bunch of real fellows who can take that old parchment and fix it up like it should have been all these years. . . . Now when they get the Constitution all fixed up they are going to start in on the Ten Commandments, just as soon as they find somebody in Washington who has read them.

Constitutional change is always political. The press of events and the emergence of different attitudes on the part of leaders and the populace occasionally create a need to alter a nation's fundamental framework. Every democratic system must provide a mechanism to achieve such accommodations, or run the risk that frustrated individuals and groups will turn to violence to achieve their goals. The question, therefore, is not whether a democratic constitution will be changed, but how. The U.S. Constitution can be changed through a formal amending process and through a number of other processes as well.

Formal Amendments

One important method of changing the Constitution is the process of formal amendment. This process consists of two distinct stages: (1) the proposal of the amendment and (2) the ratification of the amendment. The Constitution provides two options for each stage.

The two methods of proposing amendments are a two-thirds vote in both houses of Congress and a national convention called by Congress at the request of two-thirds of the states (34 of the 50 states). To date, the only method that has ever been used to propose any amendment is the first, a two-thirds vote in Congress.[4] The authority to propose amendments under this method rests exclusively with Congress; the president has neither the responsibility to sign amendments nor the authority to veto them. But the president is not prohibited from politically supporting or opposing proposed amendments. During his administration, for example, President Clinton actively lobbied members of Congress to defeat a balanced budget amendment and urged them to propose an amendment granting Washington, DC, full representation in Congress.

---

[4]The requirement is two-thirds of those present and voting, not two-thirds of the chamber's entire membership. Since amendments typically involve very important issues, however, few members miss these votes.

Since the convention method has never been used, the details of this process are largely unknown. Do two-thirds of the state legislatures have to pass resolutions with exactly the same wording, or are similar resolutions on the same issue sufficient? Is there a time limit on how long it takes for two-thirds of the states to request a convention? If a convention is called, how many delegates will attend the convention, and how will they be apportioned among the states? How will delegates be selected? Will they be popularly elected, appointed by state legislatures, or selected by state governors? Will the convention require a simple majority or a super majority (two-thirds or three-fourths) to propose amendments? Is the convention limited to proposing the amendment for which it was called, or can delegates propose additional amendments—or perhaps even become a runaway convention and rewrite the Constitution entirely, as happened in 1787?

Congress has the constitutional authority to resolve these issues, and the answers will inevitably involve political choices, not strictly legal or constitutional ones. Although the convention method of proposing amendments has never been used, it is important because the Constitution provides states with the means to initiate the formal amending process. Yet, Congress retains considerable authority to determine exactly how a convention would be called and how it would operate. (See the Promise and Policy feature "Efforts to Call a Constitutional Convention" for a brief history of this yet-to-be-used method of changing the Constitution.) Thus, proposing

The Anti-Federalists fought to establish the first ten amendments (the Bill of Rights) to the Constitution in order to protect individuals against arbitrary government action and promote political equality. Many of the later amendments are also concerned with equality, but the fight to achieve these rights was long and difficult. In the mid-1800s, Susan B. Anthony and Elizabeth Cady Stanton began what would be a fifty-year campaign to secure the right of women to vote, and both died before the Nineteenth Amendment to the Constitution was passed in 1920.

PROMISE AND POLICY
Efforts to Call a Constitutional Convention

Since the Constitution was ratified in 1789, there have been more than 400 applications from states to call a convention to propose amendments. In the first century following ratification, there were relatively few such petitions. In the last half of the twentieth century, however, applications to call constitutional conventions proliferated, with more than 90 percent of all requests being made during that time period. About half have come since the 1960s.

Applications in the last half-century have been motivated almost exclusively by conservatives outraged by liberal Supreme Court decisions on such issues as busing to achieve integration of public schools, reapportionment of congressional districts, school prayer, and abortion. Most of the time, only a handful of state legislatures pass resolutions requesting a convention, far less than the two-thirds of states necessary to oblige Congress to act. In fact, no issue has yet garnered requests from the required two-thirds of states to start the amending process. Given the difficulties of coordinating political action across a large number of state legislatures, it is perhaps not surprising that all of the amendments proposed to date have been initiated by Congress.

Some issues have come close to mustering requests from the required number of states. One is the movement to call a convention to propose an amendment requiring a balanced federal budget. Indiana was the first state to call for a convention on a balanced budget amendment in 1957. Thirty-one other states submitted similar applications, just two states short of the 34 required. The effort appeared to have stalled and seemed to be moving in reverse when Alabama rescinded its 1976 application in April 1988.

Although it has never been used, this provision of giving states the power to initiate the process of amending the constitution is important. Even if an effort falls short, the threat of a constitutional convention may pressure Congress to act, especially if the number of states calling for a convention nears the required two-thirds mark. For example, Congress proposed the amendment to allow for the direct election of senators in response to the pressure of states requesting a convention. Moreover, such calls have been instrumental in raising public consciousness about issues and have increased the pressure on politicians to propose remedies other than constitutional amendments.

Source: Weber, Paul J., and Barbara A. Perry. 1989. *Unfounded Fears: Myths and Realities of a Constitutional Convention.* Westport, CT: Greenwood Press, 2–7, 56, 74.

amendments is ultimately a political process, and Congress plays a key role regardless of the proposal method used.

Ratification is also a political process, and states determine whether a proposed amendment will be ratified. After an amendment has been proposed, it must be ratified by three-fourths of states (38) before it can become part of the Constitution. There are two ways for states to ratify amendments: by votes of state legislatures and by conventions held in the states. Congress specifies which ratification method is to be used. Only the Twenty-First Amendment (repeal of prohibition) was ratified by state conventions. In this case, there was concern that political forces favoring prohibition controlled key leadership positions in state legislatures and might be able to thwart popular support for repeal. Congress specified state conventions, apparently in the hope that they would more accurately reflect popular sentiment.

Most successful amendments were ratified within three years of being proposed (see Table 2.1). While some amendments took longer, in most cases if there is not sufficient support in the states to ratify in two to three years, the amendment is likely to die. (For a look at some proposals that did not succeed with ratification, see the Promise and Policy feature "Proposed Amendments That Were Not Ratified.") The Constitution does not

Table 2.1

Length of Time between Congressional Approval and Actual Ratification of the Twenty-Seven Amendments to the U.S. Constitution

AMENDMENT		TIME REQUIRED FOR RATIFICATION	YEAR RATIFIED
1–10	Bill of Rights	26.5 months	1791
11	Lawsuits against states	11 months	1795
12	Presidential elections	6.5 months	1804
13	Abolition of slavery	10 months	1865
14	Civil rights	25 months	1868
15	Suffrage for all races	11 months	1870
16	Income tax	42.5 months	1913
17	Senatorial elections	11 months	1913
18	Prohibition	13 months	1919
19	Women's suffrage	14 months	1920
20	Terms of office	11 months	1933
21	Repeal of prohibition	9.5 months	1933
22	Limit on presidential terms	47 months	1951
23	Washington, DC, vote	9 months	1961
24	Abolition of poll taxes	16 months	1964
25	Presidential succession	22 months	1967
26	18-year-old suffrage	3 months	1971
27	Congressional salaries	2438 months	1992
Median		**25 months**	

Sources: Congressional Research Service, *The Constitution of the United States: Analysis and Interpretation* (Washington, DC: U.S. Government Printing Office, 1973), 23–44 (92d Cong., 2d sess., S. Doc. 92–82); *Congressional Quarterly Weekly Report* (1992), 1,423.

Table adapted from Stanley, Harold W., and Richard G. Niemi. 2001. *Vital Statistics on American Politics 2001–2002.* Washington, DC: CQ Press, 303.

specify a time limit for states to act on proposed amendments, although beginning with the Eighteenth Amendment (proposed in 1917) Congress instituted a seven-year deadline on ratification.[5] Amendments proposed before 1917 had no time limits; it was generally considered that such proposals were dead if the states did not act within a reasonable time so a "contemporaneous consensus" would be reflected in the decision.

[5]Initially, Congress placed the time limit in the body of the amendment. With the proposal of the Twenty-Third Amendment in 1960, the deadline was placed in the submission resolution. The importance of the change is that resolutions are not bound by the two-thirds rule in order to pass; a simple majority is enough because they are not a formal part of the amendment. Thus, when the seven-year limit on the Equal Rights Amendment (proposed in 1971) was about to expire, Congress extended it for three more years on a simple majority vote. In 1978, when Congress proposed an amendment to treat Washington, DC, like a state for purposes of representation, it reverted to the practice of placing the time limit in the body of the amendment.

PROMISE AND POLICY
Proposed Amendments That Were Not Ratified

Only thirty-three of the thousands of constitutional amendments introduced in Congress since 1789 were submitted to the states for ratification. Twenty-seven of these were ratified and added to the Constitution. Six have not become amendments. Congress set a time limit of seven years for the required three-fourths of states to ratify most of these proposals. But there are still four proposals with no time-limit provisions that theoretically could be ratified. It is unlikely that any of these will surface again because their central issues have been addressed in statutes passed by Congress or by other amendments. The other two proposals failed when their time limits expired.

The four proposed amendments with no time limits deal with apportionment of U.S. representatives, the issue of titles of nobility for citizens, slavery, and child labor. One of these was among a total of twelve proposals submitted by the First Congress. It dealt with apportionment of House districts, providing for one representative for every 30,000 people until there were 100 members in the House, at which time Congress would regulate the proportion until the size reached 200 members. At that point, Congress could increase the size beyond 200 so that each representative would represent no more than 50,000 people. The last recorded action on this amendment was ratification by Connecticut and Georgia in 1939; to date, only 12 states have ratified the amendment. Today, membership in the House is capped at 435 by a statute

passed by Congress. Every ten years, after the census, the 435 House seats are reapportioned among the states, with some states losing and others gaining seats depending on whether the state's population has grown or declined. Once the seats are reapportioned, the actual drawing of congressional districts is the responsibility of state legislatures. With the size of the House fixed at 435, each member represents a district containing about 620,000 people. If the proposed limit of 50,000 constituents per member of Congress were followed, the House would need about 5,400 members to represent a population of 270 million.

Another amendment without a time limit concerns U.S. citizens' use of titles of nobility and other honors bestowed by foreign governments and monarchs. The proposed amendment, passed by Congress on May 1, 1810, would have denationalized any U.S. citizen who accepted honors or titles of nobility without prior congressional approval. Twelve states ratified this amendment, one short of the 13 required at the time it was submitted. As more states were admitted to the Union, the number required to validate the amendment increased: Louisiana became the eighteenth state in 1812, increasing to 14 the number of additional states necessary to reach the three-fourths requirement. The issue has subsequently been dealt with by statute. For example, naturalized citizens must renounce titles or orders of nobility according to a law passed in 1906. An 1881 law limited congressional approval of honors to the

acceptance of a "decoration or other thing," since the awarding of such honors by other governments cannot be prevented. In 1958, Congress passed a law authorizing retired U.S. government personnel "to accept and wear . . . decorations, orders, medals, emblems, presents and other things" (Private Law 85–704).

Congress proposed another constitutional amendment with no time limit on March 2, 1861. It stated that no constitutional amendments could authorize Congress to interfere with state laws regarding slavery. This amendment was proposed as a gesture of compromise in an effort to avert the attempted secession of southern states. Only three states ratified it. It was rendered moot by the conclusion of the Civil War and ratification of the Thirteenth Amendment abolishing slavery. Two interesting procedural details are associated with this proposal. One is that President James Buchanan signed the amendment, but presidential approval of constitutional amendments is unnecessary. Another is that although Congress specified that the state legislatures were to decide about ratification, Illinois ratified the amendment in a constitutional convention. This irregularity did not generate much controversy, since the number of states ratifying was so far short of the required number.

The last amendment with no time limit was proposed on June 2, 1924. It would have given Congress power to regulate child labor. Although Congress established the practice of attaching time limits in 1917, it did not attach a time limit to this proposal. Only 28 states have ratified the proposal. The ratification process provoked controversy that ended up in the Supreme Court when the state of Kansas first rejected the amendment in 1925 but then reconsidered and ratified it

continued

continued

twelve years later. In the case of *Coleman v. Miller* (1939), the Supreme Court held that Congress has the ultimate authority to decide whether there will be a time limit and whether a proposed amendment has been properly ratified by the requisite number of states. The record of state actions on proposed amendments reflects changing attitudes about child labor. Both state and federal statutes now regulate child labor.

Two proposals failed when the time limit set by Congress expired. One of these, known as the Equal Rights Amendment (ERA), was submitted to the states in 1972 with a seven-year time limit. The core provision was a mere twenty-two words: "Equality of rights under the law shall not be denied by the United States or by any State on account of sex." The proposal had wide initial support, and 22 of the necessary 38 states ratified it in the first year after it was proposed. But momentum stalled as opponents organized.

When the time limit expired in 1979, only 13 more states had ratified the amendment, three short of the necessary number. Some states that had ratified the amendment passed resolutions rescinding the earlier action, although given the ruling in *Coleman*, it is not clear that states may retract ratification. Just as time was about to expire, Congress extended the limit to 1982. No additional states ratified the proposal in this period. Some supporters of the ERA argue that if three more states were to ratify the amendment, Congress could certify that it has been ratified by the required number of states even though the time limit has expired. Such action seems unlikely and would certainly provoke controversy.

The final proposal that failed to be ratified concerned congressional representation for Washington, DC. Since the citizens of Washington, DC, are not part of any state, they have no voting representatives in Congress. The House allows the

citizens of the nation's capital to send a nonvoting delegate, but they have no voice in the Senate. The amendment proposed in 1978 would have treated the District of Columbia as if it were a state for purposes of representation and in voting for president and vice president. This means that the residents would have had two senators, at least one representative, and the same number of electoral votes as states with similar populations. When the time limit expired in 1985, only a handful of states had ratified the amendment. Congress had inserted the time limit in the amendment itself, rather than putting it in a separate transmittal resolution as was done with the ERA. Any extension of the time, therefore, would require a two-thirds vote.

Source: Virginia Commission on Constitutional Government. 1961. *The Constitution of the United States of America.* Richmond, VA: Virginia Commission on Constitutional Government.

The absence of a deadline presented an interesting political dilemma in one case. Reacting to a political furor over congressional pay hikes in the 1990s, Michigan and New Jersey dusted off an old proposal and became the thirty-eighth and thirty-ninth states to approve the Twenty-Seventh Amendment, which requires an election to intervene before a congressional pay raise can take effect. This amendment was originally submitted to the states along with other proposals that became the Bill of Rights, and its May 7, 1992, ratification came 203 years after its proposal!

The anti-Federalists were primarily responsible for the first ten amendments, which are mostly concerned with political freedom and political equality. They were concerned with **civil liberties,** protecting individuals against arbitrary government action. Many of the remaining amendments revolve around the central democratic value of equality. The Thirteenth, Fourteenth, and Fifteenth Amendments relate to race, while the Nineteenth, Twenty-Third, Twenty-Fourth, and Twenty-Sixth govern the voting rights of women, residents of the District of Columbia, people who live in jurisdictions where a poll tax is levied, and citizens between the ages of 18 and 21. These amendments were designed to safeguard disadvantaged groups' access to the political process and the social and economic life of the United States. It is important to note that this set of amendments primarily affects the states, not the national government.

The Seventeenth and Twenty-Second Amendments also relate to political participation, but they deal with the suffrage rights of all voters, not particular groups. The Seventeenth Amendment provides for direct election of senators, thus allowing all voters to choose members of the upper house of the national legislature. The Twenty-Second Amendment limits the length of presidential terms by preventing voters from choosing the same person more than twice. The two amendments are based on somewhat different assumptions about human capacities: the Seventeenth expresses faith in the electorate's ability to choose good senators; the Twenty-Second reflects a fear that voters may fall victim to the entreaties of a demagogue.

Four of the amendments—the Eleventh, Twelfth, Twentieth, and Twenty-Fifth—bear no particular imprint of group influence or political philosophy. Rather, these amendments relate to changes brought about by the press of particular historical events and primarily deal with the structure and procedures of government. For example, the Twelfth Amendment specifies that members of the electoral college cast separate ballots for president and vice president. This amendment was a direct result of the election of 1800, in which Thomas Jefferson and Aaron Burr—the presidential and vice presidential candidates of the same party—received the same number of votes in the electoral college; the Twelfth Amendment clarifies that electors cast separate votes for president and vice president. The Twentieth Amendment reduces the time between the election and inauguration of the president and vice president.

Two other amendments alter powers and procedures of the national government. The Sixteenth allows the federal government to levy an income tax, and, as already discussed, the Twenty-Seventh limits the authority of members of Congress to give themselves a pay raise by requiring an election to intervene before the raise can go into effect. The remaining two amendments—the Eighteenth and Twenty-First—result in no net change by first establishing and then repealing prohibition of alcohol.

Although amendments have produced important changes in the Constitution, only twenty-seven amendments have made it past the hurdles embedded in the process, and of these, ten came at once and two counteract each other. Thus, in more than two centuries, the Constitution has undergone lasting formal alteration on only fifteen occasions. But the formal amendment process does not begin to tell the full story of the vast changes that have occurred in the functions, procedures, and structure of the American political system over this period. These changes have been a result of processes other than amending the Constitution—specifically, of custom and usage and of interpretation by officials of the three branches of the national government.

Custom and Usage

Constitutional change through **custom and usage** occurs when practices and institutions not mentioned in the formal document evolve in response to political needs and alter the operation of the political system. For example, political parties are not mentioned in the Constitution. Indeed, the Founders probably viewed parties as examples of the factions Madison discussed in *Federalist* Number 10. Nonetheless, political parties developed soon after ratification in response to the demands of electoral politics. Although not formal government institutions, parties have fundamentally altered the way government works. For example, members of Congress are chosen in partisan elections, and Congress itself is organized along party lines.

Political parties have also changed the way the electoral college operates. The Founders created the electoral college in part because they did not trust ordinary citizens to exercise sound judgment in choosing a president. The Constitution mandated that "Each state shall appoint, in such manner as the Legislature thereof may direct" a number of electors equal to its number of senators and representatives (Article II, Section 1). Each state originally appointed one slate of electors. As political parties developed, they began nominating slates of partisan electors, and the popular vote in a state now determines which party's electors cast that state's electoral votes for president. Thus, while the constitutional provisions governing the electoral college have not been significantly altered by formal amendment,[6] the operation of the electoral college has changed significantly from the original intent of the Founders; it has become more democratic through a process of custom and usage.

Executive Interpretation

The Constitution contains three types of powers. **Enumerated powers** are powers that are explicitly granted to government or to a particular institution. Article I, Section 8, for example, lists the powers of Congress (power to declare war, raise an army and navy, coin money, regulate interstate commerce, and so on), and Article II enumerates specific powers of the chief executive (commander-in-chief of the army and navy, the power to make treaties—with the advice and consent of the Senate—to see that the laws are faithfully executed, to receive ambassadors and other public ministers, and so forth). **Implied powers** are those not formally specified by the Constitution but rather are inferred from the powers that are formally specified. Implied powers flow from the "necessary and proper" clause in Article I, Section 8, which empowers the national government to make other laws that are "necessary and proper for carrying into Execution the foregoing Powers and all other Powers vested by this Constitution in the Government of the United States, or in any Department or Officer thereof." **Inherent powers** (or *prerogative powers*) are not derived from either enumerated or implied powers but are those that are essential to the functioning of government or a particular office.

Although the formal powers of the president have changed little since George Washington first exercised them, the political powers of the presidency have expanded significantly through executive interpretation. Such interpretation derives mainly from the concept of inherent or prerogative powers; presidents have claimed them as an essential characteristic of the executive office. An early example of executive interpretation occurred when George Washington interpreted the power to "receive ambassadors and other public ministers" to mean that the president also had the authority to

---

[6]The Twelfth Amendment specified that electors were to cast separate votes for president and vice president, but this provision did not change the goal of removing selection of the president from direct popular control.

recognize foreign governments. This interpretation significantly expanded presidential powers beyond those specifically enumerated. Perhaps the best-known example is **executive privilege,** the right of the president to withhold information on matters of national sensitivity or personal privacy. Another example is the president's ability to dismiss high-ranking members of the executive branch. There is nothing in the Constitution about the procedure for removing executive branch officials. Does the president have the power to do this unilaterally as part of his power as chief executive, or is the Senate's approval also required? That issue surfaced as a factor in the impeachment action against President Andrew Johnson shortly after the Civil War and eventually led to a number of court decisions after Presidents Woodrow Wilson and Franklin Roosevelt also removed key executive officials.

Legislative Interpretation

Each time Congress enacts legislation, it must interpret the Constitution. Some laws passed by Congress are so far-reaching that they fundamentally alter the responsibility and functions of the government. For example, the Social Security Act of 1935 involved the federal government in basic social welfare services, and the Employment Act of 1946 gave the national government responsibility to use its power to promote economic prosperity and full employment. Both laws were highly controversial when first enacted, and opponents argued that they were beyond the constitutional scope of government. Congress's interpretation prevailed. Today, government's responsibility in these areas is generally accepted.

Judicial Interpretation

Judicial review refers to the power of courts to declare the acts and actions of legislatures and executives unconstitutional. It is an extraordinary power that seems to challenge the democratic values of popular sovereignty and majority rule. And nowhere does the Constitution explicitly grant courts the authority to nullify the actions of elected officials. In a prime example of constitutional change through judicial interpretation, the Supreme Court itself claimed the power of judicial review in 1803 in the case of *Marbury v. Madison,* which is discussed in detail in Chapter 15.

It is hard to overstate the importance of judicial interpretation on the American political process. For example, Supreme Court interpretations of the "equal protection of the laws" clause of the Fourteenth Amendment has altered the composition of both the House of Representatives and state legislatures and also revolutionized race relations in this nation. Judicial interpretation has promoted political and social equality in American life.

Thus, the U.S. Constitution has contributed both to the stability and the flexibility of the American political system. The relative difficulty of the formal amendment process has helped ensure that fundamental aspects of governmental functions, procedures, and structure will not be easily altered. At the same time, the brevity and ambiguity of many parts of the document have enabled the constitutional system to change through custom and usage and interpretation, thus allowing it to adapt to the new challenges that arise over time.

Performance Assessment

The U.S. Constitution is a remarkable piece of political engineering that well deserves its common description as a living document. It has provided an enduring institutional foundation for the political process in the United States, while retaining a remarkable degree of adaptability to the shifting needs of the polity.

The original document reflected two of the Founders' concerns. The first was national unity—the necessity for drawing together the disparate interests of the states. In this respect, the United States was faced with the same major problem that preoccupies leaders of most emerging democracies: providing some sense of national identity for a people with deep economic, regional, and social divisions. Such divisions or factions, to use Madison's terminology, threatened the very existence of the American political system.

The second concern was the protection of private property against the incursion of majority rule. For the Founders, property ownership was linked to individual liberty, their most cherished value. They clearly perceived that the most significant threat to this value, and the great danger of democratic rule, was the power of an unchecked majority. In essence they were centrally concerned with how two core democratic values—majority rule and political freedom—could be accommodated in a political system. The Constitution tends to emphasize political freedom over majority rule. At a minimum, it clearly reflects the desire to place obstacles in the path of majority factions.

Debates over which of these concerns—national unity or property rights—was most important to the Founders are largely meaningless. The two were inexorably linked in their thinking. They believed that a young nation could not survive interstate commercial rivalries, uncertainties involving the collection of debts, and a worthless currency. The charges raised by some scholars that the Founders' prime motivation in writing the Constitution was to protect their own personal property interests rather than to promote the public good thus miss an important point. To the Founders, there was no real difference between personal property rights and the public good. They believed that the ownership of property gave people a stake in society and hence made them better citizens. Like most people, they tended to identify their own interests with the interests of society as a whole. Property rights for the Founders were the cornerstone of individual liberty, and as the basis of individual liberty they were necessarily the foundation for political freedom. It is political freedom and minority rights that the Constitution champions above all else.

To some extent, the constitutional movement represented a reaction against some of the democratic values and assumptions of the Revolutionary period. Ironically, the same political philosopher, John Locke, provided much of the intellectual ammunition for both movements. The earlier era espoused Locke's concepts of majority rule and legislative supremacy. The Founders stressed Locke's concern with property rights and his recognition of executive prerogatives.

In place of government dominated by legislatures that were closely tied to the public by short terms of office, forced rotation in office, and recall, the Founders sought to substitute a political system with three rival branches that were removed in different degrees from direct public control and that were responsive to different interests. They favored a mixed government reflecting the interests of both the few with property and the many without. Although they rejected the principles of direct democracy, they also turned their backs on monarchy and on oligarchic control of society by members of the upper class. Even given the flaws that are obvious to the modern eye—the perpetuation of slavery being the most obvious and notable—the system created by the Founders was still the most democratic of its day.

An analysis of the American constitutional system thus indicates that the original rules were written primarily by groups interested in protecting property rights (seen as the basis of political freedom) and avoiding what they viewed as the harmful effects of direct democracy. The major changes that have been made to the original constitutional system over the years have tended to come from groups concerned with civil liberties and from those who desire to grant historically excluded groups greater access to the democratic process. In other words, political equality—the core value perhaps least stressed by the framers of the Constitution—has dominated much of the political debate concerning changes to the Constitution.

Summary

- The constitution of a democratic nation provides the basic principles that determine the conduct of its political affairs. Generally, constitutions lay down the institutional framework of government and specify the government's powers and responsibilities and the procedures used in exercising or fulfilling these powers and responsibilities. Constitutions establish a set of legal relationships between the leaders and the led by determining the rules for access and exercising political power.
- The Articles of Confederation served as the first constitution of the United States. Ratified in 1777, the Articles of Confederation established a political system with a weak central government headed by the Continental Congress and strong state governments. Legislatures tended to be the dominant political institutions.
- Civil unrest and the inability of the national government to respond to economic priorities fueled a movement to create a stronger national government. Those who favored a new constitution giving more power to the national government were called Federalists; those opposed were known as anti-Federalists.
- Two events in the fall of 1786 provided the Federalists with the opportunity to create a stronger national government. First, state delegates at an interstate trade meeting sent a report to the Continental Congress calling for a convention to revise the Articles of Confederation. Second, Shays' Rebellion, an armed insurrection by Massachusetts farmers, raised fears that the republic would dissolve without stronger central authority.
- In February 1787, the Continental Congress called on the states to send delegates to a convention in Philadelphia for the purpose of amending the Articles of Confederation. Delegates quickly abandoned the attempt to revise the Articles of Confederation and decided to write a new constitution.
- The key characteristic of the delegates is that they were primarily Federalists. They constituted a political elite who agreed that the national government should be more powerful. Although there was disagreement about specifics, there was enough common ground for acceptable compromises to be reached.

- The Constitution produced by the delegates was characterized by the principles of republican (or representative) government, separation of power, and checks and balances. These principles were designed to prevent a single faction from controlling the government and abusing its power, thus preserving individual liberty and preventing tyranny of the majority.
- A stronger national government was created, with power divided among three coequal branches. The legislative, executive, and judicial branches each had some ability to check abuses of power by the other branches.
- Power was also decentralized by creating a federal system in which the national government was granted limited powers and states retained sovereignty in other jurisdictions. This was formalized by the Tenth Amendment, adopted after the Constitution was ratified.
- The Constitution had to be approved by nine states to be ratified. The ratification battle was a bruising political contest. The Federalists just managed to pull out majorities in several key states. Rhode Island was the last state to ratify in May 1790, and the Constitution was officially ratified and took force in May 1791.
- There are several ways to change the Constitution. It can be changed by formal amendment; by custom and usage; and through legislative, executive, and judicial interpretation.

Key Terms

anti-Federalists 38	Federalist Papers 43
Articles of Confederation 35	Federalists 37
bicameral 41	implied powers 56
check and balance 46	inherent powers (prerogative
civil liberties 54	powers) 56
Connecticut Compromise	judicial review 57
(Great Compromise) 41	Madisonian dilemma 44
constituency 46	mixed government 48
constitution 32	New Jersey plan 41
custom and usage 55	reciprocity 32
enumerated powers 56	republican form of government 44
executive privilege 57	separation of powers 46
faction 44	Virginia plan 40
federalism 47	

Selected Readings

Bowen, Catherine Drinker. 1966. *Miracle at Philadelphia: The Story of the Constitutional Convention.* Boston: Little, Brown. One of the most accessible and thorough treatments of the Constitutional Convention, including the events that led up to it and the battles that followed.

Collier, Christopher, and James Lincoln Collier. 1986. *Decision in Philadelphia. The Constitutional Convention of 1787.* New York: Ballantine. A highly readable account of the struggle to create the Constitution. It includes an explanation of the events leading up to the convention, includes portraits of the key figures, and provides rich detail about issues and controversies.

Morgan, Edmund S. 1992. *The Birth of the Republic: 1763–89.* Chicago: University of Chicago Press. A succinct and informative introduction to the historical context that led to independence and the formation of a new country and political system.

Webster, Mary E., ed. 1999. *The Federalist Papers. In Modern Language, Indexed for Today's Political Issues.* Bellevue, MA: Merrill Press. This book attempts to translate the arguments of the Federalist Papers into contemporary language more accessible to the modern reader. It also seeks to highlight the continuing relevance of these arguments by linking them to contemporary political issues.

3 | Federalism

In March 2003, John Anthony and Russell Smith, both of Beaumont, Texas, went before state District Judge Tom Mulvaney with an unusual request: The two men wanted a divorce. Anthony and Smith had entered into a civil union under the laws of Vermont in 2002, a legal arrangement between same-sex couples that provides some of the same benefits of marriage. Texas law, however, recognizes marriage only as a union between a man and a woman and does not recognize civil unions at all. This presented Judge Mulvaney with a dilemma: If Anthony and Smith were not married in the eyes of Texas law, could they get a divorce?

Yes, said Mulvaney. Texas was obligated to recognize contracts entered into in other states as legal and binding. Even though civil unions were not recognized by Texas, the state had to recognize the lawful standing of the domestic partnership. He issued a divorce decree.

No, said Texas Attorney General Greg Abbott, whose office intervened in the proceeding to protest Mulvaney's decision. If there is no marriage or any other legalized domestic partnership according to Texas law, Texas courts have no jurisdiction and thus cannot issue divorce decrees for gay couples, even if their relationship is legally recognized according to the laws of another state. Mulvaney bowed to the pressure of the attorney general and vacated his decision (Cox 2003).

During the past decade the question of gay marriage/unions has precipitated a flurry of legislative activity in dozens of state capitals, led to confusion and conflicting decisions in state courts, impelled the U.S. Congress to intervene in a legal matter historically the province of the states, and prompted politicians at all levels of government to raise public defenses of traditional family arrangements (Kersh 1997). Many believe that government sanction of same-sex unions is a threat to the legal, economic, and social standing of traditional families. Many others believe that denying same-sex couples the legal benefits of marriage amounts to little more than discrimination. But viewing the fight as either a defense of traditional family values or as a struggle to achieve equality before the law is only half the story: The underlying issue is the obligation one state has to honor and enforce legal agreements made under the laws of another state.

In practical terms, the legal status of same-sex unions boils down to a question of portability: If gay unions are recognized by the laws of one state, must those unions have legal standing in all states? If the answer is yes, only one state has to legally recognize gay marriage or some form of equivalent domestic partnership for same-sex unions to have legal standing everywhere. Thus, the gay marriage controversy in large measure turns on a matter of federalism, specifically Article IV, Section 1 of the U.S. Constitution. This section, under the "full faith and credit" clause, requires that every state uphold the "public acts, records and judicial proceedings" of all the other states, and it gives Congress the power to "prescribe the manner in which such acts, records and proceedings shall be proved." Under the "full faith and credit" clause, if 1 state sanctions gay marriages, the remaining 49 states might also have to recognize those unions as legal and binding. Thus, Mulvaney faced the question: If a gay couple goes to Vermont and enters into a civil union, does whatever state they return to have to recognize that union as legal even if same-sex unions are specifically outlawed by the state they reside in?

The federal government has tried to make sure that the answer to this question is no. In 1996 Congress passed the Defense of Marriage Act, which places limits on the "full faith and credit" clause (*Congressional Digest* 1996, 263). In effect, the federal government said the "full faith and credit" clause did not apply to marriages that involved two people of the same sex. Yet the Supreme Court has struck down laws designed to allow states to find loopholes in the "full faith and credit" clause. As this is written, the question of gay marriage—and divorce—is very much unresolved.

Who wins the debate hinges on the federalism issue. Same-sex marriages are almost certainly not what the Founders had in mind when they created the organizational framework of U.S. government. Nonetheless, the gay marriage controversy serves as an apt metaphor for the consequences of that framework: a complicated and politically charged give-and-take between governments over who gets to decide public policy.

 ## The Promise of Federalism

Federalism is a political system where regional governments share power with the national government. It is the primary institutional feature of the United States Constitution. According to the Tenth Amendment, powers "not delegated to the United States by the Constitution, nor prohibited by it to the states, are reserved to the states respectively, or to the people." Essentially, what this provision means is that states are sovereign governments. They get their power from their citizens and are not subordinate to the national government. At least in legal principle, states are coequal and independent partners in the governing process. As long as they do not contravene other sections of the Constitution, they are free to enact laws as they see fit. Thus, they are not prohibited from allowing same-sex marriages (Massachusetts actually became the first state to legally sanction gay marriages in 2004). In practice, as the politics surrounding gay marriage demonstrates, the division of power in the United States is a complicated and contentious business.

In a very real sense, the argument about the appropriate roles of state and national governments that lay at the heart of the struggle between Federalists and anti-Federalists has never been fully resolved. Defining those roles is at the center of many important political struggles. States still seek to protect their independence from one another and from federal encroachment, and the federal government still struggles to provide the regulatory uniformity that characterizes a nation-state.

The relationship between levels of government can be characterized as a struggle over what level of government has the constitutional authority to decide who gets what. Both conservatives and liberals can take one side or the other of the issue, depending on what is at stake. Some conservatives, for example, often echo anti-Federalist arguments championing states rights. Yet on some issues, like gay marriage, they are quick to support sweeping legal intervention by the federal government. Some liberals turn to the federal government to provide uniform solutions to important issues, such as civil rights, but prefer leaving other issues, like gay marriage, with the states.

Understanding the division of power in the United States and how it affects relationships among the institutional actors in the political system is an important prerequisite to understanding the sometimes-complicated nature of American politics. The performance of American democracy is wedded to the promises embedded in the federalist system. To that end, this chapter provides a basic grounding in federalism by outlining the various ways political power can be divided, detailing the federal system adopted in the United States, tracing the evolution of state–federal relationships, and examining the consequences of these arrangements.

In the United States the basic promise of federalism is to preserve the right of the states to be autonomous and independent governments that are accountable to their own citizens rather than to the national government. This means the states share with

Same-sex marriages performed in California and Massachusetts in 2004 caused great controversy. Although marriage laws have traditionally been under the control of the states, many push for federal control over the same-sex marriage issue in the form of a constitutional amendment.

the national government the responsibility for living up to the promise of democracy. In other words, the four core values must be upheld not just in Washington, DC, but in all 50 state capitals. There are a number of reasons why the Founders wanted states to share this responsibility, to be partners of the federal government rather than its subordinates. Key among these was the idea that having strong and independent states would help prevent the federal government from gaining too much power and threatening the rights of citizens. Americans have always feared concentrations of power, and dividing power between the states and the federal government was an attempt to provide balance. If the states remained sovereign governments, power remained closer to the people and thus less likely to be used against their will. Thus, in its general design, this system of sharing power is based on upholding core democratic values.

Dividing Political Power

All political systems divide and delegate power. What distinguishes these systems is how power is divided. There are three basic ways to divide power between a central (national) government and regional governments, and these produce three distinct methods of organizing a political system: confederal, unitary, and federal.

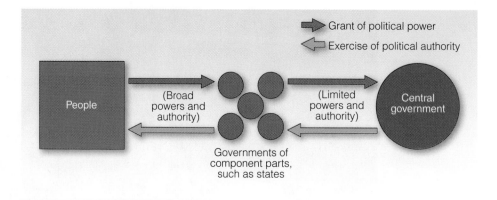

Figure 3.1
Confederation

Confederation

In a **confederation,** the central government is not sovereign. In other words, it receives no direct grant of power from citizens. It can only exercise the authority granted to it by regional governments. Thus, in a confederal system, the central government is subordinate to the regional governments. A familiar example of a confederal system is the United States under the Articles of Confederation. The original Congress could not exercise direct control over people or states in order to enforce its authority. It had to rely on state governments to provide money and troops for the Revolutionary War, and it needed state courts to enforce its laws. Figure 3.1 illustrates relationships in a confederation.

Besides a relatively weak central government, two other features are usually associated with a confederation. One is the right of a component government to voluntarily withdraw from the larger union. The second is a requirement for all members of the union to consent to any change in the division of powers between the two levels of government.

A modern-day example of a confederation is the United Nations. In this body, nation-states—such as the United States, Mexico, and Kenya—are the component governments, while the United Nations itself is the central political unit. The UN possesses the basic features of a confederation: It exercises only those powers granted to it by its members; its authority is small compared to that retained by the nation-states; it depends on voluntary contributions of money and military forces for its operations; it cannot force its provisions on individual members; and nations are free to withdraw from it at any time.

Unitary Government

In a **unitary system,** only the central government is sovereign. The central government may create regional governments, but these local units can exercise only the powers delegated and authorized by the central government (Figure 3.2). The central government retains the most extensive and important powers, and it may reduce or take

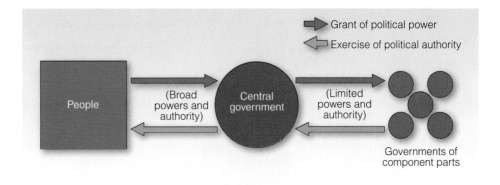

Figure 3.2
Unitary System

back any powers it grants to the lower political units. Most countries have unitary governments, as do the individual states of our own nation. Villages, cities, counties, and school districts in the United States are not sovereign; they exercise only the powers allowed them by state government. These local governments do not have the power to block any changes in state–local relationships, nor can they legally withdraw from the jurisdiction of state government.

Federalism

Standing somewhere between the confederate and unitary options is federalism, a system in which central and regional governments share sovereignty. Each level of government has its own jurisdiction and set of responsibilities. In the American system, for example, neither the national government nor the government of any individual state is dependent on the other for its political power. The same is true of other federal systems. Provinces in Canada, cantons in Sweden, and *lander* in Germany all have power bases independent of their national governments. Figure 3.3 illustrates federal relationships.

The most important features of a federal system are (1) that each level of government is granted power directly by the constitution and (2) that each level possesses and exercises some powers that are legally independent of the other. A federal system has two other essential characteristics. First, both levels of government must participate in any decision to change the division of powers between them. For example, in the United States the states must play a role in amending the federal Constitution. Second, the component parts are not free to voluntarily leave the union. This was the major legal issue underlying the American Civil War. The southern states claimed that they had the right to secede from the Union, while the northern states disagreed. The question was decided in favor of the North both on the battlefield and in the courtroom.

Though confederal, unitary, and federal systems are clearly distinct from one another, there is considerable variation in how power is distributed within each of these categories. As weak as the national government was under the Articles of Confederation, it had much more power than the United Nations has today. Both France and Great Britain have unitary governments, but counties and towns exercise more power in

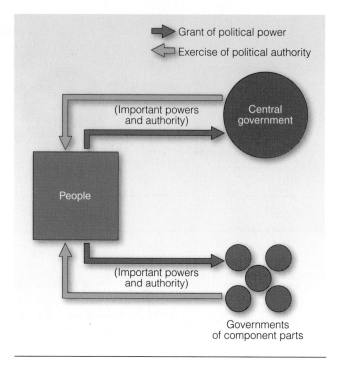

Figure 3.3
Federalism

Great Britain than in France because of the British tradition of local self-government. What keeps the categories distinct is the basis of power; the government that is sovereign reigns supreme. Technically, the powers that the central authorities in Great Britain grant to local governments today can be legally withdrawn tomorrow. The national government of the United States has no legal basis to remove the power of the states.

Advantages and Disadvantages of Federalism

For the Founders, a federal system was not just a principled philosophical choice; it was the only option that made sense given their experience and the demands of their political environment. The difficulties in waging a war and founding a nation under the Articles of Confederation made clear to them the limitations of a confederacy. And most of the Founders had no intention of reestablishing a unitary system along British lines; as colonists, they had learned to fear the concentration of power that is a central characteristic of unitary government. Also, as anti-Federalist sentiments ran high in many states, politically it was clear that if the Constitution stood any chance of ratification, the states would have to retain a good deal of independence from the central government.

In opting for a federal system, however, the Founders were doing more than bowing to the demands of their political environment. They made a conscious choice to create a political system that trades off some goals against others.

Advantages of Federalism

Dispersal of Power   A key objective for the Founders was to disperse power, and a two-level system that divided power not just among branches of government, but also between levels of government, helped accomplish this goal. Federalism thus institutionalizes and safeguards the division of powers the Founders believed to be so critical to a well-constructed republic.

Accommodation of Diverse Interests   Giving regional governments independent grants of political power means local interests and political priorities are respected and represented. States are given broad latitude to pursue their own policy paths, allowing them to respond to the wishes of their citizens rather than to the dictates of the federal government.

Policy Experimentation   Variation in laws and public policy across states is one of the most commonly cited advantages of federalism. As Supreme Court Justice Louis Brandeis observed, state governments are the "laboratories of democracy." Public policy experimentation provides important lessons not only for other states, but also for the national government, and even for democracy in other countries. Expanding the vote to women is one example of a policy that was implemented in some states before it became a national policy.

Disadvantages of Federalism

Institutionalizing a division of power, accommodating diverse interests, and allowing state and local experimentation are clear advantages of the American system of federalism. But there are also some disadvantages.

Factions   Smaller political units tend to be politically, socially, and economically more alike than the larger nation of which they are a part. As a result, these political units are more likely to be dominated by factions; and because of their sensitivity to local interests, state governments may be more vulnerable to a tyranny of the majority. The nation's history is replete with examples of dominant factions appropriating the power of state and local governments and denying minority groups equal rights—exactly the sort of behavior Madison feared. One example is the systematic disenfranchisement of blacks following the Civil War, especially in southern states. Segregation and Jim Crow laws were supported by majority whites in many of these states who used their majority status to deny blacks equal political, social, and economic opportunities.

Complexity and Inefficiency   While experimentation in public policy has advantages, it also leads to bewildering variation in state laws. In West Virginia dogs are taxed; in New Jersey they are not. Texas routinely executes dozens of murderers annually; Wisconsin would not execute Jeffrey Dahmer, one of the most notorious serial murderers in the nation's history. In Nebraska the speed limit is 75 miles per hour; cross into neighboring Iowa or Kansas at that velocity and you immediately break the law (Mooney 1998). In other words, the simple act of crossing a state line means entering a different political jurisdiction with different legal standards. All this variation makes coordinating intergovernmental action difficult, creates headaches for those who engage in interstate business and must deal with a patchwork of regulatory requirements, and can catch even a conscientiously law-abiding citizen unaware. Your status as a traffic scofflaw or tax dodger depends not only on what you do but where you do it.

Accountability   The variation can also make it harder for the citizen to hold government accountable. Who is really responsible for, say, welfare policy? The states have a good deal of freedom in deciding policy specifics, but much of the funding comes from the federal government, and the money comes with strings attached. Who gets the credit for success or the blame for failure? Such questions can be frustratingly hard to answer in a federal system.

Division of Powers in the American Federal System

Federations differ on the particular methods they use to divide political power. The American approach is to use a written constitution to divide political power, with specific grants of authority going to the national government and the rest being reserved to the states. In the United States, the central operative question in politics is not just who gets what, but also what level of government gets to decide who gets what. The answer to the second question often influences the answer to the first. Understanding how the Constitution divides power between state and federal governments is thus a basic requirement for formulating answers to questions about which level of government is responsible for a given policy action or inaction.

The Powers of the National Government

Article I, Section 8 spells out certain powers given to Congress. These include the power to levy and collect taxes, to borrow money, to regulate interstate commerce, to coin money, to declare war, and to raise and support an army and a navy. The specific grants of power given to the national government are called *enumerated powers.* But the national government's powers are not limited to these. Also included in Article I, Section 8 is a vague and sweeping grant giving Congress the power "to make all laws which shall be necessary and proper for carrying into execution the foregoing powers" (this is often called the "elastic" clause of the Constitution). With this statement, the Founders expanded the authority of the national government beyond its enumerated powers by giving it *implied powers.* Madison strongly favored implied powers; the logic behind these powers is the impossibility of listing in detail every specific power the national government would be authorized to take in every conceivable situation.

While enumerated powers make it clear that the power of the national government is to be limited, the potential for increasing central government influence through the doctrine of implied powers is hard to overestimate. The scope of this potential was first tested in the case of *McCulloch v. Maryland* (1819), which involved a dispute over whether the central government had the power to create a national bank. The national bank was created in the first year of the new national government as part of a broad economic program formulated by Secretary of the Treasury

Alexander Hamilton. President Washington had some doubts about the constitutionality of this proposal and got conflicting advice from two key members of his cabinet—Hamilton and Thomas Jefferson.

Hamilton maintained that though establishing a bank was not one of the national government's enumerated powers, the "necessary and proper" clause gave it the implied power to do so because the bank would be a convenient way to keep and administer the revenues Congress raised by taxing and borrowing. He thus interpreted *necessary* as "convenient" or "appropriate." Jefferson, in contrast, interpreted *necessary* as "indispensable." A national bank was not indispensable to safeguarding federal funds (they could be deposited in state banks, for instance) and was accordingly beyond the authority of the national government. Washington sided with Hamilton and signed the national bank bill into law. A quarter-century later, the bank again became the center of a constitutional controversy when the state of Maryland taxed a branch of the national bank located within its borders. On instructions from his superiors, the bank's cashier, James McCulloch, refused to pay the tax on the grounds that it constituted state interference with a legitimate activity of the national government. The case was eventually appealed to the U.S. Supreme Court, again raising the basic issue first argued between Jefferson and Hamilton: Does the national government have the constitutional authority to create a bank? The Court affirmed Hamilton's interpretation that *necessary* meant "appropriate," not "indispensable" or "absolutely necessary."

This early judicial test of the powers of the national government resulted in a broad interpretation of its authority and opened the door to the expansion of its activities through the use of implied powers. Yet enumerated powers have also been broadly interpreted and have, if anything, given the federal government even greater opportunities for expanding its influence. This is especially true of the power to regulate interstate commerce and the power to tax and spend for the general welfare.

The constitutional issue boils down to the same thing in both instances: how narrow or broad an interpretation to give the applicable phrases. The Supreme Court has interpreted the interstate commerce clause to give the national government the power to license the operation of boats on New York State waters (*Gibbons v. Ogden* 1824), to regulate what farmers can feed chickens (*Wickard v. Filburn* 1942), and to prohibit private acts of racial discrimination (*Heart of Atlanta Motel v. United States* 1964 and *Katzenbach v. McClung* 1964). Passenger vessels were considered interstate commerce even if they were not directly engaged in the buying and selling of goods; what farmers feed chickens was reasoned to be an activity that economically affected the interstate market for wheat; and individuals who racially discriminate while serving substantial numbers of interstate travelers or relying on interstate commerce for their supplies were held to interfere with the rights of minorities to travel and engage in interstate commerce.

The Court has not always been consistent in its interpretation of the interstate commerce clause, but until recently the general pattern of court decisions has led students of constitutional law to conclude that, given the interdependent nature of American economic and social activities, there is almost no activity that the Supreme Court would consider beyond the scope of the interstate commerce power. Recent decisions, however, have limited the use of the commerce clause. For example, in *United States v. Morrison* (2000), the Supreme Court ruled the federal government did not have the power to provide a civil remedy for sexual assault. The case turned on the 1994 Violence against Women Act, which gave rape victims the right to sue their attackers in federal court. Congress justified its intrusion into what is traditionally an area of law left wholly to the states, using the interstate commerce clause. The argument was that fear of violence prevented women from activities like traveling alone and going out at night. As these actions are often associated with work obligations and may also involve crossing state lines, Congress could invoke the interstate commerce clause. The Supreme Court disagreed, and for the first time since the 1930s rejected a congressional argument that a popular activity constituted interstate commerce.

As was the case with the "necessary and proper" clause, the power of the national government to tax and spend for the general welfare provoked a debate between two of the nation's early leaders—this time Hamilton and Madison. These coauthors of *The Federalist* disagreed about what the national government had the power to tax and spend money on. Madison argued that the national government could tax and spend only for the activities it is specifically authorized to undertake. Hamilton held that the power to tax and spend is independent of the other enumerated powers. In other words, in Hamilton's view, Congress had the power to tax and spend money for functions it could not otherwise control.

Again, a series of Supreme Court decisions decided the issue on Hamilton's terms. The implications for the expansion of federal power are considerable; this means Congress can use its taxing power as an indirect method of regulating an activity, such as by taxing gambling. Since the meaning of "the general welfare" has undergone a similarly broad interpretation, the taxing and spending power of Congress has evolved into a very powerful tool.

Interstate commerce and taxation—the two powers the Founders thought most crucial to the operation of a national government—thus have become the major bases for the constitutional expansion of national government. There is little doubt that the federal government has significantly expanded its power since its founding.

The Powers, Rights, and Obligations of State Governments

The Constitution focuses more on the national government than on states. Nonetheless, states are granted certain powers and rights under the Constitution, and states are required to fulfill certain obligations to one another.

State Powers   In contrast to the federal government, state governments receive no specific grant of powers by the Constitution. In fact, in its original form the Constitution made no mention at all of state prerogatives. The Federalists implied that all powers not granted to the national government would remain with the states, but the lack of explicit guarantees was a sore point with anti-Federalists. During the ratification battle, the Federalists promised that if the Constitution was adopted, it would be amended to include a guarantee of states rights. This promise was kept with the Tenth Amendment pledge that "the powers not delegated to the United States by the Constitution, nor prohibited by it to the states, are reserved to the states respectively, or to the people."

The constitutional questions raised by the Tenth Amendment center on the scope of national powers. Supporters of a strong central government have long argued that the Tenth Amendment is superfluous due to what is already implied in the original document; that is, that the states have authority over any matter not delegated to the national government or prohibited to the states. Advocates of states rights argue that the

© David Sailors/Corbis

The source for political authority for the states comes mainly from their own constitutions, which specify their powers and limitations. One power held by all states is police power, or the authority to pass laws for the health, safety, and morals of their citizens. The influence of this sovereignty can be seen in many aspects of our day-to-day lives, including taxation, law enforcement, medical systems, record-keeping, and even something as mundane as the regulation of traffic.

amendment is an important limit on the expansion of the federal government. For much of the 20th century, judicial interpretation tended to side with the national government and provided legal support for almost any activity the federal government wished to undertake. This interpretation provided an important nationalizing influence on American federalism. However, a shift on the Supreme Court during the 1990s reversed the trend. For example, in *United States v. Lopez* (1995), the Supreme Court ruled that the 1990 Gun-Free School Zones Act, which banned possession of firearms within a thousand feet of any school, was unconstitutional. The Court ruled that this regulation had nothing to do with commerce and therefore exceeded the federal government's authority. In other words, the states had jurisdiction, not the federal government.

Although such court decisions show that the Tenth Amendment still provides important protections for state independence, the general source of political authority for the states comes from their own constitutions. These specify each state's powers and limitations. As long as the powers and limitations do not contravene the U.S. Constitution or conflict with legitimate federal statutes and treaties, each state is generally free to establish its own form of government and responsibilities.

As already mentioned, state laws vary. Still, there are important commonalties. In general, states possess **police power,** the authority to pass laws for the health, safety, and morals of their citizens. This grant of political authority is in many ways much broader than any given the national government. The only activities that a state may not legislate are those specifically forbidden by the national or its own state constitutions or considered by the courts to be an unreasonable use of police powers, such as permitting men, but not women, to be licensed motorists. States also share **concurrent powers,** or powers that both the national and state governments can exercise. These include the authority to tax and to borrow money.

The large jurisdictional overlap and the vaguely defined divisions between state and federal authority arising from the Tenth Amendment, the "necessary and proper" clause, and the broad interpretation of enumerated powers means that relations within the American federal system are often marked by tension. Who has the authority to do what? The ability and authority to answer that question is the key to power in the American political system. Yet given the wide range of possible interpretations of both national and state constitutions, it is often a frustratingly hard question to answer.

States Rights   The Constitution guarantees the states certain rights in the American federal system. First, the Constitution guarantees the states that the central government will protect them from invasion and insurrection. National defense is a responsibility of the central government, and Article IV, Section 4 declares that the invasion of any state is an invasion of the United States. States are thus freed from the obligation of maintaining standing military forces. If local authorities are unable to maintain law and order, the governor may ask the president to send federal military troops to assist.

Second, the Constitution guarantees the states a *republican form of government.* The term is not precisely defined by the Constitution but is generally taken to mean the government is based on consent of the governed and representative institutions. The enforcement of this constitutional guarantee is political rather than legal. The federal courts generally have declined jurisdiction when questions have arisen and have deferred to Congress to determine whether a state has a republican government. Senator Charles Sumner of Massachusetts once expressed concern that this clause is a "sleeping giant" because it potentially gives Congress authority to intervene (some might say meddle) in local affairs. Politics rather than legal limitations constrain this type of congressional intrusion.

A third constitutional guarantee to the states is equal representation in the Senate. This system of representation is inconsistent with the principle of political equality because sparsely populated states have more than their fair share of representation in the Senate, while the most populous states have less than their fair share. For example, the least populous state, Wyoming, has 0.18 percent of the nation's population, while the most populous, California, has 12 percent, but each state has two senators (or 2 percent). Thus, Wyoming's representation is over eleven times greater than its share of the population, while California's is only one-sixth of its share. Equal representation in the Senate is a constitutional recognition that states are units of government that have special status not possessed by counties or cities.

Fourth, under the Constitution all states are equal after admission. Every state has the same degree of sovereignty with the same rights and powers. The president or Congress has occasionally tried to mandate certain conditions of statehood. But such requirements are not enforceable if they would give the new state more or less power than other states. For example, President Taft vetoed legislation admitting Arizona as a state because he objected to a provision in the proposed state constitution permitting voters to recall state judges. Once the offending clause was deleted, Taft signed the act, and Arizona became the forty-eighth state in 1912. The new state promptly restored the recall provision (Peltason 1982, 122). Similarly, in 1907

Congress attached a provision to the enabling act passed prior to Oklahoma's admission as a state prohibiting Oklahoma from moving its state capital from Guthrie for ten years. Two years later, the voters of the state approved a referendum to move the capital to Oklahoma City. When the residents of Guthrie sued in federal court to enforce the provision of the enabling act, the Supreme Court held that the provision could not be enforced because once Oklahoma became a state, it was on equal footing with all other states and thus had control over the location of the seat of government (*Coyle v. Smith* 1911). There is no seniority when it comes to state power and sovereignty: Once a territory achieves the constitutional status of statehood, it is equal to all other states.

Finally, states have the right to decide how or if the Constitution is to be changed. At least three-fourths (38) of the states must agree to any changes in the Constitution. This requirement is a major protection of states rights and sovereignty because amendments must be approved by the states acting as governmental units either through state legislatures or state conventions. In other words, the Constitution gives the states, not the people, the power to approve amendments. This means that the 13 least populous states, which represent about 4 percent of the nation's population, can block a change favored by the other 37 states, which represent the other 96 percent of the nation's people.

Obligations of States The Constitution also imposes certain obligations on the states. As discussed in the introduction to this chapter, Article IV, Section 1 requires states to grant **"full faith and credit"** to one another's public acts and records. This provision ensures that such important civil obligations as property rights, wills, and marriages (with the possible exception of gay marriages) will be valid and honored in all states.

Note that this provision applies only to civil proceedings. Because states have the right to establish their own criminal laws and punishments, one state would be precluded from enforcing criminal laws of another state. The constitutional obligation of one state to another in the area of criminal law is limited to **interstate rendition.** If a person accused of a crime flees across state lines, Article IV, Section 2 indicates that the governor of the state to which the criminal has fled shall deliver the criminal back to the state with jurisdiction over the crime.

The Addition of New States. New states were added to the original 13 states by congressional action as specified in Article IV, Section 3. New states cannot be formed by combining or dividing existing states without their consent.[1] Once admitted, states have equal sovereignty and powers.

The typical procedure is as follows:

- Congress forms an incorporated territory.
- Residents of the territory petition Congress for admission as a state.

---

[1]Five states were formed from other states with consent of both Congress and the legislatures of the affected states: Vermont from New York in 1791, Kentucky from Virginia in 1792, Tennessee from North Carolina in 1796, Maine from Massachusetts in 1820, and West Virginia from Virginia in 1863 (Peltason 1982, 122). The West Virginia case is a little different from the others. The Virginia legislature voted to secede and join the Confederacy. Several counties wanted to remain in the Union, and representatives from those counties formed a new Virginia legislature that approved the formation of West Virginia during the Civil War.

- Congress passes a resolution called an **enabling act** authorizing the residents of the territory to draft a state constitution and hold a referendum to approve it. The resolution must be approved by the president.
- When the proposed state constitution is approved by the majority vote of both houses of Congress and signed by the president, the territory becomes a state on equal footing with all other states.

Texas is a special case because it began as an independent nation, the Republic of Texas, that negotiated with Congress for statehood. The congressional resolution admitting Texas as a state contains a provision authorizing Texas to divide itself into five states if the state legislature desires. Although some Texans claim this could be done unilaterally without congressional approval, the Civil War and several Supreme Court rulings establish that Texas has the same rights and powers as other states, so such action would require consent of Congress as well.

The most recent discussion about adding a new state involves Puerto Rico. Puerto Rico is an unincorporated territory of the United States. Its residents are U.S. citizens, but they pay no federal income tax. Puerto Rico's special commonwealth status gives it greater control over local matters than such territories as Guam, American Samoa, and the Virgin Islands. At 3.8 million, Puerto Rico's population is similar to that of Oklahoma and Oregon (at 3.4 million), and greater than 24 states. Yet citizens of Puerto Rico cannot vote in presidential elections, and they have no voting representatives in Congress. They do have a nonvoting delegate to the House, but no voice at all in the Senate. The status of Puerto Rico in the federal system is hotly debated in local politics, with residents about equally divided between the current commonwealth status and statehood, and with a small fraction favoring independence. In a popular referendum on the status of Puerto Rico in 1998, supporters of statehood garnered about 46 percent of the vote, while those favoring continuation of the status quo got about 50.3 percent. Statehood was an issue in the 2000 Republican presidential primary; Texas Governor George W. Bush supported statehood, while his challenger, Senator John McCain, favored a status **plebiscite** in which Puerto Ricans would have a chance to decide.[2] In November 2000, Sila Calderon was elected governor; she is from the pro-commonwealth Popular Democratic Party (PDP) and is the first female governor of Puerto Rico. Her immediate predecessor, Governor Pedro Rossello, was pro-statehood. Without strong local support, it is unlikely that Puerto Rico will become the fifty-first state in the near future.

Washington, DC, poses difficult issues relating to statehood and representation. Since passage of the Twenty-Third Amendment, the U.S. citizens who reside in the nation's capital vote for president, but they have no voting representation in Congress (like Puerto Rico and the territories, they have a nonvoting delegate in the House and none in the Senate). Yet, about 572,000 people live in the District of Columbia, as compared with about 494,000 in Wyoming.

Because the Constitution establishes Washington, DC, as the seat of the national government, it is neither a state nor a part of a state. Consequently, Congress cannot extend full representation by statute. In 1978, Congress proposed an amendment that would have treated DC as a state for purposes of representation in Congress and in the

---

[2]The presidential nominating process is discussed in more detail in Chapter 7. Although residents of U.S. territories do not vote in presidential elections, both the Republican and Democratic parties allow them to send delegates to the national conventions.

Because it is not a state or a part of a state, citizens of Washington, DC, are not represented in Congress. Here, Washington, DC, Mayor Anthony Williams addresses a "Taxes Paid, Representation Denied" rally. In 1998 DC Vote was founded to serve as an umbrella organization for the numerous groups in DC fighting to win full voting rights for the residents of the District of Columbia.

electoral college, but the necessary three-fourths of the states did not ratify the proposal within the seven-year time limit. Given the current political situation, it is unlikely that a proposal to grant the District of Columbia the equivalent of statehood for purposes of representation could muster the necessary support among the states. Equally unlikely is the option of having Congress cede all land that is not federal property in DC back to Maryland, which would at least make District residents part of a state and allow them to participate in electing members of Congress. Given the lukewarm southern and Republican support for granting the mostly African American and overwhelmingly Democratic District more political influence than it already has, DC seems likely to remain in its unique representational limbo for some time (Ponessa 1995).

Admitting new states has always been an inherently political process. In the early years of the republic, the politics of gaining admission to the Union tended to revolve around the issue of slavery. The Civil War resolved this issue, but it did nothing to end the intensely political conflicts that surround application for statehood. For example, Utah's battle to gain statehood was stymied by an ongoing political fight over polygamy and the role of Mormon religious leaders in public life. In 1849 Mormon settlers took the initial step toward statehood by seeking congressional recognition of the provisional state then called Deseret. These initial appeals were rebuffed because the territory did not have the 60,000 eligible voters usually set as a minimum requirement for statehood. Between this beginning and the time statehood was finally achieved in 1896, the political obstacles centered largely on suspicion about the Mormon Church and its adherents' way of life. These were finally overcome when Wilford Woodruff, president of the Church of Jesus Christ of Latter-Day Saints, issued a manifesto declaring that the Mormon Church would no longer teach, sanction, or permit its members to practice plural marriage. In effect, the federal government required the church to alter its views on marriage as a condition of statehood, thus regulating intimate relationships a century before the question of gay marriages arose. Even after the question of polygamy was resolved, Utah's statehood was accepted not simply on the merits of the case, but also because of a power struggle between the Democratic and Republican parties, both of which were maneuvering to gain an advantage by admitting new states (Lyman 1986, 1–5).

The politics that surround statehood are amply demonstrated by examining the last two states to gain admission to the Union: Hawaii and Alaska. Originally a colonial possession, Hawaii took the unusual route of seeking—and eventually gaining—political equality within the system that annexed it. As was the case with Utah, Hawaii's statehood was long delayed, partly because of suspicion of a "foreign" culture. Hawaii underwent a slow process of Americanization in which the traditional political, cultural, social, and economic systems of a Polynesian kingdom gave way to the competing norms and values of the mainland. Never far from the center of the struggle for statehood was the question of absorbing a minority culture into the political mainstream. Granting Hawaii statehood presented Congress "with an unprecedented dilemma: it raised unavoidably the question of equality under the nation's Constitution for a non-contiguous area with an essentially nonwhite population" (Bell 1984, 5). Such was the sensitivity of this question that it took at least a half-century to resolve. After 1919, bills petitioning for statehood were routinely introduced by the islands' nonvoting delegates to Congress. Hawaii was finally admitted to the Union in 1959.

Alaska was also admitted to the Union that year. Alaska's fight for statehood epitomizes the basic politics that surround any proposal of statehood. Some members of Congress were reluctant to support Alaska's bid because of the potential to upset the balance of political power. According to the 1950 census, Alaska's population was 127,000, and some members of large states publicly questioned the fairness of giving such a small number of people disproportionate representation. For example, Alaska would get the same number of U.S. senators as New York State with its 15 million people. Some in the Texas delegation resisted Alaska's statehood simply because it meant ceding bragging rights as the largest state in the Union (Gruening 1967, 100–101). On such questions has the fate of states risen and fallen.

Refereeing Power Conflicts

The Constitution makes some provisions for settling conflicts between state and federal operations. Article VI declares that the U.S. Constitution, laws passed by Congress, and treaties made by the national government shall be the **"supreme law of the land."** State constitutions and laws are subordinate to the supreme law, and if there is a conflict between a state provision and a federal provision, the latter is enforced. The Constitution thus establishes a hierarchy of law; the U.S. Constitution is superior to both national laws and state laws and constitutions, and national laws and treaties are superior to state constitutions and laws. Given the vague and broad constitutional language, this means that the ultimate umpire in the federal system is

© Getty Images

Federal troops were called in to help desegregate Central High School in Little Rock, Arkansas, in 1957 (as shown here). Desegregation was opposed by many at the local and state levels. When segregation was ruled unconstitutional by the U.S. Supreme Court, however, state laws mandating racially separate schools were invalidated. State laws cannot violate the U.S. Constitution, which is the law of the land.

the U.S. Supreme Court, which has the final say on how the Constitution is interpreted. As discussed earlier, the Supreme Court has made such rulings on a number of important issues respecting federal and state power.

Although the Supreme Court has historically tended to favor the federal government in apportioning powers, the states are far from helpless in conflicts. For example, the federal system ensures that state interests play an important role in the national government. Although Congress is the lawmaking branch of the national government, members of Congress are elected to represent state and local—not necessarily national—interests. Most members of Congress—at least those interested in reelection—have a fundamental interest in making sure that national legislation either positively benefits their constituents or, at least, does not harm them. Representatives who face a choice between backing national or local interests ignore the latter at their peril. A famous example is the case of Representative Marjorie Margolies-Mezvinsky, a freshman Democrat in 1993, who provided a critical vote to help pass President Clinton's first budget bill. The bill included a series of tax increases and spending cuts aimed at bringing enormous federal deficits under control. The taxes and spending cuts were not popular with Margolies-Mezvinsky's suburban Philadelphia constituents, and she initially opposed the bill. She provided a key swing vote only after the president appealed to her responsibilities to the nation. Her constituents responded to her actions by booting her from office in the next election (Barone and Ujifusa 1994, 1108–1109).

Public opinion polls show strong support for state rather than federal leadership on a wide variety of issues, including welfare, transportation, education, crime, and agriculture, to name a few. It thus makes good political sense for candidates seeking national office to at least rhetorically align themselves with the cause of states rights. Following popular opinion, most major party presidential candidates in the past three or four presidential electoral cycles have expressed support for **devolution**—policies that shift power back to states and localities (Donahue 1997, 18). The political framework set up by the Founders ensures that state and local interests will always have a strong influence on the national government, and these interests play a significant role in determining which level of government should have the responsibility and authority to carry out public policy.

The Evolution of Federalism

A historical analysis of governmental development in the United States points to one overriding pattern: the growth of activities at *all levels* of the political system. While the fortunes of both state and federal governments have waxed and waned in their relationship with each other, taken as a whole, local, state, and national governments are all providing more services and regulating the actions of their citizens to a greater extent today than at any time in the past. Government expenditures tell this story clearly: At the beginning of the 20th century, the total expenditure of all levels of government was less than $2 billion; at the beginning of the 21st century that figure had increased to roughly $3 trillion. That latter number is a 3 followed by twelve 0s and amounts to a 1,500-fold increase.

One of the key reasons for this increase is the greater role of the federal government. While government spending at all levels has risen, the proportion of total government expenditures accounted for by the federal government has increased, while the proportion accounted for by states has decreased. At the beginning of the 20th century, the federal government accounted for about 35 percent of all government expenditures. At the turn of the 21st century, the federal government accounted for more than 50 percent of all government expenditures. The figures for states were roughly reversed: They started out the 20th century accounting for about 60 percent of government spending and finished the century accounting for 30 percent (Advisory Commission on Intergovernmental Relations 1994; U.S. Census Bureau 2001).

Three historical events drove these long-term trends: World War I and its aftermath (roughly 1914 to 1922); the New Deal response to the Great Depression (roughly 1933 to 1938); and the buildup and aftermath of World War II (roughly 1938 to 1948). War and economic depression meant the federal government's growth was, at least to some extent, expansion by default. Military matters have always been the primary concern of the national government, and World Wars I and II required harnessing a large portion of the nation's resources to the military effort. As the Great Depression worsened during the early 1930s, the national government was in a better position to respond to the crisis than were state or local governments. The federal government had power over currency, the banking system, and the regulation of interstate economic activities. It also had a superior tax base, since the Sixteenth Amendment, ratified in 1913, had given Congress the authority to levy an income tax. Led by President Franklin Roosevelt, the national government in the 1930s used these resources to embark on an ambitious and expensive series of new programs designed to lead the country to recovery. Thus military and economic crises combined with fiscal and political capacities to radically alter the division of government activities, with the federal government taking on many responsibilities previously left to states and localities.

Though the federal government's role has significantly increased over the past century, it would be inaccurate to conclude that the history of federalism is a story of federal expansion at the expense of state and local governments. States and localities remain the primary regulatory powers for such major domestic activities as education and law enforcement. Moreover, aggregate spending patterns do not reveal the more complex issue of intergovernmental relationships that have accompanied changes in expenditure patterns. States and localities are not slowly disappearing into the shadows cast by the fiscal power of the federal government. Their capabilities and responsibilities have increased dramatically during the history of the nation, and they have not by any means evolved into supplicants of the federal government. At times states have fiercely fought to maintain independence from the federal government, and states have established a broad set of working relationships with the federal government that account for a great deal of the domestic policy we take for granted. Roads, schools, utilities, and much more are built and maintained as a result of combined federal, state, and local policy.

Although attempting to systematically describe the evolution of federalism is likely to provoke some debate, it is possible to categorize federalism into three reasonably distinct eras. Each is characterized by a different model of federalism: dual federalism, cooperative federalism, and new federalism.

Dual Federalism

Dual federalism is the notion that the federal and state governments are sovereign powers with separate and distinct jurisdictions. The central government has jurisdiction over national concerns, such as providing national defense, coining money, and regulating interstate and foreign commerce, while the states have responsibility for local concerns—that is, police powers, including public safety, education, health, and welfare.

In theory, the line between national and state responsibilities is clear. Each level of government is supreme in its own policy arena, and the other level has no constitutional basis to enter the arena uninvited. During the 19th century, the Supreme Court adopted the doctrine of dual federalism as a guiding principle to referee conflicts between state and federal governments. And at least compared to contemporary times, dual federalism was practiced to some extent. The federal government, for example, was much less involved in the daily lives of its citizens during the formative years of the republic than it is today.

Still, intense controversies have always marked federalism. As discussed earlier, the ink was barely dry on the Constitution before Alexander Hamilton, one of its authors, began to loosely interpret its provisions to expand the federal government's power. In the first few decades after the adoption of the Constitution, Federalist sentiments dominated politics, and the federal government established itself as a central force.

This early expansion of national government fortunes underwent a sharp decline when Andrew Jackson became president in 1829 and set about resurrecting the anti-Federalist states rights platform. Jackson appointed Roger B. Taney as chief justice of the Supreme Court. Taney is generally acknowledged as the author of the dual federalism doctrine, and his rulings represented a clear philosophical break from those of his predecessor, John Marshall, who had been much more receptive to Federalist arguments.

While the federal government may have been less involved in the daily lives of its citizens, it was often involved in standoffs with state governments. These conflicts sometimes became so intense that even Jackson found himself on the nationalist side. For example, in the 1830s states rights advocates favored the doctrine of **nullification,** the act of declaring a national law null and void within a state's borders. This policy was especially attractive to southerners who objected to tariffs they believed threatened their agricultural economy. In 1832, South Carolina not only nullified a set of national tariffs but also threatened to secede from the Union. Jackson responded by threatening to use federal troops, and South Carolina dropped its secessionist stand.

South Carolina was not the only state to threaten to leave the Union because of disagreements with federal policy. The New England states threatened to secede en masse in response to a federally ordered embargo during the War of 1812. The most notable of these conflicts was, of course, the Civil War, when 11 southern states actually seceded from the Union. The Civil War settled the lingering questions of nullification and secession, and for a time power came back to the federal government. The Thirteenth Amendment outlawing slavery, the Fourteenth Amendment guaranteeing due process and equal protection of the law, and the Fifteenth Amendment prohibiting denying the right to vote on the basis of "race, color, or previous condition of servitude" served to limit state power in these areas. During Reconstruction, the federal government became the dominant partner in the politics of many southern states.

Toward the end of the 19th century, the country entered a period of explosive economic growth fueled by freewheeling capitalism sometimes referred to as the Gilded Age. The doctrine of dual federalism strongly reasserted itself, even in areas traditionally considered the domain of the national government. For example, the dominant industrial capitalists of the day were not overly supportive of strong central government regulation of business, interstate or otherwise. These sentiments were often reflected by the Supreme Court, which declared unconstitutional federal laws establishing a minimum wage and regulating the use of child labor. Still, the newly industrialized economy provided the impetus for greater federal regulatory powers, and the movement to give the national government a more prominent role was accelerated by World War I. Although this expansion of federal power blurred the line separating state and federal jurisdictions, dual federalism lingered as the operative model until a severe economic crisis pushed the federal government into a much more central role.

Cooperative Federalism

In contrast to dual federalism, **cooperative federalism** is the notion that the distinction between state and national responsibilities is blurry, and the different levels of government share responsibility in many policy areas. Accordingly, state and federal governments coordinate their actions to serve and respond to the needs of citizens.

The impetus for the cooperative model of federalism was the Great Depression, although it had been practiced in rudimentary form even before the Constitutional Convention. For example, in 1785 Congress passed a statute, supplemented by the Northwest Ordinance of 1787, that gave the states large sections of public lands to be developed for educational purposes. The basic form of this legislation—a grant from the federal government so that the states could achieve a desired policy end—remains the basic mechanism of cooperative federalism.

Initially, federal grant programs to the states mostly involved a resource that the national government had in abundance—land. Toward the end of the 19th century, the form of grants shifted from land to cash, and instead of being once-only gifts, the grants came in the form of continuing appropriations. This new form of subsidy became known as **grants-in-aid,** and it is the reason cooperative federalism is sometimes called *fiscal federalism,* in recognition that cooperation among the levels of government is often characterized by financial relationships.

Grants-in-aid became more common in the early 20th century as the federal government tapped the lucrative new revenue source of the income tax and became more willing to involve itself in regulating the economy. Federal grant-in-aid expenditures jumped from $5 million in 1912 to almost $34 million in 1920. Most of these funds went for education, highways, and agricultural extension programs, but Congress also laid the basis for modern assistance programs by providing money for maternal and child healthcare.

During the New Deal the use of grants-in-aid exploded and became a—perhaps the—central characteristic of American federalism. State and local governments were ill prepared to deal with the massive economic dislocation of the 1930s. Facing a social disaster of unprecedented proportions, the federal government stepped into the breach. Between 1932 and 1935, grant-in-aid expenditures swelled from $200 million to more than $2 billion. Rather than having the federal government administer burgeoning new programs in welfare, health, employment security, and public housing, President Franklin Roosevelt chose to funnel the money and much of the program responsibility through state and local governments.

The outbreak of World War II temporarily slowed grant-in-aid programs, as the national government conserved its resources for the military effort. But the war also propelled the federal government into unprecedented centralizing of power. Among other things, the federal government regulated wages, prices, and industrial production. Beginning in 1948, grant expenditures began to rise again, and by 1954 they had reached their prewar level of $3 billion. During the administration of Dwight Eisenhower in the 1950s, the amount of grant-in-aid money began to creep upward as an explicit attempt to counter the centralization of domestic programs in Washington.

The 1960s and early 1970s witnessed a major surge in grant-in-aid programs similar to that of the 1930s. As part of President Lyndon Johnson's Great Society initiative, roughly two dozen grant-in-aid programs were enacted in 1964 and 1965 alone. During the next two presidential administrations, more than a hundred grant programs were created. These programs tended to concentrate on the problems of large metropolitan areas and covered a broad range of policy issues dealing with economic development, education, and race relations. They also brought another important feature to the evolution of grants-in-aid: Some grants went directly to private groups, bypassing both state and local governments.

© Ralf-Finn Hestoft/Corbis

Since its beginning in 1965, Head Start has been a successful federally funded program that has brought education and health programs to underprivileged children all over the country. Administered jointly by the Administration on Children, Youth, and Families; the Administration for Children and Families; and the Department of Health and Human Services, it operates with a paid staff of just under 200,000 and a volunteer staff of nearly 1.5 million workers. In addition to its general outreach to communities, it funds grants to the American Indian and Migrant Programs in order to further help these special needs groups.

By the early 1980s, the federal government was funneling huge amounts of money to states and localities, which in turn used them to finance an enormous expansion of the programs and policies they provided to citizens. Federalism was now characterized by the politics of grants-in-aid—a struggle between state and national government not over whether the federal government should be involved in policy areas traditionally the responsibility of the states, but over how the involvement should be conducted.

The political battles over grants-in-aid reflect how policy priorities have shifted over the past half-century. In the 1940s and 1950s, for example, federal assistance for health programs accounted for less than 10 percent of all federal grants to states and communities. Since the mid-1990s, health programs have been the largest single category, accounting for more than 40 percent of federal grants-in-aid. In total, federal grants to state and local governments came to more than $350 billion in 2002, or roughly 18 percent of federal expenditures. (See Figures 3.4 and 3.5.)

States tend to favor **general revenue sharing,** a type of grant that originated in the early 1970s that comes with no strings attached. In general revenue sharing, the federal government simply turns money over to states and localities to use as they wish. Policymakers at the federal level tend to favor **categorical grants,** programs that not only provide funds for a defined area of activity, such as education or public housing, but also specify how the programs are to be carried out. Categorical grants allow the

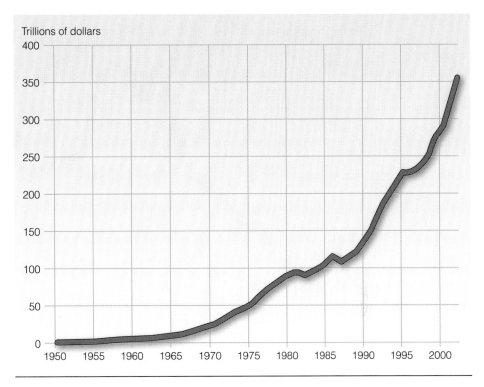

Figure 3.4
Federal Grants-in-Aid, 1950–2002
Source: Office of Management and Budget: *www.whitehouse.gov/omb/budget/fy2004*

federal government to use the power of the purse to exercise maximum control over various policy responsibilities of state and local governments. Somewhere between general revenue sharing and categorical grants are **block grants.** Block grants provide funds for a general policy area, but they allow states and localities greater discretion than categorical grants in designing the programs being funded.

As grant-in-aid programs multiplied, they produced major problems of coordination and control for all levels of government. There is no single, centralized control mechanism for grants-in-aid. Instead, they are controlled piecemeal by a dizzying array of departments and bureaus, many of which operate according to their own rules and regulations. The compartmentalization of hundreds of programs sometimes means that the federal left hand does not know what the federal right hand is doing. The Department of Transportation, for example, might help develop a highway that displaces low-income urban residents, creating a shortage of low-income housing that ultimately becomes a major concern of officials in the Department of Housing and Urban Development. Legislators, governors, mayors, council members, and other officials charged with viewing overall public needs find it very difficult to control the activities of specialized agencies and establish priorities among them.

Though these problems are far from insignificant, the two central drawbacks associated with cooperative federalism are its expense and its tendency to concentrate

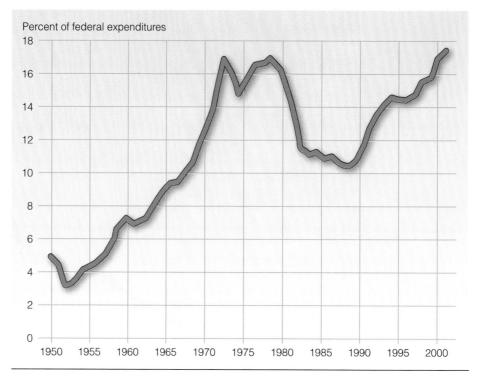

Figure 3.5
Grants as Percentage of Federal Spending
Source: Office of Management and Budget: *www.whitehouse.gov/omb/budget/fy2004*

power in the hands of the federal government. Intergovernmental transfers account for as much as 20 percent of state and local government revenues. And that money comes with strings attached. For example, the national government in effect set the national minimum drinking age at 21 by threatening to withhold highway funds from states that did not adopt this policy. Constitutionally speaking, setting the legal drinking age is the legislative province of the states. But the Supreme Court ruled that the federal government was allowed to place conditions on offers of financial aid as long as the states had the right to refuse the aid. These so-called **crossover sanctions,** or conditions placed on the receipt of grant money that have nothing to do with the original purpose of the grant, constitute the fee exacted for entrance to the federal treasury. The other options—raising taxes or going without—were largely unpalatable to state politicians and the electorate. So the states accepted the conditions and the money. There has been a uniform drinking age of 21 in all states since the mid-1980s.

The New Federalism

New federalism is a movement to take power from the federal government and return it to the states. Just as the era of cooperative federalism overlapped the era of dual federalism, there is no clear date that marks the beginning of new federalism.

The term *new federalism* was first used by President Richard Nixon to describe an early 1970s plan to reverse the trend of federal government expansion triggered by the Great Society programs of the 1960s. Nixon had mixed success. The main policy associated with Nixon's new federalism was general revenue sharing. As already indicated, this was very popular with state and local governments, but it hardly promoted their independence from the federal government.

The first president to seriously attempt a systematic reversal of cooperative federalism was Ronald Reagan. He campaigned vigorously against the concentration of power in Washington and promised to cut states free from the regulatory thicket that bound them to federal government dictates. His push to make federalism more state-centered quickly ran into several problems. First, along with cutting regulations, Reagan also cut grants-in-aid. General revenue sharing was eliminated completely, and Reagan proposed a radical restructuring of program and funding responsibilities between national and state governments. These proposals were opposed by both Congress and state officials.

Second, many of Reagan's supporters began to realize that there were advantages to federal regulation, and they started to oppose the effort to turn regulatory power over to the states. Such reconsideration was especially true of business groups. Facing the prospect of fifty systems of regulation in areas such as consumer product safety and the environment, businesses began lobbying Congress for uniform and standardized federal laws. Congress responded. During the Reagan administration, Congress aggressively used the principle of **preemption,** expressly giving national law precedence over state and local laws in a variety of policy areas.

The third set of problems with Reagan's proposals resulted from Supreme Court rulings that continued to uphold federal expansion. In *Garcia v. San Antonio Metropolitan Transport Authority* (1985), for example, the Court seemed to place Tenth Amendment guarantees in the hands of the federal government. The Court said that since the states are represented in the federal government (directly in the Senate, indirectly in the House), their interests should be protected there.

Arguments in favor of new federalism also began to pick up steam in the 1990s with the election of Bill Clinton, a former Democratic governor sympathetic to state interests, and a Republican Congress that made taking power away from Washington its campaign battle cry. The most dramatic of the new federalism initiatives of this era was the 1996 welfare reform law that ended the Aid to Families with Dependent Children (AFDC) program and gave states much more flexibility to design and run their own welfare programs. The drive by Congress and the president to push more responsibilities toward the states was supported by a series of Supreme Court decisions that reversed the direction set by *Garcia* and put more teeth into the Tenth Amendment:

- In *New York v. United States* (1992), the Court ruled that a federal law unconstitutionally coerced states into becoming responsible for disposing of low-level radioactive waste.
- In *Printz v. United States* (1997), the Court said that the federal government could not force local law enforcement agencies to perform the criminal background checks required by the Brady Handgun Control Act of 1994.
- In *Alden v. Maine* (1999), the Court set clear boundaries on decades-old federal labor law, ruling that a citizen cannot use a federal law to sue a state in state court.

- In *Kimmel v. Florida Board of Regents* (2000), the Court ruled that state workers cannot bring age-based discrimination suits in federal court, a ruling that essentially meant that Congress cannot make states liable for age-based discrimination claims by state employees. These claims can still be pursued in state court.

By the beginning of the 21st century, however, it became clear that the commitment to new federalism was suspect in at least some areas and that the unintended consequences of turning power over to the states could be negative. New federalism represented a rethinking of what level of government should bear primary responsibility for a particular policy area and what level of government should pay for the programs in that area. Many observers of American politics saw this as potentially constructive; the give-and-take over program and funding responsibility allowed governments in the federal system to experiment with the best mix of functional responsibilities. Some argued that the best division of responsibilities would leave redistributive policies (policies that take something from one group and give it to another, such as Social Security and welfare programs) to the federal government, and developmental policies (roads, education, and the like) to the states (Peterson 1995).

The problem is that new federalism is not necessarily producing that sort of division. If anything, states are getting more responsibility for redistributive policies, which carries some disturbing implications. A high-profile example is welfare, a redistributive policy where responsibility has shifted significantly away from the federal and toward the state level. The concern here is that states will be pressured to adopt increasingly stingier welfare programs, because more generous state welfare programs may attract disadvantaged people from less generous states. This incentive structure is beneficial for the disadvantaged, who get larger benefits, and good for the states they leave, because it reduces their welfare costs. It is bad for the states they move to—generous benefits acting as a "welfare magnet"—leaving those taxpayers to shoulder a disproportionate share of the burden in providing a social safety net. The obvious way to avoid being the sucker in this scenario is for a state to slash its welfare benefits. Doing so will encourage surrounding states to do the same, and the net result is a "race to the bottom."

There are also downsides to the states taking primary responsibility for developmental policy. For example, to attract business they may offer special tax breaks or engage in developmental projects designed to lure a specific company to relocate. This competition is good for business but may not be so good for taxpayers who have to fund these projects and take on a greater share of the overall tax burden. In essence, states end up trying to poach one another's tax base—and not tax it (Donahue 1997). There is a vigorous debate over the seriousness of such problems, but their potential is enough for some to question whether the costs of new federalism outweigh its benefits.

The new federalism movement is not just sorting out who should do what and grappling with the problem of unhealthy competition among the states. The commitment to its philosophical underpinnings is suspect, especially at the federal level. The federal government continues to pass unfunded mandates; in other words, it requires states and localities to take on certain responsibilities without covering any of the associated expenses. High-profile examples of unfunded mandates include federal laws requiring state and local governments to make all public buildings handicapped accessible and the No Child Left Behind (NCLB) law, which not only requires state and local government to pay for large portions of a federally mandated program but shifts power over education—constitutionally a responsibility of state governments—toward the national government.

LIVING THE PROMISE
Post-9/11 Federalism

Historically, war and recession tend to promote the role of the federal government. This tendency is understandable: If the crisis is national, only the national government, not states and localities, can comprehensively respond. The predictable result is a centralization of power at the federal level as the president and Congress seek the tools and authority to respond to the threat.

The terrorist attacks of September 11, 2001, prompted just such a predictable response. Following the hijacking of four commercial airliners in a single day, and the subsequent devastation at the World Trade Center in New York City and at the Pentagon very near Washington, DC, the nation found itself thrust into a war with terrorist organizations. Fighting that war placed the policy focus squarely on the national government, which responded with new laws, new agencies, and military action. The Patriot Act granted sweeping new powers to federal law enforcement officials. The Department of Homeland Security (DHS) created one of the most massive bureaucratic reorganizations in thirty or more years. Military action in Afghanistan and Iraq left the U.S. armed forces fighting more difficult than expected guerrilla campaigns.

There were, however, several things that made the attacks of 9/11—and the government response—different from previous wars. For one thing, it was an attack on U.S. soil, meaning the first priority was not to respond to the attackers militarily but to ensure domestic security. Second, the attack was by a non-state terrorist organization, meaning there was no obvious enemy to retaliate against. The attacks were carried out by people living in the United States, not by the military forces of a foreign nation.

The end result of these differences is that states and localities bore much of the responsibility for homeland security, even as the federal government naturally took a central role. Consider that the initial response to the terrorist attacks were by state and local agencies. It was the New York police and fire departments that responded to the World Trade Center attack. First responders to the Pentagon attack were the Arlington County Fire Department and the Fairfax County Search and Rescue Team. The federal government simply has no effective nationwide law enforcement and emergency first response capabilities; under federalism, this responsibility falls to state and local governments as part of their police powers. This means state and local governments, whether they want to or not, are on the front lines of the war on terrorism.

That role has been recognized by the federal government, but perhaps not fully appreciated. The 9/11 attacks created an urgent need to develop a comprehensive counterterrorism plan to coordinate federal, state, and local efforts of ensuring homeland security. The Homeland Security Council (HSC) was created to take on this responsibility. Its members included the president, vice president, attorney general, and various cabinet secretaries and heads of federal law enforcement and intelligence agencies. Notably absent from the council were any representatives of state and local government—a glaring omission given that the HSC policy is heavily dependent upon state and local resources.

In the wake of 9/11 it is governors and mayors who are charged with providing security for much of the public infrastructure, not the Department of Defense or the Federal Bureau of Investigation. The DHS endures considerable criticism for its inability to coordinate a comprehensive homeland security program. Governors and mayors chastise the DHS for issuing alerts and pressuring local agencies to protect a long list of potential terrorist targets without providing specific information or money. For example, governors and mayors have learned about potential terrorist threats not directly from the DHS but from television news. Other local officials have had a hard time coordinating their emergency response plans with federal policy because they cannot get federal officials to return their phone calls.

Bearing the brunt of the on-the-ground responsibility for homeland security is also fantastically expensive for state and local governments. Dallas spent an estimated $6 million on extra security measures in the last three months of 2001, New Orleans $10 million. Baltimore was spending $100,000 a week just on overtime pay for police. All of these expenses were particularly hard to bear because of a recession that was straining state and local budgets. The federal government's primary response to the recession (tax cuts) worsened, if anything, the financial position of states and localities. This is because the tax systems of states and localities are often linked to the federal system, and changes in the latter automatically produces changes in

continued

continued

the former. The federal government did provide grants-in-aid for homeland security purposes, but these covered only a portion of the expenses involved, and the entire budget dedicated to homeland security ($38 billion in 2002) was less than the new funds awarded the Defense Department ($47 billion).

The response to 9/11 demonstrates both the best and the worst aspects of federalism. The best is the actions of particular branches of government—especially the emergency response agencies. For the most part, these agencies were created, trained, and maintained by local governments, and their professionalism under extreme conditions deserves the highest praise. The worst is the struggle to create a clear homeland security plan and coordinate the kaleidoscopic elements of the federal system into a focused and coherent implementation of its goals. This is not necessarily a failure of government officials; it is simply part of the price of a federal system. War and recession may change some things, but the basic nature of federalism remains the same.

Sources: Comfort, Louise K. 2002. "Managing Intergovernmental Responses to Terrorism and Other Extreme Events." *Publius: The Journal of Federalism.* 32: 29–49; Krane, Dale A. 2002. "The State of American Federalism, 2001–2002: Resilience in Response to Crisis." *Publius: The Journal of Federalism,* 32: 1–28.

President George W. Bush provides a good example of the mixed commitment to new federalism. A former governor, he appeared to be a strong supporter of new federalism philosophy. For example, soon after arriving at the White House, Bush established the Interagency Working Group on Federalism, a group whose responsibilities included identifying programs that could be turned over to the states and cutting the red tape that surrounded grants-in-aid. Yet Bush's commitment to new federalism was uneven, partly because of circumstances, but also because of politics. The first years of his presidency were marked by a sagging economy and devastating terrorist attacks in New York City and Washington, DC; early military successes in Afghanistan and Iraq were followed by unexpectedly difficult guerrilla campaigns. Recession and war traditionally focus power on the national government because it is simply better equipped to deal with such challenges. Here it was no different: States and localities followed the lead of the federal government (see the Living the Promise feature "Post-9/11 Federalism").

Yet Bush's own agenda, not just the demands of recession and war, also checked the new federalism drive. The NCLB was a Bush administration initiative that significantly shifted power from states and localities to the national government. The NCLB, at least at the time of its adoption, was hugely popular, but philosophically it was in direct contrast to the principles of new federalism (see the Promise and Policy feature "The No Child Left Behind Law"). Rather than new federalism, some observers suggest what is emerging in the 21st century is **ad hoc federalism.** This term describes the process of adopting a state- or nation-centered view of federalism on the basis of political convenience. Rather than a commitment to a particular vision of what state and federal governments should or should not do, the issue at hand (and who supports it) determines whether a policymaker makes the states rights or federal supremacy argument. One early review of the new federalism movement concluded that "If there is a 'New Federal Order' emerging, [recent] developments . . . suggest that it is not as revolutionary as advocates might have hoped" (Schramm and Wiessert 1997, 1). This was an accurate piece of political fortune telling: The political struggle that has always characterized state and federal relationships continues.

PROMISE AND POLICY
The No Child Left Behind Law

A revolution in public education occurred at an old wooden desk in the gymnasium of Ohio's Hamilton High School in early 2002. At that desk, and with much foot-stomping fanfare, President George W. Bush signed into law the No Child Left Behind (NCLB) Act. With his signature, the power over public education took a significant step away from state legislatures and local school boards and toward the federal government in Washington, DC.

Traditionally, public education has been treated almost wholly as a state and local policy responsibility. Public education systems exist mostly because they are mandated by state constitutions; in most states the constitution gives the state legislature the responsibility and power to govern education, though most choose to delegate a good portion of that duty to local school boards. States and localities pay most of the money, build the schools, hire the teachers, and set the standards.

The NCLB puts the federal government into the last part of that equation in a big way: In essence, it extends federal control over education standards and accountability. The key provisions of the massive 1,100-page law set annual testing requirements for grades 3 through 8, requires states to adopt a set of ambitious perform-ance goals and fully achieve them,

and gives parents the right to remove their children from schools not meet-ing these standards and transfer them to other schools or receive federal aid for private tutoring.

In principle most agree with the act's general goals: that is, to improve public education and make it more accountable. Yet in practice the NCLB has been harshly criticized for sticking the federal government's nose into state and local business by mandating a sweeping set of changes that many see as at best confusing and at worst harmful.

Consider the law's testing require-ments. Many states and school systems already have in place effective testing and accountability systems that are more demanding than those envisioned by NCLB. These systems may have to be aban-doned or at least significantly modi-fied. The net effect is to potentially weaken, rather than strengthen, stan-dards. The performance goals are criticized as all but impossible to meet because they, in effect, require all students to be above average. What this means is that schools con-sidered exemplary by every measure except those set by the NCLB could end up being labeled as underper-forming or even failing. In other words, rather than making bad schools better, the law has the poten-tial to make good schools look bad.

The choice provisions of the legis-lation also have come in for harsh

criticism. California, New York, and many other states already have school choice laws allowing students to transfer from one public school to another. The problem in these states is not lack of choice but lack of space. In many metropolitan areas, the schools with a reputation for excel-lence are already overcrowded. In rural areas, choice is unrealistic. As many as two-thirds of rural schools are in communities where there is no other school in commuting distance.

For critics of the NCLB, it repre-sents exactly what can go wrong when the national government decides to extend its powers into the policy responsibilities traditionally delegated to states and localities: The law misidentifies key problems, sets unrealistic goals, mandates policy solutions that already exist, and bur-dens regional governments with a one-size-fits-all approach that may be inappropriate for local situations. For the critics, the fact that the federal government has failed to meet all its NCLB-related funding promises, but not backed off of the NCLB man-dates, only adds insult to injury.

The NCLB was one of the key pol-icy priorities of the Bush administra-tion, and it passed Congress with large bipartisan majorities. It turns out, though, that what looks good in Washington, DC, often looks very dif-ferent at the state and local level.

Sources: Krane, Dale A. 2002. "The State of American Federalism, 2001–2002: Resilience in Response to Crisis." *Publius: The Journal of Federalism,* 32: 1–28; National Education Association. 2003. "No Child Left Behind?" *NEA Today: http://www.nea.org/neatoday/0305/ cover.html.* Accessed September 16, 2003.

Performance Assessment

The federal system has a mixed record in upholding the core values of democracy. For example, if majority rule is a key principle of democracy, there is no doubt that our federal system is in some ways an affront to this prized value. The system allows interests that are a national minority, but a local majority, to have their way on certain matters, at least for some period of time. The classic example is the states rights rationale adopted in the South to pursue what in practice amounted to a prolonged policy of racial apartheid.

The questionable performance of American democracy can often be traced to the unclear promises of the federal system. Yet the federal system has not given the states a permanent veto on any issue. The South was unable to prevent all three branches of the national government from pursuing policies guaranteeing civil rights and liberties to minorities and forcing the states to comply with them. The legal powers of the national government, in addition to its revenue sources, are large enough that almost no issue is beyond its scope, provided that national officials have the political will to deal with it.

A federal system also reflects a conflict between two other basic democratic values: liberty and equality. When states are responsible for a policy area, they are free to experiment, and successful innovations can be copied by others. But because states vary widely in financial resources and governmental capacities, some are in a position to provide much better governmental services than others. As a result, the quality of the services citizens receive varies widely, depending on the state in which they reside.

One of the advantages of federal grant-in-aid programs is that they permit states to operate their own programs while helping to ensure that a minimum level of service will be provided to all citizens nationwide. The expansion of federal power that accompanied the rise of fiscal-based federalism has also enabled the national government to push policy innovations in areas that the states ignored for a long time. Congressional legislation on air and water pollution, meat inspection, and disclosure of full credit information to consumers, among others, requires state governments to bring their regulatory controls up to national standards or face federal preemption of the problems. Such legislation thus attempts to protect all citizens in all states.

But federalism also has a dark side, and it can serve the ulterior purposes of people who seek to prevent action on a problem. Some, for example, have argued that social welfare programs should be the responsibility of the states, knowing that some states either could not or would not make the financial sacrifices necessary to provide such services. One of the most commonly voiced concerns about the "devolution revolution" is that states will engage in a "race to the bottom." With money from the federal government under tight constraints, and engaged in fierce competition to attract business and promote economic expansion, states are unlikely to raise taxes in order to support social welfare programs. The result will be a shrinking safety net under the neediest citizens, especially poor children. Proponents of devolution counter that the greater flexibility given to states under devolution policies gives them the room to innovate and find efficient as well as effective programs. The result will be better services for those who truly need them and a lighter burden for the taxpayer. The jury is still out on which of these arguments is correct, but it is clear that failures of such experiments have the potential to exact enormous costs on the most vulnerable in society.

The rise of the new federalism and devolution movements also counters fears that the federal government is inexorably expanding and centralizing power. While it is undeniable that the federal government has steadily expanded its reach into a wide variety of areas traditionally the responsibility of states and cities, states are a long way from being the lackeys of Washington. Public opinion polls indicate that people place greater faith in states on a long list of issues, and all three branches of the federal government recognize that the Tenth Amendment gives states the broad authority to act independently. Many states have highly professional government operations, with full-time legislatures and governors who, in some areas, wield more executive power than the president. For example, several governors have the power of a line item veto. Yet it is also true that the commitment to the principles of new federalism seems shaky, especially at the national level. Some of the most vocal proponents of states rights, such as President George W. Bush, are the same people leading the charge to pass laws expanding the national government's influence over traditionally state and local responsibilities.

Perhaps what ultimately characterizes the relationship between federal and state governments is not the creeping dominance of one level of government over the other but cyclical swings in which one level takes precedence during one era, and another takes the lead during a different era. The theory of **cyclical federalism** argues that the national government becomes the major policy player during liberal periods of American history, such as the New Deal in the 1930s and the Great Society efforts of the 1960s. In conservative periods, the national government retrenches, and states become the sources of major policy innovations. Such swings occurred in the 1920s and the 1990s. The inauguration of a conservative president in 2001, the terrorist attacks later that same year, and the fiscal crisis faced by the states in 2002 and 2003 managed the unique feat of trying to push the pendulum of cyclical federalism both ways. The end result seems to be ad hoc federalism—policymakers picking and choosing a state or national perspective based on what is convenient for their favored agenda. While this raises questions about the philosophical commitments of policymakers, it serves to underline the point that the determination of whether the state or national government plays the dominant role is driven as much by the issue at hand and the contemporary political context as by the continuation of any inexorable historical trend.

Summary

- Federalism is a political system in which regional governments share power with the national government, and it is the primary institutional feature of the U. S. Constitution. In the system established by the Constitution, states are sovereign powers and are partners of, rather than subordinates to, the federal government.
- There are two other primary means of dividing power in a political system. In a confederation, the central government is subordinate to the regional governments. In a unitary system, power is concentrated in the central government, and regional governments can exercise only the power granted to them by central authority.
- Federalism offers some general advantages. It allows experimentation and gives regional governments the ability to tailor policy more closely to local preferences.

It also has disadvantages, creating an often confusing patchwork of laws and regulations across a nation.

- The Constitution grants the national government enumerated and implied powers. Enumerated powers are specified in the Constitution. Implied powers come from broad constitutional clauses such as the power to "make all laws which shall be necessary and proper" (Article I, Section 8). Both enumerated and implied powers have been interpreted broadly and have allowed the constitutional expansion of the national government.

- The Constitution gives no specific powers to state governments, and state prerogatives were not spelled out in the original document. State powers are concentrated in the Tenth Amendment, which provides that the powers not given to the national government nor prohibited to the states "are reserved to the states respectively, or to the people." The general source of political authority for the states comes from their own constitutions, which specify each state's powers and limitations.

- The Constitution guarantees certain rights to the states. These include protection by the federal government against insurrection and invasion, a republican form of government, equal representation in the Senate, equality with other states, and the right to approve any changes to the Constitution.

- The Constitution places obligations on the states. States are required to extend "full faith and credit" to the public acts and records of other states and to deliver criminals who cross state lines to the state with jurisdiction over the crime.

- The Constitution makes some provisions for settling conflicts between federal and state governments. It makes all state and federal law, including state constitutions, subordinate to the Constitution, in effect making the U.S. Supreme Court the ultimate umpire of the federal system.

- Federal and state governments and the relationship between them have evolved considerably in the two centuries the Constitution has been in force. All levels of government have gotten larger and have played a more prominent role in the lives of citizens.

- The federal government has tended to have the upper hand in the cooperative relationship with the states by using grants-in-aid to fund programs. In recent decades, the new federalism movement has begun to alter the cooperative relationship based on grants-in-aid. Essentially, new federalism seeks to devolve power back to the states and give them more autonomy from federal preferences. Although policy and court decisions have given some teeth to the new federalism movement, there remain strong pressures for federal preemption on a number of key policy issues.

Key Terms

ad hoc federalism 90	crossover sanctions 86
block grants 85	cyclical federalism 93
categorical grants 84	devolution 80
concurrent powers 74	dual federalism 81
confederation 66	enabling act 76
cooperative federalism 82	"full faith and credit" 75

Selected Readings

Elazar, Daniel. 1984. *American Federalism: A View from the States.* 3rd ed. New York: Harper & Row. A classic analysis of American federalism that is particularly strong on the origins of regional political cultures and on their effect on policy and political behavior.

Peterson, Paul E. 1995. *The Price of Federalism.* Washington, DC: Brookings. A comprehensive look at how federalism operates in the United States. Peterson traces the evolution of the relationships between state and federal governments and provides an in-depth look at what works and what does not.

Rivlin, Alice. 1992. *Reinventing the American Dream: The Economy, the States, and the Federal Government.* Washington, DC: Brookings. An examination of the fiscal relationship between the state and federal governments. The author was a budget director during the Clinton administration.

Van Horn, Carl, ed. *The State of the States.* 1996. Washington, DC: CQ Press. Each chapter in this book examines a feature of state political systems and traces its evolution and performance through the contemporary period.

Weber, Ronald E., and Paul Brace, eds. 1999. *American State and Local Politics: Directions for the 21st Century.* New York: Chatham House. A comprehensive reader that looks at the institutional changes affecting state and local politics and examines challenges facing governments within the federal system today.

4 | Civil Liberties

Brianna LaHara is not the sort of person you would normally expect to go on a smash-and-grab looting spree. Yet that, more or less, is what the 12-year-old New York City honors student was charged with in a September 2003 lawsuit filed by the Recording Industry Association of America (RIAA). According to the RIAA, Brianna's crime was downloading copyrighted songs—more than a thousand of them—without paying. What she "stole" were electronic files containing tunes like "If You're Happy and You Know It (Clap Your Hands)."

The RIAA took a public relations hit for suing Brianna and hundreds of others for illegally downloading and sharing music files. Yet it was largely unrepentant. Roughly 2.6 billion copyrighted songs are illegally downloaded every month, and to the recording industry that translates into very real losses. Suing your own customers is rarely a good business move, but the RIAA claims it had little choice. It was one of the few options they had to discourage people from taking their products without paying. Grandparents, grade-schoolers, and college undergraduates were targeted by the RIAA, and, thus far, the courts have mostly sided with the RIAA, even if public opinion has not (CBS News 2004).

The controversy over music file sharing highlights one of the central tensions in democratic societies: the need to balance individual freedom with social order. Few people believe that suing 12-year-olds for music piracy serves the broader interests of society. Yet neither is letting people use the Internet to take what, by legal right, is not

theirs. If there are no rules limiting personal freedom, cyberspace devolves into anarchy. Substitute music files for pirated term papers, medical records, or hardcore pornography. Instead of downloading files, think of individuals secretly putting spyware on hard drives to track the surfing habits of unsuspecting computer users. Should people be free to do any or all of these things? If freedom is not absolute in cyberspace, where should the government or the law limit what individuals can freely choose to access, post, or download?

There are no universally approved answers to these questions, and they extend into the real world, not just the virtual one. The central problem here is the need to balance the freedom of the individual with the need for social order—a dilemma that cuts to the heart of the core democratic value of political freedom. If a democratic system can guarantee citizens considerable individual freedom while retaining order and the preservation of communal values, it has gone a long way toward delivering on the promise of democracy. Yet delivering this promise is a tough balancing act that requires squarely facing the Madisonian dilemma discussed in Chapter 2. How do you give government enough authority to preserve social order and communal values, but not so much that it places unfair and inappropriate limits on individual freedom of choice? In this chapter we explore how the United States has struggled with this question by examining civil liberties—the freedom of individual citizens—and the constitutional principles that protect them.

© Kim Kumenich/San Francisco Chronicle/Corbis Saba

Raymond Maalouf (left) and daughters Kristina (center) and
Michelle (right) might have to pay the Recording Industry
Association of America thousands of dollars after the association
sued them for illegal downloading of copyrighted material.
Ironically, the girls say they are part of a Pepsi Super Bowl TV
ad that touts the Apple iTunes music downloading service, as
seen on the computer screen.

The Promise of Civil Liberties

The promise of civil liberty is, in essence, the promise of political freedom. **Civil liberties**
can be defined as the freedoms enjoyed by individuals in democratic society. They constitute the choices individuals are free to make with little or no interference from governmental authority. Choosing and practicing religious beliefs, speaking our minds, and
seeking to form associations of like-minded people are examples of freedoms American
citizens are granted by the Constitution. Civil liberties thus boil down to a promise to
deliver on the core democratic value of political freedom: They represent a basic guarantee that individual citizens are free to make their own choices, to select their own goals
and the means to achieve them.

Yet civil liberties cannot be absolute. Even in democratic systems, governments
impose restrictions on individual liberties in the name of the public interest. For

example, Americans are guaranteed the rights of free speech and assembly by the First Amendment. Yet there are restrictions on these rights. For example, you cannot use your right of free speech to incite a riot. If you exercise your right to assemble by organizing a mass demonstration, you may be required by government authorities to obtain permits and satisfy health, safety, and sanitary regulations. Most people see these as a reasonable way to balance the freedoms of the individual with the need to maintain social order.

Liberty and Authority

Balancing the liberty of the individual with the authority of government is not always easy. Consider the government's response to the terrorist attacks of September 11; 2001. This included rounding up hundreds of Middle Eastern men for questioning; declaring two U.S. citizens as "enemy combatants" and putting them in a military prison without charging them or giving them access to U.S. courts; allowing FBI agents to enter houses of religious worship or attend political meetings; and passing the Patriot Act, which gave the government sweeping new powers to spy on its own citizens. The aggressive response to ensure security and social order was, at least initially, popular. Yet many of these efforts clearly ran into, and sometimes over, civil liberties. Under the provisions of the Patriot Act, for example, government agencies can secretly search your house or even your library records. Compare these powers with the individual freedoms guaranteed by the Fourth Amendment, which gives individual citizens the right to be secure in their "persons, houses, papers, and effects" and free from "unreasonable searches and seizures." If the government is conducting a "sneak and peak" search of your records to make sure you are not taking an unhealthy interest in extremist religious groups, and doing it without your knowledge, do you still have all the liberties guaranteed by the Constitution? Critics from the left and the right have argued no, and have criticized the Patriot Act for giving government too much power to infringe upon the freedom and liberty of the individual (Eggen 2003). How much of our civil liberties are we willing to give up for greater assurances of security? Should the government be able to detain people indefinitely without charges? Conduct secret searches? Target groups for surveillance based on their religious or political beliefs? Engage in racial profiling in the hunt for terrorists? (See the Promise and Policy feature "Civil Liberty and the War on Terror.")

These are not easy questions because the issue is not liberty *or* authority; rather, it is liberty *and* authority. Government must have some authority to set and enforce limits on freedom of choice to maintain social order because without social order, individual liberties are meaningless. Our individual freedoms have to be backed by some central authority. Without that authority, one individual's freedom extends only to the willingness of the next individual to respect those freedoms. Inevitably, some will use their freedom to deprive others of their liberties, their property, or even their lives. Hence the need for central authority; without it social order is replaced by anarchy. Yet democracy does not require complete social order, because this would mean individual behavior being dictated to a large extent by the state. This too would threaten individual freedom. The government, for example, could almost certainly make the country more secure from the threat of terrorism through increased monitoring of individual activities, restricting the freedom to travel, and outlawing certain political

PROMISE AND POLICY
Civil Liberty and the War on Terror

Most citizens accused of a crime in the United States are given the presumption of innocence, access to a lawyer, and the right to a speedy trial. Not so Jose Padilla, who was served with a warrant in May 2002, designated an enemy combatant two months later, and tossed into a military prison in South Carolina. And there he sat, without being formally charged, without access to a lawyer, with no trial . . . for a year and a half.

Padilla's alleged crime was involvement in a plot to make a so-called dirty bomb, which is a conventional bomb salted with radioactive material. There is little evidence that Padilla did anything more than think about building such a device, with even the intent behind that thought a matter of significant debate.

Padilla was the most famous of dozens of people rounded up under a seldom used material witness law that gives the government the authority to detain people for extended periods of time without charging them with a crime. In designating Padilla an "enemy combatant," the government went a significant step further—actually seeking to strip Padilla of a number of constitutional rights by putting him under the authority of military rather than civilian law.

The government made a number of similar aggressive moves to increase its authority to deal with suspected terrorists. It created military tribunals to deal with noncitizens, thus cutting them off from the regular court system and its constitutional guarantees. It declared the right to hold 650 Taliban and al-Qaeda operatives in military custody at a naval base for the duration of the war on terror, effectively declaring they would be kept behind barbed wire indefinitely. It rounded up hundreds of Middle Eastern men for questioning and detained them (again without access to a lawyer) for extended periods of time. It changed Department of Justice rules to allow FBI agents to enter houses of worship to check up on suspected terrorist-related activities.

It also passed the Patriot Act, which gives government sweeping new authority to search records and anonymously eavesdrop on phone calls and emails and requires businesses to keep tabs on customers whose transactions seem "suspicious"—for any reason at all—and might arouse the interest of any federal law enforcement agency.

The government's justification for doing this is that they are trying to round up the bad guys in the war on terror. There is little doubt that some, perhaps most, of those caught in this antiterror net are, by some definition, "bad guys." Yet these activities clearly represent a shift toward authority over liberty and have sounded alarms across the ideological spectrum from civil libertarians.

The basic question raised by civil libertarians is whether we as a society are willing to trade our individual liberties for collective security. Stripping suspected terrorists of their constitutional rights, letting the government lock people up more or less at will, and allowing law enforcement agencies to snoop through our private records and communications looking for signs of lawbreaking might well make us all safer. It will almost certainly make it harder to plan and execute terrorist acts.

Yet it also will also make us less free. In engaging in these activities, the government is consciously making a trade: the rights of individuals for the authority of government. In the name of collective security, some compromise along these lines has to be made. Yet how much is too much? How much individual freedom are we willing to give up to gain greater security? There are no universal answers or agreements in response to these questions. It is a classic case of balancing liberty with authority, the rights of the individual with the need for social order. At some point trading liberty for authority goes too far and breaks the promise of political freedom. Some argue that the government's war on terror strikes a reasonable balance; others argue it has already broken the promise.

Sources: Eggen, Dan. 2003. "Anti-Terror Law Power Used Broadly." *Washington Post.* May 21, p. 12A; Locy, Toni. 2004. "Patriot Act Blurred in the Public Mind." *USA Today.* February 26, p. 5A.

groups or beliefs. Doing so, however, breaks the promise of political freedom. The crux of the issue is how a free and secure society can achieve an acceptable balance between the values of individual freedom and the authority needed to maintain social order.

Resolving the conflicts that arise over these two values is difficult and complex, especially when individual liberties conflict. One group or individual exercising its rights may infringe on the rights and liberties of others. The old cliché that a person can exercise rights only as long as they do not interfere with someone else's rights is incorrect. When an individual exercises a right, it inevitably comes into conflict with someone else's right. A classic case is a newspaper editor who exercises freedom of the press by publishing information about a crime that jeopardizes the right of the accused to a fair trail. Is freedom of the press more important than a fair trial? Or does the right to a fair trial justify limiting freedom of the press? In such cases the authority of government has to choose, in effect, which individual's freedoms are more important. How does a democratic society go about choosing which individual freedoms take precedent over others?

Restrictions on the Government

The basic approach to dealing with civil liberties in the United States begins with the assumption that citizens should have as much freedom as possible to make individual choices. The rights and freedoms of individual Americans are embodied in the Bill of Rights to the Constitution. The Bill of Rights provides a starting point for establishing what individuals are free to do without government interference. These freedoms have undergone a considerable evolution over the past two centuries.

The Bill of Rights

A central concern of those who took the initiative in calling the Constitutional Convention was the protection of individual property rights from state governments. They gave almost no consideration to safeguarding civil liberties from the actions of national authorities. Although one of the main reasons for splitting from Great Britain was the lack of guaranteed individual rights, the notion of formally including such rights in the Constitution was brought up only toward the end of the convention, and even then in a halfhearted way. As originally written, there was virtually no mention of guaranteed civil liberties in the Constitution (Collier and Collier 1986, 338).

The absence of a guaranteed set of civil liberties—a so-called Bill of Rights— became one of the central issues raised by opponents to the Constitution during the ratification campaign. Even leaders like Thomas Jefferson, who favored the adoption of the Constitution, were unhappy that the convention had not included a statement of rights. The absence of a Bill of Rights "nearly sank the Constitution" (Collier and Collier 1986, 342). In response, the Federalists backing adoption of the Constitution agreed to make fashioning a Bill of Rights one of the first orders of business of the new government formed after ratification. Acting under a moral rather than a legal obligation, Washington, in his inaugural address, asked Congress to give careful attention to the demands to amend the Constitution to include a statement of rights.

James Madison took the lead in coordinating the suggestions of state ratifying conventions and introduced the amendments into the House of Representatives. Congress pared down the list to twelve, and ten of the resulting amendments were eventually ratified. These first ten amendments constitute the Bill of Rights, which became the legal basis of civil liberties in the United States. Both the anti-Federalists and the Federalists gained from the process. The former saw their initial support for a Bill of Rights vindicated, while the latter gained additional popular support for the Constitution they authored.

Restrictions on State Violations of Civil Liberties

The Bill of Rights originally was interpreted to apply only to the federal government, not to state governments. In the early years of the republic, restricting the Bill of Rights to the federal government made sense for the simple reason that states were well ahead of the federal government in guaranteeing basic civil liberties. Virginia's Declaration of Rights, for example, guaranteed that state's citizens basic freedoms of press and religion and the right to a trial by jury, and it was passed years before the Constitutional Convention. In fact, all the early state constitutions either contained a separate bill of rights or incorporated similar provisions as part of the basic document.

Given that state governments already incorporated basic guarantees of civil liberties, it is not surprising that Congress focused on the national government when developing the Bill of Rights. Nowhere did Congress specifically state that the amendments in the Bill of Rights applied only to the national government, but this was undoubtedly the intention of those who drafted them in the early 1790s.[1] This view was explicitly confirmed by the Supreme Court four decades later in the case of *Barron v. Baltimore* (1833).

The application of the Bill of Rights to state governments, however, gradually became an increasingly important question in guaranteeing civil liberties. This question was especially the case in the South during much of the 19th and 20th centuries, where a number of state governments passed laws systematically denying racial minorities civil liberties. The Civil War ended slavery, thus freeing African Americans from involuntary servitude, but state laws prevented many from enjoying the full rights and freedoms of citizenship. Following the Civil War, the Thirteenth, Fourteenth, and Fifteenth Amendments had seemed to take a large step toward making the Bill of Rights apply to state governments as well as the federal government. Of particular importance is the Fourteenth Amendment, which reads in part: "No state shall make or enforce any law which shall . . . deprive any person of life, liberty, or property, without due process of law." The Fifth Amendment contains a "due process of law" clause that applies to the national government, and the same clause in the Fourteenth Amendment applies to the states. The same clause appearing in both amendments implies that at least part—and perhaps all—of the Bill of Rights is binding on state governments.

These parallel provisions sparked a running debate over what is known as the **incorporation doctrine,** or the notion of what specific guarantees in the Bill of Rights are applied to state governments through the due process clause of the Fourteenth Amendment. Some argued that the Fourteenth Amendment, in effect, applied the entire Bill of Rights to state governments. Others disagreed, arguing the due process

---

[1]The First Amendment states "Congress shall make no law," and presumably this phrase is read into the amendments that follow, although this is never clarified.

clause applied the Bill of Rights more selectively to the states, and their application and limitations should be worked out on a case-by-case basis. The Supreme Court followed the latter course and only slowly began using the Fourteenth Amendment to apply the Bill of Rights to the states.

An important early example of this piecemeal approach to incorporating the Bill of Rights to apply to states as well as to the national government came in the 1925 case of *Gitlow v. New York*. Here the Supreme Court ruled that freedoms of speech and the press are such fundamental rights that the Fourteenth Amendment prevents states from unduly limiting these freedoms. Using similar reasoning, rulings in other cases added the other First Amendment freedoms to the liberties so protected. Over the years much of the Bill of Rights has, provision by provision, been applied to the states. Table 4.1 lists provisions in the Bill of Rights that have been incorporated. Today, most, but not all, of the limitations on government in the Bill of Rights apply to the states as well as to the national government.

Applied to all governments, the Bill of Rights now provides a common yardstick to judge the civil liberties shared by all citizens. In essence, what this means is that the most important dilemmas pitting liberty against authority, or liberty against liberty, are resolved by the Supreme Court interpreting and applying the Bill of Rights to specific cases. It is here, in the cases that come before the Supreme Court, where the promise of political freedom is ultimately judged. To learn how these decisions have balanced liberty with authority and kept or broken the promise of political freedom, it is helpful to look at the specifics of particular cases. Accordingly, the next sections discuss controversies and Supreme Court decisions surrounding a particular set of freedoms and rights guaranteed by the Bill of Rights and considered fundamental civil liberties: freedom of religion, freedom of expression, privacy, and the protections offered people accused of committing crimes.

Freedom of Religion

Many Americans assume that freedom from government interference in religious matters is a right that predates the founding of the republic. Tradition has Puritans fleeing England in the early 1620s to escape the dictates of the official Anglican Church and that the right of individuals to worship as they saw fit was a characteristic of the Massachusetts Bay Colony. In reality, the Puritans wanted only the freedom to impose their religious views on others. They quickly established the Congregational Church and forced all inhabitants under their jurisdiction to follow its religious precepts. Other colonies followed similar practices, and as late as the Revolutionary War most of them had what were known as established churches, or a particular set of religious beliefs that were favored by the government.

For the most part, these established churches did not survive the Revolutionary period. Rather than a single established church, some of the Founders (notably George Washington) wanted all Christian churches to be state religions of equal standing and to be supported by taxation. This notion was opposed by others who thought it unwise to mix church and state and sought an official separation between the two (those favoring this position included James Madison, Thomas Jefferson, and George Mason). The latter position was written into state law in 1786 in the Virginia Statute of Religious Liberty, which mandated that state government could force no one to frequent or support any religion or religious practice. This general attitude about church–state

Table 4.1

Incorporation of the Bill of Rights to Apply to State Governments

YEAR	ISSUE AND AMENDMENT	SUPREME COURT CASE	VOTE
1868	Fourteenth Amendment to Constitution ratified		
1897	Just compensation in taking of private property by government (V)	Chicago, Burlington & Quincy RR v. Chicago 166 U.S. 266	9:0
1925	Freedom of speech and press (I)	Gitlow v. New York 268 U.S. 652	7:2
1927	Freedom of speech (I)	Fiske v. Kansas 274 U.S. 380	9:0
1931	Freedom of press (I)	Near v. Minnesota 283 U.S. 697	5:4
1932	Counsel in capital criminal cases (VI)	Powell v. Alabama 287 U.S. 45	7:2
1934	Free exercise of religion (I)	Hamilton v. Regents of the U. of California 293 U.S. 245	9:0
1937	Freedom of assembly and petition (I)	De Jonge v. Oregon 299 U.S. 253	8:0
1940	Free exercise of religion (I)	Cantwell v. Connecticut 310 U.S. 296	9:0
1947	Separation of church and state (I)	Everson v. Board of Education 330 U.S. 1	5:4
1948	Public trial (VI)	In re Oliver 33 U.S. 257	7:2
1949	Unreasonable searches and seizures (IV)	Wolf v. Colorado 338 U.S. 25	6:3
1961	Exclusionary rule of evidence from unreasonable searches and seizures (IV)	Mapp v. Ohio 367 U.S. 643	6:3
1962	Cruel and unusual punishment (VIII)	Robinson v. California 370 U.S. 660	6:2
1963	Counsel in all criminal cases (VI)	Gideon v. Wainwright 372 U.S. 335	9:0
1964	Self-incrimination (V)	Malloy v. Hogan 378 U.S. 1	5:4
		Murphy v. Waterfront Commission 378 U.S. 52	9:0
1965	Right to confront adverse witnesses (VI)	Pointer v. Texas 380 U.S. 400	7:2
1965	Right to privacy (IX)	Griswold v. Connecticut 381 U.S. 479	7:2
1967	Impartial jury (VI)	Parker v. Gladden 385 U.S. 363	8:1
1967	Obtaining and confronting favorable witnesses (VI)	Washington v. Texas 388 U.S. 14	9:0
1967	Speedy trial (VI)	Klopfer v. North Carolina 386 U.S. 213	9:0
1968	Jury trial in non-petty criminal cases (VI)	Duncan v. Louisiana 391 U.S. 145	7:2
1969	Double jeopardy (V)	Benton v. Maryland 395 U.S. 784	7:2

Note: The Fourteenth Amendment's due process clause is the basis for applying the Bill of Rights to the states. Enumerated rights not incorporated: Second Amendment right to bear arms; Third Amendment safeguards against quartering troops in private homes; Fifth Amendment provision for grand jury indictment; Seventh Amendment trial by jury in civil cases; and Eighth Amendment right against excessive fines and bail.

Sources: Stanley, Harold W., and Richard G. Niemi. 2001. Vital Statistics on American Politics 1999–2000. Washington, DC: Congressional Quarterly Press, 304; Abraham, Henry J. 1994. The Judiciary: The Supreme Court in the Governmental Process. 9th ed. Dubuque, IA: William C. Brown; Feeley, Malcolm M., and Samuel Krislov. 1990. Constitutional Law. 2nd ed. Glenview, IL: Scott, Foresman, 382; United States Reports. Washington, DC: U.S. Government Printing Office, various years.

relations became dominant in other states. Two sections of the Constitution made this attitude national policy. Article VI prohibits the use of a religious test as a requirement for public office, and the First Amendment mandates that "Congress shall make no law respecting an establishment of religion, or prohibiting the free exercise thereof." In *Cantwell v. Connecticut* (1940), the Supreme Court incorporated this clause of the First Amendment, ruling that it represented a fundamental liberty and was applicable to state governments through the due process clause of the Fourteenth Amendment.

In making the religious provisions of the First Amendment apply to all governments, the Supreme Court was in effect passing on two separate guarantees. The first is that government cannot establish a religion. The second is that government cannot prohibit the free exercise of religion. Though obviously related, these are two different ideas, and the Supreme Court has made a point of keeping them distinct.

Prohibition against the Establishment of Religion

Controversies over the establishment clause deal with whether public authorities can sanction religious activities or favor a particular religious group or belief. The Supreme Court has generally said public authorities cannot do this directly, although it has allowed public authorities considerable leeway in indirectly supporting secular activities undertaken by religious organizations. Public education provides an excellent case study of how these issues have evolved over the past century.

An early case involving public education and the establishment clause was *Everson v. Board of Education* (1947). This case originated in New Jersey, where state law authorized local school boards to reimburse parents for costs incurred in transporting their children to parochial schools. The key question was whether the expenditures showed favoritism that constituted an establishment of religion. In its majority opinion the Court for the first time directly articulated the principle of **separation of church and state,** meaning neither federal nor state government could pass any law supporting one religion or all religions, or any law preferring one religion over another. Though the *Everson* ruling called for a sharp separation between church and state, the Court concluded that the transportation expenditures did not support any religious activity and were therefore allowable. In directly articulating the concept of separation of church and state, however, the Court laid the foundation for several other cases that had a much broader and controversial impact on education.

One of the most significant of these cases is *Engel v. Vitale* (1962), which decided public schools could not officially sanction prayer. The heart of the case involved a prayer written by New York State officials that was read aloud by teachers and students in public schools: "Almighty God, we acknowledge our dependence upon Thee, and we beg Thy blessings upon us, our parents, our teachers, and our country." In a blunt majority opinion, the Court declared that "the constitutional prohibition against laws respecting an establishment of religion must at least mean that in this country it is no part of the business of government to compose official prayers for any group of the American people to recite as part of a religious program carried on by government." A year later, in *Abington Township v. Schempp* (1963), the Court extended this line of reasoning by prohibiting states from requiring Bible reading or recitation of the Lord's Prayer in public schools.

The Supreme Court has struck down state- or school-sanctioned religious activities in most subsequent cases. In *Stone v. Graham* (1980) a Kentucky statute requiring the

© David H. Wells/Corbis

The free exercise of religion is a constitutional right familiar to Americans, but the interpretations of how to uphold that right are often controversial, especially with regard to religion in schools. The Supreme Court has consistently ruled that when a public authority supports an activity with religious content (such as prayer in public schools), it is favoring a belief system, which is prohibited by the First Amendment. On the other hand, it has also ruled that government support of secular activities by parochial schools is legal if it does not promote excessive relations between church and state and does not impede or promote religion. What difficulties do you see in comparing these types of rulings?

Ten Commandments be posted in every public school classroom was ruled unconstitutional. An Alabama statute authorizing a 1-minute period of silence in public schools for "meditation or voluntary prayer" met a similar fate in *Wallace v. Jaffree* (1985). In *Lee v. Weisman* (1992) the court ruled having clergy offer prayers at public school ceremonies that students were required to attend was similarly a violation of separation of church and state and thus a violation of the establishment clause.

What all these cases have in common is some form of governmental authority (state law, school district, public official) sanctioning or supporting some form of religious expression or activity. The Court has consistently ruled that when a public authority organizes, requires, or officially approves any activity with religious content, it is favoring a particular belief system. This, the Supreme Court has ruled, constitutes establishment of religion and is prohibited by the First Amendment. This ban has been extended to encompass everything from drawing school district boundaries to create public schools with a particular religious majority (*Board of Education Kiryas Joel Village v. Grumet* 1994) to student-led prayer at high school football games (*Santa Fe Independent School District v. Doe* 2000).

All of these decisions are based on the idea that the First Amendment clearly states what government cannot do: It cannot establish a religion. But what can the government do? The First Amendment is much less clear on this point. Parochial schools engage in a wide range of educational activities that have no direct religious component. Can government support some of these activities, even though that support would indirectly benefit an organization that promotes a particular religion? Permitting indirect support clearly was the implication of the *Everson* case, which allowed reimbursement for the costs of traveling to a religious school, even as the ruling affirmed the separation of church and state. The Supreme Court has generally ruled that as long as an activity related to a religious school has a secular purpose, does not impede or promote religion, and does not promote excessive entanglement between church and state, public authorities can support that activity without violating the establishment clause of the First Amendment.

Even so, attempts to use public money or other resources to support activities at religious schools are controversial. Behind these disputes is a more fundamental difference concerning the role that schools, especially parochial schools, should play in a democratic society. Those who support public expenditures for parochial schools argue that they educate a lot of children and thereby save the public school system a good deal of money. Furthermore, say proponents, it is not fair to tax parents for the public schools while they are paying parochial school tuition; such parents are in effect paying twice to educate their children. Finally, supporters of parochial schools argue that such schools do not raise serious religious problems in American society because they devote most of their activities to educating students in secular rather than sectarian subjects.

Opponents argue that separation of children into schools on the basis of religion is democratically undesirable. A primary advantage of public schools is their democratizing influence, and this includes bringing children of various religious backgrounds together during their formative years. This diversity is seen as particularly important because religious differences are often associated with differences in ethnicity and socioeconomic background. Opponents, therefore, do not want to see government take any action that would foster parochial schools at the expense of public ones. If parents wish to send their children to church-supported schools rather than to public schools, that is their prerogative. But they must assume the financial burden of that choice and not expect the rest of society to assist them. Just as those who choose to hire private security firms are not exempt from paying taxes to support local law enforcement, those who choose to send their children to private schools are still required to contribute to public schools. Finally, opponents believe it is not possible to draw clear distinctions between sectarian and secular matters and that religious points of view have an effect on the way that many nonreligious subjects are taught.

The most recent Supreme Court ruling on this issue sided with proponents of programs that result in tax dollars going to religious schools. The issue in *Zelman v. Simmons-Harris* (2002) was the constitutionality of a school voucher program in Cleveland, Ohio. The publicly funded vouchers were given to disadvantaged students who could use them to pay for tuition at private schools. The overwhelming majority of vouchers (more than 90 percent) were redeemed at religiously affiliated schools. Opponents argued the vouchers represented little more than a way to subsidize religious institutions. Proponents argued that rather than the vouchers representing government favoring religion, the program was designed to help students by giving them a means to leave failing public schools. The financial boon to religious schools thus was not a policy goal but simply a by-product of individual choice that was neither required nor encouraged by government. In a 5 to 4 decision, the Court sided with proponents of vouchers. While such subsidies can (and in some cases are) prohibited by state constitutions, the *Zelman* ruling means including parochial schools in voucher programs does not violate the separation of church and state mandated by the First Amendment. This clears the way for millions of tax dollars to be used to pay tuition at religiously affiliated schools.

Free Exercise of Religion

Controversies involving the free exercise of religion deal with the extent to which the state can regulate individual religious practices. In the late 1870s, the Supreme Court had to decide whether a federal law banning polygamy in the territories violated the First Amendment rights of Mormons who practiced plural marriages. In

Reynolds v. United States (1879), the court made a clear distinction between religious beliefs and actions stemming from those beliefs. The justices reasoned that Mormons had every right to believe that God permits men to have as many wives as possible but that Mormons had no right to implement this belief because it violates social duty and order.

As *Reynolds* indicates, the free exercise of religion is a liberty subject to some restrictions by government. But the Court has frequently acted to protect individual religious choices from government restrictions. For example, a series of cases in the 1930s and 1940s dealt with Jehovah's Witnesses who acted on their belief that each member of the group is a minister with a duty to spread the gospel. In distributing religious literature in the public streets, Jehovah's Witnesses ran afoul of state and local laws relating to permits, fees, and taxes. The Court ruled that Jehovah's Witnesses had the right to pass out tracts in residential areas. The Court in effect had to balance the right of Jehovah's Witnesses to propagate their faith with the right of individuals to privacy—in this case, to not be bothered by people seeking to convert them (*Cantwell v. Connecticut* 1940; *Minersville School District v. Gobitis* 1940; *West Virginia State Board of Education v. Barnette* 1943).

Few issues better highlight the delicate balance between the right to free exercise of religion and the broader interests of society than religious exercises in state-supported schools. This issue actually spans both the establishment and the free exercise clauses. Since its initial ruling banning mandatory prayer in public schools in 1962, the Supreme Court has consistently ruled that because public schools are government institutions, the Constitution prohibits state and local authorities from commanding schoolchildren to pray aloud or silently, or to engage in other activities that could be construed as having a religious purpose. Yet none of these decisions prevents an individual from praying in school. The government has no right—and, as a practical matter, no ability—to interfere with such practices. Nor can public authorities prevent religious groups from using public facilities if such access is available to others (*Lamb's Chapel v. Center Moriches School District* 1993; *Good News Club v. Milford Central School District* 2001).

While the government cannot limit individuals or groups from practicing their religious beliefs, the Supreme Court has also ruled that public authorities are not obligated to subsidize how individuals choose to exercise those rights. In *Locke v. Davey* (2004), the Supreme Court said state governments are allowed to withhold taxpayer-funded scholarships for those who choose to study for the ministry. At issue in this case was the constitutionality of Washington State's so-called Blaine amendment. Blaine amendments (named for the congressman who tried, and failed, to get the U.S. Constitution amended) are included in some state constitutions. They specifically prohibit state governments from funding religious activities. Joshua Davey was a college student who won a publicly funded scholarship and decided to study for the ministry. The state rescinded the scholarship on the grounds that paying to train someone to lead a congregation constituted support of a religious activity. Davey sued, arguing withholding the scholarship—available to students studying in any other field—amounted to religious discrimination. The Supreme Court held that Washington State was under no First Amendment obligation to provide the scholarship.

Davey makes an interesting companion case to the *Zelman v. Simmons-Harris* (2002) ruling on school vouchers. In *Zelman* the Supreme Court said state governments could, at least indirectly, support activities undertaken by religious organizations. In *Davey,* the Court ruled that just because state governments *could* support such activities, they were not *obligated* to do so. Withholding financial support from religious education imposes no criminal or civil limitations on the free exercise of religion, and states are free to mandate that tax dollars not be used to support any religious activity.

Freedom of Expression

In addition to freedom of religion, the First Amendment spells out a number of other liberties that government may not interfere with: freedom of speech and the press, the right of peaceful assembly, and the right to petition the government for redress of grievances. Together these constitute means by which individuals and groups can express their views and communicate them to one another as well as to public officials.

Like religious freedom, the First Amendment liberties relating to expression did not become a matter of major concern for the Supreme Court until the 20th century. It was not until the 1950s that social and political changes prompted a series of vital First Amendment issues to be decided by the Supreme Court.

General Approaches

There are several basic approaches to dealing with issues of freedom of expression. One is to treat this freedom as absolute. This **absolutist approach** argues that the Founders wanted the words of the First Amendment to be taken literally; in other words, the phrase that Congress shall make "no law" means that government cannot take any action that interferes with the free expression of views, no matter how offensive, hurtful, or even harmful they may be. Absolutists do recognize that society has a right to place limits on the freedom of expression, but they want those limits kept to a minimum.

Other approaches to freedom of expression issues differ from the absolutist position in degree rather than kind. Some justices adopted the **preferred freedoms doctrine** approach to freedom of expression. According to this doctrine, First Amendment rights are considered so fundamental to achieving a free society that courts have a greater obligation to protect these freedoms than other rights. Justice Oliver Wendell Holmes first expressed this view in the early 1900s. This doctrine supports an argument that courts should take a more active role in First Amendment controversies, rather than defer to the Congress and the president.

Other justices have avoided trying to treat freedom of expression issues with a universal philosophy. For example, Justice Felix Frankfurter was known for a pragmatic **balancing test** approach to free expression. Essentially, this approach called for weighing competing values on a case-by-case basis to determine when restrictions on freedom of expression are warranted in order to protect society or the rights of other individuals or groups. The significant difference between the balancing test approach and the absolutist and preferred freedoms approaches is that the former rejects the idea that freedom of expression is an absolute value that is to take precedence over other legitimate concerns.

Specific Tests

Although the general approaches to freedom of expression reflect important basic attitudes, in practice none has been particularly helpful in dealing with the wide variety of freedom of expression issues the Supreme Court has faced in the past half century or so.

The basic problem is that while most justices advocate the greatest degree of freedom possible in matters of individual expression, it has proven difficult to balance that freedom with society's need for order and authority. The Supreme Court has devised various tests to provide a basic rule about when freedom of expression can legitimately be regulated.

The **"clear and present danger" test** was articulated by Justice Oliver Wendell Holmes, Jr., in *Schenck v. United States* (1919) and follows from his preferred freedoms doctrine. The case involved a socialist convicted of violating the Espionage Act by circulating antiwar leaflets to members of the armed forces. According to Holmes, the central issue was whether the leaflets constituted a "clear and present danger" of bringing about "substantive evils" that Congress had a right to prevent. Schenck's activities were deemed to meet this test; the possibility of soldiers' refusing to fight was considered a substantive evil, and his conviction was upheld.

The **bad tendency rule** was articulated just a year after the *Schenck* case in *Pierce v. United States* (1920). This case also involved socialists distributing antiwar pamphlets, though there was no indication that any of this literature reached members of the armed forces or had an immediate effect on the war. The case is notable because it eased the "clear and present danger" test for restricting freedom of speech. Instead of requiring speech to raise the probability of an immediate evil before it could be restricted, the bad tendency rule simply required that speech might tend to bring about an evil at some time in the future.

This ruling raised the question of when to use the "clear and present danger" test and when to use the bad tendency rule, a question the Court sought to answer in *Dennis v. United States* (1951). This case revolved around communists charged with conspiring to overthrow the government. In deciding whether expression advocating the overthrow of the government was protected by the First Amendment, the Supreme Court indicated that the nature of the evil to be avoided had to be taken into account. If the evil was grave enough, such as the violent overthrow of the government, then it was not necessary to demonstrate that the expression would probably result in the immediate occurrence of the evil. But if the evil was less grave, such as a local disturbance, then those seeking to regulate expression must meet the thresholds established earlier. In this case, the Court seemed to say if the evil is serious enough, the bad tendency test should be employed; if the evil is less serious, the "clear and present danger" standard is applicable.

The difficulty with all these tests, as well as with those applied to other areas of free expression, is that verbal formulas cannot possibly capture all the complexities of social situations. In other words, judges ultimately exercise considerable discretion in deciding freedom of expression issues. This discretion is sometimes used to defend individual liberty against the authority of the state. For example, in *Texas v. Johnson* (1989), the Supreme Court ruled that burning the American flag was a form of expression that had constitutional protection. Despite widespread support for laws outlawing desecration of the flag, the Court ruled that a "bedrock principle" of the First Amendment is that the government has no authority to prevent the expression of an idea simply because it is offensive. In short, the Court reaffirmed that the purpose of the First Amendment is to protect the expression of ideas and views that others find disagreeable. Yet while the Supreme Court said burning flags was protected speech, they ruled that burning crosses was not in *Virginia v. Black* (2003). The key issue in this case was a Virginia law making it a felony to burn a cross for the purpose of intimidating any person or group. The

The rapper Eminem has come under severe criticism for his violent and derogatory lyrics. A wide variety of groups have called for suppressing or censoring his lyrics, but Eminem claims the right to freedom of speech and refers to the provisions of the First Amendment to the Constitution for support. The Supreme Court, while admitting that some obscene speech should be regulated, has not been able to provide guidelines for what specific types of speech can be regulated, making enforcement nearly impossible.

Supreme Court rejected the argument that cross burning with the intent of racial intimidation was constitutionally protected free speech. In this case the Supreme Court used its discretionary power to limit the freedom of the individual in the name of protecting security and social order.

In *McConnell v. Federal Election Commission* (2003), the Supreme Court also gave Congress the right to limit some forms of political speech immediately before an election. The issue here was not what was said or how it was said, but where it was said. The McCain-Feingold Act of 2002 banned special interest groups from running issue ads within sixty days of a federal election. Opponents of the law sued, arguing the law violated First Amendment rights in a way that was particularly offensive; in effect, the law served to weaken the voice of citizens when they are most likely to be heard, that is, right before an election. The court disagreed, ruling that the money underlying these ad campaigns raised the possibility of perceived or actual corruption and that the government had a basic interest in preventing both. That interest overrode the right of special interest groups to speak loudly in an election.

Unprotected Speech

The Supreme Court has ruled that some forms of expression are always beyond constitutional protection and can be outlawed or strictly regulated by the government. Yet even in these cases, the Court has struggled to strike an appropriate balance of competing values and clear standards that government and individuals can understand and follow.

Obscenity   Few civil liberty issues have given the Supreme Court more difficulty than obscenity. Rulings in two key 1957 cases, *Roth v. United States* and *Alberts v. California,* clearly articulated that obscenity was not protected speech but was instead a form of expression that could be outlawed by the state. Yet while outlawing obscenity, neither case produced a clear definition of obscenity.

In *Roth,* the test of obscenity was whether an "average person, applying contemporary community standards" would find that the dominant theme of the material in question would appeal to prurient interest. The ruling made clear that isolated passages from a film or a literary work could not be used to judge whether the work was obscene; the dominant theme of the entire work had to be judged. The test caused enormous problems in application. There was huge variation in what people considered obscene under this definition, and this variation existed not simply from community to community but also from state to state and even from court to court.

The frustration caused by the Court's inability to provide a clear and universally applicable definition of obscenity was most famously articulated by Justice Potter Stewart in *Jacobellis v. Ohio* (1964). In a concurring opinion, Stewart wrote: "perhaps I could never succeed in intelligibly [defining obscenity]. But I know it when I see it." Stewart's statement points out a basic problem with enforcing restrictions on sexually explicit expression: Those who engage in such expression often do not know if they are breaking the law because of the elasticity of the definition of obscenity.

In *Miller v. California* (1973), the Supreme Court set three criteria for judging whether a work was obscene:

1.   The average person applying contemporary standards finds that the work as a whole appeals to prurient interests (the *Roth* test).
2.   The work "depicts or describes in a patently offensive way, sexual conduct specifically defined by the applicable state law."
3.   The work lacks any "serious literary, artistic, political or scientific value."

These guidelines have subsequently been incorporated into federal and state statutes, but thus far they have not surmounted the problem articulated by Stewart. In recent years, the enforcement of obscenity statutes seems to have been driven by the subjective moral judgments of policymakers and politically active groups rather than by any objective standard of obscenity (Smith 1999). The problem is that if government is going to be given the authority to completely outlaw some forms of expression, citizens must know exactly what the forms of expression are. If the state has the authority to arbitrarily or inconsistently declare some forms of expression beyond constitutional protection, this clearly threatens individual liberty.

The advent of the Internet and the World Wide Web—where pornographic material is but a mouse click away for anyone with an online connection—has given new relevance to the debate over sexually explicit materials and free speech. In *Reno v. ACLU* (1997) the Supreme Court ruled unconstitutional key provisions of the Communications Decency Act, a law passed by Congress that sought to define and regulate the Internet as a broadcast rather than a print medium. The law argued that even sexually explicit materials constitutionally protected as free speech cannot be legally sold to minors. In the name of protecting minors, television networks are not allowed to broadcast X-rated movies over the open air waves. Why should the Internet be any different? The Supreme Court saw things differently. Who is going to decide what is indecent and therefore illegal to post on the Web? Rather than create another endless definitional debate about what is or is not "indecent," "pornographic," or "obscene," the Court ruled the Internet to be the equivalent of a print medium or public forum. That meant the Court was obligated to provide that medium the broadest First Amendment protection, and it struck down the Communications Decency Act. Yet the Court has also ruled that government can seek to limit minors accessing sexually explicit materials on the Internet. In *United States v.*

American Library Association (2004), the Court ruled Congress was not unduly restricting free speech rights by requiring libraries to install filtering software on computers as a condition of receiving federal funds. Again, we see the Supreme Court engaged in a delicate balancing act: on the one hand, trying to maximize civil liberty and restrict government interference with individual choices; on the other, trying to ensure the government has enough authority to ensure free exercise of those liberties does not threaten social order.

Libel and Slander   Other forms of unprotected speech have run into the same problem. Making false and defaming statements about someone is **slander** when done orally and **libel** when done in print or other media. The Court has ruled that an individual's right to free speech does not extend to using that right to harm others, so slander and libel do not have constitutional protection. This principle has raised concerns about the First Amendment's guarantee of freedom of the press.

The basic requirements for proving libel are

- Publication—the statements must be communicated such that third parties can observe them.
- Identification—the aggrieved party is clearly specified.
- Harm—the aggrieved party suffers as a result of the libel.

The basic defense in a libel suit is truth. If a communication is defamatory but is also completely factual, the aggrieved party generally does not have the basis for a successful libel suit. The problem for the press is that the news media often report on issues that portray public figures in an unfavorable light, and under the pressure of deadlines or because they are not privy to crucial information, they could unwittingly libel someone.

There are different standards for public officials than for people who are not in the spotlight, and public officials have a more difficult time winning libel cases than private citizens. In *New York Times Co. v. Sullivan* (1964), the Supreme Court ruled that in order to win a libel suit, a public official who is defamed in press reports must prove not only that a report was false and defamatory but also that it was issued with "actual malice." In other words, false and harmful reports about public officials are not libelous unless it can be proved that the reports were known to be false when they were published or were published with a "reckless disregard" for the truth. However, public officials have discovered that proving malice is a comparable legal hurdle to defining obscenity. In later rulings, the Supreme Court extended the principle in *Sullivan* to include public figures such as movie stars, athletes, and other celebrities (*Curtis Publishing Company v. Butts* 1967; *Associated Press v. Walker* 1967). As a result, this standard gives the press broad liberties to report on public figures in order to inform the public, while public figures have limited recourse if this freedom is used to issue false and misleading statements about them.

The Right to Privacy

Nowhere does the Constitution explicitly articulate a right of privacy. Yet there is nothing new about **privacy** as a fundamental civil liberty. The Constitution does include numerous amendments and clauses upholding an individual's right to be free of government interference without due cause or due process. Combined, these can be seen as a right to be left alone.

Privacy became the focus of controversy in the latter half of the 20th century when the Supreme Court expanded the right of privacy beyond its link with the traditional protections actually spelled out in the Constitution and granted it independent status. Over a series of decisions, the right to privacy, in essence, became a part of the Bill of Rights. The lead case in this movement was *Griswold v. Connecticut* (1965). In ruling that Connecticut could not prohibit the use of contraceptives by married couples, the Court enumerated a right of marital privacy, even though it conceded that no such right was specifically provided for in the Constitution. Lacking a specific constitutional guideline, the Court argued that various guarantees in the First, Third, Fourth, Fifth, and Ninth Amendments create "zones of privacy" that the government had no right to invade.

In the years following *Griswold,* the Court signaled a willingness to expand this right to privacy. In *Eisenstadt v. Baird* (1972), the Court ruled that it was unconstitutional to prevent the dissemination of birth control information and devices to unmarried people. "If the right of privacy means anything," wrote Justice William J. Brennan, Jr., for the majority, "it is the right of the individual, married or single, to be free from unwarranted governmental intrusion into matters so fundamentally affecting a person as the decision to whether to bear or beget a child."

The most controversial expansion of the right to privacy came in two 1973 decisions, *Roe v. Wade* and *Doe v. Bolton,* invalidating laws in Texas and Georgia regulating abortions. The Court reaffirmed the right of privacy enumerated in *Griswold,* balancing the mother's right to privacy against the state's interest in protecting the unborn fetus. Justice Harry Blackmun's decision divided pregnancy into three periods. During the first trimester of pregnancy, the decision about whether to have an abortion belongs to the woman and her attending physician without interference from the state. During the second trimester, when abortion poses a greater threat to a woman's health, states can enact regulations to protect the health of the mother. Only during the final stage of pregnancy is the state's interest in protecting the fetus great enough to warrant severe restrictions on abortion, and even then the state must permit abortions to save the life of the mother.

Since *Roe,* the Court has ruled on a number of restrictions on abortion rights enacted by states and municipalities. It has invalidated those requiring the consent of the father and those that require the abortion be performed only in a hospital. Since the1980s, however, the Court signaled a willingness to permit restrictions on abortion rights. In *Webster v. Reproductive Health Services* (1989), the Court upheld a Missouri law that prohibited abortion in a publicly funded facility. In *Planned Parenthood v. Casey* (1992), the Court upheld a Pennsylvania law that mandated counseling and a 24-hour waiting period prior to an abortion and also required a minor seeking an abortion to obtain parental or judicial permission in order to get an abortion. Although these decisions seem to chip away at the broad privacy rights articulated in *Roe,* the Court has thus far declined to overturn the substance of that ruling.

While the Court has extended the right to privacy to cover some personal areas of an individual's life, it has also ruled that other behaviors are beyond this protection. For example, it struck down a Georgia law allowing news reporters to be sued for publishing or broadcasting the names of rape victims, ruling that states may not impose sanctions for the publication of truthful information contained in court records that are open to the public (*Cox Broadcasting v. Cohn* 1975). In balancing one liberty against another, the Court has generally favored the right to free expression over the right to privacy. The Court has also chosen government authority over individual privacy in certain issues.

In *U.S. v. Miller* (1976), the Court refused to extend the right of privacy to individual bank accounts, ruling that the government has the right to obtain records of checks and other transactions. Similarly, the Court has ruled that state laws prohibiting physician-assisted suicide are constitutional (*Washington v. Glucksberg* 1997).

Some of the most controversial questions about an individual's right to privacy have focused on state laws outlawing consensual sodomy between homosexuals. In effect, these cases try to decide the question of whether the government has the right to regulate what consenting adults can do in the privacy of their own bedrooms. In *Bowers v. Hardwick* (1986), the Court upheld a Georgia law that made it a crime to engage in homosexual sex. In *Lawrence v. Texas* (2003), however, the Court over-turned this decision and ruled that the government had no right to regulate or control consenting personal relationships. In both *Bowers* and *Lawrence,* police officers had entered the homes of gay men and caught them having sex. In the former case, the Court ruled that state bans against homosexual acts had deep cultural roots, and the government had the right to enforce these bans in the name of social order. In *Lawrence,* the Court rejected that reasoning and came down firmly on the side of indi-vidual liberty, justifying its shift on the grounds that the government had no legitimate reason to intrude into the personal and private life of individuals.

Though the right to privacy has been greatly expanded and refined since the *Griswold* decisions, broader social movement and issues continually pressure this right. Wendy Kaminer (1999) observed that such individual liberties as freedom of expression and the right to privacy are quick to be subordinated when they conflict with other val-ues central to a particular ideological point of view. On the left, some feminists want indi-vidual freedom of expression limited when it is sexually explicit because they believe that sexually explicit material perpetuates second-class status for women and encourages vio-lent crimes against women. On the right, some conservatives back the "imposition of moral absolutes," such as making homosexual acts a crime, even in the most private realm of individual behavior. The initial popularity of the Patriot Act shows that a broad cross-section of Americans were willing to give up at least some of their rights to privacy in exchange for greater assurances of security in the wake of terrorist attacks. What all this shows is that balancing an individual's right to privacy and society's broader interest is not easy and is often contentious. Individual choices and behaviors—even if they are conducted in the privacy of the bedroom—may be seen as threats to other people's value systems. The need for social order may require citizens to give government at least some limited authority to intrude upon their private lives.

Criminal Procedure

One area in which privacy rights are usually respected is criminal procedure. Generally speaking, democracies go out of their way to protect the citizen from the state because government is a powerful institution, and the individuals are seldom of equal strength in criminal cases. The state can marshal its vast resources against a single person, who must struggle to defend himself or herself against charges of having committed a wrong against society. To ensure that government does not abuse this power and unnecessarily intrude on civil liberties, the rights of a person to privacy and freedom from arbitrary governmental action are basic values in democracies in general and in American society in particular. It has long been a central feature of Anglo-American legal systems that an individual cannot be subject to criminal sanctions arbitrarily. As early as the 14th century, English courts provided that no one could be imprisoned or put to death except by "due process of law." English settlers in America brought a concern for the rights of the accused and a determination to protect those rights in criminal procedures.

This solicitude for the rights of the accused in criminal cases has continued to be a hallmark of the American legal system, and it is explicitly codified in the Constitution and in subsequent court rulings. The government is specifically forbidden to violate the privacy of the individual through unreasonable searches and seizures of home or person. The government is also prohibited from arbitrarily arresting people, and in a trial the burden is on the government to prove its charges against the individual "beyond a reasonable doubt." Such prohibitions and requirements are deliberately designed to make it difficult for the government to succeed in any attempt to deny a citizen property, freedom of movement, or the right to life itself. Such protections favor the accused in order to protect the innocent; to lessen the chances that government will punish an innocent person, the Constitution establishes rules and procedures that make it difficult to punish anyone.

The federal system in the United States has resulted in separate legal systems with separate lists of criminal offenses and trial procedures for the nation as a whole and each of the fifty states. Most "major crimes"—murder, rape, assault, robbery, burglary, and the like—are violations of state rather than federal law and are thus tried in the state courts. Criminal violations of federal law include certain drug trafficking activities, transporting a stolen automobile across state lines, and plotting to assassinate federal officials, among others.

The rules governing criminal procedure and spelling out the rights of the accused in federal cases spring from several sources. The most important is the Constitution, particularly the Fourth, Fifth, Sixth, and Eighth Amendments:

- The Fourth Amendment protects individuals from unreasonable searches and seizures of personal property.
- The Fifth Amendment contains the historic English guarantee that a person cannot be denied life, liberty, or property without due process of law and also includes specific protections from coerced confessions and from being tried twice for the same offense.
- The Sixth Amendment lays down specific guidelines for a fair trial, requiring a speedy and public trial by a jury of one's peers, the right to confront witnesses, and the right to be represented by counsel.
- The Eighth Amendment prohibits cruel and unusual punishment.

Through various cases, most of these rights have been applied to people being tried in state as well as federal courts.[2] Thus, regardless of which level of government charges an individual with a crime, it must abide by a set of basic safeguards and guarantees in these constitutional clauses.

These rights were the source of significant controversy in the 20th century. A series of rulings expanded the rights of the accused and imposed increased burdens and responsibilities on government. In general, the Court has expanded rights through interpretation of the Constitution, has applied them to the states through the

[2]The Fifth Amendment's provision requiring indictment by a grand jury and the Eighth Amendment's prohibition of excessive bail have not been applied to trials in state courts.

Fourteenth Amendment, and in later rulings has placed limitations on the expanded rights. The swing of the judicial pendulum demonstrates that achieving the "right" balance between individual liberties and social order is an extraordinarily difficult objective that periodically must be reconsidered in a process that is political.

Exclusionary Rule

One of the most controversial interpretations of the Fourth Amendment's protections against unreasonable searches and seizures is the **exclusionary rule** first articulated in *Weeks v. U.S.* in 1914. This ruling said that evidence obtained through an unreasonable search and seizure cannot be used in federal trials. The case of *Mapp v. Ohio* (1961) extended the exclusionary rule to state trials. Excluding evidence of a crime is a controversial way to protect individuals' rights against unreasonable search and seizure. The goal is to deter police from infringing on the rights of innocent people, but it is frustrating to be prevented from using evidence to punish guilty people.

The courts have been unable to find a better way to protect the innocent from overzealous police, but court rulings in the past two decades have backed away from the exclusionary rule somewhat. In *Nix v. Williams* (1984), the Supreme Court granted an **inevitable discovery** exception, ruling that illegally acquired evidence can be used in court if it would have been eventually discovered through legal means. In *United States v. Leon* (1984), the Court granted another significant exception to the exclusionary rule, allowing evidence gathered in "good faith" to be used against defendants. As long as a law officer believes that the warrant authorizing a search is valid, evidence obtained in the search is admissible even if the warrant is later found to be flawed. This ruling is viewed as a significant weakening of the exclusionary rule because what constitutes good faith is open to broad interpretation.

Right to Counsel

One of the most basic rights to guarantee a fair trial is the Sixth Amendment right to assistance of counsel in mounting a defense against a criminal charge. As early as 1790, Congress passed a law providing legal counsel for all people charged with capital crimes (those punishable by death), but generally speaking, the ability to exercise this right was limited to people who could afford it. This practice changed in federal cases in 1938, when the Court required provision of counsel to anyone accused of a federal crime (*Johnson v. Zerbst*).

The obligation of state governments to provide an attorney was not firmly established until almost thirty years later. In *Gideon v. Wainwright* (1963), the Supreme Court ruled that the right to counsel is a fundamental part of a fair system of criminal justice, reasoning that without the assistance of counsel a trial is stacked in favor of the government. *Gideon* was a landmark case that opened the door to a series of specific questions involving the right to counsel. Most fundamental was what kind of criminal cases initiated the state's obligation to provide a lawyer. In a series of later rulings, notably *Argersinger v. Hamlin* (1972) and *Scott v. Illinois* (1979), the Supreme Court ruled that any charge that carried a potential loss of liberty was serious enough to trigger the state obligation under *Gideon*.

Right against Self-Incrimination

Probably the most famous expansion of the Fifth Amendment right against self-incrimination came in *Miranda v. Arizona* (1966). At issue was a confession to the crimes of kidnapping and rape that Ernesto Miranda made to police officers during a 2-hour interrogation. The Court ruled the confession inadmissible on the grounds that once Miranda had been taken into custody or deprived of his freedom of action in any significant way, law enforcement officials were under an obligation to inform him that he had the right to remain silent and that if he gave up this right anything he said could be used against him in court. This ruling also shifted the Sixth Amendment right to counsel from the trial stage to the police station: *Miranda* required police to inform suspects of their rights to counsel and to have an attorney appointed if they could not afford one.

The basic reasoning behind the *Miranda* ruling was that confessions can be coerced in ways other than beatings. Just being in custody in a strange environment and being questioned by police is a psychologically coercive situation. Furthermore, criminal laws are often complex, and an accused individual may unwittingly admit to criminal acts. Individuals cannot exercise their constitutional right against self-incrimination if they are unaware of it, and they need the help of an attorney to protect their rights.

The *Miranda* decision provoked a storm of protest. Law enforcement officials complained that it would handcuff them in dealing with criminals. The ruling seemed to be placing the rights of criminals above the public interest. Subsequent rulings

Ernesto Miranda (right) and his attorney John Flynn leaving the U.S. Supreme Court in June 1966 after it overturned the Arizona State court's decision of guilt and a jail sentence of twenty years.

© Bettman/Corbis

LIVING THE PROMISE
The Strange Fate of Ernesto Miranda

Ernesto Miranda is best remembered for the landmark Supreme Court case that overturned his rape conviction and obligated law enforcement officers to inform suspects of their right against self-incrimination. What is less remembered about Miranda is that his victory did him little good and may even have helped his killer escape justice.

Miranda was a school dropout who grew up in and around Phoenix, Arizona. He had amassed a considerable criminal record by March 1963, when he was arrested and accused of kidnapping and raping a woman he had picked up in his car. Taken into custody, Miranda confessed to this crime and to other charges of kidnapping and robbery.

Although he had confessed to the crimes, Miranda pleaded not guilty in court, and his lawyer unsuccessfully sought to suppress the confessions. Miranda was found guilty and sentenced to twenty-five to thirty years in prison. He appealed the convic-tion, seeking a new trial in which the confessions would not be allowed into evidence. His appeal gradually wended its way through the court system, and it was one of six cases bundled together by the U.S. Supreme Court in a review of how police obtained confessions. Because his name was listed first, these cases collectively became known as "Miranda."

The court ruled that in order to exercise their rights, citizens must first be aware of what those rights are, and that it was the responsibility of law enforcement personnel to expressly inform people suspected of crimes of their rights against self-incrimination and to legal representation. On this basis, Miranda's confession was excluded from evidence, and his conviction was overturned.

The standard warning that emerged from this ruling has been immortalized in innumerable movies and television shows: "You have the right to remain silent. Anything you say can be held against you in a court of law. You have the right to an attorney to assist you prior to questioning and to be with you during questioning. If you cannot afford an attorney, one will be provided for you."

Miranda's victory was fleeting. He was retried in state court and again convicted, even though the confessions were excluded from his second trial. He went back to prison and served until he was paroled in 1972.

Miranda returned to Phoenix and sold autographed copies of Miranda warning cards from the courthouse steps for $2 each. In January 1976, while playing cards in a Phoenix bar, he got involved in a fight over a $3 bet. As he left the bar, he was attacked by two men and fatally stabbed.

The police tracked down one suspect and read him his rights in accordance with the Miranda ruling. The suspect refused to answer questions, and he went free for lack of evidence.

Source: Simonich, Milan. 2000. "Miranda's Life Ended with Warning, No Conviction." http://www.post-gazette.com/healines/20000110miran-daside2.asp. Accessed October 25, 2000.

have placed some limits on the *Miranda* decision. For example, in *Michigan v. Mosley* (1975), the Court ruled that if a defendant exercises the right to be silent when originally questioned about a crime, but voluntarily makes statements about a different crime during a subsequent interrogation, the later statements are not protected by the original decision to remain silent and can be used as evidence in a trial. In *New York v. Quarles* (1984), the Court ruled that the police are allowed to interrogate a suspect before advising him or her of rights if "public safety" is at risk. This was considered a significant erosion of the rights established by earlier rulings. Although having to let a guilty person go free on a legal technicality is frustrating, *Miranda's* role in adding to such frustrations is debatable. Ernesto Miranda, for example, was retried and convicted of rape on the basis of evidence other than the coerced confession. (See the Living the Promise feature "The Strange Fate of Ernesto Miranda.")

Capital Punishment

Capital punishment is one of the most divisive controversies in American jurisprudence. At one time, it appeared that the forfeit of life would be ruled a violation of the Eighth Amendment's protection against "cruel and unusual punishment." In *Furman v. Georgia* (1972), the Supreme Court outlawed the death penalty as it was then implemented by the states. Only Justices William Brennan and Thurgood Marshall stated that the death penalty was inherently unconstitutional. Other justices claimed that the problem was not the penalty itself but rather how it was applied; it seemed to be applied arbitrarily and was disproportionately used on defendants who were socioeconomically disadvantaged.

Furman thus left open the possibility that new death penalty statutes could pass constitutional muster if they avoided imposing the sentence in a capricious manner. Between 1972 and 1975, some 30 states passed new statutes that did exactly that. Figure 4.1 shows which states make use of the death penalty and the number of executions that have taken place since 1976.

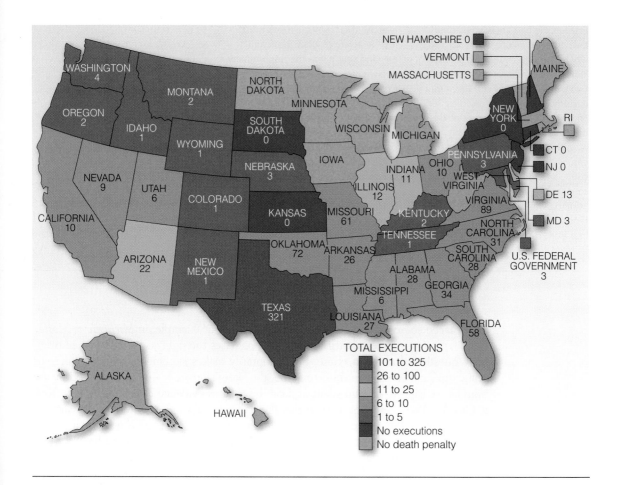

Figure 4.1

Executions by State, 1976–2004

Source: The Death Penalty Information Center: *http://deathpenaltyinfo.org/article.php?scid=8&did=186.* Accessed March 10, 2004.

The states used one of two basic approaches to avoid imposing the sentence in an arbitrary and capricious way. One was to make the death penalty mandatory for certain offences, such as the murder of a police officer. The second was to establish separate procedures for determining guilt and passing sentence, thus essentially holding two trials in cases involving capital crimes: one to determine guilt or innocence and the other to determine whether to apply the death penalty.

In 1976, the Supreme Court heard five related cases involving the constitutionality of death penalty laws in Georgia, Texas, Florida, North Carolina, and Louisiana. It upheld the laws of the first three states and invalidated those of the latter two. While there were a number of differences in these laws, all of those upheld contained a two-part procedure for determining guilt and sentencing. In contrast, the two that were struck down set mandatory death penalties for certain crimes. The most important of these cases was *Gregg v. Georgia,* where the Court ruled that the death penalty does not, by itself violate the Constitution. As long as the states took steps to ensure that death sentences were not automatically awarded upon conviction, but came after due deliberation by the sentencing authorities, it was not considered cruel and unusual punishment.

Even though it the Supreme Court ruled the death penalty constitutional, its application has continued to raise controversy and concern. The case for the death penalty rests on the argument that some crimes are so repugnant and heinous that, in the name of the greater good, society has a right to assume the ultimate authority and take someone's life. Yet for a system that tries to maximize individual liberty and minimize government authority, the basic problem with the death penalty is the potential for executing the innocent. In such cases, authority completely and obviously squashes individual liberty and breaks the democratic promise of political freedom. A second objection to the death penalty is that its application is racially biased—minorities tend to be disproportionately represented on death row. These concerns have driven a long-running battle between opponents and proponents of the death penalty. In 2003, Illinois Governor George Ryan, citing a system "fraught with error," commuted the death sentences of 167 death row inmates. Ryan's decision came after investigations showed at least thirteen men convicted and sentenced to death were later exonerated and set free. His decision was celebrated by death penalty opponents and harshly criticized by proponents who argued the net result of the action was to literally let people get away with murder while trampling the rights of victims.

 ## Performance Assessment

Reconciling liberty and authority is a difficult and delicate balancing act. Like most conflicts that pit one fundamental value against another, trying to find the right mix of liberty and authority is more likely to produce controversy than a universally approved equilibrium. Perhaps the true test of how democratic performance equates with the democratic promise is a never-ending search for such an equilibrium rather than its actual achievement. The perfect balance between liberty and authority has not, does not, and probably will never exist. A continued struggle toward that goal, however, shows a society truly committed to upholding the core value of political freedom.

By that yardstick, the democracy in the United States measures up reasonably well. From the beginning, a central concern of the political system has been to safeguard individual liberties against government encroachment. This concern was a major issue in the battle to ratify the Constitution, one of the first pieces of business attended to by the first Congress, and the subject of constitutional amendments, laws, regulations, and court cases ever since. If nothing else, the fact that the courts continue to be asked to resolve conflicts between liberty and authority is testament that the political system is receptive to people who believe a government action intolerably disrupts the equilibrium between these values.

On the other hand, there have been instances when the equilibrium has clearly tilted toward one extreme or the other. Most recently, the war on terror has raised fears and alarms from civil libertarians. All agree that the government needs the necessary authority to effectively wage the war on terror. But must this authority include the right to jail people without charges and deny them access to legal representation and the court system? Does it really require giving government the power to anonymously spy on its own citizens? If you answer either of these questions negatively, you have just argued that the U.S. government has, at least in some small way, broken the promise of political freedom. On the other hand, if you answer these questions in the affirmative, you indicate support for the notion that a greater assurance of security and social order is worth the price of a little less political freedom. Which of these viewpoints is correct? Both and neither. There is no way to objectively determine the appropriate balance of liberty and authority; the often-impassioned debate continues.

In the absence of clear and objective boundaries on individual liberty and government authority, those limits have been, and will continue to be, revisited and changed by the Supreme Court. The civil liberties enjoyed by citizens in the 1930s, the 1960s, and the 1990s were different in significant ways, and the difference is not attributable to a uniformly expanding set of individual liberties at the cost of shrinking authority. The Supreme Court has favored liberty at some periods and in some cases, and authority in others. It is fair to say that the enormous attention devoted by the political system to conflict between liberty and authority over the years indicates that many believe the United States has consistently fallen short of the democratic promise of political freedom. Yet that same attention also shows that the system has always been aware of this shortfall and has continued to work for that elusive balance.

Summary

- Civil liberties are the freedoms enjoyed by individuals in a democratic society. They constitute the choices individuals are free to make with little or no interference from governmental authority. The Constitution grants individuals the freedom to choose religious beliefs and practices, to form associations of like-minded people, and to freely express opinions and preferences.
- These liberties are not absolute, and there remains a need for constraints on them to preserve social order.
- Finding an appropriate balance between liberty and authority is difficult and is one of the central dilemmas of democratic societies. Authority is required for social order; without social order, individual liberties are meaningless because the state cannot ensure them. But complete social order requires individual behavior to be dictated by the state, which also eliminates individual liberty. The goal is to achieve an acceptable balance between these two values.

- Reconciling liberty and authority was a major issue in the battle to ratify the Constitution. It was largely resolved by the Federalist promise to amend the Constitution to guarantee individual rights. This promise was fulfilled in the first ten amendments to the Constitution, which are collectively known as the Bill of Rights.
- The basic assumption in the American polity is that individuals should have as much liberty as possible, and numerous individual liberties have been specified in constitutional amendments, especially in the Bill of Rights.
- Originally, the Bill of Rights was held to place restrictions only on the federal government. The Supreme Court made much of the Bill of Rights binding on state governments in key rulings on freedom of religion, separation of church and state, freedom of expression, the right to privacy, and criminal procedure.
- Most of the civil liberties guaranteed by the Bill of Rights have gone through a process of expansion and change as Supreme Court decisions continue to redefine the limits of individual freedom and political authority.

Key Terms

absolutist approach 109	inevitable discovery 117
bad tendency rule 110	libel 113
balancing test 109	preferred freedoms doctrine 109
civil liberties 98	privacy 113
"clear and present danger" test 110	separation of church and state 105
exclusionary rule 117	slander 113
incorporation doctrine 102	

Selected Readings

Abraham, Henry. 2003. *Freedom and the Court: Civil Rights and Liberties in the United States.* 8th ed. Lawrence: University Press of Kansas. An excellent historical overview of civil rights and liberties.

Cole, David. 2003. *Enemy Aliens.* New York: New Press. A civil liberties lawyer argues that the government's response to terrorism after September 11, 2001, encroaches on political freedom.

Lewis, Anthony. 1964. *Gideon's Trumpet.* New York: Random House. The classic study of *Gideon v. Wainwright* and an excellent examination of specific civil liberties.

Strossen, Nadine. 1995. *Defending Pornography: Free Speech, Sex, and the Fight for Women's Rights.* New York: Scribner. Strossen, the head of the American Civil Liberties Union, presents a feminist case for protecting sexually explicit materials as free speech.

5 | Civil Rights

Jennifer Gratz was determined to gain admittance into the University of Michigan at Ann Arbor, an institution not far from her home in Southgate, a working-class suburb of Detroit. Founded in 1817, its motto—"An uncommon education for the common man"—seemed particularly apt for the blue-collar Gratz. Neither of her parents, a retired police sergeant and a secretary, were college graduates, and she would have to bootstrap her way into one of the most prestigious public universities in the nation.

She was willing to put in the work to achieve this dream. She finished high school ranked 13th in her class of 298, with a GPA of 3.76. She did well on the ACT (83rd percentile). She was the vice president of the student council, homecoming queen, a math tutor, and participated in athletics. She was so focused on Michigan she did not even bother applying anywhere else. When she was rejected, she was stunned. Rejections from major universities are not uncommon, and upon receiving them most students try to make the best of their other options. Not Gratz. She made a federal case of her rejection. Literally.

Gratz believed that what kept her out of the University of Michigan was not her record, but her race. Gratz is white, and the University of Michigan's admissions system gave preference to minorities. At the time, applicants to Michigan were ranked on a point system. A total of 150 points were possible, and a minimum 100 points were required to be considered for admission. Of these, 110 points were awarded on the basis of academic achievement. The other 40 points came under the heading of "other factors." These included things like personal achievement and public service, but they also were awarded on the basis of certain group characteristics. These included state residents (extra points for applicants from Michigan), legacies (points if your parents or stepparents went to the university), scholarship athletes, and those from socioeconomically disadvantaged backgrounds. They also included race. At the heart of the Gratz lawsuit was the claim that this latter category amounted to an unfair and unconstitutional racial preference.

The university disagreed. Of the roughly 25,000 students who apply for admission every year, there are only about 5,000 slots open. How to choose the 5,000? All agree the primary emphasis should be on academics, but should other things—like race and ethnicity—be taken into consideration? The university argued yes. All students benefit from a diverse campus, said university officials, pointing to a number of studies showing that students at racially diverse campuses learn better and are more civically involved citizens when they leave. And even if race were not taken into consideration, the university suggested Gratz's chances of admission were unlikely to change. So few minorities actually applied to the University of Michigan that they had virtually no effect on the probability of a white student being accepted. Even if Michigan accepted not a single minority student, the rejection rate for whites would still be 70 percent. Elite universities, after all, are by definition elite. Michigan claimed the net effect of eliminating their admissions system would not be to get people like Gratz in but to keep minorities out.

Others disagreed, and Gratz's lawsuit attracted some powerful supporters, including President George W. Bush. His administration saw the university as operating a quota system that unfairly judged prospective students on the basis of their race. The administration's argument was that acceptance into college should not be based on your parentage, a claim that university supporters pointed out was ironic, if not downright hypocritical, for Bush to make (being a C student who got into Yale on the basis of parental-based preferential treatment and as a legacy). Regardless of the pros and cons of both sides to this argument, it ultimately ended up in the Supreme Court (Younge 2003).

At stake was not just the University of Michigan's admissions policy, but the broader concept of

affirmative action, or governmental actions designed to help minorities compete on an equal basis and overcome the effects of past discrimination. Throughout the Republic's history, numerous groups have been systematically excluded from the political and social mainstream, meaning the core democratic values of political equality and minority rights have been denied to people based on characteristics such as race and religion. Affirmative action is one means to help restore and uphold the democratic promise embedded in those values.

Yet some see affirmative action not as a way to restore the promise of democracy but as a means to break that promise. This view was the underlying issue that had to be resolved in the Gratz lawsuit and in a companion case that examined the admissions process for Michigan's law school. There was a delicate balancing act here. Most agreed that a diverse student body served a greater social good; the question was whether this could be achieved without discriminating on the basis of race.

The court's response was to strike down the points system but also to uphold the right of public universities to use race as a factor in the admissions process. Universities can continue to use race as an admission criterion, but only if they can demonstrate that doing so promotes the educational benefits that flow from a diverse student body (Biskupic 2003). The practical result was to strike down the specific process that kept Gratz out of Michigan but to reject her overall argument. Bruised and somewhat diminished, affirmative action nonetheless remained constitutional.

This somewhat mixed decision represents just one more chapter in America's long-running debate over **civil rights,** which are the rights of all citizens to legal, social, and economic equality. How those rights are guaranteed by government, and what government does when those rights are denied, has been the basis of heated debate, and these conflicts cut to the heart of the core democratic values of political equality and minority rights. In this chapter we explore the struggles undertaken by several groups in an attempt to achieve equality in American life. These struggles have often been divisive and bitter, and, as the controversy over the University of Michigan's admissions process shows, the debate over whether they have fully delivered on the value of political equality continues to this day.

Hundreds of students at the University of Michigan rally to support the claim of admissions discrimination made by Jennifer Gratz. While the Supreme Court found affirmative action constitutional, controversy over its use is still strongly debated as a civil rights issue.

The Promise of Civil Rights

The promise of civil rights is essentially the promise that government has a duty to take action to protect political equality and minority rights. In Chapter 4 we learned that civil liberties ensure that government cannot arbitrarily deny citizens the freedom to make the individual choices they please. Civil rights ensure that government will take some action to ensure those freedoms are not arbitrarily denied to certain categories of citizens. The metaphor of the "shield and sword" (*Pollock v. Williams* 1944) serves to clarify the distinction between civil liberties and civil rights. Questions of civil liberties center on the issue of when government is prevented from acting in order to protect individual freedom. Questions of civil rights center on the issue of when government is required to act to protect that freedom. Robert Carr has noted that this figure of speech has important implications for civil liberties and civil rights. The shield is a negative safeguard: "It enables a person whose freedom is endangered to invoke the Constitution" to invalidate government action (1947, 3). This shield is civil liberties. By contrast, the sword is a "positive weapon wielded by the federal government, which takes the initiative in protecting helpless individuals by bringing criminal charges against persons who are encroaching upon their rights" (Carr 1947, 5).

The struggle for civil rights—in other words, the struggle to make sure that all groups share equally in the privileges and rights of citizenship—has a long history in the United States. Historically, both federal and state governments have tolerated unequal treatment of citizens based on characteristics such as race, gender, and religion. The most notorious example is the treatment of African Americans. In the name of political pragmatism, the Founders accepted the institution of slavery and enshrined in the Constitution the value of slaves (referred to as "other persons") as three-fifths of a person for purposes of taxation and representation (Article I, Section 2). Since most blacks were slaves at the time, the Constitution itself violated the civil rights of a large section of the population on the basis of race. Even for free African Americans and even after the abolition of slavery, such basic liberties as the right to vote were systematically denied on the basis of race.

African Americans are not the only group that has waged an extended battle to get the federal government to take positive action to prevent their freedoms from being arbitrarily denied. Other minorities—including Native Americans, Latinos, and Asian Americans—have suffered like discrimination and have faced similar obstacles. So have women, the disabled, and gays and lesbians. Age has been a battleground for civil rights. During the Vietnam War, young people were angry that their government could draft them into military service and send them to fight in a war but would not let them vote and have input into the decision to wage war. This concern was the driving force behind the Twenty-Sixth Amendment, adopted in 1971, that guarantees all citizens aged 18 or older the right to vote. On the other end of the spectrum, advocates for the elderly have fought against mandatory retirement and age discrimination in employment. Other groups with civil rights agendas include nonsmokers, who have advocated a ban on smoking in public places, and smokers, who have fought for designated smoking areas; the terminally ill, who want the right to die with dignity; and welfare recipients, who seek the opportunity to make more of the decisions about how they will live their lives.

In short, the quest for greater freedom and equality neither begins nor ends with a discussion of the civil rights campaigns of racial and ethnic minorities, women, the disabled, and homosexuals. The quest for greater freedom and equality—the drive to get the federal government to end a group's arbitrary exclusion from full participation in public, social, or economic activities—is a central component of American political life. These stories represent democracy's attempt to live up to the values of political equality and minority rights in the United States. We cannot do justice to every group that has struggled to gain equal access to the rights and privileges of citizenship in one chapter of a textbook, but we can examine some representative cases reflecting the best-known civil rights movements. These should provide a basic foundation for judging whether the promise of political equality and the promise of minority rights are reflected in the performance of the American political system.

African Americans

The institution of slavery systematically denied civil rights to large numbers of African Americans for almost the first century of the Republic's history. The end of the Civil War brought with it a constitutional ban on slavery. In the postwar period, the federal government embarked on a program to bring liberated slaves, who were concentrated in the South, into the mainstream of American life. Congress passed legislation granting African Americans the right to sue, to give evidence in court, and to buy, sell, and inherit property. New federal laws also outlawed segregation in transportation, schools, and public accommodations. The Fifteenth Amendment specifically prohibited states from denying any adult male the right to vote on the basis of race, color, or previous condition of servitude.

Benefiting from the newfound political rights guaranteed by the federal government, African Americans initially seemed to be poised on the threshold of political equality. African Americans were elected to Congress and to numerous state and local offices. This brief period of hope for securing the civil rights of African Americans ended with a political deal struck between northern Republicans and southern Democrats in the disputed election of 1876. The Democrats acquiesced in the selection of Republican Rutherford B. Hayes over their candidate, Samuel J. Tilden, in return for Hayes' agreement to withdraw troops from the South when he came to office. Hayes fulfilled the pledge in 1877, in essence removing federal influence from southern political life.

Racial Segregation

As a result of the federal government's retreat, African Americans began to be systematically denied civil and political rights in the South. Initially, **racial segregation,** or the separation of people based on their race, was based on tradition. Gradually, however, state laws segregated public schools, transportation, and accommodations by race. Other laws politically disenfranchised African Americans through a series of legal techniques such as **poll taxes** (fees required for casting a ballot), literacy tests, and the exclusion of African Americans from Democratic Party primaries. Lynching was not uncommon in the last two decades of the 19th century. By the early years of the 20th century, segregation of African Americans through intimidation and disenfranchisement was complete in the southern states.

At about the same time, however, the locus of race problems began to shift. The overwhelming proportion of African Americans had been concentrated in the rural South. But millions began migrating to urban areas in the North to try to escape oppression and to improve their lives economically. Northern cities were less than welcoming. African Americans were often shut out of white neighborhoods by residential segregation ordinances and restrictive covenants forbidding the sale of property to nonwhites. These legal means of oppression were sometimes augmented by beatings and bombings. The end result was that African Americans were often concentrated in low-rent, racially exclusive ghettoes. In terms of day-to-day life, northern ghettoes were probably better than southern plantations, but discrimination and segregation remained a central fact of life in the North as well as the South.

African Americans' reaction to being systematically denied their civil rights varied. Some, like Booker T. Washington, urged accommodation. Others, especially a group of northern intellectuals, argued for a more active pursuit of political equality. Among the best known of this latter group is W. E. B. Du Bois, who in 1909 joined with prominent white intellectuals like philosopher John Dewey and lawyer Clarence Darrow, among others, to form the National Association for the Advancement of Colored People (NAACP).

The Judicial Strategy to End Segregation

Because African Americans were often prevented from exercising their right to vote, elected officials in the state legislatures and governors' mansions were unresponsive and even hostile to demands for racial equality. Excluded from the electoral process, African Americans turned to the federal courts for help in securing fundamental constitutional rights.

The NAACP became the major group fighting for civil rights and led the way in court battles to end segregation and disenfranchisement. Soon after its founding, the NAACP began a successful series of test cases on several legal fronts. Its initial victory came in *Guinn v. United States* (1915), in which the Supreme Court invalidated the **grandfather clause** of the Oklahoma constitution, a clause that exempted people whose ancestors were entitled to vote in 1866 from the literacy test. Only whites had the right to vote that year.

In the three decades following *Guinn,* the NAACP scored a number of other notable victories. The most significant was the fight to get equal treatment in public facilities like schools. The Fourteenth Amendment prohibits states from passing or enforcing any law that would deny "any person within its jurisdiction the equal protection of the laws." Southern states responded by passing laws requiring **separate but equal** accommodations for blacks and whites in public facilities such as public transportation. An 1896 Supreme Court decision, *Plessy v. Ferguson,* ruled that separate public facilities for people of different races satisfied the Fourteenth Amendment's equal protection clause, provided they were "equal."

Initially, the NAACP tried to chip away at the "separate but equal" doctrine on a case-by-case basis. The first big victory came in *Missouri ex rel Gaines v. Canada* (1938). The University of Missouri had refused to admit a qualified African American student to its law school, but the state offered to pay his expenses at a school in a neighboring state that admitted blacks. The Supreme Court ruled that this policy did not satisfy the state's constitutional responsibilities. "Separate but equal," in other words, meant separate but equal within the state.

As a result of this case, the Supreme Court began to pay closer attention to whether separate facilities were actually equal. In the early 1950s, NAACP lawyers decided to abandon the policy of chipping away at the "separate but equal" doctrine and to advance the argument that separate facilities for different races in and of themselves violated the equal protection of the law clause of the Fourteenth Amendment. The strategy was vindicated in *Brown v. Board of Education* (1954), one of the most important civil rights decisions ever made by the Supreme Court. Speaking for a unanimous Court, Chief Justice Earl Warren declared that separate educational facilities are inherently unequal. Even if all the tangible characteristics of schools—such as classrooms, libraries, curricula, teachers' salaries, and teachers' qualifications—are equal, wrote Warren, the intangible quality of education is not equal in racially segregated schools. Racial segregation of public schools deprives African American children of equal protection of the laws because "To separate them from others of similar age and qualifications solely because of their race generates a feeling of inferiority . . . that may affect their hearts and minds in a way unlikely ever to be undone." The following year, the Court ordered states to dismantle the system of segregated schools "with all deliberate speed" and entrusted the federal district courts to require local school boards to comply.

The Revolution in Race Relations

While the NAACP scored significant victories in court, the legislative and executive branches of government initially did little to ensure the rights of African Americans. Southern senators successfully filibustered the attempt to enact anti-lynching legislation. Even the liberal presidents of the first half of the twentieth century showed little commitment to the civil rights of African Americans. Franklin Roosevelt, for example, introduced no major civil rights legislation; he issued an executive order establishing a Committee on Fair Employment Practices in 1941 only after being threatened with a march on Washington to secure job opportunities for minorities.

The first significant steps for racial equality were taken shortly after World War II, when President Harry Truman outlawed segregation of the armed services and of civilian jobs in national government and mandated that the federal government would do business only with firms that did not discriminate in hiring. Truman also proposed a broad civil rights program to Congress and appointed a committee to study race relations. Truman's successor, Dwight Eisenhower, followed up on the process of desegregating the armed forces and pushed for ending segregation in the District of Columbia. The Civil Rights Act of 1957 created the U.S. Civil Rights Commission and was the first civil rights law to be passed by the federal government since the Reconstruction period following the Civil War.

Thus, by the mid-1950s, the judicial, executive, and legislative branches of the federal government had finally begun to take proactive steps to uphold the civil rights of African Americans. At about the same time, the civil rights movement abruptly rejected the status quo in race relations, and a large segment of the African American community refused to accommodate itself to the inferior position African Americans had been assigned in American society. The civil rights movement began engaging in acts of **civil disobedience,** or deliberately disobeying laws viewed as morally repugnant. An event that epitomized this development was the December 1955 arrest of Rosa Parks, an African American seamstress who refused to move to the back of a municipal bus in Montgomery, Alabama. The arrest sparked a bus boycott led by a young minister, Dr. Martin Luther King, Jr., and ultimately led to government action to outlaw racial segregation.

What had been a battle waged by a relatively few well-educated, middle-class African Americans became a broad movement that cut across social and economic lines. The legal battles and conciliatory negotiations with government and white leaders that had been used by groups such as the NAACP and the National Urban League came in for sharp criticism. According to Martin Luther King, Jr., and others of a new generation of civil rights leaders, what was needed was direct action by the masses, including peaceful boycotts, sit-ins, and protest marches. People were no longer willing to wait for the outcome of lengthy courtroom campaigns to win rights for their children. They wanted those rights for themselves, and they wanted them soon. (See the Living the Promise feature "I Have a Dream.")

On August 28, 1963 Martin Luther King, Jr. delivered his "I Have a Dream" speech to over 200,000 people who marched on Washington, DC that summer.

© Bettman/Corbis

The reasons for this sudden shift are varied. World War II contributed in a number of ways. Many African Americans serving in the armed forces had the novel experience of being treated with respect by white people in France and Great Britain who gave them social acceptance they had never enjoyed in their own country. Returning from military service, they naturally resented returning to an inferior position in civilian life and desired to do something about it. Furthermore, many were keenly aware of the irony of a country's fighting a war against the racist philosophy of Nazi Germany while at the same time practicing its own brand of **racism.**

The attitudes of whites, though far from uniform, also began to change. Supreme Court decisions and executive actions indicated that the political system was either responding to or promoting more tolerant racial attitudes in the white mainstream.

LIVING THE PROMISE
"I Have a Dream"

Address delivered by Dr. Martin Luther King, Jr., at the March on Washington for Jobs and Freedom, August 28, 1963.

I am happy to join with you today in what will go down in history as the greatest demonstration for freedom in the history of our nation.

Five score years ago, a great American, in whose symbolic shadow we stand today, signed the Emancipation Proclamation. This momentous decree came as a great beacon light of hope to millions of Negro slaves who had been seared in the flames of withering injustice. It came as a joyous daybreak to end the long night of their captivity.

But one hundred years later, the Negro still is not free. One hundred years later, the life of the Negro is still sadly crippled by the manacles of segregation and the chains of discrimination. One hundred years later, the Negro lives on a lonely island of poverty in the midst of a vast ocean of material prosperity. One hundred years later, the Negro is still languished in the comers of American society and finds himself an exile in his own land. And so we've come here today to dramatize a shameful condition.

In a sense we've come to our nation's capital to cash a check. When the architects of our republic wrote the magnificent words of the Constitution and the Declaration of Independence, they were signing a promissory note to which every American was to fall heir. This note was a promise that all men, yes, black men as well as white men, would be guaranteed the "unalienable Rights of Life, Liberty, and the pursuit of Happiness." It is obvious today that America has defaulted on this promissory note insofar as her citizens of color are concerned. Instead of honoring this sacred obligation, America has given the Negro people a bad check, a check which has come back marked "insufficient funds."

But we refuse to believe that the bank of justice is bankrupt. We refuse to believe that there are insufficient funds in the great vaults of opportunity of this nation. And so we've come to cash this check, a check that will give us upon demand the riches of freedom and the security of justice.

We have also come to this hallowed spot to remind America of the fierce urgency of now. This is no time to engage in the luxury of cooling off or to take the tranquilizing drug of gradualism. Now is the time to make real the promises of democracy. Now is the time to rise from the dark and desolate valley of segregation to the sunlit path of racial justice. Now is the time to lift our nation from the quicksands of racial injustice to the solid rock of brotherhood. Now is the time to make justice a reality for all of God's children.

It would be fatal for the nation to overlook the urgency of the moment. This sweltering summer of the Negro's legitimate discontent will not pass until there is an invigorating autumn of freedom and equality. Nineteen sixty-three is not an end, but a beginning. And those who hope that the Negro needed to blow off steam and will now be content will have a rude awakening if the nation returns to business as usual. There will be neither rest nor tranquility in America until the Negro is granted his citizenship rights. The whirlwinds of revolt will continue to shake the foundations of our nation until the bright day of justice emerges.

But there is something that I must say to my people, who stand on the warm threshold which leads into the palace of justice: In the process of gaining our rightful place, we must not be guilty of wrongful deeds. Let us not seek to satisfy our thirst for freedom by drinking from the cup of bitterness and hatred. We must forever conduct our struggle on the high plane of dignity and discipline. We must not allow our creative protest to degenerate into physical violence. Again and again, we must rise to the majestic heights of meeting physical force with soul force. The marvelous new militancy which has engulfed the Negro community must not lead us to a distrust of all white people, for many of our white brothers, as evidenced by their presence here today, have come to realize that their destiny is tied up with our destiny. And they have come to realize that their freedom is inextricably bound to our freedom. We cannot walk alone.

And as we walk, we must make the pledge that we shall always march ahead. We cannot turn back. There are those who are asking the devotees of civil rights, "When will you be satisfied?"

We can never be satisfied as long as the Negro is the victim of the unspeakable horrors of police brutality. We can never be satisfied as long as our bodies, heavy with the fatigue of travel, cannot gain lodging in the motels of the highways and the hotels of the cities. We cannot be satisfied as long as the Negro's basic mobility is from a smaller ghetto to a larger one. We can never be satisfied as long as our children are stripped of their selfhood and robbed of their dignity by signs stating "for whites only." We cannot be satisfied as long as a Negro in Mississippi cannot vote and a Negro in New York believes he has nothing for which to vote. No, no, we are not satisfied and we will not be satisfied until "justice rolls down like waters and righteousness like a mighty stream."

I am not unmindful that some of you have come here out of great trials and tribulations. Some of you have come fresh from narrow jail cells. Some of you have come from areas where your quest for freedom left you battered by the storms of persecution and staggered by the winds of police brutality. You have been the veterans of creative suffering. Continue to work with the faith that unearned suffering is redemptive. Go back to Mississippi, go back to Alabama, go back to South Carolina, go back to Georgia, go back to Louisiana, go back to the slums and ghettos of our northern cities, knowing that somehow this situation can and will be changed. Let us not wallow in the valley of despair.

I say to you today, my friends, so even though we face the difficulties of today and tomorrow, I still have a dream. It is a dream deeply rooted in the American dream.

I have a dream that one day this nation will rise up and live out the true meaning of its creed: "We hold these truths to be self-evident, that all men are created equal."

I have a dream that one day on the red hills of Georgia, the sons of former slaves and the sons of former slave owners will be able to sit down together at the table of brotherhood.

I have a dream that one day even the state of Mississippi, a state sweltering with the heat of injustice, sweltering with the heat of oppression, will be transformed into an oasis of freedom and justice.

I have a dream that my four little children will one day live in a nation where they will not be judged by the color of their skin but by the content of their character. I have a dream today.

I have a dream that one day down in Alabama, with its vicious racists, with its governor having his lips dripping with the words of "interposition" and "nullification," one day right there in Alabama little black boys and black girls will be able to join hands with little white boys and white girls as sisters and brothers. I have a dream today.

I have a dream that one day "every valley shall be exalted, and every hill and mountain shall be made low; the rough places will be made plain, and the crooked places will be made straight; and the glory of the Lord shall be revealed, and all flesh shall see it together."

This is our hope. This is the faith that I go back to the South with. With this faith we will be able to hew out of the mountain of despair a stone of hope. With this faith we will be able to transform the jangling discords of our nation into a beautiful symphony of brotherhood. With this faith we will be able to work together, to pray together, to struggle together, to go to jail together, to stand up for freedom together, knowing that we will be free one day. This will be the day, this will be the day when all of God's children will be able to sing with new meaning:

My country, 'tis of thee, sweet land of liberty, of thee I sing. Land where my fathers died, land of the pilgrim's pride, From every mountainside, let freedom ring!

And if America is to be a great nation, this must become true.

And so let freedom ring from the prodigious hilltops of New Hampshire.

Let freedom ring from the mighty mountains of New York.

Let freedom ring from the heightening Alleghenies of Pennsylvania.

Let freedom ring from the snow-capped Rockies of Colorado.

Let freedom ring from the curvaceous slopes of California.

But not only that: Let freedom ring from Stone Mountain of Georgia.

Let freedom ring from Lookout Mountain of Tennessee.

Let freedom ring from every hill and molehill of Mississippi.

From every mountainside, let freedom ring.

And when this happens, when we allow freedom to ring, when we let it ring from every village and every hamlet, from every state and every city, we will be able to speed up that day when all of God's children, black men and white men, Jews and Gentiles, Protestants and Catholics, will be able to join hands and sing in the words of the old Negro spiritual:

Free at last! Free at last! Thank God Almighty, we are free at last!

Capitalizing on these changes, leaders such as King began to push for full integration in all aspects of American life. King favored nonviolent tactics, or what was termed **passive resistance,** a technique used successfully by Mahatma Gandhi to obtain India's independence from Britain. A broad coalition of new groups emerged, including the Southern Christian Leadership Conference, the Student Nonviolent Coordinating Committee, and the Congress of Racial Equality. Sympathetic whites lent support, particularly college students who went to the South to assist in registering African American voters and integrating public facilities.

By the mid-1960s, some African Americans began to feel that nonviolent direct action was too slow a method of achieving their goals, and some advocated taking civil disobedience a step further and pursuing change through violence. Leaders of the Black Muslims, a group founded in the 1930s, and the Black Panthers, an organization founded in 1966 in Oakland, California, to protect African Americans from police brutality, openly advocated violent revolution. Race riots in Los Angeles, Detroit, Washington, DC, and other major cities in the mid-to-late 1960s seemed to have been spontaneous mass reactions to police brutality or to the assassination of King, not organized actions coordinated with a particular group's agenda.

Government's Response to the Race Revolution

Although the social turmoil of race relations in the 1950s and 1960s was not pretty, it did seem to affect the political system. In the summer of 1963, more than 200,000 people marched on Washington, where Martin Luther King delivered his famous speech, "I Have a Dream." This march pressured the Kennedy administration into supporting the expansion of the 1957 Civil Rights Act. After Kennedy was assassinated in November 1963, Lyndon Johnson, acting with the moral authority bestowed by the shadow of the slain president, picked up Kennedy's civil rights bill, strengthened it, and submitted it to Congress. The Civil Rights Act of 1964 is seen as a major victory in the struggle for racial equality. Title II of the law barred racial segregation in public accommodations; Title VI outlawed racial discrimination in any program that received assistance from the federal government; and Title VII banned discrimination by employers and unions. That same year also saw the ratification of the Twenty-Fourth Amendment, which made poll taxes unconstitutional and strengthened the voting rights of African Americans.

A year later, Johnson signed the 1965 Voting Rights Act into law. This act targeted **Jim Crow** laws used mainly by southern states to disenfranchise African Americans by requiring them to pass literacy tests, pay poll taxes, and be of "good moral character," among other things, as prerequisites to voting. Significantly, the law authorized the federal government to ensure that eligible voters were not denied access to the ballot. For the first time, the Fifteenth Amendment rights of African Americans were actively being protected by the federal government. In the wake of the Voting Rights Act, millions of African Americans registered to vote, making it harder for elected officials to ignore their concerns and pressuring the political system to provide them with full political equality.

Affirmative Action

The values expressed in the Civil Rights Act and the Voting Rights act are now firmly embedded in the American political system, and it is generally accepted that people should not be denied political equality or denied the rights of citizenship on the basis of their race. Accepting these values, however, has not ended the civil rights movement for African Americans. To help minorities who experienced **discrimination** (unequal or unfair treatment), affirmative action programs began to be implemented in the 1970s. This shift from eliminating the legal obstacles to political equality to pursuing programs that actively seek to counter past or present effects of discrimination created a second, long-running political dispute.

The basic argument for affirmative action policies is that inequality cannot be wiped out by removing ***de jure* discrimination,** or discrimination by law. The effects of discrimination linger long past their official sanction in law. As President Lyndon Johnson put it, "You do not wipe away the scars of centuries by saying: Now you are free to go where you want, do as you desire, and choose the leaders you please . . . [W]e seek not just freedom but opportunity—not just legal equity but human ability—not just equality as a right and a theory, but equality as a fact and as a result" (Americans United for Affirmative Action 1999). In other words, equality before the law was not enough. To combat the lasting effects of discrimination—in hiring, college admissions, and promotions—government needed to take proactive steps to help those groups that had been systematically excluded from the full rights and privileges of citizenship.

The argument against affirmative action is that it replaces one form of discrimination with another. Rather than promote equality, opponents argue, affirmative action actually promotes political inequality because it creates **reverse discrimination,** which simply means punishing whites on the basis of their race. Critics argue that if any race is discriminated against, political equality suffers. Equality before the law, however imperfect, *is* enough to deliver on the value of political equality.

The big disagreement in civil rights has boiled down to the conflict embodied in these two points of view. Over the past thirty years, the Supreme Court has repeatedly tried to strike a balance that allows policies to promote diversity in the name of the greater social good, without promoting outright quotas or favoritism. A key early case was *Regents of the University of California v. Bakke* (1978). Allan Bakke was denied admission to medical school at the University of California, Davis, which had designated a set-aside quota for minority students. Bakke's academic record was superior to all of the students admitted under the quota, and he sued, claiming the school violated his Fourteenth Amendment right to equal protection of the law. The Court agreed, ruling that racial quotas violated federal law. However, the Court also said that race could be used as a factor in deciding admissions, even though it could not be the sole criterion.

In later cases, the Court ruled that racial set-asides were constitutional under some circumstances. For example, in *United Steelworkers of America v. Weber* (1979), the Court upheld an affirmative action plan voluntarily agreed to by Kaiser Aluminum Chemical Corporation and a union representing its employees. The plan guaranteed a certain number of jobs to African Americans until the racial makeup of the company's employees reflected the racial breakdown of the local labor force. The Court said that this plan did not violate federal statute because its purpose was to redress the effect of past discrimination. The *Weber* decision was enormously controversial, and racial quotas became a divisive political issue.

Throughout the 1980s and 1990s, affirmative action programs were increasingly criticized for providing unfair advantages to minorities and for unduly downgrading merit as the basis of social economic opportunities. In 1996 a solid majority of

California voters approved Proposition 209, which prevented race from being a criterion in determining school admissions, employment, government contracts, and the like. This law effectively eliminated the state's affirmative action policy, and the Supreme Court refused to hear a legal challenge to Proposition 209, rejecting opponents' arguments that government has a duty to use racial preferences to make up for past discrimination. Other states also began to dismantle their affirmative action policies without attracting Supreme Court intervention. In 1998 Washington passed Initiative 200, which was very similar to Proposition 209. The Supreme Court also let stand a lower court ruling in *Hopwood v. Texas* (1994) that prohibited the use of race and gender in public college admissions policies in Texas, Louisiana, and Mississippi. All of these actions were broadly popular, and the survival of affirmative action seemed to be in doubt.

Then came the lawsuit against the University of Michigan admissions policies detailed at the beginning of this chapter. The key case here was not that of Jennifer Gratz (in which the ruling was to strike down the points system for undergraduate admissions) but that of Barbra Gruttner, who was denied admission to the university's law school. The law school did not use a points system for admission but did use race as one of several admissions factors. In *Gruttner v. Bollinger* (2004), the Supreme Court ruled that this type of affirmative action was allowable: As long as the university had a compelling interest in promoting the educational benefits of a diverse student body, it could continue to use race as a factor in admissions. The broader impact of *Gruttner* was to breathe new life into affirmative action. Many opponents of affirmative action viewed this case as an opportunity for the Court to declare that affirmative action had served its purpose and should be abandoned. Instead, the Court endorsed affirmative action as a still-needed corrective to the past effects of discrimination.

Thus the debate over affirmative action — the conflict over whether it represents a commitment to political equality or an obstacle to political equality — continues. The scholarly record suggests that, at least in higher education, affirmative action policies have more benefits than costs. Derek Bok and William Bowen (1998), for example, examined the academic performance and the postgraduate activities of students admitted under such programs. They found that students admitted under affirmative action policies performed well in even the most selective schools and that after graduation these students went on to have positive roles in the broader community. Bok and Bowen concluded that affirmative action had a positive effect on people who had historically been denied equality of opportunity, and they rejected critics' claims that affirmative action punished the deserving to boost the unqualified.

Such studies are provocative but do little to mollify critics of affirmative action who see policies that promote racial preferences as inherently unfair. Proponents of affirmative action reply that African Americans still are not on an even playing field; four decades after the federal government first took positive steps to address historical discrimination, African Americans still lag behind the white majority on a broad variety of measures ranging from per capita income to educational achievement. Do these disparities reflect an inequality of opportunity that lingers as a result of discrimination? Do they reflect continued **de facto** (literally, "by fact") **discrimination** — patterns of segregation and social opportunity? Or are the issues more complex? There are no easy answers to such questions, and the struggle for the civil rights of African Americans has yet to begin its final chapter.

Latinos and Native Americans

African Americans are not the only group to have been systematically denied the full rights and privileges of citizenship on the basis of race and ethnicity. Though no other group has suffered the wholesale indignity of being reduced to property or singled out as counting for only three-fifths of a person in the Constitution, other racial and ethnic minorities have also long struggled for political equality. Two of the most notable of these groups are Latinos, the single largest ethnic and racial minority in the U.S. population, and Native Americans.

Latinos

Latinos, or people who came or whose ancestors came from Spanish-speaking nations, are the fastest-growing ethnic minority in the United States. They are also the largest. In 2003 the U.S. Census Bureau estimated that Latinos passed African Americans as the largest minority group, accounting for 38.8 million people, or 13 percent of the population. Latinos now account for roughly half of all population growth in the United States (El Nasser 2003). Mexican Americans are the most numerous, and their political power has been increasing in many states, particularly in the Southwest.

The initial experience of Mexican Americans with American society was as a conquered people. The Treaty of Guadalupe Hidalgo, which ended the Mexican-American War in 1848, ceded parts of what are now seven southwestern and western states to the United States. The treaty guaranteed Mexican Americans living in these areas citizenship and certain land grants and rights. These rights were rapidly abrogated as land was seized by both legal and illegal means by cotton plantation owners, cattle and sheep ranchers, miners, and farmers. Some Mexican Americans struck back with armed raids, and even after the violence subsided, the divisions remained well into the 20th century.

During the Great Depression, the government succeeded in deporting some Mexican Americans, and groups like the League of United Latin American Citizens (LULAC) had to work hard to gain even a semblance of integration into mainstream American life. About a million Mexican Americans fought in World War II, and Mexican American combat units were often highly decorated. The industrial war effort drew many others into urban centers where, for the first time, they obtained high-paying, skilled jobs. The GI Bill of Rights enabled Mexican American veterans to go to college and receive other benefits, such as housing and expanded economic opportunities. As a result, Mexican Americans increasingly refused to accept second-class status and, like African Americans, began to demand equality. Significant progress has been made, but even after decades of civil rights progress, Mexican Americans still lag behind whites in income and education, and they often face the additional burden of language barriers.

The civil rights struggle of Latinos combined litigation and political activism. Among the groups spearheading these efforts during the past four decades are the Mexican American Legal Defense and Educational Fund (MALDEF) and the Puerto Rican Legal Defense and Education Fund (PRLDEF). These groups often modeled their tactics on the litigation pursued by the NAACP, and they have focused their efforts on issues related to education. They scored notable successes in lawsuits seeking more equitable distribution of resources for schools, implementation of bilingual programs, and gaining equal access to higher education. They have also aggressively fought to protect Latinos' voting rights and to increase their representation in the political process. For example, in *White v. Register* (1973), a test case brought by MALDEF, the Supreme Court overturned multi-member electoral districts in Texas, agreeing with arguments that such districts unfairly stacked the deck by making it harder for minority candidates to win a majority.

These sorts of victories, combined with their numbers, have made Latinos an important political force in recent decades, especially in the Southwest. Yet their representation in elected and appointive office still does not reflect their relative proportion of the population. Consequently, issues that resonate in Latino communities, such as bilingual programs and access to educational opportunities, are not always fully represented in the policymaking process. Even when these issues are pushed into the political process, they often are perceived as attempts to limit the rights of Latinos rather than expand them. Immigrant access to public services is perhaps the best-known recent example of this. Much of the growth in the Latino population is being driven by immigration, and immigrants—especially illegals—have faced a backlash. This backlash is ironic as the United States views itself as a nation of immigrants, evidenced by the inscription on the base of the Statue of Liberty welcoming prospective Americans with the words, "Give me your tired, your poor . . . your huddled masses." Political developments over the past decade or two have sent a clear message that the welcome does not apply to illegals (who often end up existing on the margins of the economy and are thus often tired and almost always poor).

Protested strongly by minority groups and those supporting the needs of illegal immigrants, Proposition 187 was seen by its proponents as a solution to the huge expense of education and healthcare for the illegal immigrant population in California. Overturned in 1998 by a federal court as unconstitutional, its supporters still hope to get new legislation in place that will carry the same mandates. Because both Governors Gray Davis and Arnold Schwarzenegger have successively supported this issue, it is not likely to disappear from public attention.

This message was perhaps most forcefully made by Proposition 187, passed by California voters in 1994. Proposition 187 requires California law enforcement, healthcare, and social welfare agencies to check and verify citizenship status, report illegal immigrants to federal authorities, and deny illegal immigrants access to services. LULAC, among others, spearheaded efforts to overturn Proposition 187 in the courts, and it was eventually ruled unconstitutional. It became a political litmus test for the Latino community, however, and may have contributed to the downturn in the fortunes of the Republican Party in California in the 1990s (the initiative's most prominent backer was Republican Governor Pete Wilson). Certainly a candidate's position on Proposition 187 remains an issue of importance in California politics (*San Jose Mercury News* 2004).

Native Americans

Native Americans, or American Indians, are the original settlers of the land that became the United States. As the European settlers moved westward, tribe after tribe was chased off its land, and the remaining tribes were moved onto reservations, mostly in the West. Some scholars and critics have equated the treatment of Native Americans by the U.S. government with **genocide,** which is the deliberate destruction of a population.

Historically, native tribes were considered independent nations, and the U.S. government's legal relationship with individuals in the tribes operated through the tribal governments. These relationships were codified in a confusing legal tangle of hundreds of treaties made with different tribal authorities. This government-to-government relationship differentiates the struggle for civil rights for Native Americans from that of other racial and ethnic minorities. The rights of Native Americans derive from their legal status as members or descendants of a tribe that is a separate nation rather than from their race (Strickland 1992).

Government policies toward Native Americans have changed repeatedly. Overall, the 19th century saw systematic campaigns to rob Native Americans of their traditional ways of life. In the 20th century, Native Americans were treated as second-class citizens and did not actually become U.S. citizens with universal voting rights until Congress passed legislation granting them citizenship in 1924. Like African Americans, Native Americans turned to the courts in their fight for civil rights, and in the past few decades, they have managed to score a number of important victories regarding treaty violations, including rulings granting hunting and fishing rights and awarding substantial financial compensation for past wrongs. Congress has passed laws guaranteeing First Amendment rights and criminal due process protection to Native Americans living in federally supported housing and has also provided welfare, education, and food-stamp programs, community development grants, and federal funds for tribally controlled colleges.

One of the problems Native Americans have faced in their struggle for civil rights is that separate tribal identities, the geographical separation of tribes, and the literally hundreds of separate treaties governing tribal relationships with the federal government have worked against the creation of a coordinated, broad-scale civil rights movement. It was not until the 1960s that Native Americans began to take coordinated action. In 1970, the Native American Rights Fund (NARF) was founded to pursue the litigation tactics proven successful by the NAACP and MALDEF. NARF's legal advocates, who are Native Americans with expertise in Indian law, have successfully used the courts to secure fishing and hunting rights, support tribal land claims, and advance Native American rights in a broad variety of areas.

Other Native American groups engaged in more radical activities. The best-known incident that focused national attention on the plight of Native Americans was the 71-day occupation of Wounded Knee, South Dakota, in 1973 by 200 members of the American Indian Movement (AIM). AIM wanted, among other things, a federal investigation into the condition of Native American tribal communities and a review of the 300 treaties between tribes and the federal government.

Native American groups have had numerous important successes, particularly in reclaiming lands confiscated by the federal government in treaty violations or legit-imized by one-sided agreements. However, Native Americans still face a number of challenges. Litigation to protect sacred sites and to gain the right to engage in reli-gious practices involving, for example, ceremonial consumption of peyote has fre-quently been unsuccessful. A movement to fight negative stereotyping by challenging the practice of using epithets and tribal names as names of sports teams and mascots has also met with mixed success. Some schools have renamed their teams, while others have refused to do so. There have also been vigorous legal challenges over trademark disputes from the National Football League's Washington Redskins and Major League Baseball's Atlanta Braves and Cleveland Indians.

Women

Women differ significantly from the other groups discussed in this chapter; they are not a minority in terms of numbers. Females make up a little more than 50 percent of the U.S. population, and in recent elections, more than 50 percent of voters. But this apparent advantage in numbers has failed to protect women from many of the same types of discrimination suffered by minorities. In the past, women were prevented from voting and owning property and denied political, social, and economic opportu-nities. Although many of these barriers have fallen, significant obstacles remain.

Historical Background

The struggle for women's rights in the United States has been tied to the cause of equality for African Americans. Women made significant contributions to the abolitionist move-ment that sought to end slavery. Ironically, they discovered that many men who were vehemently opposed to slavery did not extend such passions to the rights of women.

Women were refused the right to participate in the 1833 Philadelphia convention to form the American Anti-Slavery Society, a snub that was repeated at the 1840 World Anti-Slavery convention in London. Among the women in the American delegation to the latter were Lucretia Mott and Elizabeth Cady Stanton. Outraged at being denied par-ticipation on the basis of their gender, Mott and Stanton organized a women's rights con-vention in 1848 at Seneca Falls, New York. The 300 delegates at this meeting approved a Declaration of Sentiments modeled after the Declaration of Independence: "We hold these truths to be self-evident, that all men and women are created equal; that they are endowed by their Creator with certain inalienable rights; that among these are life, lib-erty, and the pursuit of happiness" (quoted in McGlen and O'Connor 1983, 389). The convention marked the beginning of the women's rights movement in the United States.

Conventions similar to Seneca Falls met in different cities in the East and Midwest nearly every year until the Civil War. Although Susan B. Anthony and others argued that the struggle for the rights of African Americans and the rights of women were inseparable, the women's rights movement temporarily suspended during the Civil War. When the movement commenced shortly after the war, it became clear that although African Americans and women shared a number of mutual interests, they would fight separate battles. Some militant feminists wanted to add the word *sex* to the statement in the Fifteenth Amendment about "race, color, or previous condition of servitude." Frederick Douglass and other African American leaders opposed linking **suffrage** (the right to vote) for women and African Americans, fearing it would make it easier to defeat the amendment. Some in the women's movement agreed. They argued that if African American men were given voting rights first, it would make gaining the vote for women easier. Ultimately this argument prevailed, and the women's rights movement separated itself from the cause of racial equality.

The women's rights movement was hampered by division. Advocates agreed that female suffrage was important but disagreed about broader goals. In 1869, Anthony and Stanton organized the National Suffrage Association, which advocated the broad cause of women's rights and regarded the vote as the means to a general improvement of women's place in society. The same year, Lucy Stone helped form the American Women Suffrage Association to concentrate on suffrage as an end rather than a means and seek change on a state-by-state basis. The National Suffrage Association was more militant, advocating an amendment to the federal Constitution. The American Women Suffrage Association tried to appear "respectable" and avoided taking stands on controversial issues involving marriage and religion. Over time, Stone's more conservative organization gained supporters, and the women's rights movement increasingly focused on the suffrage issue. In 1890, the two groups merged into the National American Women Suffrage Association, which evolved into a single-issue organization pursuing suffrage. In 1890, Wyoming gave women the right to vote, and by 1918, 15 states allowed women to vote (Figure 5.1).

In time, a new generation of women suffragists threw off the conservative constraints of the National American Women Suffrage Association. Particularly important was Alice Paul, a militant feminist who formed a small radical group called the Congressional Union in 1913. Its members were generally dissatisfied with the slow and uneven progress in the state-by-state strategy. They sought an amendment to the Constitution and were willing to use unorthodox means to achieve it, including parades, picketing of the White House, mass demonstrations, and hunger strikes. Some were willing to be jailed in order to get the issue onto the public agenda.

World War I helped promote the arguments of the Congressional Union. Women made many critical contributions to the war effort, and women's rights advocates argued that they should be rewarded with the right to vote. Under pressure from the Congressional Union, Congress proposed an amendment giving women the vote in 1919. It was ratified a year later and officially became the Nineteenth Amendment. More than seventy years after the Seneca Falls convention, the Constitution finally guaranteed that citizens' right to vote could not be "denied or abridged" on the basis of sex.

The cause of women's rights won some important victories in the years immediately following passage of the Nineteenth Amendment, notably a federal law granting women citizenship independent of their husbands. But in general, the broad-based coalition that had grown around the suffrage issue dissolved. Only a few groups continued to actively push for women's rights. Key among them was the National

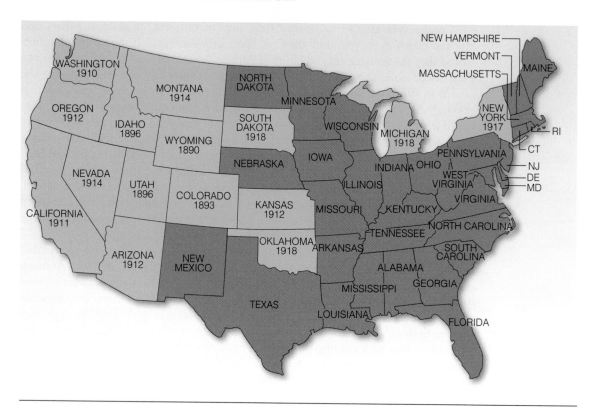

Figure 5.1
States (in yellow) that Allowed Women to Vote before the Nineteenth Amendment
Note: The Nineteenth Amendment was ratified on August 26, 1920.

Women's Party (NWP), which had evolved from the Congressional Union. In 1923, the NWP drafted an equal rights amendment (ERA), secured its introduction to Congress, and lobbied vigorously for its passage. The NWP met with little success. The proposal was reintroduced year after year but made little headway.

The movement for women's rights had some modest successes in the broader political arena. The National Federation of Business and Professional Women's Clubs (BPW), for example, actively campaigned to open up the federal civil service to women, lobbied for equal pay legislation, and came out in favor of the Equal Rights Amendment in 1937. But for the most part, women's rights advocates like the NWP and BPW spent the years between World War I and World War II laboring in vain, because they lacked political allies, public support, and a dramatic rallying issue like suffrage.

The Reemergence of Women's Rights

The struggle for women's rights reemerged in American life in the 1960s. This reemergence was not a result of pressure from interest groups outside the political system but rather was prompted by initiatives from within the federal government. When

President Kennedy took office in 1961, he appointed Esther Peterson, a long-time labor lobbyist, to head the Women's Bureau in the Department of Labor. Peterson convinced Kennedy to establish the President's Commission on the Status of Women, a body consisting of thirteen women and eleven men and headed by Eleanor Roosevelt. In October 1962, the commission issued *American Women,* a factual report on the status of women in employment and education that also contained recommendations for government action. The report was moderate in tone and achieved some concrete results. President Kennedy revised an 1870 law that had banned women from high-level federal employment, and in 1963 Congress passed the Equal Pay Act, which mandated equal pay for equal work performed under equal conditions. Both actions had been recommended by the commission.

Although these represented significant advances, some feminists had serious doubts about the way the reforms were achieved and the slow pace toward ensuring broader equality for women. The Commission on the Status of Women was seen as an easy way for Kennedy to repay his political obligations to women who were active in his campaign. Some feminists even suggested that Kennedy's actions were meant to take any remaining political steam out of the drive for an Equal Rights Amendment, which the commission opposed in its final report. The 1963 Equal Pay Act was interpreted by some critics as increasing the job security of men by preventing their replacement with lower-paid women.

In the mid-1960s, a series of events converged to stimulate the formation of a new type of interest group to press for women's rights. Betty Friedan's *The Feminine Mystique* (1963), led many women to begin questioning their general situation in society. While commuting to Washington to gather material for a second book, Friedan began talking with women who worked in Congress, the executive branch, and the Citizen's Advisory Council. Many of these women wanted the Equal Employment Opportunity Commission (EEOC) to take sex discrimination in private employment as seriously as it did racial discrimination. A number of them were frustrated with groups like the National Federation of Business and Professional Women's Clubs and the League of Women Voters, which had refused to launch campaigns against sex discrimination for fear of being labeled "militant" or "feminist."

Within this general atmosphere, a specific issue and a particular event combined to spur the creation of a new feminist interest group. The issue was the EEOC's failure to prevent newspapers from running separate job listings for men and women; the event was the third annual conference of State Commissions on the Status of Women. When the latter met in June 1966, many women wanted the group to pass a strongly worded resolution condemning sex discrimination in employment, but they were informed that the conference was not allowed to pass resolutions or take action. Outraged by the failure of the EEOC to act and disappointed in existing organizations, a group of women formed the National Organization for Women (NOW).

Incorporated in October 1966 with Betty Friedan as its first elected president, NOW passed a strongly worded resolution calling for action to bring women into the mainstream of American society. Instead of shrinking from the feminist label, this group embraced it. NOW pressured the EEOC for favorable rulings, opposed confirmation of Supreme Court nominee G. Harrold Carswell for his antifeminist positions, filed suit against the nation's largest corporations for sex discrimination, lobbied for funds for childcare centers, and picketed all-male bars.

Women's rights advocates scored a number of important victories in the 1960s and the 1970s:

- The Equal Opportunity Act of 1972 extended the coverage of the antidiscrimination provisions of the 1964 Civil Rights Act to educational institutions and state and local governments.
- The Education Amendment Act, also passed in 1972, prohibited sex discrimination in all federally aided education programs.
- A 1974 law extended the jurisdiction of the U.S. Commission on Civil Rights, which was originally set up to study problems of minorities, to include sex discrimination.

The most dramatic congressional victory was the passage of a proposal that had been doggedly building support for a half-century—the Equal Rights Amendment. After the original introduction of the amendment in 1923, it took two decades before first the Republicans and then the Democrats endorsed the measure as part of their party platforms. In the 1950s, the amendment twice passed the Senate but failed to gain approval of the House. By the 1970s, the pressure to pass the ERA had become overwhelming. The amendment was backed by virtually every women's rights group, President Richard Nixon, and a bipartisan group of members of Congress. In March 1972, the ERA finally received the required two-thirds vote in both the House and the Senate and was ready for ratification by three-fourths of the states.

Initially, the ERA had easy sailing at the state level, and 28 state legislatures ratified the amendment in the first year. But in 1973, the Stop ERA campaign began a national drive against the measure. Led by Phyllis Schlafly, an articulate spokeswoman for conservative causes, the campaign drew support from a number of right-leaning organizations, including the John Birch Society, the Christian Crusade, and Young Americans for Freedom. Opponents claimed that the ERA would make women eligible for the draft, deny wives the support of their husbands, and remove children from the custody of their mothers. State legislatures soon felt serious pressure to oppose the ERA, and the ratification movement lost momentum. The deadline for ratification expired in 1979, but women's groups persuaded Congress to extend it until 1982. The extra time did not help, and the ERA movement was halted just three states short of the 38 needed for ratification.

Although the ERA failed, women's rights advanced significantly in the 1980s and 1990s. Among changes made to the 1964 Civil Rights Act in 1972 were the denial of federal funds to any public or private program that discriminated on the basis of sex and the inclusion of Title IX, which required giving women's athletics equal standing with men's athletics in schools. In 1984, Representative Geraldine A. Ferraro became the first woman to run for the vice presidency on a major-party ticket. The courts became more open to claims of sex discrimination. In 1994, Congress passed the Violence against Women Act. In 1996, the Virginia Military Institute was required to admit women or lose state funding, ending more than 150 years as an all-male state-supported college. In 2002, Representative Nancy Pelosi (D-CA) became minority party whip and later that same year, minority party leader. These are the highest offices ever held by a woman in the U.S. Congress, and this breakthrough placed her in line to be speaker of the House if the Democrats should regain control of the House during her tenure. These examples are suggestive of a political system responsive to concerns of sex-based discrimination.

© Getty Images

Representative Nancy Pelosi (D-CA) joins hands with fellow Democratic Representative Robert Menendez (D-NJ) and Representative James Clyburn (D-SC) to celebrate her 2002 victory in becoming the House minority leader. She is the first woman to lead a party in Congress. While women achieving positions of high authority are becoming more commonplace, men still dominate national political institutions; women are more likely to be below the poverty line, and there remains a persistent pay gap between males and females.

During the same period, women also began to play a greater role in the political, social, and economic life of the nation. Only one senator and sixteen members of the House of Representatives in the Ninety-Sixth Congress (1979–1980) were women. The 108th Congress (2003–2004) included a record seventy-six women, sixty-two in the House of Representatives and fourteen in the Senate. Women continue to be a minority in elected office at the national level, but the days have passed when a female in a high-ranking public office is a novelty.

Women have also made advances in the economic arena. Women make up roughly half the U.S. labor force, and nearly 70 percent of women work full time. Women are making significant inroads into traditionally male-dominated career fields, inroads that are reflected in the shifting patterns of education: The percentage of women who are studying medicine or law is approaching parity with the percentage of men (Institute for Women's Policy Research 1996, 18–25).

Nevertheless, full equality between the sexes remains an elusive goal. Men still dominate national political institutions; women are more likely to be below the poverty line than men; and some career fields remain largely segregated by sex. There also remains a persistent pay gap between males and females, with women earning roughly 80 percent of what men earn. Much of this gap can be explained by work patterns; women, for example, tend to work fewer hours per year and have less full-time work experience than men. These factors cannot account for the entire gap,

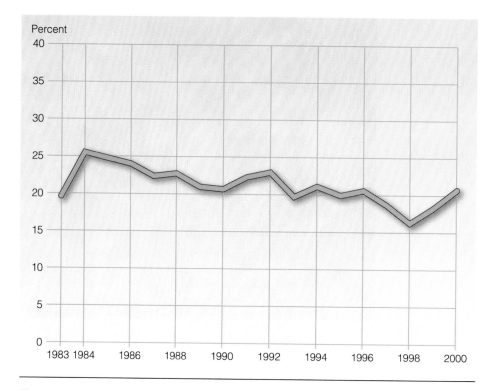

Figure 5.2
Percentage of Men's and Women's Earnings Difference
As the graph shows, there were fluctuations in the earnings difference for each year studied. Over the time period, there was a small but statistically significant decline in the average earnings difference between men and women.
Source: GAO analysis of Panel Study of Income Dynamics data.
Note: Percentages reflect earnings differences after accounting for factors that affect earnings. Data were collected annually through 1997 and then biennially starting in 1999.

however, and some experts suggest discrimination still plays a role in gender-based wage differences (General Accounting Office 2003). Figure 5.2 demonstrates the earnings gap, even after accounting for other factors.

To some extent, the broad-based movement promoting women's rights has been a victim of its own success. As one report put it, after three decades of tearing down barriers in employment, education, sports, and other areas of social life, many women are increasingly skeptical of the activism that did so much to achieve these breakthroughs. Indeed, many women now reject the label "feminist" because "they fear being stereotyped as strident, humorless and anti-male, or worry that feminists downgrade the importance of motherhood" (*CQ Researcher* 1997a, 169).

After achieving a series of significant victories, the women's movement has decentralized into often-conflicting camps that pursue contradictory political goals. Victim feminism, power feminism, radical feminism, and liberal feminism take differing stands on abortion, pornography, sexual harassment, and homemaking. (See the Living the Promise feature "Nanny's Rights?") Some even suggest an element of

LIVING THE PROMISE
Nanny's Rights?

Though straightforward in the abstract, achieving political equality in practice is complicated. It is not just a matter of overcoming ingrained prejudice or persuading some to give up positions of privilege. As it turns out, achieving political equality for one group can raise questions about the civil rights of another.

Take, for example, nannies.

The women's rights movement is one of the most successful civil rights stories of modern times. Though it is debatable whether women have achieved full equality with men, nowadays there is at least broad recognition that political, economic, and social opportunity should not be determined by gender. Certainly, in terms of gaining access to education and career opportunities, women have made significant strides compared to their forebears.

Yet as more women have taken advantage of those opportunities and entered the workforce, it has created a large demand for childcare and for the household services— cooking, cleaning, and general homemaking—traditionally performed by wives and mothers. Attempts to draft men into shouldering an equal burden of these chores have met with mixed success. Men do more than they used to around the house but still not as much as women. Even if men do pick up a fair share, the household burden creates a time and energy squeeze for dual-career couples. For single mothers,

that crunch can be severe. Who can society get to take on the grunt household labor?

Well . . . women.

Highly educated and well-paid women in professional careers are often turning to the nanny solution to this problem. Those nannies are overwhelmingly female, and they are often poorly paid and receive no benefits. This practice has created an uncomfortable paradox that several feminist writers have recognized: Some of those who have benefited most from the victories of the women's rights movement are exploiting women.

As Caitlin Flanagan puts it, the overwhelmingly female, largely nonwhite and immigrant population that serves as nannies has been embraced not by "a highly organized and politically powerful group of American women intent on bettering the lot of their sex but, rather, by an equally large army of educated professional-class women with booming careers who needed their children looked after and their houses cleaned" (114). It is the most-educated and powerful women who are most likely to employ nannies, "and when they do so, it is very often on the most undesirable terms" (121–122).

The most notorious example of this is Zoe Baird, nominated by President Bill Clinton for the post of attorney general. Baird's nomination fell afoul of "Nannygate;" her chances of becoming the nation's top

lawyer ruined by the revelation that she had employed two illegal Peruvians as domestic workers without paying Social Security taxes on their wages. Some argued, not without justification, that Baird was unfairly treated. Yet that does not remove the uncomfortable fact that Baird and her husband made more than $500,000 annually, while their nanny and housekeeper was paid $6 an hour with no benefits.

The real problem here is not the hypocrisy that has accompanied some of the advances in women's opportunities but the undeniable fact that American society has not and does not economically value the physically exhausting and emotionally draining work of raising kids and cleaning house. Males quite rightly bear a large share of the blame for undervaluing traditionally female work that by any measure other than money represents some of the most important responsibilities in society. Yet according to writers like Flanagan, women are on the giving as well as the receiving end of these unfair expectations.

Achieving equal rights is not easy. In some ways, it is painless to address the most egregious and obvious inequalities because they are so inequitable and so obvious. It is obviously unjust for women to be treated as economic and social inferiors to men. Yet recognizing that fact does not automatically provide uncomplicated answers to the problem. Indeed, sometimes it just raises hard questions. And hard work. Just ask a nanny.

Source: Flanagan, Caitlin. 2004. "How Serfdom Saved the Women's Movement." *The Atlantic,* 293 (March): 109–128.

contradiction has crept into parts of the feminist camp. For example, affordable child-care—a critical issue for working women—is dependent largely upon keeping wages low for childcare workers, who are also predominantly female. In other words, the economic prospects of the former group of women is working at cross purposes with the latter (Flanagan 2004). There appears to be little consensus on how, or even whether, the federal government should act to address such issues. Having made enormous advances, the movement for women's rights seems to be undergoing a reassessment while still far short of the goal of full equality.

The Disabled

People with mental or physical disabilities have often been the target of particularly virulent forms of discrimination. Their handicaps have been viewed as divine retribution for the sins of families and individuals or as a sign of spiritual uncleanliness. They were marked for persecution, and many were prevented from fully participating in social, political, and economic life (Humphries and Wright 1992). In the United States, basic care for the disabled was seen largely as the responsibility of family and private initiative, and the government made little effort to overcome the barriers that physical or mental disabilities presented to citizens seeking to exercise their rights.

Wounded war veterans were the first group of disabled citizens targeted for assistance from the federal government. The Smith-Sears Veterans' Rehabilitation Act was passed in 1918 to help veterans disabled in World War I. It was followed by the Smith-Fess Act in 1920, which was the first law to provide broad-based government assistance to the disabled. The federal government provided grants to state vocational rehabilitation programs, and states were required to match the funds on a dollar-for-dollar basis. These programs, which were aimed at boosting the economic self-sufficiency of military veterans disabled as a result of their service, had a limited effect. Nonetheless, assistance programs for the disabled slowly began to expand. All states had rehabilitation operations by the end of the 1930s, and the Social Security Act of 1935 made the federal government's role in supporting these programs permanent. The reach of government policy began to expand to include medical assistance to the mentally handicapped and broader support for the families of disabled citizens. The range of services and people covered by such programs was expanded even further by the Barden-LaFollette Act of 1943.

World War II created more pressure for the federal government to increase its involvement in assisting disabled citizens. In 1947, President Harry Truman helped establish the President's Commission on the Handicapped, which became a vocal advocate for disabled people. In 1954, the Vocational Rehabilitation Act substantially expanded the government's involvement in assisting the disabled, providing support for a wide range of physical and mental disorders. Such initiatives were significant, but they were not part of a cohesive civil rights agenda. Rather, they were viewed as extensions of moral obligations.

This view began to change in the late 1950s, when the government began to seriously examine the problems of access for the first time. **Access** is the ability to get into and make use of public facilities, and it became a focal point for the development of a true civil rights campaign for the disabled. Disabled groups pointed out that they were being segregated from the broader society and denied equal opportunity.

A report by the National Commission on Architectural Barriers issued in 1968 estimated that more than 20 million Americans were "built out of normal living by unnecessary barriers: a stairway, a too-narrow door, a too-high telephone" (Percy 1989, 50). Pressure began to build for the federal government to take action to ensure access to public facilities to the greatest extent possible. This pressure resulted in the Architectural Barriers Act of 1968, a law that mandated designing public buildings to allow handicapped access. This law shifted public policy from a service orientation to a focus on rights.

The new focus on the civil rights of the disabled began to bear fruit in the 1970s. First were two important legal victories. *Pennsylvania Association for Retarded Children (PARC) v. Pennsylvania* (1971) contended that the state was arbitrarily denying mentally disabled students a right to an education because state law assumed that children with mental handicaps were incapable of being educated and did not provide due process in excluding mentally disabled students from the public school system. As part of an agreement to settle the suit in 1972, the state acknowledged that it had an obligation to provide a free and appropriate education to mentally disabled students. In *Mills v. Board of Education of the District of Columbia* (1972), parents of mentally disabled students sued the education authorities in the nation's capital using a similar argument. The court ruled in the plaintiffs' favor and ordered school authorities to provide "a free and suitable publicly supported education regardless of the child's mental, physical, or emotional disability or impairment." Although neither case reached the Supreme Court, both were important civil rights victories for the disabled because they established a legal precedent for civil rights action (Percy 1989, 56–57).

The legal victories were followed by important legislation. The 1973 Rehabilitation Act provided some of the same protections to the disabled as had been granted earlier to minorities and women, including a prohibition on discrimination on the basis of handicap by any program receiving federal funds. The legislation was complex and controversial. It was passed during the tenure of Richard Nixon, but was not implemented by either Nixon or his successor, Gerald Ford. When Jimmy Carter also sought to delay implementation, his foot-dragging prompted a public outcry. The regulations putting the law into practice were finally signed by Secretary of Health, Education, and Welfare Joseph Califano, Jr., in April 1977. Califano said that the law represented "the first federal civil rights law protecting the rights of handicapped persons and reflects a national commitment to end discrimination on the basis of handicap" (Worsnop 1996).

In 1975 Congress approved the Education for All Handicapped Children Act, which required all states to provide a "free appropriate public education" to disabled children, thus writing into law the decisions in *PARC* and *Mills*. Like the Rehabilitation Act, this legislation was controversial because of its cost and complexity and its increased federal preemption of what traditionally had been an area under state and local government control. President Ford threatened to veto the bill, but it passed Congress with enough votes to override a veto. The Education for All Handicapped Children Act evolved into the Individuals with Disabilities Education Act in 1992. In essence, this law guaranteed the disabled the right to a public education and obligated schools to protect and support that right regardless of the costs they incur in doing so (Biskupic 1999).

The costs associated with the Rehabilitation Act and the Education for All Handicapped Children Act were particularly worrisome to institutions such as schools. They had to invest in such physical improvements as installing elevators and building

The Americans with Disabilities Act of 1990 extended to disabled citizens a formal recognition of their civil rights and protections. It also brought the issue of access, which had formally been enforced only in public institutions and facilities, into the private sector.

wheelchair ramps to make their facilities handicapped accessible, and they had to make a greater commitment to expensive special education programs. The federal government did make funds available to help cover some of these costs, but it quickly became apparent that part of the financial burden was being passed on to local governments.

The federal government expanded the civil rights protection of the disabled in 1988 with the Fair Housing Amendments Act, which was aimed at preventing discrimination in housing. Then, in 1990, Congress passed the Americans with Disabilities Act (ADA), which specifically extended to disabled citizens the civil rights and protections that were the cornerstone of the 1964 Civil Rights Act. Although a landmark victory, the law "was notable more for its sweep than its novelty" (Worsnop 1996, 1,118). It largely codified existing laws and regulations and extended them to the private sector.

Like the laws it superceded, the ADA was controversial. It required private companies to assume "reasonable" expenditures to meet the legislation's requirements. Businesses complained that the federal government was now able to dictate the width of hallways in a private office building, where a store can display its merchandise, and much more. Although the federal government had the power to make such mandates, it assumed little or none of the cost of actually following through on them (Ferguson 1995).

In enforcing the ADA, the government has tended to concentrate on guaranteeing access to public and civic life and has preferred to negotiate compliance with public and private organizations that have been the target of complaints. For example, the city of Waukesha, Wisconsin, responded to pressure from the federal government to make city hall handicapped accessible. The complaint was initiated by a city alderman who used a wheelchair and had difficulty getting into city facilities, including the room where the council held closed meetings (U.S. Department of Justice 2000). The Supreme Court, however, has also signaled a willingness to set limits on the rights of the disabled. For example, in *Board of Trustees v. Garrett* (2001), the court ruled that employees of state agencies could not pursue discrimination claims by using the ADA to sue their employers in federal court. In this case the Supreme Court ruled against the civil rights of the disabled and upheld the sovereign immunity of states, which restricts the rights of individuals to sue states in federal court.

Gays and Lesbians

Ethnicity, gender, and disability are far from the only classifications used to arbitrarily deny American citizens full participation in political life. Sexual orientation has also served as a basis for systematic discrimination. Homosexuals have fought to get state and local governments to enact policies preventing systematic discrimination against gays and lesbians and to get the federal government to prohibit denying employment opportunities for the same reason.

The fight over gay rights has become increasingly partisan in recent years. Many Americans perceive homosexuality as a threat to mainstream family values (Haider-Markel and Meier 1996). The adoption of policies prohibiting discrimination on the basis of sexual orientation has provoked a political backlash, succeeding in some states and localities, failing in others. In *Lawrence v. Texas* (2003), a case discussed in the previous chapter, the Supreme Court ruled unconstitutional state laws criminalizing homosexual sex conducted between consenting adults in the privacy of their own bedrooms. This represented a significant step forward for the gay rights movement because, in essence, it said that gays had the same right to privacy as everyone else. Yet in upholding this right, the Court stopped considerably short of granting homosexuals full political equality. Nowhere is this more apparent—or more controversial—than in the conflict over gay marriage.

The debate over whether gays should be able to gain the same legal rights available to married heterosexual couples was pushed onto the public agenda as far back as 1993, when the Hawaii Supreme Court ruled that denying same-sex couples a marriage license denied them equal protection rights under the Hawaii constitution. Congress and many states moved quickly to not only squash such laws but also to prevent recognition of homosexual marriages altogether. Congress passed the Defense of Marriage Act, and President Clinton signed the bill into law in 1996. About 30 states have passed similar statutes. These laws stipulate that other states are not obligated to recognize same-sex marriages. Even Hawaii amended its state constitution in 1998 to authorize limiting marriage to couples of the opposite sex.

This did not end the drive for gay marriage, however. In 2004 the Massachusetts Supreme Court ruled that denying same-sex couples the right to marry violated the equal protection guarantees of the state's constitution. That same year, local authorities in San Francisco began issuing marriage licenses to same-sex couples, a move that was followed by a handful of other local governments across the country. These actions prompted immediate legal challenges. In Massachusetts lawmakers began considering a constitutional amendment to counter the state's high court ruling, and the California Supreme Court ordered San Francisco to stop sanctioning gay marriages. Seeking to end the question once and for all, opponents of gay marriage began pushing for an amendment to the U.S. Constitution banning gay marriage nationwide. This attracted powerful support, including that of President Bush, and became an issue in the 2004 presidential campaign. The proposal, at least initially, met with a mixed response. Though public opinion was not behind legalizing gay marriage, an amendment banning such unions would gain the dubious distinction of being the first time the Constitution was changed specifically to deny a group rights that are enjoyed by others. The latter concern seemed to give even gay marriage opponents second thoughts on addressing the issue by seeking a constitutional amendment.

State and local governments have actually been grappling for some time with the question of gay unions and related issues, such as whether employers should extend insurance benefits to same-sex partners of employees. In 2000, Vermont passed a law recognizing civil unions between gay and lesbian couples. A civil union is not technically or legally a marriage, but the Vermont law gives gay and lesbian couples almost all of the same legal benefits enjoyed by married couples, including:

- Automatic inheritance rights without having to write a will and broad protections for the surviving partner under probate laws
- Preference for becoming the partner's guardian if the partner is incapacitated
- The right to visit the partner in the hospital and to make healthcare decisions
- Communication privileges, so that a partner cannot be forced to testify against the other partner
- Leave from work under family medical leave laws to care for an ill partner or if one partner gives birth to or adopts a child
- Rights as a stepparent for a child of the other partner
- Protection from discrimination in insurance and credit (for example, to obtain joint car insurance)
- Greater access to health insurance coverage to partners in a civil union
- Potential responsibility to provide support (alimony) to the other partner upon dissolution (Vermont Freedom to Marry Action Committee 2000)

To form a civil union in Vermont, the couple simply gets a license from a town clerk and participates in a union ceremony conducted by a justice of the peace or clergy member. The license is then filed with the town clerk, creating a public record of the union. A couple wishing to terminate a civil union must file a dissolution proceeding in family court that follows the same procedures and applies the same laws as when a married couple goes through a divorce. The major marriage benefit missing from these civil unions is portability. Marriages between heterosexual couples are generally recognized by all other states under the "full faith and credit" provision of the U.S. Constitution (see Chapter 3). But legal experts have said that other states would not necessarily be required to recognize a civil union between a same-sex couple, an opinion underlined in federal law by the Defense of Marriage Act. As of 2004 the Defense of Marriage Act had not faced a direct constitutional challenge, and it was matter of some debate and confusion as to whether states would ultimately be obligated to recognize the gay marriage laws of any other state as legal and binding (this issue was discussed at the beginning of Chapter 3).

While equality in terms of the legal rights and status of marriage remains an issue of fierce debate and no small amount of confusion, advocates of homosexual rights have scored some notable successes in other areas. In *Romer v. Evans* (1996), for example, the Supreme Court struck down an amendment to Colorado's constitution that invalidated local ordinances seeking to protect homosexual rights and outlawed similar regulations. This marked the first time the equal protection clause of the Fourteenth Amendment had been extended to homosexuals. Numerous companies and municipalities have taken it upon themselves to extend fringe benefits, such as health and life insurance coverage, to unmarried domestic partners—including same-sex partners—of their employees. States like Hawaii and California have domestic partnership systems in place statewide (Goldberg 2000).

The development of gay and lesbian civil rights is in its early stages compared to similar movements for ethnic minorities and women. Whether homosexuals can secure the same sorts of successes in gaining civil rights remains unclear.

Performance Assessment

The government's orientation toward civil rights is a litmus test of whether the political system is making good on the democratic promise. Does the government take on the obligation to ensure that groups of citizens are not arbitrarily prohibited from exercising the liberties and freedoms enjoyed by others? Another way of putting this is simply to ask whether the government upholds the core democratic values of political equality and minority rights.

In the case of the United States, the answers are mixed. There is absolutely no doubt that some Americans have been systematically denied such basic freedoms as the right to vote and own property based on group classification. African Americans were denied pretty much all personal freedom during the formative years of the republic. Women were not universally guaranteed the vote until 1920. Native Americans, the nation's original inhabitants, did not win even the rights of citizenship until several years after that. It was not until the last two or three decades that disabled citizens were accorded the right to full access to public services and facilities. If you are gay, the law denies you the rights and privileges of marriage enjoyed by heterosexuals. Although all these groups have undoubtedly made significant advances in gaining political, social, and economic equality, many of their advocates argue that their struggle for civil rights still goes on. Numerous other groups have similar tales to tell, all of which seem to show that government has much left to do if it is to meet its obligation to act as a sword in protecting civil rights.

Part of the problem is that while legal and legislative victories are important, they create only the means to achieve equality, not equality itself. These victories may establish legal recognition of the rights of a minority group, but they do not automatically protect those rights in practice. A successful civil rights agenda thus virtually requires an organized and sustained political effort; movements without such sustained efforts might get discriminatory laws struck down, but they will have a hard time getting nondiscrimination laws implemented. The importance of endurance was succinctly summed up by political scientists Charles Bullock and Charles Lamb in their study of problems with implementing civil rights laws: "While recognition by the federal government that a right existed was an important step, it alone provided but a light nudge toward attainment of the right" (1984, 205).

Though the American political system's record on the core democratic values of political equality and minority rights leaves much to be desired, it is also true that the general historical trend in the United States has been toward greater guarantees of civil rights. The democratic promise here has been imperfectly fulfilled, but the political system has also been responsive to some of the most egregious differences in equality, even if the response has sometimes been grudging and slow.

Setting aside the historical record, some argue that contemporary government is, if anything, too sensitive to civil rights. From this perspective, the government and the law is seen as so sensitive to claims of inequality by minority groups it is willing to deny political equality to the majority. A common argument employed by opponents of affirmative action and antidiscrimination policies is that legitimate complaints of inequality have largely been addressed, and what remains is little more than demands for preferential treatment. Shelby Steele, an African American scholar, is one of the more eloquent voices to weigh in against affirmative action, saying that it has shifted from the laudable aim of antidiscrimination enforcement to "social engineering by means of quotas, goals, timetables, set-asides, and other forms of preferential treatment" (Steele 1990, 46). The net result, argues Steele, not only creates the possibility of reverse discrimination, it condemns minorities to second-class status. The implication of affirmative action, Steele argues, is that African Americans cannot succeed on merit alone. In other words, minorities have exchanged a system of legal inequality for a system of implied inferiority. The ironic result is that affirmative action in some way validates the discriminatory laws that denied minorities civil rights because minorities who gain high social or economic positions are seen as tokens of favoritism, not as individuals who achieved such station through hard work and ability.

Pro and con, the civil rights debates will continue. This debate is good in the sense that, regardless of whether you agree or disagree with the outcome, the very act of discussion and debate indicates that political equality and minority rights are not taken for granted.

Summary

- Civil liberties ensure that citizens are free to make the individual choices they please. Civil rights ensure that those freedoms are not arbitrarily denied to certain categories of citizens. Civil rights are thus the rights of all citizens to legal, social, and economic equality.
- Numerous groups have been systematically excluded from the political and social mainstream. Both federal and state governments have tolerated unequal treatment of citizens based on characteristics such as race, gender, and religion. Many of these groups have fought long battles to get the government to ensure that they enjoy the same democratic rights and privileges enjoyed by others.
- The most notorious example of government tolerance of inequality is the historical treatment of African Americans. In the name of political pragmatism, the Founders accepted the institution of slavery and enshrined in the Constitution the value of slaves as three-fifths of a person for purposes of taxation and representation. It took the better part of two centuries to get the federal government to guarantee civil rights to African Americans, and this remains a contentious political issue today.

- A long list of ethnic minority groups have suffered discrimination and faced numerous obstacles to achieving equal status. These include Native Americans, Latinos, and Asian Americans. Other groups that have faced systematic discrimination include women, the elderly, the young, and gays and lesbians.
- Most of the groups that have waged extensive battles for civil rights have won important victories. These range from the abolishment of slavery to the elimination of poll taxes, from affirmative action programs to the reformation of discriminatory representation systems, from reclaiming ownership of tribal lands to guaranteeing equal access to public buildings and places. Nonetheless, many groups believe that their struggles for civil rights are far from over. The quest for greater freedom and equality—the drive to get the federal government to protect groups from arbitrary exclusion from full participation in public, social, and economic activities—continues to be a central component of American political life.
- Although the historical record on civil rights in the United States suggests performance has been a long way from the democratic promise, the general trend during the nation's history has been toward greater guarantees of civil rights. The political system has been responsive to egregious differences in equality, although that response has at times been grudging and very slow in coming.

Key Terms

access   148
affirmative action   126
civil disobedience   131
civil rights   126
discrimination   135
de facto discrimination   136
de jure discrimination   135
genocide   139
grandfather clause   129

Jim Crow   134
passive resistance   134
poll taxes   128
racial segregation   128
racism   131
reverse discrimination   135
separate but equal   129
suffrage   141

Selected Readings

Beckwith, Francis J., and Todd E. Jones, eds. 1997. *Affirmative Action: Social Justice or Reverse Discrimination?* New York: Prometheus. Supporters and opponents of affirmative action present their positions on this politically difficult issue.

Koppelman, Andrew. 1998. *Anti-Discrimination Law and Social Equality.* New Haven, CT: Yale University Press. An examination of the sometimes competing desires among Americans to preserve individual liberty and merit-based access to social and economic opportunity, and the commitment to eliminating discrimination within society.

Shipler, David. 1998. *A Country of Strangers.* New York: Vintage. A *New York Times* reporter takes an in-depth look at what separates blacks and whites—perspectives as well as issues—and what might bring them together.

Sommers, Christine Hoff. 1995. *Who Stole Feminism?* New York: Simon & Schuster. A tough and pointed critique of the modern feminist movement.

6 | Interest Groups

© Getty Images

On March 13, 1996, a gunman stalked onto the grounds of a school in Dunblane, Scotland, and killed sixteen students, their teacher, and, finally, himself. One month later, at the other end of the world, another man used a semiautomatic rifle to kill thirty-five people in Tasmania, an island state off the coast of Australia. A year later and an ocean away, the violence was echoed in a disturbing series of shootings by students in American schools. In October 1997, two were killed and seven wounded at Pearl High School in Mississippi. In March 1998, two underage boys staged a deliberate sniper attack on their classmates in Jonesboro, Arkansas, killing five and wounding ten. In May 1998, a student went on a shooting spree in a Springfield, Oregon, school cafeteria, where he killed two and injured twenty-two. In April 1999, two high school seniors gunned down twelve classmates and a teacher before killing themselves in a murderous rampage at Columbine High School in Littleton, Colorado.

These unrelated incidents triggered public outrage and prompted differing government reactions. The British government banned the private possession of handguns. The Australian government outlawed the sale and possession of all automatic and semiautomatic firearms (CQ Researcher 1997b). The U.S. government passed no major gun control laws. On July 22, 1998, the U.S. Senate tabled legislation requiring child safety locks on handguns. A day later, it tabled legislation that would have made adult gun owners legally responsible for restricting children's access to their firearms. Tanya K. Metaksa, a gun-rights lobbyist, called the Senate's inaction "A great day for gun safety in America" (NRA 1998). But July 24, 1998, the day Metaksa's remarks were released, turned out to be a very bad day for gun safety on Capitol Hill when Russell Weston, Jr., a man with a history of mental instability, shot his way into the offices of the House of Representatives, killing two police officers before being wounded himself (Gibbs 1998). Even a gun battle within its own walls did not prompt Congress to enact stricter gun-control laws.

What accounts for this reluctance to push for tighter gun regulations? One possibility is that Americans tend to be more supportive and protective of gun ownership than people in other countries. Consequently, legislators may be justifiably leery of opposing the right to own personal firearms. But even accounting for such cultural differences, public opinion in the United States overwhelmingly supports gun-control laws. Polls by the *Wall Street Journal* and the Hearst news organization showed majorities of 75 percent or more supporting the legislation tabled (and effectively killed) by the U.S. Senate in the wake of the school shootings (Handgun Control 1998). In fact, public opinion polls show American citizens have overwhelmingly approved stricter gun-control laws for more than six decades (Wright, Rossi, and Daly 1983). Why has the government largely failed to respond?

The answer is that, in general, the American political system is not designed to detect the will of the people and translate it into government action. The government responds to the people who are involved in the process; and motivated and well-organized groups like the NRA can be more effectively involved than individuals or less well-organized groups. The American political system is characterized by a variety of interest groups battling for government action and public support and employing a number of different techniques to achieve their goals. Groups' abilities to achieve their objectives depend not only on having political resources but also on how well they use the resources. Understanding how groups go about achieving their goals and how and why the government responds to these efforts is the purpose of this chapter. The chapter thus examines what interest groups are, who joins them and why, their sources of power and influence, and their place in American politics. (See the Promise and Policy feature "Guns and Interest Groups.")

The Promise of Interest Groups

The basic promise of interest groups is found in the First Amendment "right of the people peaceably to assemble, and to petition the Government for a redress of grievances." This is a straightforward expression of the core democratic value of political freedom. Political freedom means, in part, having the right to join with others to pursue shared interests. This is a right Americans enthusiastically embrace. Alexis de Tocqueville, a French aristocrat and political thinker, commented on 19th-century Americans' proclivity to form associations in his book, *Democracy in America* (1835). He observed that Americans exercised the right to form associations more often than citizens of other nations at the time. Even today, Americans are still joiners.

Political scientists have long recognized that interest groups play a key role in a pluralist democratic process: Formation and mobilization of interest groups is a natural result of like-minded individuals coming together to pursue a common goal (Truman 1951). Yet there is debate over exactly what an interest group is and how its membership is defined (see Baumgartner and Leech 1998, 22–33). For our purposes, an **interest group** is a politically oriented organization of people who share common interests and make demands on others in society with respect to those interests.

Not every group fits this definition. People who have red hair or who are college students share certain characteristics but have different interests. They comprise what sociologists call *categorical groups*. The first basic requirement of an interest group is a shared interest, not simply a common characteristic.

This definition also excludes groups that are not political in nature. Some interest groups do not make demands on society or seek to influence collective decisions about who gets what. For example, people who share a common interest in classical music may meet to listen to CDs, attend concerts, or sponsor a touring orchestra. This group is not an interest group. If that same group demands that a rock music radio station devote an hour a day to Mozart and Beethoven, then the group meets the second basic requirement and can be defined as an interest group because it now makes demands on others in society.

This example illustrates that groups can engage in political action without involving government. For example, though labor unions exert extensive influence in and on government, they also make demands on employers and the general public through strikes and picketing. Other groups also seek to satisfy their demands by dealing directly with private individuals and organizations. Students, for example, have sought to bring about major changes in universities through negotiation and confrontation with school officials.

Political action, nonetheless, frequently does involve government. Getting the government involved offers significant advantages because government has coercive power. If, for example, the classical music lovers are unsuccessful in convincing the owners of radio stations to play classical music, they might ask the Federal Communications Commission (FCC), the federal agency that grants licenses to radio stations, to require stations to devote a certain percentage of air time to serve the public interest in order to keep their broadcast licenses. The harassed radio station owner may decide that it is easier to cooperate with the music lovers than to defend its programming decisions before the FCC. Furthermore, these classical music radicals

PROMISE AND POLICY
Guns and Interest Groups

Opponents of gun control often base their arguments on the rights and liberties guaranteed by the U.S. Constitution. They argue that the Second Amendment guarantees individuals the right to "keep and bear arms" and that even a majority of citizens has no legitimate basis to restrict this right. The Constitution, in other words, makes a clear promise that government will not interfere with the private possession of firearms.

Yet it is not that simple. There is relatively little case law on the Second Amendment, but what does exist often contradicts the gun-rights position. Quoted in full, the amendment states: "A well-regulated militia, being necessary to the security of a free state, the right of the people to keep and bear arms, shall not be infringed." The courts have generally interpreted this provision to mean that the right of an individual to bear arms is subordinate to the government's regulatory power to use a "well-regulated" citizen militia, which is a citizen-based military organization formed for the purpose of common defense under state or federal government control.

This position was most clearly expressed in *U.S. v. Miller* (1939), in which the Supreme Court held that the Second Amendment's "obvious purpose" was ensuring the effectiveness of a well-regulated militia and not to broadly guarantee the individual right to gun ownership. The interpretation was reaffirmed in

Lewis v. United States (1980), in which the Court held: "The Second Amendment guarantees no right to keep and bear a firearm that does not have 'some reasonable relationship to the preservation or efficiency of a well-regulated militia.' "

A central reason for the government's tardiness in enacting gun control legislation is the political effectiveness of a single organization—the National Rifle Association (NRA). With its annual revenues approaching $150 million, the NRA maintains a paid staff of more than 300 employees and is the center of a network of roughly 10,000 local gun clubs distributed across all 50 states. It has an entire division, the Institute for Legislative Action, which specializes in lobbying, maintaining government contacts, and providing money to political candidates who support its political goals. The NRA maintains computerized databases on its millions of members and on state and national legislators. In a few hours, the organization can coordinate an impressive display of political action, prompting thousands—even tens of thousands—of people to mail letters and make phone calls to their government representatives. These resources make the NRA a potent political force. Few members of Congress relish the prospect of being targeted for electoral defeat by the NRA, and the political risks involved in doing so are considerable.

Accusations of extremism have to some extent blunted the NRA's

effectiveness. For example, the NRA damaged its ties to the law enforcement community—traditionally a strong backer—by strenuously opposing a ban on so-called cop killer bullets. There is also organized opposition to the NRA. A number of antigun groups routinely battle the NRA for legislative influence and have scored some important victories. These include the passage in 1993 of the Brady Bill, named after Jim Brady, a former presidential press secretary who was seriously injured in an assassination attempt on President Ronald Reagan. The Brady Bill mandates a 5-day waiting period and background check before completion of the purchase of a handgun.

The best-known antigun groups are Handgun Control, Inc., and the Coalition to Stop Gun Violence. Both organizations have worked effectively to assemble the congressional coalition necessary to act on gun-control proposals. But, even combined, these organizations have only a fraction of the membership and resources of the NRA. And because they generally face the task of passing legislation, such groups have a built-in political disadvantage: It is much easier to kill proposed legislation than it is to pass it.

This explains why the U.S. government has a difficult time passing gun-control legislation: A motivated, well-organized minority can prevail over the will of the majority. The preferences of the majority can eventually find their way into public policy, but this is neither easy nor guaranteed. The Brady Bill was overwhelmingly supported by the public in almost every poll taken on the issue, yet it took six years of concerted political activity across three presidential administrations for Congress to actually pass the bill.

might persuade the city council to subsidize a local orchestra with public funds so that its performances could be broadcast. This politically savvy set of Mozart lovers would thus have taken advantage of the government's ability to require radio stations to conform to certain rules and would have gained tax money taken from people who do not necessarily like classical music.

Comparison of Interest Groups and Political Parties

Political parties are in some ways similar to interest groups: Both are organizations that engage in political action to achieve goals. Despite these similarities, however, there are important differences between interest groups and political parties. That is, political parties (discussed in greater depth in Chapter 7) are not just a special type of interest group.

The most important difference distinguishing these types of organizations is that they use fundamentally different methods to influence the political process: Political parties run candidates for office under a party label; interest groups do not. In contrast to special interest groups, political parties seek to staff government positions by recruiting and nominating candidates for office, and they work to get their candidates elected to important government positions.

A second major difference is that interest groups tend to focus on a narrower set of issues than political parties. If political parties are too narrowly focused, they will not be able to appeal to the broad electorate that determines campaign outcomes. In contrast, interest groups are more effective if they limit their attention to the few specific concerns of their members. Individuals participate in interest groups because they share a set of attitudes on some specific matter, such as classical music. All members agree on their love for classical music and will support group activities to promote it. But classical music lovers do not necessarily agree on gun control, and if the group takes a position on such an issue, it risks splintering the group.

A third difference is that interest groups are private organizations, while parties are quasi-public. This is important because private organizations can establish whatever membership requirements they wish. Being private organizations, interest groups can restrict membership by income, professional qualifications, age, or even gender or race. Public organizations are legally prohibited from enacting such restrictions. Although political parties are not part of government, the U.S. Supreme Court has held that they are quasi-public organizations because they perform a "state function." Thus, according to the Court, the Texas Democratic Party could not declare itself a private club and limit participation in its primaries to white voters because such action prevented citizens of other races from effective participation in the political process (*Smith v. Allwright* 1944).

Interest Group Goals

Political interest groups pursue two basic objectives:

1. They seek new positive benefits to *promote* the group's interest.
2. They defend current benefits to *protect* the group's interest.

Engaging in political action to persuade a radio station to play classical music and trying to convince a city council to subsidize a local orchestra are examples of seeking new positive benefits. Groups that are generally satisfied with the present distribution of resources take defensive actions in the political arena to preserve the status quo. Interest groups thus attempt to achieve their objectives by trying to get their group and its goals to be the answer to the question of who gets what.

Interest Group Membership

Political activity in the United States has always been shaped by organized group activity. James Madison was fully cognizant of the role interest groups played in American politics; what he called "factions" in *Federalist* Number 10 fits the definition of political interest groups. As Figure 6.1 illustrates, most Americans belong to some form of voluntary organization—about 79 percent in one study. Although many organizations are not political interest groups as we define them in this chapter, on average 61 percent of the members of these organizations reported that the organization took stands on political issues (Verba, Schlozman, and Brady 1995, 62–65).

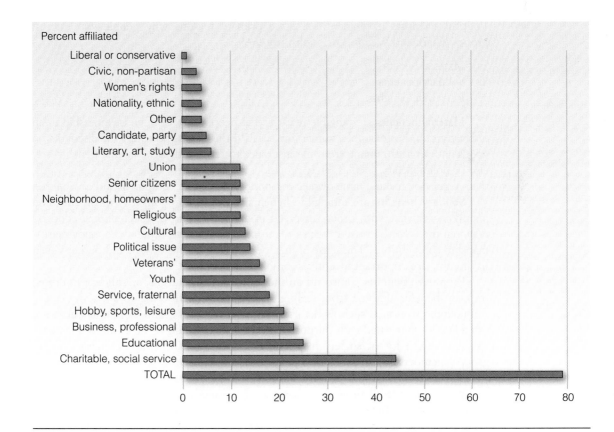

Figure 6.1
Percentage of Americans Affiliated with Voluntary Organizations
Source: Verba, Schlozman, and Brady 1995, 62–65; adapted from Lowery and Brasher 2004, 33.

At the very least, the vast majority of Americans are not far removed from an interest group. For example, many are members of, or have parents or grandparents in, the American Association of Retired Persons (AARP), one of the largest and most powerful interest groups in the nation. AARP has more than 35 million members, a significant portion of the adult population, and a 2003 budget of about $690 million. Among the many issues it addresses are laws to protect pensions, fight age discrimination, and provide prescription drug coverage in Medicare. Other Americans are members or are related to members of labor or teachers' unions, the American Bar Association, the American Medical Association, or other business or professional groups that lobby some level of government on behalf of their members. Students may be involved in campus or school organizations that make demands on the university for facilities, funding, or recognition. It is likely that some students who read this text are members of the NRA or Handgun Control, Inc., or another group that shares a common interest and makes demands on others with respect to that interest.

Why People Join Interest Groups

Political scientists have identified three primary reasons why people join interest groups (Clark and Wilson 1961; Salisbury 1969):

1. Material benefits
2. Solidary benefits
3. Purposive benefits

Material benefits are tangible rewards that people gain through membership in an interest group. For example, joining the AARP brings an opportunity for discounts on goods and services ranging from life insurance to travel lodging. Material benefits may also be nonmonetary, such as safety provisions for coal miners achieved through government regulation making mine owners responsible for certain equipment and procedures.

Solidary benefits are intangible benefits. Farmers may join a farm organization mainly to socialize with others involved in agricultural work. Recreational shooters may join the NRA because it brings them into contact with others who enjoy marksmanship competitions. The sense of membership and identification, and perhaps even having fun, are important incentives for joining a group.

Purposive benefits transcend an individual's own material or solidary interests; they are benefits derived from feeling good about contributing to a worthy cause. Public-interest groups such as the government watchdog group Common Cause are often largely concerned with purposive benefits. They channel the desire of members to improve the lot of society in general, not just the individual concerns of the group's members.

Material, solidary, and purposive benefits are not mutually exclusive. An interest group may provide all three. For example, the United Automobile Workers (UAW) provides material benefits to its members in the form of higher wages obtained through contract negotiations, it sponsors recreational and other activities, and it may push for social and economic reforms to benefit groups beyond its membership. Thus, the UAW provides different kinds of incentives to appeal to different interests or requirements of its members.

© AP/Wide World Photos

Although many people are drawn to issues for personal reasons, interest groups can provide purposive benefits. Wendy Hamilton, whose sister and young nephew were killed by a drunk driver, is the current president of Mothers Against Drunk Driving (MADD); here she stands before a display of people killed by drunk drivers in Louisiana. Established in 1980, the special interest nonprofit group has grown to more than 600 affiliates and 2 million members nation-wide, and it has successfully sponsored more than 2,300 anti–drunk driving laws. MADD works closely with the National Highway Traffic Safety Administration (NHTSA) to expand programs with the goal of saving lives.

This explanation of interest group membership assumes that individuals voluntarily join interest groups because it is **rational** to do so (Olson 1965). Rationality is defined in terms of an individual's self-interest: A rational being makes choices that maximize benefits and minimize costs. Applied to interest groups, the assumption that people are rational actors means that they join because the material, solidary, or purposive benefits they receive from membership are greater than the costs (membership dues, time commitments, and so forth).

Public Goods and Free Riders

Although the assumption of rational action is at the heart of mainstream explanations of why people join interest groups, it has a well-known problem: It is not rational to join an interest group if the benefit it produces is a public good (Olson 1965). A **public good** is a benefit that is provided to everyone; it cannot be withheld from people who are not group members and who do not contribute to the cost of providing the good. For example, an environmental group that pushes for clean air laws is seeking a public good—pleasant outdoor activities, better health, lower medical costs—that will be available to everyone. A rational actor who supports these goals may decline to join the group because he or she will get the benefits of the group's activities without paying any of the costs. In other words, if a group is providing a public good that is available to everyone, it is rational to be a **free rider.** *Free rider* simply describes a rational actor who chooses to enjoy the benefits of group activity without incurring any of the costs.

Thus, it may be rational *not* to join a group if the goal is a public good. The paradox is that securing a public good requires collective action; that is, a lot of people have to get involved in order to get the desired government action. This collective action problem presents something of a Catch-22: A public good requires organized group action; but if the goal is a public good, a rational actor has less incentive join in. Interest groups that can overcome this barrier are more likely to play a significant role in deciding who gets what. The challenge is to make it more attractive to join than to ride for free.

Overcoming the Free Rider Problem

Groups have several ways to overcome the free rider problem. One is to get government to require membership. For example, workers in some states are required to join a union if a majority of workers vote to let the union represent them. This arrangement is called a *union shop* or *closed shop.* But federal law also permits states to legislate an open shop so that workers are not required to join a union. Not surprisingly, labor unions in open-shop states are weaker than those in closed-shop states because of the free rider problem. Why join the union if everyone gets the benefits regardless? The problem is that because the unions are smaller and weaker in open-shop states, they lack the political muscle to achieve the collective goals. Open-shop states with weak unions tend to have lower wages and less job security—the very benefits the free riders may want the most.

Labor unions are not the only group that seeks to use the government to overcome the free rider problem. Some states require lawyers to join the state bar in order to practice law, and many universities require students to pay fees to support student government and other student organizations. (See the Promise and Policy feature "Student Activity Fees.") This remedy to the free rider problem, however, is relatively unusual and can be used only if the conditions are right.

Another way to discourage free riding is to use peer pressure to persuade others to do their part in achieving group goals—in other words, the group can threaten to ostracize people who do not join in. Ostracizing people who do not contribute tends to be more effective in small populations in which individuals have frequent face-to-face contact. In small groups, an individual's failure to contribute is more likely to be noticed because each individual contribution is a relatively large part of the collective group effort. In such settings, ostracism can be a powerful behavioral influence. Most people desire a sense of identification with a group, and the possibility of group disapproval, or even exclusion, is an important counter to the temptation to free ride.

The third and most common approach to entice people to join an organization is to utilize **selective benefits** restricted to members. These benefits are generally material

PROMISE AND POLICY
Student Activity Fees

Should a Jewish student be compelled to contribute to funding a Nazi group? Should an African American student be forced to help support a Ku Klux Klan organization? Many colleges and universities require students to pay a general activity fee that is used to fund a variety of student organizations. Some students have objected when the money supports organizations that espouse social or political views they find objectionable or speech they find offensive. Supporters of the general activity fee counter by pointing out that colleges should support the free and open exchange of ideas, even objectionable ideas, because it contributes to the growth of knowledge—a public good.

In 1996 a University of Wisconsin student, Scott Southworth, organized

a group of conservative Christian students and sued the university for mandating the payment of student activity fees. These fees subsidized a variety of student organizations, including the Lesbian, Gay, Bisexual Campus Center; the Campus Women's Center; the Madison AIDS Support Network; the International Socialist Organization; Amnesty International; and Students of National Organization for Women. Southworth argued that these groups engaged in political and ideological advocacy for causes he did not support and that he should therefore not be forced to contribute to them. A federal judge ruled that students may opt out of paying the portion of the fee that funds organizations they find objectionable, and a U.S. appeals

court in Chicago upheld the ruling (*Southworth v. Grebe* 1998).

But in March 2000, the Supreme Court reversed these decisions and unanimously voted to uphold the University of Wisconsin's student-fee system (*Board of Regents of the University of Wisconsin v. Southworth* 2000). "The University may determine that its mission is well served if students have the means to engage in dynamic discussions of philosophical, religious, scientific, social, and political subjects in their extracurricular campus life outside the lecture hall. If the University reaches this conclusion, it is entitled to impose a mandatory fee to sustain an open dialogue to these ends," wrote Justice Anthony M. Kennedy in the Court's opinion. As Justice Ruth Bader Ginsburg noted, "People are compelled to pay for all kinds of things being taught that they might not believe in." The Supreme Court's ruling also means that colleges and universities can compel students to not be free riders, at least when it comes to student organizations.

incentives, such as low-cost life insurance and health plans for union members and technical journals and newsletters for professionals. By using selective benefits to encourage membership, groups can overcome the free rider problem and secure a large enough base to engage in collective action to secure public benefits.

The Origins and Growth of Interest Groups

Interest groups have long played an important role in the American political system. For example, the Chamber of Commerce of the United States, an organization designed to advance the interests of the nation's business community, was formed in 1912. A related group, the National Association of Manufacturers, was established in 1895. The American Farm Bureau Federation dates back to 1919; today it is one of the largest agricultural interest groups in the nation, with membership of more than 3 million. These groups and others like them have been actively making demands on others in society through government action for the better part of a century. But what drives people to form interest groups?

Theoretical Perspectives on the Formation of Interest Groups

Political scientists have suggested several explanations for why interest groups form.

Pluralist Theory   The **pluralist explanation** of **interest groups** is that they form in reaction to problems created by particular social or economic events (Truman 1951). For example, the National Association of Manufacturers was formed in response to an economic depression.

Groups may also form as a result of government activity (Lowi 1969). When the national government expanded its role in the economy and in social welfare, numerous groups formed seeking social and political recognition or favors, including civil rights groups and groups representing the poor, the elderly, the disabled, gays, and consumers.

Exchange Theory   Political scientist Robert Salisbury (1969) proposed a more general **exchange theory** of interest groups. The basic idea is that groups form as a result of a deal—an exchange—between a group entrepreneur and an unorganized interest that may be underrepresented or not represented at all. The initiator of the exchange is a **group entrepreneur** who invests resources (such as time, money, and organizational skill) to create and build an organization that offers various types of benefits (material, solidary, and purposive) to entice others to join the group. Individuals with a common, but unorganized, interest join the group in exchange for the benefits of membership.

Niche Theory   One of the latest explanations for growth in interest groups is niche theory, formulated by political scientists Virginia Gray and David Lowery (1996). They applied biological concepts (such as population ecology and carrying capacity) to interest groups. Just as a biological environment has a certain carrying capacity to support various species that compete for resources (for example, food and nesting space), a political environment has a capacity to support interest groups that compete for the resources they need to survive (such as members and financial contributions). An environment—biological or political—is composed of various **niches**—spaces that contain an array of resources necessary for survival. A key insight of niche theory is that it is not competition from predators that threatens the survival of a species; instead, it is competition from similar species for the same resources in the niche. A species of finches, for example, is unlikely to be hunted to extinction by raptors, but the survival of these finches may be threatened by other species of finches that compete for the same resources (food and nesting space) to the point that they are excluded from the niche. Niche theory uses the concept of *partitioning* to explain how competing species resolve the conflict. **Partitioning** occurs when competitors in effect segment the available resources in the niche and use them in a way that excludes having to compete with the other species. One species of finches, for example, might feed only at the top of the trees in the morning, while another species feeds at the bottom of the trees later in the day (Lowery and Brasher 2004, 50–51).

In the same way, the explosion of interest groups can be explained as the partitioning of a policy niche into groups representing narrower and narrower interests.

For example, there is a long list of environmental organizations, ranging from the Environmental Defense Fund to the Sierra Club to Ducks Unlimited. We might think that the main competitors to environmental groups would be organizations representing industrial manufactures and land developers that pollute the environment and threaten wetlands. Although these oppose policies favored by environmentalists, they do not threaten the survival of environmental groups. Indeed, threats to the environment energize and mobilize environmentalists. The real threat to any particular environmental group's survival is other environmental groups competing for the same members and contributions. These organizations avoid conflict by appealing to different kinds of environmentalists and different parts of the policy niche.

New techniques and technologies have led to more efficient partitioning and expanded the carrying capacity for the number of interest groups. For example, changes in communications technology and the growing importance of money in mounting competitive political campaigns have provided opportunities for entrepreneurs to identify and reach particular constituencies, to make their interests known, and to make them a potent political force through fundraising activities. Emily's List, the nationwide network of political donors that backs pro-choice female Democratic candidates, is a good example of how such niche organizations have grown. In 1986, 1,155 members raised $350,000; in 1996, its almost 45,000 members contributed $6.5 million; in 2002, membership had grown to almost 73,000 members, and contributions totaled nearly $9.7 million.

Changes in techniques and opportunities for building organizations may have also redefined what it means to be a member of an interest group. In the past, associations were more likely to be national in scale, to be centered on social cleavages like race or gender, and to involve face-to-face activity with other members of the group. In the last thirty or forty years, special interest groups have become centralized, and membership involvement is more distant. Groups tend to locate their headquarters in the national or state capitals, and the primary role of membership is to send funds to a group of professionals whose full-time job is advocacy of a relatively narrow agenda.

And while the number of interest groups has grown, the average number of members per group has generally declined. With few exceptions (AARP being a notable example), groups with national membership bases tend to be much smaller in scale and have a different type of structure and orientation than earlier organizations designed as civic and political associations. At its 1993 peak, for example, the National Organization for Women (NOW) had 280,000 members in 800 local chapters, with no administrative or organizational levels between the local and national groups. By contrast, in 1955 an earlier women's advocacy group, the General Federation of Women's Clubs (GFWC), had 826,000 members in 15,168 local clubs that were divided into organizational networks with hierarchies in each state (Skocpol 1999). The GFWC had a very different orientation than NOW. Unlike the GFWC, NOW is oriented toward advocacy of a tightly defined political agenda and is much less involved in channeling the activism of educated wives and mothers into community-based good deeds. A broad set of social and technological changes—including economic, social, and political opportunities for women—seems to have hurt old-style organizations like the GFWC, while groups like NOW have been created and have prospered.

The Recent Growth of Interest Groups

In recent decades, the role of interest groups has expanded considerably. The 1960s through the 1980s saw an explosion of interest group activity in the nation's capital. According to reliable estimates, 70 percent of all interest groups operating in Washington, DC, in the mid-1980s had opened their offices after 1960 (Schlozman and Tierney 1983). Growth of some categories of interest groups has been particularly spectacular. For example, as shown in Table 6.1, there were 117 public affairs associations listed in the Encyclopedia of Associations in 1959. By 1995 the number had increased to 2,178.

Table 6.1

Uneven Patterns of Growth among Interest Groups of Various Types

TYPE OF ASSOCIATION	NUMBER OF ASSOCIATIONS LISTED		RATIO OF GROWTH
	1959	1995	
Public affairs	117	2,178	18.62
Hobby and avocational	98	1,579	16.11
Social welfare	241	1,938	8.04
Athletic and sports	123	850	6.91
Veterans, hereditary, and patriotic	109	740	6.78
Educational[a]	563	1,312	5.77
Cultural	-	1,938	-
Health and medical	433	2,426	5.60
Legal, governmental, public administration, and military	164	781	4.76
Engineering, technological, and natural and social science	294	1,383	4.70
Fraternal, foreign interest, nationality, and ethnic	122	555	4.59
Religious	295	1,243	4.21
Environmental and agricultural	331	1,136	3.43
Trade, business, and commercial	2,309	3,973	1.72
Chambers of commerce, trade, and tourism[b]	100	168	1.68
Labor unions, associations, and federations	226	246	1.09
Greek and non-Greek letter societies	318	338	1.06
Fan clubs[c]	-	514	-
Total	5,843	23,298	3.99

[a]The educational and cultural categories were combined before 1972. Their combined growth rate is presented in the last column.
[b]Before 1970, thousands of local chambers of commerce were also listed in the national *Encyclopedia.* Since 1970, they have been listed separately. The 1959 figure is an estimate for the number of national groups in that year.
[c]Fan clubs was not a category before 1987. No growth rate is calculated.

Sources: Baumgartner, Frank R., and Beth Leech. 1998. *Basic Interests: The Importance of Groups and Politics in Political Science.* Princeton, NJ: Princeton University Press, 103; *Encyclopedia of Associations,* years indicated. For 1995, the CD-ROM version; for 1959, printed volumes.

Although groups are active across a broad range of issues, some interests are more prominent than others. A study of Washington lobbying groups by Frank Baumgartner and Beth Leech (2001), for example, found that business groups were a dominant force among the Washington lobbying community—over 59 percent of registered lobbyists were from business and trade associations, while unions accounted for less than 2 percent, and nonprofit citizens' groups accounted for less than 10 percent (see Figure 6.2).

Activity and competition across issues also is highly skewed. Only a small number of issues attract the attention of a large number of groups presenting opposing views, while on many issues there is only one group actively lobbying. Differential success in overcoming the collective action problem may account for some of the differences in activity. Another likely explanation for uneven group activity is that groups successfully stake out their own little niche that is partitioned from other groups. Baumgartner and Leech (2001, 1204) found that business, trade associations, and representatives of state and local governments were active on all types of issues, but on issues "where only one or two groups were active, participation was almost exclusively limited to" these interests. Unions, nonprofits, and citizens' groups were likely to be active on highly visible issues in conflict with many other groups including business.

Thus, group influence tends to be greatest on issues that attract little attention and conflict because there is no one to present an opposing point of view. Those big, controversial issues where we see intense conflict from opposing groups are the issues that Americans see—it is these issues that Americans see on TV or read about in the papers. As important as these issues are, they are just a tiny fraction of the issues on which groups seek to influence who gets what. The most common type of group influence occurs on small, noncontroversial issues where only one perspective is presented and outside the view of the media and most citizens.

Growth in numbers has been accompanied by a shift in the nature of interest groups. One matter of concern is the rise of **single-issue groups**—groups that take positions and are active on only one specific issue (such as abortion, guns, homosexuality, the environment). There are often single-issue groups on both sides of an issue (for example, pro-life and pro-choice groups on the abortion issue), but these groups are similar in that they tend to take extreme, uncompromising positions on a single emotional issue. Critics complain that these groups undermine the democratic process by polarizing the issues and making compromise more difficult. Others respond that these groups just provide a different type of representation. Traditional interest groups represent some economic or occupational interest (such as

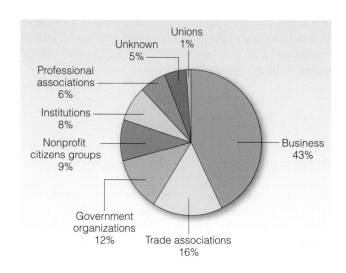

Figure 6.2
Lobbying Group Registrations
Source: Baumgartner and Leech (2001, 1,196); figure format adapted from Lowery and Brasher (2004, 91).

farmers, businesspeople, or lawyers); these so-called single-interest groups represent ideas about a specific issue (such as protecting the environment, promoting peace, or achieving racial equality). These issues are not necessarily narrow, and such groups are not new to American politics (Tesh 1984). Groups advocating abolition of slavery, the prohibition of alcohol, and women's suffrage were politically active early in our nation's history. The intense conflict over abortion in contemporary politics is not nearly as divisive, or as violent, as the slavery issue was in the 1860s.

Another troubling form of interest group activity is the rise of so-called think tanks that blur the line between research and advocacy. Traditionally, think tanks have been institutions dedicated to the scholarly examination of policy issues of national importance. Although some have a partisan perspective, organizations like the Brookings Institution and the American Enterprise Institute have long been recognized as sources of creative and independent thinking on policy matters of national importance, not as advocates of a narrow set of interests.

The new generation of think tanks is much more ideological and partisan, and much more aggressive in trying to influence policy decisions. Some of them are financially dependent on organizations with a vested interest in the outcome of their research and have been accused of providing scholarly cover to blatantly self-interested agendas (Jacobson 1995). These ideological think tanks predominantly espouse libertarian or conservative agendas. Examples are the Citizens for a Sound Economy, which focuses on taxes and regulation, and the Institute for Justice, which has drafted legislative proposals to end affirmative action programs.

Interest Group Resources and Activities

The ability of interest groups to affect decisions about who gets what depends on a number of factors. To determine whether the role of an interest group is positive or negative, it is necessary to understand where the political power of interest groups comes from and how it is exercised. The sources of interest group power can be divided into two broad categories: political resources and tactics.

Political Resources

Political resources are the tools interest groups have at their disposal to influence the political process. They include membership, money, leadership, and expertise.

Membership The most basic political resource of an interest group is its membership. Several aspects of group membership can provide muscle in the political arena. One is sheer size. Groups that can potentially shift large blocks of voters behind a candidate or a policy proposal often have an advantage over those that cannot. A group like AARP, representing millions of senior citizens who are likely to turn out to vote, has a good deal of clout from size alone.

Numbers are not everything. The geographic distribution of the membership is also important. Groups with membership spread out over the entire country are likely to have an advantage over groups with a membership largely confined to a single region. One reason teachers unions are formidable political players is the wide geographic distribution of their membership. Schools are a recognizable and central component of nearly every community in the nation. Collective action by teachers can bring pressure on the government from all points simply because every congressional representative has a large number of teachers as constituents.

In addition to size and geographic distribution, the status of a group's membership is also a valuable political resource. The American Medical Association and the National Academy of Sciences, for example, do not represent huge blocks of voters, but physicians and scientists have high social status and are respected, so their collective voice is treated with deference.

Money   Perhaps the most popularly recognized political resource of interest groups is money. A well-financed group no doubt has an easier time in the political arena than one short of cash. But money is a tool, not a guarantee. It is not just how much money a group has but what the group does with the money. Spending money on an unpopular campaign, for example, can diminish a group's political clout rather than enhance it. Such was the case in April 1995, when the NRA mailed a fundraising letter signed by NRA Executive Vice President Wayne LaPierre describing federal agents as fascist thugs who wore "Nazi bucket helmets and black storm trooper uniforms" and who "harass, intimidate, and even murder law-abiding citizens." Former President George H. W. Bush was outraged and called the letter a "vicious slander on good people." Bush turned in his lifetime NRA membership (Spitzer 1998). The letter designed to bolster support for the NRA's position turned out to be a public relations disaster that may have benefited the NRA's opponents.

In order to spend money, groups first have to raise it, and this can be hard work. Interest groups get their money from a variety of sources, including membership dues, fundraising campaigns, special events, endowments, and return on investments, to mention just a few. All these require a significant investment of interest group resources. Even a stable membership base requires careful tending. For a national organization, staying in contact with members through newsletters, journals, and direct mailings can be expensive. Setting dues that are high enough to defray costs but low enough to retain existing members and attract new ones is a delicate balancing act.

Leadership and Expertise   The most important sources of political clout are a group's leadership and expertise. With dynamic and forceful leadership, clear objectives, and a well-prepared plan on how to achieve them, a small group operating on a shoestring can be as effective as a much larger and well-financed operation lacking such leadership. When these assets are combined with a large membership and operating budget, the group can be a potent political force. Groups like the Sierra Club and the National Organization for Women enroll less than 1 percent of the adult population as members, but they have committed leaders, chapters operating in all 50 states, and an active membership base (Skocpol 1999). Combined, these assets give them influence in the political arena above and beyond that provided by membership or money alone.

Perhaps the most commonly overlooked source of interest group power is the knowledge and expertise of a group. On matters of health policy, for example, the American Medical Association often has clout not only because of its members' status

© Getty Images

NOW (National Organization for Women) has long been a powerful special interest group, involved in many issues. The largest women's rights organization in the United States, it has a membership of over 500,000 men and women. The group's combination of strong leadership, chapters in all 50 states, and active membership make it an influential political force.

but also because it represents the collective voice of medical experts. Interest groups are not shy about using their expertise as a political tool. A primary objective of interest group lobbying is to provide policymakers with information they can use in decision making. For example, the American Bar Association routinely issues ratings of nominees to the federal judiciary.

Political Tactics

It is one thing to have political resources; it is quite another to exercise political influence or power. **Tactics** are the ways groups use their political resources to achieve their goals. In order to influence public policy, a political interest group must have **access** to official decision makers. That is, it must have some means of presenting its point of view to them.

Access is more than just the ability to contact decision makers; it also implies willingness on the part of a decision maker to consider the group's views, whether or not the official ultimately decides to adopt them. To successfully make demands on others in society through government action, a political interest group is largely concerned with deploying its resources to gain access to decision makers. This process is generically referred to as *lobbying.* The term originated from a literal lobby, the entrance hall to the House of Commons, where people who were not part of the government could meet and discuss their concerns with members of Parliament. Today, **lobbying** is more broadly defined and refers to any activity in which a person or group attempts to influence public policymaking on behalf of themselves or other people or groups (Baumgartner and Leech 1998, 33–34). Lobbying takes on a number of forms, uses a number of tactics, and is aimed at a number of targets.

Professional Lobbyists   A common approach is to hire a **lobbyist,** an individual whose job is to contact government officials on behalf of someone else. Some groups—such as trade unions, large trade associations, and corporations with offices in Washington—use their own executives as lobbyists. But many others hire a professional lobbyist to look after their interests in the nation's capital.

Professional lobbyists often work for several clients. Some Washington law firms not only carry on standard legal practices but also represent clients on political matters before legislative and executive officials. And while some firms tend to be associated with a particular political party, some large lobbying firms hire highly visible lobbyists from both parties to increase access for whoever their client might be. Other lobbyist-entrepreneurs specialize in matters that do not require legal expertise and provide services on a fee basis. Often founders and leaders of groups with purposive goals, such as eliminating handguns, serve as lobbyists for their organizations.

Whatever the arrangement, interest groups look for people who possess the information, skills, and access that make them effective in transmitting group views to decision makers. Former members of Congress, for example, are sought after as lobbyists because they understand the complexities of legislation, have contacts among former colleagues and staff, and have the right to go onto the floor of the legislative chambers—a privilege that may give them a special type of access to policymakers. However, more lobbyists come from the executive branch than from the legislative branch. There are more former executive branch employees to draw from, and many crucial decisions are made by administrative agencies. It may be more important for an interest group to have a conduit to an agency that implements a law than to the legislature that passes it.

Direct and Indirect Lobbying   Interest groups and their lobbyists employ a variety of approaches to communicate their viewpoints to decision makers. Some involve direct contacts with public officials—called **direct lobbying.** Others make use of intermediaries to make the contact, which is **indirect lobbying.**

Lobbyists trying to influence Congress have a number of direct lobbying options. As the fate of legislative proposals largely depends on the committees that initially consider them, lobbyists routinely appear before these committees to express their groups' viewpoints on pending legislation. Speaking before a congressional committee allows a lobbyist to have direct contact with more than one legislator and makes the group's views a matter of record in the transcripts of committee hearings that are routinely distributed to interested parties. One-on-one contact with individual representatives is usually considered more effective than appearing before a committee. Members of Congress are frequently absent from committee meetings and may be distracted by other business when they are present. A personal visit ensures attention and is more likely to convey the impression that the lobbyist considers the representative important enough to merit special consultation.

Lobbyists often find it advantageous to work through others who enjoy special relationships with a decision maker they hope to influence. Personal friends or relatives of officials, of course, may provide an entree. One of the most effective ways to reach senators and representatives is through their constituents, especially constituents who can affect their political careers. If a lobbyist can convince, say, a major campaign contributor or a newspaper editor in a legislator's home state to present the group's point in a favorable light, the message is likely to be well-received.

Another way to effectively use the indirect approach is to draw on a group's membership. Members of Congress take note of letters, phone calls, and email about issues, and enough contacts—especially from a member's own constituents—can gain a legislator's attention. A flood of mail and calls can alert a decision maker to the importance of an issue. Such tactics, however, are sometimes ineffective because legislators can usually detect a contrived campaign that is pretending to be a grass-roots effort (that is, a spontaneous outpouring of sentiment from voters). Letters that contain the same wording, that were sent on the same day, and that disproportion-ately come from a few zip codes indicate that constituents' expressions of concern are not spontaneous. Some political consulting firms specialize in such campaigns, which are called AstroTurf® to distinguish them from true grassroots campaigns.

A more subtle form of indirect lobbying is to inform voters about a legislator's positions and votes, rather than informing the legislator about voter preferences. Interest groups frequently provide rank-and-file members with "report cards" on leg-islators. The report lists the percentage of the time a legislator opposed or supported the group's preferences. Table 6.2 shows how several different groups rated some prominent members of Congress.

Other possibilities for effective indirect lobbying include having group mem-bers talk to their representatives when they are back home campaigning or visiting, having members who are visiting Washington call on their legislators, and holding a conference in the nation's capital to let lawmakers know firsthand how concerned individuals and groups are about an issue. A less frequently used method is to stage a dramatic demonstration in Washington. Civil rights and antiwar groups used this tactic in the 1960s, members of the American Agricultural Movement in the 1970s, and groups involved on both sides of the abortion debate from the 1980s to the 2000s.

Coalition Building   One way to effectively extend a group's influence in the political arena is to join forces with other groups. This process of **coalition building** is a form of indirect lobbying that signals to politicians that an issue is of concern to more than just an isolated segment of the public.

One basis for forming a coalition is common and overlapping interests. Even groups that oppose each other occasionally find common interests. The major auto-mobile manufacturers, for example, banded together with the United Auto Workers to delay the imposition of emission standards. Despite their differing positions on labor–management issues, all feared that they would be economically harmed by having to meet the timetable favored by environmental groups.

A second type of coalition comes through a process called **logrolling.** This is an exchange of support in which one group essentially tells another, "You support me on my issue, and I'll support you on yours." Logrolling may result in a coalition of uncommon interests—that is, a coalition of groups whose interests do not necessarily overlap but are not directly in opposition. For example, the Chamber of Commerce of the United States typically sides with the American Farm Bureau Federation on agricultural policy issues, while the latter takes the chamber's side on business issues.

Shaping Public Opinion   Perhaps the most appealing coalition is the public itself. If an interest group can make enough people sympathetic to its desires and persuade them to convey their sentiments to those in public office, it achieves a major strategic objective: Other people are lobbying on its behalf. Efforts to shape public attitudes have become an increasingly important tactic.

Table 6.2

Interest Group Ratings of Some Members of Congress

	ADA	ACLU	AFS	LCV	NTU	COC	ACU	CHC
Republicans								
Representative Dennis Hastert (IL), Speaker of the House*	0	6	0	23	51	100	100	100
Representative Tom DeLay (TX), House Majority Leader	0	7	0	0	59	95	92	100
Representative Ileana Ros-Lehtinen (FL)	10	14	0	25	56	75	88	58
Representative Sue Kelly (NY)	20	33	0	63	53	85	88	67
Senator Bill Frist (TN) Majority Leader	10	20	0	0	67	100	100	100
Senator Mitch McConnell (KY) Majority Whip	0	20	13	6	64	95	100	100
Senator Kay Bailey Hutchison (TX)	5	25	13	6	68	95	97	100
Senator John McCain (AZ)	20	0	29	41	64	79	78	60
Senator Olympia Snowe (ME)	30	60	50	82	41	85	65	40
Democrats								
Representative Nancy Pelosi (CA), House Minority Leader	100	87	100	100	21	37	0	0
Representative Steny Hoyer (MD), Minority Whip	95	87	100	88	18	42	4	0
Representative Jesse L. Jackson, Jr. (IL)	90	93	100	100	24	25	0	0
Representative Charles Gonzalez (TX)	100	86	100	75	17	45	0	0
Representative Collin Peterson (MN)	45	57	56	25	26	70	48	58
Senator Harry Reid (NV), Minority Leader	85	40	100	94	11	45	10	0
Senator Richard Durbin (IL), Minority Whip	95	60	100	88	9	50	0	0
Senator Ted Kennedy (MA)	100	60	100	82	13	29	0	0
Senator Hillary Clinton (NY)	95	60	100	88	17	45	10	0
Senator Robert Byrd (WV)	75	20	88	47	15	40	15	60
Independents								
Representative Bernie Sanders (VT)	95	60	86	76	18	16	6	40
Senator Jim Jeffords (VT)	95	93	100	88	22	53	0	8

*The speaker of the House does not vote. Hastert's ratings are from before he became speaker in 1998. Entries are the percentage of the time that the member voted in agreement with the group's position in 2001 or 2002:

ADA Americans for Democratic Action (liberal)
ACLU American Civil Liberties Union (pro-individual liberties)
AFS American Federation of State, County, and Municipal Employees (liberal labor)
LCV League of Conservation Voters (environmental)
NTU National Taxpayers Union (pro-taxpayer rights)
COC Chamber of Commerce of the United States (pro-business)
ACU American Conservative Union (conservative)
CHC Christian Coalition (conservative pro-family)

Source: Barone and Ujifusa. *The Almanac of American Politics 2004*. (1571, 1477, 430, 1153, 669, 100, 1515, 727, 186, 756, 539, 1566, 1460, 986, 773, 1098, 1713, 1630, 1627).

A group's membership can be used as one vehicle to shape public opinion. For example, in a fight against healthcare proposals they considered to be "socialized medicine," the American Medical Association got doctors to distribute literature and talk to patients about the issue. This activity capitalized on patients' tendency to respect their own physicians and to view them as experts. Another tactic is to

Well-known public figures can bring considerable attention to interest groups and garner support for them. Here, actress Sharon Stone speaks on behalf of the American Foundation for AIDS Research (amfAR) at a World AIDS Day conference. The group is the nation's leading nonprofit organization dedicated to the support of HIV/AIDS research, AIDS prevention, treatment education, and the advocacy of sound AIDS-related public policy.

use well-regarded experts or trusted figures to persuade the public to support a group's cause. For example, NRA members elected Charlton Heston president in 1998. Heston had a long record of Second Amendment activism prior to this election. But Heston is most famous as an actor, especially for his portrayal of Moses in the 1956 movie *The Ten Commandments.* Heston's name recognition and the moral authority identified with the characters he played in movies gives the NRA a powerful public champion.

Ultimately, though, probably the most powerful way to shape public opinion and attitude is through the mass media. Appeals can and sometimes do camouflage the partisan self-interest that is their source. For example, letters to the editor may be statements drafted by lobbyists for individual signatures. A similar practice is the provision of "canned" editorials, prepared statements on public issues distributed freely to the press. A harried newspaper editor may welcome such materials; not only may they reflect the editor's own views, but they also come free of charge.

Television is another natural outlet for interest groups that seek to shape public attitudes. Public service announcements touting a company's commitment to the environment, for example, may serve as an effective counter to the corporate image being portrayed by environmentalist groups.

Campaign Support   The most basic support an interest group can provide any public official is help winning office. If the candidate seeks an appointive office, the group's representatives can use their political influence to see to it that those responsible for making the appointment are aware of the nominee's qualifications and the high esteem in which the nominee is held by the organization. Many interest groups become involved in appointments to major executive posts and seats on the federal bench.

Interest groups can also provide important political support for a person running for an elective office. This support can take many forms: financial contributions; providing information for political speeches and audiences to hear the speeches; favorable coverage in the organization's newsletter; helping get voters registered and to the polls. The earlier a group provides political support and the more extensive that support, the more likely the public official is to grant the access that is all-important to the organization (Austin-Smith 1995; Grier et al. 1994).

There are also dangers when a group irrevocably commits itself to single party's candidates. The group is unlikely to have much influence if the candidate it supports loses. To minimize this risk, it is not uncommon for groups to contribute money to more than one candidate and to both major political parties. The presumption is that regardless of the outcome, the group will have lent enough support to gain the access it desires.

Lobbying in Court   Interest groups also use the judicial process to further their interests. Groups pursue a judicial strategy because court decisions are binding public policies about who gets what. For example, when the Supreme Court ruled that states cannot ban abortion early in a pregnancy (*Roe v. Wade* 1973), it was setting an important national policy. This type of lobbying is governed by different rules and expectations than efforts to influence members of the legislative or executive branches. Lobbyists cannot go to a judge's office and try to persuade the judge to give them a favorable ruling in an important case.

Nonetheless, interest groups can influence judicial policymaking in two legal and legitimate ways: filing test cases and filing *amicus curiae* **briefs.** A **test case** is a lawsuit filed to test the constitutionality of some government policy. The lawsuit must be filed by someone who has actually been injured by the policy, and the court's ruling technically applies only to the parties involved in the suit. But because judicial rulings serve as precedents to guide rulings in future cases, some cases represent major policy victories for certain interests. Perhaps the most famous test case is *Brown v. Board of Education* (1954). The Reverend Oliver Brown filed suit on behalf of his 7-year-old daughter Linda, challenging the constitutionality of the policy of the Topeka, Kansas, school board requiring her to attend an all-black school. The *Brown* case was one of several similar suits posing the same question: Do racially segregated schools violate the equal protection clause of the Fourteenth Amendment? Where did citizens of modest means get the huge sums of money required to take this case through the judicial system all the way to the Supreme Court? How did it come about that they would file such similar suits all at the same time? An interest group—the National Association for the Advancement of Colored People (NAACP)—provided the resources and the strategy to challenge the segregation policy in the courts. Although the NAACP was not a party in this case (the parties were the plaintiff, Mr. Brown, and the defendant, the Board of Education), the interest group made this suit a test case as part of a political strategy. Since the *Brown* decision, other interest groups have pursued a judicial strategy to promote or protect their interests.

Interest groups can also try to influence judicial decisions by filing an ***amicus curiae* brief,** which is a legal brief filed by someone or some organization with an interest in a case but not an actual party. In a lawsuit, the plaintiff and the defendant each file legal briefs making arguments about how the case should be decided. Sometimes other organizations would like to present arguments even though they are not a party in the suit. This procedure is a way for interest groups to present arguments and information *amicus curiae* (Latin for "friend of the court"). The Supreme Court sometimes quotes from these briefs in their written opinions, indicating the arguments in *amicus curiae* brief were persuasive.

The Power and Regulation of Interest Groups

Understanding what interest groups are, who joins them, and what they do is important. But the central concern most citizens have about interest groups is the extent of their influence on political decision making. Are they too powerful? Do they make a positive or negative contribution to the democratic process? To answer these questions, keep in mind that interest groups, as Madison recognized, are a natural by-product of a free and open democratic process. Interest group activity, in essence, is the core value of political freedom being put into practice: In a free and democratic society, people with shared interests must have the freedom and opportunity to band together in order to advance their common preferences. A system of divided powers, such as that of the United States, with multiple venues to seek a response from the government is especially conducive to group action. At least in theory, this group activity contributes to greater democratic responsiveness. Government has a hard time responding to input such as an individual vote in a presidential or congressional election. It is much easier to get a response with collective input like an endorsement from the 35 million-member AARP. So, interest group activities make a positive contribution to the performance of democracy by helping make good on the promise to act on the will of the people.

Some political scientists argue that interest groups act as a more general stimulant to political involvement and activity by giving individuals an opportunity to develop the skills necessary for political participation. This contribution has been called *unintentional mobilization* because it is an unintended by-product of group involvement (Leighley 1996). Also, organized group action on one side of an issue often spawns another interest group taking the opposite position, so interest groups can be seen as promoting pluralism. Interest groups can thus be viewed as making important contributions to a healthy democratic system.

But interest groups are exactly what Madison had in mind in his discussion of factions in *Federalist* Number 10. All the dangers Madison associated with factions potentially apply to politically active interest groups. Many may seek to advance their agendas by suppressing the preferences of others. As a result, interest groups may contribute to low levels of satisfaction with the performance of democracy. It is important to realize that not all interest groups are equal. Some have more resources and more influence. Some interest groups exercise power in very specific policy niches where they do not have to compete with other interests to influence who gets what.

Interest Group Power and Influence

Have interest groups become too powerful? Do a handful of groups exercise undue influence? Is the result a political process that is elitist rather than pluralist? Researchers have found evidence to support both affirmative and negative answers to such questions.

On the one hand, it is clear that well-organized, well-financed groups have enough political muscle to hinder adoption of visible, controversial policies they oppose. And the groups may themselves be dominated by a small number of elites who are less concerned with compromise than are other members. Although most interest groups look democratic in the sense that rank-and-file members have some say over policy decisions and the election of officers, in practice an active minority usually runs the organization. Attendance at an annual convention by rank-and-file members who have limited knowledge of the group's operations does not place a meaningful check on the actions of the group's leadership. There is no group of officeholders to counter the ruling clique, so rarely is there any organized opposition to the current leadership. Unlike the broader political arena, the internal operation of interest groups is not governed by a system of checks and balances.

Of particular concern is the organized collection and disbursement of huge amounts of money into the political arena. Businesses and labor unions are prohibited from making campaign contributions directly to candidates. But these and other interests can form **political action committees (PACs)** to raise funds and make political contributions on a group's behalf. Over the last several decades, the number of PACs and the amount of money they pump into the electoral process has exploded. Currently thousands of PACs spend hundreds of millions of dollars every national election cycle (see Figures 6.3 and 6.4).

On the other hand, the way that the power and influence of interest groups works in reality generally does not fit common public perceptions. More than fifty years ago, Will Rogers quipped, "America has the best politicians money can buy" (quoted in Sterling 1979, 63). Many Americans share this sentiment today. Lobbyists are typically

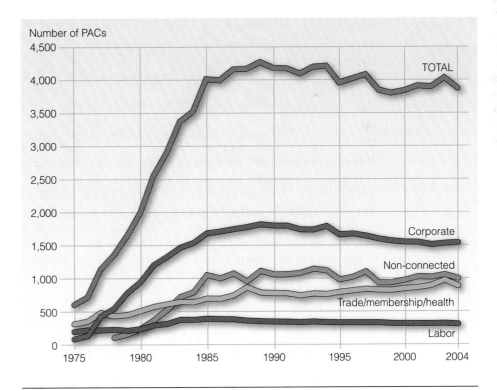

Figure 6.3
Number of PACs, 1975–2004

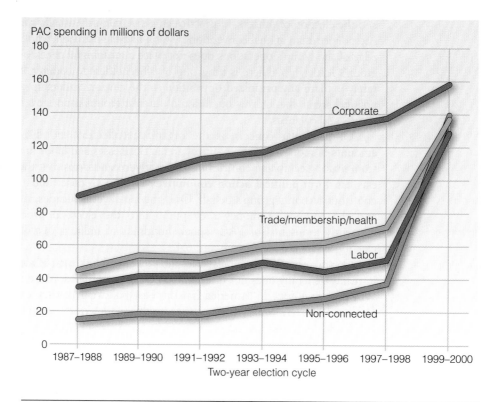

Figure 6.4
PAC Spending, 1987–2000

pictured as stealthy figures carrying little black satchels stuffed with money with which to bribe government officials for favors. Although there certainly are instances of public officials taking bribes, such corrupt dealings are the exception rather than the rule. If relationships between interest groups and public officials have changed over time, they are probably less corrupt now than was the case in the past.

Political scientists who have studied this issue have generally found a remarkably weak connection between financial contributions and decision making. Numerous studies looking for a correlation between campaign contributions and roll-call votes have found little evidence that votes in Congress are purchased (Baumgartner and Leech 1998, 14–15).

Even if there is no direct connection between money and votes, the primary goal of interest groups is to gain access, and some studies find evidence that contributions do help groups get a foot in the door (Austin-Smith 1995; Grier, Munger, and Roberts 1994; Wright 1990). But other research shows that groups associated with PACs do not have an advantage over constituents in gaining access to elected representatives. A study of who gets appointments with members of the House of Representatives found that "members give priority to constituent requests over PACs" (Chin, Bond, and Geva 2000, 545).

The NAACP (National Association for the Advancement of Colored People) has served as a communication vehicle between minority groups and government officials for more than ninety-five years. Because of its long history, the group seeks to protect the advances it has already achieved while still working to eliminate the current adverse effects of racial prejudice and discrimination. Here members prepare for a march to honor the late Rev. Dr. Martin Luther King, Jr., on the forty-year anniversary of his "I Have a Dream" speech in Washington, DC.

Researchers studying the details of how bills are crafted in committee have found evidence that interest group activity does influence public policymaking. This influence, however, turns out to be much less clear-cut than the quid pro quo, or money-for-favors, process often imagined by the general public (Smith 1995). Contributions, direct lobbying, and the various other tactics employed by interest groups can indeed influence what sort of bill comes out of a committee (Hall 1996). But an interest group's chance of getting what it wants depends much more on opposing interest group activity than on the money given to a campaign and the number of direct contacts with an official. A clash of interests and their associated lobbying efforts puts a significant constraint on group influence.

Indeed, a clash of interests can elevate the role of public officials as independent decision makers. Groups opposed to gun control, for example, were able to block or defeat legislation in Congress for many years in part because there was no organized group supporting the legislation. Passage of the Brady Law, requiring a 5-day waiting period to purchase a handgun, came about at least to some extent because lobbying by Handgun Control, Inc. countered efforts by the NRA (Spitzer 1995, chap. 4). Political scientist Diana Evans (1996) concludes that "Far from viewing members of Congress as their pawns, a stereotype evidently cherished by much of the public, lobbyists saw committee leaders as powerful decision-makers, especially in cases of conflict." But most issues are not like gun control or abortion, attracting a lot of attention and controversy from opposing interests. Rather, most issues draw the focus of a tiny number of groups that may not disagree; on these issues, well-heeled groups use their access to quietly push through specific policy provisions favorable to their interest (Baumgartner and Leech 2001).

Furthermore, interest group success is affected by whether the group is trying to get some new benefit from government or trying to protect benefits it already has. Because governmental power is fragmented and the policymaking requires not one, but many, decisions, groups defending the status quo have an advantage over groups pushing for new benefits. A proposal to provide new benefits must survive multiple decision points in Congress, a possible presidential veto, a likely legal challenge, and numerous decisions in the bureaucracy that will implement the policy. In contrast, groups that would be harmed by the change can defeat, or at least delay, the new policy if they prevail with just one of the many decision points in the process.

A discussion of power in a democratic society also needs to recognize that the relationship between interest groups and public officials is a two-way process: Private groups not only make demands on officials, they also serve as potential bases of support for the officials. In other words, interest groups and their lobbyists act as an effective communications vehicle between the broader electorate and government officials. They provide a way for citizens with similar interests to make sure that the government is aware of and responds to their preferences. Interest groups often perform important services for those who are in office, including furnishing factual information, proposed drafts of legislation, and written speeches that can be delivered to constituents.

Regulation of Interest Group Activity

Despite concerns about their political influence, special interests are lightly regulated. Lobbying is regarded as a legitimate method of influencing public policy and is considered part of the rights of free speech, assembly, and petition protected by the First and Fourteenth Amendments. Congress has placed two types of restrictions on lobbying: (1) limits on the kinds of activities in which interest groups may engage and (2) requirements that lobbyists and organizations disclose their identity and certain basic facts about their operations.

Federal law prohibits bribery; it is unlawful to offer a member of Congress "anything of value" for the purpose of buying a vote or otherwise trying to influence his or her official actions. Legislators who sell their votes are subject to criminal charges. Although the law prohibiting such activity is fairly clear, in practice it is hard to enforce. It is difficult to prove that a favor was tendered for the purposes forbidden by law. For example, it does not constitute bribery for a lobbyist to promise future political support in an attempt to influence how a member of Congress votes. Informing a politician that group members will be happy if the politician votes a particular way is an act of free speech protected by the First Amendment. There are few things more valuable to officeholders than votes.

Lobbyists for certain groups—among them those representing foreign governments, shipping firms, and public utility holding companies—were singled out by Congress in the 1930s and made to disclose information about themselves and their clients. In 1946, Congress passed legislation requiring similar information from lobbyists and interest groups in general. Enacted as part of a broad statute dealing with the reorganization of Congress, the Federal Regulation of Lobbying Act (FRLA) requires any person or group hired by someone else for the "principal purpose" of influencing congressional legislation to register with both the secretary of the Senate and the clerk of the House and to file quarterly reports with the latter on receipts and expenditures for lobbying.

Critics argue, however, that this approach contains so many loopholes that it is largely ineffective. Groups avoided FRLA requirements, for example, by claiming that they spend their own funds for lobbying and do not solicit funds from outside sources, or that the outside funds they do collect are not raised for the "principal purpose" of influencing Congress. The 1977 Foreign Agent Registration Act

(FARA) prohibits foreign nationals from making political contributions, but it does not prohibit resident aliens or the domestic operations of foreign companies from doing so.

In the 1970s, Congress passed legislation requiring lobbyists and interest groups with business before the national legislature to make their financial arrangements a matter of public record. That is, the primary approach is to illuminate lobbying activities rather than prohibit them. The Federal Election Campaign Act (FECA) in 1971 allowed unions and corporations to form political action committees to raise and contribute campaign funds to candidates. In 1974, Congress amended FECA to create the Federal Election Commission (FEC) to collect and report information on campaign contributions. These amendments limited individual contributions to $1,000 and PAC contributions to $5,000 in each election.[1] The law also tried to place limits on how much a candidate could spend, but the Supreme Court held that mandatory limits on candidate spending violated the First Amendment (*Buckley v. Valeo* 1976). In 1979, campaign finance laws were changed to permit unlimited contributions to political parties for "party-building" activities.

Thus, individual and PAC contributions to candidates were limited; these direct contributions to candidates are known as **hard money.** But candidates—millionaires, for example—could spend as much of their own money as they wanted, and all candidates were free to raise unlimited amounts of hard money as long as it was from individuals and groups that had not already given the maximum. Groups could spend as much money as they wanted for advertising on political issues as long as the ads were not coordinated with a particular candidate. And contributions to political parties for party building were unlimited; these contributions are called **soft money.**

These efforts to reduce the amount of money spent on campaigns were largely ineffective. Soft money contributions soared in the 1980s and 1990s, and the total amount of hard money contributions also went up as candidates used new techniques like direct mail solicitations to raise huge amounts of money from many small contributions. The most effective feature of FECA was the disclosure requirements: Contributions had to be reported to the FEC, and campaign spending by interest groups and political parties also had to be reported.

Concern over the potentially corrupting influence of all this money in the political arena led to the most recent attempt at reform—the Bipartisan Campaign Reform Act (BCRA) of 2002, better known as the McCain-Feingold Law for its main Senate sponsors John McCain (R-AZ) and Russell Feingold (D-WI). This law raises limits on hard money contributions during each election cycle to $2,000 from individuals and $5,000 from PACS. The main target of the reform is soft money, which the BCRA bans outright. It also restricts "issue ads" run immediately before an election. *Issue ads* are political commercials run by interest groups that support or oppose some issue (such as abortion, gun rights, or protecting the environment). Numerous interest groups on both the left and the right strongly opposed this provision.

A strange coalition of interests (including the National Rifle Association, the National Right to Life Committee, the American Civil Liberties Union, the AFL-CIO, the Republican National Committee, and the California Democratic Party) challenged the law in court, arguing that it unconstitutionally infringed on basic First Amendment

---

[1]These are contributions to candidates for Congress. Regulations for presidential campaigns are treated differently, which we discuss in Chapter 10.

rights of free speech and association. The Supreme Court rejected these claims and upheld the law's major provisions (*McConnell v. Federal Election Commission* 2003). Although passage of this law was a major victory for supporters of campaign finance reform, interest groups and political parties are already finding loopholes. In the first elections conducted under the new restrictions, enormous sums of money were raised and spent.

Despite the lack of effective legal regulation of lobbying, there are certain informal codes of behavior that most lobbyists follow. Aside from matters of individual conscience, lobbyists desire to protect their reputations with their colleagues and, more importantly, with public officials. Lobbyists who provide false or misleading information to public officials quickly lose the very thing they have worked so hard to achieve: access to those officials. A lobbyist who steps over the informally agreed-on line between legitimate advocacy and false or misleading polemics is quickly cut off from important people who make vital decisions affecting the lobbyist's group. Denial of access is a powerful deterrent to lobbyists who may be tempted to engage in improper activities to try to influence public decisions.

 Performance Assessment

Interest group activity provides evidence of the core value of political action. It also makes a valuable contribution to the American political system. By channeling citizens' demands to those in positions of public authority, interest groups help link the will of the people to the actions of government. Lobbying efforts help alert public officials that at least some sections of the electorate consider particular issues important, and they also help educate officials by providing factual information and arguments relating to the issues. Although each interest group naturally presents its own side, legislative and executive officials are able to examine a wide range of views from competing interest groups and coalitions. This political competition allows them to balance the pros and cons of different sides in making decisions.

The major weakness in the way interest groups work in the United States is that not all interests participate equally. Well-educated upper- and middle-class people are more inclined to join organizations than the less educated and the poor. This upper-class tilt raises questions of unbalanced representation in the political system.

Even setting aside such concerns, business and professional organizations have more financial resources to spend on lobbying than do other interest groups, and they benefit from the prestige and deference accorded their members by officeholders and the general public. The result is that upper- and middle-class Americans are more likely to have their demands satisfied than those with fewer advantages. And although opposing groups challenge the power of these groups on some highly visible controversial issues, these are only a small part of the full range of issues on the agenda. Most issues attract the attention of only one or two groups lobbying on some specific benefit relevant for their niche.

The have-nots in American society are better organized today than they were in the past. For example, a number of groups represent the poor and ethnic minorities. This development has reduced, but not eliminated, the gap between the advantaged and the disadvantaged.

The most significant resource that disadvantaged interests have to draw on is the sheer size of their potential membership. Translating those numbers into cohesive action, however, is tough. Much of the difficulty is a result of the free rider problem. There might be vastly more poor people than rich people, but rich people are more likely to be aware of their common interests and to see the benefits of collective action. Hence, they are more likely to join and actively participate in interest group activity, and government is more likely to respond to those who participate.

There is mounting criticism about how interest groups affect the political process. The number of single-issue interest groups that focus exclusively and intensely on one narrow issue has increased significantly in the past few decades. These groups often form around some of the most controversial issues, such as abortion and gun control, and frame their activities in moral rather than political terms. Critics worry that the net effect of this activity is to shift politics from a search for common ground to a battle between "good" and "evil" in which compromise is unlikely to be sought or accepted. Absolutism does not fit well with the promise of democracy to focus on process rather than outcome.

Other critics have argued that interest groups have put a stranglehold on government by fighting for programs that, once secured, are defended at all costs. In an article in the *National Journal,* contributing editor Jonathan Rauch (1994) coined the term *demosclerosis* to describe the result: Government cannot engage in effective decision making because it is too committed to doling out the favors and entitlements that thousands of interest groups have secured for their members. In other words, interest groups have been charged with a negative effect on the performance of the democratic system as well as its promise.

Yet interest group activity is also evidence of the core value of political freedom being put into action. Given the explosion of interest groups and interest group activity over the last few decades, organized interests are probably promoting the inclusion of more preferences from more people rather than excluding the main preferences of most people. The result may not be pretty, but in and of itself, it is not breaking the promise of democracy.

Summary

- Government responds to people who participate in the political process. Motivated and well-organized groups can be more effectively involved than individuals or less well-organized groups.
- An interest group is a politically oriented organization of people who share common attitudes on some matter and make demands on society with respect to that matter.
- Political interest groups pursue two basic objectives: (1) They seek new benefits to promote the group's interest; (2) they defend current benefits from outside threats to protect the group's interest.
- Most citizens belong to voluntary organizations, many of which can be classified as interest groups. These include groups such as the AARP, the NRA, labor unions, and professional organizations like the ABA and the AMA.
- People join interest groups for (1) material benefits, which are tangible benefits such as discounts on goods or services; (2) solidary benefits, which are intangible

benefits such as the pleasure of socializing with like-minded people; and (3) purposive benefits, which are benefits that transcend the individual and the group and are aimed at others.

- A central problem interest groups face is free riders. People can often receive the benefits of group activity without joining the group or contributing to its operation. Groups seek to avoid free riders through laws that require group membership, selective benefits provided only to group members, and social pressure.

- The rational perspective that underlies the major explanations for joining interest groups may overstate the role of tangible benefits in providing incentives to join and in reducing the incentive to free ride. Group membership often seems to be a product of social context, not just an individual rational decision.

- Interest groups form in reaction to social or economic events, because of the activities of organization entrepreneurs, and in response to the carrying capacity of the political environment.

- The large increase in the number of interest groups in recent years may be a result of the partitioning of a policy niche into groups representing narrower and narrower interests. The partitioning of policy niches increases the carrying capacity of a political environment so that it can support more interest groups competing for the resources they need to survive (such as members and financial contributions).

- The ability of interest groups to achieve their objectives depends on political resources (membership size, geographical distribution, status, financial capacity, leadership, and expertise) and the success of political tactics (directly lobbying public officials; indirectly lobbying through third parties; mobilization of membership and voter education campaigns; coalition building; shaping public opinion; and involvement in electoral campaigns).

- Many citizens are concerned about the power of interest groups, and there is a widespread perception that well-organized and well-funded interest groups have undue influence over lawmakers. Most academic research finds little evidence of a quid pro quo, or money-for-votes, relationship between interest groups and policymakers. What powerful interest groups gain is access to policymakers and the opportunity to argue their case.

- Only a tiny fraction of issues attract the attention of many competing interests on different sides. Most issues are largely invisible to the public and attract the attention of only a few groups that may have similar interests. Interest groups are more successful on these issues than on the highly controversial ones.

- It is difficult to regulate interest group activity, and the regulations that do exist are hard to enforce. Constitutional guarantees of freedom of speech, freedom of assembly, and the right to petition government for redress of grievances virtually invite organized interest group activity and provide strong protections for it.

- Rather than preventing or constraining certain actions or behaviors, laws regulating interest groups generally seek to make interest group activity a matter of public record through rules such as financial disclosure requirements.

- Informal codes of behavior, rather than formal regulation, tend to restrain flagrantly unethical behavior such as offering bribes to public officials or providing false or misleading information. Such behavior is as likely to result in reducing access to public officials as in guaranteeing it, and denial of access is a powerful deterrent to improper lobbying activities.

Key Terms

access 172
amicus curiae brief 177
coalition building 174
direct lobbying 173
exchange theory 166
free rider 164
group entrepreneur 166
hard money 183
indirect lobbying 173
interest group 159
lobbying 172
lobbyist 172
logrolling 174
material benefits 163
niches 166

partitioning 166
pluralist explanation of interest
  groups 166
political action committees (PACs) 179
political resources 170
public good 163
purposive benefits 163
rational 163
selective benefits 164
single-issue groups 169
soft money 183
solidary benefits 163
tactics 172
test case 177

Selected Readings

Baumgartner, Frank, and Beth Leech. 1998. *Basic Interest: The Importance of Groups in Politics and in Political Science.* Princeton, NJ: Princeton University Press. A comprehensive introduction to virtually all the major themes of interest group scholarship.

Cigler, Allan, and Burdett Loomis, eds. 2002. *Interest Group Politics.* 6th ed. Washington, DC: CQ Press. An edited volume of essays presenting the latest scholarship on interest groups.

Gray, Virginia, and David Lowery. 1996. *The Population Ecology of Interest Representation.* Ann Arbor: University of Michigan Press. Lays out the basic population ecology theory of interest group representation.

Olson, Mancur. 1965. *The Logic of Collective Action.* Cambridge, MA: Harvard University Press. The classic treatise on interest group formation and activity from the rational choice perspective. One of the most influential scholarly works on interest groups.

7 Political Parties

In September 1796, six months before the end of his second term as president, George Washington announced that he would not be a candidate in the upcoming election. In what became known as his Farewell Address, he set forth his hopes and fears for the young republic and expressed his concern that the nation would be destroyed by the "baneful effects of the spirit of party." He acknowledged that parties might help preserve liberty "in Governments of a Monarchical cast," but "in those of the popular character, in Governments purely elective, it is a spirit not to be encouraged." He feared that "the spirit of party" in the new American republic would agitate "the community with ill-founded jealousies and false alarms," spread animosity between groups, and foment "occasionally riot and insurrection."

Washington's plea for the political system to turn away from parties went unheeded. As early as the Second Congress (1791–1793), officeholders had splintered into two factions. The Federalists coalesced around the political ideas and agenda of Alexander Hamilton, and the Democratic-Republicans around the ideas and agenda of Thomas Jefferson and James Madison. Midway into Washington's second term, both factions were sufficiently organized "to coordinate presidential elections, extend their concern over issues, and capture the affiliation of essentially all national politicians" (Aldrich 1995, 82).

Between the end of Washington's second term and the start of Jefferson's first, the Federalists and the Democratic-Republicans transformed themselves from loosely identifiable factions into the progenitors of modern political parties.

Historically, public sentiment about political parties in the United States has largely reflected Washington's initial suspicion and distrust. Scholars and professional political observers, however, argue that in organizing the first recognizable parties, Hamilton, Jefferson, and Madison contributed to the long-term health of the democratic process. Political scientists in particular have largely accepted that parties are a central, and probably necessary, democratic institution. Morris Fiorina (1980) argues that the only way collective responsibility can exist in a democratic political system such as the United States is through political parties. E. E. Schattschneider, one of the best-known political party scholars, put the matter more bluntly: "democracy is unthinkable save in terms of parties" (1942, 1).

A full understanding of the U.S. political system must account for the roles and functions of political parties. What are political parties? What do they do, how do they do it, and why? Ultimately, do they help match the performance with the promise of democracy? These are the questions this chapter seeks to answer.

The Promise of Political Parties

The basic promise of political parties is to help transmit the wishes of the people to government and to help ordinary citizens determine how well the actions of government respond to their wishes. By aiding this connection, political parties contribute to achieving the core democratic values of popular sovereignty and majority rule. But what, exactly, are political parties?

The Challenge of Defining American Political Parties

An immediate problem in studying political parties, especially in the context of American politics, is deciding what exactly is being studied. Students of government have experienced much difficulty defining a political party. Particularly confusing is identifying the features of a political party that distinguish it from related concepts, such as interest groups and factions, that also help connect citizens to government.

Political Parties, Interest Groups, and Factions

The definition problem is not new; the writings of some of the Founders illustrate the dilemma. In *Federalist* Number 10, Madison used three different terms to describe divisions in society. One is *faction,* a concept explored in Chapter 2. Another is *interest,* which Madison calls the most durable source of factions, using as illustrations a manufacturing interest, a mercantile interest, and the like. Madison also refers to the conflict of *parties.* Washington's Farewell Address is similarly vague; his condemnation of the "spirit of party" seems to reflect a general unhappiness with the divisiveness and bickering among citizens rather than a criticism of a particular kind of political organization.

A basic way to distinguish parties from other political groupings is to define a **political party** as an organization that nominates and runs candidates for public office under its own label. As discussed in Chapter 6, running candidates for office under a party label is the most important difference that distinguishes parties from interest groups. Other differences are that parties tend to focus on a broader range of issues than interest groups do, and political parties are quasi-public institutions that cannot restrict eligible voters from participating in party activities based on race (or other such criteria as gender or income).

Parties also differ from factions. Historically, factions preceded political parties; they were groups of people who joined together on an ad hoc basis to win some political advantage. In the days of a restricted electorate and relatively few elective offices, factions formed around candidates, and they were able to control elections fairly effectively. As the right to vote expanded to include a greater diversity of social groups, more inclusive and permanent organizations became necessary. Particularly important was the task of making clear to voters which candidate represented which group. The crucial step that turned factions into political parties was running candidates for office under a common label.

Today, the term *faction* refers to a group that is part of a larger political entity. The term commonly identifies a segment within a political party based on a personality, philosophy, or geographical region. Thus, people speak of the religious right faction of the Republican Party or the southern faction of the Democratic Party. In this sense, *faction* is synonymous with *wing* or *division.*

Membership in American Political Parties

Another difficulty in studying parties is the problem of identifying the membership. In contrast to interest groups and political parties in other countries, most Americans do not formally join a political party and pay dues. The French Socialist party and the American Farm Bureau Federation can quantify with fairly rigorous accuracy their membership; the Republican and Democratic parties cannot.

A useful attempt to overcome these difficulties was formulated by political scientist V. O. Key (1964). Key identified three major divisions of political parties associated with different activities and different people:

- Party in the electorate
- Party in government
- Party organization

The **party in the electorate** consists of ordinary citizens who identify with the party and who usually support the party's candidates with votes and campaign contributions. Although these partisan supporters are most active at election time, they tend to hold similar views on many political issues in periods between elections.

The **party in government** is the elected and appointed officeholders at the national, state, and local levels who are considered representatives of the party. Because partisans in different branches and levels of government share a party label and have similar views on many issues, they often use their official powers to pursue common policies.

The **party organization** is made up of party professionals who hold official positions in the party and the other people who are active in running and maintaining the party's organizational apparatus. These individuals carry out the major campaign activities of the party, contributing their time, money, skills, and effort. Party organizations exist at the national, state, and local levels.

Viewing parties from this perspective is useful because it specifies the relationship between individuals and the party they support. It also highlights the broad and diffuse nature of political parties in the United States. Basically, American political parties are not centralized organizations with formalized memberships and rigid hierarchies, but rather fairly loose coalitions operating at all levels of the political system.

Functions of Political Parties

Defining what parties are and knowing who is in them is the first step to understanding, but what, exactly, do they do? Recall that political parties are organizations that run candidates for office under a common label. As they run candidates for office, parties engage in a number of specific activities—they recruit and nominate candidates, develop party positions on issues, disseminate party "propaganda," provide campaign support to their candidates, sponsor get-out-the-vote drives to encourage potential supporters to vote, and other activities. Note that parties engage in these activities for mostly selfish reasons. But as parties pursue their own political self-interest, they perform several broader functions that contribute to the democratic process. Political scientists have identified four major functions political parties perform in democratic governments:

- Facilitate participation of large numbers of people
- Promote government responsiveness
- Promote government accountability
- Promote stability and the peaceful resolution of conflict

Political parties facilitate participation by ordinary people like Ilana Wexler, 12, who was invited to speak at the Democratic National Convention on behalf of the organization she founded: Kids for Kerry. After hearing her parents' comments about a speech by Teresa Heinz Kerry, Ilana decided that she too could campaign to elect the man she wanted to see as president. She has successfully enrolled kids from all over the country to support her efforts and has an interactive website where kids can voice their opinions.

© Paul J. Richards/AFP/Getty Images

Facilitate Participation

Democratic government relies on the participation of ordinary people. Political parties help make it possible for large numbers of people to participate, and they help make that participation more effective and meaningful. Party activities facilitate participation in several ways.

Aggregating Interests First, political parties facilitate participation because they aggregate interests and act as intermediaries between citizens and government. Parties seek to put together broad coalitions of different interests for purely selfish reasons—they want people to vote for their candidates. But as parties put these electoral coalitions together, they also aggregate individual preferences into coherent policy agendas that can serve as a plan of action for government (Bibby 1996).

This aggregation of interests provides a more-or-less organized way to resolve differences about what we ought to do. Like interest groups, political parties channel the views and demands of individuals and groups to public officials. But unlike interest groups that transmit relatively narrow positions, parties aggregate multiple and often conflicting demands into broader, more coherent messages by combining shared and overlapping interests and accommodating differences through compromise. Aggregating diverse interests into a party coalition helps ordinary people participate in a meaningful way.

Simplifying Alternatives   Second, parties facilitate participation by simplifying alternatives for voters. Parties run candidates for public office under their label. To have a realistic chance to win national and most state elections, a candidate must run under one of the major party labels—either Democrat or Republican.[1] Although party leaders sometimes actively recruit candidates, most candidates for national offices (the presidency and Congress) are self-starters who decide on their own to become candidates. To win a major party nomination, a candidate must survive an often grueling nomination process (discussed in more depth in Chapter 10) that chooses a single party standard-bearer from among several candidates vying for the party's nomination. These nominating contests winnow out weaker candidates so that on election day voters choose between at most two viable candidates—one Democrat and one Republican—for the various offices.

Although some citizens complain about the limited choice, for many it serves a useful purpose: It reduces the amount of information necessary to decide which candidate is most likely to serve their interest. It is much easier to keep up with the issues and positions of two candidates than it would be for many. Suppose that in the 2004 election for president, rather than choosing either Republican George W. Bush or Democrat John F. Kerry, voters could choose from a long list of candidates. Some voters no doubt would welcome the opportunity to sort out the different qualifications and issue positions of dozens of candidates and find the one closest to their interest. Most Americans, however, are not inclined to invest the time and effort required to dig up information for a lengthy roster of candidates. Without relevant information about the candidates, many citizens would be confused and deterred from voting.[2] Moreover, because most voters identify with one of the two major parties, there is some very useful information printed right on the ballot—namely, each candidate's party affiliation. Simplifying the alternatives reduces information costs and helps many voters—over 100 million in the 2000 presidential election—to participate in the electoral process in a meaningful way.

Stimulating Interest in Politics and Government   Third, the parties' campaign activities facilitate participation by stimulating interest in politics. Parties contest elections and mobilize voters. They fund candidates, engage in media campaigns promoting partisan agendas, and help get their supporters registered and to the polls. That is, political parties have a fundamental interest in promoting political participation among their supporters. Although these activities are self-serving, as parties engage in these campaigns, they raise awareness and interest in politics among mostly disinterested citizens.

---

[1]Independent and minor party candidates do compete in elections, and they occasionally win seats in Congress, though this is rare. Socialist Bernie Sanders, for example, won Vermont's single House seat running as an independent in 1992. With rare exceptions, only major party nominees have a realistic chance of winning a seat in Congress.

[2]Many local elections are nonpartisan in that no label appears on the ballot. Judges in some states and state legislators in Nebraska are also elected this way. The intent of removing party labels is to remove politics from the election process, though removing party labels changes politics rather than eliminates it. Specifically, interest groups and the media become more influential in recruiting and electing candidates. And turnout in these nonpartisan elections tends to be low, at least in part because voters have a more difficult time distinguishing among the candidates.

Promote Government Responsiveness

Another major function that parties perform is to promote government responsiveness. Government must be responsive to the demands of ordinary citizens to achieving the core democratic value of popular sovereignty. Parties help achieve this goal as they organize government and seek to pass a policy agenda (Bibby 1996).

Parties serve as the basis for organizing and operating the national government. Representatives in Congress split into majority party and minority party members. Members of the majority party hold the major leadership positions in Congress (for example, the speaker of the House), and they chair and have a majority of the seats of all standing committees. This organizational control gives the majority party leverage to advance its agenda and suppress the minority party's agenda. The president is also an important policymaker who pursues a partisan agenda. Success in enacting this agenda is greatly influenced by whether the president's party controls Congress (what political scientists refer to as unified government), or it is controlled by the opposition party (divided government).

Voter choices determine which party wins control of the institutions of government. Because voters base their choices at least in part on party agendas, officeholders are responding to preferences of ordinary citizens when they seek to advance a party agenda. Although government responsiveness may be somewhat clearer under unified government, even divided government may be a reflection of voters' preferences. Morris Fiorina (1996, 72–81) suggests that at least some voters prefer divided government to check and moderate the extremes of each party's agenda.

Promote Government Accountability

Popular sovereignty requires not only responsiveness, but also the means to hold government officials accountable if they are not responsive. Parties act as agents of accountability (Bibby 1996). Particularly important here is the role of the minority party in keeping an eye on the majority. There is, of course, a large degree of self-interest in performing this watchdog function. Uncovering and publicizing questionable actions or broken campaign promises of the party in power may produce electoral benefits for the out party in future elections. But this self-interested scrutiny also serves a broader civic function in that the minority party helps to check any abuse of power by the majority, and it aids citizens in holding unresponsive policymakers accountable.

Promote Stability and Peaceful Resolution of Conflict

Finally, some scholars suggest that political parties promote stability and the peaceful resolution of conflict. The process of reconciling and accommodating a broad spectrum of views assists in settling social conflict and developing significant areas of agreement among citizens of various backgrounds and perspectives. The creation of such a consensus contributes to a basic feature of a democratic society: the pursuit and maintenance of political power by peaceful means and, when the populace so desires, the peaceful transfer of that power into other hands. For example, after a bitter campaign in the 2004 election, Senator John Kerry expressed disappointment but accepted his loss with grace: "I wish that things had turned out a little differently. But in an American election, there are no losers, because whether or not our candidates are successful, the next morning we all wake up as Americans. That is the greatest privilege . . . that can come to us on Earth. With that gift also comes obligation. We are required now to work together for the good of our country. . . . We must join in common effort, without remorse or recrimination, without anger or rancor."

The Responsible Party Model

The extent to which political parties perform these functions varies across different political systems. Political scientists use the phrase **responsible party model** to describe democracies with strong, competitive parties in which one party wins control of the government based on its policy proposals, enacts those proposals once it is in control, and stands or falls in the next election based on its performance in delivering on its promises. The party out of power (sometimes referred to as the loyal opposition) notes every policy failure and every action at odds with popular sentiment; it then uses these failures to formulate new policy agendas and to provide points of contrast and debate in the next electoral cycle. The disciplined political parties of Great Britain are a close approximation of the responsible party model. The parliamentary system unifies control of the executive and legislative branches of government under the prime minister, who is the majority party leader. When the prime minister presents legislation to Parliament, members of the governing party are expected to support it, and members of the loyal opposition are expected to oppose it. A party member who does not vote along party lines is subject to sanctions that might include losing his or her seat.

In theory, this competition over policy encourages government responsive to the will of the people. Moreover, competition between disciplined parties helps citizens assign responsibility for government performance. Offering clear policy choices and making it easy to assign credit or blame provides voters with the means to hold an unresponsive government accountable. If parties behave according to the theory, they play a critical role in delivering democratic performance that fits with the democratic promise.

Critics, however, have long suspected that the responsible party model is an idealized depiction of the role political parties play and one that rarely occurs, particularly in the United States. American political parties are weak and undisciplined. They have no centralized controlling body and few options for enforcing **party discipline**—that is, the means to require party members in public office to promote or carry through on a partisan agenda and to punish those who do not toe the party line. American political parties sometimes offer similar policy agendas, and officeholders often choose their constituencies or their consciences over their party's policy preferences. Moreover, the American electoral system frequently results in **divided government**—when one party wins the presidency and another party wins a majority of seats in one or both houses of Congress. Divided government makes it hard for voters to assign responsibility and to hold public officials accountable. If a Democratic president signs a law passed by a Republican Congress, who gets the credit or blame? Although there have been periods in American history when parties were stronger, the U.S. party system generally falls far short of the party discipline required by the responsible party model. Nonetheless, party strength in America has varied considerably over time.

The Strength of Political Parties

The potential of political parties to fulfill these broader functions in a democratic society depends on their viability as institutions. A number of political scientists have argued that parties have been declining since the 1950s. If party decline is in fact the case, it raises important questions about the performance and stability of the political system. Specifically, what or who will take over the vitally important functions traditionally performed by parties? The party decline thesis rests on several pieces of evidence:

- The electorate's attachment to political parties is not as strong as it once was.
- The central role of parties in the electoral process has been eclipsed by the rise of candidate-centered campaigns in which a candidate's electoral chances rest heavily on his or her personal organization rather than on the party's.
- Party-line voting in Congress occurs less frequently than it once did.
- Party organizations no longer have the power to determine who runs under their party's label.

Other scholars argue that political parties are not likely to fade from a central role in American politics. Parties may be changing, but they still contribute to the democratic process. These researchers present evidence that the trend toward partisan decline reached a low point in the 1970s but then reversed in the mid-1980s. The party in the electorate and party in government show signs of increasing strength that have persisted into the 21st century. Party organizations may no longer unilaterally pick candidates to run under their label, but they have become an important supplier of the resources necessary to run a successful campaign: money, logistical support, and connections to a broad and supportive political network.

In short, the issue of party decline seems to rest heavily on which of the three divisions of political parties we examine—party in the electorate, party in government, or party organization—and at what time.

The Strength of Party in the Electorate

The argument that parties are in decline begins with the observation that the electorate is becoming less partisan. Scholars who favor this point of view focus on three indicators:

1. A decline in the percentage of the electorate referring to themselves as strong partisans
2. An increase in the percentage of the electorate calling themselves independents
3. A decline in straight-ticket voting (voting for the same party's candidates for president and Congress)

Several explanations may account for the decline of the party in the electorate. Perhaps the most intuitive explanation is that, as political scientist Martin Wattenberg (1990) argues, political parties are simply less relevant to voters than they once were. Rather than being loyal to a political party, voters are increasingly influenced by issues and candidate image. A candidate's character, views, and appearance increasingly influence voting, while the importance of the party label has declined (also see Aldrich 1995, 17). (Chapter 11 discusses the effect of party on voting behavior in more detail.)

A closer look at the evidence indicates that the trend toward weaker partisanship in the electorate characterized the period from the 1950s to the 1970s, but the trend reversed in the 1980s and continued to rise through the 1990s. Political scientists typically measure party identification in the electorate on a scale that identifies strong Democrats, weak Democrats, independents, weak Republicans, and strong Republicans. Figure 7.1 shows the percentage of strong partisans (that is, strong Democrats plus strong Republicans) since 1952. In the 1950s, about 36 percent of the electorate were strong partisans. The percentage fell to 32 percent in the 1960s and to 25 percent in the 1970s. But in the 1980s and 1990s, strong partisans increased to about 30 percent. Thus, "the slide toward weaker partisanship . . . seems to have stalled" (Fleisher and Bond 2000b).

Another indication that the electorate is becoming less partisan focuses on the rise in the number of independents. Figure 7.2 plots trends in the percentage of Democrats, Independents, and Republicans in the electorate. To understand this evidence, we need to consider the definition of *partisans* and *independents*. Studies of partisanship in the electorate consistently show that about two-thirds of individuals who initially say they are "independent" admit that they think of themselves "as

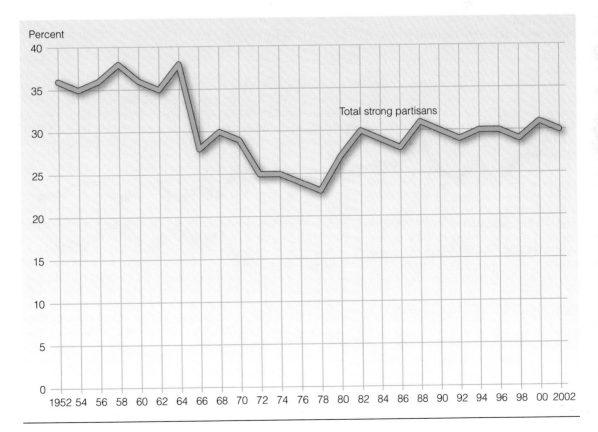

Figure 7.1
Strong Partisans in the Electorate, 1952–2002
Source: National Election Studies, 1995–2002, www.umich.edu/~nes/nesguide

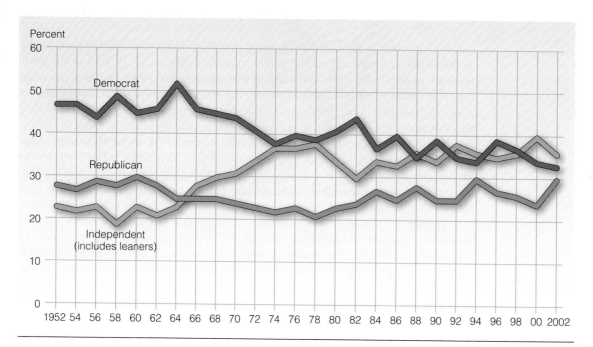

Figure 7.2A
Party Identification in the Electorate (Independent Includes Leaners), 1952–2002

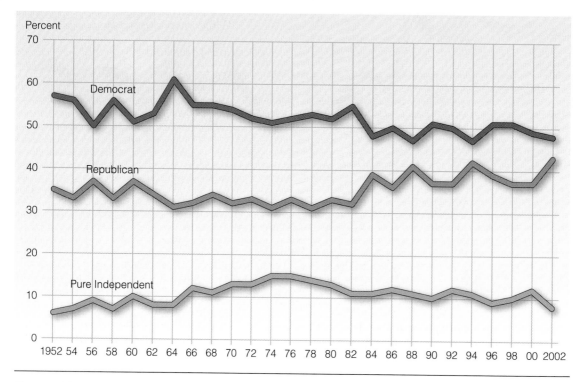

Figure 7.2B
Party Identification in the Electorate (Independent Excludes Leaners), 1952–2002

closer to the Republican or Democratic party" (see Stanley and Neimi 2003, 116). This group is referred to as independent leaners because they lean toward preferring one party or the other. Should we count leaners as independents or as partisans? The choice makes a big difference in whether we find a growing number of independents.

Figure 7.2A shows the trends if independents include all those who say they are independents (that is, independent leaners count as independents), and partisans are those who express a party preference (strong plus weak partisans in each party). Using this definition, there appears to be a gradual long-term decline in the percentage of Democrats and Republicans and a concurrent increase in the percentage of independents. Indeed, there appear to have been more independents than Republicans since 1966 and more independents than Democrats since 2000.

But it is important not to overstate the decline of party and the rise of independents in the electorate. Independents who lean toward the Democrats or the Republicans exhibit partisan voting patterns. In presidential elections, for example, independents who lean toward one party or the other vote for the candidate of the party they favor at about the same (and sometimes higher) rate as weak partisans. This behavior supports the argument that these voters are not true independents, regardless of their initial self-identification as such. Figure 7.2B shows the trends if independents include only those who do not favor one party or the other (pure independents), and partisans include independent leaners along with strong and weak partisans. About 90 percent of the electorate identify themselves as either Democrats or Republicans, and the percentage of pure independents increased only slightly. About 7 percent of the electorate identified as independent in the 1950s and 1960s; the number of independents doubled to about 14 percent in the 1970s but then declined to about 10 percent in the 1980s and 1990s.

Another indicator of partisanship in the electorate is the percentage of **straight-ticket voters**—that is, voting for the same party's candidates for president and Congress. Figure 7.3 shows that the percentage of straight-ticket voters decreased considerably from the 1950s through the 1970s but then climbed in the 1980s and 1990s.

Although issues and candidate image have increasingly influenced voting decisions over time, the effects of party identification remain strong. Party identification was a stronger influence on the vote in the 1984 presidential election than in any election since the 1950s, and the relationship remained strong in the next four presidential elections—1988, 1992, 1996, and 2000 (Abramson, Aldrich, and Rohde 2003, 178). When Larry Bartels analyzed the effect of partisanship on voting in both presidential and congressional elections from the 1950s to the 1990s, he concluded that the "conventional wisdom regarding the 'decline of parties' is both exaggerated and outdated" (2000, 35).

Partisan identification, therefore, remains a significant predictor of vote choice and even seems to help shape how voters perceive candidates and issues. As Morris Fiorina observed, arguments about "issue voting" versus "party voting" miss the point: "the 'issues' are in party identification" (1981, 200). Democrats and Republicans tend to express different issue positions, and the level of polarization between partisans (even weak and independent partisans) increased in the 1990s (Fleisher and Bond 2000b). Thus, the trend toward declining partisanship from

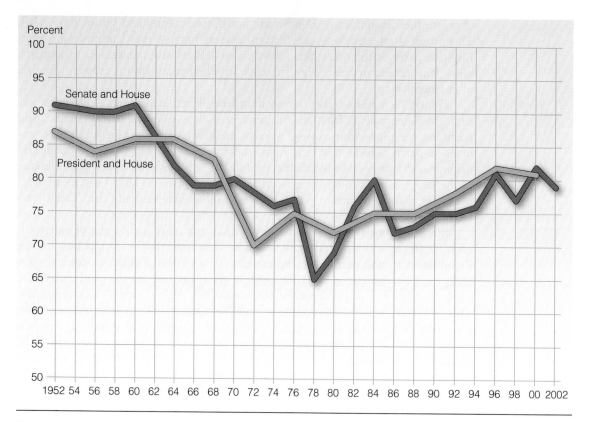

Figure 7.3
Straight-Ticket Voting, 1952–2002

the 1950s to the 1970s turned around, and the electorate became somewhat more partisan in the 1980s and 1990s.

The Strength of Party in Government

A number of observers have also found evidence of decline of party in government. Two common pieces of evidence to support this perspective are the rise of divided government and a decline in party-line voting in Congress.

The strength of party in government depends in large part on the strength of partisanship in the electorate. According to political scientists David Brady, Joseph Cooper, and Patricia Hurley (1979), a partisan electorate is a key requirement for partisan voting in Congress. When voters elect representatives on the basis of partisanship, members of Congress are more likely to be tied to a common party-centered electoral fate. Thus, as the party in the electorate declines, it also erodes the party in government. As the electorate attaches its loyalties to individual candidates rather than to parties, officeholders have more freedom to resist the party line when it conflicts with constituent preferences. Recall that divided government occurs when one party wins the presidency and another party wins a majority of seats in one or both

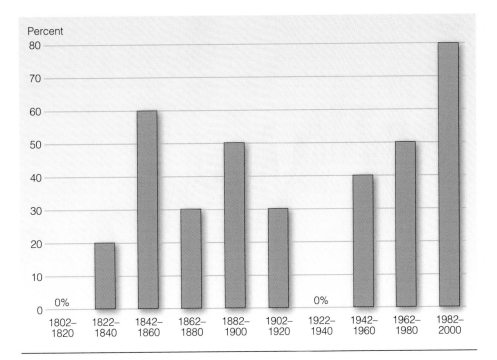

Figure 7.4
Elections Producing Divided Government

houses of Congress. Figure 7.4 shows the frequency of divided government in the 19th and 20th centuries. Although divided government has been common in earlier periods of American history, the last two decades of the 20th century stand out. Eight of the ten elections from 1982 to 2000 resulted in divided party control of the presidency and Congress.

Some scholars see divided government as a symptom of weak parties because it hinders the exercise of coordinated government action (Jacobson 2001). In order to approach the responsible party model, parties must exercise enough control to get government to at least attempt to follow through on partisan policy agendas. If the major parties split control of the legislature and executive, they may be able to conduct the business of government, but they can hardly claim the sole partisan responsibility for it. Voters have difficulty assigning credit or blame when party control of national governing institutions is split.

Although divided government certainly detracts from the system of government envisioned by the responsible party model, it does not necessarily indicate that parties are weak. Instead, divided government could be viewed as sign of two competitive parties with different strengths—one party strong enough to win the presidency and the other party strong enough to win control of Congress.

The argument that party in government has declined is bolstered by evidence that party unity within the legislative branch has eroded. Partisanship in the U.S. Congress has never reached the levels common in most parliamentary democracies, although there

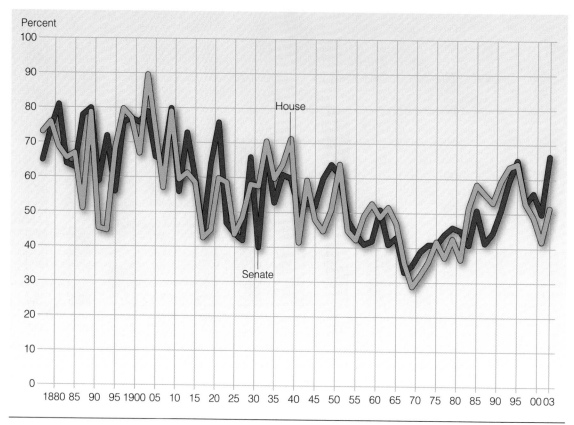

Figure 7.5
Party-Line Votes in Congress, 1877–2003

have been periods when Congress was characterized by high levels of party voting. A **party-line vote** is commonly defined as one on which a majority of Democrats vote on one side of an issue and a majority of Republicans on the other. As Figure 7.5 shows, party-line votes were common from the 1870s to the early 1900s, occurring 80 to 90 percent of the time in some years. The frequency of party votes declined somewhat during the 1920s, rebounded briefly during the New Deal years of the 1930s, and then began a long-term slide, reaching a low point in the late 1960s. In recent decades, however, party in government has become stronger. The proportion of party-line votes in both the House and Senate increased gradually through the 1970s and then accelerated dramatically in the late 1980s (Fleisher and Bond 2000a). The trend toward increased partisanship in Congress continued through the 1990s and into the early years of the 21st century.

The rise of partisanship in Congress resulted in part from electoral changes. The most dramatic change occurred in the South. Implementation of the 1965 Voting Rights Act brought large numbers of African Americans into the electorate, and white southern Democrats in Congress became more responsive to the interests of their African American constituents. As a result, southern Democrats in the House and Senate became more liberal and began voting more like their northern colleagues

(Fleisher 1993; Rohde 1991). At the same time, the most conservative white southern voters began to leave the Democratic Party, contributing to the election of an increasing number of conservative southern Republicans to Congress. Most of the remaining southern Democrats are almost as liberal as northern Democrats. According to David Rohde (1991), when northern and southern Democrats in Congress became more similar ideologically, the Democratic caucus adopted reforms that strengthened the Democratic leadership's ability to promote party discipline.

Another factor contributing to elevated partisanship in the 1980s and 1990s was the election of Ronald Reagan and the Republican takeover of the Senate in the 1980 elections. Republicans interpreted their electoral victory as a mandate to enact a conservative agenda. When House Democrats began to use the rules to prevent votes on the Republican agenda, Republicans turned to conservative activists like Newt Gingrich. Under Gingrich's leadership, the Republican Party campaigned on the "Contract with America," a coherent policy agenda, in the 1994 elections. Republicans won control of both houses of Congress for the first time in forty years.

In the House of Representatives, the new Republican leadership made use of disciplined voting patterns to push through many provisions of the Contract. Republican electoral success was aided by redistricting after the 1990 census. States were encouraged to draw districts so as to increase the number of African Americans elected to Congress. These efforts removed large blocs of reliably Democratic voters from the constituencies of white southern Democratic incumbents. A side effect of drawing districts to elect more African American representatives was the defeat of several moderate white Democrats by conservative Republicans in 1992 and 1994 (Hill 1995). The resulting large turnover of members created large freshman classes that were more likely to vote the party line than were the members they replaced (Hurley and Kerr 1997).

Thus, electoral changes, rules, and leadership of Congress all have contributed to more partisan voting behavior. Although party discipline in the United States has never attained the levels typical of parliamentary systems, parties remain the primary mechanism for organizing Congress, and party unity remains relatively high even in the face of divided government.

The Strength of Party Organizations

The thesis that parties have declined in strength also rests on some important historical evidence about the decline of party organizations. There is no doubt that modern party organizations have considerably less power than the political machines that once controlled politics in numerous cities and some states. A **political machine** is a party organization, headed by a "party boss"; political machines and party bosses maintained their power and control over government offices with such techniques as control over nominations, patronage, graft and bribery, vote buying, and rigging elections (Plano 2002, 111). Roughly a hundred years ago, reformers disgusted by powerful and corrupt party machines began pursuing reforms specifically designed to weaken party organizations. One such reform was nonpartisan elections. Numerous cities and one state (Nebraska) adopted nonpartisan elections. The absence of party labels on the ballot made it more difficult for party bosses to mobilize voters in support of their candidates.

Another successful reform was reducing **political patronage,** that is, government jobs and contracts that elected officeholders handed out to those who supported the party. Reformers advocated using a merit system—hiring government workers based on their skills and qualifications to do the job rather than party loyalty. In place of awarding government contracts to party supporters (who often inflated the cost of doing the job and gave kickbacks to the party machine), reformers proposed a system of competitive bids to award contracts for government work to the lowest bidder who was qualified to do the job. Losing control of patronage diminished the role of parties in many voters' political, social, and economic lives. No longer could parties use government jobs and contracts to recruit supporters and maintain their loyalty.

By far the most important of the reforms was the direct primary. The **direct primary**—an election in which rank-and-file voters choose the party's nominees for various offices—transferred the key power of determining who has the right to use the party label in an election from party bosses to voters. Before the direct primary, elected officials would heed the party line or face the threat that party leaders would withhold the party label from them in the next election. Without the party machine's endorsement, candidates had little prospect of getting elected.

Rank-and-file voters are less likely than party leaders to choose candidates on the basis of party loyalty. For example, in recent years, both major parties have been embarrassed by fringe candidates who won party nominations in direct primaries. David Duke, an activist with ties to the Ku Klux Klan, ran as the Republican nominee for governor of Louisiana. And a supporter of political extremist Lyndon LaRouche won the Democratic nomination for lieutenant governor in Illinois. The Republican Party condemned Duke, and the Democratic Party did the same to the LaRouche backer, but neither party could stop the candidate from claiming the party label in the general election. Although these are extreme examples, they illustrate that the direct primary made officeholders much more independent of their parties.

There is, however, evidence that although they differ from the old political machines, modern party organizations are alive and well. A group of political scientists undertook an extensive analysis of party organizations at local, state, and national levels in the 1960s, 1970s, and 1980s (Cotter et al. 1989; Gibson et al. 1985, 1989; Huckshorn et al. 1986). In contrast to those who forecast imminent party demise, these researchers saw active organizations busily reinventing themselves as central players in American politics. They found that party organizations at all levels had become more professional. Parties were key sources of funding and logistical support for candidates running under their labels and linked party members in differing levels of government and different offices. The research also indicated that parties still remain capable of coherent policy platforms. Furthermore, party organization influences party in the electorate. John Coleman (1996, 821) finds that "strong, competitive party organizations contribute to generalized support for parties" among ordinary citizens.

These scholars do not deny that the reforms adopted around the turn of the 20th century affected party organization. They argue, however, that the reforms did not permanently diminish the relevance of parties but rather obliged them to deal with a new political environment. Parties responded to these changes not by collapsing, but by adapting. For example, the new electoral environment may make candidates more independent in one sense, but they still need campaign funds, a clear message, a way to get the message to the voters, tracking polls, and the host of administrative and logistical services required to run a successful modern campaign. Parties provide all of this and more. By strategically deploying these resources, parties make themselves central players in electoral politics. Indeed, Cotter and his associates (1989, 168) conclude that parties operate in "a framework of public regulation and support which protects more than weakens the existing parties."

Cycles of Party Strength

Thus, we see that party strength rises and falls in cycles over time. At some points, parties have played prominent roles in structuring citizens' vote choice and in making public policy; at other times, their influence has waned. Parties seem to assume heightened importance during critical elections and periods of electoral realignment.

A **critical election** is the first election that clearly reflects a new partisan alignment and produces a new partisan majority. An **electoral realignment** is a new and stable (or long-term) pattern of partisan loyalties in the electorate and government. During periods of electoral realignment, party loyalties in the electorate are in a state of flux. New issues emerge that have not been integrated into the philosophies of the existing parties, which puts pressure on existing parties to adapt and encourages the formation of new parties.

The last major realignment in American history occurred during the Great Depression. Many voters thought that the Republicans were not doing enough to address problems caused by the Depression. A coalition formed consisting of traditional Democratic groups such as southerners, the working class, and Catholic voters plus members of historically Republican groups such as African Americans and organized labor. In the critical election of 1932, Democrat Franklin Roosevelt won the White House, and the Democrats won an overwhelming majority of congressional seats. The change in the partisan makeup of government led to the large-scale changes in policy, known as Roosevelt's New Deal.

America may also have experienced a partisan realignment in the 1990s. A number of studies offer evidence that elections in the 1990s reflected the culmination of a long-term process of ideological shift, with conservative Democrats moving steadily into the Republican fold. By the mid-1990s, the parties had become more polarized along ideological lines, making it easier for citizens to match their ideology with a party and signaling a new era of party strength. In 1994, this change produced the first Republican Congress in four decades and a decidedly conservative shift in government policy (Abramowitz and Saunders 1998). Republicans managed to maintain control of Congress for the next decade. In the 2004 elections, Republicans added to their slim majorities in both the House and Senate.

In sum, rather than steadily declining over time, political parties have adapted to changes in the political landscape and have retained a central, albeit altered, place in the political system. As long as political parties continue to attract adherents, they remain viable institutions central to the democratic process, and they have the potential to fulfill their broader functions in the political system.

Incentives for Associating with Political Parties

The general incentives for associating with political parties are similar to those previously described for interest groups: material benefits, solidary benefits, and purposive benefits. Political scientist James Q. Wilson (1962) divided the people who participate in party activities into two major categories: (1) **professionals,** whose incentives for participating are primarily material and social in nature, and (2) **amateurs,** whose incentives are primarily purposive and social. These two types of party activists hold different views about compromise, political patronage, and the internal governance of the party. (See the Living the Promise feature "Party Chairs and Political Science Majors" on pages 208–209.)

The material incentives that motivate party professionals to participate in politics include tangible rewards, such as patronage jobs and government contracts. These individuals are also motivated by social incentives. In general, they get satisfaction from the game of politics for its own sake—the quest for victory, the maneuvering for advantage, and the camaraderie of working and socializing with other party members. They like the exercise of political power and the deference paid to them because of the positions they hold and the influence they wield.

The professionals tend to place great emphasis on winning elections. Although they may personally favor a particular program, party professionals evaluate policy primarily in terms of whether it can attract political support. If a policy threatens to cost the party an electoral victory, professionals will work to moderate the party's position or even abandon it altogether. Professionals understand the importance of compromise in politics and are tolerant of people who differ on political matters. As for the internal operation of the political party, professionals expect it to be an oligarchy in which the people in top positions make the decisions.

The prototype of a party organization run by professionals was the old-time political machine. As noted earlier, the party boss used political influence to get supporters and their families and friends public jobs, government contracts, loans, gifts, and help when they ran afoul of the law or public regulations. The political organization also sponsored picnics, beer parties, and other events for supporters, many of whom were immigrants looking for new friends and social outlets. In return, the boss received votes from the recipients of this largess, political contributions from those on the public payroll (usually a set percentage of their salary known as a "lug"), and kickbacks from those with government contracts.

In contrast, political amateurs are less concerned with using political parties to further their own interests; instead, they want to use parties to help other individuals or groups or society in general. They believe in certain principles and are dedicated to implementing those principles in public policies—for example, banning abortion or protecting the environment. The devotion to principle means that amateurs are less concerned with winning elections than they are with doing the right thing. All else being equal, amateurs prefer to be on the winning side, but they would rather support a loser who espouses their principles than a winner who does not. Compared to professionals, amateurs are less willing to compromise their principles and the policies that follow from them. Political scientists have sometimes referred to political amateurs as purists who believe that it is better to remain true to their principles and stay out of office than to compromise them as the price of winning power (Polsby and Wildavsky 2000, 44; Wildavsky 1965).

In actual party organizations, few individuals perfectly fit either category. So-called political professionals, for example, are interested in political programs, and most amateurs will compromise on some things. In addition, the tools and activities of party professionals have changed over the years. Machine politics have waned as a result of reform movements. Modern party leaders continue to focus on winning elections, but they use public polling, computer technology, modern fundraising techniques, and media campaigns to build and maintain party organizations. And just as parties change, so do individuals: Amateurs evolve into professionals.

Nonetheless, the primary political orientation of many people and organizations can be characterized as essentially professional or amateur in nature. Assessments of American political parties often turn on whether they are judged by the standards of a political professional or an amateur.

The History and Development of American Political Parties

The beginning of this chapter indicated that American parties were founded on a paradox: a conviction that parties would be ultimately harmful and the simultaneous organization of embryonic parties by many of the same men who espoused those convictions. Madison and Washington were particularly concerned that internal divisions could imperil national unity at the very time the young republic was dealing with the disruptive forces of regional and economic rivalries. Hamilton, who showed little faith in common people, spurned political organizations that would enable the public at large to influence decisions he believed were best left to those of superior intellect and training.

Ironically, what precipitated the formation of two parties was the economic program that Hamilton, as the first secretary of the treasury in the Washington administration, submitted to Congress in 1790. Hamilton's plan rested on two controversial proposals: (1) that the national government should assume the debts owed by the states and (2) that Congress should create a national bank. Madison, who was serving in Congress, led the fight to oppose the debt proposal, arguing that many of the southern states had paid their debts and should not be taxed to pay off the unmet obligations of the North. Jefferson, who was then Washington's secretary of state, worked out a compromise in which the debts would be assumed by the national government in return for locating the nation's capital in the South (what was to become Washington, DC). Jefferson opposed creation of a national bank. He considered it a dangerous monopoly that would benefit mercantile interests rather than the interests of the yeoman farmers, and his supporters joined Madison's to try to quash the movement for a national bank.

Other issues contributed to the growing split between these former allies. Hamilton's economic program included taxes that clearly favored the industrial sections of the nation. Farmers who purchased manufactured goods bore the brunt of such taxes. Especially vexing to farmers was an excise tax on liquor. Commercial distilleries could pass this tax on to consumers. But many farmers made liquor for their own use, and for them, the tax amounted to a personal levy by the federal government. Farmers in western Pennsylvania were so outraged that they refused to pay the tax. This precipitated the so-called Whiskey Rebellion of 1794, which ended when Washington sent a military force over the Alleghenies to put down the threat to the legitimacy of the new government.

As domestic and economic concerns contributed to a growing split, ideology and foreign policy widened the cleavage. The eruption of the French Revolution in 1789 and the war between the new French regime and Great Britain four years later polarized Americans. Followers of Jefferson viewed the French Revolution as

continued on page 210

LIVING THE PROMISE
Party Chairs and Political Science Majors

Political science majors study politics in college, but they seldom go on to practice politics as party leaders. In 2004, however, two graduates of Catholic University's political science department were chairs of the Republican and Democratic National Committees. This article by Ann Gerhart of the *Washington Post* describes the combative campaign process of the two major parties in animated detail.

With an eight-month campaign, you need an undercard. It can't be all Ali-Frazier all the time. Which is how

we got to last night at Catholic University, with a couple of light heavyweights in the ring. Eddie "The Kid" Gillespie and Terry "The Terror" McAuliffe, no holds barred, in a post-Saint Paddy's Day smack-down of two Irish scrappers.

The chairmen of the Republican National Committee and the Democratic National Committee are both proud alums of this college's political science department, Class of '83 and Class of '79, respectively. University President the Rev. David M. O'Connell, perhaps

aware of a proud tradition of Catholic boxers, persuaded them to debate, with bantamweight George Stephanopoulos refereeing.

Right in the opening round, Democrat McAuliffe couldn't resist a kidney punch. Republican Gillespie said he had returned to campus a year ago and was "surprised to see they had closed the Rat," a longtime student pub. "If the Rat had been closed when we were here, we could have graduated summa cum laude," said Gillespie, and McAuliffe immediately interjected, "I did."

"Oooooo," said the capacity crowd of 750 alums and students in the Pryz, formally known as the Edward J. Pryzbyla University Center.

Gillespie countered with a glancing blow. He had become the

Political party professionals are motivated by material and social incentives. Sometimes these individuals take a very public role, especially during a presidential election. Here Ed Gillespie (left), chairman of the Republican National Committee, and Terry McAuliffe, chairman of the Democratic National Committee, debate the issues at their alma mater, Catholic University, with George Stephanopoulos (center) moderating.

© Getty Images

chairman of the Republican Party, he said, "because I had better professors."

Credibility and leadership dominated the early rounds, with the bout disintegrating in later minutes into a series of punches and counterpunches over which side is uglier in its attacks.

McAuliffe, who was a student government vice president for three years, gave President Bush credit for pulling the nation together immediately after the Sept. 11, 2001, attacks, then hammered him on for dispensing "faulty information" shortly thereafter. Charges of an African nation selling yellowcake uranium "turned out to be fake"; warnings that Iraq could launch chemical or biological weapons within 45 minutes "turned out to be false."

Gillespie, who served for a time as sports editor of the college paper, acknowledged that "we can continue to improve" on making America safer. He then threw some jabs at Democratic contender John Kerry for his "constant reversal of positions," noting that the Massachusetts senator voted for the Iraq war resolution based on the same intelligence that was available to the administration.

Stephanopoulos at that point pried the two apart, and asked them to sign a "joint declaration of unity" to work toward a bipartisan framework in continuing the war on terror. Nice try, ref! This is blood sport!

"I have no doubt that Terry cares deeply about fighting terrorism," Gillespie said. "The difference is how you do it."

"Then you'd be willing to sign it?" asked Stephanopoulos. "I'd like

to see it," said Gillespie. "If it's a statement supporting the policies of John Kerry, I won't."

McAuliffe immediately threw a right hook. "We went in on false pretenses," he said of the decision to overthrow Saddam Hussein. "I would be glad to sign anything to make sure we stop terrorism in America. It goes to credibility."

And so it went, for an hour, word blows flying, McAuliffe dancing and darting, jabbing over Medicare, striking over Social Security, quick on his feet. Gillespie wobbled a little, but he never went down, pounding his point that tax relief stimulates the economy.

Anytime Kerry "says he will raise taxes for the rich," said Gillespie, "anybody in the middle class needs to grab an umbrella, because that [tax increase] is coming your way."

"No wonder you didn't graduate summa cum laude," said McAuliffe. "You would have gotten an F in economics."

"Ooooo," said the audience.

This being an upstanding religious institution, there were no women in hot pants carrying the round cards. Playing to his audience, and a question about appealing to Catholic voters, Gillespie quickly moved for what McAuliffe called the wedge issues. Catholics "tend to oppose the heinous practice known as partial-birth abortion," which Bush signed a law prohibiting, Gillespie said. Kerry, said the RNC head, was one of only 14 senators who voted against limits on gay marriage as spelled out in the Defense of Marriage Act, which Bill Clinton signed into law.

Toward the end of the fight, words like "liars" and "crooks" and

"thugs" and "felon" began flying fiercely. Each contender got a chance to ask the other a question. McAuliffe used his to ask Gillespie to sign a joint letter to the Justice Department demanding an investigation into allegations that a Republican congressman was threatened by a member of his own party in connection with a vote and that a Medicare actuary was threatened with firing if he released higher cost figures for prescription drug legislation.

Gillespie then went to his cut man, who turned out to be the Minnesota Democratic state party chairman. He waved an e-mail from the operative that said the president "and his party of thugs" have made a career "of lying, cheating and misleading the public," according to Gillespie.

"That is not worthy," he said, promising he would repudiate any Republican chairman who took such a tone, and calling on McAuliffe to do the same. He then walked over to McAuliffe's corner and handed over the e-mail, in triumph. The crowd clapped and cheered.

The crowd appeared to have a real thirst for political fisticuffs and an appreciation for the finer points of rhetorical nastiness. For those who don't, even the undercard gets numbing. But it's only March, too early to go down for the count, so expect a rematch soon.

Source: "At Gillespie vs. McAuliffe, a Left for Every Right," by Ann Gerhart, *Washington Post,* March 19, 2004, p. C01. Reprinted by permission of the Washington Post Writers Group.

a logical extension of the American Revolution; Hamiltonians thought that the stability of society was threatened by the excesses of the French mob.

Injected into this increasingly ideological climate was a controversial treaty negotiated with the British in 1794—called the Jay Treaty, after John Jay who negotiated the treaty for the Washington administration. This treaty resolved some lingering controversies from the Revolutionary War, but it failed to satisfy two American grievances: compensation for slaves the British carried off during the hostilities and the impressment of American sailors. The latter practice, in which the British seized ships engaged in trade with the French and forced their crews into British service, was considered particularly onerous by Americans. Washington was forced to use his considerable prestige to win ratification in the Senate.

These political controversies led to the creation of the Federalist and Democratic-Republican parties.[3] Party voting patterns appeared in Congress first, and "by 1800 elections were publicly and undeniably partisan" (Aldrich 1995, 77). In the executive branch, the divisions were apparent in the campaign to succeed Washington, and Federalist candidate John Adams defeated Democratic-Republican Jefferson in 1796.

The driving force behind the political and policy agenda of the Federalists was Hamilton, and Washington was its popular leader. Madison and Jefferson, who resigned from the Washington administration in 1793 over the national bank issue, organized the Democratic-Republican opposition. Partisan battles quickly turned nasty. The Alien and Sedition Laws, passed in 1798, made it a crime to criticize the government or government officials, and the Federalists used these laws to jail or fine about twenty-five Democratic-Republicans who criticized President Adams. Many of those jailed were newspaper editors. These actions helped trigger a backlash, and the Democratic-Republican ticket of Jefferson and Aaron Burr decisively defeated the Federalist team of Adams and Charles Pinckney in the presidential election of 1800. The Democratic-Republicans also won control of both the Senate and the House.

Thus, within two decades of forming, the United States went through crucial stages of political development that led to the establishment of a more-or-less permanent party system. Washington was initially viewed as a patriot king who would rule in the interests of the people. But it quickly became apparent there were major differences of opinion on important issues that could not be settled by a neutral political figure, no matter how fair-minded or popular. Equally apparent was that traditional electoral organizations—factions based on local or state political personalities—did not have sufficient scope to capture control of Congress and the presidency. Permanent, visible, and broad-based organizations were required for such a task. So the world's first democratic parties came into being. When the Federalists grudgingly gave up power after the election of 1800, they established another crucial political first: the peaceful transfer of power from one party to another. Orderly, nonviolent competition has characterized the American party system ever since.

---

[3]The Democratic-Republican label is somewhat confusing. The party has also been referred to as the anti-Federalist Party, the Jeffersonian Republican Party, and the Republican Party. The label used here is traced to a later incarnation of the Democratic Party during the Jackson administration that claimed to resurrect the Republican principles of Jefferson and Madison (Aldrich 1995, 305, fn10).

The parties themselves changed over the years. The Federalists operated for more than a decade after the election of 1800, but the party never again captured the presidency or control of Congress. It slowly disintegrated, disappearing completely around 1816. The demise has variously been ascribed to differences between Hamilton and John Adams, its elitist political philosophy that precluded recruitment of broad-based support, and the pro-British attitude of many Federalists during the War of 1812. There was a brief period of one-party government following the demise of the Federalists, a so-called era of good feeling that culminated in the near-unanimous election of James Monroe to the presidency in 1820. The good feeling was short-lived, and the Democratic-Republican Party divided into competing factions, one organized around John Quincy Adams and the other around Andrew Jackson. These competing wings gradually became independent and evolved into genuine parties in their own right. The followers of Adams became known as the National Republicans and those of Jackson as Democrats.

The National Republicans were eclipsed by the Whigs in the late 1830s. The Whigs were initially organized not from any coherent set of principles or a single personality, but from a coalition that sprang up to oppose Martin Van Buren, who succeeded Jackson as the Democratic Party's leading figure in the mid-1830s. A Whig candidate, William Henry Harrison, won the presidency in 1840. This election marked the return of true two-party competition.

Competition between Whigs and Democrats continued into the middle 1850s, when the Whig party disappeared and was replaced by the Republican Party. The Republican Party ran its first presidential candidate, General John Fremont, in 1856. Since then, the Democratic and Republican parties have dominated American politics in the oldest continuous two-party competition in the world.

Party Competition

Figure 7.6 is an overview of American political parties since 1789. Except for initial Federalist dominance under Washington and Democratic-Republican dominance during the era of good feeling in the 1820s, American politics has been characterized by competition between two major parties. Although a variety of minor parties have run candidates and have occasionally had an important influence, none has seriously threatened to replace a major party.

The General Types of Party Systems

Political scientists distinguish three types of electoral situations based on the number of parties—one party, multiple parties, or two parties—that effectively compete for power. In a **one-party system,** representatives of a single political party hold all or almost all the major offices in government. This condition may prevail where only one party is legally permitted to run candidates, such as was the case in Nazi Germany and fascist Italy in the 1930s. Political systems that use government coercion to prevent opposition parties from competing for power are not democratic. There are instances of political systems in which opposition parties are legally recognized, but one party dominates electoral contests. In Mexico, for example, the

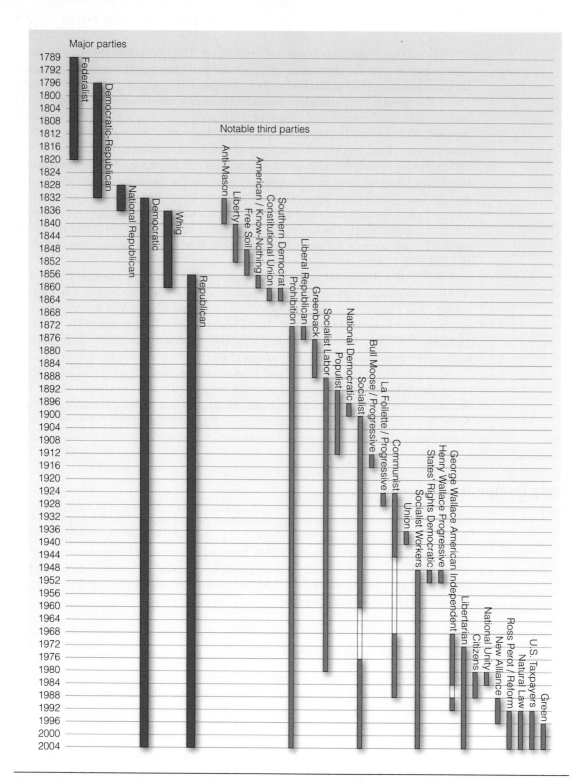

Figure 7.6
American Political Parties since 1789

Institutional Revolutionary Party (PRI) won election after election against weak opposition for about seventy years until Vicente Fox Quesada of the National Action Party (PAN) won the presidency in 2000. Democrats enjoyed the same sort of electoral dominance in southern states from the end of Reconstruction until the 1970s. Electoral competition in one-party democracies tends to be among factions within the dominant party.

Most contemporary democracies are **multiparty systems,** in which three or more parties effectively compete for political offices, and no single party can win sole control of the government. Multiparty systems are common in parliamentary systems in which the legislature chooses the leaders of the executive branch. These political systems are typically characterized by ruling coalitions. In other words, parties combine to form a government and divide up cabinet seats among all the parties in the governing coalition. Examples of such systems are Germany, Japan, and Israel.

Under a **two-party system,** only two political parties have a realistic chance of winning control of a significant number of major political offices. Both parties seek total political power, but neither can eliminate its rival at the ballot box. Each party is capable of capturing enough offices to govern, but the opposition party continues to obtain a sufficiently large enough vote to threaten the tenure of the majority party. The result is that public officials of either stripe must take public wishes and sentiments into account or risk losing to the opposition party in the next election. Such a system works best if the opposition threat is at least occasionally successful, so that the parties alternate in governing. Two-party competition characterizes fewer than 30 percent of the world's democracies. In a widely respected comparative study of political parties, Arend Lijphart (1984) found that only six of the twenty-one nations that have been continuously democratic since the end of World War II have two-party systems: Australia, Austria, Canada, Great Britain, New Zealand, and the United States.

American Party Competition at the National Level

The long-term rivalry between the Republican and Democratic parties clearly meets the requirements of two-party competition. From 1856 to the present, each of these two parties, and only these two, won control of the major institutions of the national government—the presidency, House, and Senate—and sometimes all three at the same time. Figure 7.7 illustrates this close competition with plots of the percentage of elections won in 10-year increments.

In presidential elections, Republicans were successful in 61 percent and Democrats in 39 percent. The competition every two years for control of Congress has also been relatively close: Republicans won 43 percent of House elections to the Democrats' 57 percent in Senate elections, Republicans won 56 percent of the elections to the Democrats' 44 percent. During this period, Republicans won unified party control of the presidency and both houses of Congress 25 times, and Democrats won unified control 21 times. Thus, both Republicans and Democrats have been able to win political power in both the executive and legislative branches of government.

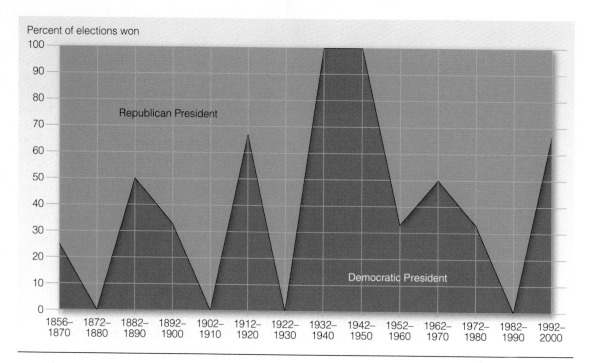

Figure 7.7A
Party Competition for the Presidency, 1856–2000

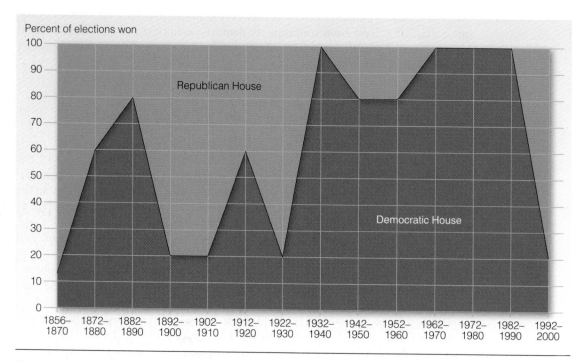

Figure 7.7B
Party Competition for Control of the House of Representatives, 1856–2000

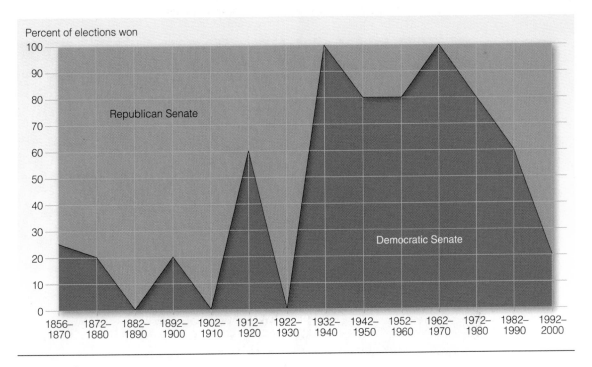

Figure 7.7C
Party Competition for Control of the Senate, 1856–2000

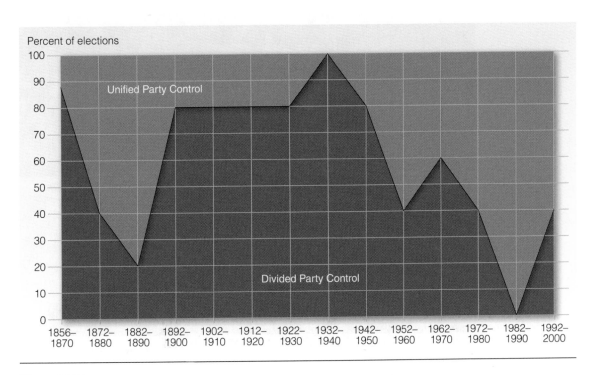

Figure 7.7D
Competition for Unified Party Control, 1856–2000

The Democratic and Republican parties have won control over major governmental institutions for nearly 150 years, creating a two-party system in the United States. At their respective 2004 national conventions, the parties nominated their candidates for president: Democrat John F. Kerry (top) and Republican George W. Bush.

Even in defeat, the major parties still muster substantial political support. Landslide presidential elections in which the winner gets more than 60 percent of the vote were rare in the 20th century. There were only four: Warren Harding in 1920, Franklin Roosevelt in 1936, Lyndon Johnson in 1964, and Richard Nixon in 1972.[4] The popular vote for control of the House has been even closer. The losing party received less than 40 percent of the vote only twice—one was the Democrats in 1920, and the other was the Republicans in 1936.

Although Democrats and Republicans have been able to oust each other from office at fairly frequent intervals, there have been notable periods of one-party dominance. The Republicans largely dominated the executive from 1860 until 1932, with only two Democrats, Grover Cleveland and Woodrow Wilson, winning the presidency during that period. For the next twenty years, Democrats held the presidency. Similar one-party eras occurred in Congress. Most notably, the Democrats had majorities in the House of Representatives from 1955 to 1994. On balance, however, the American system at the national level is rightly considered two party. The roughly equal division of major party victories throughout nearly 150 years of competition, the close split of popular votes, and relatively frequent alternation in power place the system squarely in the two-party category.

Reasons for the National Two-Party System

If most democracies are multiparty systems, why does the United States have a two-party system? Scholars have identified several possible causes.

Historical Factors One reason for the formation of a two-party system in the United States is the early division of political loyalties into two broad groups. As discussed in Chapter 2, two basic constellations of interests battled over the Constitution: the Federalists and the anti-Federalists. The Federalists tended to be people who relied on trade for their livelihood (manufacturers, merchants, and the like), while the anti-Federalists tended to be those who did not (subsistence farmers, artisans, and mechanics). Later, the commercial classes supported the Hamiltonian economic program, and agricultural interests opposed it. The first two parties formed around these two disparate groups: The Federalists represented business and commercial interests, and the Democratic-Republicans represented agricultural interests.[5] The division was also geographical; commercial interests were concentrated along the coasts in the North and agricultural interests in the South and the interior.

Two broad divisions of interests have continued to characterize political parties in the United States. In the Jacksonian era, western frontier forces faced off against eastern moneyed interests. As slavery became a political flashpoint, this East–West schism was replaced by a new sectionalism along North–South lines, reflecting the differing economies of the industrial Northeast and the agricultural South.

---

[4]A landslide victory is generally defined as receiving 60 percent or more of the vote. Ronald Reagan came close with 59.2 percent in 1984, and that election is also generally considered a landslide.

[5]Not all individuals followed this pattern. Madison and Jefferson, for example, supported the Constitution but founded the Democratic-Republican Party. Still, most leaders who favored the Constitution became members of the Federalist Party, while anti-Federalists typically became Democratic-Republicans.

Lingering memories of the Civil War and the problems of race made North–South differences a major factor in American politics well into the 20th century. The period from the Civil War until the 1920s was a time of sectional politics, with Republicans in the Northeast, Democrats in the South, and both vying for support in the West and Midwest, regions that held the balance of political power between the two parties.

Beginning in the late 1920s, increasing urbanization and the industrialization of the South and West began to erode this sectionalism. The result was the development of class politics, as the Republicans gathered the support of affluent and upper-middle-class economic groups, while working-class people, immigrants from central and southern Europe and their children, and African Americans increasingly moved into the Democratic camp. This pattern continues to prevail today, but it is complicated by the reemergence of race as a major issue in American politics. As a result of increased African American participation, Democratic officeholders are likely to support their generally liberal policy preferences; conservative white southerners and some working-class whites in the North have swung their support to Republicans.

This simplified description indicates that for much of our history, two parties have been able to aggregate many of the major interests in society into broad coalitions.

Electoral Rules   Once political conflicts divide into two camps, the rules of the game—particularly electoral rules—tend to reinforce that initial division. Electoral rules are seldom neutral; they almost always favor some interests over others. In the United States, the rules have undoubtedly given the two major parties important advantages over minor parties.

The system used to elect representatives has a strong effect on whether a democracy will have two parties or multiple parties. Most liberal democracies use a system of multimember constituencies and **proportional representation,** both of which facilitate multiple parties. In such electoral systems, seats are allocated to the parties on the basis of their share of the popular vote. In contrast, the United States uses the **single-member-district-plurality system,** a winner-take-all system that makes it hard for minor parties to win office.

To illustrate the electoral implications of these two systems, imagine a state entitled to elect ten members to the House of Representatives. In a multimember constituency system, all ten members would be elected statewide, and all ten would represent the same constituency. With proportional representation, the ten seats would be allocated to parties on the basis of their statewide share of the popular vote. A party that got 20 percent of the vote would get two of the seats. In a single-member-district-plurality system, by contrast, the state would be carved up into ten separate districts, and voters in each district would choose one representative. The candidate in each district with a plurality of the votes (that is, more than anyone else) wins the seat. This system clearly hinders the development of third parties. Although a minor party may have the support of a substantial minority of voters in the state, it would gain no representation in Congress unless one of its candidates won a plurality in a district. Without at least some success at the ballot box, it is difficult to keep supporters. Lijphart's (1984) comparative study found that five of the six democracies that use the plurality method to choose representatives have two-party systems, whereas fourteen of the fifteen that use proportional representation have multiparty systems.

The way the chief executive is elected also influences the number of parties. The parliamentary system typical of other democracies encourages multiple parties. In a **parliamentary system,** the party that controls the majority of legislative seats chooses the chief executive, who is usually called the prime minister or premier. The prime minister then forms a government by appointing individuals to run the various government departments or ministries—a secretary of defense, a foreign secretary, a secretary of education, and so on. Since minor parties often win seats in parliament, sometimes no party controls a majority of the seats. When no party has a majority of the seats, the leader of one of the parties will try to form a coalition government by offering cabinet seats to other parties in return for their support. As partners in majority coalitions, minor party representatives can end up in posts of central importance in running the government. In contrast, the United States uses a **presidential system,** in which the chief executive and the legislature are elected independently.

The system used to choose the president in the United States offers a distinct advantage to the two major parties. As we explain more completely in Chapter 10, the president is not chosen directly by the popular vote but by the electoral college. The Constitution allocates electoral votes to each state; to win the presidency, a candidate must receive a majority of electoral votes. Each state's electoral votes are allocated on a winner-take-all basis to the candidate who wins a plurality of the votes in the state. Although third party and independent candidates occasionally attract significant popular support nationwide, they often receive no electoral votes because they do not win a plurality of the popular vote in any state. For example, Ross Perot received roughly 19 percent of the popular vote in 1992 but not a single electoral vote. A party that has no chance of winning the nation's highest office is unlikely to be an enduring force in the nation's politics.

Two other types of electoral rules also favor the two-party system. First, state laws regulating access to the ballot are a considerable obstacle to minor parties. Candidates of the two major parties automatically appear on the ballot in every state. Minor parties do not get automatic access to the ballot. In order to appear on the ballot, minor parties must satisfy state laws that typically require them to file a candidacy petition signed by a specific number of registered voters by a certain time prior to the election. This procedure requires considerable organizational and financial resources. If a minor party does qualify for access to the ballot in a state, it may have to repeat this arduous process if it fails to draw a minimum percentage of the vote (usually 5 percent to 10 percent). Laws regulating who is listed on the ballot are thus a significant handicap for third parties.[6]

Second, public financing of presidential campaigns benefits the major parties. As discussed in Chapter 10, presidential nominees of the two major parties receive full financing of their general election campaigns, while those representing minor parties receive partial funding or none at all. And minor party candidates routinely find it difficult to raise funds, since contributors are reluctant to give to candidates who have little chance of winning.

The legal obstacles facing minor parties are typically justified as means for protecting the electoral process from frivolous candidates and parties. Making it difficult for

---

[6]A party that fails to qualify to have its candidates listed on the ballot can encourage write-in votes, but it is hard to get voters to support candidates who are not listed on the ballot.

"nuts and crackpots" to get on the ballot is not considered to be a serious threat to democracy. Giving free ballot access to anyone who wants to run for office would increase the costs of administering elections and confuse voters rather than offering real choices. But minor party candidates obviously do not consider their proposals frivolous. They claim that Democrats and Republicans who control the institutions that write the rules have used that power to maintain the status quo and protect themselves.

Natural Perpetuation of the Two-Party System   Another cause of the two-party system is a set of mechanisms that tend to make it self-perpetuating. As we will see in Chapter 9, people often develop an attachment to a political party at an early age, and the attachment deepens during their adult lives. In a society where two parties have been dominant for more than a century, it is natural for most citizens to think of themselves as Republican or Democrat. In other words, traditional party patterns embedded in the political socialization process perpetuate the two-party system.

Since only Republican and Democratic parties have a realistic chance of winning any offices, these two major parties attract the best political and leadership talent. Those who aspire to political office realize that without one of these labels, their chances of fulfilling their ambitions are small. Not surprisingly, political talent gravitates toward the two major parties rather than to minor parties.

The two-party system also perpetuates itself by channeling political conflict into two major outlets: the organization in power and the one out of power. Support and opposition to the government thus coalesce into two distinct groups. Citizens unhappy with the status quo vote not only against present officeholders but also for candidates of the other major party because that is the only viable alternative to replace the party in power.

Minor Political Parties

Although America is clearly a two-party system, minor or **third parties**[7] have appeared often throughout our history (as Figure 7.6 demonstrated). Despite never capturing a significant number of national offices, third parties have occasionally had a considerable effect on American politics.

As political scientists John Bibby and L. Sandy Maisel point out, two-party politics is not mandated by the Constitution, and public opinion polls consistently find that "voters express a distaste for the major parties" and want an alternative (1998, 3–4). In the 1990s, voters awarded independent presidential candidate Ross Perot significant portions of the popular vote in two consecutive elections, and they elected minor party governors in Maine (Angus King), Connecticut (Lowell Weicker), Alaska (Walter Hickel), and Minnesota (Jesse Ventura).

American political history is littered with minor parties and independent candidacies. Some, like the anti-Masonic party of the 1830s, contested a single presidential election and disappeared almost immediately. Others, like the Socialist

---

[7]Although minor parties are commonly referred to by this term, it would be more precise to label them "third," "fourth," or "fifth" parties depending on their relative electoral strength.

Party, have fielded candidates in a hopeless electoral cause for a number of years. The Prohibition Party, whose members focused on the evils of alcohol, began running presidential candidates in 1872 and was still contesting the nation's highest office in the mid-1990s. The Communist Party of the 1920s sought a radical overhaul of the entire economic and political structure. The Libertarians, who have had a presidential candidate on the ballot in all 50 states in every election since 1972, seek a drastic reduction of the level of governmental involvement in the economy and individual lives.

Probably the most notable recent third party movement sprang from Ross Perot's presidential bid in 1992. Perot ran as an independent in that election. The organizational effort associated with this candidacy served as the genesis of a genuine third party—the Reform Party—that backed Perot's run for the presidency in 1996, and it ran twenty-two congressional candidates in the 1998 elections. Although it failed to elect any members to Congress, former professional wrestler Jesse Ventura was elected governor of Minnesota. The initial promise of the Reform Party as a legitimate contender to the major parties has largely fizzled. Its major issue—out-of-control government spending—evaporated with the appearance of balanced federal budgets, and its *"angry* middle" constituency disappeared in the economic good times of the mid-1990s (Sifry 1998). Nonetheless, the Reform Party is a good example of the primary characteristic shared by minor parties in American politics: a feeling that certain values or interests are not being properly represented by the two major parties (see the Promise and Policy feature "The Rise and Fall of the Reform Party").

Goals and Types of Minor Parties

Some minor parties have promoted ideologies foreign to the nation's traditional beliefs, notably parties introduced into the United States from Europe that failed to adapt to the political reality of free-enterprise economics. Included here are the Socialist Party, which has advocated public ownership of basic industries; the Socialist Labor Party, which seeks to eliminate the capitalist system through essentially peaceful means; and the Communist Party, a group founded in 1919 and notable for its close ties to the now-defunct Soviet Union. Of the three, the Socialist Labor Party has been the longest lived, running a presidential candidate in every election between 1896 and 1976. The Socialist Party has been the biggest vote-getter, pulling in 6 percent of the popular vote in 1912. The Communist Party's electoral forays have been sporadic and uniformly hopeless. Its highest vote total was 100,000 in 1932, but this pales in comparison to the 23 million voters who chose the Democratic candidate, Franklin Roosevelt.

The most successful minor parties have, like the Marxist parties, protested economic injustices. But their ideology has been indigenous rather than imported from foreign sources. The Populists, for example, emerged during the 1890s proposing free and unlimited coinage of silver, a graduated income tax, public ownership of railroads, an expansion of the money supply, and a number of other measures designed to break the financial hold of the industrial East over the producers of raw materials. In 1892, the Populists received 8.5 percent of the popular vote and 22 electoral votes.

PROMISE AND POLICY
The Rise and Fall of the Reform Party

To get his name on the ballot in all 50 states for the 1992 presidential election, businessman Ross Perot organized a group that he named United We Stand America (UWSA) to collect petition signatures. After the election in which Perot won 19 percent of the popular vote, Perot and UWSA began the process of organizing as a third political party, the Reform Party USA. By 1996, the Reform Party had qualified for party status under the separate laws of 50 states and the District of Columbia, and Perot joined the presidential campaign as its presidential nominee. He won 8.4 percent of the popular vote, which exceeded the 5 percent threshold necessary to ensure that candidates for the 2000 Reform Party presidential nomination would be eligible for nearly $12.6 million in federal matching funds.

Almost immediately after the Reform Party qualified for party status, some Reform Party members became dissatisfied with Perot's leadership. A splinter group known as the American Reform Party backed the former governor of Colorado, Dick Lamm, over Perot for the 1996 presidential nomination. The following year, the split became permanent. Nevertheless, in 1998, 184 candidates ran under the Reform Party label for federal and state offices. Perhaps the most famous candidate to win election that year was the candidate for Minnesota governor, Jesse Ventura.

Ventura's upset victory over his better-known Republican and Democrat opponents strengthened the perception that the Reform Party was a growing progressive political movement. The power base of the party shifted from Perot's headquarters in Dallas to St. Paul, Minnesota, where Governor Ventura's aides began recruiting candidates and planning strategy for challenges to the two major parties. Although Ventura decided not to seek the 2000 presidential nomination, his aides expected him to consider a bid in 2004. But shortly after conservative presidential hopeful Patrick Buchanan left the Republican Party and announced his intention to seek the Reform Party's nomination, Ventura severed his ties with the party.

The future of the Reform Party is unclear at this time. While the party has managed to field candidates and win offices at the local level, it continues to be plagued by factions and party leadership disputes. At a contentious meeting in February 2000, Perot supporters voted to remove Jack Gargan, an ally of Governor Ventura, as party chairman. Gargan turned to the courts, but he lost the case. Fights continued, however, with party members arguing over a location for the 2000 nominating convention and over efforts by Buchanan supporters to replace key party officers with Buchanan loyalists.

At the national convention in the summer of 2000, the party openly split into two factions. Buchanan had the most delegates, and he was selected as the presidential candidate. A minority faction loyal to Ross Perot left the convention and nominated John Hagelin, who was also the candidate of the Natural Law Party. The Federal Election Commission (FEC) decided that Buchanan was the "real" Reform Party nominee and awarded him the federal matching funds. Although Buchanan's name was on the Reform Party line of the ballot in most states, John Hagelin was listed on both the Natural Law Party and Reform Party lines in at least one state.

Buchanan's candidacy attracted support from a number of extremely conservative organizations, some of them intensely prejudiced against African Americans, Jews, and immigrants. Although the Buchanan campaign denied that he was racist or anti-Semitic, his candidacy transformed the Reform Party from an organization appealing to centrist voters concerned about trade, campaign finance reform, and balancing the federal budget to one drawing voters on the extreme right. Buchanan received about 450,000 votes nationwide, less than one-half of 1 percent of the more than 100 million votes cast. Green Party candidate Ralph Nader ran best among the minor parties in 2000, receiving more than 2.5 million votes, about 3 percent of the popular vote. Nader ran again in the 2004 presidential election as an independent candidate. The Reform Party did nominate a candidate, but endorsed Nader. Even with this endorsement, Nader polled less than 500,000 votes nationwide.

Sources: Allen, Mike. 2000. "Reform Party's New Leaders Are Planning New Direction." New York Times Online. http://www.nytimes.com/library/politics/camp/080399wh-ref-candidate.html; American Reform Party. 2000. "ARP Applauds Governor Jesse Ventura for Cutting Ties with Reform Party." http://www.americanreform.org/press/ventura-bolts-rp.html; Breaux, Ma Shant'e. 2000. "Judge to Rule Monday in Reform Party Power Struggle." CNN Online. http://www.cnn.com/2000/ALLPOLITICS/stories/03/24/reform.ap/index.html; Edsall, Thomas B. 2000. "Buchanan's Bid Transforms the Reform Party." Washington Post, July 23, p. A04; Kellman, Laurie. 2000. "Reform Party Convention Site Still Not Nailed Down." CNN Online. http://www.cnn.com/2000/ALLPOLITICS/stories/03/29/reform.ap/index.html; Verney, Russell. 2000. "Reform Party History." http://www.reformparty.org/history.html.

The Progressives were probably the most successful third party movement of the 20th century. The genesis for the Progressive movement came from the liberal wing of the Republican Party, and the group is best known for attacks on abuses of both economic and political power. It proposed government regulation of monopolies and championed the adoption of direct democracy reforms such as the initiative (a way for citizens to propose and enact legislation), the referendum (referring proposed laws to the electorate for the ultimate decision), and the recall (permitting citizens to oust unsatisfactory officeholders between elections). There was a second Progressive movement that focused on the farmer and echoed the earlier Populist movement. Both Theodore Roosevelt (1912) and Robert La Follette (1924) ran for president under the Progressive label with some success. Roosevelt received 88 electoral votes, and La Follette picked up 16.6 percent of the popular vote.

Racial conflict spawned party competition in the decades following World War II. In 1948, a group of dissident Democrats bolted from their party's national nominating convention over the issue of civil rights. They formed the States' Rights Democratic Party, which was widely known as the Dixiecrat Party, and nominated J. Strom Thurmond of South Carolina and Fielding Wright of Mississippi as candidates for president and vice president. Twenty years later, a third party with similar racial views headed by former Alabama Governor George Wallace ran candidates under the label of the American Independent Party. Both of these minor parties carried several southern states in presidential elections. The Dixiecrat ticket received 39 electoral votes in 1948, and Wallace captured 46 in 1968.

Effects of Minor Parties

It may appear that third parties have been of little significance in American politics. The most successful minor party foray into presidential politics—Theodore Roosevelt's 1912 run as a Progressive—attracted a little more than a quarter of the popular vote but nowhere near enough electoral votes to be considered a serious threat to win the White House. Third parties have not only failed to capture the main prize in American politics, they have also had little success in attaining other national offices.

The significance of minor parties lies not in the offices they have won, but in their effect on the other two parties. Judged from this perspective, some third party movements precipitated seismic shifts in the American political landscape, up to and including deciding the fate of the presidency. For example, Roosevelt's Progressive candidacy in 1912 contributed to Republican William Howard Taft's loss in his bid for a second term and helped elect Democrat Woodrow Wilson. The Progressives split Republican loyalties between the traditional party structure and its radical offshoot. George Wallace's strategy in his presidential bid in 1968 was not to win outright; he was a savvy politician who knew that his appeal was largely regional and that his chances of ending up in the White House were slim. His objective was to get enough electoral votes from the South to prevent either the Democrat Hubert Humphrey or the Republican Richard Nixon from winning the majority of electoral votes. This would allow him to be the king-maker who would

© Ramin Talaie/Corbis

Minor parties have played a major role in deciding who gets the electoral votes of certain states. Many believe that Ralph Nader's Green Party campaign in 2000 cost Al Gore the presidential election. Despite being asked not to run in 2004, Nader again put in his bid for the presidency.

instruct his electors to vote for the candidate he favored. The idea was to negotiate with Humphrey and Nixon for policy positions in return for the presidency. Nixon got a majority of electoral votes, so Wallace's strategy was never put into action, but it was considered plausible (Bibby and Maisel 1998, 96–97).

Even if they do not decide who ends up in the White House, minor parties have certainly played a major role in deciding who gets the electoral votes of particular states. Rather than take the laborious third party route of gaining ballot access, the 1948 Dixiecrats presented Thurmond and Wright as the official Democratic nominees in Alabama, Louisiana, Mississippi, and South Carolina. This tactic paid off, and they largely carried these states. In 2000, Green Party candidate Ralph Nader received more than 97,000 votes in Florida, where a margin of a few hundred votes gave Republican George W. Bush the state's 25 electoral votes, which made him president. Had Nader not been on the ballot, challenger Al Gore would probably have received enough support from Nader voters to win Florida and the presidency. Several prominent Democrats and even some who voted for Nader in 2000 begged him not to run in 2004 and risk helping to reelect President George W. Bush. Nader ignored these pleas and ran again, but he polled fewer than 500,000 votes and had no apparent effect on the outcome.

The effects of minor parties are not only felt in vote totals. They can help shape the policy orientation of the major parties, which adopt their ideas as a way to attract more voters. The Democrats did this in 1896, when William Jennings Bryan adopted the Populists' call for free and unlimited coinage of silver. This position pushed the Democratic Party to the left and separated it from the "sound money" policies of the Republicans. In the aftermath of strong Progressive showings in 1912 and 1924, the Democratic Party absorbed some of the central campaign themes of Roosevelt and La Follette, such as the regulation of large corporations and the promotion of labor interests, which held little attraction for Republicans. The Republicans under Nixon picked up on some of Wallace's

American Independent Party's civil rights positions, distinguishing itself on racial issues from the Democratic Party.

This process of absorbing appealing minor party themes has often led to the demise of the organizations that initially espoused them. The Populists were essentially assimilated by the Democrats; the Progressives eventually trudged home to the Republican Party; and the Dixiecrats returned to the Democratic fold or became Republicans. (Dixiecrat Strom Thurmond, for example, switched to the Republican Party.)

Thus, rather than being viable alternatives to the major parties, minor parties have had a more lasting effect by helping shape the composition of the major parties. Factions within a major party that believe they are losing internal conflicts over key issues may defect to the other major party or may begin an independent movement. These movements can have important electoral consequences that prompt a response from the major party. Some third party supporters are not overly distressed if that response signals the demise of their movement: The rationale for the party's formation no longer exists because the values that were formerly ignored now have major party representation.

Students of political parties see few signs that two-party dominance will end in the near future. Minor parties are likely to have important political roles from time to time. If nothing else, they can signal dissatisfaction with the performance or policy stands of the two major parties. If this signal is strong enough, the major parties will respond.

 ## Performance Assessment

Historically, American political parties have generally made a positive contribution to the democratic process. They appeared in the early years of the republic to become the world's first permanent electoral organizations, and they have served as models for other democratic countries. Persisting as a central feature of American politics for more than two centuries indicates that the party system has performed at least some of its functions successfully.

This success is due in large part to a favorable political environment characterized by a general consensus on basic social, economic, and political values and institutions. These broad areas of agreement have spared American political parties from having to represent and reconcile deep cleavages. The expanding economy has made it possible for a wide variety of groups to satisfy their demands through the rival parties without resorting to an all-out do-or-die struggle.

American political parties, in turn, have contributed to the successful operation of democratic institutions. They have recruited and backed many able men and women for public office. They have provided voters with significant choices of personnel and policies, especially during key historical periods when party competition reflected and advanced differing economic and social interests.

American political parties have also had some notable failures. Their inability to deal with the race issue resulted in a bloody Civil War and, a century later, a bitter fight for civil rights. Racial issues still permeate contemporary politics and continue to affect party divisions.

A number of political scientists have criticized the institutional structure of American parties and have called for the creation of responsible parties along the lines discussed earlier in this chapter. In 1950, the Committee on Political Parties of the American Political Science Association issued a report entitled "Towards a More Responsible Two-Party System." The report advocates strong national party organizations that present alternative policy programs in their platforms and that have the capability to discipline their members in Congress to get such programs enacted into law. Such proposals have been periodically advocated by political scientists ever since.

Not all scholars agree with the advocates of responsible party government. Defenders of the existing party system criticize the reformers on three grounds. One is that their goals are undesirable: If the two major parties did present very different programs to Americans, and if the winning party then proceeded to carry out these programs, political conflict would increase because the losers would resist implementation of public policies that threatened their basic values and interests. Also, more intraparty democracy means that the selection of candidates and the adoption of policies would be made by rank-and-file party members who are not as knowledgeable and skilled as party leaders. Second, even if the goals of the reformers are desirable, they cannot be attained: It is unrealistic to expect programmatic national parties to develop in the United States with its federal system of government, a presidential system with separation of powers, and a tradition of pragmatism and protecting minority rights. Third, some of the charges leveled against the American party system are untrue: Parties sometimes do present alternative programs in their platforms, and party members in Congress see to it that such programs are enacted into law.

Which of these arguments is correct remains a matter of some debate. Regardless, keep both in mind as we examine the part that political parties play in various aspects of American politics. In Chapters 9, 10, and 11 we focus on their role in the electoral process. In subsequent chapters, we analyze the role of the party in the government in making public policy.

Summary

- Although political parties were not envisioned by the Founders and have been viewed with suspicion and distrust since their emergence in the early days of the republic, political scientists tend to view political parties as organizations that play an important role in promoting the long-term health and stability of the democratic process.
- A political party is an organization that nominates and runs candidates for public office under its own label. This characteristic sets parties apart from interest groups, which often try to influence policy but do not run candidates for office under their own labels.
- Political parties are relatively weak and decentralized in the United States. They have no controlling centralized body and few options for requiring party members holding public office to support or carry through a partisan agenda.

- Parties can be thought of as consisting of three overlapping groups: (1) the party in the electorate, consisting of ordinary citizens who identify with the party; (2) the party in government, consisting of the elected and appointed officeholders who share a party label; and (3) the party organization, consisting of the party professionals who hold official positions in the party.
- Political parties link citizens and government by facilitating participation. Parties facilitate participation in three ways: (1) They aggregate individual policy preferences into coherent policy agendas; (2) they structure and simplify alternatives for voters; and (3) their campaign activities stimulate interest in politics and government.
- Political parties promote government responsiveness as they organize government and seek to pass a policy agenda.
- Political parties promote accountability when parties out of power scrutinize activities of the party in power and report mistakes and abuses.
- Political parties promote stability and the peaceful resolution of conflict as they reconcile and accommodate a diverse spectrum of views to build broad coalitions.
- Some observers argue that parties are in decline based on a decrease in partisanship within the electorate, a drop in straight-ticket voting, and a decline of party voting in Congress.
- Others argue that this evidence is time bound. Although there is evidence of party decline from the 1950s and 1960s with a low point in the 1970s, during the 1980s and continuing through the 1990s there is evidence of rising partisanship in the electorate and in government. Party organizations remain active and vibrant as they have adapted to changes in the political environment.
- Professionals participate in party activities for tangible rewards, such as patronage jobs and government contracts, and for social incentives, such as the satisfaction from a victory and the camaraderie of working with other party members. Their main goal is to win elections, and they tend to evaluate policy proposals in terms of how much political support they will attract.
- Amateurs are more committed to a core set of principles and are dedicated to implementing those principles in public policy. The devotion to principle means that amateurs are less concerned with winning elections than they are with doing the right thing.
- Although some of the Founders believed that parties would be harmful to the republic, the same men who espoused these convictions laid the foundation for political parties. The Federalist Party coalesced around the ideas of Hamilton with Washington as its popular leader. Madison and Jefferson resigned from the Washington administration in 1793 and organized the Democratic-Republican opposition. Within two decades of its founding, the United States had a fairly permanent party system.
- Party systems are classified according to the number of parties that effectively compete for power: one party, multiparty, or two party. American politics has been characterized by two-party competition through most if its

history. Democrats and Republicans dominated political competition in the United States from 1856 to the present in the oldest continuous two-party competition in the world.

- Reasons for the two-party system in the United States include historical factors, electoral rules (including the single-member-district-plurality system, the electoral college, state laws regulating access to the ballot, and public financing of presidential elections), and a set of mechanisms that tend to make it self-perpetuating.
- Minor or third parties do exist in the United States and have periodically had an important effect on American politics. By siphoning off votes from the major parties, minor parties sometimes influence who wins an election. Minor party issues that attract significant support tend to be absorbed by the major parties.

Key Terms

amateurs 206
critical election 205
direct primary 204
divided government 195
electoral realignment 205
multiparty system 213
one-party system 211
parliamentary system 219
party discipline 195
party in government 191
party in the electorate 191
party organization 191
party-line vote 202

political machine 203
political party 190
political patronage 203
presidential system 219
professionals 206
proportional
  representation 218
responsible party model 195
single-member-district-plurality
  system 218
straight-ticket voters 199
third parties 220
two-party system 213

Selected Readings

Aldrich, John J. 1995. *Why Parties?* Chicago: University of Chicago Press. Includes excellent surveys of the scholarship analyzing the historical formation and role of political parties as well as their contemporary evolution and effects.

Bibby, John F., and L. Sandy Maisel. 1998. *Two Parties—Or More? The American Party System.* Boulder, CO: Westview Press. An accessible and comprehensive primer on political parties that pays particular attention to the role of third parties.

Chambers, William. 1963. *Political Parties in a New Nation: The American Experience.* New York: Oxford University Press. One of the best books on the historical foundations and development of political parties in America.

Sabato, Larry. 1988. *The Party's Just Begun.* Glenview, IL: Scott, Foresman. A comprehensive overview of the advantages and disadvantages of the two-party system in the United States.

Stonecash, Jeffrey M. 2003. *Diverging Parties: Social Change, Realignment, and Party Polarization.* Boulder, CO: Westview Press. Presents evidence that polarization of parties in Congress results from the realignment of the electoral bases of the parties.

Wattenberg, Martin. 1998. *The Decline of American Political Parties, 1952–1996.* Cambridge, MA: Harvard University Press. One of the most comprehensive arguments on the decline of American political parties.

8 | The Mass Media and Politics

The central tenet of the First Church of George Herbert Walker Christ is the belief that the forty-first president of the United States is the reincarnation of Jesus Christ. Sound a little goofy? Read on, because it gets even stranger.

The church was founded by a handful of evangelicals who saw the first Gulf War as the start of Armageddon and Saddam Hussein as the anti-Christ. Bush, who put together the international coalition that fought Gulf One, was seen as the logical nominee for supreme spiritual savior. The congregation's religious practices are as unorthodox as its founding. For example, though nominally Christian, the congregation keeps kosher, or at least follows a set of eating guidelines similar to the Jewish dietary rules. There are some differences. Bush was known for his dislike of broccoli, so that is prohibited. Bush's equally well-known fondness for pork rinds sparked something of a theological controversy. Pork is not kosher (Glass 1997).

There's one more thing you should probably know about the First Church of George Herbert Walker Christ: It doesn't exist. Never has. At least, it never existed in reality. It did exist in the fertile imagination of Stephen Glass, who in the 1990s was a star reporter for the *New Republic* magazine. The whole notion of the church turned out to be just as absurd as it sounds. Yet Glass reported its existence, its beliefs, even the size of its congregation, as fact. He did so in the cover story of a nationally known and journalistically respected magazine.

This fabrication was not the only one Glass wove into his reporting. In truth, there was as much fiction as fact in many of his stories. And Glass is not the only high-profile journalist to get caught fibbing. In recent years, Jayson Blair of *The New York Times* and Jack Kelley of *USA Today* sullied the reputations of these newspapers after getting caught leaving a trail of lies and deception in their reporting.

Glass and Kelley and Blair are bad enough, but at least they can be viewed as bad apples in organizations that,

for the most part, try to get their facts straight and that took some responsibility for untruths told. In these cases, reporters were fired, editors lost their jobs, internal investigations were conducted, policies were changed, and scathing reviews were compiled and dutifully reported by the publications they targeted.

What about other media organizations and media personalities—those whose reward for occasional (and sometimes frequent) factual errors is a bigger audience? Critics of conservative talk radio host Rush Limbaugh and conservative Fox News television hosts Bill O'Reilly and Sean Hannity have certainly been charged with taking a very "liberal" attitude with facts (Franken 2003). Should their broadcasts be subject to the fine-tooth comb investigation endured by Glass, Blair, and Kelley? If there is any pattern of factual inaccuracies, should they be punished?

Muddled facts, political spin, voices with more volume than substance—surely this cannot be good for the civic life that is at the heart of a democracy. Although this point is debatable, a more important issue is that it would be unequivocally worse for democracy if government tried to prevent or regulate these voices. As we shall see shortly, a free press is absolutely crucial to the functioning of a healthy democracy and plays a critical role in upholding the core value of political freedom.

Yet a free press means exactly that—it is free and unregulated. Free does not mean fair, unbiased, or even accurate. It means free, and how people use that freedom, with few exceptions, is up to them. The result is not always pretty; at times it can be downright infuriating. Democracy, though, is dependent on that freedom in important ways. Limit that freedom, and you limit the promise of democracy.

We live in a media-soaked culture, with virtually unlimited access to information. Supplying that information is the **mass media,** a term describing all the means used to transmit information to masses of people. These include the **print media,** which consist of newspapers, magazines, and books; and the **electronic media,** which consist of television, radio, movies, records, and the Internet. Of particular importance to politics is the **news media:** organizations and journalists that cover the news. **News** is defined as accounts of timely and specific events. The print and electronic media that are partially or wholly devoted to collecting and reporting news in the United States consist of roughly 1,500 daily newspapers; 6,700 weekly newspapers; 1,700 television stations; 13,000 radio stations; and hundreds of magazines; as well as their Internet-based counterparts (Newspaper Association of America 2003; Federal Communications Commission 2004). Generically, these are all known as the **press.**

In this chapter we explore the role of the press in a democratic society. As it turns out, it is the freedom of the media—not its fairness or accuracy—that is most critical in delivering on the promise of democracy.

 ## The Promise of the Press

The basic promise of a free press is just that—to be free. Allowing the press to investigate and criticize government, to promote a diverse set of perspectives and viewpoints, and to collect and distribute information with little government censorship or regulation is considered a central characteristic of a democratic society. A free press promotes the core democratic value of political freedom.

The media make good on the promise of political freedom by helping to create what Jürgen Habermas (1991) termed a **public sphere,** a forum where information on matters important to civic life can be freely accessed and exchanged. A free marketplace of perspectives and ideas is critically important because a healthy democracy not only requires citizens to be able to express their opinions and preferences, but to be knowledgeable and informed when they make political choices.

For example, in a representative democracy elections are the primary way to connect the preferences of citizens to the actions of government. Elections will not achieve this goal if citizens have no information about what their government is doing, what issues are important, and what options exist to address those issues. It is difficult, after all, to have preferences about issues, proposals, or candidates if you are unaware they exist. In any society with a free press, finding out what the government is doing, identifying the important issues of the day, and getting a broad sense of what is being proposed to address those issues is easy. All this information and much, much, more is delivered to doorsteps every morning, and it is available with the flick of a switch or click of a mouse pretty much any hour of the day.

Allowing that free flow of information is critical to a functioning democracy, not only because it helps inform voters but because it serves as an important check on government officials. Public officeholders are aware that their proposals and their actions will be recorded and transmitted through the mass media, and they also know there are consequences if that information creates a negative impression on their constituents. As Thomas Jefferson (1823) put it: "The only security of all is in a free press. The force of public opinion cannot be resisted when permitted freely to be expressed."

The media creates a public sphere and helps uphold the core value of political freedom by serving a number of specific roles in democratic societies. These functions include information and education, agenda setting, and watchdog and public advocate.

Information and Education

The news media see their primary role as informing and educating the public. They monitor what the government is doing, report its activities to the public, and try to put these activities into context by seeking to explain the meaning and significance of government decisions or actions.

This information and education function has become increasingly important over the last half century as the media have taken on some of the roles traditionally held by political parties. For example, prior to the widespread adoption of primary elections, the job of nominating candidates for office was controlled by relatively small groups of party elites. The rise of the direct primary took the power to nominate candidates from party leaders and placed it in the hands of the voting public.[1] Because voters largely rely on the mass media for information about candidates, this shift in nomination procedures thrust the media into a more prominent role in connecting citizens to government.

The mass media have also taken over some of the traditional party roles for candidates. Historically, candidates relied on party organizations to connect with voters. To reach voters during campaigns, teams of party volunteers banged on doors, organized rallies where candidates gave speeches, and handed out campaign literature. Yet even the most dedicated party machine is an ineffective means of communication compared with the mass media. A television speaks to voters every day, right in their living rooms.

The net effect of these changes is, "a new form of campaigning in which the mass media have replaced the political party as the main intermediary between voters and candidates" (Iyengar 1997, 144). Rather than political parties, most voters now connect with candidates through their television screens, newspapers, radios, and the Internet. Candidates are fully aware that the best way to communicate with large numbers of people is through the press, and they engage in sophisticated media marketing campaigns to get their messages out (Patterson 1984).

Although there is little doubt that the mass media can reach a much larger percentage of the electorate than even the most dedicated party effort, its impact on the information and education role of the media is mixed. In terms of quantity, the shift to media-based campaigns undoubtedly led to the availability of more information for citizens and gave candidates the opportunity to get their message to large numbers of voters. The content of those messages, however, is no less partisan. Rather than seeking to educate citizens with civil debate, candidates for office often seek to point out the faults of their opponents. There is nothing new about this; as long as there have been elections in the United States, candidates have engaged in mudslinging. The rise of the mass media, especially the electronic media, however, provided the opportunity to do this on a grand scale.

If anything, mass media campaigns have provided a boon for the negative electioneering that has always been part and parcel of democratic politics in America. As one political scientist observed, "More often than not, candidates use their media opportunities to criticize, discredit, or ridicule their opponents rather than to promote their own ideas and programs" (Iyengar 1997, 145). Such has been the case since the Founding, but mass literacy and the rise of daily newspapers, not to mention radio, television, and the Internet, make it easier than ever to sling more mud over a wider audience. Many bemoan the attack ads and scathing sound bites,

---

[1]The direct primary is discussed in more detail in Chapter 10.

but there is a simple reason for such negativity: It works. Tearing down your opponent can create doubt among voters, making it less likely they will vote for the other candidate. It may make them less likely to vote, period.

Different Media, Different Information   Given the media's increasingly important role as a central connection between voters and government, the job of informing and educating the public has emerged as a fundamental service to the democratic process. The political freedom of citizens—their ability to make choices—is tied to the information they have about government officials, actions, and issues. This connection raises the question of how well the media do this all-important job. It turns out that not all media are equal in terms of their ability to convey political information, and not all are equal in their ability to convey political information accurately.

Television, by far, is the dominant mass medium in the United States. Access to television is nearly universal—virtually every household has a TV—and the potential audience for television news encompasses just about every single citizen. Americans get most of their political information from television (Figure 8.1). For example, roughly 66 percent of voters get information about elections from television news (Pew Research Center 2003).

After television, newspapers are the next major source of political information. About a third of voters get election information from newspapers. The rest of the news media—radio, magazines, and the Internet—are used much less frequently, though the Internet is growing as a medium for political news (Pew Research Center 2003).

These different media have different capabilities to convey information. Television is a passive medium; it requires little effort or active involvement on the part of the viewer to get information. You do not even have to be literate to follow a television news broadcast. Yet while television makes it easy to access information, it also has drawbacks.

Most importantly, television has tight limits on the amount and depth of information it can convey. A minute of air time, for example, constitutes a major story on a national network newscast. Even a more in-depth report, such as those found on TV shows such as *60 Minutes,* cannot contain the same amount of information as an in-depth article in a newspaper or newsmagazine. The print media are less accessible because they require literacy, and the reader must be willing to follow stories as they jump from page to page. Yet, these media can convey not only more information but more detailed information.

Academic studies show that people who rely more on newspapers tend to be better informed and more knowledgeable about politics than those who rely

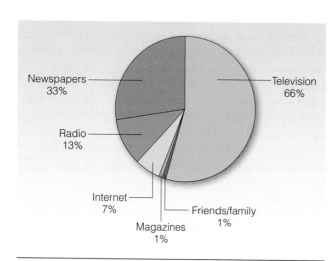

Figure 8.1

Where Americans Get Election News

Note: Percentages add up to more than 100 percent because respondents could list up to two primary sources.

Source: Compiled from Pew Research Center. 2003. "Political Sites Gain, but Major Sites Still Dominant." *http://people-press.org/reports.*

© Syracuse Newspapers/John Berry/The Image Works

Students in a government studies class watch a live TV press conference by President George W. Bush as he announces the invasion of Iraq in March 2003. Despite spending a good deal of time paying attention to the news, Americans tend to remain politically uninformed, possibly due to their primary news source, television, which is less effective at conveying information than newspapers.

more on television. This finding is something of a concern because it means some people will be better informed—and thus in a better position to make informed political choices—than others. Young people, immigrants, the less educated, and the poor tend to be more reliant on television as a primary source of political news; these are also groups that tend to be less politically informed and less politically active (Chaffee and Frank 1996).

Compared with other industrialized democracies, Americans tend to have low levels of political knowledge and information, for which the mass media must bear at least some responsibility. For example, political scientists Michael Dimock and Samuel Popkin (1997) conducted a study based on a political knowledge quiz given to representative samples of citizens from the United States, Canada, Britain, France, Germany, Italy, and Spain. Americans scored poorly on this quiz, with more than half unable to answer a single question correctly.

This finding is somewhat surprising. As a group, Americans are better educated than their counterparts in other countries (higher levels of education are usually associated with higher levels of political knowledge). Americans also spent more time paying attention to the news: an average of 52 minutes a day on television news and newspapers. Given this greater attention, why were Americans so poorly informed?

Dimock and Popkin concluded that the low levels of knowledge were at least partially attributable to television. Television is less effective at conveying information than newspapers, yet it is the primary news source for most Americans. Furthermore, televised news in the United States seems particularly ineffective compared to broadcast news programming in other countries. Noncommercial, nonprofit news organizations such as the British Broadcasting Company (BBC), which are largely free of government control, are widely recognized for the quality of their reporting and are prominent features of the media landscapes in other democracies. Not so the United States, where the news media are dominated by for-profit networks. One of the conclusions of the Dimock and Popkin study is that the former are simply better at informing and educating viewers than the latter.

It is not just that some media do a better job of informing voters; some media actually lead to **misinformation,** or the belief that incorrect information is true. Several studies have found that heavy consumers of political talk radio not only tend to be more misinformed, they tend to have more confidence in the political viewpoints their misinformation supports. In other words, they not only are more likely to have inaccurate information about politics and government, they are more likely to base their political beliefs and actions on that misinformation (Hofstetter et al. 1999).

Trust and Information   Americans tend to be skeptical about the quality of information they get from the mass media. More than half believe that news organizations often print or broadcast stories that are factually inaccurate. Roughly the same proportion also believes the press covers up their mistakes rather than admitting them (Pew Research Center 2002a).

Despite this skepticism, Americans seem willing to accept much of what appears in the mainstream media as reasonably accurate, though some news sources are seen as more accurate than others. Most mainstream print and electronic news media—the major television news networks and national daily newspapers, for example—are seen as reasonably credible. Tabloids like the *National Enquirer* are viewed as less believable. Some individual news figures are also seen as better sources of information than others. The major network news anchors—Peter Jennings, Dan Rather, and Tom Brokaw—are seen as being a little more believable than Brit Hume (managing editor of Fox News) and Bill O'Reilly (cable talk show host). All of these are seen as more credible than television journalist and talk show host Geraldo Rivera (Pew Research Center 2002a). Figures 8.2 and 8.3 illustrate the levels of trust Americans have in their various news sources and media personalities.

Americans, then, give the media mixed grades for its information and education role. On the one hand, Americans consume enormous amounts of information, and they are plugged in to the mass media. Daily newspapers, for example, have a total circulation of nearly 50 million (Singhania 2002). The average American spends 4 hours a day watching television (TV-Turnoff Network 2004). Millions more tune in to political radio talk shows, and millions read magazines like *Time* and *Newsweek*. At any given hour of any given day, millions more plug directly in to Internet-based news outlets, chat rooms, and politically oriented Web sites.

Yet, this huge quantity of information consumed is of mixed quality—a fact that Americans seem to acknowledge. Seeing, reading, or hearing is not necessarily believing.

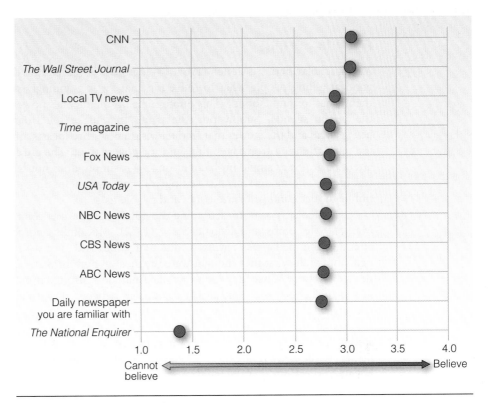

Figure 8.2
American News Sources and Levels of Trust
Source: Compiled from Pew Research Center. 2002a. "News Media's Improved Image Proves Short-Lived."
http://people-press.org/reports.

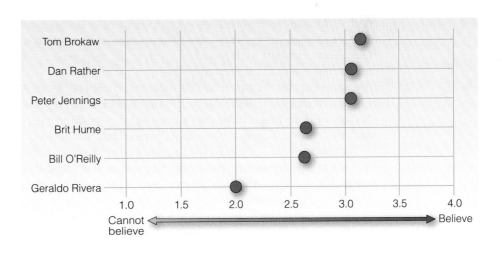

Figure 8.3
American Media Personalities and Levels of Trust
Source: Compiled from Pew Research Center. 2002a. "News Media's Improved Image Proves Short-Lived."
http://people-press.org/reports.

Agenda Setting

Media scholar Bernard Cohen (1963, 13) famously observed that the press is not very good at telling people what to think but that "it is stunningly successful in telling them what to think about." This quote sums up the media's powerful role in shaping the public agenda. Simply put, the issues that make the front page of national newspapers and the stories that lead television news broadcasts are the issues that get the most attention from the public and the government. The government cannot pay attention to every single problem at once—it simply does not have the time or the resources. The media's agenda-setting role means it helps the government and the public to focus and prioritize issues and problems.

The media's power to determine the public agenda was confirmed in a study by Maxwell McCombs and Donald Shaw (1972). McCombs and Shaw measured the attention the media was paying to different issues and then asked a group of independent voters what they thought were the most important issues in an ongoing presidential election. What they found was a remarkably strong correlation; in fact, there was virtually no way to statistically distinguish between the prominence of an issue's coverage in the media and how important the issue was ranked by voters.

Yet though McCombs and Shaw showed Cohen was essentially correct, other studies have shown that this view of **agenda setting** underestimates the impact of the media. While news reports are unlikely to make us change our fundamental political beliefs, it turns out that the media do play a more complex—and in some ways more influential role—than the quote by Cohen implies.

The media's agenda-setting role goes beyond simply identifying and ordering the list of topics that make up the public agenda. The media also frames these issues for the public. **Framing** means emphasizing certain aspects of a story to make them more important (Iyengar and Kinder 1987). Framing helps shape how we think about issues or topics.

For example, in 1995 a terrorist bomb gutted the federal building in Oklahoma City and killed 168 people. Initially, the media concentrated on the possibility that this was an attack by Middle Eastern terrorists—it fit the pattern of similar bombings carried out by foreign extremist groups, and some of these groups had vowed to attack the United States. These elements were played up in the initial news reports, and that became how the bombing was originally viewed by the public: as an attack by foreign terrorists. When it became clear that the bomb had been detonated not only by an American citizen but by a war veteran—Timothy McVeigh—the media reframed the story. Emphasizing McVeigh's ties to fringe right-wing groups led the public to view the bombing as an attack by the domestic militia movement (Rogers, Hart, and Dearing 1997).

By framing stories, the mass media gives a particular perspective on issues and topics. That perspective is not necessarily fair, nor as the Oklahoma bombing example shows, even accurate. Although framing may not tell us what to think, media framing suggests what to think about as well as from what perspective our thoughts are generated.

By choosing which aspects of a story to emphasize, the media also influence the criteria people use to judge issues. This process is known as **priming** (Iyengar 1991, 133). For example, if the media emphasize rising healthcare costs as the most important current problem facing the nation, people will likely judge presidential performance on how effectively the president has tackled healthcare policy. If the emphasis shifts to the economy, a shift in what people use to judge presidential performance will likely follow (Rogers, Hart, and Dearing 1997, 235).

The agenda-setting role of the media, ultimately, comes down to what Walter Lippmann (1922) called "the pictures in our heads." What issues are emphasized in media coverage, and how these issues are framed, helps shape our mental picture of those issues.

Watchdog and Public Advocate

Representative democracy has been described as a government in which the many are watching the few. Yet few citizens in modern representative democracies can afford to devote much time to watching government officials. Similarly, not many people have the time or resources to monitor whether the public interest is represented when government decides who gets what, when, and how. If citizens are not watching, who watches to see if government officials are competent and truthful, and who blows the whistle if they are not? Who makes sure that the public's interests, not just special interests, are represented in official decision making? The press has traditionally embraced the role of government watchdog, monitoring government officials for signs of corruption or deceit. Increasingly, the press has also taken on the role of public advocate and representative.

The most famous example of the press acting as watchdog is the Watergate scandal, where two *Washington Post* reporters effectively ended a presidency.[2] In a months-long investigation, Bob Woodward and Carl Bernstein uncovered that high-ranking officials in President Richard Nixon's administration were connected to a burglary of the Democratic National Committee's headquarters during the 1972 presidential election and that they had illegally tried to cover up their involvement. The news was sensational, and other media outlets began covering the story. When it became clear that the wrong-doing went all the way to the Oval Office, Nixon resigned rather than face impeachment.

Woodward and Bernstein won a Pulitzer Prize (journalism's highest honor) for their Watergate reporting, and they became role models for the next generation of journalists. Today, most U.S. news organizations see themselves as agents of accountability in the Woodward and Bernstein sense. As *Washington Post* writers Leonard Downie and Robert Kaiser (2002, 8) put it, "Anyone tempted to abuse power looks over his or her shoulder to see if someone else is watching. Ideally, there should be a reporter in the rearview mirror."

Journalists not only keep an eye on government, they also see themselves as representatives of the public interest. The public does not send delegates to presidential press conferences, and the public galleries in legislatures are empty much of the time. Reporters, though, invariably are there. One of the roles the press takes upon itself is to use its unique presence and access to stand in for the public, asking questions and probing officials on behalf of the public interest.

Threats to a Free Press

Democracy presumes the existence of a public sphere where information can be freely accessed and transmitted. Without a public sphere, the core values of political freedom and popular sovereignty are difficult to uphold: Unless the people have the

---

[2]The term *Watergate* refers to the Watergate Hotel in Washington, DC, where the Democratic Party was headquartered when it was broken into during the 1972 presidential campaign.

means to inform and develop their opinions and points of view, they cannot be truly free, and the will of the people cannot be the highest political authority. The need to maintain a public sphere makes keeping the press free of regulation and censorship a critical issue for democracy.

Yet, it is often tempting to place limits on the free access of information. Government officials do not want their misdeeds publicized; entrenched special interests would rather not have the negative side of their agendas broadcast and publicly dissected. Even though the press is seen as a primary defense of political freedom, most Americans seem to favor at least some forms of media censorship. One survey showed roughly 60 percent of Americans favored giving the military more power to control how the press reports the war in Afghanistan (Pew Research Center 2001).

Given that majority sentiment may favor some government regulation of the mass media, protecting the public sphere and keeping the media free of government regulation can be difficult. Majority rule is also a core democratic value, and as we learned in Chapter 1, democracy requires a balancing act when these values come into conflict. Majority sentiment can threaten a free press in two ways: government control and private control. Either threat is capable of shrinking the public sphere, reducing the effectiveness of the media's democratic roles, and in doing so, limiting political freedom.

Keeping the media free of government regulation can be difficult despite strong limitations like the First Amendment. This image of slain Iraq War soldiers and 359 other photos taken by the Air Force at Dover Air Force Base in Delaware were not released by the Pentagon for publication until an organization (*www.thememoryhol.org*) requested them under the Freedom of Information Act.

Government Control

In the United States, government's authority to control the press is limited. The primary limitation is the First Amendment, which states in part that, "Congress shall make no law . . . abridging the freedom of speech, or of the press." The courts have consistently interpreted this provision to mean that the news media have great freedom to report on politics as they choose.

A governmental order to prohibit or censor a news story prior to publication or broadcast is known as **prior restraint,** and the Supreme Court has consistently ruled that, except in extraordinary circumstances, prior constraint violates the First Amendment. The only basis on which the government can prevent publication or

LIVING THE PROMISE
Politicians and the Press: Who's Using Whom?

Politicians and journalists have a love–hate relationship: They need each other, but for different reasons.

Journalists need politicians because they are a primary source of news. Politicians decide policy, run for office, and make decisions that can involve the health and safety of citizens, not to mention billions of taxpayer dollars. All this adds up to news, and journalists are heavily dependent on politicians to get the stories.

Politicians need journalists for different reasons: They want to get their message out, they need to connect with their constituents, and they need to persuade voters to back their stand on the issues.

Daniel Schorr, senior news analyst for National Public Radio, says the end result of these competing goals is that politicians and journalists end up using each other. Take, for instance, the leak. A *leak* is traditionally defined as revealing information that officials would prefer to keep secret. Yet there are leaks, and then there are leaks.

Some leaks are done with the full knowledge and even cooperation of the officials who supposedly want the information kept secret. Public officials know journalists have a hard time resisting a leak, or information that is not designated for public consumption. Officials use this knowledge to try to manipulate the news.

As Schorr puts it, "First, you leak something to the press. You feed the press, then you get feedback." If the feedback is not what you wanted, you make some changes. Then you leak again. The end result is that when a policy proposal is "officially" announced, it is pretty much what everyone expected and wanted to hear.

Leaking is just one subset of what is generically known as *spin*, or trying to get a message framed in a particular way. Politicians try to get the media to frame issues so that it puts the most positive light on themselves and the issues they favor. The press resists these attempts at manipulation . . . unless it means an exclusive story or information that is going to lead to a news broadcast or make the front page.

This dance between the media and politicians "has become so ingrained as to make governing seem like a form of theater." Schorr is harshly critical of the end result of politician and journalist feeding off of each other's needs: "We journalists have tried so hard to serve as guardians of reality, only to be no longer sure there is a reality or whether our bosses care if there is a reality."

Source: Schorr, Daniel. 1997. "Who Uses Whom?" In *Do the Media Govern?* Shanto Iyengar and Richard Reeves, eds. Thousand Oaks, CA: Sage.

---

broadcast of a news story is if the government can convince a court that the story would harm national security, an exception that is exceedingly rare.

Perhaps the best-known court case dealing with prior restraint is *New York Times v. United States* (1971), which dealt with what became known as the Pentagon Papers. The Pentagon Papers referred to a secret government study of U.S. involvement in Southeast Asia that revealed, among other things, that the government had deliberately deceived the public about the impact and success of military operations in Vietnam. In 1971, a copy of the study was leaked to *The New York Times*. A **leak** is revealing information that officials want kept secret. (See the Living the Promise feature "Politicians and the Press: Who's Using Whom?")

President Richard Nixon sought—and received—a court order preventing the newspaper from publishing its stories about the study. The administration argued that publication of the study would threaten national security by undermining the war effort. The Supreme Court ruled that this potential threat to national security was not serious enough to justify a prior restraint order, and the story was published.

Congress has occasionally attempted to place some legal restraints on the freedom of the press, but these are notable more for their failures than their successes. For example, in 1798, Congress passed the Alien and Sedition Acts, which in part made publishing any "false, scandalous, and malicious writing" a crime. This law was mainly used as a legal tool by the Federalist Party to intimidate and silence critical newspaper editors. Opposition to the law was widespread, and after the Federalists were swept from office in the election of 1800, the law was repealed, those convicted of breaking the law were pardoned, and fines were repaid with interest.

The federal government, however, has been given considerably more leeway in regulating broadcast media than in regulating print media. The reason is that the broadcast media, unlike the print media, relies on a public good to transmit information: the airwaves. There are a limited number of broadcast frequencies, and government began regulating their use in 1934 with the passage of the Communications Act.

Prior to this law, something akin to anarchy prevailed on the nation's radio airwaves, with stations broadcasting on the same frequencies and drowning out one another's transmissions. In the name of the public interest, the Communications Act regulated the nation's airwaves, required broadcast licenses, and established a set of performance standards as prerequisites for obtaining or maintaining a license.

The law also established the Federal Communications Commission (FCC), an independent agency that was empowered to enforce the Communications Act. Today, the FCC is charged with regulating interstate and international communications by radio, television, wire, satellite, and cable. There is no print equivalent of the FCC, and the primary justification for regulating the electronic media is that it is heavily based on a limited, public resource: broadcast frequencies.

There has been a heated debate over whether the Internet should be treated as a broadcast or as a print medium. The Communications Decency Act, passed by the 104th Congress, sought to regulate the Internet as a broadcast medium by placing restrictions on indecent content. In *Reno v. ACLU* (1997), the Supreme Court rejected this approach by striking down key provisions of the law. The Court characterized the Internet as a print medium and extended to it the full protections of the First Amendment.

In practice, the regulations imposed on the electronic media are not particularly onerous, though in theory the FCC has the power to revoke licenses and to shut down television and radio stations. Such drastic action is rarely even considered, mainly because such a move would almost certainly provoke a public outcry. Freedom of the press is so embedded as a fundamental value of American society that the government is wary of restricting that freedom even when it has the legal power to do so.

Private Control

Although there are well-established limits on government control of the press, freedom of the press can also be limited by private control. Left unchecked, market forces can also limit the free flow of information. This restriction occurs in two basic ways.

The first is concentration of ownership. The public sphere presumes a marketplace of ideas, where numerous interests and points of view compete for attention. But what if the mass media are largely in the hands of a few narrow interests? If control of the news media belongs to only a specific few, what prevents them from censoring or distorting information that harms their interests?

The concentration of media ownership into a small number of powerful hands is not just idle speculation. Since the 1980s, there has been a significant change in the patterns of ownership in the mass media industry. Spurred on by new laws that deregulated

Comcast president and CEO Brian L. Roberts discusses his company's launch of an unsolicited bid to buy the Walt Disney Company for more than $54 billion in stock in February 2004. The offer was later dropped, but the bid exemplifies the current move toward consolidation of media control in the hands of just a few major corporations. Private control may limit the flow of information because corporations' main objective is to make money, not help realize a core value of political freedom.

the telecommunications industry, and the widespread adoption of new technologies such as cable television and the Internet, mass media companies began to recognize and pursue multimedia strategies that allowed them to take advantage of shared resources and economies in scale. By the early 21st century, just a handful of corporations control a dominant share of the mass media industry in the United States. Rupert Murdoch's News Corporation, for example, controls 132 newspapers, 20th Century Fox movie studio, Fox television broadcasting network, roughly two dozen magazines (including *TV Guide*), and several book publishers (News Corporation 2004). Time Warner owns America Online Internet service (with 24 million subscribers in the United States), 130 magazines (everything from *Time* and *Sports Illustrated* to *Practical Boat Owner*), a large number of television and cable companies (from CNN to the Cartoon Network), as well as Warner Brothers film and television studio (Time Warner 2004). Figure 8.4 illustrates the concentration of the media industry ownership over the past twenty years. This concentration of so many media outlets into so few corporate families set off alarm bells for critics concerned with the impact on the public sphere. For example, would a news organization vigorously pursue a story that reflected negatively on its corporate owner?

The second reason private control may limit the free flow of information is money. Giant media conglomerates like News Corporation and Time Warner are not in business to promote a public sphere or to help realize the core value of political freedom. Like most other businesses, they exist to make money. Profits in the print and electronic media

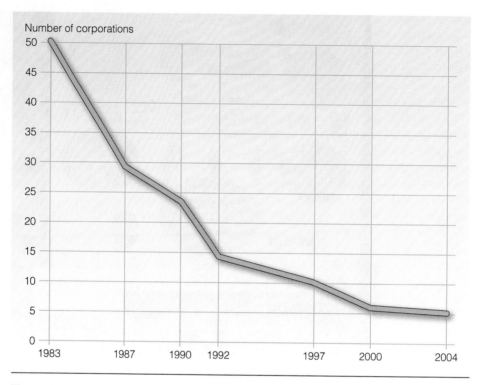

Figure 8.4
Number of Corporations that Control a Majority of U.S. Media, 1983–2004
Source: Media Reform Information Center. *http://www.corporations.org/media/.* Accessed June 5, 2004.

are driven largely by advertising, and the larger the audience delivered to advertisers, the more money it is possible to make. Minority and marginalized voices get little attention from corporate media giants—not because big business wants their viewpoints silenced but because there is less money in a smaller audience. Some advertisers go beyond simply being interested in media that reach the largest audience: They actually try to influence the information carried by those media. For example, some advertisers have strict policies against buying advertising from media companies whose programming presents their sponsors in a negative light (Herman and McChesney 1997, 7).

News itself has become a commodity—a product that is shaped by the forces of supply and demand and packaged to appeal to certain audiences (Hamilton 2004, 7). **Hard news,** stories that focus on factual information about important decisions or events, is increasingly deemphasized in favor of **soft news,** stories characterized by opinion, human interest, and often entertainment value. Why? Soft news sells. News has become less focused on the give-and-take of politics or the major events of the day and more on whatever will appeal to audience interests. Ratings and circulation, after all, drive advertising revenues.

Among those who are worried about the impact of the profit motive on news gathering are journalists. Most reporters, especially those working for television or radio, believe that the quality of news coverage is being diluted by profit pressures. Opinions among journalists are notable for their contrast with the executives who handle the

© Cheryl Diaz/Meyer/Dallas Morning News/Corbis

Uniss Mohammad Salman, 10, on his first day at the reopened Baghdad Elementary school, April 2003. This kind of human interest story, or soft news, is being increasingly emphasized over coverage of factual information and important decisions or events (hard news) because it appeals to wider audiences.

business side of news organizations. The latter acknowledge that the profit motive is changing what news organizations do and what they report, but they do not see this as a bad thing (Johnson 2004). Political scientists are not so sure. For example, newspapers have been reducing the number of reporters covering state legislatures, even as their importance as key policymaking institutions is increasing. Why cut coverage of an increasingly important part of government? Budgets and marketing. As political scientist Alan Rosenthal puts it, "Papers want to find stuff that connects with their audience . . . news that is more entertainment-oriented." The fact is that covering state government does not pad the bottom line like covering Hollywood (quoted in Boulard 1999).

Ultimately, the danger to the public sphere of private control is not that voices will be legally censored or that there will be government regulation of what can be broadcast or printed. The danger is that the information and messages that cannot attract a profit-making audience will simply be ignored. (See the Promise and Policy feature "Censorship and Wardrobe Malfunction.")

Media Bias

Most people do not perceive government censorship or corporate ownership to be the biggest problem with the mass media. Most people believe the biggest problem is media bias. **Media bias** is the tendency to present an unbalanced perspective so that information is conveyed in such a way that consistently favors one set of interests over another.

PROMISE AND POLICY
Censorship and Wardrobe Malfunction

It takes a lot to get the United States government to promote censorship of the press. For example, Janet Jackson's underwear (or lack thereof).

When Jackson had her infamous "wardrobe malfunction" during the 2004 Super Bowl halftime show and bared a breast to a worldwide television audience, the Federal Communications Commission (FCC) and broadcaster CBS received hundreds of thousands of complaints.

Now, if Jackson had appeared partially nude on the front page of *The Rolling Stone,* or even *The New York Times,* the government would have a hard time taking any action in response to reader complaints. The First Amendment, after all, says Congress "shall make no law" regarding the freedom of the press, not Congress "shall make no law . . . except if it involves pop divas exposing themselves."

But Jackson's exposure, because it came on television, makes things a little different. Unlike the print media, television springs from a public resource—the broadcast spectrum— which is regulated in the public interest by the FCC. As part of its charge to make sure this public resource is used in the public interest, the FCC has rules against indecency.

CBS was well aware of this. The network got a lot of bad press, a lot of complaints, and was duly apologetic. Congress proposed upping the fines for broadcasting indecency, and the FCC promised to look into the matter and hinted it just might levy one of those big fines. CBS, though, never faced a serious threat of censorship because of Jackson's bared breast. No, if the wardrobe malfunction led to the censoring of anyone, it was Howard Stern.

Controversial shock jock Stern had nothing to do with the halftime show that caused all the fuss. No, he was just broadcasting on his radio show what he's being doing for years—fart jokes, porn stars, and very frank interviews of the rich and famous. Very frank interviews of the not rich and famous, too.

Stern, though, got caught between the twin pressures of the newly vigilant FCC and a radio corporation nervous about profits and the political implications of having Stern on the airwaves. Clear Channel Communications is a corporation that owns more than a thousand radio stations in the US, including six that broadcast Stern. In February 2004, they suspended Stern's show for violating the company's policy of "zero tolerance" of indecency. In April 2004, the FCC fined Clear Channel nearly $500,000 for comments made on the Howard Stern show that same month. In response, Clear Channel permanently booted Stern from their radio stations.

Stern was not happy, arguing that he was the victim of a "McCarthy-type witch hunt." That is debatable. Yet what clearly seems to be the case is that Stern was censored—he was, after all, taken off the air in several media markets—by a mix of government and corporate pressure. Regardless of your stance on Stern and his, uh, eclectic mix of material, perhaps that should be a concern if you are interested in a free press.

Source: Steinberg, Jacques. 2004. "FCC to Fine Clear Channel $495,000 for Sex Talk." *New York Times,* April 9.

Virtually everyone believes the media are biased. Asked to supply a one-word description of the national news media, the most frequent response is "biased" (Pew Research Center 1998b, 22). This view of media bias was not always the case. Several decades ago most people regarded the news media as trustworthy and journalists as professionals who did their best to present information in a fair and balanced manner (Erskine 1970). Today, a large majority of people—as many as 80 percent—believe that members of the news media let their own views influence the way they report the news (Niven 2002, 39). There is no single or universally accepted answer to why this change has occurred. In general, though, trust in society's institutions has fallen across the board, and the media have shown no immunity to this trend.

Although most people see the media as biased, they see bias in different ways. There are indeed different sorts of media bias, and the evidence on whether bias exists—and if it does, whether it has any negative impact on civic life—varies according to the type of bias being considered.

Political Bias

When most people think of media bias they are usually referring to **political bias,** or the tendency to favor a political party or ideological point of view. Political bias has a long history in the American media.

Prior to the advent of electronic media, most print media were openly partisan. For the first hundred years of the republic, newspapers were often little more than propaganda organs for political parties or other organized interests. The Founding Fathers, for example, endured scathing attacks in the press that make the most negative contemporary news stories look mild in comparison.

Consider the career of James Callender, a newspaper editor who made no secret of his political preferences. Writing in the *Richmond Examiner,* Callender called President George Washington a traitor, a liar, and a robber. He referred in print to Washington's successor, John Adams, as a "repulsive pedant," a "gross hypocrite," and a "strange compound of ignorance and ferocity, of deceit and weakness." Callender was put up to some of these character assassinations by none other than Thomas Jefferson, who not only reviewed and approved some of these stories but probably paid their author to write them (Daniels 1965, 62–67; McCulloch 2001, 537).

The partisan press gradually yielded to the vision of **objective journalism,** which seeks to report facts rather than promote a partisan point of view and seeks balance by reporting both sides of any given story (Alger 1996, 122–123). An early promoter of objective journalism was Albert Ochs, publisher of *The New York Times,* who made it the basis for his paper's news coverage at the turn of the 20th century. This approach gradually became the standard for the mainstream print press and was adopted by the news organizations of the electronic media.

Today, however, few people seem to believe that the news media abide by the standards set by objective journalism. Most people agree that the press has a distinct partisan and ideological tilt. What they disagree on is which party or ideology the media actually favors. Conservatives tend to make the most consistent and loudest complaints of media bias, and they see the media as distinctly favoring Democrats and a liberal point of view. This claim is buttressed by research finding that reporters tend to be more liberal and more likely to vote Democratic than the average American. For example, reporters are roughly three times as likely to identify themselves as liberals than average members of the American public (Dautrich and Hartley 1996, 96–97).

Liberals reject the notion of a liberal slant in the media; indeed, they see quite the opposite: a media so cowed and intimidated by conservative critics that it is afraid to give right-leaning issues and candidates the same tough scrutiny it gives to the left. Liberals point not to reporters, but to the owners of the dominant media outlets. As we have already seen, these are mostly giant media corporations headed by conservative-leaning businessmen.

The problem with political bias in the media is that it is critics with a liberal or conservative bias of their own who make the charges. Although both the left and the right are convinced that the media systematically favor their ideological and partisan opponents, academic scholars have found virtually no evidence of ideological or partisan bias in the mainstream media. David Niven (2002) conducted one of the more exhaustive recent studies of media bias. His approach was to examine whether the tone and type of coverage of specific issues systematically changes based on whether they involved Democratic or Republican officeholders. His conclusion was that no such systematic differences existed: "In a comparison of coverage of two presidents, 200 governors, the mayors of eight cities, and 266 members of Congress, all matched to a member of the opposite party who had the same outcome in office, there is simply no evidence for partisan bias" (Niven 2002, 93).

Though other scholarly studies consistently come to similar conclusions, these do little to mollify partisans on either side. Perhaps the best evidence that there is no consistent, systemic partisan bias in the mainstream news media is that partisans on one side see the other as being favored.

Racial and Gender Bias

Although it receives considerably less attention, there is actually a much better case for racial and gender bias in the press, rather than partisan bias. A number of scholarly studies, for example, have found that female candidates for elective office are covered differently in the news media than male candidates. Compared to their male counterparts, females tend to get less news coverage. The coverage of female candidates also tends to disproportionately focus on women's issues such as abortion and places less emphasis on professional experience and accomplishments than personality, appearance, and fashion decisions (Kahn 1992, 1996).

Compared to their white counterparts, academic studies have also found a systematic imbalance in the portrayals of African American political leaders. In addition to looking at partisan bias, Niven's study (2002) also compared the coverage of African American and white mayors. Niven found that, compared to white mayors, African American mayors are less prominently covered in stories reporting good outcomes and are more prominently covered in stories reporting bad outcomes. For example, African American mayors get more coverage than comparable white mayors when a city's murder rate is increasing and less coverage when it is decreasing (Niven 2002, 105).

Communications scholars believe these imbalances are a product of the demographic makeup of newsrooms. While conservatives complain that reporters are too liberal and liberals complain that media owners are too conservative, both tend to miss what the majority of reporters, anchors, editors, producers, owners, and shareholders have in common: They are overwhelmingly white males.

For example, stories written by male reporters and published in *The New York Times* outnumber the stories written by females by a ratio of roughly 5 to 1 (Mills 1997). Of the nation's twelve most popular politically oriented talk shows, all twelve are hosted by white males, and eleven of the twelve are self-described conservatives, libertarians, and Republicans (Numbers USA 2004).

Negativity Bias

Perhaps the most open and obvious bias of the media is a tendency to favor stories that emphasize the negative aspects of politics and government. In presidential campaigns, for example, the large majority of candidates' comments are devoted to making a positive case for their candidacies. The large majority of the media's coverage of presidential campaigns, however, focuses on the negative attacks the candidates make on each other (Morin 2000).

In the media's defense, there are some good reasons for the bias toward negativity. The watchdog function of the press discussed earlier tends to promote an emphasis on reporting incompetence or wrongdoing in government. The press believes that it is its responsibility, at least in part, to alert the public to government misconduct, and the logical consequence is that stories emphasizing the negative get more coverage and more prominence.

Moreover, most of what government does is rarely considered news by journalists and editors. Imagine a front-page story headlined, "Government Agency Run Competently, Does Job Well." This is what actually goes on the vast majority of the time. It is the exception to this general rule that gets the attention of the press. There is an old cliché in journalism that says "dog bites man" is not news, but "man bites dog" is. The news media tend to focus on the unusual and the extreme, not on the mundane and the common.

The media's bias toward the negative may prompt people to be negative and cynical about politics. For example, the media tend to emphasize **strategic framing,** or giving prominence in its stories to who is gaining or losing on an issue. This focus can create a cynical and view of the political process, even when the people involved in that process are not being adversarial.

For example, Joseph Capella and Kathleen Hall Jamieson (1997) examined how the media frames political news by looking at a high-profile public meeting that occurred in 1995 between President Bill Clinton and House Speaker Newt Gingrich. The New Hampshire meeting was an unusual opportunity for two powerful policymakers to engage in a frank public give-and-take about the major issues facing the nation. Though they disagreed on many points, Clinton and Gingrich were mutually respectful and friendly toward each other. Yet media reports of this meeting did not stress the issues they discussed or the civility Clinton and Gingrich showed to each other. Instead, news stories emphasized the strategic elements of the meeting: Who scored political points? Who stumbled? Who won? Capella and Jamieson concluded that the media's relentless focus on the competitive aspects of politics promotes public cynicism about the entire process. Media bias not only seems to exist, but it also has the potential to do long-term harm to the public sphere.

Changes in the Public Sphere

Why has public trust in the media eroded, and why are so many Americans convinced that the media is biased? These are complicated questions that have a number of answers. As mentioned above, there has been a general decline in trust in most of society's major institutions during the past three or four decades, and the media are no exception to this overall trend.

Yet the revolution in communications technology has had a particularly notable impact on the media. This revolution occurred at the same time as a number of broad-reaching changes in the political environment. The net result is that compared to the media of the 1960s, 1970s, and 1980s, today a very different media are shaping a very different public sphere.

The technological changes include the rise of cable television and the introduction and widespread use of the Internet. These technologies altered a long period of stability in the media that were primarily associated with political news and information. Prior to the 1980s, political news was dominated by the three major television network news organizations, daily newspapers, newsmagazines like *Time* and *Newsweek* to a lesser extent, and radio news organizations such as National Public Radio.

This relative stability in the media context began eroding in the late 1970s and 1980s, and by the 1990s it was shattered. Cable television helped foster the creation of new television networks, including the rise of 24-hour cable news organizations such as Cable News Network (CNN), Fox News, and MSNBC. Political talk radio evolved into a major media presence, with personalities such as Rush Limbaugh broadcasting shows heard by millions and audience interaction with the hosts live on the air.

Then there is the Internet, which created a whole new communications medium. Web sites, email, listservs, and chat rooms—these create a medium that has the visual aspects of television combined with the potential for in-depth information of newspapers, along with the interactive features of a telephone. Table 8.1 demonstrates the market penetration of various media today.

These technological changes were accompanied by significant developments in the broader social and political environment. For example, the information revolution helped foster the rise of multinational corporations, organizations that defied traditional political boundaries. Japanese companies now make cars in America with components imported from China and Mexico. Multinationals may have tremendous economic clout in a state or country, but they are not bound to the laws of any single nation; it is profit, not patriotism or ideology or the canon of journalistic values, that is their guiding force. Media companies were not excluded from this trend. Companies like Time Warner and News Corporation are international conglomerates.

The past twenty years have also seen the rapid expansion of single-issue interest groups, which have taken advantage of the new communications opportunities to aggressively promote narrowly focused agendas. Groups such as the National Rifle Association can (and do) raise and spend millions backing candidates who support their policy preferences. Many of those millions are poured into sophisticated media campaigns that focus on narrowly targeted interests.

These sorts of developments had important consequences for the public sphere. Notably, they resulted in the decline of the media as gatekeepers and the potential for new technology to reshape civic engagement.

The Decline of the Gatekeepers

A **gatekeeper** is someone or some institution that controls access to something. In the mass media, the people who actually make decisions about what to print or what to broadcast (journalists, editors, and producers) and the organizations they work for have traditionally been considered gatekeepers of information.

Thirty or forty years ago, editors and producers at major news organizations could realistically be viewed as society's information gatekeepers—a relatively small group of people decided what political information reached a mass audience. That is no longer the case. Control over information has been pushed downward and made more diverse.

Individuals now have numerous choices to get very specialized and specific information. The Internet, in particular, gives individuals enormous control over the sorts of information they gather and consume. In some respects, this development

Table 8.1

Market Penetration of Different Media (in percentage)

YEAR	DAILY NEWSPAPER READERS AS % OF U.S. ADULT POPULATION	TELEVISION HOUSEHOLDS AS % OF U.S. HOUSEHOLDS	CABLE TV HOUSEHOLDS AS % OF TV HOUSEHOLDS	RADIO HOUSEHOLDS AS % OF U.S. HOUSEHOLDS
1970	77.6	95.3	6.7	98.6
1975	NA	97.1	12.6	98.6
1980	66.9	97.9	19.9	99
1985	64.2	98.1	42.8	99
1990	62.4	98.2	56.4	99
1995	64.2	98.3	63.4	99
1996	58.8	98.3	65.3	99
1997	58.7	98.4	66.5	99
1998	58.6	98.3	67.2	99
1999	56.9	98.2	67.5	99
2000	55.1	98.2	68	99
2001	54.3	98.2	68	
2002	55.4	98.2	69.4	

INTERNET USAGE CHARACTERISTICS

YEAR	INTERNET USAGE PER PERSON PER YEAR (HOURS)
1992	2
1993	2
1994	3
1995	7
1996	16
1997	22
1998	30
1999	33
2000	37

Source: Media InfoCenter, 2004 "Audience Penetration." *www.mediainfocenter.org/compare/penetration.*

has a positive impact on promoting the public sphere. Citizens now have virtually unlimited access to information, and they are much less reliant on a small number of gatekeepers to decide what information they will or will not get. As the new technology is often highly interactive (chat rooms and email, for example), some political scientists are optimistic that it will make it easier for the average citizen to participate meaningfully in the exchange of ideas and opinions that make up the public sphere (Kreuger 2002).

Yet there is also a downside to these developments. The rise of cable television and the Internet has also fueled fierce competition among media organizations, which now have to fight harder to attract and maintain an audience that has an abundance of information options. Some see this cutthroat competition as having profoundly negative effects on the quality of information produced by news organizations. Political scientist David Swanson (2000, 411), for example, argues the intense competition to find an audience "has led to a loosening of commitments to traditional journalistic values and canons of practice, resulting in news that is more sensationalized . . . and less governed by serious news values."

In other words, the old mass media filtered information on the basis of quality as well as its ability to attract an audience. The new media, largely controlled by profit-oriented corporations, is much more focused on the latter (profits) than the former. News has become a commodity, "a product shaped by the forces of supply and demand" (Hamilton 2004, 8). The end result is a public sphere that is at least as dominated by celebrity profiles or the latest diet fad than by important policy issues ranging from taxes to war. Media organizations have discovered that entertaining, rather than educating and informing, gets the bigger audiences and thus the bigger profits.

Information and Civic Engagement

Whatever the negative consequences of changes in communication technology, political scientists are increasingly interested in the potential impact on civic engagement. Internet chat rooms, email, and the like dramatically lower the cost of exchanging information. Will lowering the barriers and costs of exchanging information expand the public sphere in a positive way? Perhaps.

In theory, new information technologies hold the potential to draw more citizens into the public sphere. As one scholar argued, computer-based communication options provide "an inviting opportunity for democratic dialogue" (Benson 1996, 61). By creating a virtual commons where people can exchange ideas and opinions in a "spirit of community and civility," the Internet provides a unique way to expand and improve the public sphere (Benson 1996, 61).

In practice, though, the new communications technology may have contributed to a reduction rather than an expansion in civic interaction. People rarely surf the Web to have their opinions and beliefs challenged; quite the contrary, they tend to seek out sites and forums that fit their interests and preexisting preferences. Interactive forums do not automatically promote civil exchange. One study's conclusions about online media forums is succinctly summed up by quote taken directly from a forum post: "Destroy the scum, and then neuter their families" (Coffey and Woolworth 2003). Hardly the stuff of civil debate.

There are clearly tradeoffs in the rise of new media and how they are employed by a changing democratic society. On the one hand, "More citizens have more ready access to more information and opinion than ever before . . . concerning more topics of both public and personal interest" (Swanson 2000, 412). On the other hand: "The Internet is filled with advocacy masked as information, with rumor and innuendo, and with the simply outrageous." The burden of judging information for its reliability and importance to the public sphere has shifted toward the individual citizen and away from gatekeepers who served the old media model using a set of professional standards (Swanson 2000, 412).

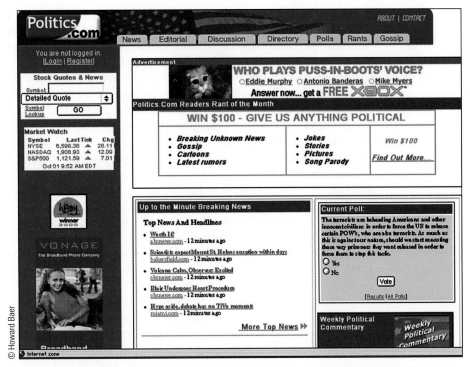

One of the most comprehensive and "newspaperlike" sites to offer information and news is *www.politics.com,* established by Howard Baer. It is intended, according to the site, "for a public disenfranchised with mainstream media," and it offers a directory with links to government and public organizations, radio and TV media, and statistics and polls on current issues, as well as opinion and discussion forums. However, unlimited access to information on the Web and interactivity do not necessarily promote civil exchange, and chat rooms can become venues for gossip or venting instead.

Thus, some argue that these developments are a good thing, because they expand the political freedom of the individual. If unlimited access to information and access to a virtual press is within the grasp of every citizen, this is a good thing for democracy. Others are not so sure. Rather than building democratic community, some see the new media environment as dividing the public sphere.

Performance Assessment

As we discussed in Chapter 1, the necessary ingredients for political freedom include the right to criticize current governmental leaders and policies, the right to propose new courses of action for government to follow, and the right to discuss political issues free from government censorship. The media give us the information to responsibly and effectively exercise all of these rights and thereby play a crucial role in connecting citizens to government.

At its best, the media help create a public sphere, which in the modern world encompasses newspapers, the airwaves, and the virtual information superhighway. Across these media travels a vast amount of information—messages and facts that connect government to citizen and citizen to government. When that information flows freely and with little government interference, the media contribute to the democratic promise. The government, with few exceptions, has mostly kept its end of the bargain by leaving the media in the United States unregulated and uncensored.

Yet there is much to criticize about the media and its role in civic life. Media critics conclude that intense competition, the concentration of media ownership, and the news-as-commodity approach produced by profit pressures have diluted the quality of news reporting, blurred the division between news and entertainment, and coarsened civic discourse. New communications technology has, if anything, exacerbated this trend.

The public sphere probably is bigger and almost certainly encompasses a greater portion of the population than at any time in history. Television and radio are all but universal. A virtual press is available to anyone who can cobble together a Web site. Email, online surveys, and forums offer fast, low-cost ways for anyone to get involved in just about any issue.

It is questionable, however, whether all this adds up to a more informed and more involved public. While the government does not censor, the market increasingly does. Or if the media market does not censor content, it at least segments into narrower and narrower niches. Information that cannot find a large audience holds little interest to profit-driven media giants. To avoid confronting opposing opinions and viewpoints, many people simply choose media outlets that confirm the beliefs they hold. Rather than a common space to hash out differences, the public sphere sometimes seems to dissolve into separate camps that yell noisily about the shortcomings of those with whom they disagree but rarely try to engage them in any meaningful way.

This segmentation reflects poorly on the performance of the mass media and on the performance of Americans as democratic citizens. The relative lack of government censorship and regulation means the system is upholding the core value of political freedom. What the media—and citizens—choose to do with that freedom is a matter of some concern for those interested in the promise of democracy.

Summary

- The mass media are the means used to transmit information to masses of people. The mass media include the print media, the electronic media, and the news media. Generically, all are known as the press.
- The press plays an important role in supporting the key democratic value of political freedom by helping to create a public sphere, a forum where information on issues important to civic life can be freely accessed and exchanged. It performs this role by giving us the information necessary to effectively and responsibly criticize governmental policies and leaders, propose new courses of action, and discuss political issues.
- The media has several specific roles in a democratic society that help promote the core value of political freedom. This role includes providing information and education, agenda setting, and acting as a watchdog and public advocate.

- The media has taken over several of the traditional roles of political parties and are now a primary connection between citizens and government.
- There are two basic threats to a free press: government control and private control. In the United States, government has always had a limited ability to control the press because of the First Amendment. Private control is more of a concern because profit pressures lead the mass media to ignore opinions and issues that will not attract large audiences.
- Most people believe the media are biased, though scholarly evidence supporting these beliefs is inconclusive. There is little evidence of systematic political bias in the media, although there is more evidence to support the idea of racial and gender bias. Negativity bias is largely supported by systematic research.
- Changes in communications technology coupled with changes in the broader social, political, and economic environment have changed the mass media in important ways. Technology has increased the size of the public sphere and lowered the costs of participation. Competitive pressures, concentration of ownership, and other trends have diluted the media's gatekeeper function, and some critics argue the quality of news reporting has been lowered as well.

Key Terms

agenda setting 238
electronic media 232
framing 238
gatekeeper 250
hard news 244
leak 241
mass media 231
media bias 245
misinformation 236
news 232

news media 232
objective journalism 247
political bias 247
press 232
priming 238
print media 231
prior restraint 240
public sphere 232
soft news 244
strategic framing 249

Selected Readings

Franken, Al. 2003. *Lies and the Lying Liars Who Tell Them.* New York: Dutton. A liberal satirist dissects the messages of the conservative media.

Goldberg, Bernard. 2001. *Bias: A CBS Insider Exposes How the Media Distort the News.* New York: HarperCollins. A longtime CBS journalist argues that the media put a liberal spin on the news.

Graber, Doris. 2001. *Mass Media and American Politics.* 6th ed. Washington, DC: CQ Press. An excellent overview of the media's role in American politics, written by one of the best-known political communication scholars.

Jamieson, Kathleen Hall, and Paul Waldman. 2002. *The Press Effect.* New York: Oxford University Press. A forceful critique of the media role in politics. Particularly insightful on the impact of framing.

Niven, David. 2002. *Tilt?* Westport, CT: Praeger. A scholarly study of media bias. Provides a good overview of academic research on media bias—along with many original insights.

9

Public Opinion and Political Socialization

Abraham Lincoln once said that "What I want to get done is what the people desire to have done, and the question for me is how to find that out exactly" (Crispi 1989, 1–2). Although many people would consider this a worthy and democratic sentiment, others might consider it naïve, foolish, and perhaps even dangerous. It is both.

Given what we learned in Chapter 1, the democratic appeal of Lincoln's words should be obvious. Lincoln is expressing a straightforward desire to put two core democratic values into action: popular sovereignty and majority rule. Popular sovereignty means that the highest source of political authority is the will of the people, and majority rule means the government follows the course of action preferred by most people. Thus, in a democracy, we should expect to find government responding to the demands and preferences of citizens.

Yet there are two problems with following up on Lincoln's desire to have the government do the people's bidding. The first is practical: How do you find out what the people want? This problem is far from trivial. In most democracies, and certainly in the United States, citizens are rarely of one mind about anything. The people want government doing different things on everything from taxes to military operations in Iraq. Ask the people whether they support Policy X to address Problem A and the answer will always be yes. And no. And maybe. It all depends on what particular group of people you talk to.

Public opinion is the sum of individual attitudes or beliefs about an issue or question. How is it possible to add up the disagreements and different attitudes into a clear expression of the people's will? Lincoln had no systematic answer to this question. Seventy years after Lincoln's death, Elmo Roper, George Gallup, and Archibald Crossley proposed such a systematic answer. These individuals—a journalism professor, a jewelry salesman, and a market researcher—pioneered the creation of scientific public opinion polling (Crispi 1989). Scientific polling provided the first reliable way to assess how citizens felt about a particular issue or question. As such, public opinion polling is viewed by some as an expression of the will of the people and as a means to measure the preferences of the majority.

Using public opinion as an expression of the popular will, however, raises a second problem: Should the government really do what the people want? Even if the answer is yes, how quickly must government respond to the expressed popular will to be democratic? Public opinion is a debatable basis for making policy—it is often uninformed and subject to dramatic swings. Most Americans, for example, cannot name their representatives in government, have little information about political issues, and are mostly ignorant about how government can or should translate their demands into action (Campbell et al. 1960, chap. 8; Jacobson 2001, 111). And on most issues, public opinion is fickle: It is subject to sudden shifts and provides contradictory signals about the preferences of the majority. If government responds too quickly, it will find itself out of step with popular sentiment.

Thus, the contradiction: On the one hand, citizens rightfully expect government to act on their preferences; doing so is the heart of the democratic promise. Yet doing so could (and does) lead to ineffective, irresponsible, and even undemocratic answers to the question of who gets what.

Though the Founders had no knowledge of scientific polling, they felt strongly that the whims of the masses should not guide government decision making. Accordingly, the Constitution did not establish a government that would quickly translate the will of the people into public policy. Indeed, as discussed in Chapters 2 and 3, it does exactly the opposite. It is designed both to frustrate the will of a majority when it threatens the rights of a minority and to keep key policymakers at arm's length from popular passions.

Yet the Founders also wanted to create a system that would govern with the consent of the governed. Popular governments existed long before scientific polling. In these early popular governments, the public relied on political participation to make preferences known to government leaders. Political participation has multiple forms, including voting, lobbying, circulating petitions, and mail and email to public officials.

The Founders tried to balance the contradiction between the core values of democracy and the desire for reasoned deliberation by shielding much of government from the stormy winds of public opinion; at the same time, political sovereignty rested with the people. The idea was to design a government that responded to the public will but acted in the public interest. That is a tough challenge because public opinion and public interest are not necessarily the same thing.

How well the political system achieves this balancing act is critical to understanding the promise and perform-

ance of American democracy. The link between the will of the public and the actions of government is the point where promise and performance are balanced. There must be a strong relationship between the will of the people and government action for performance to match up to the democratic promise. Yet effective governance requires decisions that serve the public interest, not just public opinion.

In this chapter we examine how well the American political system achieves this difficult balancing act by looking at what public opinion is, where it comes from, and the central role it plays in the American political system. This analysis provides a context for an examination of how political participation translates individual opinions, attitudes, and beliefs into action to influence public policy.

The Promise of Public Opinion

The basic promise of public opinion is to help connect the will of the people to the actions of government. By making this connection, public opinion helps deliver on the core democratic values of popular sovereignty and majority rule. As an aggregate measure of attitudes and beliefs, public opinion is one expression of the will of the people. When public opinion is strongly for or against a particular something, it signals to the government the preferences of the majority.

As such, public opinion carries enormous weight in decision making in a democracy. Public opinion provides legitimacy to proposed policies, serves as an important check on politicians, and forces the political system to be responsive to the wishes of the governed. No politician, political party, or interest group wants to be on the wrong side of public opinion. All of these political actors invest great time and effort into trying to persuade public opinion to their point of view, because it is much easier to advance a political agenda with the backing of public opinion.

Although public opinion is important in all democracies, it seems to have a special importance in the United States. As political scientist Anthony King (1997, 46) put it, "American politicians run scared—and are right to do so." King argues that Americans are much more insistent that their elected representatives be obedient to public opinion than citizens in other Western democracies. Americans express a strong preference for the **delegate model of representative democracy.** This notion of democracy holds that the job of elected officials is *not* to act independently, making whatever decisions they feel are in the best interests of the community or society. Rather, their job is to translate the views of the majority, whatever those views may be, into government action. The American political system is so focused on public opinion that the result has been described as a **hyperdemocracy,** a place where policymakers have become largely subservient "to every passing gust of public opinion" (Schell 1996, 72).

The delegate model of representative democracy makes clear the importance of public opinion; it is a primary means used to connect the wishes of the governed to the actions of government. But implementing the delegate model of representative democracy is much harder in practice than in theory. The problem is that public opinion is a good deal more complex than our original definition implies. This complexity means that public opinion can often be a poor basis for deciding who gets what.

The Elements of Public Opinion

The basic definition of public opinion as the sum of individual attitudes or beliefs about an issue or a question is simple, straightforward, and mostly accurate. But this definition oversimplifies what turns out to be a complex concept. What citizens think or feel about an issue depends upon a variety of factors, most of which can change quickly. Summing up the public's feelings on any given issue is more than just a problem of arithmetic—adding up who is for or against a proposed policy. To fully appreciate what public opinion is, it is useful to break it down into its basic elements: direction, stability, intensity, and salience.

Public opinion does not provide the government with clear guidance for making decisions related to abortion. Although attitudes and intensity have remained strong and stable, direction has been evenly balanced between for and against for many years and the topic's saliency wanes unless a specific issue becomes prominent.

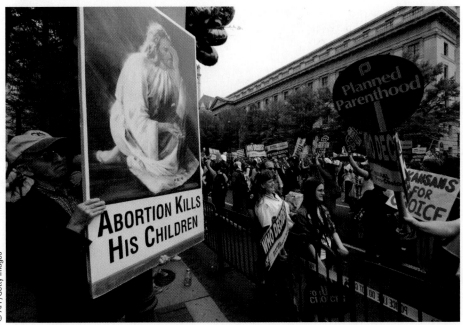

© AFP/Getty Images

Direction   The term **direction** refers to whether public opinion is positive or negative (favorable or unfavorable) about a given issue. On some issues, public opinion has no clear direction. Consider abortion for example. Public policy on abortion is a controversial issue, and the government is frequently pressured to defend or restrict abortion rights. What should the government do in order to follow the will of the people on this issue?

As it turns out, public opinion is of little help in getting a clear answer to this question. As Figure 9.1 shows, positive and negative attitudes about abortion are more or less evenly balanced, with a slight majority favoring some limits but against an outright ban. This division leaves government with no clear signal from public opinion, with each specific proposal to place limits on abortion the subject of its own controversial debate.

Stability   The factor of **stability** is the likelihood of changes in the direction of public opinion. On some issues, public opinion retains a clear direction (or lack of direction) over long periods of time. Strongly pro-choice and pro-life attitudes, for example, have remained relatively stable in the U.S. population for the last quarter century. During this time, roughly a quarter of Americans believed abortion should be legal in all circumstances, and a slightly smaller proportion believed it should be illegal

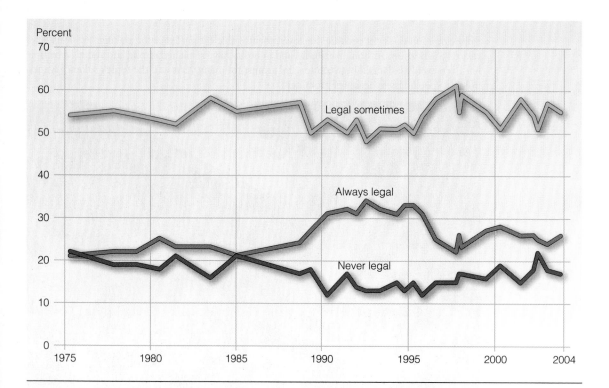

Figure 9.1

Trends in Public Opinion on Abortion, 1975–2004

Source: Gallup Poll News Service. *http://www.gallup.com/content/?ci = 11461.* Accessed July 25, 2004.

in all circumstances. The majority of Americans consistently put themselves between these two extremes. Notice that the trend line of opinions for the middle position in Figure 9.1 is essentially flat. The trends for the extreme positions diverge somewhat in the mid-1990s, but neither position has tended to greatly increase or decrease over more than a quarter century.

On other issues, however, attitudes and beliefs are more volatile, with the direction of public opinion subject to shifts because of new information or experiences. Contrast the stability of abortion attitudes with public support for the Iraq war. Figure 9.2 shows that support for military action in Iraq varied greatly over a relatively brief time span, moving from a large majority supporting the war in April 2003 to a majority opposed 15 months later in July 2004.

Intensity How strongly people hold the attitudes and beliefs that make up public opinion is the **intensity.** Low intensity tends to make public opinion less stable because people are more willing to change their minds if they are not strongly attached to one point of view. Public opinion on issues where large numbers of people have intensely

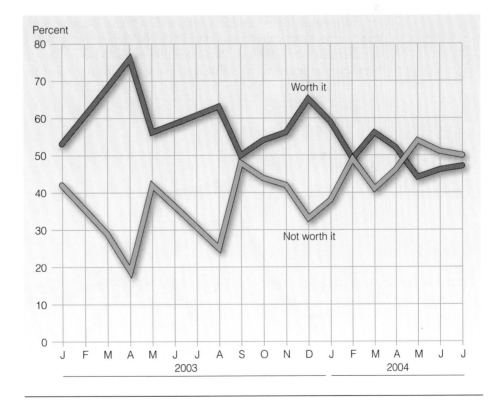

Figure 9.2

Public Support for the War in Iraq, January 2003–July 2004

Sources: *www.pollingreport.com; http://www.gallup.com/poll/focus/sr030610.asp?ci=10024.*

Note: Respondents were asked, "Do you think the result of the war with Iraq was worth the loss of American life and other costs of attacking Iraq, or not worth it?"

held views tends to be more stable. People with strong pro-choice or pro-life views, for example, tend to be very firm in their beliefs and are resistant to arguments or information coming from the other side.

Salience   The term **salience** refers to the prominence and visibility of an issue and how important the issue is to the public. Individuals differ in their opinions about what issues are most important—or salient. Some citizens may view abortion as the most important issue, while others view economic problems or crime or war as most important. If we add up all the differing views about what issues are most salient, we have an indication of what issues are most salient to the public in general at a given point in time. Abortion may be salient periodically if a proposal to limit abortion rights or a court case is prominently covered by the news media. For much of the time, however, most people do not view abortion as one of the most important issues facing the nation. Instead, the economy and crime consistently show up as two of the most important issues. Other issues, such as healthcare or war, sometimes arise if there is a great deal of media attention or political debate among policymakers. Figure 9.3 shows which issues are most important in recent years. Notice that abortion does not appear on the chart. Although some citizens feel very strongly about this issue, very few mention abortion as one of the most important problems for government to address.

To provide the government with a clear signal on what it is expected to do in response to a particular question or issue, the elements of public opinion must come together in a particular way. Public opinion needs to have a clear direction and reflect high levels of intensity, be stable across a reasonable period of time, and concern an issue of high salience. The concurrence of all four elements is rare. On most issues the

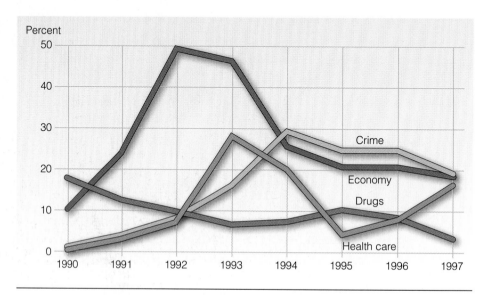

Figure 9.3
Public Opinion on the Most Important Problems Facing the Nation, 1990–1997
Source: *The Gallup Poll Monthly.* 1997. August, 44.

LIVING THE PROMISE
Public Opinion and the War in Iraq

What a difference a year makes. In April 2003, public opinion was firmly behind the war in Iraq, and Americans expressed high levels of support for President George Bush and his decision to take military action against the regime of Saddam Hussein. Iraq's army was quickly beaten, Hussein overthrown, and the dramatic early image of the war was the dictator's statue being pulled down by joyful Iraqis.

By April 2004, things had changed considerably. President Bush's approval ratings had dropped by nearly a third, and Americans were increasingly of the opinion that the war was a mistake.

What happened?

The obvious answer is that the quick military victory over Hussein's army became a long, bloody guerrilla war, taking a steady toll on U.S. troops and Iraqi civilians. Rather than welcomed as liberators, Americans increasingly came to be viewed by Iraqis as an occupying military force.

Political scientist and public opinion expert Ruy Teixeira argues that the opinion shifted so dramatically in the course of twelve months because of more than that. He argues that as the war unfolded, two questions slowly began to take hold in the public mind—two questions the Bush administration had difficulty answering.

The first question was, how do we get out of Iraq? As the war shifted from a quick and convincing win over Hussein's military to an open-ended guerrilla conflict, public opinion began to increasingly question what the United States was doing in Iraq. The Americans went into Iraq with only token support from other countries, and outright opposition from many (the United Kingdom being the major exception), meaning the costs in terms of lives and money were borne largely by the United States. Americans wanted to know how long they had to foot the bill in terms of blood and treasure, and there was no clear answer.

The second question was, how do we stop terrorism? The invasion of Iraq was justified by the Bush ad-ministration as a central front in the war on terrorism, backed up by claims that Hussein had weapons of mass destruction and significant contacts with terrorist groups. In the aftermath of the war, it appeared both claims were seriously inflated or even completely wrong. Terrorists continued their bloody work, bombing a Spanish train station, kidnapping and killing civilians in Iraq, while Iran turned out to have more of a connection with the September 11 plotters than Iraq did. No nuclear, biological, or chemical arsenal was found. In short, it became less clear that invading Iraq was critical to slowing terrorism or to protecting U.S. national security.

The result was the Bush administration's Iraq policies lost public support. While Iraq remained a salient issue, and one that many had intense opinions about, public opinion on Iraq turned out to be unstable, and its direction reversed.

Sources: Teixeira, Ruy. 2004. "The Big Shift: How Public Opinion Has Changed on Iraq." Center for American Progress; *http://www.americanprogress.org/site/ pp.asp?c=biJRJ8OVF&b=38980*. Accessed June 19, 2004.

government faces, one or more elements is missing; pubic opinion is divided or unstable, attitudes are not strongly held, or the issue is of low interest to most people.

Thus, rather than offering clear guidance, public opinion can often create difficult choices for government leaders. If the public knows little about a complex issue, considers it of little importance, and has no strong feelings one way or the other, public opinion can be a poor basis for deciding questions of who gets what. Public ignorance or indifference creates an obvious problem for a system with a strong preference for the delegate model. If public opinion cannot provide a competent basis for making sound decisions, a system premised on following the dictates of public opinion is going to reflect that incompetence. (See the Living the Promise feature "Public Opinion and the War in Iraq.")

The Competence of Public Opinion

The appropriate role of public opinion in democratic government has been the subject of debate for a long time. Some, like George Gallup, believe that public opinion is a scientifically valid measure of the will of the people. As a direct expression of one of the core values of democracy, they believe public opinion should play an important role in guiding political decisions. Others disagree, arguing that this view is not only naïve, but dangerous.

Walter Lippmann, a contemporary of Gallup's, expressed this contrary view. He famously argued that public opinion is little more than a collection of individual biases that rest as much on ignorance and prejudice as on knowledge and rational thought. His great fear was that unless citizens are well informed about political issues, public opinion could be easily manipulated by groups promoting narrow interests. Prejudice, ignorance, and the self-interested campaigns of interest groups are hardly the best basis for making policy that serves the public interest. Lippmann argued that rather than a delegate model of democracy, the political system would be better served by a **trustee system of democracy.** In a trustee system, public officials are expected to be to be experts on the issues, and they make decisions they believe to be in the public interest whether or not they are supported by public opinion. In effect, Lippmann argued that public opinion was too ill informed and too biased to be a guide for policies and laws that were effective and served the public interest. Governing was best left to an elite that was knowledgeable enough to see beyond its own interests (Lippmann 1949, 195).

Political scientists have found a good deal of evidence to support Lippmann's criticism's of public opinion. People often express strong opinions about issues, candidates, and parties, even though they have little factual information about these matters (Sears and Valentino 1997). Political scientist John Zaller found that "Most people aren't sure what their opinions are on most political matters, including even such completely personal matters as their level of interest in politics" (1992, 76). To back his argument, Zaller cites the work of another researcher, George Bishop, who studied the accuracy and reliability of public opinion by looking at self-reported levels of interest in politics. Bishop conducted an experiment where one group of people was asked whether they remembered a legislative bill that their congressional representative had voted on in the last twelve years. Only 12 percent could. When this group was asked to describe their level of interest in politics, 45 percent indicated low levels of interest. A second group was asked about their levels of interest in politics, but was not asked questions about their congressional representative. In this group only 22 percent indicated low levels of interest in politics. Zaller argues these sorts of findings lead inevitably to the conclusion that people are "heavily influenced by whatever ideas happen to be at the top of their minds. Thus what was most salient to many of the respondents in the Bishop experiment, who had just had an opportunity to observe how little they knew about politics, was that they were apparently not very interested in politics" (1992, 76).

Students of public opinion have long known that responses to public opinion polls are influenced by the wording and the order of the questions. This knowledge can lead to attempts to manipulate public opinion to support a particular issue or candidate. For example, a **push poll** deliberately feeds respondents misleading information or leading questions in an effort to "push" them into favoring a particular candidate or issue. In a push poll, the interviewer might ask the respondent which candidate he or she favors in an upcoming election. If the response is "wrong"—in other words, the respondent favors the candidate opposed by whoever is backing the push poll—there will be a followup question designed to push support away from this candidate. For example, the next question might be, "Would you still support this candidate if you knew he favored tax increases?"

The broader point here is that if public opinion is so ill informed, and easily manipulated, can it really serve as a competent guide for making public policy?

Elite Opinion and Issue Publics

The argument that public opinion is a poor basis for answering questions of who gets what obviously has some merit. Yet it can also be argued that, in at least some ways, public opinion is an informed and reliable basis for guiding government action.

Public opinion can be reasonably judged as informed and reliable in two basic ways—both involving the opinions of smaller, more select groups rather than of the public as a whole. One group that typically has high levels of information backing their opinions is elites, or people with influential positions within society. **Elite opinion** is the attitudes of people with large measures of political influence or expertise.

There is clear and convincing evidence that the opinions of elites are more informed than those of the general public (Erikson and Tedin 2002). It is also clear that the opinions of some help shape the opinions of others. For example, I may have little information about an issue, but if an official I admire, or my priest, or my boss, or a prominent member of my peer group is against it, I may be willing to follow their lead. Yet while acknowledging that elite opinion is more informed and serves as a guide for the opinions of others, using it as the primary basis for political decision making presents a clear conflict with the notion of popular sovereignty. This core democratic value is about the will of the people, not about the will of a small minority of elites.

The second approach to viewing public opinion as more competent than its critics suggest is to divide opinions by issue, rather than looking at opinions of elites or of the general public. While most Americans know little about the details of lawmaking and have low levels of information about most issues, many have clear preferences about the issues that are most salient to them. People tend to have higher levels of information on the issues about which they care the most.

Recognizing that people have well-informed opinions only on the issues that are most salient to them suggests that there is not just one general public opinion, but rather opinions held by numerous issue publics. An **issue public** is simply the section of the population with a strong interest in a particular issue. Issue publics tend to be well informed about the policy area in question and are capable of making sophisticated choices, even if the issue is complex. They are much more likely to be knowledgeable about the voting records of elected officials and the positions of candidates on the issues with which they are concerned. Armed with this base level of information, citizens can effectively monitor their representatives and the policy actions of government. They do not have to keep up with every decision and action by all elected officials, all of the time. All they need to do is keep alert to any unexpected actions related to the issues that interest them. For example, citizens involved on either side of the gay rights debate do not have to keep up with all the votes and decisions of their representatives. Knowing when representatives vote contrary to their views on same-sex marriage provides an informed basis for political opinion that is sufficient to keep government accountable (Hutchings 2003).

Because issue publics can offer an informed perspective on policy, these opinions should be recognized and respected in a representative democratic system. Although measuring opinions of numerous issue publics presents challenges, some argue that these challenges also offer an "exciting opportunity for more often engaging American voters in direct debates on policy priorities and direction. Such debates . . . are a sign of a vibrant democracy" (Lake and Sosin 1998, 70).

Despite the problems, public opinion polls can make a positive contribution to democratic governance. Many support "the common-sense view that when effective public opinion polls came on stream they positively added to the other modes of citizen expression" (Converse 1996, 649). Even the confusion created by the muddled and mixed messages that opinion polls often provide is not necessarily a bad thing. Instability and mixed direction show political leaders that the policy choices are not as clear, nor the stakes as high, as are often portrayed in partisan debate. Low levels of intensity and salience can demonstrate the need to transmit a clear and understandable message to the voters.

In short, even if they lack clarity, polls can still service a positive democratic purpose by prodding politicians into making a better case for their policy agendas. The backing of public opinion provides a large measure of legitimacy to government action. If polling does nothing else, it forces public officials to fight for and justify that legitimacy rather than simply assume it exists.

Interpreting Public Opinion

Obviously, public opinion is complex and contradictory. Even a minimal exposure to the U.S. political system is convincing evidence that many groups seek to measure and influence the public mood by putting a particular spin on everything from the president's job performance to whether it was worth invading Iraq. The net result is that public opinion often produces more confusion than clarity about the will of the people. Can public opinion be fully and broadly understood?

The short answer is no—assessing public opinion is an interpretive art, and on most issues there is plenty of room for disagreement about the real state of the public's preferences. It is possible, however, to have an understanding of how public opinion polls work. Such an understanding is important knowledge for any citizen because it can provide a realistic assessment of the meaning and value of the results being reported or promoted.

Polling expert Brad Edmondson suggests that whenever "a poker-faced person tries to give you the latest news about how Americans feel," you should ask some questions of your own (1996, 10). Edmondson suggests that getting the answers to four basic questions can help you decide whether a poll is a reliable indicator of public opinion:

1. Did the poll ask the right people?
2. What is the margin of error?
3. What was the question?
4. Which question came first?

Did the Poll Ask the Right People?   The validity of a poll, or its ability to accurately represent what it claims, is tied to the people who answered the questions. Practically, it is not possible to ask all Americans their opinion of a particular candidate or issue. When a poll finds that a certain percentage of Americans are for or against something, that percentage is an estimate. Pollsters make that estimate by selecting a relatively small group of people, called a sample, to represent the entire population.

There are many ways to go about getting a sample, and the poll's accuracy depends on the sample type. Scientific polls are based on the concept of random sampling. Although the mathematics used to calculate a random sample can get complicated, the concept itself is easy to understand: To use a small group to figure out the opinions and attitudes of a large group, everyone in the large group must have an equal chance of being in the small group. A **random sample** is thus one in which every person in the target population has an equal chance of being a poll respondent. If the target population is, say, Republican women, then the target population includes every woman who is a Republican. A random sample of Republican women would be a small group randomly chosen from the entire target population of Republican women. With random sampling, it is possible to get a reasonably accurate assessment of the opinions and attitudes of hundreds of millions of people—the entire population of the country—using a group that consists of a thousand or less.

Other ways to select a group of poll respondents run the risk of creating a **biased sample,** which is a group that does not accurately represent the target population and thus provides inaccurate estimates of the true opinions and attitudes of the target population. Common examples of polls based on biased samples are radio and television surveys based on viewers who are asked to call or email or vote online in response to a particular question. Such polls only reflect the views of those who were tuned into the television or radio program and felt strongly enough about the question to register their views. Because people who were not tuned in had no chance of expressing their views, such polls are not based on a random sample, and they are unlikely to produce an accurate picture of broader public opinion. Polls based on nonrandom samples are often referred to as **straw polls,** which also include "man on the street" interviews and mail-in surveys placed in magazines.

Even a very large nonrandom sample can produce misleading results. The classic example is a 1936 poll conducted by the editors of *Literary Digest* on the presidential contest between incumbent President Franklin Roosevelt, the Democratic candidate, and Alf Landon, the Republican nominee. The sample for this survey was put together using telephone books and automobile registrations, and more than 10 million ballots were sent out by the magazine. The resulting sample was huge—more than 2 million people responded to the survey. The survey results indicated the winner would be Alf Landon, and the magazine used the poll to predict a Landon victory. Never heard of President Alf Landon? Not surprising—Roosevelt won the election by a landslide, while Landon could barely muster a third of the popular vote.

Why was a poll based on a sample of 2 million so wrong? However large the sample, it was a biased sample. In the mid-1930s, the country was still in the grip of the Great Depression, and only the relatively prosperous had an automobile or a telephone. The well-off were much more likely to be Republicans. *Literary Digest* had essentially taken a massive straw poll of Republicans about who they were going to vote for. Not surprisingly, Republicans responded they were going to vote for the Republican candidate. Underrepresented in the sample were Democrats, who tended to be less well-off and much more numerous. Though fewer Democrats were asked their opinion, this did not stop them from voting.

What Is the Margin of Error?   Even a scientifically selected random sample will not be perfectly representative of a larger population. A well-selected sample approximates the target's populations, but it is almost always a little bit off. Fortunately, another useful feature of random samples is that statisticians can calculate the margin of error. **Margin of error** (sometimes called *sampling error*) is the amount the sample responses are likely to differ from those of the population within very tight boundaries that are known as the confidence level of a survey.

Reputable and reliable surveys always report a margin of error and a confidence level. Although the math behind them may seem complicated, margin of error and confidence levels are easy and intuitive to interpret. A poll with a margin of error of 5 percentage points and a confidence level of 95 percent means that there is a 95 percent chance that the sample responses are within plus or minus 5 percentage points of the target population's real opinions.

The size of the random sample determines how large the margin of error is: The larger the random sample, the smaller the margin of error. A useful guide to determining the approximate error of a random sample is shown in Table 9.1. Note that it is the size of the random sample, not the size of the population, that is important. A random sample of 1,000 will have a margin of error of plus or minus 3 percentage points in any large population, regardless of whether the sample is drawn from a population of 2 million, 20 million, or even 200 million.

There are two important points to keep in mind. First, the margin of error means that pinpoint precision about public opinion is unlikely; even a well-done poll can only show the likely range of public opinion. For example, a poll showing 47 percent of likely voters supporting candidate A and 44 percent supporting candidate B does not necessarily mean that candidate A is ahead. If the margin of error is 3 percent, it means candidate A's support ranges somewhere between 44 percent and 50 percent,

Table 9.1
Guide for Determining Margin of Error

SAMPLING SIZE	MARGIN OF ERROR
250	±6.0%
500	±4.5%
1000	±3.0%
2000	±2.0%

Source: Traugott, Michael W., and Paul J. Lavrakas. 2000. *The Voter's Guide to Election Polls.* 2nd ed. New York: Seven Bridges Press, 123.

and candidate B's support is somewhere between 41 percent and 47 percent. In other words, it is possible that candidate B has more support than candidate A.

The second point deals with the **confidence level.** As discussed earlier, a 95 percent confidence level means that there is a 95 percent chance that the true opinion of the population falls somewhere within the boundaries set by the margin of error. That means there is a 5 percent probability that the true opinion of the population falls outside that range. In other words, there is a 1 in 20 chance that the results of the poll are wrong and that the true opinion of the population is outside the margin of error.

These odds mean the probability of a well-done poll being wrong is very low, but they cannot be completely dismissed. To make a reasoned judgment on what a poll says about public preferences, it is important, at a minimum, to know the margin of error. Any poll that does not report a margin of error should be treated with skepticism. Without the margin of error, it is hard to judge whether a poll is an accurate barometer of broader opinion.

What Was the Question?   In order to judge the validity of a poll, it is important to know not only about the sample on which it was based and the associated margin of error, but also the wording of the questions asked. Pollsters have long known that how a question is worded can help determine how a question is answered. Consider this example taken from a real survey: "Do you want union officials in effect to decide how many municipal employees you, the taxpayer, must support?" (Edmondson 1996, 14). This is a leading question, meaning it is worded so as to prompt a particular answer or opinion—in this case, opposition to municipal unions. Such questions do not produce accurate estimates of true opinions.

The process of designing survey questionnaires is known as **instrumentation.** Reputable pollsters are aware of the potential pitfalls of writing questions that mislead, confuse, or prompt off-topic responses. Technical wording that is hard to understand, or questions that provoke strong negative or positive biases can easily threaten the validity of a survey. For example, asking whether people support welfare is likely to elicit a more negative response than asking whether people support programs to help the needy. The word *welfare* tends to prompt a negative image of individuals working the system and looking for handouts. The phrase "help the needy" conjures up an image of people in genuine distress through no fault of their own. These sorts of wording issues can determine whether a poll shows support or opposition to particular issue or candidate.

Instrumentation involves not just the wording of questions, but how they are structured. Many surveys rely on closed-ended questions, or multiple-choice questions. The advantage of closed-ended questions is that they ensure a degree of uniformity in responses, which makes data processing and analysis easier. Their disadvantage is that they prevent respondents from answering in their own words. By limiting the response options, a survey may miss important information and unanticipated trends (Manheim and Rich 1991, 115–123). For example, limiting respondents to the major-party presidential candidates in a presidential election poll will fail to gauge support for minority-party candidates.

Which Question Came First?   The order of questions in a survey can also affect answers. Edmondson (1996) looks at two polls taken at virtually the same time that used almost identical questions about tax cuts and the federal deficit. One poll reported 55 percent of Americans believed tax cuts and deficit reduction could be accomplished simultaneously while the other poll reported only 46 percent of Americans believed this to be possible. This difference, which is well outside the margin of error of the surveys, has to do with the order in which the questions were asked. One poll first asked if respondents favored a tax cut, then asked if they would still favor a tax cut if it meant no deficit reduction, and only then were asked whether a tax cut and deficit reduction could be achieved at the same time. The other poll only asked the latter question, that is, whether they thought tax cuts and deficit reduction could happen simultaneously.

What is probably going on here is that respondents in the first poll expressed support for a tax cut in the first question and then were reluctant to back away from that position when questions about the deficit were introduced, even if they favored deficit reduction. Respondents in the second poll had no question setting up a specific position on tax cuts and so were less boxed in by their own previously expressed preferences when the question of tax cuts and deficits came up. This example shows that the order of questions is critical; without knowing the order in which they were asked, it is hard to form a solid judgment about the validity of the results.

Getting satisfactory answers to the four questions suggested by Edmondson can help determine whether a poll is providing a real reflection of public opinion or is simply a collection of largely meaningless numbers. Of course, it is often hard to get the information required to answer all these questions. Few news reports include all the technical details of polls, especially on matters such as question order. At a minimum, however, it is critical to get answers to the first two questions (whether a random sample was used and the margin of error); without this information, it is wise not to invest any faith in poll numbers. (See the Living the Promise feature "Peasants under Glass.")

The Origins of Public Opinion

Many people do not base their opinions on information or rational analysis. Where do people get their opinions? Are they simply random thoughts plucked from whatever is foremost on people's minds when they are asked a question? If so, the consequences for democratic governance in a delegate system are not appealing. Making decisions on the basis of random impulse is not a good basis for effective governance.

However, from another perspective, public opinion is a complex product of many forces, and some researchers believe it may be quite competent. These forces can be classified into three broad categories: political culture, ideology, and political socialization.

Political Culture

A stable political system rests on a set of shared beliefs that include a broad agreement about basic political values, the legitimacy of political institutions, and broad acceptance of the process government uses to make policy. These shared beliefs constitute **political culture.**

LIVING THE PROMISE
Peasants under Glass

There is more than one way to uncover the views and preferences of the man or woman on the street. Opinion polls based on random sampling are the most reliable, but pollsters are also increasingly using another technique that has been nicknamed "peasants under glass."

This technique is the focus group. Focus groups are, in essence, an in-depth conversation with a small number of people (typically six to twelve). Unlike most polls, in a focus group it is practical to ask open-ended questions, let people take the conversation where they want to take it, and give them the freedom to make the responses that they want to make. It is not unusual for a focus group to be asked if there were any questions they felt should have been asked, but were not.

Thus, the big advantage of a focus group is that, unlike most surveys, it sets up a two-way flow of information. A focus group consists of a carefully chosen set of people who respond not just to the questions of an interviewer but to one another's thoughts and comments. Leading a focus group is a moderator, whose job is not to complete a survey questionnaire but to keep the group conversation focused on the issue of interest.

Because focus groups are usually chosen to bring together a group of similar people, participants feel more at ease in expressing their true beliefs and attitudes. This approach can offer useful information to political strategists who are trying to figure out what particular groups like or dislike a particular candidate or issue or how they will respond to particular proposals or arguments.

According to former Republican campaign strategist Lee Atwater, focus groups are useful because they give "you a sense of what makes people tick and a sense of what is going on with people's minds that you simply can't get with survey data." In other words, focus groups do not just help determine what people think but also why they think that way.

Two advantages of focus groups are their ability to gather a lot of useful information in a relatively short time and their ability to follow up on unanticipated responses or group beliefs. Because of this second advantage, focus groups are increasingly popular for those who want to "test run" arguments or proposals before they are made to the general public. For example, rather that make a major policy proposal in stump speech, a presidential candidate may test the proposal through various focus groups. Based on the response, the

proposal can be packaged for the maximum desired effect. Focus groups then, are ultimately a way to observe the responses of the man and woman on the street under controlled circumstances, almost like a scientist observing reactions under a microscope (hence, "peasants under glass").

Focus groups, however, also have disadvantages. The largest and most obvious is that they are not based on a random sample. This means that what a focus group says is not necessarily reflective of the beliefs and attitudes of the population it was chosen to represent. In fact, different focus groups taken from the same population may give different responses to the same general questions.

A second disadvantage is the need for a skilled moderator. A well-done survey instrument can be administered by anyone with minimal training and a telephone. However, getting useful information from a focus group requires a moderator skilled in group dynamics who knows when to take the lead and when to step back.

Yet, these disadvantages are outweighed by the potential to obtain personal and in-depth information about beliefs and attitudes, why people have those beliefs and attitudes, and how those beliefs and attitudes shape responses to candidates and issues.

Source: American Statistical Association. 1997. *What Are Focus Groups?* Alexandria, VA: American Statistical Association, Section on Survey Research Methods.

Political culture helps tie a polity together by providing a basic sense of what the nation is, what it stands for, and what political actions will be considered acceptable. A consensus on fundamentals does not mean people agree on specific outcomes. It means that people share a general sense of how those outcomes should be achieved and what those outcomes should not include. Most Americans, for example, express a strong "tribal loyalty" to the political system. At least in the abstract, Americans believe in the democratic process and believe the political system set up by the Constitution is the best way to run things. Support for our system does not mean everyone likes particular officeholders or that we all approve of how particular parts of the system (Congress, the courts) are doing their jobs. Americans may dislike—even loathe—officeholders and the policies they produce, but the people generally accept the officeholders as legitimate as long as they are perceived as holding their positions and passing laws in accordance with the basic principles of the democratic process.

This broad agreement on how decisions should be made has important implications for public opinion. One of the significant characteristics about the beliefs that make up political culture is that they are stable and enduring: direction, saliency, intensity, and stability are no problem at this level. Although Americans have occasionally quarreled over specifics, in general they have maintained a strong belief in and commitment to democratic institutions and processes as the appropriate means to political order. Anything that smacks of authoritarianism or oligarchy tends to find itself on the wrong side of public opinion. Well-heeled special interest groups, for example, are widely believed to wield too much influence, and Americans tend to have negative attitudes toward them—even though many belong to such organizations.

Political culture, then, acts as a unifying force. It sets the boundaries for what opinions, attitudes, and beliefs are considered legitimate. A positive or a negative opinion of presidential performance, for example, is "in bounds" even though these attitudes reflect fundamental disagreements among citizens. Getting rid of the presidency and replacing the system of divided powers with a parliamentary system would likely be considered "out of bounds" as this attitude does not fit with the political culture's broad commitment expressed in the Constitution.

Policies and actions that contradict the beliefs central to political culture tend to be rejected quickly, if they are considered at all. Political culture is the more-or-less stable channel through which the changing currents of public opinion flow.

Ideology

While political culture can help explain very broad patterns in public opinion, it does little to help us understand where opinions on specific issues come from. Abortion rights and the war in Iraq evoke conflicting responses from people who share the same fundamental beliefs that make up political culture. Young people tend to have different views than older people. What is the source of these differing attitudes?

One answer is ideology. As discussed in Chapter 1, ideology is a consistent set of values, attitudes, and beliefs about the appropriate role of government in society (Campbell et al. 1960). Ideology is critical to understanding public opinion because it gives people preferences about issues even if they have no individual stake in them. Heterosexual civilians, for example, will have strong opinions about gays in the military. Men have strong opinions about abortion rights. The opinions produced by ideology have important political consequences; they help drive political participation by prompting people to vote, join interest groups, and contact public officials (Bawn 1999).

While political scientists have convincingly demonstrated that ideology plays an important role in determining individual opinions on a wide range of issues, this knowledge redefines rather than answers the question of where public opinion comes from. If opinion comes from ideology, where does ideology come from?

There is no unanimous answer to this question. Some argue that ideology is an outgrowth of national traditions and political culture. Others argue that it is a product of electoral systems, group interests, historical events, religious beliefs, family background, life experience, or some combination of these factors (Gerring 1997).

Regardless of where ideology comes from, there is little doubt of its powerful role in shaping individual opinions. On many issues, all you need to form an opinion is whether you consider yourself a liberal or a conservative. This is because the key characteristic of ideology is a consistent, stable, and interconnected set of beliefs about politics and government. Individuals who view politics ideologically tend to have very coherent and consistent views on political matters, adopting regular and predictable patterns on issue positions, regardless of their levels of information.

Most Americans view themselves as "moderate" on political issues; very few consider themselves to be "very" liberal or conservative (fewer than 10 percent in each extreme). But young adults (18–29 years old) tend to have somewhat less conservative ideology than older Americans (those over 30). Table 9.2 shows the results of a Gallup poll conducted in October 2003, which confirms these assertions.

Table 9.2

Ideological Views on Social and Economic Issues

	VERY CONSERVATIVE OR CONSERVATIVE	MODERATE	VERY LIBERAL OR LIBERAL
	%	%	%
Social Issues			
18- to 29-year-olds	32	39	27
30 years and older	39	35	23
Difference	*−7*	*+4*	*+4*
Economic Issues			
18- to 29-year-olds	32	42	24
30 years and older	45	40	12
Difference	*−13*	*+2*	*+12*

Source: The Gallup Organization. *http://www.gallup.com/poll/releases/pr031105.asp.* Accessed November 8, 2003.

Political Socialization

Ideology emerges from a broader process called political socialization, which is the process of acquiring political values. More precisely, **political socialization** is the process through which a younger generation learns political values from previous generations.

Political socialization thus involves the transmission of values from one generation to another. These values help determine not just ideology but our opinions on specific issues. Traditionally, political scientists have organized the major agents of political socialization into five general categories: family, schools, peers, events and experiences, and the media (Erikson and Luttbeg 1973).

Some of these agents, like family, have an effect early in life. Others, like coworkers or fellow students, can influence political opinions as an adult. Some of these agents involve groups where there are face-to-face relationships over long periods of time (family or church, for example). Others involve secondary groups like labor unions or professional associations where contact among members is more limited and involves different people across time.

The broader point is that political socialization is a lifelong process—the agents of political socialization can shape our opinions about political matters at any age. Understanding the agents of political socialization offers a way to understand where public opinion comes from.

© AFP/Getty Images

Political socialization involves the transmission of values from one generation to another. Hip-hop star Sean "P. Diddy" Combs (shown here at the 2004 Democratic National Convention) has created a non-partisan coalition called Citizen Change to entice youths and minorities to vote in the 2004 election. He says he wants to make voting and participation in the political process "cool."

Family The family is the most influential agent in shaping individual political attitudes, and it exercises its major effect during the individual's most impressionable years. For most people, the family enjoys a near monopoly over a person's political attention during the early years of life, and children often learn to orient themselves toward politics and government by imitating their parents. For example, if parents think and speak well of the president, children tend to echo that support. If parents are cynical about government and politics, believing that politics and politicians are corrupt, their children tend to adopt those beliefs. As well, children tend to espouse the political party affiliation of their parents.

Political scientists have long recognized that the family's influence becomes less monopolistic as people are exposed to other agents of political socialization, but political attitudes do tend to persist across generations within families

(Jennings and Niemi 1975). How a child is politically socialized by the family generally has a lasting effect on his or her opinions.

Schools   Schools also play a major role in shaping political attitudes. Like family, schools are an important part of a child's life. In fact, one of the reasons for establishing public school systems is to ensure the transmission of the "right" political values to the next generation. Yet there are important differences between schools and family as agents of political socialization.

A major difference is that schools have less influence on fundamental political orientations such as ideology and partisanship. In the United States, there has always "existed a tradition of strong dissent to a public system of education that teaches political doctrines" (Spring 1998, 10). And while any number of groups and individuals may try to use public schools to promote their political agendas, the ability of schools to actually influence specific ideological or partisan political opinions of students seems limited.

Rather than instilling particular attitudes about particular issues, candidates, or parties, schools play a more central role in reinforcing the broader set of beliefs that make up political culture. For example, in school children learn to salute the flag, recite the pledge of allegiance, sing patriotic songs, and honor the nation's heroes. The very notion of public school systems in the United States was based, at least in part, on the desire to promote democratic attributes such as a tolerance of different opinions. This sort of socialization is more likely to promote positive feelings about the nation and its system of government, rather than turn children into fervent Democrats, Republicans, or supporters of abortion rights or gun control.

Schools do play a direct role in opinion formation, but this is because they are places where people from different backgrounds and different ideas come into frequent contact with one another. Postsecondary education in particular exposes young adults to political and cultural diversity. Exposure to diverse ideas is a central characteristic of higher education, and students often change their attitudes and opinions about political issues while in college. This change is at least partially due to college faculties and student populations that tend to be more politically, ethnically, and socially diverse than their counterparts in high school. Change of opinion in college tends to have less to do with professors brainwashing easily swayed undergraduates than with exposure to different peer groups with different political perspectives. Classmates are particularly influential because students are in constant association with one another. Close physical proximity to people with different attitudes—coupled with the feeling of many students that they have broken with the past—helps promote the formation of new political attitudes and new ways of looking at the political world.

Peers   Peer groups are important agents of political socialization, not just in school but throughout life. The political attitudes of adults can be influenced by peers from formal or informal networks where common interests are shared. These networks include churches, clubs, ethnic groups, neighborhoods, and professional and recreational associations. Peer influence on political attitudes depends on how important political concerns are within the group, the extent of agreement on such matters among group members, and how closely an individual identifies with the group.

Individuals' political attitudes may also be shaped by groups to which they do not belong, at least not in any formal sense. Such groups are called **reference groups** because they provide signals that people use to get their social and psychological bearings. For example, a white liberal may identify with the National Association for the Advancement of Colored People (NAACP), which promotes policies designed to help African Americans, without personally joining the group or receiving any material benefits from the policies the group supports. Reference groups can provide negative as well as positive symbols. A candidate's association with radical groups, such as the Ku Klux Klan or fundamentalist groups that refuse to condemn acts of terrorism, may be enough to turn opinions and votes away.

Events and Experiences   Our own experiences and the larger political context in which they take place can have a powerful effect on our opinions and attitudes. Someone who has just been mugged, for example, is unlikely to be convinced by statistics showing that crime is declining.

A powerful example of how an event can shape public opinion was the terrorist attacks of September 11, 2001. Prior to the attacks, President George Bush had middling job approval ratings from the public, and opinion polls showed little evidence the public considered conducting a sustained campaign against terrorism a policy priority. Following the attacks, opinions of the president's job performance became overwhelmingly positive as people reflexively drew together and backed the nation's leader in a time of crisis. This effect is known as a "rally' round the flag" response of public opinion. The campaign against terrorism became priority number one in most opinion polls, and the public expressed strong support for actions such as the Patriot Act and the invasions of Afghanistan and Iraq.

Yet other experiences helped drag down President Bush's approval ratings and support for the policies his administration pursued as part of the war on terror. The prolonged, bloody guerrilla campaign that followed toppling of Saddam Hussein's government in Iraq, the Abu Ghraib prison abuse scandal, and official acknowledgment that the administration had made mistakes in building its case for war with Iraq shifted opinions both on Bush and on support for the war. Figure 9.4 shows President George W. Bush's job approval ratings throughout this time.

Events and experiences do not have to be as dramatic as a mugging or a war to shape opinions. Routine events within the political system such as elections can also influence opinions and attitudes. Political scientists David Sears and Nicholas Valentino (1997) found that presidential campaigns increase levels of political information among young people and help shape their attitudes toward candidates, political parties, and particular issues. The central conclusion of this study was that people are socialized by political events, with their views on political matters shaped and strengthened by political campaigns.

The Mass Media   Another way to influence political opinion is through the mass media—television, radio, newspapers, magazines, and the Internet. The Internet has become an increasingly important tool of political and partisan persuasion (Browning 1996; Hill and Hughes 1997), yet it is television that is the most important source of political information for most Americans (Stanley and Niemi 2001).

Regardless of the media form, a number of scholars have expressed concern that the media shapes public opinion in a negative way. The concern rests on the media's

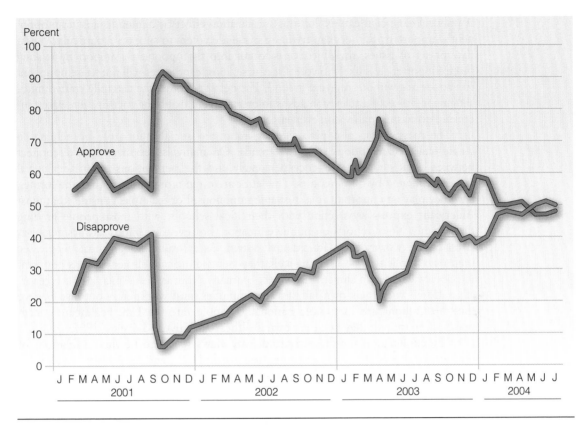

Figure 9.4

President George W. Bush's Job Approval Rating, February 2001–July 2004

Source: Washington Post Poll. July 8–11, 2004. *www.pollingreport.com.*

Note: N = 850 adults nationwide. MoE ± 3. Fieldwork by TNS. Trend includes ABC News and ABC News/*Washington Post* polls.

Respondents were asked, "Do you approve or disapprove of the way George W. Bush is handling his job as president?"

potential to make people skeptical and cynical about politics and government in general. Scandal, corruption, and incompetence are a staple of media reports on politicians and government. Some believe the strong focus on the negative helps make Americans more distrustful of government and more cynical about politics, even though federal officeholders operate under strict ethical guidelines and almost certainly engage in less unethical behavior than in other historical periods (Harris 1995, 61–62). Although studies indicate that the media only reinforce what people already believe to be true, the negative tone about politics, especially in television news programs, tends to promote negative opinions about government institutions, and these opinions persist even when more objective measures of government's job performance are positive (Hibbing and Theiss-Morse 1998a).

Political campaigns may take advantage of the negative socialization effects of television by running negative ads. Viewers of these ads become more cynical about the political system and the ability of an average citizen to influence the democratic process (Ansolabehere et al. 1994). This increased cynicism makes people less likely to vote.

A political campaign can exploit this socialization effect by aiming its ads at an opponent's supporters. Rather than trying to persuade voters to support a particular candidate or set of issues, the objective is to cut into the opponent's support by making those supporters less likely to vote. Of course, most candidates will not let an opponent run attack ads without replying in kind. The net effect of all the carefully crafted mudslinging in 30-second television ads is to create a very troubling socialization effect: increased cynicism, apathy, and even anger.

The mass media also play another important socialization role by helping to create shared perceptions of social trends. On many issues there is a disconnect between what people experience personally and the perceptions of broader social trends generated by news reports. The latter are often more negative than the former, and they play an important role in shaping opinions. For example, consider that most Americans express satisfaction with their local schools, with most people grading them highly. News reports on public education, however, are almost always negative, stressing the worst of the educational system. As a result, though most people see their own public schools as doing well, they view public schools generally as performing poorly. There is a similar disconnect on many other issues: Americans are generally satisfied with their own families, communities, and workplaces but also believe these institutions are in trouble nationally; people rate the U.S. healthcare system poorly, even though they rate their own healthcare positively (Loveless 1997).

The explanation for these contradictory views seems to be that evaluations of our local schools, families, communities, workplaces, and healthcare system are based on what we personally experience. Evaluations of these same institutions nationally are shaped more by the media. The contradictory opinions generated by these different agents of socialization present policymakers with a dilemma: Citizens want things to change based on the negative perceptions of broader social trends, but they also want to keep the status quo in their personal lives because they are relatively satisfied.

Public Opinion and Participation

Neither the government nor citizens have to rely on confusing public opinion polls to assess the will of the people. The attitudes and beliefs that make up public opinion can also be expressed through **political participation,** or the translation of a personal preference into a voluntary action designed to influence public policy. In other words, political participation is the process of turning an opinion into a direct contribution of determining who gets what.

Rather than wait for a pollster to ask their opinion, trust that the poll is well done and fairly represents their views, then hope that government acts on the results, the people can express their will directly through involvement in the political system. The causes and consequences of political participation are addressed in Chapter 11. What is important for the purposes of this chapter is to recognize that public opinion polls are not the only way to connect the attitudes and preferences of citizens to the actions of government.

Political participation involves everything from voting, to writing letters or emails to government officials, to joining an interest group. These activities may seem like a better guide to the will of the people than a public opinion poll. If an attitude

Political participation is the transformation of personal preferences into an action meant to influence policy. For Donna Ladd, Editor-in-Chief of the Jackson Free Press, editing an alternative weekly newspaper is about listening to the voices that are not being heard. Her newspaper offers both its own commentary and comments on articles from other newspapers across the country. Readers are invited to take an active role in the website, and to offer commentary. Lists of sites Ladd feels are important and of interest to her readers are a popular feature as well as the paper's news and op-ed columns.

or belief provides enough motivation to get someone to go vote or join an interest group, it certainly seems to indicate that an issue is salient and that an attitude is intensely held. The problem with participation is that not all people participate equally. As a result, some groups and their preferences exert a disproportionate influence on the political process. Some Americans do not participate at all; others limit their participation to occasionally casting a ballot; and still others concentrate on specific types of political involvement.

Scholars who study political participation as a means to connect the will of the people to the actions of government have raised persistent concerns that varying rates of participation across racial, ethnic, and socioeconomic lines mean that some preferences will be given more weight than others. This concern is consistent with the elitist perspective of the American political system.

Political scientists have found strong evidence that the voting rates of particular groups can determine election outcomes (Jackson 1997) and that disproportionate participation of those higher on the socioeconomic scale results in policies that favor their interests at the expense of those on the lower end of the scale (Bennett and Resnick 1990; Gant and Lyons 1993; Hill and Leighley 1992). But all research findings do not support this elitist perspective on participation. There is some systematic evidence that government can and does manage to respond to the broader currents of public opinion, not just to those who participate (Erikson, Wright, and McIver 1993).

Thus, participation may or may not be an accurate indicator of "what the people desire to have done," as Lincoln suggested. It indicates what the people who participate desire to have done, but even in a presidential election that adds up to little more than half of eligible voters. Moreover, those who do participate tend to be distinct from the broader electorate in a number of important ways: They are older, better educated, and more prosperous; they are less racially and ethnically diverse than the public at large; and they are more likely to be dissatisfied with the status quo, distrustful of government, more partisan, and more confident that their views not only deserve to be respected but should receive a satisfactory response from the government (Verba, Schlozman, and Brady 1995).

We have come full circle, right back to the lament of Lincoln that opened the chapter. Varying rates of participation mean that elections cannot be counted on to reveal what the people—all the people—really want. Although estimated turnout in the 1860 presidential election was a remarkable 82 percent of eligible voters, Lincoln won the presidency with less than 40 percent of the popular vote. Even with near universal participation, how could Lincoln respond to the preferences of "all the people," when over 60 percent of them expressed a preference for one of his three opponents? If scientific polling had been available then, Lincoln still would have found it difficult to determine what "the people" want done. Public opinion turns out to be more complex than Lincoln imagined.

 ## Performance Assessment

If aligning public policy with the will of the people is a basic promise of democracy, the United States should get relatively good marks for its performance. Studies repeatedly find a fairly good match between public preferences and government policies.

Despite the shifting tides of public opinion, the government does seem to "get done what the people desire to have done," as Lincoln put it. The government does this despite the jumbled, confusing, perhaps even elitist signals that public opinion sends.

Being responsive, however, does not seem to be enough, and the public often gives government little credit for this accomplishment. Americans remain cynical about and mistrustful of government. It takes an extreme set of circumstances to overcome citizens' skepticism toward government, and even then any reduction in mistrust and cynicism tends to be temporary. For example, in the wake of the terrorist attacks of September 11, 2001, public opinion rallied behind the government, and people expressed high levels of confidence and trust in the nation's political institutions and their leaders. That trust and confidence soon dissolved as people began to worry about the tradeoffs between civil rights and civil security, and some suspected that the Bush administration had oversold its case for war with Iraq.

The paradox of public opinion is that though people believe elected officials and special interests ignore their views, the exact opposite seems to be the case. Politicians, political parties, interest groups, and the mass media are engaged in a constant examination and analysis of public attitudes and are highly attuned to the public mood. If politicians are out of touch with the will of the people, this disconnect comes "in spite of relentless, assiduous, hugely expensive efforts to be *in* touch" (Schell 1996, 72).

The real problem with public opinion is not the decisions of government but the complex nature of the will of the people. In reality, on most issues there is no such thing as *the* will of the people—public opinion is plural rather than singular. And those wills are often vague and prone to change. Government does not ignore the will of the people; rather, it somehow manages to discover and act on what the people want done.

Few Americans are knowledgeable about or interested in a broad range of political issues, and for good reason. The average voter has no big incentive to be steeped in the intricacies of every issue on the public agenda. On a daily basis, most people (even political scientists!) have more pressing concerns: family, career, school, life.

The American democratic system has been successful not because it requires voters to be political experts but because it expects them to be capable of exercising prudence and common sense when appropriately informed. On this basis, the electorate is considered to be the most secure and least harmful repository of political power. As Thomas Jefferson put it: "I know of no safe depository of the ultimate powers of society but the people themselves; and if we think them not enlightened enough to exercise their control with wholesome discretion, the remedy is not to take it from them, but to inform their discretion by education" (Padover 1939).

The responsibility to educate people on the issues rests as much with political leaders as it does with voters. Governing by public opinion poll is not leading; it is following. Leadership involves staking out a direction and persuading voters that it is the direction worth taking. Political scientist E. E. Schattschneider once pointed out the importance of leadership in democratic politics with this analogy: "What people can do spontaneously, on their own initiative, is not much more than a locomotive can do without rails" (1960, 139). In other words, public opinion is an engine that will pull a policy train, but it is only useful if someone has a direction and has taken the time to prepare the ground.

The point here is not that the public is unqualified to exercise the power of popular sovereignty. Rather, the point is that lacking a clear articulation of the public will, government will have a hard time translating it into action. It is not simply a case of finding out what the people want and putting it into action. The public will has to be informed, cajoled, and persuaded to get behind an agenda or an issue.

Summary

- Public opinion is the sum of attitudes or beliefs about an issue or question and is seen as one expression of the will of the people. Most people believe public opinion should play a significant role in guiding government decision making in democratic systems because a basic promise of democracy is to align public policy with the will of the people.
- The problem with public opinion is that it is often ill informed, fragmented, and subject to rapid change. The government of the United States is designed to shield policymakers from the excesses of public opinion.
- Public opinion has four elements: direction, stability, intensity, and salience.
- Opinions are typically not the product of rational or knowledgeable analysis. They tend to be products of ideology, socialization, and political culture.
- There is a disagreement about the appropriate role of public opinion. Some believe public opinion is too poorly informed to make competent judgments about complex issues. Others argue that public opinion has a rightful place in the broader democratic debate and is more informed and sophisticated than its critics give it credit for.
- Public opinion polls are not the only way the people can make their will known to the government. Political participation sends a direct message by translating personal preference into voluntary action.
- Political participation is an imperfect reflection of the will of the people because different groups participate at different rates. Generally speaking, the well-off, the better educated, and the middle-aged are more likely to participate than the poor, the poorly educated, and the young.

Key Terms

biased sample   267
confidence level   269
delegate model of representative
   democracy   258
direction   260
elite opinion   265
hyperdemocracy   258
instrumentation   269
intensity   261
issue public   265
margin of error   268

political culture   270
political participation   278
political socialization   274
public opinion   257
push poll   264
random sample   267
reference groups   276
salience   262
stability   260
straw poll   267
trustee system of democracy   264

Suggested Readings

Hutchings, Vincent. 2003. *Public Opinion and Democratic Accountability: How Citizens Learn about Politics.* Princeton, NJ: Princeton University Press. A new study that tackles in-depth the notion of issue publics and how they provide a good basis for contributing to democratic policymaking and holding government accountable.

Lippmann, Walter. 1997. *Public Opinion.* New York: Free Press. Lippmann's classic work on the role of citizens in a democratic society and the problems with using public opinion as a basis for making public policy.

Putnam, Robert. 1993. *Making Democracy Work.* New York: Princeton University Press. A highly acclaimed study examining how political culture shapes and supports democratic governance.

Zaller, John R. 1992. *The Nature and Origins of Mass Opinion.* Cambridge, New York: Cambridge University Press. A classic scholarly study on where public opinion comes from.

10 | Elections

The 2000 and 2004 presidential elections were nail-biters. The campaigns were so competitive that polls could not identify a likely winner in the weeks before the vote. Arguments about who "really" won continued even after all the votes were counted (and recounted), the chads scrutinized, the lawsuits settled, and the voting machines praised and damned. These presidential contests, however, send a somewhat misleading signal about elections in the United States. Truth is, most elections, most of the time, are not very competitive at all.

Even presidential races are not competitive in most places. Yes, the contests between George W. Bush and Al Gore in 2000 and between Bush and John Kerry in 2004 split the national vote almost evenly. Look at things state by state, though, and a different picture emerges. In both 2000 and 2004, the Democratic candidate took California (the nation's most populous state) and New York without much trouble. Bush won big in his home state of Texas and in numerous other southern and mountain states. Only in a handful of states—Florida, Ohio, New Mexico, Pennsylvania, and perhaps a few others—was there any real doubt about who would win. In most of the country, there was not much competition at all.

Yet at least the presidential election was competitive and interesting, even if it was only in a few geographic pockets. Congressional contests, on the other hand, are typically snoozers. In 2000 and 2002, more than 80 percent of House members coasted to victory with more than 60 percent of the vote. Senate elections are a tad more interesting, but not by much. Of the more than 30 U.S. Senate seats up in each of these electoral cycles, only a handful was truly competitive.

Lack of competition is a concern because elections play a critical role in upholding the promise of democracy. Elections cannot deliver on the promise unless there is vigorous competition that allows voters to choose between at least two viable alternatives. In a representative democracy, deciding who gets what begins by choosing who wins office—the voters do not make policy decisions, but elect people to make decisions on their behalf. Elections thus amount to choosing the decision makers, and those are the most critical choices citizens make in terms of shaping government policy and holding it accountable for its actions. Yet elections in the United States, as we have just seen, are mostly one-sided affairs. Where is the choice if the outcome is in the bag before a vote is cast?

In this chapter we explore how candidates are elected to office. To fully understand what elections mean to the promise of democracy, we first need to understand the rules and procedures that structure the electoral process. Providing that understanding is the goal of this chapter.

The Promise of Elections

Elections connect the ultimate source of sovereignty in a democracy (the people) to actions of the institution with authority to decide who gets what (the government). The promise of elections is to make government responsive and accountable to the will of the people. Elections also help uphold the core values of popular sovereignty, majority rule, and political equality.

Elections to choose national representatives in the United States—that is, the president and members of Congress—consist of two steps: nomination and the general election. Nominating candidates is the responsibility of political parties. In general, **nomination** is the process through which political parties winnow down a field of candidates to a single one who will be the party's standard-bearer in the general election. In the **general election,** voters choose their representatives from among the parties' nominees.[1]

Methods of Nominating Candidates

How candidates are selected has important consequences for both the promise and performance of democracy. William Marcy "Boss" Tweed, who headed the powerful Tammany machine in New York during the 1850s and 1860s, once said, "I don't care who does the electing as long as I do the nominating" (Thomsett and Thomsett 1994, 14). A sure way to influence a general election is to determine the choices available to voters. Parties in the United States have used three methods of nominating candidates—legislative caucus, conventions, and direct primaries. The method of nominating candidates has varied over time and for president and Congress.

Legislative Caucus

The need for a mechanism to choose who would carry party labels into the electoral arena arose with the development of political parties. Races for local offices, state legislatures, and even the House of Representatives presented no great difficulty. These elections involved a limited number of voters living in a reasonably compact political district. Parties simply held meetings, called **caucuses,** of their most active supporters to nominate candidates.

Selecting candidates for statewide offices presented more of a problem. Transportation and communication were primitive, and it was no easy task to assemble party activists from all over a state. Nominating candidates for president and vice president presented the same difficulty on an even larger scale. The initial solution to this problem was to give the **legislative caucus** responsibility for choosing nominees for state and national offices. The party's members in a state legislature assembled to select candidates for statewide office, and party members in the House of

---

[1]Although independent and minor party candidates may also be choices on the general election ballot, in the United States only the major party candidates—Democrats and Republicans—are likely to have a realistic chance of winning office.

Representatives caucused to select candidates for president and vice president. In short, members of the party in government chose candidates for offices representing large constituencies.[2]

Although convenient, allowing members of Congress to select presidential and vice presidential nominees presented several problems: It violated separation of powers; it did not represent elements of the party in states where the party had lost; and party activists who were not members of Congress had no voice in choosing the party's nominee for president.

Convention

The nomination method that emerged to tackle the drawbacks of the caucus approach to nominations was the **national party convention,** a meeting composed of delegates from various states. In 1832, the Democratic Party under Andrew Jackson became the first major party to use the national convention.[3] The convention quickly evolved into the dominant means of choosing candidates at both the state and national levels. Delegates to state conventions were sometimes chosen directly by local party members. More commonly, delegates were selected by county conventions, whose delegates had in turn been selected by party members in smaller political units. The state convention then chose candidates for statewide office and the delegates to the national presidential convention. This system allowed rank-and-file party members to participate in choosing delegates, but the delegates, not the rank-and-file, made the key decisions. Candidate selection, in other words, shifted from party in government to the party organization, but it still excluded the party in the electorate.

Disillusionment with the convention began to grow in the early 20th century as powerful party insiders learned how to manipulate the system to their own advantage. Meetings to choose delegates were often called without notifying all interested people and were packed with ineligible participants. Disputes between rival delegations from the same area were common, and the convention that ultimately decided which was the "real" delegation often did so unfairly or without full knowledge of the facts. Foes of the convention began pushing for an entirely new way to nominate candidates that would shift power from the party organization to the party in the electorate.

The Direct Primary

The direct primary allows voters to choose party nominees for public office. In the convention system, voters have an indirect role—they choose the delegates who choose the nominee. A direct primary removes the go-between, allowing voters to select the nominee. Wisconsin passed the first law for a statewide direct primary in 1903. Today, all 50 states use the direct primary for some, if not all, nominations.

Primary laws vary from state to state. Some states, for example, hold **closed primaries** in which only registered party members may vote in a party's primary. That is,

---

[2]Chapter 7 explains the three elements of a political party: party in electorate, party in government, and party organization.
[3]A minor party, the anti-Masons, was actually first to employ a national convention, in 1831. The anti-Masons had no appreciable representation in Congress and could not use the legislative caucus effectively.

only registered Democrats may vote in the Democratic primary and only registered Republicans in the Republican primary; voters who register as independents may vote in the general election, but they cannot participate in party primaries. Other states hold **open primaries** in which independents, and in some cases voters from other parties, participate in a party's primary.[4]

Direct primaries increase the influence of rank-and-file voters at the expense of party leaders. The shift in power away from party leaders, however, is less in closed primaries than in open ones. Proponents of open primaries argue that they are more democratic because they allow all interested citizens to participate in the selection of candidates, and they criticize closed primaries as infringing on citizens' ability to participate in the electoral process. Defenders of closed primaries argue that participation by independents may undermine a party's chances by supporting candidates who are unacceptable to most party members. In open primaries, supporters of the opposing party also have an incentive to cross over and try to get weak candidates nominated so they will be easier to defeat in the general election.

Nominating Presidential Candidates

Both major parties nominate their candidates for president and vice president in national party conventions composed of delegates from the states. To win a party's nomination, a candidate must get the support of a majority of delegates at the convention. The rules that govern the nominating contests that choose the delegates influence the participants' strategies and tactics. Rules are not neutral. Because rules inevitably advantage some interests at the expense of others, they can determine outcomes.

The Allocation of National Convention Delegates

Both parties use similar criteria to decide how many delegates each state party is entitled to send to the convention: state population and support for the party's candidates in the state. Table 10.1 shows the number of delegates each state party sent to their national conventions in 2004. The most important determinant of the size of a state's delegation is population—large states get more delegates than small states. California, for example, had 441 delegates at the 2004 Democratic convention while Alaska had only 18 delegates. In addition, both parties give extra delegates to states with a record of supporting their candidates. Democrats use votes cast for the Democratic presidential candidate to award these extra delegates, whereas the Republicans reward states for electing a Republican governor, congressional delegation, and presidential electors. Oklahoma and Oregon, for example, are nearly equal in population, but strongly Republican Oklahoma has a larger delegation at the Republican convention while strongly Democratic Oregon has a larger delegation at the Democratic convention.

---

[4]Another option used in Alaska, California, and Washington is a "blanket primary" in which voters can vote for some offices in one party's primary and other offices in another party's primary. The Supreme Court invalidated this type of primary in *California Democratic Party v. Jones* (2000) because it violates the political parties' right to freedom of association. The Court upheld Louisiana's nonpartisan primary, which is discussed later in this chapter.

Table 10.1
Size of State Delegations at the 2004 National Party Conventions

STATE	DEMOCRATIC CONVENTION	REPUBLICAN CONVENTION
Alabama	62	48
Alaska	**18**	**29**
Arizona	64	52
Arkansas	47	35
California	**441**	**173**
Colorado	63	50
Connecticut	62	30
Delaware	23	18
Florida	201	112
Georgia	101	69
Hawaii	29	20
Idaho	23	32
Illinois	186	73
Indiana	81	55
Iowa	57	32
Kansas	41	39
Kentucky	57	46
Louisiana	72	45
Maine	35	21
Maryland	99	39
Massachusetts	121	44
Michigan	155	61
Minnesota	86	41
Mississippi	41	38
Missouri	88	57
Montana	21	28
Nebraska	31	35
Nevada	32	33
New Hampshire	27	32
New Jersey	128	52
New Mexico	37	24
New York	284	102
North Carolina	107	67
North Dakota	22	26
Ohio	159	91
Oklahoma	**47**	**41**
Oregon	**59**	**31**
Pennsylvania	178	75
Rhode Island	32	21
South Carolina	55	46
South Dakota	22	27

(continued)

Table 10.1   (continued)

STATE	DEMOCRATIC CONVENTION	REPUBLICAN CONVENTION
Tennessee	85	55
Texas	232	138
Utah	29	36
Vermont	22	18
Virginia	98	64
Washington	95	41
West Virginia	39	30
Wisconsin	87	40
Wyoming	19	28
Washington, DC	39	19
American Samoa	6	9
Democrats Abroad	9	
Guam	5	9
Puerto Rico	57	23
Virgin Islands	6	9
Totals	**4,322**	**2,509**

Source: The Green Papers, *http://www.thegreenpapers.com/.*

The Selection of Delegates

The parties select national convention delegates in two basic ways:[5]

1. The **caucus method,** in which national convention delegates are chosen at a state convention
2. A **state presidential primary,** in which voters directly elect delegates

State law determines which method state parties use to select delegates, whether the process will be open or closed, and the date when the parties select delegates.

Over time, there has been a trend of increasing use of primaries to choose national convention delegates. Figures 10.1a and 10.1b show the number of presidential primaries and the percentage of national convention delegates chosen in primaries. The first time a presidential candidate used primaries as a major part of a nomination strategy was 1912. Although relatively few delegates were chosen in primaries over the next fifty years, states began switching to primaries in the 1970s. In the last several elections, more than two-thirds of delegates at party conventions were chosen in primaries. With the rise of the direct primary, power over the nomination process has shifted away from professionals and toward amateurs.

[5]Delegates were once handpicked by party officials, but this method has largely disappeared. Although the Democratic Party continues to set aside a number of delegate slots for party and elected officials—governors, members of Congress, and party officials—these are a small proportion of delegates at the national Democratic convention.

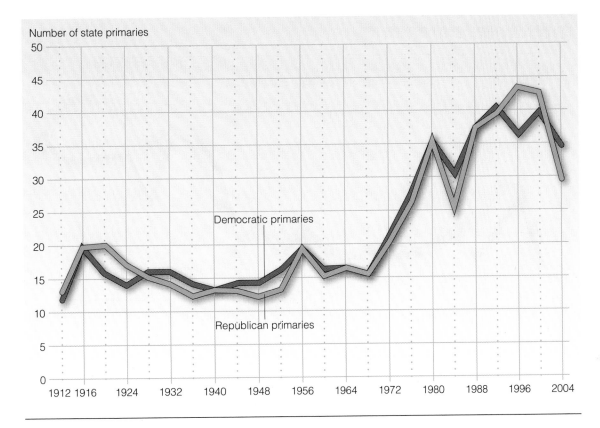

Number of state primaries

Figure 10.1a
Number of States Using Primaries
Source: Stanley and Niemi 2003, 66; 2004 calculated by the authors from *www.thegreenpapers.com/p04*

This shift in power has had a profound effect on nomination campaigns. First, the nomination calendar is now critically important. To attract the media attention and broader support necessary to be considered serious contenders, presidential candidates have to do well in the early competitions for delegates. The first two nominating contests are the New Hampshire primary and the Iowa caucuses, where only a relative handful of delegates are at stake. Yet these contests have enormous influence on the fate of presidential nominees. A poor showing in these contests can severely wound a campaign. The importance of these early contests has led to **frontloading,** in which states leapfrog their primaries to earlier dates in an effort to gain more influence in the choice of a presidential nominee.

Second, frontloading has made it critical for candidates to lay the groundwork early. A candidate must be familiar with the relevant laws and selection methods in all 50 states and understand the political situation in each. This requires political expertise, a well-administered national organization, time, and an enormous amount of money.

Third, candidates need to raise a lot of money early. The availability of money does not guarantee that a candidate will win the nomination, but the absence of money guarantees a loss. Frontloading has so shortened the time available to select delegates that candidates who do not have national name recognition, a national

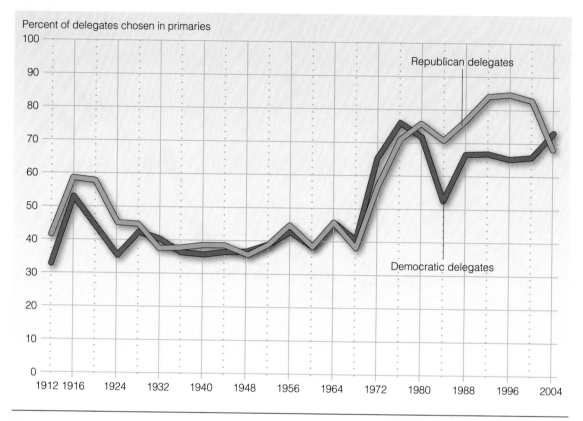

Percent of delegates chosen in primaries

Figure 10.1b
Percent of Convention Delegates Chosen in Primaries
Source: Stanley and Niemi 2003, 66; 2004 calculated by the authors from *www.thegreenpapers.com/p04*

organization, and huge sums of money at the start of the nominating contests have little chance of winning the nomination.

The Nomination Campaign

As political scientist John Haskell observed, "Everything important in the presidential nomination campaigns revolves around the selection of delegates who will get to the national convention" (1996, 33). To gain a party's nomination, a candidate must get the support of an absolute majority of the delegates at the convention—that is, 50 percent plus one of all delegates. The number of delegate votes needed to win is called the **magic number.** In 2004, for example, the Republican National Convention was composed of 2,509 delegates, so the magic number needed to win the nomination was 1,255. The Democratic convention was larger, consisting of 4,322 delegates, and the magic number to win the Democratic nomination was 2,162. Candidates compete for delegates in the caucuses and primaries, hoping to win the magic number of delegates. The nomination campaign is a winnowing process to determine which one of several candidates will win enough delegates to be a party's presidential nominee.

The nomination campaign is a winnowing process to determine which one of several candidates will win enough delegates to be a party's presidential nominee. Sitting presidents running for reelection typically have few, if any, challengers for the nomination. The party not in power, however, will have numerous candidates competing for the nomination. In 2004 several Democrats competed for the privilege of running against President Bush—nine of them are shown here at the New Hampshire Democratic Candidates Debate at the University of New Hampshire in Durham, New Hampshire, December 2003.

Sitting presidents running for reelection typically have few if any challengers for the nomination. Bill Clinton had no opposition for the Democratic nomination in 1996, and George W. Bush had no opposition for the Republican nomination in 2004. The party not in power, however, will have numerous candidates competing for the nomination. In 2004, for example, more than a dozen Democrats competed for the privilege of running against President G. W. Bush.

This winnowing process has a number of filter points that cull out weaker candidates. Political scientist John Kessel (1992) identified four stages of presidential nomination campaigns:

- Early days
- Initial contests
- Mist clearing
- Convention

The four phases blend together in the real world, but they are distinct enough to provide analytic clarity to aid understanding of how a nomination campaign progresses.

Early Days   The unofficial official nomination process begins long before the New Hampshire primary and the Iowa caucuses. The period between the election of one president and the first contest to pick the next one has been described as the **invisible primary** (Hadley 1976). During this period, candidates decide whether to enter the race. They begin raising funds, putting together an organization, and maneuvering for political advantage. The invisible primary takes place largely behind the scenes—there are no delegates chosen and few if any formal rules. In this stage, potential candidates compete for attention, money, and position.

The invisible primary serves to sort out and begin solidifying the field of serious contenders who will wage the battle for delegates. The chief criteria for assessing the strength of the potential candidates are standing in the polls and money. The early poll standings reflect mostly name recognition. For example, the two most popular Democrats in the early polls—former Vice President Al Gore, the 2000 Democratic presidential nominee, and Senator Hillary Clinton—did not run. Lesser-known individuals engage in activities to get mentioned in the media as potentially good presidential contenders. As early as two years before the 2004 election, for example, more than a dozen Democrats were mentioned as possible presidential candidates. During this time, potential candidates decide not to run and others enter the race.

Money to finance a campaign is an equally important indicator of a candidate's strength during the invisible primary. Although Kerry and Edwards were the early leaders in fundraising in the 2004 Democratic nomination contest, former Vermont Governor Howard Dean used the Internet to overtake his rivals in fundraising. Another innovation in 2004 was the "Internet primary" held by MoveOn.org, a liberal-leaning organization. Howard Dean's first-place finish along with his successful Internet fundraising made him the frontrunner as the invisible primary drew to a close, and the Democratic nomination contest continued to the next stage.

Initial Contests   The first official contests that actually begin the process of choosing convention delegates are the Iowa caucuses and New Hampshire primary. These initial contests are important only because they are first. The number of delegates at stake is small; in 2004, the two states combined had 84 of the 4,322 Democratic delegates and 64 of the 2,509 Republicans. These contests, however, provide the first major opportunity to generate some favorable national publicity and establish momentum for future contests. They also serve to begin culling out weak candidates. (See the Promise and Policy feature "How the Iowa Caucuses Work.")

All the candidates enter these contests, and the media devote much time reporting how the contestants fared, granting favorable free publicity to the perceived winner. The perceived winner is not necessarily the candidate who finishes first but rather the candidate who does better than the pundits expected. The perceived winner gets headlines across the nation, becomes an instant topic of talk shows, is granted the image of being a winner, and is the recipient of additional campaign contributions.

In the 2004 Democratic contest, for example, Howard Dean's impressive rise to frontrunner status in the invisible primary created high expectations in Iowa. His third-place finish behind John Kerry and John Edwards took away his frontrunner status and put more pressure on him to win in New Hampshire. Richard Gephardt, from neighboring Missouri, had campaigned hard in Iowa; his disappointing fourth-place finish prompted him to drop out of the race. Kerry won the New Hampshire primary the following week, cementing his status as the new frontrunner.

Mist Clearing   The mist-clearing phase is not a precise point in time. Rather, it is an ongoing process analogous to the lifting of an early morning fog, slowly bringing surroundings into focus (Kessel 1992, 9). This phase is characterized by a reduction in uncertainty as weaker candidates are sifted out in the contests that occur in the following weeks, and the major contenders emerge. The criteria for assessing success at

PROMISE AND POLICY
How the Iowa Caucuses Work

The Iowa caucuses traditionally serve as an all-important preliminary heat in the race for a presidential nomination. The winner does not get much in the way of convention delegates, because Iowa sends a miniscule fraction of the delegates needed to clinch a nomination at a national party convention. Instead, what a candidate gets is media attention and momentum.

Yet while the Iowa caucuses are recognized every four years as the first serious competition among candidates jockeying for their party's presidential nomination, they can be confusing to outsiders. The caucuses are not a primary election, but rather a rolling series of party meetings that start at the local level and culminate in district and state conventions that decide which delegates will go to the national party convention.

Both Republicans and Democrats organize their Iowa caucuses in the same basic four-step fashion:

1. *Caucuses in local precincts:* These are meetings in each of Iowa's 2,166 precincts, and the main function of these caucuses is to come up with 1,500 delegates to send to county conventions.
2. *County conventions:* Iowa has 99 counties, and each has its own party convention. The job of the county conventions is to choose 3,000 delegates to send to the congressional district conventions.
3. *Congressional district conventions:* In 2000, Iowa had six congressional districts. Each had its own convention, which chose district-level candidates to attend the national party convention and the state party convention.
4. *State convention:* The party's state convention selects at-large delegates to the national party convention.

At each of these stages, presidential hopefuls compete for delegates backing their candidacy, though exactly how these are chosen varies slightly for Democrats and Republicans.

In the all-important first round (the precinct caucuses), Democrats only allow registered Democrats who live in the precinct and are eligible to vote to participate. At the precinct caucuses, attendees join preference groups for candidates. A group must have at least 15 percent of those in attendance. Groups that do not meet the threshold are dissolved, and their members are free to join other groups. Delegates chosen to go to the next level are allocated to candidates proportionally based on the size of their group at each precinct caucus.

Republicans require attendees at the precinct caucuses to be eligible to vote but do not require them to be registered Republicans. Attendees at the Republican precinct caucuses first conduct a secret ballot to see who are the top choices among the candidates, and then delegates to the county convention are chosen by direct election (the winner gets all the delegates) or proportionally on the basis of a straw vote.

Okay, got all that? No? Well, don't worry. Just hope the good folks in Iowa get all the nuances. What they do in the caucuses every four years goes a long way to determining the choice the rest of the electorate gets in the general election.

Source: Wayne, Stephen. 2000. *The Road to the White House 2000.* Boston: Bedford/St. Martin's, 107.

---

this stage shifts from perceptions of who exceeded expectations to more objective indicators such as delegate counts.

In 1980, several states began holding their primaries on a single day in early March. Because these states chose a significant portion of delegates to the national convention, this is called Super Tuesday. In subsequent presidential elections, more states moved their nominating contests earlier, frontloading the process. In both 2000 and 2004, party nominations were settled by Super Tuesday, six weeks after the initial contests.

The National Convention   The national convention, composed of the delegates selected in the state primaries and caucuses, is the supreme governing authority of the party. The conventions meet for four days once every four years to nominate candidates for president and vice president and to conduct other party business.

Conventions now serve somewhat different purposes than they once did. As political scientists John Jackson and William Crotty observed, both the media and the public in general have become increasingly disinterested and cynical about national conventions. They argue that conventions have become little more than "marketing devices for the parties, the candidates and the issues and images they want to sell the public in the general election" (1996, 63). The state primaries and caucuses select the presidential nominee, and the convention simply acts as a ratifying body.

Although it is clear that modern conventions are carefully scripted to appeal to a mass television audience, such criticism may be overstated. Conventions have five major functions:

1. They officially nominate the party's candidates for president and vice president, which ratifies and legitimizes the results of the primaries and caucuses.
2. They approve a platform for the nominees to run on.
3. They provide a mechanism to encourage the losing candidates and disparate party factions to unify in preparation for the general election.
4. They showcase the party and its candidates on national television and create a favorable image with the public.
5. They adopt rules and regulations to govern the party at the convention and in the interim between elections.

The most important function of the national convention continues to be to choose the party's nominees for president and vice president. Whatever may have happened before, the actual nomination occurs at the convention. In recent nomination contests in both parties, the conventions ratified the winner who had secured a majority of the delegates in the primaries and caucuses: The convention has become a body that *legitimizes* the decision about the presidential nominee made before the delegates gather.

The convention typically ratifies the presidential nominee's choice of a vice presidential running mate. A number of considerations go into the choice of a running mate. Generally, there has been an attempt to balance the ticket with someone who differs in important ways from the presidential nominee to unify the party and appeal to key segments of voters. The most common characteristics to balance are region, ideology, and political experience inside and outside of Washington, DC. In 2000, Republican nominee George W. Bush selected Dick Cheney, a former congressman and secretary of defense, to balance his lack of national-level experience. Cheney's solid conservative record also balanced Bush's more moderate image. In 2004, John Kerry from Massachusetts picked fellow Senator John Edwards from North Carolina. This ticket has the traditional regional balance, but another consideration was Edwards' exciting populist campaign style to balance the more cerebral Kerry.

A second important function is adopting the platform, which is the central policy document of the party and a statement of its general philosophy. Platforms serve as campaign documents, and they provide a reasonably good indication of what the candidates will do as president. Although they do not deliver on all their promises, presidents attempt to follow through on the broad outlines of the party's basic document.

A third function of the national convention is to promote party unity. Candidates seeking a party nomination generally agree on policy. Unable to differentiate themselves on policy, nomination campaigns sometimes become contentious and personal. The partisan spirit at the convention gives the contestants an opportunity to put aside their personal disagreements and work together to defeat the other party's ticket. If disagreements prevent the party from unifying, its nominee will be in a weaker position in the general election. Byron Shafer (1988) found that since 1968, the party with the most harmonious convention was victorious over a party with a more contentious convention.

A fourth function of conventions is to present a favorable image on national television—what Stephen Wayne calls the "pep rally goal" (2000, 156). As reforms in delegate selection reduced the chance that conventions would exercise independent choice, this pep rally function has assumed greater importance. According to Wayne, party leaders and the nominee now view the convention "primarily as a launching pad for the general election" (2000, 156).

Both party conventions in 2000 and 2004 made the pep rally goal paramount. The Republicans abandoned the traditional roll call in which the state delegations cast their votes for the nominee in one evening in favor of a roll call that extended over several nights. The convention adopted a different theme for each night and chose speakers to present a favorable message and image to television viewers. Traditional party business, such as adopting rules and the platform, were relegated to the background. The Democrats also hosted highly scripted conventions intended to present a favorable and harmonious image to television viewers.

One function of party conventions is to present a favorable image on national television. California Governor Arnold Schwarzenegger helped achieve this "pep-rally goal" by giving a rousing speech at the Republican National Convention in August 2004.

© Getty Images

The final function of the convention is to adopt rules to govern the party. As the supreme governing authority of the party, the convention's rules may affect the party's future operation. The elimination in 1936 of the Democratic Party rule requiring a two-thirds majority to nominate a candidate reduced the likelihood of a deadlocked convention. Another controversial rule used by Democrats until 1968 was the **unit rule,** in which a majority of a state delegation could require the entire delegation to vote the same way on nominations and other issues, thereby disenfranchising the minority.

Electing the President

The presidency is the single greatest electoral prize in the United States, and it is the only office with a truly national constituency. The presidential election is the focus of more attention, more money, and more effort than any other election. The complex mechanism established to choose the president—the electoral college—is unique to the American political system.

The Electoral College

More Americans cast ballots for president than in any other election, yet the president is not chosen by popular vote. The race for the presidency is not a single contest for a national vote, but rather 51 separate elections in the states and the District of Columbia to choose slates of partisan electors. These electors elect the president according to rules and procedures specified in the Constitution.

The **electoral college,** a system "jerry-rigged out of odds and ends of parliamentary junk pressed together by contending interests" (Collier and Collier 1986, 303), reflects disagreement among the Founders about how to choose the executive. For example, some wanted direct popular election of the president; others wanted Congress or the state legislatures to have the responsibility. The electoral college was the bargain struck to satisfy these competing preferences (Jackson and Crotty 1996, 104).

The electoral college is not democratic, nor was it intended to be. Some of the Founders had a profound distrust of ordinary citizens' abilities to make sound judgments about choosing the president. Convention delegate George Mason, for example, argued that to allow the people to make such a choice made no more sense than "to refer a trial of colors to a blind man" (Benton 1986, 1,128). But even Madison, Hamilton, and others who believed that the president ought to reflect the will of the people suggested that this popular will should be filtered through intermediaries who would have superior knowledge and judgment. As John Jay explained in *Federalist* 64, "the select assemblies [that is, the electors] . . . will in general be composed of the most enlightened and respectable citizens."

The 2000 presidential election dramatically highlights the importance of counting electoral votes rather than the national popular vote. The outcome hung in the balance for more than a month after election day while the candidates contested a razor-thin margin in Florida. Democrat Al Gore's victory in the national popular vote over Republican George W. Bush had no bearing on who won the presidency. Neither candidate could win without Florida's 25 electoral votes, so choice of president thus came down to a postelection struggle to win a single state largely fought in the courts. Bush won the battle, received Florida's electoral votes, and became president. And the convoluted process of electing presidents became the focus of intense popular interest.

How the Electoral College Works   The electoral college is an awkward electoral device that has attracted its share of critics. The Twelfth and Twenty-Third Amendments, adopted to address some of the criticisms, made only modest changes. The basic legal structure and requirements of the process remain relatively unaltered.

The Constitution provides that each state legislature choose, by whatever means it desires, a number of electors equal to its total number of senators and House members. Although a state's total representation in Congress determines the number of electoral votes it has, members of Congress and those who hold other national offices are not eligible to serve as electors.

The minimum number of electoral votes a state can have is 3—every state has two senators and at least one representative in the House. Seven states—Alaska, Delaware, Montana, North Dakota, South Dakota, Vermont, and Wyoming—have the minimum. Larger states with more representatives have more electoral votes; California is the largest with 55 electoral votes. The total number of electoral votes is 538, the sum of 100 senators, 435 House members, and 3 for Washington, DC, as mandated by the Twenty-Third Amendment.

The electors meet in their respective state capitals in December and, as mandated by the Twelfth Amendment, cast separate votes for president and vice president. These votes are transmitted to the nation's capital, to be opened and counted in a joint session of Congress in January. To be elected president or vice president, a candidate must receive an absolute majority of electoral votes—that is, 270 of the 538 votes. The incumbent vice president, who is the presiding officer of the Senate, announces the outcome before the joint session of Congress. One candidate usually receives a majority of the electoral votes, and the vice president officially declares that candidate to be president. This procedure has produced its share of irony. In January 2001, Vice President Al Gore declared his opponent, George W. Bush, to be president. (See the Promise and Policy feature "The Strange Story of the Twelfth Amendment and the Death of Alexander Hamilton.")

If no presidential candidate receives a majority of electoral votes, the House of Representatives, voting by states, chooses the president from among the top three candidates. Each state has one vote; the state's representatives collectively agree on how to cast that vote. A candidate must receive 26 votes, a majority, to be elected. If no vice presidential candidate receives a majority of electoral votes, the Senate, voting as individuals, elects the vice president from among the two highest candidates. An absolute majority, or 51 senators, is required to elect the vice president.

The original idea behind this convoluted process was to have politically savvy electors, typically chosen by state legislatures, exercise their independent judgment to select the president. If this was the intent, it was quickly dashed. In the first two presidential elections, most state legislatures chose electors, although four states used popular elections to select them. Regardless, there was no division: In 1789 and again in 1793, George Washington got every electoral vote cast. Consensus disappeared with Washington's decision to retire from public office and with the emergence of political parties. More states began having popular elections to choose electors. The

PROMISE AND POLICY
The Strange Story of the Twelfth Amendment and the Death of Alexander Hamilton

The Twelfth Amendment to the Constitution was a direct result of the development of political parties. Originally, each elector cast two votes for president, and the candidate who received the most votes was declared president as long as the vote tally constituted a majority. If no candidate received a majority, the House of Representatives, voting by states (one state delegation, one vote), would choose the president from among the five candidates receiving the highest number of electoral votes. After the choice of president was made, the person with the next highest number of electoral votes would be declared vice president. If two or more contenders received an equal number of electoral votes, the Senate would choose the vice president from among them.

The formation and organization of political parties proceeded at such a rapid pace that, by the election of 1800, the electors no longer served as independent people exercising personal judgment about candidates' capabilities; rather, they acted as the agents of political parties and the general public. In fact, party discipline was so complete that all Republican electors in 1800 cast their two votes for Thomas Jefferson and

Aaron Burr. Although it was generally understood that Jefferson was the Democratic-Republican candidate for president and that Burr was the candidate for vice president, the Constitution provided no means for the electors to make that distinction on their ballots. The result was a tie between Jefferson and Burr, and as neither won a majority, the matter of deciding a president was thrown to the House of Representatives.

Ironically, the Federalists, despite their crushing defeat in the congressional elections of 1800 at the hands of the Democratic-Republicans, still controlled the lame-duck Congress, which did not expire until March 1801. They were therefore in a position to help decide which Republican would serve as president and which as vice president. Alexander Hamilton had a good deal of influence in the Federalist caucus and played a decisive role. Although friendly with Burr, he did not believe Burr could be trusted with the nation's highest office. In spite of disagreeing with Jefferson on policy matters, Hamilton swung the New York vote behind Jefferson, who became the third president on the House's 36th vote.

One result of this bizarre chain of events was the ratification in 1804 of

the Twelfth Amendment, stipulating that electors cast separate ballots for president and vice president. The amendment also provides that, if no presidential candidate receives a majority of the electoral votes, the House of Representatives, balloting by states, will select the president by majority vote from among the three candidates receiving the highest number of electoral votes. If no vice presidential candidate receives a majority of electoral votes, similar procedures are to be used by the Senate in choosing between the two people with the highest number of electoral votes.

A second, albeit indirect, result of this odd presidential election was the death of Alexander Hamilton at the hands of Aaron Burr. Although the two had long been friends, their relationship quickly soured after Hamilton deliberately rejected Burr in the House's presidential balloting of 1800. In 1804, the same year the Twelfth Amendment was ratified, Burr became a New York gubernatorial candidate, and Hamilton once again moved to block Burr's political ambitions. By this time, the relationship between the two men had become so acrimonious that Burr formally challenged Hamilton to a duel to settle their disagreements. In the early morning of July 11, 1804, Burr and Hamilton faced each other with pistols at twenty paces. Hamilton was mortally wounded in the encounter and died a day later, at the age of 47.

Founders' original vision of a body of wise men insulated from the winds of public opinion who judiciously picked the nation's highest official faded.

In each state and Washington, DC, the political parties nominate a slate of partisan electors. In November, citizens in each jurisdiction cast votes for president. But the voters are actually deciding which party's slate of electors will win the privilege of casting the state's electoral votes. Except for an occasional elector who is unfaithful, these electors do not exercise independent judgment. Instead, they are chosen by parties to vote for the party's nominee, and they almost always vote that way.[6]

How the Electoral College Violates Core Democratic Values

The electoral college violates the core democratic principle of political equality and has the potential to violate majority rule and popular sovereignty. Although choosing electors by direct popular vote rather than by the state legislatures is more democratic, this reform does not prevent the electoral college from violating these core democratic values.

The basic structure of the electoral college violates political equality because the value of a vote for president depends on where it is cast. To achieve political equality in the electoral college, each state's percentage of electoral votes must equal its percentage of the population. Recall that the number of representatives a state has in the House and Senate determines how many electoral votes it has. Because all states have two senators and at least one representative, no state can have fewer than three electoral votes. As a result, the electoral college gives the smallest states more voting weight and the largest states less weight compared to their populations (Table 10.2). At 55, California's share of the 538 electoral votes is about 15 percent less than its share of the U.S. population. In contrast, Wyoming's share of the electoral college—3 electoral votes—is over 200 percent greater than Wyoming's share of the population.

In addition, in every state some votes count more than others. In most cases, all of a state's electoral votes go to the candidate who wins a plurality of the popular votes. This winner-take-all feature means that the preferences of voters who supported a losing candidate are not represented in the electoral college. In 2004, for example, John Kerry won the popular vote in California and got all 55 of its electoral votes, while George Bush won all 34 electoral votes in Texas. The preferences of millions who voted for Bush in California and Kerry in Texas were not represented in their state's electoral vote.

Election of the president by the House of Representatives when no candidate has a majority in the electoral college also violates the concept of political equality. Because the House votes by state to select the president, the decision is not made according to the "one person, one vote" principle. The House has twice been called on to elect the president, in 1800 and 1824.[7]

Nor does the electoral college ensure that the majority will rule. Five times in the nation's history, the candidate who received the most popular votes failed to get a majority in the electoral college: John Quincy Adams in 1824, Rutherford B. Hayes in

---

[6]Because the parties choose individuals who have proven their loyalty, unfaithful electors are rare. Between 1820 and 2004, only 18 electors failed to vote for their party's candidates for president and vice president. In 1988, a West Virginia Democratic elector who was supposed to vote for Michael Dukakis for president and Lloyd Bentsen for vice president cast her presidential vote for Bentsen and her vice presidential vote for Dukakis. In 2004, a Democratic elector from Minnesota voted for John Edwards for president. There is speculation that this may have been an error because this elector also voted for Edwards for vice president. About one-half of the states have laws that attempt to bind the electors to vote for the winner, but there is some question whether such laws are constitutional because the Constitution clearly intends electors to exercise independent judgment.

[7]The Senate was called on to select the vice president in 1837. Martin Van Buren won a majority of electoral votes for president against four other candidates who received some electoral votes. But Democratic electors from Virginia withheld their votes from Van Buren's running mate, Richard M. Johnson, denying him a majority for vice president. The Senate elected Johnson vice president over the runner-up.

Table 10.2

Allocation of Electors, 2004

STATE	ELECTORS	POPULATION	% UNDER-/OVER-REPRESENTED*
California	55	33,930,798	−15.0
Texas	34	20,903,994	−14.7
New York	31	19,004,973	−14.5
Florida	27	16,028,890	−11.6
Illinois	21	12,439,042	−11.6
Pennsylvania	21	12,300,670	−10.6
Ohio	20	11,374,540	−7.7
Michigan	17	9,955,829	−10.5
New Jersey	15	8,424,354	−6.7
Georgia	15	8,206,975	−4.1
North Carolina	15	8,067,673	−2.4
Virginia	13	7,100,702	−4.0
Massachusetts	12	6,355,568	−0.9
Indiana	11	6,090,782	−5.6
Washington	11	5,908,684	−2.9
Tennessee	11	5,700,037	1.0
Missouri	11	5,606,260	2.5
Wisconsin	10	5,371,210	−2.1
Maryland	10	5,307,886	−1.1
Arizona	10	5,140,683	2.2
Minnesota	10	4,925,670	6.3
Louisiana	9	4,480,271	5.0
Alabama	9	4,461,130	5.7
Colorado	9	4,311,882	9.2
Kentucky	8	4,049,431	3.5
South Carolina	8	4,025,061	4.2
Oklahoma	7	3,458,819	5.7
Oregon	7	3,428,543	6.6
Connecticut	7	3,409,535	7.4
Iowa	7	2,931,923	25.0
Mississippi	6	2,852,927	10.9
Kansas	6	2,693,824	16.7
Arkansas	6	2,679,733	17.9
Utah	5	2,236,714	17.7
Nevada	5	2,002,032	31.0
New Mexico	5	1,823,821	43.1
West Virginia	5	1,813,077	45.3
Nebraska	5	1,715,369	52.5
Idaho	4	1,297,274	60.9
Maine	4	1,277,731	64.4
New Hampshire	4	1,238,415	68.2

(continued)

Hawaii	4	1,216,642	72.1
Rhode Island	4	1,049,662	100.0
Montana	3	905,316	75.0
Delaware	3	785,068	100.0
South Dakota	3	756,874	107.4
North Dakota	3	643,756	143.5
Alaska	3	628,933	154.5
Vermont	3	609,890	154.5
District of Columbia	3	574,096	180.0
Wyoming	3	495,304	211.1
Totals	**538**	**281,998,273**	

*Percentage difference between a state's share of the electoral college and its share of the U.S. population. Negative numbers indicate states that are under-represented; positive numbers indicate states that are over-represented.

1876, Benjamin Harrison in 1888, John Kennedy[8] in 1960, and George W. Bush in 2000. The electoral college may fail to choose the winner of the national popular vote even if every elector votes for the candidate he or she was chosen to vote for. This can occur because electoral votes are allocated on a winner-take-all basis, regardless of how close or lopsided the vote is in the state. Table 10.3 illustrates an extreme example in which a candidate is on the ballot in only the 11 largest states. If this candidate were to win the popular vote in these states even by a one-vote margin and get no votes in any other states, he or she would be elected president with 271 electoral votes. Although the other candidate would have had a larger popular vote margin nationally, this popular candidate would receive only 267 electoral votes from the other 39 states.

The mathematical advantage of the small states can also cause the electoral college to fail to choose the popular winner. In the 2000 presidential election, George W. Bush lost the popular vote nationwide, but he won a majority of electoral votes in part because of his success in the smallest states. Bush won 54 electoral votes from 13 of the 19 smallest states, where his popular vote total was about 2.7 million. More than twice as many people—5.7 million—voted for Al Gore in California to give him the same number of electoral votes.

Proposals to Reform the Electoral College   These defects in the electoral college have led to several reform proposals. In recent years, attention has focused on three basic plans:

1.   The proportional plan
2.   The district plan
3.   The direct popular election plan

[8]Kennedy is typically credited with a small popular vote victory over Nixon. Political scientists question this result. Kennedy's name did not appear on the ballot in Alabama. Instead, only the names of Democratic electors appeared on the ballot, and 6 of the 11 chosen did not support Kennedy. Reports listing Kennedy as the popular vote winner nationwide count all votes for Democratic electors as popular votes for Kennedy, even though some of these popular votes clearly were not for Kennedy. If the popular vote in Alabama is divided in proportion to how the electors voted, Nixon turns out to be the popular vote winner nation wide by a small margin (Gaines 2001).

Table 10.3
How the Popular Vote Winner Can Lose in the Electoral College

STATE	ELECTORAL VOTES	TOTAL VOTES CAST IN STATE	MINIMUM VOTES NEEDED TO WIN STATE'S ELECTORAL VOTES
California	55	9,830,550	4,915,276
Texas	34	7,346,779	3,673,391
New York	31	6,779,917	3,389,960
Florida	27	7,514,166	3,757,084
Illinois	21	5,140,172	2,570,087
Pennsylvania	21	5,640,194	2,820,098
Ohio	20	5,455,811	2,727,907
Michigan	17	4,778,322	2,389,162
New Jersey	15	3,386,814	1,693,408
Georgia	15	3,235,030	1,617,516
North Carolina	15	3,395,094	1,697,548
Subtotal for 11 Largest States	**271**	62,502,849	31,251,436
Percent of Total	50.4%		**(27.0%)**
Other 39 States	267	53,046,542	
Total	538	115,549,391	

Source: Calculated by Jon Bond and Kevin Smith.
Note: Popular votes cast for the two major party candidates in 2004. Minimum number of votes needed to win a state's electoral votes is 50 percent plus 1 of the two-party vote.

The **proportional plan** would divide each state's electoral votes in proportion to the division of the popular vote. For example, a candidate receiving 60 percent of the popular vote in a state would get 60 percent of its electoral votes. Other features of the electoral college would remain, such as requiring a majority of electoral votes for a candidate to be elected, and having Congress choose the president if no candidate receives a majority.

The **district plan** would return to the method some states used early in the nation's history. The district plan allocates one electoral vote to the presidential candidate who receives a plurality in a House district; the state's remaining two electoral votes go to the candidate who wins a plurality statewide.

Neither of these reforms would require amending the Constitution. The Constitution says that state legislatures can choose electors however they wish, so any state legislature could choose to allocate the state's electoral votes in proportion to the statewide percentages or by congressional district. Maine and Nebraska currently use the district plan, and a number of states have considered adopting the proportional plan.

The **direct popular election plan** would abolish the electoral college and permit voters in the 50 states and the District of Columbia to choose the president. A majority of the public has consistently supported direct election for several decades (Edwards 2004). Implementing this reform, however, has proved remarkably difficult. Adopting this reform would require a constitutional amendment to abolish the electoral college, and thus far it has proved impossible to muster the two-thirds majorities in both houses of Congress to propose an amendment. Even if Congress were to pass such an amendment, it is unlikely that it would be ratified by three-fourths of state legislatures.

If the goal of reform is to ensure that the winner of the national popular vote is elected president, only direct popular election guarantees it. Table 10.4 shows what would have happened in the last thirteen presidential elections if electoral votes had been allocated under the various reforms. At least in some cases, reform of the electoral college would have changed who won the presidency.

Table 10.4
Winner of the Presidency under the Various Electoral College Reforms

	ELECTION YEAR	POPULAR VOTE WINNER	ELECTORAL COLLEGE WINNER	PROPORTIONAL PLAN WINNER	DISTRICT PLAN WINNER
Eisenhower (R)	1956	Eisenhower (R) 57.4%	Eisenhower (R) 457	Eisenhower (R) 296.7	Eisenhower (R) 411
Kennedy (D)	**1960**	**Nixon (R)***	**Kennedy (D) 219 to 303**	**Uncertain/House 266.1**	Nixon (R) 278
Johnson (D)	1964	Johnson (D) 61.0%	Johnson (D) 486	Johnson (D) 320.0	Johnson (D) 466
Nixon (R)	**1968**	**Nixon (R) 43.2% plurality**	Nixon (R) 301	**Uncertain/House 231.5**	Nixon (R) 289
Nixon (R)	1972	Nixon (R) 60.7%	Nixon (R) 520	Nixon (R) 330.3	Nixon (R) 474
Carter (D)	**1976**	**Carter (D) 50.1%**	Carter (D) 297	**Uncertain/House 269.7**	**Uncertain/House 269**
Reagan (R)	1980	Reagan (R) 50.7	Reagan (R) 489	Reagan (R) 272.9	Reagan (R) 396
Reagan (R)	1984	Reagan (R) 58.8%	Reagan (R) 525	Reagan (R) 317.6	Reagan (R) 468
Bush (R)	1988	Bush (R) 53.4%	Bush (R) 426	Bush (R) 287.8	Bush (R) 379
Clinton (D)	**1992**	**Clinton (D) 43.0% plurality**	Clinton (D) 370	**Uncertain/House 231.6**	Clinton (D) 324
Clinton (D)	**1996**	**Clinton (D) 49.2% plurality**	Clinton (D) 379	**Uncertain/House 262.0**	Clinton (D) 345
Bush, G.W. (R)	**2000**	**Gore (D) 48.3% plurality**	**Bush, G.W. (R) 266 to 273**	**Uncertain/House 258.3**	**Bush, G.W. (R) 250 to 288**
Bush, G.W. (R)	2004	Bush, G.W. (R) 51.5%	Bush, G.W. (R) 286	Bush, G.W. (R) 274.92	Bush, G.W. (R) N/A

Source: Adapted from Wayne (2000, 313-14) for 1956 to 1996 elections; 2000 and 2004 results calculated by the authors.
*Note: Kennedy is typically credited with a national popular vote victory in 1960. Footnote 8 explains why political scientists believe that Nixon actually won the popular vote.

Under the proportional plan, no candidate would have received a majority of electoral votes in half of these elections. If other features of the electoral college were maintained, these elections would have been decided by the House. The House would probably have chosen the popular vote winners in most of these elections, but there is no guarantee. For example, in 1996, Ross Perot and other minor party candidates would have received enough electoral votes under the proportional plan to deny Clinton, the popular winner, a majority in the electoral college. Republicans controlled the House of Representatives in 1996, increasing the chances that the House would have chosen Bob Dole, who finished second in the popular vote. The district plan fares slightly better, though in 1976, Gerald Ford and Jimmy Carter would have tied in electoral votes, throwing the election to the House.

Neither the proportional plan nor the district plan will fully correct the electoral college's violation of the core value of political equality. The district plan consistently prevents equal weighting of votes because every state regardless of population gets two electoral votes for its two senators and the district plan awards two electoral votes to the statewide winner. And since the electoral votes awarded by congressional district go the plurality winner in the district, the preferences of voters who support the losing candidate in every district are not represented in the electoral vote. The proportional plan does a better job of weighting votes equally, but this plan frequently sends the election to the House. Recall that if the House elects the president, the voting is by state—each state has one vote, and it takes a majority of states to elect the president. Voting by state means that Wyoming, with fewer than 500,000 people, has the same influence in electing the president as California, with over 30 million people. Thus, neither the proportional plan nor the district plan would successfully reform the electoral college to ensure results consistent with the principles of democracy. Only direct popular election would ensure democratic results.

The electoral college system does have some advantages. By making the presidency a race for states, it preserves the principle of federalism that is the bedrock of the American political system. While it presents an enormous obstacle to third-party candidates, it also helps promote a stable two-party system. And, however imperfectly, it institutionalizes a check on the tyranny of the majority; demagogues may be able to attract a lot of votes, but they have no guarantee of actually governing unless they win states. As political scientist Judith Best puts it, "the electoral vote system is a model of our federal Constitution . . . that creates one society out of many societies" (1996, 72). Research by George Edwards (2004), however, shows that the electoral college has little to do with preserving federalism—equal representation in the Senate is more important on that score.

The Campaign

Strategy and money are important components of a successful presidential campaign. Strategy is driven not just by the issues but also by electoral rules. Due to a unique system of public financing, presidential candidates tend to be on a more-or-less equal financial footing in the general election.

How the Electoral-College System Affects Campaign Decisions   The ultimate goal of presidential candidates is get 270 electoral votes. Consequently, campaign efforts focus on states with a lot of electoral votes and on **swing states** in which the outcome could go either way. Although the presidential campaign is indeed a race for states, only a small number of large and competitive states receive any attention from the candidates' campaigns. Table 10.5 shows the number of times the presidential candidates visited each state in 2000. The presidential campaigns focused disproportionately on 10 states: California, Florida, Pennsylvania, Illinois, Ohio, Michigan, Wisconsin, Missouri, Tennessee, and Iowa. These states were highly competitive and, except for Iowa, had

Table 10.5
Presidential Campaign Visits in 2000

STATE	ELECTORAL VOTES	PRESIDENTIAL CANDIDATES' CAMPAIGN STOPS	PRESIDENTIAL & VICE PRESIDENTIAL CAMPAIGN STOPS
California	54	31	44
Florida	25	26	61
Pennsylvania	23	22	42
Illinois	22	20	36
Ohio	21	14	33
Michigan	18	31	43
Wisconsin	11	18	36
Missouri	11	17	31
Tennessee	11	14	24
Iowa	7	19	26
	203	**212 (72% of visits)**	**376 (66% of visits)**
New York	33	7	16
North Carolina	14	5	6
Massachusetts	12	6	6
Washington	11	9	18
Louisiana	9	7	10
Oregon	7	7	15
Arkansas	6	5	13
New Mexico	5	8	15
Texas	32	3	10
New Jersey	15	2	9
Georgia	13	1	2
Virginia	13	0	0
Indiana	12	2	4
Maryland	10	3	4
Minnesota	10	2	9
Alabama	9	1	1
Kentucky	8	3	12
Arizona	8	1	1
Colorado	8	0	2
Connecticut	8	0	8

(continued)

Table 10.5 (continued)

STATE	ELECTORAL VOTES	PRESIDENTIAL CANDIDATES' CAMPAIGN STOPS	PRESIDENTIAL & VICE PRESIDENTIAL CAMPAIGN STOPS
Oklahoma	8	0	0
South Carolina	8	0	0
Mississippi	7	0	1
Kansas	6	0	0
West Virginia	5	3	5
Nebraska	5	0	0
Utah	5	0	0
Maine	4	3	8
New Hampshire	4	3	7
Nevada	4	1	5
Hawaii	4	0	0
Idaho	4	0	2
Rhode Island	4	0	0
Delaware	3	1	2
Alaska	3	0	0
Montana	3	0	0
North Dakota	3	0	0
South Dakota	3	0	0
Vermont	3	0	3
Wyoming	3	0	1
	235	29 (10% of visits)	96 (17% of visits)
Total		295	571

Source: Adapted from George C. Edwards III, 2004. *Why the Electoral College Is Bad for America*. New Haven, CT: Yale University Press, 104–105.

large blocs of electoral votes. More than two-thirds of presidential and vice presidential candidates' campaign visits were to these 10 states. In contrast, 32 states in which one of the candidates had an insurmountable lead received few, if any, campaign visits.

Not only do the rules help determine *where* candidates will campaign, they also determine to a considerable extent *how* they will campaign. Unlike the long invisible primary associated with the nomination campaign, the general election has tight time limits. After the parties' nominating conventions, there are only 10 to 15 weeks until the general election. This time limit determines the entire strategy of a campaign. As political scientists John Jackson and William Crotty put it, "all the strategic plans, all marshaling and deployment of resources, all the advertising, and every facet of the entire campaign effort works backward from the election date" (1996, 99). The time constraint places enormous pressure on the candidates and their organizations to get their messages out, mobilize their party bases, and attract undecided voters. The option of a front porch campaign in which the candidate stays at home rather than going out to engage the voters has long since receded into history.

Financing the Presidential Election

Running for president is an expensive proposition. Even with the advantage of incumbency and facing no opposition for the 2004 Republican nomination, George W. Bush spent more than $220 million campaigning before the national convention. Facing a crowded field, John Kerry, the eventual Democratic nominee, spent more than $197 million (Center for Responsive Politics n.d.).

Although many observers express concern about the corrupting influence of money in politics, efforts to regulate campaign spending must be balanced against constitutional guarantees protecting the rights of free speech and free association. Historically, restrictions on contributions to presidential campaigns have been ineffective. Although Congress enacted several laws in the first half of the 20th century to prevent corporations and labor unions from contributing money to presidential elections, these laws were circumvented by channeling money through intermediaries and political action committees. Candidates and political parties have also found loopholes in more recent efforts to regulate campaign contributions.

Presidential campaign finance is regulated by the Federal Election Campaign Act (FECA). Its key provisions include:

- Public financing of presidential campaigns and overall expenditure limits
- Contribution limits for candidates who accept public financing
- Public disclosure requirements
- Creation of the Federal Election Commission (FEC) to enforce the law

In 1976 the Supreme Court ruled that overall spending limits violated individuals' First Amendment free speech rights; that is, wealthy candidates have the right to spend as much of their own money as they wish on their campaigns. Contribution and expenditures of candidates who accept public funds were ruled constitutionally acceptable (*Buckley v. Valeo* 1976).

Candidates become eligible for public funds as soon as they raise at least $5,000 in contributions of $250 or less in each of 20 states, for a total of $100,000. Once qualified, they receive public funds on a dollar-for-dollar basis for the first $250 received from an individual. In 2004, those who accepted public financing were bound to a spending limit of about $40 million in the campaign for party nominations. Candidates are not required to accept public financing and the spending limits that come with it. In the 2004 nomination contest, for example, President Bush, John Kerry and Howard Dean declined public financing so they could raise more than the $40 million limit.

Campaigns have developed creative methods to avoid the spirit, if not the letter, of campaign finance laws. Campaign contributions can be characterized as either hard money or soft money. The contribution limits established by FECA applied to *hard money*—that is money given to expressly support or oppose a candidate. FECA did not regulate *soft money,* which is contributions given to party organizations rather than to individual candidates. Parties used soft money for general party building and for such political purposes as voter registration drives and to run issue ads advocating some cause or issue. Although political activities supported by soft money are not supposed to directly support or oppose a candidate, many observers viewed them as a loophole used to circumvent the contribution limits to indirectly benefit party standard-bearers. In 2002, Congress passed the Bipartisan Campaign Reform Act

(BCRA), better known as the McCain-Feingold Law for its main Senate sponsors John McCain (R-AZ) and Russell Feingold (D-WI) to address this problem. The BCRA bans soft money outright, and it restricts "issue ads" run immediately before an election. This law also raised limits on hard money contributions during each election cycle to $2,000 from individuals and $5,000 from political action committees (PACs). But this latest reform also has loopholes that the candidates used in the 2004 presidential election.

Changes in campaign finance legislation have important consequences for presidential nominations. Candidates can no longer turn to a few "fat cats" to bankroll their campaigns (unless they themselves are the fat cats). In the absence of a personal fortune, candidates have to raise a lot of small individual contributions. This time-consuming logistical challenge rewards early starters.

Public campaign financing is also available in the general election. Nominees of the parties that received 25 percent or more of the popular vote in the previous presidential election—that is, the Democratic and Republican candidates—are eligible for full public financing; candidates of parties that received between 5 and 25 percent of the vote in the previous election are eligible to receive partial public financing. The major party candidates receive equal funding, about $74 million in 2004. Public financing of the general election "has leveled the playing field between the two major parties in the money available to support their" campaigns (Jackson and Crotty 1996, 186).

Nominating Candidates for Congress

Congressional elections differ from presidential elections in a number of ways. There are different rules for winning, smaller constituencies, shifting political jurisdictions, distinct advantages for incumbents, and no public campaign financing. The Constitution leaves the method of selecting congressional candidates to the individual states, so how candidates for the House and Senate gain their party's nomination depends on state law.

Primary Laws

State parties nominate candidates for the Senate and House of Representatives in a direct primary or, at most, a primary and a **run-off primary.** In most states, the candidate receiving a plurality wins the nomination. Ten states, primarily in the South, require a majority vote to win the nomination, and if no candidate receives a majority, a run-off primary is held between the two with the most votes. Southern states adopted the run-off primary because of one-party Democratic dominance following Reconstruction. With no viable Republican party to nominate candidates, winning the Democratic nomination was tantamount to election.

Each state's election law spells out the particulars of how and when the primary is conducted. There are three types of primary elections used to nominate congressional candidates: closed primary, open primary, and nonpartisan primary. A little more than half of the states nominate congressional candidates in closed primaries, and most other states have open primaries. In both cases, voters are limited to casting votes in only one party's primary. Both open and closed primaries produce the same outcome: separate nominees, one Democrat, one Republican, and one candidate from each minor party, if any, to run for each office in the general election.

The single exception to this rule occurs in Louisiana, which has a unique **nonpartisan primary.** In that state, all candidates run in the same primary election. A candidate who gets a majority of the primary vote wins the office. If no candidate gains a majority, the top two vote getters face off in the general election. This means that two Republicans or two Democrats can end up competing against each other in the run-off election. Strictly speaking, the Louisiana primary is not wholly nonpartisan because candidates list a party affiliation on the primary ballot. It is called nonpartisan because of its structure: It "throws all comers into the pot" and presumably dilutes the importance of partisanship (Kuzenski 1997). The Supreme Court ruled this practice unconstitutional because in effect it changed the official election day for federal elections set by Congress (*Foster v. Love* 1997). Louisiana got around the ruling by moving the primary to the regular election day and holding a run-off in December if no candidate wins a majority of votes cast. With this modification, it might be more accurate to refer to Louisiana's system as an "all-party election with a run-off."[9]

The Politics of Choosing Congressional Candidates

Generalizing about the politics of congressional nominations is difficult because of the unique and idiosyncratic forces that tend to be present in each nomination contest. Nonetheless, it is possible to identify some general patterns in congressional nominations. The first is the source of the candidates themselves. Senatorial candidates traditionally have been members of the House of Representatives or state governors. Political scientist David Canon (1990) has shown that from 1913, when the Seventeenth Amendment instituted direct election of senators, to 1987, 34 percent of senators were former House members and 20 percent were former governors. In the 108th Congress (2003–2004), 99 of the 100 senators had served in the House.

The candidate pool of the House of Representatives is less structured, reflecting the lower prestige of the House relative to the Senate. In general, however, service in the state legislature or in local offices is a stepping-stone to Congress. Since the 1930s, the proportion of House members with state legislative experience has increased (Canon 1990, 59). While governors and House members consider the Senate a move up the political ladder, senators and governors generally express little interest in serving in the House.

Perhaps the most important generalization about congressional nominations is that incumbents seldom lose. Figure 10.2 shows the number of incumbent representatives and senators defeated in primaries. In elections since the 1950s, an average of six incumbents lost their bid for renomination, about 1.5 percent of those running. As we will see below, Senate races are more competitive than those for the House in the general election, but recent senatorial primaries have been no more competitive than those for the House. Senate incumbents rarely lose in the primary—only two incumbent senators have been defeated in primaries in the last twenty years.

[9]A few states still use conventions as part of the nomination process, although the ability of the party organization to override the party in the electorate is limited in these cases.

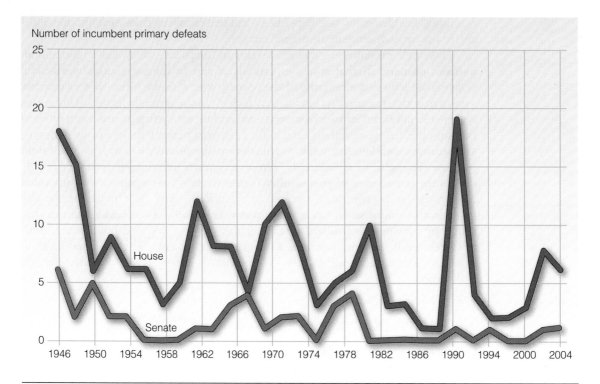

Number of incumbent primary defeats

Figure 10.2
Incumbents Defeated in Primaries
Source: Stanley, Harold W., and Richard G. Niemi. *Vital Statistics on American Politics 2003–2004.*
Washington, DC: CQ Press, 51–52.

Unless there are indications that an incumbent is vulnerable, experienced candidates of the other party do not battle vigorously for the honor of going down to defeat in the general election. Previous campaign experience, close relationships with voters, greater knowledge of issues, and superior financial resources give the veteran legislator enormous advantages over his or her opponents. While surmounting these obstacles in a primary race is not impossible, it is rare enough to constitute the exception that underlines the rule.

Vigorous primary competition does occasionally occur. If the incumbent is perceived to be vulnerable or is not seeking reelection, competitive candidates are likely to jump into the nomination fray. Scandal, a weak showing in the previous election, or a voting record out of tune with the partisan base in the state or district can make an incumbent vulnerable. So can other factors beyond the incumbent's control. For example, House incumbents are more likely to suffer primary defeats in election years ending in two—1962, 1972, 1982, 1992, 2002—because these elections follow the decennial census, which triggers the reapportionment of House seats among states. The resulting redistricting contributes to more defeats because some incumbents must run in altered districts; in some cases, redistricting puts two incumbents in the same district.

Electing Members of Congress

Unlike presidential aspirants, congressional candidates do not face complex electoral college rules; they do not need a majority of votes to be elected, nor do they have to contend with contingency procedures in the event that they fail to receive a specified proportion of the vote. All they need to do is win a plurality of the popular vote. Senatorial aspirants and House candidates in states with only one representative have an easily defined constituency—the entire population of the state. However, House candidates in states with multiple congressional districts are affected by the way the geographical limits of their constituencies are determined.

Apportionment

The Constitution provides for members of the House of Representatives to be apportioned among the states according to population. To keep the allocation of House seats current with changes in state populations, the Constitution requires a national head count—a census—every ten years. The census has taken place each decade since 1790.

The Constitution does not establish a permanent size for the House of Representatives, leaving the matter to Congress. Following the 1790 census, the membership of the House was set at 105. As both the population and the number of states grew, the size of the House gradually expanded until it reached 435 following the 1910 census. The size of the House was permanently fixed at 435 at that time (Jacobson 2001, 7).[10]

Apportioning seats in a legislature with a fixed size means that, after each census, each state gains, loses, or retains seats depending on how its population changed in relation to the national average. The process of adjusting the number of House seats among the states to reflect population shifts is called **reapportionment.** Over the last several decades, population has been shifting away from the Northeast and Midwest to the South and West. From 1942 to 2002, New York and Pennsylvania lost 16 and 14 House seats respectively, while California gained 30 seats and Florida gained 19.

Congressional Districts

For congressional candidates, perhaps a more salient issue is not how many House seats a state gets, but how congressional constituencies are defined within a state. For the first half-century of the nation's existence, each state was free to determine how congressional seats were to be apportioned internally. Many states elected their representatives at large, which means that all were elected statewide. This arrangement, in which more than one member is elected from the same constituency, is the **multimember district** election system. Another way to choose representatives is the **single-member district** system, in which the state is carved up into the number of districts equal to the number of representatives the state has in the House, and voters in each district choose one representative.

---

[10]When Alaska and Hawaii were admitted into the Union in the 1950s, one seat for each of the new states was temporarily added to the House. After the 1960 census, the membership was again reduced to 435.

Since 1842, federal law has required representatives to be elected from single-member districts. After each reapportionment, state legislatures must redraw congressional district lines to accommodate changes in the number of seats and to reflect population shifts within the state. The process of redrawing the district lines within a state is called **redistricting.** State legislatures have the responsibility of redistricting.

The partisan stakes are high in redistricting, and they often result in **gerrymandering,** which means drawing district boundaries to benefit one interest and hinder another. The term was coined in honor of Elbridge Gerry, a Massachusetts governor who supposedly designed a district in 1812 shaped like a salamander in order to gain a partisan advantage (Figure 10.3). Gerrymanders can benefit several kinds of political interests:

1. Partisan gerrymanders benefit the majority party.
2. Incumbent gerrymanders benefit current officeholders regardless of party.
3. Racial gerrymanders benefit citizens of a particular race or deny representation to a particular race.

Gerrymandering is accomplished through a process of "packing and cracking." In packing, voters who support the disadvantaged interest are concentrated in a few legislative districts, which means that minority candidates are likely to win those districts by overwhelming margins, but the number of seats they win is smaller than their share of the population. In cracking, such voters are spread out over many districts so that minority candidates are unlikely to win at all because their supporters are spread too thinly to muster a plurality in any district.

As a result of population shifts from rural areas to cities from the 1930s to the 1970s, the distribution of seats in the legislature did not fairly reflect the distribution of

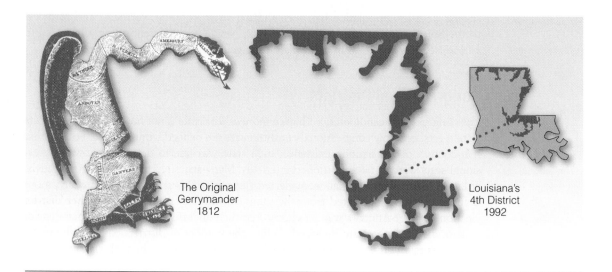

The Original
Gerrymander
1812

Louisiana's
4th District
1992

Figure 10.3
Gerrymandering, Then and Now
Source: Louisiana's 4th District: Engstrom, Richard L., and Jason Kirksey. 1998. "Race and Representational Districting ʲsiana." In *Race and Redistricting in the1980s*, Bernard Grofman, ed. New York: Agathon Press.

the population, and many state legislatures came to be **malapportioned** (badly apportioned). Disparities in the populations of legislative districts became particularly pronounced in states whose constitutions granted towns and counties representation in the state legislature, frequently without regard to their size. In 1960, for example, the most populous district of the California State Senate had 422 times more people than the smallest one. The ratio between the largest and smallest congressional districts in Texas was four to one. Yet neither state legislatures nor successive Congresses were disposed to change the situation. It was asking a lot to expect representatives who came from malapportioned and gerrymandered districts to risk their political careers by changing the system.

Faced with the unwillingness of legislative bodies to remedy the situation, aggrieved parties turned to the courts for assistance. The basis for the court challenge was that the Constitution mandates reapportionment of congressional seats among the states after every census, and the Fourteenth amendment's guarantee of equal protection of the law requires these new districts to be about equal in population. If legislative districts are not equal in size, then citizens are denied equal protection because every person's vote does not have equal weight—in effect, malapportionment violates the core democratic value of political equality.

The federal courts initially refused to deal with unequally sized districts and gerrymandering, on the grounds that legislative apportionment was a political question that they did not have jurisdiction to decide; instead, the remedy of political questions lay with the state legislatures and Congress (*Colgrove v. Green* 1946). Then in *Baker v. Carr* (1962), the Supreme Court overturned the political question doctrine, holding that legislative apportionment was a **justiciable issue** that the courts had jurisdiction to hear and decide.[11]

The ruling in *Baker* led to a number of landmark cases addressing the issue of political equality in legislative apportionment. In *Wesberry v. Sanders* (1964), the Supreme Court invalidated unequal congressional districts in Georgia. Citing language in the Constitution mandating that representatives be apportioned among the states according to population and that they be chosen by the people of the states, the Court ruled that "as nearly as practicable, one [person's] vote in a congressional election is to be worth as much as another's." The ruling is popularly known as the principle of **one person, one vote.** It means that all legislative districts must contain about equal numbers of people. The same year, in *Reynolds v. Sims* (1964), the Court extended the principle to state legislatures, holding that the equal protection of the laws clause of the Fourteenth Amendment requires state legislative districts to be substantially equal and seats in both houses of a bicameral state legislature to be apportioned on the basis of population.

These rulings, however, did not end gerrymandering. It is possible for a state legislature to distribute residents equally among districts but still benefit the majority party or an incumbent legislator. Perhaps the most controversial redistricting issue of recent years is racial gerrymandering, in which district boundaries are drawn with the explicit goal of creating a majority block of ethnic minority voters within them. Following the 1990 census, a number of states in the South and Southwest drew up black-majority and

---

[11]It may seem strange that legislative apportionment was a political question in 1946 and was not in 1962. As discussed in Chapter 15, the federal courts are political institutions that make public policy. The apportionment issue was political throughout the debate. In 1962 it was a political question the Court was willing to deal with; in 1946 it was not.

© Getty Images

How best to represent the interests of minorities in Congress remains the subject of debate. One side argues that ethnic minorities ought to be represented by members of their own ethnic groups. The other side of the debate contends that a representative does not have to be African American, Latino, Asian, or female to represent those interests. Barack Obama, who ran for a Senate seat in Illinois in the 2004 election, managed to appeal to voters in his state across racial lines, achieving a balance between substantive and descriptive representation.

Latino-majority districts, which are referred to as **majority-minority districts.** Both the U.S. Department of Justice and various civil rights groups supported such districts as a way to maximize the number of African American and Latino representatives in Congress.[12] Many of the resulting districts did not correspond to local political geography. Some divided towns and communities, while others sprawled across states in a bewildering pattern of spikes and curls that flicked out toward concentrations of minority populations and skirted predominantly white areas. For example, Louisiana's 4th Congressional District, shown in Figure 10.3, was designed to elect an African American to the House. The strange shape resulted from linking widely dispersed communities of African Americans into one district.

In subsequent lawsuits, federal courts began striking these new districts down. In the case of *Shaw v. Reno* (1993), the Supreme Court held that race may not be the sole criterion used in drawing congressional districts.

How best to represent the interests of minorities remains the subject of fierce debate. One side argues that ethnic minorities ought to be represented by members of their own ethnic groups. This view suggests that districts should be drawn to maximize the number of minority representatives elected to achieve **descriptive representation,** in which the racial makeup of Congress reflects the racial makeup of the nation. In other words, if 12 percent of the population is African American, 12 percent of the representatives in Congress should be African American.

The other side of the debate contends that a representative does not have to be African American, Latino, Asian, or female to represent those interests. Rather, **substantive representation** of the basic interests of various groups is more important than descriptive representation. Political scientist Carol Swain (1995) argues that increasing the representation of African American interests by creating additional majority-minority

---

[12]Racial gerrymanders have not always been used to benefit minorities. During the period between Reconstruction and the 1970s, racial gerrymanders were often used to prevent the election of black representatives.

districts is ineffective and shortsighted because there are a limited number of places where such districts can be drawn.[13] And there is evidence that packing so many African American voters into majority-minority districts may actually decrease their influence in Congress. Research found that when large numbers of African American voters were removed from the districts of white representatives during redistricting, the voting records of the representatives indicated less support of minority interests (Overby and Cosgrove 1996). After redistricting removed African American voters from their districts, several moderate southern Democrats who often supported minority interests were defeated in the 1992 and 1994 elections by conservative Republicans who were less supportive (Hill 1995).

Incumbency Advantage in Congressional Elections

Congressional campaigns resemble presidential campaigns in several ways. Congressional candidates make the same basic political appeals involving personal image, party label, pleas for group support, general positions on issues, and the development of campaign themes. Presidential and congressional candidates have the same basic strategic options and the same basic objectives—to acquire and allocate scarce political resources in an attempt to maximize votes.

There are also important differences between the two types of campaigns. Perhaps the most basic and distinguishing feature of congressional elections is the great advantage congressional incumbents enjoy over challengers. Presidential incumbents do not have a great electoral advantage. Of the seven incumbent presidents who ran for reelection since 1972, only four (47 percent) were successful. But as Figure 10.4 shows, congressional incumbents are overwhelmingly successful when they run for reelection. Since 1972, for example, an average of 94 percent of House incumbents and 81 percent of Senate incumbents were reelected. Why are congressional incumbents so successful when they run for reelection? Why are House incumbents more successful than Senate incumbents? The reasons include the nature of congressional districts, resources, and relations with constituents, among others.

Districts, Challengers, and Resources The political makeup of a district sets the general limits of competition. Some districts are overwhelmingly Democratic or Republican, and others are more evenly balanced. Many House candidates run in districts drawn to have a distinct tilt toward one party, while candidates for the Senate and the presidency must compete for the votes of a more diverse and competitive statewide or nationwide constituency.

Within the limits set by the nature of the district, several factors determine how competitive a congressional election is likely to be. Most important is the quality of the challenger. Most House incumbents coast to easy, lopsided reelection victories because they run against challengers with no political experience who have little campaign money. Although having large sums of money does not guarantee victory, without adequate

[13]In order to draw enough single-member districts to elect a Congress that will descriptively reflect the population requires the various groups to be concentrated enough to combine into a district. In some states, African American and Latino populations are sufficiently concentrated to draw such districts. However, drawing a district that is majority female, for example, is not possible even though women are a majority of the population.

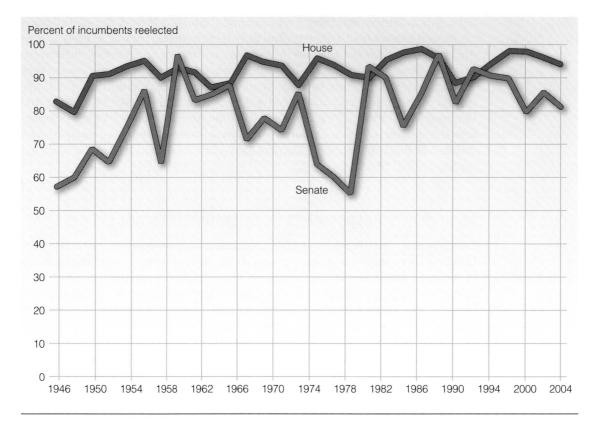

Figure 10.4
Incumbency Advantage in House and Senate Elections
Source: Stanley, Harold W., and Richard G. Niemi. *Vital Statistics on American Politics 2003–2004.*
Washington, DC: CQ Press, 51–52.

funding there is little chance of success. How much money does it take to run a competitive campaign? Political scientist Gary Jacobson suggests a figure of $600,000 as a reasonable threshold for House races (2001, 43); Senate races are typically more expensive, as much as ten times more expensive in some states. While incumbents are able to raise and spend as much as they need, few challengers can raise enough money to be competitive.

The few challengers who can raise lots of money pose a serious threat to incumbents. But incumbents spend in response to the magnitude of the threat. Paradoxically, incumbents who spend the most money are the most likely to be defeated. This is because the challengers who are best able to raise campaign money target vulnerable incumbents who respond by spending huge amounts of money in losing campaigns. In 2002, for example, losing incumbents spent an average of $2.5 million compared to winning challengers' $2.0 million (Center for Responsive Politics n.d.). As Jacobson observes, "For incumbents, spending a great deal of money on the campaign is a sign of weakness rather than strength" (2001, 43). Humorist Will Rogers showed considerable insight when he said, "Politics has got so expensive that it takes lots of money even to get beat with nowadays" (Sterling 1979, 61).

Performance, Perks, and Pork Barrel   What a representative does or fails to do over the course of the term can damage or improve the chances of reelection. Although they try to avoid it, a few incumbents are tarnished with scandal and suffer at the polls (Peters and Welch 1980; Welch and Hibbing 1997).

More typically, incumbents engage in activities intended to discourage vigorous challenges. They work to bring pork-barrel benefits to their districts, and they use the perquisites of office to appeal to constituents. As discussed in Chapter 12, pork-barrel benefits are government-sponsored projects that bring economic benefits to a member's state or district. Examples include public works projects such as dams, roads, and government buildings; grants to local government or a university; and defense contracts.

Perquisites or perks are benefits and support services that members need in order to do their jobs. These include an allowance to pay staff members to answer constituents' letters and help with their problems, the franking privilege that allows members to use their signatures instead of buying stamps to send mail to constituents, and a travel allowance so that representatives can make frequent trips home to stay in touch with constituents. (Perks and franking privilege are also discussed in Chapter 12.)

Perks are not supposed to be used in a campaign, and there are legal regulations designed to prevent incumbents from using congressional staff or the frank for campaign activities. Nonetheless, critics suspect that pork-barrel projects and the use of perks provide incumbents with considerable electoral benefits. Political scientist David Mayhew suggests that members of Congress use their offices to make three basic kinds of appeals to constituents. The first is **advertising,** defined as "any effort to disseminate one's name among constituents . . . to create a favorable image" (Mayhew 1974, 49). Advertising activities include sending out newsletters, making frequent visits to constituents, addressing high school commencements, and sending out infant-care booklets. The second is **credit claiming,** an effort to generate the belief that the representative is responsible for government actions that constituents find desirable, such as pork-barrel projects that benefit the district. The third is **position taking,** making public statements on issues that are pleasing to constituents.

These three activities are nonpartisan and are likely to win friends without making enemies. When a member of Congress votes on a controversial piece of legislation, the vote might make as many enemies as friends. But when a member helps a veteran who is having a problem with the Department of Veterans Affairs, it generates goodwill and contributes to the reputation of being a good representative.

Political scientists who have studied the electoral payoff of pork-barrel projects and the use of perquisites, however, have been unable to show that these activities make vulnerable members safe (Bickers and Stein 1996; Cain, Ferejohn, and Fiorina 1987; Feldman and Jondrow 1984). The key to competition, as noted above, is the challenger and how much money he or she has to spend.

Competitive House Races   Incumbency, however, does not guarantee reelection. Congressional elections in which numerous incumbents go down to defeat are rare, but challengers manage to pick off incumbents in at least a handful of races during every electoral cycle. An incumbent may be vulnerable because the congressional district has been greatly altered by redistricting, because he or she has lost touch with the district, or because his or her party affiliation or voting record does not match the preferences of most constituents. In such cases, a candidate with political experience and access to campaign money is likely to challenge the incumbent.

Some representatives retire or die in each election cycle. Contests for **open seats** in which no incumbent is running are much more competitive. Both parties are likely to have experienced candidates with adequate campaign money. In open-seat House races in 2002, for example, Democratic candidates raised an average of $423,000, and Republican candidates raised an average of $452,227 (Center for Responsive Politics n.d.).

Incumbency in Senate Elections   Although incumbency is an advantage in Senate elections, it is smaller than it is in House races. Unlike House districts, the boundaries of Senate constituencies (an entire state) cannot be manipulated to benefit a particular party or candidate. States also have a ready pool of ambitious, experienced House members, governors, and other statewide officeholders who want to be senators. These experienced politicians make formidable opponents because they have experience representing the same constituents as the incumbent senator and access to a campaign organization and campaign funds.

Other factors also contribute to greater vulnerability for senators. Because states tend to be larger and more diverse than House districts, senators have a harder time developing the close personal bonds with their constituents that are common in the smaller House districts. Senate campaigns receive more media attention, which means that Senate challengers are more likely to get more publicity and visibility than House challengers. All these factors make Senate races more competitive than those of the House.

Some House representatives retire or die in each election cycle. Contests for open seats in which no incumbent is running are often competitive. In 2004, Republican Jennifer Dunn retired from her 8th Congressional District post in Washington state. The race between Dave Reichert (left), a sheriff and local hero for capturing a notorious serial killer, and Dave Ross (right), a well-known local talk show host was very close. The District had been leaning left over the past several years, and Reichert's strongly right-leaning stance created a great deal of opportunity for Ross. Dave Reichert won the election.

Financing Congressional Elections

Congressional candidates must raise all their funds from private sources. Although candidates for Congress are subject to the contribution limits and the ban on soft money established by the Bipartisan Campaign Reform Act of 2002, incumbents continue to have a significant advantage over challengers. They can raise more money than challengers because people are generally not motivated to give money to probable losers.

Raising a considerable amount of money from a wide variety of donors, therefore, is a central task for anyone wishing to make a serious bid for a seat in Congress. Indeed, deciding whether a candidate is a serious contender or a sacrificial lamb often begins with an assessment of the campaign's bank balance. Often-quoted advice for those seeking congressional office is to "learn how to beg, and do it in a way that leaves you with some dignity" (Granat 1984).

The amount of money raised and spent on congressional campaigns is nothing short of staggering—expenditures in excess of $600 million in recent election cycles. Where does this money come from? Figures 10.5a and 10.5b show the sources of campaign contributions for the 2002 election cycle. Most campaign contributions are from individuals—over 65 percent in the Senate and 50 percent in the House. Another important source of campaign money is political action committees (PACs). PACs account for about one-fourth of contributions to Senate candidates and nearly 45 percent of House candidates. It is not difficult to understand why PACs have become more important to the financing of congressional campaigns. The number of PACs and the amount of money available to them have grown considerably in the past twenty-five years. Other sources of campaign money include party committees and the candidates themselves.

A variety of groups utilize PACs to channel their contributions to congressional candidates. Initially, labor was the major user of PACs, but corporate and business-related trade associations have increased their use of PACs the fastest. Generally speaking, labor PACs tend to favor Democratic candidates, and business-based PACs favor Republican

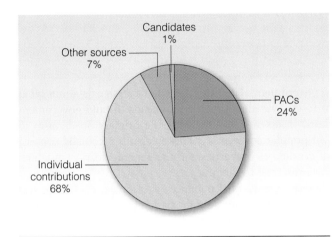

Figure 10.5a
Sources of Campaign Funding for Senate Candidates, 2002 Election Cycle
Source: Center for Responsive Politics n.d.

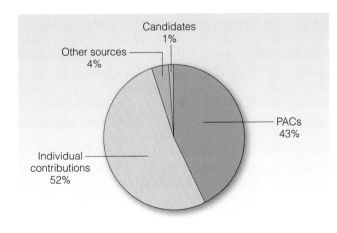

Figure 10.5b
Sources of Campaign Funding for House Candidates, 2002 Election Cycle
Source: Center for Responsive Politics n.d.

candidates, although the clearest bias of PACs is toward incumbents rather than one or the other party.

Thus, the rules of the game, campaign strategies, and available resources shape the outcome of both presidential and congressional campaigns. Winners of these contests tend to congratulate themselves for having conducted effective campaigns and praise the voters for having made wise choices. Losers are more likely to blame defeat on circumstances beyond their control: the superior financial resources of the opponent, the formidable obstacle of the opponent's incumbency, their minority party status, or other factors that even their best campaign efforts could not overcome.

 ## Performance Assessment

Elections connect citizens to government. They can provide clear signals about what people want the government to do, and they provide the means to hold government accountable for its past actions. In essence, elections are the primary mechanism to achieve the democratic goal of popular sovereignty. This mechanism actually consists of two steps—nomination of candidates by parties and the general election in which voters choose from the choices presented to them.

The current system of choosing presidential nominees is complex, confusing, and flawed. Over time, as reforms have shifted power from the party organization to the party in the electorate, the evolution of the nomination process has embraced diverse perspectives from amateurs as well as professionals and the differing voices they represent.

Flawed and confusing as it is, the existing system is an improvement compared to the past. Today the choice presented to voters in the general election is no longer shaped by a comparatively small set of elites. Instead, the choice depends on an aspirant's ability to attract organizational and financial support from a large number of activists and popular support from ordinary citizens in primaries and caucuses. At least in theory, this system stands a better chance of ensuring that the core democratic value of popular sovereignty is reflected in the quest for America's highest political office.

Yet, the electoral college consistently breaks the promise of political equality and occasionally the promise of majority rule. Proposed reforms to the electoral college system may not keep these promises either. The district plan incorporates the gerrymandering abuses still associated with manipulating House district boundaries into the presidential selection process. Neither plan guarantees that the candidate with the most popular votes will be president; neither plan achieves political equality. Only direct popular election of the president can make good on these promises.

The major objection to the popular election of the president is that it violates the principle of federalism by substituting the voters for the states in determining the outcome of the election. This is debatable. States are established as sovereign governments in their own right, and they have special protection in the composition of the Senate and in the process of amending the Constitution. They do not need special consideration in the selection of the president to retain or protect those rights.

At the congressional level, the high election rate for incumbents raises questions about whether congressional elections effectively achieve popular sovereignty. It is possible that the vast majority of incumbents win reelection because they do a good job of representing their constituencies. Although it is difficult to come up with an objective standard for measuring whether someone is doing a good job in Congress, we believe that a large majority of the incumbents who have won reelection deserve to be rewarded with another term.

Yet, there is evidence that some incumbents win reelection simply because of the incumbency advantage, regardless of whether they are doing a good job. A small number of incumbents involved in corrupt acts have won reelection. There have even been rarer cases when an incumbent who died between the time the ballots were printed and election day has been reelected. It is hard to fathom how a dead candidate can be viewed as a "good" representative.

If elections are to uphold the promise of democracy, especially in terms of following through on the core value of popular sovereignty, congressional elections need to become more competitive. Voters only get a meaningful choice if there is vigorous competition between two or more candidates who have the resources to make their respective cases to the electorate. Vigorous competition for a House seat is rare and, if anything, it is becoming rarer. Recognizing the problem, though, does not automatically present a solution.

Summary

- Elections connect the people to the government. The methods used to choose candidates have important consequences for both the promise and the performance of democracy.
- Nomination methods were needed as soon as political parties came into being. For offices in relatively small jurisdictions, this could be accomplished through meetings, called caucuses, of each party's most active members. For offices such as governors and the president, the party's legislative caucus, the party's members serving in the state or national legislature, took responsibility for nominating candidates for higher office.
- The national party convention, a meeting of delegates from all the states, replaced the caucus as the means to nominate presidential and vice presidential candidates. Today, most convention delegates are selected through primary elections. Candidates compete in the primaries to win the backing of these delegates.
- The rise of the direct primary as the main method of securing a party's presidential nomination shifted power to rank-and-file voters. To be competitive, candidates must raise enormous sums of money and have a large campaign organization in place well ahead of the primary season.
- Presidential nomination contests generally progress through a series of stages in which the field is winnowed according to success in the primary elections.
- Conventions remain important because they are the supreme governing body of the parties. Officially, they nominate presidential and vice presidential candidates, approve the party platform, and serve as a central rallying point to unify the party behind the candidate for the general election.
- The shift from nomination to general election campaigns presents candidates with a new set of political challenges. The rules, time frames, and electoral audiences change dramatically, and this requires a shift in tactics and strategy.
- Although the presidential contest is the election in which the largest number of Americans participates, the popular vote does not choose the president. The

president is chosen by the electoral college, which consists of electors chosen from the 50 states and the District of Columbia.

- The electoral college has long been criticized as an unnecessarily complex way to select a chief executive. Alternative proposals include the proportional plan, the district plan, and direct popular election. Only direct election achieves political equality and guarantees majority rule.

- Presidential general election campaigns are publicly financed, though accepting public money requires agreeing to limit other contributions.

- The nomination process for members of Congress has historically paralleled the evolution of the presidential nomination process. Congressional nominees were first chosen by caucus and convention and later by direct primary.

- Unlike presidential aspirants, congressional candidates do not face complex electoral rules, and they do not need a majority of votes to be elected. All that is required to win a congressional race is a plurality of the popular vote.

- Representation in the House is apportioned among the states every ten years following the national census. This means that the number of congressional districts within a state and the boundaries of the districts can change every ten years.

- Redistricting is done by state legislatures and is often a partisan and political undertaking.

- Money is an important factor in congressional races, with hundreds of millions of dollars spent every electoral cycle. Having lots of money does not guarantee victory, but candidates who lack adequate funding have little chance of victory. Incumbents are generally able to raise more money than challengers.

- Money for congressional campaigns mostly comes from individual donations, though a significant percentage comes from PACs.

Key Terms

advertising 319
caucuses 286
caucus method 290
closed primaries 287
credit claiming 319
descriptive representation 316
direct popular election plan 304
district plan 304
electoral college 298
frontloading 291
general election 286
gerrymandering 314
invisible primary 293
justiciable issue 315
legislative caucus 286
magic number 292
majority-minority districts 316
malapportioned 315

multimember district 313
national party convention 287
nonpartisan primary 311
nomination 286
one person, one vote 315
open primaries 288
open seats 320
position taking 319
proportional plan 304
reapportionment 313
redistricting 314
run-off primary 310
single-member district 313
state presidential primary 290
substantive representation 316
swing states 306
unit rule 298

Selected Readings

Best, Judith A. 1996. *The Choice of the People: Debating the Electoral College.* Lanham, MD: Rowman & Littlefield. A good primer on the electoral college and its advantages and disadvantages.

Edwards, George C., III. 2004. *Why the Electoral College Is Bad for America.* New Haven, CT: Yale University Press. A systematic and comprehensive case for abolishing the electoral college.

Haskell, John. 1996. *Fundamentally Flawed.* Lanham, MD: Rowman & Littlefield. A wide-ranging critique of the presidential nomination process.

Jackson, John S., and William Crotty. 1996. *The Politics of Presidential Selection.* New York: HarperCollins. A thorough and accessible introduction to the presidential nomination process.

Jacobson, Gary. 2001. *The Politics of Congressional Elections,* 5th ed. New York: Addison Wesley. A comprehensive examination of congressional elections that is periodically updated to reflect new trends and data.

Wayne, Stephen. 2000. *The Road to the White House 2000.* New York: Bedford/St. Martin's. This is representative of books that analyze nomination contests in a particular election. Books with similar titles exist for most other presidential elections from 1960 on.

11 | Voting Behavior and Political Participation

On March 2, 2004, Jeffrey Liss, a Maryland lawyer, voted in his state's Democratic primary, walked outside the polling station, and was a little taken aback to see a campaign poster for U.S. Senator Barbara Mikulski.

There was nothing unusual about the poster; Mikulski, after all, was running for her fourth term in the Senate. Liss was surprised because there were no Senate candidates listed on the ballot he had just completed.

Liss went back inside to talk to election officials. They assured him the Senate race was indeed on the ballot and that he was mistaken in his insistence that his ballot included no listing of Mikulski or any other Senate candidate. Liss finally convinced the officials to check the ballots. Sure enough, no Senate race was listed. In fact, Mikulski's race did not appear on ballots in at least three Maryland counties (Novak et al. 2004).

Leaving an entire race off a voting ballot is bad enough, but this is not a story of a printer's mix-up or an inexplicable lapse of memory by the officials who designed and approved the ballot. This was as much a technological error as a human one.

Maryland, like many other states, deployed electronic, touch-screen voting machines for the first time in 2004. The reason for putting twenty-first-century computing technology into the voting booth was to avoid a repeat of Florida's fiasco in the 2000 presidential race. The contest between George Bush and Al Gore literally came down to how Florida election officials interpreted hanging chads—the pieces of paper left behind when a paper ballot is punched.

The uncertainty over the actual vote count in Florida created enormous controversy. Bush was declared the eventual winner in Florida, and this gave him the presidency. Yet to this day some Democrats remain convinced that Bush's Florida win—which was determined by a U.S. Supreme Court decision rather than a definitive ballot count—did not truly reflect the majority preferences of Florida's voters. Electronic voting machines were considered to be a way to avoid similar controversies in the future. Computers are very good at counting numbers and keeping accurate records . . . most of the time.

A number of widely publicized glitches such as those encountered by Jeffrey Liss raised concerns that maybe computers in the voting booth were not such a good idea after all. Confidence was also shaken by the claims of some computer experts that, at least in theory, voting machines were vulnerable to computer hackers. All this worry is for naught, argue the machines' manufacturers. A few teething problems are to be expected when introducing new technology, but, overall, electronic voting machines are far better than paper ballots: They are easier to use, can be configured in several different languages, and count votes accurately.

Although this is all true, it misses the point. A representative democracy is premised largely on the notion that elections connect citizens to government. If that connection is suspect, a key promise of democracy is broken. Even if citizens only perceive that the connection is broken, it will undermine the legitimacy of government and harm the performance of democracy.

This connection can be harmed by more than technical glitches in voting machines. To a great extent, the strength of this connection is determined not by lines of computer code but by the choices and actions of citizens. In a representative democracy, voting is the fundamental form of political participation. It is the process by which citizens pass judgment on elected officials. If citizens are unhappy with what these officeholders are doing about the major problems facing society, the remedy is for voters to replace them. To make this process function as intended, the technical detail of having candidates for office actually appear on the ballot is necessary; however, the voting process is more than simply getting an accurate voting screen or punch card.

Elections in the United States are rarely decided on technicalities. Instead, they are decided by the choices voters make. Even the embarrassment of the 2000 presidential election can be seen as a product of voter choice: If more people had actually bothered to show up to the polls (only about half of those eligible showed up), maybe the most powerful office on the planet would have not hung on a few hundred contested votes in a single state.

But there is another lesson to learn from this example. Voting may be the most common way that citizens participate in a democracy, but it is not the only way. When Liss went back into the polling place to talk to election officials, he was engaging in another type of political participation—face-to-face contact with public officials. He conveyed his concern, and the officials—acting on behalf of government—responded.

What are the different forms of participation? Why do some people participate while others do not? Why is voting the most common form of participation? Are there systematic patterns in who shows up to the polls and the choices they make? What explains how voters choose between candidates? The answers to these questions actually go a lot further in explaining the functioning of the political system and the legitimacy of government than the teething problems of new voting technology. Understanding what the people are doing and why is prerequisite for judging whether elections—and the other forms of participation—are connecting the will of the people to the government.

The Promise of Political Participation

The fundamental promise of political participation is to help connect the will of the people to the actions of government. If it successfully makes this connection, participation helps uphold the core values of political freedom, popular sovereignty, and majority rule. A hallmark of a democratic political system is that it counts heads rather than breaking them. If the will of the people and the preferences of a majority are going to provide the fundamental basis for government action, then the people must participate in the political process.

Forms of Political Participation

Political scientist Sidney Verba and his associates divide political participation into four general categories:

- Voting, the most widespread and regularized form of participation
- Campaign activities, such as working for or contributing money to a party or a candidate
- Citizen-initiated contacts with government officials in which a person acts on a matter of individual concern
- Local community activities in which citizens act cooperatively to deal with social and political problems (Verba and Nie 1987; Verba, Schlozman, and Brady 1995)

The number of people engaging in these different forms of participation varies widely, depending on the cost associated with the activity. "Cost of participation" does not mean monetary cost (though that might be part of it). Rather, the term *cost* is used more broadly to indicate how easy or difficult it is to participate. Some activities, like voting, are relatively easy and require little expenditure of time and effort. That is, the costs of voting are relatively minor, and the largest number of people participate in this way. Other activities—such as writing letters to public officials, getting involved in civic organizations, attending rallies, making monetary contributions, and running for office—require greater levels of time and

© AFP/Getty Images

If the will of the people and the preferences of a majority are going to provide the fundamental basis for government action, then the people must participate in the political process. One of the main forms of political participation is to campaign for a candidate or contribute to his or her campaign fund. Here supporters of John Edwards' campaign for the 2004 Democratic vice-presidential nomination go door to door seeking support for their candidate.

effort; many fewer people engage in these more costly forms of participation. Table 11.1 shows rates of participation in these various activities at two points in time. Most people reported voting regularly in presidential elections, the least costly activity, while participation was much lower in other types of activities that require more time and effort.

Are these participation rates high or low? Answering this question requires a benchmark against which to measure the rates. In terms of one such benchmark—majority rule—these numbers appear low, with voting in presidential elections as the only activity that attracts more than half of eligible citizens. As Sidney Verba, Kay Schlozman, and Henry Brady point out, however, in a large country like the United States, even a small percentage translates into millions of people spending time to contribute to operation of government (1995, 52).

Change over time is another useful benchmark to evaluate participation. The comparison in Table 11.1 shows that voting participation declined over time. We analyze voting in more depth later in the chapter. For now, it is sufficient to note that this decline in voting is consistent with findings of other research.

The table also shows that participation in other types of activities increased over time. Substantially more people reported participating in political campaigns and contacting local government officials. Thus, except for voting, Americans are generally participating more now than in the past.

Table 11.1

Percentage Engaging in Different Types of Participation

SPECIFIC ACTIVITY	1967	1987	ABSOLUTE CHANGE	RELATIVE CHANGE
Voting				
Regular voting in presidential elections	66	58	−8	−12
Always vote in local elections	47	35	−12	−26
Campaign Activities				
Persuade others how to vote	28	32	+4	+14
Actively work for party or candidate	26	27	+1	+4
Attend political meeting or rally	19	19	0	0
Contribute money to party or candidate	13	23	+10	+77
Member of political club	8	4	−4	−50
Contacting Government				
Contact local official: issue-based	14	24	+10	+71
Contact state or national official: issue-based	11	22	+11	+100
Contact local official: particularized	7	10	+3	+43
Contact state or national official: particularized	6	7	+1	+17
Community Activities				
Work with others on local problem	30	34	+4	+13
Active membership in community problem-solving organization	31	34	+3	+10
Form group to help solve local problem	14	17	+3	+21

Sources: Verba, Sidney, Kay Lehman Schlozman, and Henry E. Brady. 1995. *Voice and Equality. Civic Volunteerism in American Politics.* Cambridge, MA: Harvard University Press, 72. 1967 data: Verba, Sidney, and Norman Nie. *Participation in America,* data file. 1987 data: National Opinion Research Center, General Social Survey.

A third useful benchmark is to compare Americans to citizens in other democracies. Figure 11.1 presents such a comparison. It shows that voting participation in the United States is much lower than that in four other representative democracies. Lower voter turnout, however, does not necessarily mean that Americans are lazy compared to citizens in other democracies. On other types of political activity, Americans are more active than citizens elsewhere, in some cases by a large margin. Compared to the average across other democracies, nearly three times more Americans participate in campaigns, and more than twice as many contact government officials and do community work. Thus, except for voting, political participation in the United States compares favorably with that in other nations and seems to be increasing over time.

Why do Americans vote less but participate more in higher cost forms of political activity than citizens in other democracies? The answer may have to do with the relative costs associated with the various forms of participation in different countries. Voting is the least costly form of participation, and it is the most common political activity in all the democracies. But, as we discuss below, there are more barriers to voting in the United States than in other democracies. When it comes to the other, more difficult forms of

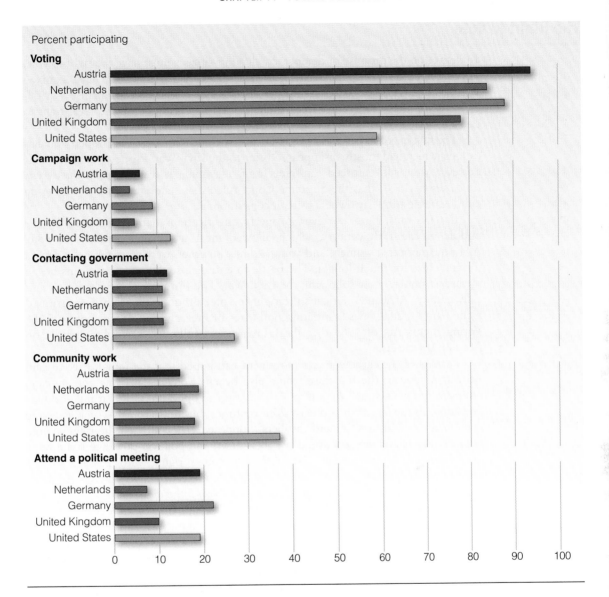

Figure 11.1
Political Participation in Five Democracies

participation, however, the barriers are not higher in the United States: it is no harder (and may be easier) to participate in campaigns, contact government officials, and participate in local community organizations in the United States than in other countries.

Of these basic forms of political participation, voting has the most visible connection to the core values of democracy. Participating in elections allows people to participate in making decisions about who gets what and allows for direct expression of the will of the people. Who has the right to participate in elections—in other words, the right to vote—thus provides an excellent starting point for judging the degree of political freedom within a democratic society.

The Right to Vote

To deliver on the promise of democracy, all adult citizens must have the right to vote. This right is known as the **franchise.** Most democracies, however, have a mixed history when it comes to voting rights. In the United States, the franchise was initially very limited, with only white, male property owners getting the legal right to cast a ballot.

The first major expansion of the franchise was the elimination of property qualifications, which had mostly disappeared prior to the Civil War. Property qualifications, however, were still enforced for some forms of voting. It was not until *Phoenix v. Kolodziejski* (1970) that the Supreme Court ruled that state laws limiting voting on bond issues to property owners were unconstitutional.

For the most part, however, property qualifications had disappeared by the middle of the 19th century, which allowed most white male citizens to vote. African Americans, women, and young adults, however, were systematically denied the franchise for much longer. The battle to enfranchise African Americans began in earnest immediately following the Civil War. The Fifteenth Amendment technically granted African Americans the right to vote, although this right was stripped from many by state laws mandating poll taxes or literacy tests. It was not until the Voting Rights Act of 1965 that the franchise was fully and securely extended to African Americans.

Leaders of the early women's movement had hoped that the initial drive to gain African Americans the franchise would also benefit women. This was not the case, however, and women had to put up with widespread opposition to their political participation. In the late 19th and early 20th centuries, business groups—such as textile manufacturers and brewers and distillers—opposed giving women the right to vote because they feared women would use their newfound political power to harm business interests. Women finally got universal voting rights with passage of the Nineteenth Amendment, ratified in 1920, which denied federal and state governments the authority to deny anyone voting rights on the basis of gender.

Young adults won the right to vote in the 1970s. The Constitution gives states the authority to set voting age requirements, and most states prior to the 1970s set this age requirement at 21. This was considered to be unfair by many. During the Vietnam War, 18- and 19-year-olds were being drafted by the government and sent into combat. If they were old enough to fight and kill for their government, reasoned the generation of the 1960s, they should be old enough to vote. Congress responded to these arguments in 1970 by passing a law that reduced the voting age to 18 in national, state, and local elections. This law was challenged, however, and the Supreme Court ruled that while Congress had the authority to set the voting age in federal elections, it had no such rights for state and local elections (*Oregon v. Mitchell* 1970).

It struck some as rather silly that an 18-year-old could vote for president but in some jurisdictions be considered too politically immature to vote for city dogcatcher. Congress proposed the Twenty-Sixth Amendment to secure the voting rights of all citizens 18 and older, which was ratified in 1971.

Eliminating property, racial, gender, and age requirements extended the franchise to most adult citizens in the United States. These changes, however, have not removed all barriers to voting, although those that remain strike most people as reasonable rather than as threat to the promise of democracy. Most states, for example, require voters to be U.S. citizens, residents of the jurisdiction where they want to cast a ballot, and registered to vote.

There are other restrictions on groups of people presumed to not to have the intelligence or moral character necessary to cast a ballot. These include the mentally ill and convicted felons. In most states felons are denied the right to vote even after they have served their sentences (Figure 11.2). This practice, though ruled constitutional by the Supreme Court, is increasingly controversial because such laws tend to disproportionately affect African American men. Though roughly 2 percent of the nation's entire voting age population has lost the right to vote because of a felony conviction, approximately 13 percent of African American men are disenfranchised because of a criminal record. In some states, almost a third of African American men have permanently lost the right to vote (Human Rights Watch and The Sentencing Project 1998). (See the Promise and Policy feature "Felons and the Franchise.")

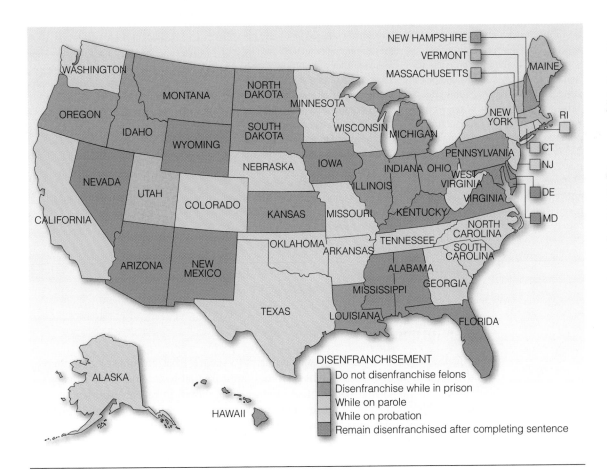

Figure 11.2
Felony Disenfranchisement Laws by State
Source: *www.hrw.org/reports98/vote/*.

PROMISE AND POLICY
Felons and the Franchise

Though most adult citizens now have the right to vote, the franchise is still withheld from one large group in U.S. society: convicted felons. Roughly 4 million Americans no longer have the right to cast a ballot because of their criminal records. This right is sometimes permanently lost to them—even after serving their time and paying their debt to society.

The voting rights of ex-prisoners are mostly governed by state statute, which means the voting rights of felons vary enormously from state to state. Forty-eight states place at least some restrictions on the voting rights of felons. Most prevent felons from voting while they are in prison or on probation. Twelve states permanently disenfranchise felons; once convicted, they can never vote again.

Some argue there is a rough justice here and that disenfranchising felons is appropriate. If you harm society through criminal activity, the theory goes, you lose the right to participate in society's decision-making process.

Others, however, argue that felony disenfranchisement is grossly unfair. It is unfair in the sense that whether you permanently lose your voting rights depends not just on what you did, but where you did it. The exact same crime in Maine and Alabama will have very different implications for individual voting rights—in Maine they are hardly affected at all, in Alabama they are gone for good.

It is also unfair, some argue, because what constitutes a felony varies considerably from state to state. For example, using a false identification card in Maryland is a felony. Two convictions of this crime will result in the state permanently revoking the person's voting rights. The exact same crime in many other states is considered a misdemeanor and will have no impact on voting

rights at all. Some argue felony disenfranchisement is unfair because it disproportionately affects one group: black males. Overall, 1 in 10 Americans have lost their right to vote because of felony convictions. For black males it is more than 1 in 10. In some states, it approaches 1 in 3. This raises serious concerns because the criminal justice system is often accused of systemic racism. It raises questions over whether the criminal law is being used as a backdoor to disenfranchise a minority that historically has been denied rights of political participation.

Finally, some argue felony disenfranchisement is unfair if it is permanent. Should individuals who serve their time, get their life together, and become law-abiding citizens have no right to cast a ballot? Should society permanently withhold suffrage for crimes (such as drug use or possession) that harmed no one but the offender? In 14 states, the answer is yes.

Source: Hull, Elizabeth. 2004. "Felons Deserve the Right to Vote." *USA Today Magazine.* January, pp. 50–52.

Voter Turnout

Ironically, having struggled for two centuries to secure a basic promise of democracy and extend to all citizens the right to vote, it appears that fewer and fewer citizens are interested in exercising that right. As Figure 11.3 shows, in recent presidential elections roughly 50 percent of those eligible cast ballots. Voter turnout for congressional races in **midterm elections** is consistently well below 50 percent.

But is **voter turnout** really declining over time? Answering this question is more complicated than you might think. First, it must be clear what proportion of voters actually vote. Yet there is more than one way to calculate this proportion. A common practice is to calculate turnout rates based on the "voting-age population"—that is, everyone of voting age who lives in one of the 50 states. But political scientists Michael McDonald and Samuel Popkin (2001) point out that not all residents older

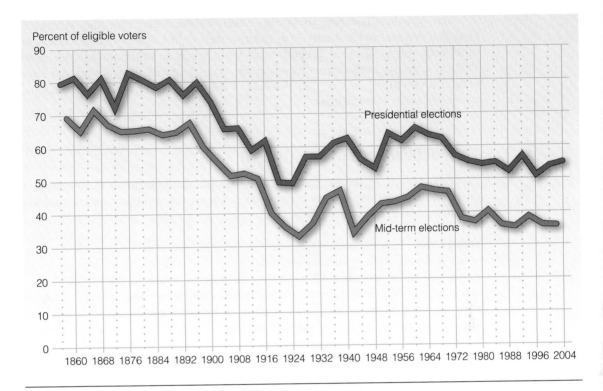

Figure 11.3
Voter Turnout, 1856–2004
Sources: Stanley and Niemi 2004 and McDonald 2004. "United States Elections Project."

than the minimum voting age are eligible to vote—for example, noncitizens cannot vote, and most states do not allow felons to vote. A more accurate estimate is the percentage voting of the "voting-eligible population" that excludes from the calculation all those who are disqualified for some reason. Since voting-age population includes people who cannot vote, it makes turnout look lower than it actually is. McDonald and Popkin argue that if ineligible people are excluded from the calculation, the apparent decline in turnout since 1972 is largely an illusion. But there continues to be debate about the appropriate baseline for calculating turnout.

Second, regardless of what baseline we use, whether we see a decline in turnout or not depends a lot on where we start. If we look at the trend for presidential elections from the 1950s forward, there seems to be a decline: Average turnout in the 1950s and 1960s was about 63 percent of eligible voters, compared to an average of about 54 percent in the 1990s. But if we go back to the early 20th century, we get a different picture: Average turnout in the 1910s and 1920s was about the same as in the 1990s—55 percent. A reasonable interpretation of the trend over this period is not that turnout is low in recent elections, but that turnout was unusually high in the 1960s. We see yet another picture if we extend our observations back to the 1860s. Turnout in the 1960s looks paltry compared to the 80 percent voting in elections around the time of the Civil War. Keep in mind, though, that the eligible electorate was more limited then—women, African Americans, and young people over 18 were excluded.

Although there is debate about the decline of turnout over time, the evidence is clear that Americans are less likely to exercise their right to vote than are citizens in other democracies. Why do proportionally fewer voters go to the polls in America? Political scientists have devoted considerable effort to explaining turnout and have arrived at two broad answers: (1) elements of the political system and (2) individual desire and ability to participate.

The Political System and Turnout

Particular aspects of the American political system that contribute to low turnout rates include voting laws, voter registration practices, the two-party system, and the scheduling and number of elections.

Voting Laws   In some countries (Australia, Belgium, and Italy are examples) voting is not optional. By law, citizens are required to vote and face fines, loss of voting rights, and social ostracism if they do not. In Italy, for example, the names of non-voters are publicly posted. In the 1880s, Bavaria came up with an innovative way to encourage voting. In order for an election to be considered valid, two-thirds of eligible citizens had to cast a ballot. If turnout fell below the two-thirds threshold, nonvoters were charged with the cost of putting on a new election (Robson 1923, 571–572).

Turnout where there are compulsory voting laws typically exceeds 70 percent and can be as high as 80 or 90 percent. Yet though turnout is clearly higher, it is obviously not universal. The punishments associated with compulsory voting laws, and the vigor with which they are enforced, undoubtedly vary considerably (Powell 1980, 9). Actually, compulsory voting laws might more accurately be termed compulsory attendance laws; these laws only require voters to pick up a ballot, not to actually use it.

Compulsory voting reflects the notion of political participation as civic duty, although its critics question whether legally forcing citizens to vote is democratic. Individual liberty and political freedom in the United States imply not just the right to vote but the right not to vote.

Voter Registration   Voter registration requires more effort in the United States than in other democracies. In European countries, it is common for 90 percent or more of those eligible to vote to actually be registered to vote. In the United States, registration rates are considerably lower.

The reason for the difference is that in the United States, registering to vote is considered an individual responsibility; it is mostly left to citizens themselves to take the initiative to register. In other democracies, government takes on the responsibility of identifying potential voters and registering them to vote.

Some political scientists argue that the burden of registration explains a big part of low voter turnout in the United States (Wolfinger 1991). The evidence underlying this argument is that turnout is much higher if it is calculated as the percentage of registered voters rather than the percentage of eligible voters. Persuaded by this logic, in 1993 Congress passed the National Voter Registration Act—the so-called motor voter law—requiring states to provide registration services when citizens go to renew their driver's license or seek other public services.

Voter registration requires more effort in the United States than in other democracies. The 2004 presidential election sparked a new drive to register people who were eligible to vote but who were either disinclined to go through the process or were not easily able to do so. The Partnership for the Homeless in New York City participated in this drive by educating the homeless about voting rights and eligibility, helping them to register, and then following up with participants by accompanying them to the polls on election day.

The bill was controversial for several reasons. First, it put the federal government directly into a role traditionally considered the province of the states, raising questions of whether Congress was overstepping its constitutional bounds. Second, there were partisan objections to the bill. Unregistered citizens tend to be poorer, less educated, and more likely to identify as Democrats. Republicans feared that they would be at an electoral disadvantage if turnout increased in this group. Research suggests the Republican fears are largely unfounded: while the motor voter law has increased registration rates, it has had, a best, a modest impact on actual turnout (Knack and White 1998).

Registration laws and procedures vary from state to state. Maine, Minnesota, and Wisconsin, for example, allow citizens to register on the day of election. Other states require voters to register a month before the election in order to vote in that election. Most states automatically cancel the registration of individuals who have not cast a ballot in a specified period of time (usually two to four years), thus forcing citizens to repeat the registration process if they do not vote on a regular basis.

The Two-Party System   Some scholars argue that because the two-party system often does not offer voters a meaningful choice, voters have less of an incentive to show up at the polls. Economist Anthony Downs (1957) famously articulated the formal explanation for the overlapping positions of the two major political parties. He argued that in two-party systems, it is rational to appeal to the average voter, which in the United States means appealing to a middle-of-the-road perspective on politics and policy.

It is perfectly rational for the parties to stake their ground in the middle of the political spectrum because that is where most voters' preferences lie. The problem is that if both parties are chasing the middle-of-the-road voter, they end up with overlapping appeals and make it hard for citizens to differentiate between them. If potential voters cannot see differences between parties or candidates, they will find it troubling to cast a ballot based on individual policy preferences. If this is the case, it is just as rational to go to the beach as to vote. As a Texas politician once said, "the only thing in the middle of the road are yella stripes and dead armadillos."

Election Schedules and Frequency   Presidential elections are held on Tuesdays, a workday for most Americans. Other democracies encourage voting by holding elections on Saturdays or Sundays. Holding national elections on weekends, or making election day a national holiday, would make it easier for working Americans to show up at the polls. (See the Living the Promise feature "Why Tuesday?")

Some have suggested that it would be fitting to hold national elections on November 11, Veterans Day. The argument here is that this would be an appropriate tribute to the members of the armed forces who have defended democracy, and it would highlight the importance of civic duty and participation (Wattenberg 1998).

It is not just the timing of elections but also the number that may depress turnout in America. Citizens in the United States are called on to vote much more often than in other democracies. The federal system means there are not just federal elections, but numerous elections at the state and local level too. Citizens in many states elect state agency heads, state and local judges, sheriffs, county officials, mayors, and city councils.

Electing candidates for these offices usually means at least two elections: a primary election and a general election. On top of that, elections are regularly held for special-purpose districts such as school districts, flood control districts, water districts, sewage districts, mosquito control districts, and park districts. In addition, voters are regularly called on to vote for proposed state constitutional amendments, ballot initiatives, and bond issues.

In short, there are a lot of elections, and the United States is far ahead of other democracies in the number of voting opportunities presented to citizens. U.S. voters may be exhausted by a virtually permanent election season. Like the mouse, they may beg, "Don't give me any more cheese; just let me out of the trap."

Individual Desire and Ability to Participate

The mix of reasons listed above may help explain why voter turnout in the United States is lower compared to other democracies. What they do not explain is why turnout has been undergoing a steady decline since the 1960s.

This decline is particularly puzzling because it has occurred at the same time as a number of reforms that, at least in theory, should have led to higher turnout. For example, although restrictive registration and voting laws keep voters away from the polls, some states have eased registration laws, set up registration booths in shopping malls, and experimented with letting people register online. Yet as registering to vote has become easier, voter turnout has continued to decline.

LIVING THE PROMISE
Why Tuesday?

Why are elections held on Tuesday? Why not Saturday or any other day of the week? In fact, there were good reasons for holding elections on Tuesday, even if those reasons are not as valid as they once were.

Originally, neither the Constitution nor federal law had much to say about when elections should be held. Article II, Section 1 of the Constitution gives Congress the authority to set a uniform election day for the United States. In 1792, the first Congress passed a bill designating the first Wednesday in December as the day on which presidential electors were to assemble and vote in their respective state capitals and requiring states to appoint the electors within 34 days prior to that date. Dates for other elections, including

elections for Congress, were not mentioned.

In 1845, Congress changed the date for the choice of electors to the "first Tuesday after the first Monday in the month of November of the year in which they are appointed." By this time, most states were choosing presidential electors in popular elections. In 1872, Congress extended this date to the election of members of the House of Representatives. In 1915, after ratification of the Seventeenth Amendment, it was extended to the election of senators.

November was chosen as the month of elections, and Tuesday chosen as election day, for practical reasons reflecting cultural and lifestyle conditions early in the nation's history. The United States

was a rural, agrarian nation. Crops were harvested by November, so farmers had free time to travel and vote, and travel was likely to be easier before the onset of winter weather in the northern states. A day's travel was necessary because most rural voters had to travel by foot or horseback to the county seat. Most of the nation strictly observed Sunday as a day of rest, which precluded travel on that day. Saturday was a workday for most people. That basically ruled out weekend elections.

Tuesday was hit upon as a way to allow for a full day of travel between Sunday and election day. Choosing the first Tuesday after the first Monday also prevented election day from falling on the first day of the month, which was frequently reserved for court business at the county seat.

Source: U.S. Congress. 1993. *Our American Government.* 102nd Congress, 2nd Session, H. Doc. 102–192, 61–62.

The puzzle of voter turnout is tied to the fundamental question of political participation: Why do some people participate while others do not? There is no single, simple answer to this question. Research has identified a number of the key elements that affect an individual's desire and ability to participate:

- Socioeconomic status (SES), which is simply the social and economic position a person occupies in society
- An individual's psychological engagement with politics
- The broader political and social context with which an individual is connected
- Resources necessary to participate—free time, money, and civic skills
- Group characteristics—age, gender, race

Socioeconomic Status Perhaps the most important determinant of any form of political participation is **socioeconomic status (SES).** Socioeconomic status is typically measured in terms of occupation, education, and income levels and serves as a baseline explanation of both the desire and the ability to participate.

Education seems to be an especially important. Well-educated people tend to hold high-status positions (business executive, doctor, lawyer) and earn high incomes.

They are likely to be aware of political matters and possess the confidence and intellectual tools to deal with them. They recognize their financial stake in politics (through taxes and fees), and they have professional, intellectual, and social skills that transfer easily to the political arena. In short, socioeconomic status helps determine whether people have the ability to participate effectively in politics. Generally speaking, higher SES citizens—those with high income, high education, and high-status occupations—are more likely to show up to the polls than low SES citizens.

Although SES clearly plays an important role in explaining why people do or do not vote, it does little to explain the puzzle of declining voter turnout. Education and income levels, for example, have risen across all levels of society during the past three decades, even as turnout was falling.

Psychological Engagement   People who believe their opinions are important and that government will respect and respond to their views are said to believe in **political efficacy.** Individuals are more likely to participate if they feel efficacious, regardless of their levels of SES (Milbrath and Goel 1977, 59). Though high SES people have the skills necessary to participate, it is the psychological engagement with politics that provides the desire to participate.

Psychological engagement, or more accurately the lack of it, may play an important role in explaining voter turnout. **Political alienation** characterizes individuals with deep-seated feelings of isolation and estrangement from the political system (Finifter 1970; Milbrath and Goel 1977; Seeman 1959). Politically alienated citizens tend to have low levels of trust in government and feel the political system does not merit their participation. **Allegiant** individuals, in contrast, express high levels of trust in government.

Although it would make sense that citizens with high levels of political efficacy would participate while politically alienated citizens would not, the relationship between psychological engagement and voter turnout is not that clear-cut. Some argue that alienation and distrust translate into voter apathy, and as alienation and distrust in government has increased, turnout has declined. Others, however, argue that this is a demonstration of "happy politics" (Eulau 1956). The notion here is that people who are happy with the process and trust government to do the right thing simply see less of a need to participate. Logically, then, people who are unhappy with the government should be more likely to vote; their dissatisfaction with the status quo provides the motivation to go to the polls to try to change things. There is research supporting both points of view, indicating both arguments have some merit, but neither can supply a full explanation for why people do, or do not, vote (Luttbeg and Gant 1995, 161; Timpone 1998).

Some scholars suggest that it is the interaction of trust and efficacy that accounts for these mixed findings (Milbrath and Goel 1977, 69–70). The premise is that efficacy provides the basic motivation to participate and that trust determines the particular form of participation. Thus, people with high levels of trust and high levels of efficacy are allegiant—they are the people most likely to be involved in all forms of political participation. Individuals with low levels of trust and low levels of efficacy are likely to withdraw from politics altogether. People with low levels of trust and high levels of efficacy, on the other hand, are more likely to engage in unconventional forms of political participation, such as protest rallies. Those with high trust and low efficacy will engage in supportive, ritualistic activities such as flying the flag and voting in presidential elections, but not much else.

Context In addition to SES and psychological attributes, participation is affected by the context in which an individual lives. The broader social network, particularly organizational memberships and the neighborhood, is important in developing civic skills. Political scientists Robert Huckfeldt and John Sprague (1995) conducted an intensive study of political activity in sixteen neighborhoods in South Bend, Indiana, during a presidential election. They found that people who live in neighborhoods that reflect and support their party identification are more likely to become politically active—not just voting, but also putting up yard signs, sporting bumper stickers, and making politics a topic of conversation.

Context, though, goes beyond the local level to include the broader impact of the political system and the experiences of the electorate as a whole. For example, the mobilization hypothesis, formulated by Steven Rosenstone and John Mark Hansen (1993), argues that participation has declined because political elites have become more sophisticated in their efforts to get people involved in politics. These elites—political parties, special interest groups, and the like—increasingly target people who have resources, have particular partisan affiliations, or are key members of social networks. In other words, they increasingly try to elicit support from the better-off and the more influential rather than targeting the mass of voters. Unsurprisingly, as political parties and special interest groups spend less effort trying to get the masses out to the polls, turnout declines.

Others argue for the generational effect hypothesis. This view suggests that the key elements of social context driving voting turnout are the events and experiences

The political and social context a person is connected to affects his or her levels of participation. People who live in neighborhoods that reflect and support their party identification are more likely to become politically active—not just by voting, but also by putting up yard signs, sporting bumper stickers, and making politics a topic of conversation.

that shape a generation's attitudes toward politics. The generation shaped by the Great Depression and World War II was more politically engaged because those events promoted a keen sense of the importance of politics and civic duty. The generations that followed experienced nothing equivalent to mass economic dislocation and a multiyear effort to fight a world war. This results in generational effect on turnout (Miller 1992). As the baby boomers and the generation Xers replace the generation born before World War II, turnout declines:

> Those born after 1932 are slower to enter the active electorate. They are voters of a different stripe, products of a system whose primary socialization has shifted from citizen duty, buttressed by partisan thinking, to a more passive, candidate-cued system. (Lyons and Alexander 2000, 1,032)

Resources   Verba, Schlozman, and Brady (1995) propose a resources model of political participation to build on the idea that SES is the main factor. Their argument is that individuals need resources in order to participate and that three types of resources are important:

1. Free time after work, household duties, and school
2. Money
3. Civic skills, such as communication and organizational abilities

Individuals who have free time, above-average family income, and the ability to speak and write well or are comfortable organizing and participating in meetings are more active and effective in politics (Verba, Schlozman, and Brady 1995). Different resources are required for different forms of participation. Contributing money to a campaign, for example, requires surplus income but not much time. Contacting a government official requires time and civic skills.

These resources are distributed unequally across the population, which helps explain why some people are more likely to participate than others. But more importantly, the different resources are not equally associated with SES. Money is associated with high SES, by definition. Free time, however, is not; low-SES individuals have as much or more of it than people with high SES.

The connection between civic skills and SES is mixed. Individuals begin acquiring civic skills early in life from the family and school. These skills develop throughout adult life in nonpolitical institutions such as the workplace, organizations, and churches and synagogues. High-SES individuals have the civic skills to participate in activities requiring them, such as working in a political campaign and contacting government officials. They probably grew up in families that valued such activity, and as adults they tend to have jobs and belong to organizations that allow them to practice writing, speaking, and organizing. But school offers opportunities to children from low-SES families to learn civic skills. For example, Verba, Brady, and Schlozman (1995) found that participation in student government contributes to an individual's civic skills. Furthermore, church attendance offers adults opportunities to develop civic skills. Church attendance is not associated with SES; individuals with low income and education have about as much opportunity to make speeches and organize meetings at church as do those with high SES. "In this way," conclude Verba and his associates, "the institutions of civil society operate, as Tocqueville noted, as the school of democracy" (Brady, Verba, and Schlozman 1995, 285).

Group Characteristics Certain group characteristics—such as race, gender, and age—are also associated with participation. The relationship between age and participation is curvilinear: Participation is highest among middle-aged people (say, those aged 45 to 65) and much lower for the very young and very old. Middle-aged people tend to have the greatest stake in the political system, to be aware of how government affects their lives, and to have the resources necessary to participate. Very young citizens participate less in politics because they are less likely to see how politics and government affect them, and they lack other attributes that encourage participation. Young people, for example, may be just starting a career or still be in school. Participation falls off among older people in part because of infirmities associated with aging. Some research indicates, however, that when differences in education and resources are accounted for, the decline in participation among the elderly is less pronounced. Retired people have the time to devote to politics, and many participate in organizations that provide them with pertinent information about politics and opportunities to develop civic skills.

Women tend to participate less than white males, but this tendency does not apply across the board. In terms of overall participation, women are less active than men, but when differences in SES and resources are taken into account, the gap in participation between men and women is reduced substantially (Verba, Schlozman, and Brady 1995). Furthermore, voter turnout in recent presidential elections has been higher among women.

African Americans and Latinos also participate less than whites. This difference, however, results mostly from other factors, particularly education, income, and resources. When SES and resources are controlled for, participation of African Americans and Latinos is not significantly different from that of whites (Verba, Schlozman, and Brady 1995). On the other hand, voter turnout of Asian Americans, another growing ethnic minority, is lower than whites even after controlling for SES and other factors (Uhlaner, Cain, and Kiewiet 1989). For other types of participation, there is no significant difference between Asian Americans and whites once the effects of SES and other factors are taken into account (Leighley and Vedlitz 1999).

Voting and Democracy

Scholars have raised concerns that turnout—or the lack of turnout—has important implications for democratic governance. If some groups participate less than others, are their preferences less likely to be accounted for in the democratic process? This concern is central to the elitist criticism of the American system. How can government truly uphold the will of the people and act on majority preferences if a majority of the people do not bother to cast a ballot?

Political scientists have approached this issue from a number of perspectives and are divided about the answer. For example, there is solid evidence that government is very responsive to broad currents of public opinion (Erikson, Wright, and McIver 1993). This suggests that people do not actually have to vote to have government respond to their preferences. It is also generally accepted that increasing turnout will not necessarily make a difference in election outcomes.

On the other hand, it is also clear that the mobilization of various groups in the electorate is an important determinant of election outcomes (Jackson 1997). Disproportionate

Voter turnout has important implications for democratic governance. Voting expresses the will of only those people who actually cast their ballots, and government policy favors those who participate.

participation by higher-class citizens logically results in policies that tend to favor their economic interests at the expense of lower-class citizens (Bennett and Resnick 1990; Gant and Lyons 1993; Hill and Leighley 1992). In other words, voting expresses the will of only a portion of the people, and government policy favors those who participate.

Models of Voting Behavior

Explaining why people do or do not vote in an election is a complex undertaking. Yet explaining voter turnout is relatively simple compared to the challenge of explaining what happens once a voter enters the voting booth. Why do some people vote Republican and others Democrat? Why do some vote for liberal candidates and others for conservative candidates?

During the past half-century, three theories have dominated the search for an explanation of vote choice: the sociological model, the social-psychological model, and the rational choice model.

The Sociological Model

Researchers at Columbia University developed the sociological model to explain voting behavior in the 1940 presidential election. Initially, the Columbia researchers tried to explain voting choices as consumer preferences. The initial idea was that political candidates could be viewed as "products" offered by political parties, and political campaigns as competing marketing efforts aimed at swaying voter preferences.

The consumer preference idea was a bust, mainly because researchers discovered that most voters decided for whom they were going to vote well in advance of the advertising campaigns (Niemi and Weisberg 1993a, 8). Casting about for an alternate explanation, the Columbia researchers noticed that sociological variables — a fancy term for the characteristics of groups—were strongly correlated with vote choice.

The result was the **sociological model** (sometimes called the *Columbia model*) of voting behavior. The sociological model uses group-level characteristics such as socioeconomic status, religion, and place of residence to explain how people vote (Lazarsfeld, Berelson, and Guadet 1944). At least in the 1940 election, this group-level approach worked well: Catholics, city dwellers, and people with low education, low income, and low-status occupations tended to vote for the Democratic candidate (Franklin Delano Roosevelt). Protestants, rural residents, and people higher up the socioeconomic chain tended to vote for the Republican candidate (Wendell Willkie).

More than sixty years later, the sociological model still provides a reasonable basis for explaining vote choice. For example, people with low income and education still tend to vote Democratic, as do African Americans, Latinos, Catholics, and Jews. Republican candidates still get higher levels of support from whites, Protestants, and people with high income. The sociological model, however, quickly fell out of favor as a comprehensive explanation of voter turnout. Although certain group characteristics—such as race, religion, and income—continue to be associated with differences in vote choice, they do not explain why those differences exist. Furthermore, there have been some changes in behavior since the Columbia study. Highly educated individuals, for example, are no longer solidly Republican: College graduates split evenly in the 2000 election, and they voted disproportionately Democratic in 1996. And in recent elections, women were more supportive of Democrats than were men. The sociological model was also formulated from a relatively small sample of voters (the sample was taken from a single county in New York State). Other studies based on larger national samples had difficulty replicating the findings. Figure 11.4 demonstrates the voting behavior of various sociological groups in recent elections.

The Social-Psychological Model

A team of researchers at the Survey Research Center of the University of Michigan began using national scientific polls to address limitations of the sociological model. Beginning with the 1948 election, they interviewed a nationwide sample of citizens to ask them how they voted and why. The findings of the Michigan team served as the basis for a new model of vote choice.

The **social-psychological model** (also known as the *Michigan model*) explains vote choice not as a product of group characteristics but individual attitudes. Specifically, the social-psychological model explains vote choice as primarily a product of three individual orientations:

1. An individual's psychological attachment to a political party, or party identification
2. Individual opinions about the candidates
3. Individual views on the issues prominent in a particular election

(a)

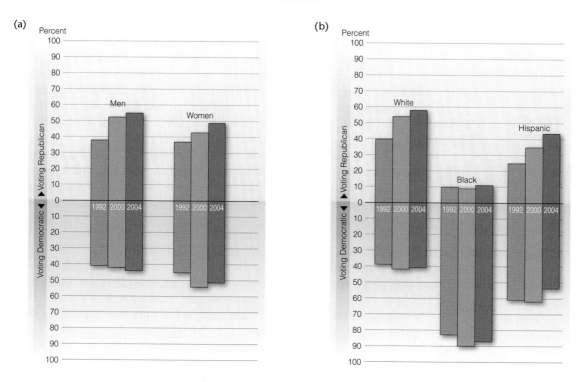

(b)

(c)

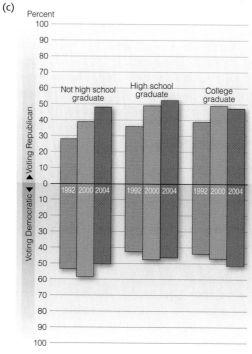

Figure 11.4

Voting Behavior of Various Sociological Groups
Source: Stanley and Niemi; 2004 *www.msnbc.msn.com/id/5297138/*

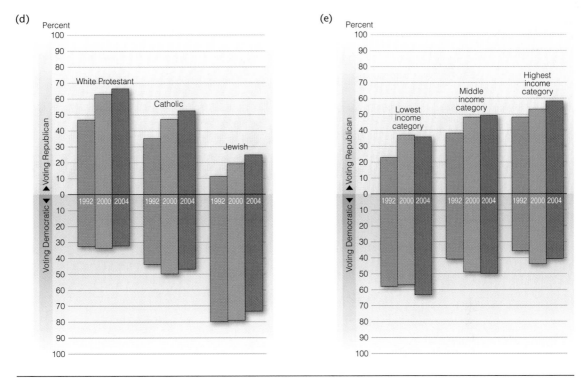

Figure 11.4   (Continued)

The best-known formulation of the social-psychological model was *The American Voter*, published in 1960. Authors Angus Campbell, Philip Converse, Warren Miller, and Donald Stokes provided what was for many years the authoritative explanation for voting behavior in the United States. It remains one of the most recognized and complete explanations of voting preferences (Niemi and Weisberg 1993a, 8).

The Michigan model did not so much refute the sociological model as extend it. The Michigan researchers used the metaphor of a "funnel of causality" to explain voter choice (see Figure 11.5). At the tip of the funnel is an individual's vote, and extending back from this are the primary influences of vote choice. At the core of the social-psychological model is party identification. Further back toward the mouth end of the funnel are factors such as SES, religion, gender, and race—these are the factors seen as driving an individual's party identification. Party identification, in turn, shapes an individual's attitudes toward candidates and issues. These three factors combined play the big role in explaining vote choice.

The model thus explains party identification as something largely inherited from parents and the same group-level characteristics dominant in the sociological model. Party identification acts as a "brand" that orients voters toward particular candidates and issues and helps them make choices. The heart of the Michigan model is its focus on party identification and individual attitudes, a focus that continues to dominate explanations of voting behavior.

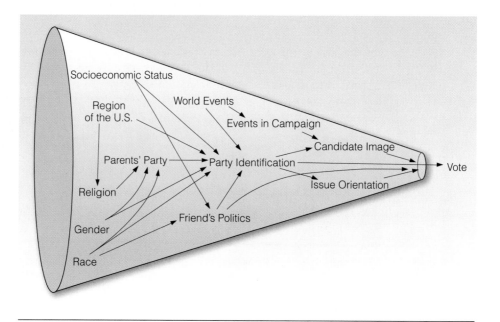

Figure 11.5
Funnel of Causality
Source: Luttbeg and Gant 1995, 13.

The Rational Choice Model

The only real rival to the Michigan model as a comprehensive explanation of voter behavior is the **rational choice model.** This model argues that the decision to show up and vote, and the particular set of choices made in the polling booth, are products of rational calculation. Broadly speaking, rational choice means that individuals will vote if the benefits of doing so outweigh the costs and will cast their ballots for candidates who are closest to sharing their views on the issues.

Unlike the Columbia and Michigan models, rational choice offers fairly precise predictions of voter behavior under different circumstances. For example, as the costs of voting increase (for example, a long line at the polling place), the rational choice model predicts a lower probability of voting. A second major contribution of the rational choice model is its focus on issues "which were submerged in the early findings of the Michigan researchers" (Niemi and Weisberg 1993a, 9).

Despite the theoretical insight provided by the rational choice model, some scholars consider its theoretical elegance to be a poor match with the reality of voting behavior. To make rational voting decisions on the basis of issues, for example, voters need some minimal level of information about those issues. A good deal of research indicates that most Americans are poorly informed about politics. Because of such practical limitations to the rational choice model, the Michigan model in various modified forms continues to provide the most accepted explanations of voting behavior.

Explaining Voter Choice

According to the Michigan model, the three primary elements that go into a decision to vote for a particular candidate are party identification, candidate image, and issues. Although it is the combination of these elements that are thought to produce a voting decision, scholars have long recognized that each plays a distinct role in shaping voter behavior.

Party Identification

The Michigan model argues that party identification is the most important determinant of vote choice (Campbell et al. 1960). In contrast to candidate image and issues, party identification is a long-term influence on voting behavior, helping to shape vote choices across many elections.

Early research suggested that an individual's general psychological attachment to a political party begins in childhood and intensifies with age (Campbell et al. 1960, 165). Party identification is also important because voters use it as a form of shorthand or a "cheat sheet." Voters rarely know everything about the specific issues a candidate supports or opposes. Indeed, they may not know anything at all about some candidates listed on a voting ballot. But most ballots are partisan ballots—they indicate the party affiliation of the candidates. Just knowing a candidate's political party can offer a rough and ready indication of what that candidate supports or opposes. So for a typical voter looking for guidance amid the complexities of personalities, issues, and events, a candidate's party label provides an important reference point. Party labels thus provide a quick and easy, if not 100-percent reliable, way of making judgments about a candidate.

Because of its central importance to explaining voter choice, political scientists have paid close attention to the partisan makeup of the electorate. It is generally recognized that levels of partisanship vary across time. In the 1950s, for example, 75 percent of the electorate identified themselves as Democrats or Republicans. By the 1990s, roughly 65 percent of voters identified themselves with one of the two major parties.

Some scholars saw this shift in party identification patterns as heralding the rise of the independent voter, a view supported by an increase in split-ticket voting. Split-ticket voters vote for one party's candidate in one race and for the other party's candidate in another. In the 1950s, straight-ticket voting was common, and party "brand loyalty" was strong across the entire ballot. That pattern changed over the next twenty years as voters became more likely to split their votes between Republican presidents and Democratic congressional candidates, or vice versa (Nie, Verba, and Petrocik 1979). As we learned in Chapter 7, however, the decline of partisanship stalled in the 1970s. Most individuals who initially claim to be independent admit to favoring one party, and they vote just like weak partisans. In the 1990s, the electorate became more partisan, and straight-ticket voting increased.

Early voting behavior studies viewed party identification as a fixed and stable political characteristic (Campbell et al. 1960). The swings over the past forty or fifty years have convinced some political scientists that party loyalty is more fluid, with party affiliation shifting not just over the course of a lifetime but even within a single electoral season (Allsop and Wiesberg 1988).

What explains the shifts in partisan loyalty? Research points to no single explanation but to a combination of factors. Key are the rise of candidate-centered election campaigns (as opposed to party-centered) and the rise of the electronic media. Candidates can make ideological and issue appeals directly to voters through television and radio ads, and this direct connection between candidate and voter may weaken party loyalties (Rapoport 1997).

Another explanation is that party loyalty underwent a period of ideological and regional realignment in the 1970s and 1980s (Abramowitz and Saunders 1998). The argument here is that conservative Democrats, especially in the South, slowly shifted to the Republican Party, which traditionally reflects a more conservative ideology. This shift was mostly complete by the mid-1990s, when the electorate became more partisan, and split-ticket voting declined. Backing up this argument is the dismal performance of Democratic presidential candidates in southern states over the last three or four presidential elections. In 1992, for example, Bill Clinton could only muster 38 percent of southern votes, even though he was a native southerner. In 2000 Al Gore, another native southerner, lost his home state of Tennessee.

Regardless of what explains the shift from periods of partisan stability to partisan instability and back again, party identification has consistently remained the most reliable predictor of voter choice in presidential elections (Abramson, Aldrich, and Rohde 1999, 174).

Candidate Image

Voter perceptions of the qualities of a candidate are known as **candidate image** (Miller and Levitin 1976). Early studies viewed candidate image as an irrational basis for vote choice because these perceptions are often based on gut-level responses to things like physical appearance, sense of humor, and family background. These factors were seen as a poor basis for making an informed, issue-based voting decision (Budesheim and DePaola 1994; Goren 1997).

Political scientists, however, also recognized that candidate image could play an incredibly important role in determining vote choice. The candidate viewed as a strong leader or having high levels of integrity is more likely to gain the confidence of citizens and their votes, regardless of the person's knowledge and experience. In the 2000 election, for example, Al Gore was seen as being very knowledgeable about the issues, but he was also seen as wooden and cold. George W. Bush did not seem to have the same grasp of policy as Gore but was widely seen as affable and approachable. Bush had the advantage of more positive candidate image.

The importance of candidate image has increased with the rise of television as the primary source of political information. Television is a passive and visual medium not well suited to in-depth coverage of policy issues and thus tends to elevate the importance of the personal and the symbolic (Carlin 1992; Patterson 1980). Not surprisingly, the personal and the symbolic have thus become a central focus of election campaigns. Television appearances and advertising are often centered on shaping image because they are a way to resonate with viewers' values and emotions and to project a suitably presidential image (Carlin 1992; Kern and Just 1995; Schutz 1995).

© AFP/Getty Images

Candidate image often plays a strong part in a voter's choice. Campaign television appearances, such as this debate between Dick Cheney and John Edwards in October of 2004, are often less about the content of the candidates' political stances than they are about shaping the image of the candidates in voters' minds. The candidate viewed as a strong leader, or having high levels of integrity, is more likely to gain the confidence of citizens and their votes, regardless of his knowledge and experience.

In 2004, for example, Democratic presidential nominee John Kerry heavily emphasized his military service in campaign ads. The idea was to contrast Kerry's (a highly decorated Vietnam veteran) military service with Bush's (a pilot in the air National Guard who never saw combat). The importance of commanding a swift boat in Vietnam or piloting a jet over Texas in the 1960s may have little relevance to being president, but the image was important to voters. The contrast was of a candidate who had volunteered for combat and risked his life for his country versus the candidate who had used family connections to sit out the Vietnam War in a cushy stateside position. This was not about issues but about character: The Kerry campaign was trying to avoid Gore's mistake and win the battle of candidate image.

In contests for Congress, candidate image is even more important than in presidential contests. People tend to evaluate members of Congress primarily on personal characteristics and qualifications, as well as devotion to district services and local issues. Those who hold office are well aware of this and devote a lot of energy to burnishing their image and "bringing home the bacon" by getting federal dollars for projects and programs in their districts. In voting terms, this adds up to a huge advantage for incumbents (Jacobson 2001). Though voters tend to dislike the institution of Congress, they tend to like their own representatives (Hibbing and Theiss-Morse 1995, 45).

Issues

In their analysis of voting behaviors in the 1950s, Angus Campbell and his associates proposed a set of criteria to gauge the importance of issues on voting choices (Campbell et al. 1960). They argued that issues can influence a voting decision only if three conditions are present:

1. The voter must be aware that the issues exist.
2. The issues must be of personal concern to the voter.
3. The voter must perceive that one candidate better represents his or her own thinking on the issues.

When they analyzed voting decisions in the 1952 and 1956 presidential elections, Campbell and his colleagues found these criteria were rarely met: They judged that less than one-third of the electorate voted on the basis of issues. Subsequent research suggests there is more potential for issue-based voting than the highly influential work of Campbell's team suggests. A key factor is how issues play out in the campaign. If there are clear issue differences between the candidates, and these issues are a central part of the campaign debate, then voters are more likely to pass the "issue test" suggested by Campbell and his colleagues (Abramson, Aldrich, and Rohde 1999, 132).

Some scholars view this issue test as an overly stringent basis for judging the importance of issues to vote choice. Morris Fiorina (1981) suggests there are two basic types of issue voting. **Retrospective voting** is based on evaluations of the past performance of the candidate; if voters feel an incumbent has done a good job, they are inclined to support that incumbent at the polls. **Prospective voting** is based on how well a voter believes a candidate will perform once he or she is in office. In practice, voters make retrospective and prospective judgments, but retrospective assessments seem to be stronger and more influential. In terms of issues, voters seem to use the performance of the incumbent "as a starting point for comparing the major contenders" (Abramson, Aldrich, and Rohde 1999, 57).

In congressional elections, issues are not as important as candidate image and party affiliation. This is because relatively few voters are familiar with the voting records of incumbents or the differences in the policy stands between incumbents and challengers.

Voting Behavior and the Operation of the American Political System

To keep the promise of democracy, the political system must balance two necessary but often conflicting qualities: stability and change. Without stability and predictability, the political system would have difficulty making binding decisions about who gets what; without change and openness to new demands, the system risks becoming stagnate and illegitimate.

Elections help the political system achieve this delicate balance because they are driven by long-term and short-term forces. Long-term forces such as party loyalties or incumbency advantage in congressional campaigns have similar effects across a number of elections; short-term forces such as dramatic events or hot new issues influence outcomes in one or two elections. The former produces stability: Most members of

Congress, for example, serve multiple terms and provide institutional memory. The latter allows the system to adapt to new events and changing issues; for example, every election brings a significant number of new representatives to Congress, and occasionally, as in 1994, a party that has been in the minority for forty years elects enough new members to become the majority.

For the most part, long-term forces prevail in elections. An election in which the long-term partisan orientation of the electorate keeps the status quo, at least in terms of which party is in power, is known as a **maintaining election.** When long-term forces give way to short-term forces, what was the minority party prior to the election can become the majority party after the election; such elections are called **deviating elections.** If the subsequent election returns the traditional majority party to power, the election that returns the traditional party to power is called a **reinstating election.**

Maintaining, deviating, and reinstating elections are all part of the ebb and flow of democracy and represent long-term stability. Occasionally, however, an election brings about long-term change. The minority party wins an election, but it is not followed by a reinstating election; instead the new majority stays in power for a number of elections. An election that brings about such a major political change is known as a **realigning election** or a critical election. Such elections are rare; they require a minority party to become the majority party and maintain that majority over the long term. Typically, realigning elections are a product of two forces: An event or crisis spawns issues that prompt blocs of voters to switch their party loyalties, and new voters are mobilized and disproportionately favor the minority party.

Political historians generally judge there have been five realigning elections in U.S. history: 1800, 1828, 1869, and 1932. During the last of these realigning elections, in 1932, the majority Republican Party was displaced by the Democratic Party for a long time. This realignment occurred because Republicans were not perceived as paying enough attention to the needs of immigrant and low-income groups who suffered mightily during the Great Depression. The latter event allowed the Democratic Party to put together a coalition of southerners, ethnic minorities, Catholics, Jews, the poor, urban blue-collar workers, and intellectuals. This coalition (known as the New Deal coalition) sustained the Democratic Party as the majority party in Congress, with relatively few interruptions, until the mid-1990s.

Contemporary Realignment?

Although there have been significant electoral changes over the last twenty-five years, there is no consensus about whether they add up to a realignment. There has clearly been a steady erosion of the New Deal coalition that has benefited Republicans. Some have argued that 1980 should be treated as a realigning election. In that year Republican Ronald Reagan defeated incumbent Democrat Jimmy Carter, while Republicans made significant gains in the House and won the Senate outright. Others argue 1980 was not a realigning election: Republicans failed to win control of both houses of Congress, and Democrats came back to win the White House with the election of Bill Clinton in 1992.

What 1980 undoubtedly did make clear is the fraying of the New Deal coalition. Groups that had traditionally voted Democratic for fifty years shifted their support to the Republican nominee in large numbers. This shift was especially noticeable in the South, where voters began to realign their traditionally conservative ideology with Republican candidates. These changes laid the foundation for a Republican resurgence. In 1994 Republicans gained control of the House and Senate for the first time since 1953. Six years later George W. Bush became the first Republican president in nearly fifty years to enjoy same-party control of both houses of Congress.

The Republican majority that emerged in the 1980s and 1990s, however, is thin. In the 2000 election, Bush actually lost the popular vote. Control of the U.S. Senate was so narrow in the early years of Bush's term that the defection of a single senator—Jim Jeffords of Vermont—from the Republican Party was enough to temporarily let Democrats regain control of the upper chamber.

Rather than a realigning election, recent electoral history points to an electorate with almost evenly matched partisan loyalties. But rather than bringing a new majority party to power, it appears that neither party has a majority—what Michael Barone dubbed "the 49% nation" (Barone and Cohen 2001, 21). George Bush won reelection in 2004 with a majority of the popular vote, and Republicans gained seats in both the House and Senate, solidifying their control of Congress. Some argue that this is evidence of a continuation of a Republican realignment that began in the 1990s. The electorate nonetheless remains closely divided between Democrats and Republicans.

 ## Performance Assessment

One of the hallmarks of a democratic society is that citizens have the right to influence important political decisions that affect their lives. Citizens participate in politics in a number of ways, but voting is the most visible and most widespread form of political participation. In a democracy, popular sovereignty and the will of the majority are exercised most forcefully through the ballot box. Who has the right to cast a ballot—or who does not have that right—provides a litmus test of the core value of political freedom.

The history of voting and voting behavior in the United States presents a curious paradox. For most of the republic's history, voting rights—and thus political freedom—have been limited. Extending the right to vote to women, African Americans, and young Americans over the age of 18—that is, virtually all adult citizens—required a long and arduous struggle. The paradox is that as the franchise expanded, turnout contracted. In recent presidential elections, barely half of eligible citizens voted; turnout in midterm congressional elections consistently falls below 50 percent. Though there are several reasonable explanations for the puzzle of turnout decline, smaller turnout stands as proof that having a right and exercising a right are two different things.

The extension of voting rights reflects the idea that individual citizens are capable of making rational judgments about their own self-interest. Though broadly accepted in the abstract, there is considerable doubt about this notion in practice. The ideal citizen visualized in most democratic utopias is highly informed, actively engaged, and bases voting decisions on issue preferences and the positions of candidates and parties. The first systematic voting behavior studies, notably *The American Voter* (Campbell et al. 1960), showed decisively that few U.S. voters approach this ideal type.

Instead of basing vote choice on a rational calculus that weighs individual preferences against the issue positions of the candidates, most voters consistently use party identification and some sort of personal connection with the image of a candidate as the basis for vote choice. This behavior hardly fits with the idealized version of a rational democratic citizen.

Some argue that describing the average voter as lacking the capacity to act rationally is overly harsh, if not inaccurate. Not voting, for example, might be perfectly rational, if you think about it. The chances of a single vote making any difference in an election (a certain presidential election in Florida excepted) are virtually zero. And, as parties and candidates tend to converge on middle-of-the-road issue positions, it is often difficult to see any difference between them. If your vote does not make a real difference and if you have to work hard to figure out the candidates' issue differences, the costs of voting are likely to be much greater than the benefits. If costs outweigh benefits, the rational choice is to spend your time doing something more fun than voting.

Others argue that voters may be more rational than assumed. A retrospective voter, for example, makes an informed vote choice, even if the choice is based on minimal information. All a retrospective voter needs is an opinion on the sort of job the incumbent has done. If the job is decent, the incumbent gets the vote; if not, consider the challenger. Retrospective voting does not require a lot of information, but it is an informed basis for deciding how to vote.

What does all this add up to? In terms of the political system, America gets good marks—at least recently. That virtually all citizens now have the franchise indicates that the system eventually was able to uphold the core value of political freedom, even if people choose not to exercise that freedom. The system, in other words, is making good on the promise. Turnout, or rather the lack of turnout, does raise questions about whether elections accurately express the will of the majority. In fact, it is voters who may be falling short in terms of performance.

These concerns raise questions of legitimacy. If more people voted, it would not necessarily change who wins or who loses. Yet the system's connection with the will of the people might appear stronger, even if the actual decisions made by government were not substantively altered. In the U.S. political system, however, the right to vote implies the right not to vote, and it is the latter right that most citizens exercise in most elections.

Summary

- Representative democracy rests on the notion that ordinary people have the right to influence decisions about who gets what. Participating in making those binding decisions upholds the core values of political freedom, popular sovereignty, and majority rule.
- There are numerous forms of political participation, including voting, campaign activities, citizen-initiated contacts with government officials, and local community activities. Voting is the most common and widespread form of political participation.
- Compared to other western-style democracies, voter turnout in American is lower, but participation in other forms is higher.

- Voter turnout in the United States has also declined over time. Turnout in presidential elections has fallen from over 60 percent of eligible voters in the 1950s and 1960s to barely half of the electorate in the 1990s. But the turnout rate in recent elections is slightly higher than it was in the 1920s. All of these rates are much lower than the 80 percent voting around the time of the Civil War (1860s).
- Various elements of the U.S. system impose higher barriers to voting than is the case in other democracies. Elements of the American political system that might cause low turnout include voting laws, voter registration practices, the two-party system, and the scheduling and number of elections.
- An individual's desire and ability to participate are affected by socioeconomic status (SES), psychological engagement with politics, political context, resources necessary to participate (free time, money, and civic skills), and group characteristics (age, gender, and race).
- Political scientists are also interested in explaining the choices voters make: For example, why do some people vote for Democrats and others vote for Republicans? Three theories have dominated the search for an explanation of vote choice: the sociological model, the social-psychological model, and the rational choice model. The sociological model uses group-level variables to explain voter behavior. The social-psychological model focuses on individual attitudes. The rational choice model views the decision to vote and the decision of who to vote for as the product of an individual cost–benefit analysis.
- Elections turn on both short-term forces (such as the candidates and issues associated with a particular race) and long-term forces (such as stable party loyalties within the electorate).
- An election that brings about major political change over the long term is called a realigning election.
- There have been significant electoral changes over the last twenty-five years that have frayed the New Deal coalition and aided Republicans. But there is no consensus about whether Republican gains add up to a realignment. It appears that in the early 21st century, the electorate is about evenly divided between Democrats and Republicans, but neither party has a majority.

Key Terms

allegiant 340	rational choice model 348
candidate image 350	realigning election 353
deviating election 353	reinstating election 353
franchise 332	retrospective voting 352
maintaining election 353	social-psychological model 345
midterm election 334	socioeconomic status (SES) 339
political alienation 340	sociological model 345
political efficacy 340	voter turnout 334
prospective voting 352	

Selected Readings

Abramson, Paul, John Aldrich, and David Rohde. 1999. *Change and Continuity in the 2000 and 2002 Elections.* Washington, DC: CQ Press. An accessible and comprehensive primer on recent congressional elections. A good example of a book that is periodically updated to track changes in voting behavior.

Campbell, Angus, Philip Converse, Warren Miller, and Donald Stokes. 1960. *The American Voter.* New York: Wiley. The classic study of voting behavior in the United States and the foundation of the social-psychological model of voting.

Jacobson, Gary. 2001. *The Politics of Congressional Elections.* 5th ed. New York: Addison-Wesley. One of the best comprehensive studies of voting in congressional elections.

Niemi, Richard, and Herbert Weisberg, eds. 2001. *Controversies in Voting Behavior.* 4th ed. Washington, DC: CQ Press. A comprehensive primer on the key issues involved in explaining why people do or do not vote.

12 | Congress

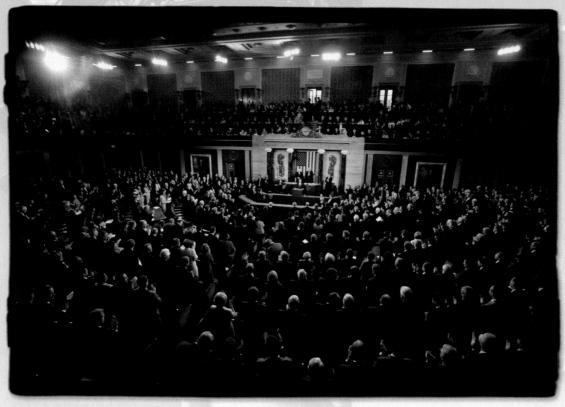

Americans tend to have low regard for Congress[1] as an institution. For example, a Gallup poll conducted in the summer of 2004 found that most Americans disapproved of the way Congress was handling its job (*http://www.gallup.com/*). Congress, especially the House of Representatives, is the government institution that is supposed to be the closest and most responsive to the will of the people. If a majority of Americans are dissatisfied with the way "the people's branch" is doing its job, does that not imply a disconnect between the promise and the performance of democracy? Maybe, but maybe not.

A study by John Hibbing and Elizabeth Theiss-Morse (1995) found that many people believe that Congress is less interested in the voice of the average citizen than in the voices of the rich and powerful. This belief seems to rest on the notion that there is broad agreement on the problems facing the nation, and all the bickering and finger pointing in Congress impedes quick action to solve these problems. Hibbing and Theiss-Morse also found that many Americans seem to lack a basic understanding of how Congress works. Its 535 members have differing goals and preferences, and they work in an institution governed by rules that could be described as Byzantine.

As discussed in Chapter 9, the voice of the people on most issues is a jarring cacophony of conflict. In short, there is no broad consensus on what government should do to solve the nation's problems, or even on what those problems are. Filtering these conflicting opinions in the public through an institution as large and as complex as the U.S. Congress will not turn discord into harmony. Perhaps all the argument and debate in Congress is just a reflection of the diverse and often conflicting opinions in the public. If so, Congress is doing exactly what it was designed to do.

Some might be surprised by this conclusion. But Americans often fail to grasp the wide variety of functions for which Congress is responsible and how the institution connects its business to the broader political arena. In this chapter, we analyze what Congress is supposed to do, who does it, and how it is done. The chapter seeks to provide a foundation for judging whether Congress is acquitting its democratic responsibilities by connecting the promise and performance of democracy.

---

[1]Although frequently used as a synonym for just the House of Representatives, the term *Congress* formally refers to both the House and the Senate.

The Promise of Congress

Congress is both a representative institution and a policymaking institution. The promise of Congress, therefore, is twofold: to represent the needs and interests of ordinary people and to translate those needs and wishes into laws that determine who gets what. If Congress keeps this dual promise, it contributes to achieving the core democratic value of popular sovereignty. To assess whether Congress is fulfilling the democratic promise, it is necessary to understand its responsibilities within the American political system.

The national legislature is charged with a dizzying number of tasks. These tasks can be grouped into primary and secondary responsibilities. Primary responsibilities are directly associated with the dual promise of representation and lawmaking. These are performed on a continuous basis and consume the greatest share of members' time. Congress also has a number of other responsibilities; these are secondary in the sense that they are handled on a sporadic basis and constitute a relatively small proportion of the legislator's heavy workload.

Primary Responsibilities of Congress

The two primary responsibilities of Congress are lawmaking and representing constituents. Lawmaking includes passing the laws and then overseeing government administration of those laws. Representation involves not only responding to constituents' needs and demands but also informing and educating the public.

Lawmaking

The legislature's foremost responsibility is lawmaking, enacting laws that address the major problems and concerns of American society. For example, in passing the Clean Air Act of 1990, Congress approved legislation "that would have a direct impact on the lives of nearly all Americans" because it "was designed to improve the quality of the air we breathe. It would have wide-ranging impacts on health, transportation, and the economy. It would affect sources of electric power, the cost and availability of consumer products, and countless other features of workplaces and homes" (Cohen 1995, 4). This particular legislation is instructive not only because of its substance, but also because it shows Congress at its best and at its worst.

On the positive side, there was clear public support for cleaning up the air, and the legislative process managed to incorporate a diverse set of viewpoints on a divisive set of topics to produce a law that had strong majority support. However, the process of lawmaking was agonizingly slow: The bill was thirteen years in the making. At several points, parochial protectionism, special interest meddling, and inter- and intra-party disagreements stalled the process. For example, the House committee with much of the responsibility for fashioning the Clean Air Act, the Energy and Commerce Committee, was the site of an ongoing struggle between Representatives John Dingell of Detroit, Michigan, and Henry Waxman of Los Angeles, California. Both Democrats, they held powerful positions, Dingell as chair of the full committee and Waxman as chair of a powerful subcommittee. Dingell was sometimes referred to as "Dirty Dingell" for his tireless attempts to insulate the auto industry from costly environmental regulations. Waxman led a strong pro-environment faction within the Democratic Party and was committed to tough regulations to help clean the air, including regulations on the auto industry. The clash between the two "produced severe tensions and near paralysis of the Energy and Commerce Committee" (Cohen 1995, 132).

Although the Dingell–Waxman face-off seems to show Congress at its worst, it is hard to distinguish hero from villain. Both members were representing their constituents: Dingell's district depended on the economic health of the auto industry; Waxman's district had a history of supporting green causes. Each representative appeared to be championing a cause he believed in: Dingell the economic health of the nation, Waxman the protection of the environment. But they were also involved in a personal struggle for political control of the powerful Energy and Commerce Committee (Cohen 1995, 77).

This example illustrates one conflict within one party on one committee. Multiply it hundreds of times to gain some insight into how hard it was to pass the Clean Air Act—or any other major piece of legislation.

Passing laws to ameliorate societal problems is a central function of Congress and an essential step in the policymaking process. The role Congress plays in the policymaking process, however, has changed over the course of the nation's history. The policymaking process (discussed in more detail in Chapter 16) involves several steps:

1. Agenda setting, which identifies the list of issues and problems to which government will pay attention
2. Policy formulation and adoption, where the government considers various alternatives and formally approves a particular one
3. Policy implementation, government translates the law into action
4. Policy evaluation, government and nongovernment actors assess the successes and problems of public policies (Ripley 1988, 48–55)

The goal of separation of powers in the Constitution was to separate legislative and executive powers. In the policymaking framework just outlined, the separation of powers principle suggests that Congress would have primary responsibility for steps one and two, and the president would have primary responsibility for steps three and four. This division of responsibilities has become less clear-cut over time.

In particular, while Congress continues to be a major agenda setter, the legislative branch has come to expect the president to take the lead in initiating policy proposals. A study of agenda setting by George Edwards and Andrew Barrett (2000, 122) found that since the 1950s, the president has initiated about one-third of the most important bills considered in Congress. Congress, of course, does not automatically pass the president's initiatives. Some presidential proposals do not pass, and those that do are often changed substantially as they work their way through the legislative process.

In addition, Congress has delegated substantial lawmaking powers to the executive branch. Congress tends to pass general laws that set broad goals and guidelines for dealing with a problem. Congress also creates administrative agencies—bureaucracies—to implement these laws. The bureaucracies set up to implement the laws have the responsibility—and power—to fill in the details. The bureaucratic procedure for filling in these details is known as *rulemaking,* which is discussed in Chapter 14.

Congress delegates the power to decide the specifics of laws to executive agencies for two basic reasons. First, members of Congress tend to be policy generalists—they can identify major problems and suggest general approaches to dealing with them, but they lack the time and expertise to deal with the complexities of issues on which they legislate. Legislators leave the technical details of policy to specialized executive branch agencies. Congress determines, for example, that the government should act to reduce air pollution, while leaving the formulation of specific air quality standards to the Environmental Protection Agency.

Second, lawmakers leave the details of policy to executive agencies for political reasons. Most people agree that no one should be free to fill the air with toxic pollutants, but there is little agreement about what or whom to regulate to achieve the desired outcome. Trying to reconcile these conflicting interests and perspectives is politically risky, and members of Congress often prefer to let others assume the risks. In some cases, the political disagreements are so intractable that even the goals of the legislation are vague. With vague goals, administrative agencies and interest groups are able to exercise considerable influence after Congress has passed legislation (Kerwin 1994; Lowi 1969).

Although Congress has delegated significant legislative power to the executive branch, it has compensated by extending its lawmaking authority to the implementation of policies. The primary way Congress has extended its lawmaking power is through legislative oversight of administration. **Legislative oversight of administration** refers to a variety of tools that Congress uses to control the administrative arm of government. These tools (discussed in more detail in Chapter 14) include the power to

- Create or abolish executive branch agencies
- Assign these agencies particular program responsibilities
- Provide or withhold funding for governmental programs
- Confirm or not confirm presidential appointments to the major administrative positions in the executive branch

Representation

The other primary responsibility of Congress is representation. **Representation** is a complex relationship involving the extent to which elected officeholders are responsive to the wants and needs of ordinary citizens.

Political scientists Heinz Eulau and Paul Karps (1977) identify four types of responsiveness that illustrate some of the complexity of representation: policy responsiveness, service responsiveness, allocation responsiveness, and symbolic responsiveness.

The first and most obvious part of representation is **policy responsiveness**—that is, the extent to which the policymaking behavior of the representative is congruent with the preferences of constituents. In the most simplistic terms, representatives are supposed to vote the way their constituents want them to vote. Political science research finds most citizens have little knowledge of how their representatives vote on issues before Congress, and partisanship and ideology are the primary predictors of how members of Congress vote on roll calls.

Do such findings mean that members of Congress are failing as representatives? Not necessarily. Members of Congress are responsive to constituents' preferences on many issues. One reason is that candidates who win election to Congress tend to reflect the politics and cultures of their constituencies. Consequently, representatives and constituents share many values, including party and policy preferences. Some districts are composed of voters who are mostly Democrats with preferences for liberal policies; these districts tend to elect liberal Democrats. Other districts are mostly Republicans with more conservative preferences, and they send conservative Republicans to Congress. Thus, representatives' party and ideology are likely to reflect broad constituency preferences. When members of Congress cast votes based on their own party and ideology, these votes are likely to be consistent with the preferences of their constituencies. Second, on the most salient issues, representatives tend to follow constituency preferences. Although constituents have very little information about policy proposals in Congress, they are likely to be aware of votes on salient issues. Failure to follow constituency preferences on salient matters invites a negative response at the polls. Thus, there is likely to be substantial policy congruence between most representatives in Congress and their constituents.

A second component of representation is **service responsiveness,** which refers to the variety of tasks that legislators perform for constituents who request assistance in dealing with the federal government. For instance, an elderly constituent might want information about Social Security benefits, or the mayor of a small city may ask for help in applying for a grant from a federal water treatment program. These activities are known as **casework.** In performing casework, members of Congress act as intermediaries between private individuals and the administrative agencies in the executive branch. Much of the actual work is done by staff members in congressional offices. Nevertheless, dealing with constituents' problems consumes a large portion of a legislator's time.

A third component of representation is **allocation responsiveness.** Members of Congress are notorious for using their position to see that their state or district gets a share of benefits of such government programs as roads, dams, government buildings, federal grants to local police and fire departments, and so on. Such allocations are often referred to as **pork-barrel benefits.** Although critics call such programs wasteful, coming up with a precise, objective definition of what is wasteful "pork" and what serves the public interest is a difficult task. The importance of this activity for representation is that by securing these allocations, a representative is anticipating and responding to the needs of his or her constituency.

The three types of representation discussed so far involve behavior intended to deliver some tangible benefit—a vote consistent with constituents' preferences, help with bureaucratic red tape, or a government expenditure to assist the district. The fourth type of representation—symbolic responsiveness—draws attention to a psychological component of representation. **Symbolic responsiveness** includes activities that use broad "political symbols in order to generate and maintain trust or support" among constituents (Eulau and Karps 1977, 246). Members of Congress develop close, cordial relations with their constituents. They spend time in the district to show that they are part of the constituency and that they are "at home" there. Richard Fenno, one of the nation's foremost authorities on Congress, refers to these activities as members' **home style,** which is the way members of Congress present themselves to the various parts of their constituency and explain their Washington activities (Fenno 1978). Typically, a member develops a home style to fit the constituency. A member who represents a strongly partisan constituency, for example, might adopt a policy-oriented home style. Another member who represents a more politically heterogeneous constituency might adopt a home style that emphasizes casework and bringing home pork-barrel benefits.

There are times, however, when a member of Congress must choose between the preferences of constituents and the dictates of conscience or what is in the best

Courtesy of Senator Dianne Feinstein

A Congressmember's home style may vary depending on with which constituents the member is communicating. Senator Dianne Feinstein maintains four California offices as well as one in Washington, DC, in order to keep in close contact with as many constituents as possible. She reaches out to many organized groups and causes as well as making a concerted effort to meet with and act as spokeswoman for individual citizens. Here the senator (center, in blue jacket) attends a groundbreaking for a new skateboard park in Orange Cove, California. In this Central Valley community, Feinstein also delivered a Washington report on current issues and met with Mayor Victor Lopez.

interest of the entire nation. A pork-barrel project might provide economic benefits and be strongly supported within the district, but what if it is an unnecessary drain on the federal treasury? Should a representative choose what constituents clearly want or what is in the best long-run interests of the nation as a whole? Such conflicts are more common than most people realize, and they raise a basic question about the exact nature of representation. Edmund Burke, a British political philosopher and member of Parliament, argued that representatives should be **trustees** who use their own judgment to make decisions they feel are appropriate for the interests first of the nation and then of their constituents. In contrast, representatives who adopt a **delegate** role simply do what their constituents want regardless of whether the representatives believe those wants are in the public interest. These contrasting philosophies suggest different decisions; the delegate will vote for the pork-barrel project, the trustee will not (and may face the electoral consequences). In reality, the philosophical divide is not quite so clear, and representatives often adopt a mix of both delegate and trustee; this type of representative is a **politico.**

Representation is a two-way concept. The four components of representation just discussed tend to view the relationship as one that flows from constituents to representative. Another aspect of representation focuses on the relationship that flows the other way, from representative to constituent. This aspect is the representative's duty to lead by informing and educating the public.

Scholars have long recognized that a central obligation of representatives is to inform the public about the major issues facing the country and the options for dealing with them (Wilson 1885). Thus, when Congress holds hearings on Social Security, pollution, drugs, or the conduct of the war in Iraq, it is helping to educate and inform the American people about the problems on the nation's agenda and the policies that might deal with them.

Members of Congress keep their constituents informed about a variety of problems, including those of special local interest. Such information is typically released in mass-produced newsletters, television broadcasts, and government publications. Such communications may be intended to produce an electoral advantage, but these activities, nonetheless, help to inform citizens about matters of public concern.

The lawmaking and representative functions together constitute the major responsibilities of Congress. Performing these functions has important side effects for society. By serving the needs of constituents, lawmakers help develop the loyalty and allegiance of the people to the political system. The give-and-take of the legislative process accommodates and compromises numerous competing demands, which helps make the final decision acceptable to the concerned parties. This accommodation process, in turn, helps

Members of Congress keep their constituents informed through mailings, state and district appearances, television broadcasts, and websites. Many of the websites, such as this one for House Representative Linda Sánchez, not only inform but also give constituents the opportunity to contact members of Congress.

Courtesy of the Office of Congresswoman Linda T. Sánchez

legitimize the political system so that citizens in general are willing to abide by the rules and regulations developed by Congress and the executive agencies.

Secondary Responsibilities of Congress

Congress performs tasks in addition to its primary responsibilities. Although these activities may be vital to the overall functioning of the government or the legislative body, they occur only sporadically. These tasks include impeachment, seating and disciplining members, and selecting leaders for the executive branch, among others.

Impeachment

In some instances, Congress acts as a quasi-judicial body by resolving disputes that are, at least in part, legal in nature. An example of this is Congress' power to remove executive and judicial officials of the national government from their positions through the impeachment process. According to the Constitution, officials subject to removal by congressional action include "the president, the vice president, and all civil officers of the United States" (Article II, Section 4). Federal judges are the only other civil officers who are likely to be subject to removal from office through impeachment. Because federal judges serve for life, there is no other practical way to remove them for wrongdoing. There are other legal procedures available to remove members of Congress and cabinet secretaries for wrongdoing.

The removal procedure set by the Constitution is a two-step process. The first step is impeachment by the House. To *impeach* means simply to charge or accuse. The House impeaches an official by passing Articles of Impeachment by a simple majority. The impeachment resolution serves as a formal charge of wrongdoing, similar to an indictment by a grand jury.

If the House passes Articles of Impeachment, the process continues to the second stage: trial in the Senate. Members of the Senate sit as a jury to hear the evidence and decide whether to acquit or remove the impeached official from office. The House sends "managers" to serve as prosecutors, and the impeached official is represented by defenders. Conviction and removal from office requires a two-thirds vote of the Senate.

As president of the Senate, the vice president would normally preside over the trial. But if it is the president who has been impeached, the Constitution designates the chief justice of the Supreme Court to preside at the trial in the Senate. The president occupies the highest, most powerful office in the government, and the chief justice of the Supreme Court adds additional dignity to the proceedings. Having the vice president preside over a trial that could elevate him or her to the presidency would be an obvious and blatant conflict of interest.[2]

---

[2]Senators take an oath to try the case impartially, but impeachment is a political process. Conflicts of interest are inevitable. In the impeachment trial of President Andrew Johnson in 1868, Senator Benjamin F. Wade (R-OH), president pro tempore of the Senate, took part in the trial and voted for conviction. Since there was no vice president, Wade was in line to become president. President Johnson's son-in-law, Senator David T. Patterson (D-TN), also participated; he voted to acquit. Senator Barbara Boxer (D-CA) participated in the recent Senate trial of President Clinton. Her daughter is married to Hillary Clinton's brother. In an ordinary judicial trial, individuals with such conflicts would be excluded.

Grounds for impeachment include "treason, bribery, or other high crimes and misdemeanors" (Article II, Section 4). Treason and bribery are straightforward but are rarely the focus of impeachment proceedings. What constitutes "high crimes and misdemeanors" is the subject of some controversy. Kenneth W. Starr, the independent prosecutor whose investigation provided the basis for the impeachment of President Bill Clinton in 1998, once argued that an official could be impeached for poisoning a neighbor's cat (Gettinger 1998). Historically, the bar for impeachment has been set considerably higher to include wrongdoing that threatens the basic functioning of government in the way that treason or bribery would. Thus, impeachable offenses would not be limited to illegal acts. If a president were to move to a Middle Eastern country so he could have several wives, such behavior would surely be impeachable, but it is not illegal (Black 1974). On the other hand, even serious illegal acts are necessarily sufficient grounds for removing a president from office. For example, when Vice President Aaron Burr shot and killed Alexander Hamilton, Burr was indicted for murder in two states, but he never faced impeachment.

Impeachment is as much a political process as a legal one. When he was a member of Congress, Republican Gerald Ford of Michigan said that an impeachable offense is "whatever a majority of the House of Representatives considers it to be at a given moment in history" (Gettinger 1998, 565). Although Ford was ridiculed at the time, the impeachment of President Clinton seems to validate this definition; the House impeached Clinton on a largely partisan vote.

The Senate is likely to prevent the bar from being lowered too far. Senators have broader constituencies than House members, and the Senate has a special status and responsibility under the Constitution that most senators take seriously. Furthermore, the super-majority vote required to convict and remove an official from office reduces the chances that a president would be removed for solely partisan purposes.

The Constitution specifies that the Senate judgment "shall not extend further than to removal from office, and disqualification to hold . . . any office of honor, trust or profit under the United States" (Article I, Section 3). Thus, after conviction by two-thirds, the Senate has the option of imposing the further penalty of disqualification to hold future office. The Senate does this with a separate vote on disqualification, which requires only a simple majority. In most cases in which officials have been removed, the Senate has declined to impose this additional penalty. Officials removed from office through impeachment are subject to punishment through normal criminal proceedings.

Impeachment is rarely employed. Since the ratification of the Constitution, only seventeen officials have been impeached. Only two presidents—Bill Clinton and Andrew Johnson—were formally impeached, and neither was removed from office. President Nixon resigned before the House vote on the Articles of Impeachment rather than face an almost-certain Senate trial. Most of the other impeached officials were federal judges; only seven were convicted and removed from office. Votes on disqualification to hold future office were held in three cases and passed in two. (See the Promise and Policy feature "The Impeachment of Judge Alcee Hastings.")

Seating and Disciplining Members

Each chamber also has power over the seating and disciplining of its members. Thus, both the House and the Senate have the authority to judge the fairness of elections. Defeated candidates sometimes challenge the results of close elections on grounds of

PROMISE AND POLICY
The Impeachment of Judge Alcee Hastings

The following is an excerpt describing the impeachment process in practice:

In the 1980s, for the first time, the Senate used a shortcut procedure first authorized in 1935 to deal with three impeachment trials of federal judges. The shortcut allowed a special 12-member committee to hear witnesses and gather evidence before the full Senate convened to try the judges. This procedure saved the Senate months of deliberation but resulted in court challenges from the judges, who claimed that their convictions were unconstitutional because the full Senate had not heard the evidence. In 1993 the Supreme Court refused to consider that argument, ruling unanimously in the case of *Nixon v. United States* that the courts could not interfere with the Senate's conduct of impeachment trials because the Constitution gave the Senate "the sole power to try all impeachments."

The Court's ruling was an important affirmation of the Senate's impeachment power, but the unique case of federal judge Alcee Hastings of Florida remained unresolved. Hastings had been impeached and convicted after having been tried and acquitted of criminal charges. In 1992 he made history by winning election to the House as a Democrat from Florida. Hastings' election raised a new constitutional question: whether conviction by the Senate was sufficient to disqualify a person from holding public office, or whether disqualification required a separate Senate vote.

The Constitution says, "judgment in cases of impeachment shall not extend further than to removal from office, and disqualification to hold and enjoy any office of honor, trust or profit under the United States." In practice the Senate had treated the punishments as distinct and held separate votes on whether to block an impeached official from holding office again. In three of its seven convictions, the Senate had taken separate votes on disqualification from future office and had twice voted to do so. A disqualification vote was not taken for Hastings, and in January 1993 a federal judge rejected a lawsuit claiming that Hastings' Senate conviction disqualified him from holding office. Hastings took his seat with the rest of the 103rd Congress.

It is not surprising that Hastings was greeted in Washington by skepticism that he would be able to work effectively with members who had voted in 1988 to impeach him. But Hastings surprised the skeptics by bearing no apparent grudges about the past and by focusing instead on building legislative influence.

"Succeeding is the best revenge," he said after nine months in office. "My goal was to get beyond people viewing me as an impeached judge. I think I've accomplished that in grand style."

Sources: Congressional Quarterly, Inc. 1993. *Congress A to Z*, 2nd ed. Washington, DC: Congressional Quarterly, 189–190; Duncan, Philip D., and Christine C. Lawrence, eds. 1998. *Politics in America 1996: The 105th Congress*. Washington, DC: CQ Press, 369.

voting irregularities. While both chambers attempt to investigate and resolve such charges impartially, historically the practice has been partisan, with the majority party seating its candidate.

The House and Senate can also **exclude** or refuse to seat individuals who win elections but do not meet the constitutional qualifications of being U.S. citizens, having residence in the state, and being at least 25 years old for House members and 30 years old for senators. Until 1969, each chamber occasionally used exclusion as a disciplinary tool against otherwise qualified individuals who were disloyal, such as those who supported secession during the Civil War or who were charged with crimes or misconduct. The Supreme Court ended this practice in *Powell v. McCormack* (1969). When the

House refused to seat Democrat Adam Clayton Powell of New York on the grounds of misuse of public funds, the Court held that a duly elected member could be excluded only for failure to meet constitutional qualifications.

Article I, Section 5 of the Constitution also authorizes both chambers to discipline sitting members for illegal or unethical behavior, though they are loath to exercise this power. Because most members do not relish the task of judging their colleagues, such formal actions are reserved for the most egregious cases. There are several penalties available, depending on the nature and seriousness of the wrongdoing: expulsion, censure, reprimand, and fine.

The most serious and least used punishment is **expulsion** from Congress. Expelling a member requires a two-thirds vote. Several members were expelled in the 1860s for supporting the Confederacy in the Civil War, but aside from that, only one House member and one senator have been expelled. Senator William Blount of Tennessee was expelled in 1876 after impeachment charges were brought against him. The House member was Ozzie Myers of New York, who was expelled in 1980 for involvement in a bribery scandal. Senator Harrison Williams, Jr., of New Jersey, who was caught in the same scandal, resigned because he was likely to be expelled.

The lesser penalties of censure, reprimand, and fines require only a simple majority to pass. **Censures and reprimands** are verbal condemnations intended to punish bad behavior by expressing public disapproval of the member's colleagues. Reprimands sometimes impose a fine. In 1997 Speaker Newt Gingrich was reprimanded for violating House ethics rules and fined $300,000 (Katz 1998). The Senate has in effect censured several members, but it uses the terms *reprimand, condemnation,* and *denouncement* interchangeably.

Selecting Leaders for the Executive Branch

The two houses of Congress are also involved on occasion in matters of leadership selection for the executive branch. As discussed in Chapter 10, if no candidate for president or vice president receives a majority of the electoral votes, the issue is decided by the House in the case of the president or the Senate in the case of the vice president. And under the Twenty-Fifth Amendment, if the vice presidency becomes vacant, both houses of Congress must approve the president's choice of a new vice president by majority vote. This procedure has been used twice. The first was when President Richard Nixon nominated Representative Gerald Ford to become vice president after the resignation of Spiro Agnew in 1973. When Nixon resigned in 1974, Ford became president and nominated Nelson Rockefeller to be vice president.

The Senate also plays an important role in staffing positions in the executive branch and judiciary. The president appoints cabinet secretaries and other high-level executive branch personnel, foreign ambassadors, and federal judges with the "advice and consent" of the Senate. There is little Senate advising before the selection, but the consent provision means that the Senate must confirm the president's appointments to these offices by majority vote. Some nominations have run into trouble and have been defeated or withdrawn. President Clinton had difficulty getting several cabinet secretaries and some ambassadors confirmed in the Senate. However, the Senate has confirmed more than 96 percent of presidents' nominations, and a recent study found that nominations enjoy a "presumption of success" (Krutz, Fleisher, and Bond 1998). The Senate is typically inclined to defer to the president's choice, and senators who are opposed to a particular nominee have a difficult time overcoming this presumption of success. In cases that are defeated, opponents have identified negative information in the nominee's background and then used the hearings and the media to expand the conflict to get other senators to change their views.

Other Policy Responsibilities

Congress also becomes involved in specialized areas of public policymaking. Both houses join in initiating constitutional amendments. The Senate also has special powers in foreign policy: The Senate must ratify treaties (by two-thirds vote) and confirm ambassadors to foreign countries appointed by the president (by a simple majority). Finally, Congress exercises legal jurisdiction over the District of Columbia.

Members of Congress and Their World

Thus far, we have examined Congress mainly from an institutional perspective. To grasp how and why Congress has such a broad social and political effect, it is important to understand not just what Congress does, but who drives the decisions of the legislature. How Congress executes its role in the political system and how it shapes the broader social fabric are determined largely by the 535 men and women who are members of one of the most exclusive clubs in the world.

The nation's legislators historically rank low in the estimation of observers. Political cartoonists portray them as possessing a surplus of hot air and scarcity of talent. Alexis de Tocqueville, the perceptive French observer of the Jacksonian period, referred to the "vulgar demeanor" of the national legislature. The aristocrats who dominated legislative assemblies in Europe, he argued, were secure in their social positions, less tied to their constituents than to their parties, and more interested in the big questions. By contrast, American legislators derived their social position from service in the assembly, were more tied to their constituents than to their parties, and as a result felt compelled to repeatedly offer the electorate confirmations of their importance and effectiveness, whether there was any basis for such claims or not. Rather than concentrate on big questions, legislators in America tacked to any inquiry deemed favorable by the democratic winds, regardless of substantive merit. "The consequence," Tocqueville wrote, "is that the debates of that great assembly are frequently vague and perplexed and that they seem to drag their slow length along rather than to advance towards a distinct object" (Tocqueville [1835] 1955, 97). To what extent does Tocqueville's analysis accurately portray Congress today? Who, exactly, are the people elected to Congress?

Backgrounds of National Legislators

Tocqueville noted that the national legislature was dominated by lawyers and businessmen, an observation that still holds true today. Lawyers are still predominant in the Senate. Although lawyers constitute less than 1 percent of the adult population in the United States, a majority of senators—59 percent—in the 108th Congress (2002–2003) were lawyers. But this is fewer than in the recent past—in the 95th (1977–1979), 68 percent of senators were lawyers. Lawyers are somewhat less prevalent in the House—37 percent of House members in the 108th Congress had a background in the law. This also is fewer than the 50 percent of House members who were attorneys in the 95th Congress (Ornstein, Mann, and Malbin 2000, 21, 27).

Attorneys are prominent in Congress for several reasons. For one thing, the tools of the lawyer's trade are the ability to analyze statutes and administrative regulations, verbal and argumentative facility, and negotiation skills—precisely the talents needed by those who legislate, control the administration, inform the public, and represent constituents. Moreover, a lawyer is a professional with specialized knowledge and training that bestows social standing in the community, and the lawyer's role is to help people with various kinds of problems. For these reasons, lawyers are often regarded as natural legislators.

Businesspeople now rival lawyers as the largest occupational group in Congress. In the 108th Congress, 45 percent of House members and 30 percent of senators listed their occupation as business, banking, or real estate. People in businesses have some of the same attributes that provide lawyers with advantages as legislators—they too tend to have social status in their communities and benefit from the high regard Americans have for entrepreneurs.

No other occupation rivals business or law in the national legislature. More than 80 percent of the 535 House members and senators serving in the 108th Congress listed their occupations as law, business, banking, or real estate. The remaining one-fifth is an eclectic mix of teachers, journalists, former congressional aides, actors, and athletes.

The similarities of the modern Congress and that of Tocqueville's time extend beyond the career background of its members. The legislature Tocqueville observed was dominated exclusively by white males. The exclusivity has diminished in the intervening years but not the dominance. The 2000 census revealed that the U.S. population was about 51 percent female, 12 percent African American, and 12.5 percent Latino. In the House of Representatives in the 108th Congress, 19 percent of members were women, 9 percent were African American, and 7 percent were Latino. The Senate was even less representative of the nation—14 percent of senators were women, but there were no African American or Latino senators. (See the Living the Promise feature "Jeannette Rankin: First Congresswoman.")

Such numbers tend to confirm that the membership of Congress reflects a narrow slice of America's citizens. The typical member today is a white male professional in his early 50s who is a Protestant, much like the typical member in Tocqueville's day. But there have been considerable changes in the composition of the legislature. Although the numbers of women and ethnic minorities are low in comparison to their proportion in the electorate, they are high in comparison to the historical representation of women and minorities in Congress. These changes suggest that the future composition of Congress may be increasingly different.

Moreover, descriptive representation, in which the legislature reflects the gender and ethnic makeup of society, is one of several types of representation. As discussed in Chapter 10, substantive representation may be more important. It is possible for

LIVING THE PROMISE
Jeannette Rankin: First Congresswoman

This excerpt describes the life and career of Jeannette Rankin (1880–1973), the first woman to serve in Congress.

A suffragist and pacifist, [Rankin] ran for the House at a time when only a handful of states allowed women to vote and as the nation was about to enter World War I.

Born into a family that believed in education for women and political activism, Rankin graduated from the University of Montana and went to study social work at the New York School of Philanthropy. She returned west and lobbied for the enfranchisement of women in the states of Washington, California, and Montana.

Rankin ran as a Republican for one of Montana's House seats in 1916 on a platform favoring Prohibition, women's rights, and federal suffrage. (The Nineteenth Amendment giving women the right to vote was not ratified until 1920.) When elected, Rankin said: "I knew the women would stand behind me. I am deeply conscious of the responsibility. I will not only represent the women of Montana, but also the women of the country . . ."

In the House Rankin worked to further the cause of women. She introduced legislation to grant women citizenship independent of their husbands and sponsored a bill providing for federally supported maternal and infant health instruction. She helped set up a House committee on women's suffrage and tried to ensure that employment generated by the legislation would include women.

In 1917 the House voted on the entry of the United States into World War I. With forty-nine other representatives Rankin voted no, saying, "I want to stand by my country but I cannot vote for war." Her vote brought national notoriety for her. . . .

After her first term in the House, Rankin ran unsuccessfully for the Senate. Out of office, she continued to work for women's rights, and in 1940 she was reelected to the House. Once again she was faced with a vote on U.S. involvement in a war. Rankin was the only member to vote against entry into World War II. Few people shared the view of Kansas newspaper editor William Allen White, who said of her pacifist stand: "It was a brave thing! And its bravery somehow discounted its folly." After the vote, she was forced to lock herself in a phone booth to escape from the curious and angry crowds.

In 1968, when she was in her late eighties, Jeannette Rankin led a Jeannette Rankin Brigade to the Capitol to protest the war in Vietnam. She died at the age of ninety-two.

Source: Congressional Quarterly, Inc. 1993. *Congress A to Z: A Ready Reference Encyclopedia.* 2nd ed. Washington, DC: Congressional Quarterly, 318–319.

---

white male professionals to understand and respond to the interests of the poor, blue-collar workers, women, and ethnic minorities and represent their substantive interests in the legislature.

Tenure and Career Patterns

Although the profile of the typical member of Congress has not changed much, the profile of the typical congressional career has changed dramatically. The most obvious change is that serving in Congress has become a career. In the 19th century, a decade was an unusually long time for anyone to be a House member, and serving in the House as a lifetime career was virtually unknown. By the latter half of the 20th century, the average member of the House of Representatives had been serving for about ten years, and some members have served much longer (Hibbing 1991).

Tenure has increased for several reasons. Members of Congress are more likely to run for reelection than in the past. In congressional elections since 1946, more than 90 percent of members of Congress ran for reelection, and they are very successful when they run—an average of about 95 percent win reelection. But it is not just a matter of the electoral advantages of incumbency. Government plays a much bigger role in social and economic life than it did before the 20th century. Serving in Congress has evolved from a part-time job in a part-time body with limited responsibilities to a full-time job in a full-time body with enormous responsibilities (Hibbing 1991, 3). As Congress has assumed ever-greater responsibilities and become more professional, it has attracted ambitious individuals who seek a career in a powerful, professional organization.

The rise of congressional careerists may have fueled cynicism toward government. A common view is that the incumbency advantage allows career politicians to ignore the needs of ordinary people and serve the interests of powerful special interests in Washington. The popularity of term limits indicates that many voters are uncomfortable with public service becoming a career unto itself.

Political scientist John Hibbing (1991) conducted a comprehensive analysis of congressional careers. Consistent with the conventional wisdom, Hibbing found that the longer a representative serves in Congress, the less attention he or she pays to constituency matters. The number of trips to the district decreases, and district offices get fewer staffers. But Hibbing also found that the more-senior members of Congress are more effective legislators. Representatives serve a sort of apprenticeship, and as they gain experience, they tend to become more active and successful legislators. First-term representatives might spend more time in the district with their constituents, but they are less likely to play a significant role in shaping legislation. Hibbing concluded that terms limits are a bad idea and "would likely result in a devastating loss of legislative acumen, expertise, and activity" (1991, 180).

A study by Jeffery Mondak (1995) supports this conclusion. Mondak developed indicators of House members' competence and integrity. He found that members serving seven terms or more scored higher than members who retired or were defeated before the seventh term (Figure 12.1). Being a member of Congress has evolved into a demanding full-time occupation. Evidence from Mondak's study suggests that electoral defeats and retirements tend to filter out individuals less able to do

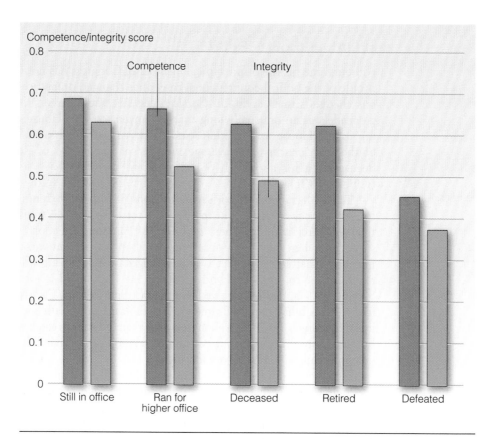

Figure 12.1
Competence and Integrity of House Members
Source: Mondak 1995, 1057.

the job well. In short, making experience and expertise a basis for disqualification from office is likely to deprive Congress of the most able legislators.

Although the length of service in Congress increased considerably from 1789 through the 1950s (Polsby 1968), this trend toward longer service has stabilized since. As Figure 12.2 shows, the average length of service in both the House and Senate has not changed much in five decades: less than ten years in one or both chambers in almost two-thirds of the Congresses since 1953. Thus, there continues to be substantial amount of turnover in Congress, which casts out deadwood and brings in fresh blood.

Thus, serving in Congress has become career oriented. It is a demanding job that requires members to serve an apprenticeship period to gain the expertise needed to play a significant role in shaping national policy. While the economic, social, and ethnic backgrounds of members of Congress may not have changed much, the job they are asked to do is drastically different from that of their historical predecessors. As a result, tenure has increased, and Congress has become more professional.

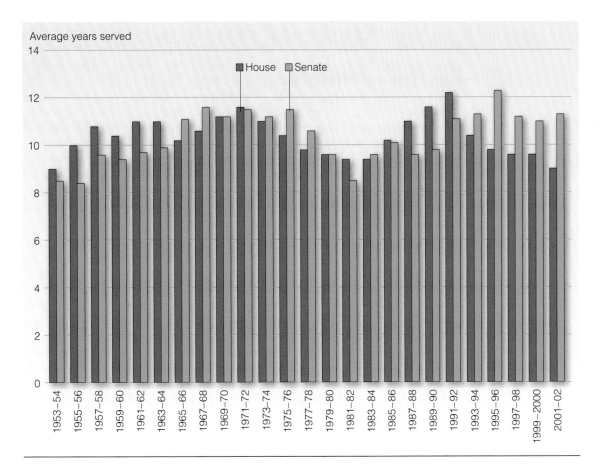

Figure 12.2
Average Length of Service in Congress
Source: Ornstein, Mann and Malbin 2002, 40–41.

Daily Life of a Member of Congress

Busy is the word to describe the typical workday of a member of Congress. One of the most accessible—and amusing—descriptions of a typical member's work routine was penned by the satirist P. J. O'Rourke (1991, 49–65). O'Rourke trailed a congressman who, as O'Rourke put it, "would just as soon not have his name in a book by me" for 11 hours one day. The day began with an 8 A.M. breakfast meeting, followed by an 8:30 A.M. breakfast meeting, followed by two committee meetings and a courtesy visit with a volunteer firefighting group from the congressman's district. There was no lunch break; perhaps the congressman was not hungry after two breakfasts.

In the afternoon, the congressman huddled with his staff for several hours to come up with coherent and defensible positions on an omnibus farm bill, the reauthorization of a commodities trading commission, a food safety act, a pesticide-control proposal, rural-development legislation, regular and supplemental appropriations bills, a number of foreign treaties, a proposed sale of fighter planes to South Korea, a housing bill, a proposal to close military bases, and a series of bills dealing with U.S. exports. There were twenty-five issues in all, representing roughly 10 percent of the items on the congressional calendar that week. The congressman had to balance the wishes of his constituents, the preferences of his party, the pressure of congressional leaders, the demands of the president, entreaties from lobbyists, and his own personal viewpoint for each issue. The congressman's position was likely to conflict with at least one of these on all of the 250 items on the calendar that week.

After 2 hours of trying to map defensible positions, the congressman was expected at a 4 P.M. meeting of party colleagues who were elected the same year he was (his so-called class). From 5:30 to 9, he was expected at the National Fire and Emergency Services dinner, and from 6 to 8, he was supposed to accompany the governor of his state to another official function. O'Rourke did not stay to see how he managed to be in two places at one time because "I was completely exhausted by 7 and went home, leaving the congressman, 20 years my senior, looking as animated and energetic as a full school bus" (1991, 63). The congressman's staff assured O'Rourke that this had been a light day for their boss.

This description is just one part the job of serving in Congress. In reality, members of Congress live in two worlds. One is Washington, DC, the world of legislating and overseeing the executive agencies of the national government. This is the world that O'Rourke was describing. The other is the district, the world of listening to constituents to learn their wants and needs and informing them of the issues before Congress.

It behooves a member of Congress who wishes to be reelected to maintain close ties with his or her district and thus to spend as much time as possible with the "folks back home." For those who live near the capital in the East, this is a minor burden, and extended weekends in the district can be the norm.[3] Those who live farther away face a formidable commuting schedule. Even they typically go back to their districts at least two or three weekends a month; few travel home less than once a month. In the district, a member often has to hit the road, visiting various parts of the district, attending such activities as high school graduations and meetings of the local Chamber of

---

[3]Congress customarily transacts official business, roll calls, and the like on Tuesday, Wednesday, and Thursday.

Commerce and veterans' groups, and holding town meetings in which constituents can discuss issues with the member. Living in these two worlds is not an easy task. It frequently means extended separation from family, balancing time and resources between Washington and home, and presenting a parochial face to constituents and a statesmanlike demeanor on questions of national import.

Congressional Pay and Perquisites

Compensation for members of Congress has been controversial since the beginning of the Republic. On one side are legislators who have a heavy workload, grave responsibilities, and limited opportunities for earnings beyond their public paychecks. On the other side are voters who are usually skeptical about claims of financial distress from officials already receiving what seems to be a generous salary and serving in a body that has the power to adjust its own pay.

The first Congress set legislative salaries at $6 a day. Even then, this was hardly a princely sum, and in 1816 Congress voted to raise its salary to $1,500 a year. The public response was swift and brutal; in the next election, 60 percent of House members were voted out of office. Congress quickly repealed the law, and legislators went back to the $6 a day stipend, which they raised shortly thereafter to $8. Congress learned early that voting itself a pay raise was electoral arsenic. Almost forty years would pass before it upped its compensation again. Annual salaries increased to $3,000 n 1855, to $5,000 a decade later, and then to $7,000 in 1873. Although congressional salaries consistently lagged behind inflation, every attempt at adjustment prompted a backlash. The 1873 increase was so controversial that it was repealed a year later, but it still cost 96 Republican supporters their seats in the next election (Harris 1995, 18).

The modern story of congressional compensation is little different. After Congress voted itself a modest increase in 1983 and again in 1984, public opposition began to grow against a third salary hike proposed in 1987. The raise passed, but in 1989 there was a huge public outcry against a further salary increase. In 1992 (203 years after it was proposed), the requisite number of states finally ratified the Twenty-Seventh Amendment requiring an election to intervene before members could receive a pay raise.

Members attempted to insulate their salary from political controversy by making annual cost of living adjustments (COLAs) for themselves, federal judges, and other federal workers. Such increases take effect automatically, without a vote, which might attract less public attention and outrage. The 1989 law instituting these adjustments provided members with a cost of living increase equal to one-half of one percentage point below the inflation index. Since 1993, Congress has voted to forgo the increase in every year except 1997. In the 108th Congress (2003–2004), the salary for members of Congress was $158,100. Many people believe that this annual salary is more than adequate, since the average wage earner's paycheck is roughly a third that of a member of Congress.

Former Senator Fred Harris (1995) of Oklahoma presents the other side of the story. Congressional salaries are often lower than those earned in comparable positions. Corporate CEOs, for example, typically earn much more than members of Congress, even though legislators arguably have much greater responsibilities and just as little job security. Unlike people in comparable positions, such as governors, university presidents, and business executives, national legislators usually must maintain two residences—one in the capital and one in the district. Harris argues that U.S. legislators are something of a bargain compared to legislators in other industrialized democracies; in general, members of Congress are paid less and work more. Keeping legislative compensation down in effect means that only the wealthy can afford to run for Congress.

In addition to a paycheck, however, members of Congress receive a number of **perquisites** (colloquially called **perks**), which are fringe benefits that go with the job. One type of perk bestows privileges that make members' lives more comfortable. Such benefits include subsidized medical care, inexpensive insurance, a generous pension plan, free parking, and access to their own gym, cafeterias, and barber shop for nominal fees.

A second type of perk is intended to help members do their jobs. Members of the House receive an allocation of about $1 million to pay for office functions, official travel, and staff. Members use the allocation for office supplies and equipment for the Washington office, setting up email and Web pages,[4] leasing and equipping one or more offices in their districts so that constituents can contact them locally, and frequent trips back home to the district.

The most expensive perk, and one of the most important, is salaries for aides to work in the Washington and district offices. Members can hire up to eighteen full-time staff to assist in various tasks. These include

- An *administrative assistant* responsible for overall management of the office
- Several *legislative assistants,* each responsible for keeping the member briefed on specific policy areas
- A *legislative director* who supervises the legislative assistants
- An *appointment secretary* to screen and maintain the member's appointments
- A *press secretary* to handle press relations
- Several *legislative correspondents* to answer constituent mail
- One or more *caseworkers* to help constituents with their problems

District offices typically have only one or two staffers; caseworkers are often placed in the district office.

Another important perk is the **franking privilege.** The frank allows members of Congress to send mail that involves official business, such as answers to constituent mail, under their signatures in lieu of postage. Since members get hundreds of letters each week, it would be unreasonable to expect them to pay for postage out of their salaries. Members also use the frank to send periodic newsletters to constituents. Some members compile specialized mailing lists of, for example, veterans, senior citizens, doctors, or real estate agents and send information and updates geared toward these interests.

These perks are paid for with tax money appropriated by Congress, and their purpose is to help representatives do their jobs by staying in touch with and responding to their constituents. Perks are not supposed to be used for political purposes, and Congress has adopted a number of rules intended to prevent members from using them in an election campaign. For example, it is illegal for a representative to assign

---

[4]Members' Web pages can be found at *http://thomas.loc.gov/.*

staff members to work in the campaign or to send campaign material out using the frank. Mass mailings cannot be sent under the frank within 60 days of an election in which the member is a candidate. In practice, however, the line between representing and campaigning is blurry. Sometimes key staff members take a leave of absence to work in the campaign, and some do campaign work after hours on their own time. The perquisites of office provide members with an undeniable political advantage; achieving widespread contact with the electorate is an expense that challengers must pay for with campaign money.

The bottom line on pay and perquisites is that members of Congress are not particularly well compensated compared to people in similar positions, particularly in the private sector, but they do get some special perks to help them perform the primary tasks of lawmaking and representing constituents. The benefits members receive must be balanced against the special demands placed on them.

Bicameralism in the American Congress

One basic and distinctive feature of the U.S. Congress is that it has two separate and independent chambers. A number of considerations explain why the Founders designed a **bicameral** legislature. One was the historical legacy from the British; Parliament was divided into the House of Commons and the House of Lords. A second was the more immediate example of the colonial legislatures, many of which were bicameral, with the upper chamber composed of emissaries appointed by the king or his representatives and the lower chamber composed of representatives elected by the colonists.

These traditions were not determinative. The national legislature under the Articles of Confederation, for example, was a **unicameral** institution. The two-house legislature is mainly a product of the conflicts discussed in Chapters 2 and 3: the political struggle between large and small states and the legal battle over whether national legislators were to represent sovereign states or individuals. Bicameralism was a compromise that settled both arguments. Also, the Founders had a strong distrust of concentrated governmental power. Dividing legislative power between two chambers was yet another way to fragment power, which the Founders believed would protect basic rights by making bargaining and compromise necessary.

The bicameral legislature was meant to serve two major purposes: (1) to represent different interests and (2) to foster deliberative, careful lawmaking. The Founders created the Senate to protect the interests of sovereign states, a function served by upper legislative chambers in other federal systems, such as in Australia, Switzerland, and Germany. The Senate was also expected to safeguard property interests. The Founders expected the prestigious nature of a Senate seat to attract an aristocratic elite that would be insulated from popular control by indirect election and a long term in office.[5] In contrast, directly elected House members with two-year terms were to reflect the interests of the many, the people who had little in the way of worldly goods. Linked to the protection of states' rights and property interest was the belief that the Senate would serve as a check on hasty legislation passed in the House.

---

[5]Election of senators by state legislatures ended in 1913 with ratification of the Seventeenth Amendment.

Table 12.1

Select House–Senate Differences

	SENATE	HOUSE
Formal		
Membership	100	435
Term of office	6 years	2 years
Minimum age for service	30 years	25 years
Electoral arena	State	District
Formal Leadership	Vice president	Speaker
Exclusive powers	Advice and consent	Raise revenue
Informal		
Most powerful leader	Majority leader	Speaker
Level of comity	Higher	Lower
Reliance on staff	Higher	Lower
Degree of hierarchy	Lower	Higher
Degree of partisanship	Lower	Higher
Member accessibility	Lower	Higher

Source: Adapted from *Contemporary Congress: A Bicameral Approach.* 1st ed., by M. Moen and G. W. Copeland 1999. Reprinted by permission of Wadsworth, an imprint of the Wadsworth Group, a division of Thomson Learning.

The Founders also had separate special functions in mind for the Senate and House. The Senate was to confirm presidential nominees for major positions in the national government and play a major role in foreign policy through its "advice and consent" power on treaties negotiated by the executive with other countries. The House was entrusted with the special and traditional prerogative of lower chambers: originating bills to raise revenue. Although constitutional changes and political reforms over the course of more than 200 years have altered Congress, the House and Senate remain separate and distinct legislative institutions. Table 12.1 summarizes some important differences.

Leadership in the U.S. Senate

The U.S. Senate has two types of leaders. The first is composed of the leaders designated by the Constitution who preside over the body and exercise essentially ceremonial duties in the chamber. Included in this group are the vice president of the United States and the Senate president pro tempore. The other type of leader occupies a party position, such as a majority leader, minority leader, or party whip. There are differences in the amount and type of power that these two types of leaders exercise in the Senate.

Article I, Section 3 of the Constitution designates the vice president as the **president of the Senate.** The vice president is entitled to preside over the chamber, exercising such parliamentary duties as recognizing speakers and ruling on points of procedure. The only voting privilege the vice president has is to cast a ballot to break a tie. Vice presidents do not have the opportunity to exercise this power very often: Vice President Al Gore (1993–2000) voted to break only four ties during his terms; Vice President Dan Quayle (1989–1992) had no opportunities. Except in the rare instances when a tie-breaking vote is necessary, the vice president is not a powerful or important figure in the Senate. And the vice president typically does not preside over the Senate because senators tend to regard the vice president as an outsider, especially if the opposition party controls the Senate.

The Constitution also provides for a **president pro tempore** chosen by the members to preside over the Senate in the absence of the vice president. The choice is largely ritualistic: The party controlling the Senate picks its most senior member to occupy the post. This office, too, is largely ceremonial and has no special influence. Because presiding over the Senate is generally of little importance, frequently neither the vice president nor the president pro tempore does so. Instead, junior members of the majority party take turns exercising the responsibility. Giving junior members the opportunity to preside helps them learn Senate rules and traditions.

The single most powerful person in the Senate is the **majority leader.** A party leader elected by members of the majority party, the majority leader's power extends to overall leadership of the Senate. Majority leaders are typically people with considerable experience in the Senate, although long tenure is not always a requirement. For example, Lyndon Johnson (D-TX), gained the post after only one term in office; Johnson held the position from 1955 to 1961 and is generally considered one of the most powerful and effective majority leaders. The majority leader of the 108th Congress (2003–2004), Republican Bill Frist of Tennessee, also won the post in his second term.

The majority leader has several tools with which to wield power in the Senate. The most important of these is control over the Senate's agenda. The majority leader is at the center of the Senate's communications network and has responsibility for legislative scheduling. The majority leader knows which senators are for and against a bill and plays a key role negotiating the rules and procedures under which bills will be debated and voted on. During consideration of legislation on the floor, the majority leader serves as floor leader to deal with complex system legislative procedures. The majority leader also influences other matters of importance, such as sought-after committee appointments, the location of certain government installations, and prime office space. The majority leader is in a unique position to see the overall workings of the Senate and thus has more influence on what the chamber does than any other individual.

The job of **minority leader** parallels in many respects that of majority leader — he or she is elected by party colleagues, usually has extensive Senate experience, is the floor leader who watches out for the minority's interest during consideration of bills on the floor, and serves as the focal point of communication among senators of the minority party. The minority leader often works closely with the majority leader in legislative scheduling and influences the committee appointments of minority members. The minority leader's power, however, is less than that of the majority leader. The minority leader cannot bestow the same level of rewards

© Roger L. Wollenberg/UPI/Landov

The majority leader's power extends to overall leadership of the Senate, the most important aspect of which is control over the Senate's agenda. Here Senate Majority Leader Bill Frist (left) and Senate Armed Services Committee Chairman John Warner speak to the media after viewing unreleased photographs of prisoner abuse in Iraq in May 2004. The Senate unanimously passed a resolution condemning the abuse and calling for a complete investigation.

and, as the head of the minority party, has a numerical disadvantage in trying to influence what the chamber does (though, as we will see, the minority can use Senate rules to block action).

Both majority and minority leaders have assistants commonly referred to as **whips** (though Senate Republicans have been using the title "assistant majority leader"). The term is a legacy from the British Parliament, which in turn borrowed it from the sport of foxhunting. A whip, or "whipper-in," was responsible for keeping the hounds from leaving the pack during the chase of the fox. By analogy, a legislative whip's job is to keep the rank-and-file members from straying from the party fold. He or she sees to it that they are present to vote on key legislative measures and that they know the party leader's desire. The whip's ability to fulfill this responsibility is limited. Unlike their counterparts in the British Parliament, party leaders in the U.S. Congress have few rewards and punishments with which to maintain party unity. In the Senate, each party's whip serves mainly as a communication link between the floor leader (a term applied to either the majority or minority leader) and rank-and-file party members. Table 12.2 lists the leaders of the 109th Congress.

Table 12.2
Congressional Leaders of the 109th Congress (2005–2006)

SENATE

President of the Senate Vice President Richard Cheney
President Pro Tempore Ted Stevens (R-AK)

Majority Bill Frist (R-TN)	Minority Leader Harry Reid (D-NV)
Majority Whip Mitch McConnell (R-KY)	Minority Whip Richard Durbin (D-IL)

HOUSE

Speaker Dennis Hastert (R-IL)

Majority Leader Tom DeLay (R-TX)	Minority Leader Nancy Pelosi (D-CA)
Majority Whip Roy Blunt (R-MO)	Minority Whip Steny Hoyer (D-MD)

Leadership in the U.S. House of Representatives

Article I, Section 2 of the Constitution provides for a **speaker of the House of Representatives.** Unlike the constitutionally designated leader of the Senate (the vice president), the speaker of the House is much more than a ceremonial figure who presides over deliberations. The speaker is the House's most powerful figure. The title was likely borrowed from the British post of speaker of the House of Commons, a strictly nonpartisan post intended to speak for Parliament before the king. The speakership in the colonial legislatures, however, was a much more political office, and colonial speakers used the office to further partisan political goals. This model from the colonial legislatures is probably what the Founders had in mind for the office.

Theoretically elected as an officer of the entire chamber, the speaker is actually selected by the majority party. The speaker, therefore, is both a House officer and a party official, combining the duties and powers shared by the vice president and the majority leader in the Senate. The speaker presides over the House, has the power to recognize members who wish to speak, rules on procedural questions, and refers bills to committee. When the House is meeting as a Committee of the Whole,[6] the speaker appoints a substitute chair (often a junior member) and may lead or participate in debate. Unlike the vice president, the speaker may vote but usually does not use this prerogative except to break a tie.

The speaker can generally use the same rewards as the Senate majority leader to influence colleagues: assistance in obtaining a favorable committee assignment, appointment to select committees, help with bills, and assistance in a tough political campaign. Like the Senate majority leader, the speaker is the center of the chamber's internal communication network and serves as a central link with the White House and the Senate.

[6]The Committee of the Whole consists of every member of the House. Its function is discussed later in this chapter.

The position of speaker became more powerful following the 1994 Republican takeover of Congress. The Republican-controlled House took several steps to curb the power of committees and committee chairs. One of the outcomes of these reforms was to effectively centralize power in the hands of Republican Speaker Newt Gingrich. Gingrich resigned after a disappointing electoral performance in the 1998 midterm elections, but his successor, Republican Dennis Hastert of Illinois, continued to consolidate power in the hands of party leaders. In the 108th Congress (2003–04), for example, Hastert limited the authority of committee chairs, and some members say that Hastert is even more powerful than Gingrich.

Next in line to the speaker in the House leadership hierarchy is the majority leader. Chosen by the majority party caucus (Republicans call their caucus a "conference"), the majority leader often has strong ties to the speaker, and the influence he or she wields is largely dependent on what the speaker wants it to be. Generally, the majority leader assists the speaker in scheduling legislation, distributes and collects information of concern to majority party members, and tries to persuade the rank-and-file to go along with the wishes of party leadership.

The position of majority leader is often a stepping-stone to the speaker's chair. The last seven Democratic speakers—William Bankhead; Sam Rayburn; John McCormack; Carl Albert; Thomas O'Neill, Jr.; Jim Wright; and Thomas Foley—were all promoted from majority leader to the top position. The Republican line of succession has been less regularized and more contentious, in part due to splits and dissatisfaction arising from Republicans' continuous minority status for forty years (1955 to 1995). Newt Gingrich had been in line to become the minority leader in the 104th Congress, but when the Republicans captured a majority in the House, he was elected speaker. Dick Armey of Texas, who had been chair of the conference, became majority leader. When Gingrich resigned in 1999, Armey faced significant opposition within the Republican conference and had to fight to retain his job as majority leader. Ultimately, Republicans passed over the party leader and the whip when they chose Dennis Hastert of Illinois to be speaker.

The nominee of the minority party caucus, who loses the election for speaker, becomes the House minority leader. This role is essentially the same as it is in the Senate: to work with the majority leader in scheduling legislation and to lead the opposition party. The majority and minority whips have the same general function in the House as in the Senate.

The Committee System

Committees are the core organizational feature of Congress, the mechanism that both chambers and parties use to handle their various tasks and responsibilities. Several different types of committees deal with legislation and oversight. In addition, party committees deal with party business.

Standing Committees   The most important committees in terms of the day-to-day handling of legislation are **standing committees,** permanent bodies with jurisdiction over particular issues and categories of legislation. The importance of standing committees in Congress is hard to overstate. Woodrow Wilson (1885) referred to them as "little legislatures" and said that they are where much of the real work of Congress is

Committees are more important and powerful in the House than in the Senate. Although this behind-the-scenes meeting of the House of Representatives Budget Committee speaks to the practical tedium of working through the details of issues, sitting on a committee is the surest way to influence House legislation.

done. In both chambers, standing committees are the primary focus of legislative business, and they wield much power within their areas of jurisdiction.

Committees exert a powerful influence over legislation within their jurisdiction for at least three reasons. First, committee members are more knowledgeable than nonmembers about the legislation in question. In Congress, knowledge and expertise are important sources of power. Committee members are more knowledgeable because they have worked on the legislation in committee for a long time, they have attended committee hearings, and they have been kept informed by committee staff. Second, committee members are more interested in the legislation. Most members can take an active interest in only a small number of policy areas and tend to seek assignment to committees with jurisdiction over policies of particular interest to them. Members of Congress with less expertise and less interest than committee members often defer to the recommendations of the committee reporting the bill. These sources of committee power are reinforced by a third reason—the **norm of reciprocity.** Among the norms and traditions of Congress is the expectation that members will respect the work and judgment of one another's committees.

Standing committee jurisdictions are defined in Senate and House rules. Committee jurisdictions roughly correspond to the major organizational divisions of the executive branch, and Senate and House committees are organized along parallel, though not identical, lines. There are seventeen standing committees in the Senate and nineteen in the House (Table 12.3).

Table 12.3

Standing Committees of the 108th Congress (2003–2004)

	TOTAL MEMBERS	PARTY RATIO	
		REPUBLICANS	DEMOCRATS
Senate			
Agriculture, Nutrition, and Forestry	21	11	10
Appropriations	29	15	14
Armed Services	25	13	12
Banking, Housing, and Urban Affairs	21	11	10
Budget	23	12	11
Commerce, Science, and Transportation	23	12	11
Energy and Natural Resources	23	12	11
Environment and Public Works	19	10	9
Finance	21	11	10
Foreign Relations	19	10	9
Governmental Affairs	17	9	8
Indian Affairs	15	8	7
Health, Education, Labor, and Pensions	21	11	10
Judiciary	19	10	9
Rules and Administration	19	10	9
Small Business and Entrepreneurship	19	10	9
Veterans' Affairs	15	8	7
House			
Agriculture	51	27	24
Appropriations	65	36	29
Armed Services	61	33	28
Financial Services	69	37	32
Budget	43	24	19
Committee on Energy and Commerce	57	31	26
Education and Workforce	49	27	22
Government Reform	43	24	19
House Administration	9	6	3
International Relations	49	26	23
Judiciary	37	21	16
Resources	52	28	24
Rules	13	9	4
Science	47	25	22
Small Business	36	19	17
Standards of Official Conduct (Ethics)	10	5	5
Transportation and Infrastructure	75	41	34
Veterans' Affairs	31	17	14
Ways and Means	41	24	17

Source: U.S. Congress. 2004. *http://www.senate.gov/clerk.house.gov*

The importance and prestige of committees varies considerably. In each chamber, there are a small number of top committees on which almost every legislator wants to serve. In both chambers, the top committees are those that deal with major taxing and spending issues: Ways and Means (House), Finance (Senate), and Appropriations (House and Senate). Other **top committees** differ according to the particular rules and responsibilities of the chamber: the House Rules Committee is a top committee, as are the Senate Foreign Relations and Armed Services committees.

Most of the remaining standing committees are considered major committees. These committees have jurisdiction over important policy areas, but members' policy and reelection interests determine which committees they deem desirable. A legislator from a district or state with a farm-based economy, for example, desires a seat on the Agriculture Committee, which deals with legislation affecting agribusiness, while a representative from New York City might prefer a seat on the Banking Committee to work on legislation dealing with Wall Street.

There are a few unrequested committees. Because very few members ask to serve on these committees, they are disproportionately populated by first-term legislators who transfer to other committees at the first opportunity. In the House, unrequested committees include the House Administration Committee and the Government Reform and Oversight Committee; in the Senate, unrequested committees include Veterans' Affairs and Rules and Administration. Members in both chambers also do not seek assignment to the Ethics Committee (officially called Standards of Official Conduct in the House). A party leader in the House expressed members' distaste for sitting in judgment of their colleagues, saying that "anyone who wants a seat on Standards doesn't deserve a seat on Standards" (quoted in Deering and Smith 1997, 77).

As shown in Table 12.3, committee size varies considerably. The size of standing committees is fixed by House and Senate rules, and the seats on each standing committee are divided between the majority and minority party according to the **party ratio** in the chamber—that is, the ratio of majority to minority party members in the chamber. Since Republicans outnumbered Democrats 229–202 in the 108th Congress, in theory Republicans would have about 53 percent of the seats on each standing committee.[7] In practice, however, the majority party often takes more seats than its ratio in the chamber, especially on the top committees. In the 108th Congress, for example, House Republicans took 59 percent of the seats on the Ways and Means Committee and 69 percent of the seats on the Rules Committee. Republicans also took a disproportionate number of seats on other key policy committees. Republicans had complained bitterly about this practice when Democrats were the majority. But since the majority party is responsible for passing legislation, Republicans discovered that they needed extra seats on key committees.

Although committees are a central organizational feature in both chambers, the committee systems in the Senate and the House differ in a number of ways. One difference is the hierarchy of committees. In the Senate, standing committees are classified as major or minor, but the four top Senate committees (Appropriations, Finance, Armed Services, and Foreign Relations) are considered elite committees. A senator can serve on only one elite committee and on no more than two major committees. According to a longstanding practice instituted by Majority Leader Lyndon Johnson in the 1950s and known as the Johnson rule, no senator can receive a second major committee assignment until every senator has one.

---

[7]The Ethics Committees are exceptions; they have an equal number of Republicans and Democrats.

The House divides committees into three formal categories: exclusive, major, and nonmajor. The top three committees in the House (Appropriations, Rules, and Ways and Means) are **exclusive committees** because members assigned to one of them receive no other significant committee assignment. Members without an exclusive committee assignment are typically given one major and one nonmajor committee assignment.

Another important difference between the committee systems in the House and Senate is the unique role performed by the House Rules Committee. When a House standing committee has completed its consideration of a proposed bill, it prepares a written report describing what the bill does, what amendments the committee has made, and why the bill should be passed. But before the committee's bill can go to the floor, it must first go to the Rules Committee, which formulates a rule under which the bill will be considered. The Rules Committee thus performs the role of a legislative traffic cop, regulating the flow of legislation from other standing committees to the floor. There is no Senate committee that performs this function.

The rule formulated by the Rules Committee sets the date the bill will be brought up on the floor for debate and specifies the conditions of the debate. These conditions normally set time limits on debate; specify which amendments, if any, can be offered; and set other rules that can significantly control the form of proposed legislation and its chances of passage. By controlling the order in which bills are considered, the Rules Committee kills some while allowing others to be decided by majority vote. Some bills are considered under an **open rule** that permits any germane amendment; others come to the floor with a **closed rule** that prohibits all amendments. Frequently, bills come to the floor with modified rules that permit only certain amendments. The speaker appoints the majority party's members, so the Rules Committee is a tool the majority party leadership uses to help meet policy objectives, keep debate under control, and prevent the minority party from scoring political points by offering amendments that would place majority party members in an awkward position.

Finally, committees are more important and powerful in the House than in Senate. The larger membership of the House means that House members have fewer committee assignments than senators; the scarcity makes committee assignments more highly valued. The surest way to influence legislation in the House is by serving on a committee. Senators have more options to influence legislation from the floor, so committees are less important. Senate rules allow individual senators opportunities to offer amendments that are not related to the bill under consideration, in some cases bypassing committee action. Such **nongermane amendments** are generally prohibited in the House. These amendments are commonly known as **riders** because they are attached to popular bills in an effort to get a free ride through the legislative process.

Constituency differences also create incentives for House members to become policy specialists and for senators to become policy generalists. Except for states that have only one House member, House constituencies are smaller and less diverse than Senate constituencies. With only a few interests dominating many House districts, a House member benefits from working on one or two committees with jurisdiction over policies important to the district. Senators representing an entire state with a wide range of interests can benefit from serving on several committees.

The standing committee system in the House has undergone significant reform. When Republicans gained majority control of the House in 1995, they eliminated a number of committees and subcommittees, changed jurisdictions, imposed term limits on committee and subcommittee chairs, eliminated proxy voting, and cut committee staffs. A primary motivation of these reforms was to shake up the power structure in the House. Committee chairs and ranking minority members on the standing committees are important party leaders in Congress.

Traditionally, committee chairs were chosen on the basis of seniority. The relevant consideration was not seniority in Congress. Instead, the practice was to appoint the member of the majority party with the longest continuous service on the committee. Automatic selection based on seniority insulated committee chairs from pressure from their party caucus and party leaders. The reforms sought to place limits on such political power. Republicans ceased using seniority as the primary qualification for chairing a committee, as Speaker Gingrich skipped over the senior Republican on several key committees and handpicked trusted lieutenants as chairs. The Republicans limited committee chairs to three terms, which further weakened the seniority system. Because the Republicans maintained control of the House in the 2000 elections, the term limits went into effect, setting off the political equivalent of musical committee chairs, and applicants had to present their agendas for running the committees to Speaker Dennis Hastert and the Republican leadership in interviews. While these reforms weakened the role of seniority in selecting committee chairs in the House, they did not eliminate it. The competition to chair committees involves mostly senior members, so committee chairs are still relatively senior majority party members. But such criteria as competence, party loyalty, and a record of raising campaign money to help fellow Republicans have become important considerations.

Other Legislative Committees In addition to standing committees, both chambers have other committees to help fulfill their legislative responsibilities. Most important are the subcommittees of the standing committees. Most standing committees have a number of subcommittees with jurisdiction over smaller slices of policy. Subcommittees are an additional division of labor. They help Congress cope with a large workload, and they permit members to develop specialized policy expertise.

Another type of committee is a select committee, a temporary organization formed to deal with a specific issue. In the 108th Congress, the House had a Select Committee on Homeland Security and a Select Committee on Intelligence.

Joint committees consist of members from both chambers. Membership generally reflects the party ratio in each chamber, and the chair generally alternates between a House member and a senator every two years. Unlike select committees, joint committees are usually permanent panels. Two joint committees, the Joint Economic Committee and the Joint Committee on Taxation, have policy roles; they study problems and make recommendations, but they cannot report legislation to the floors. Two other joint committees, the joint Committee on the Library of Congress and the Joint Committee on Printing, deal with administrative matters affecting both chambers.

The last type of legislative committee is the **conference committee,** a temporary committee composed of House and Senate members that meets to reconcile differences in a bill that has passed both chambers. Members of a conference committee are called *conferees,* and they are typically selected from among the members of the standing committee that reported the bill. A bill cannot be sent to the president until it has passed both chambers in identical form. If the House and Senate pass different versions of the same bill and neither chamber is willing to accept the other's version, a conference committee meets to iron out the differences. They play such an important role that conference committees are sometimes called the "third house of Congress."

Party Committees   In addition to committees with legislative responsibilities, several party committees handle the administration and logistics of party activity within the chamber. Each party has a caucus or conference composed of all members of the party in the chamber. Each party caucus appoints committees to make committee assignments, which is an important function because of electoral considerations and the desire to influence lawmaking. The party caucus also develops a policy agenda for the party and raises campaign money for House and Senate candidates.

The Distribution of Power

Congress is a collegial rather than a hierarchical institution. Power is widely dispersed, and leaders do not have the authority to command rank-and-file members to do their bidding. The committee system institutionalizes the diffusion of power by giving small groups of legislators disproportionate influence over legislation. Although parties and party leaders exert a centralizing force through their control of the legislative agenda, influencing their colleagues through persuasion is usually more effective than coercion.

Under House rules, a persistent and cohesive majority can usually get its way. Power is dispersed among committees, but reforms in the 1970s under Democratic majorities and in the 1990s under Republican majorities have obliged committee chairs and party leaders to be responsive to the preferences of the majority party caucus—at least on issues on which there is consensus in the party. David Rohde (1991) calls this situation **conditional party government**—when the "condition" of cohesion on policy preferences among rank-and-file party members is met, the majority party gives more power to party leaders and expects them to use the power to enact the party's legislative agenda. But the underlying power relationship is more bottom-up than top-down in that party leaders take strong action on behalf of a cohesive majority in the party.

Power is more diffuse in the Senate than in the House. Senate rules and traditions disperse power to all senators. As noted above, senators have more opportunity to influence legislation from the chamber floor through the amending process than do their House colleagues. In addition, Senate rules permitting unlimited debate give each senator the power to filibuster objectionable legislation favored by the majority. A **filibuster** is an effort by one or a few senators to delay action on a bill by making long speeches and using parliamentary tactics. The goal is to pressure the majority to give up and pull the bill from the floor or at least make changes to remove objectionable provisions. Any senator also may put a **hold** on a bill, that is, make a formal request to be notified before a bill comes to the floor. In essence, a hold tells the leadership there are objections to the legislation that need to be addressed to prevent tactics like a filibuster. A filibuster can be stopped if the Senate votes to invoke **cloture**—that is, end debate on a bill. Under Senate rules, it takes 60 votes to invoke cloture.

Historically, filibusters were rare, but they have become much more common in recent decades. Once used by individual senators to block legislation they intensely opposed, filibusters have become part of a partisan strategy that the minority party uses to influence legislation (Binder and Smith 1997, 148). In the 1950s, there was

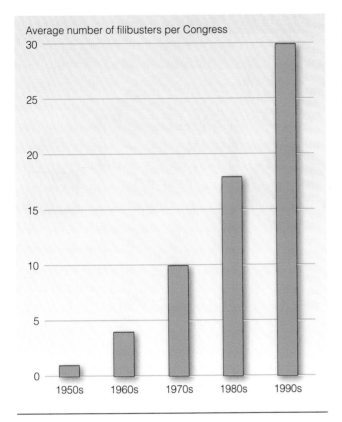

Average number of filibusters per Congress

Figure 12.3

Increasing Use of the Filibuster

Source: Democratic Study Group. 1994. "A Look at the Senate Filibuster." DSG Special Report, No. 103-28, June 13. Washington, DC: Democratic Study Group.

an average of about one filibuster per Congress; in the 1990s, the average number of filibusters per Congress increased to about thirty (Figure 12.3). Although the filibuster has been used in the Senate for more than 150 years, "nearly half of all identifiable filibusters . . . have occurred since 1980" (Democratic Study Group 1994, 1).

Most bills are not filibustered. The Senate conducts much of its legislative business under **unanimous consent agreements** (UCAs) negotiated by party leaders. These agreements define the procedures and conditions under which bills will be considered on the Senate floor. Unanimous consent agreements in the Senate perform a function similar to the rules from the Rules Committee in the House; they set limits on debate, specify which amendments will be in order, and set a schedule for the vote. But there is a big difference. Adoption of the rule in the House takes a simple majority, and the majority party leadership rarely loses a vote on a rule. Unanimous consent in the Senate means just what it says: Any one Senator can stop the agreement. Without a unanimous consent agreement, it takes 60 votes, rather than a simple majority, to pass a bill on the Senate floor.

Running the Legislative Obstacle Course

There is no legislative train track along which all bills move to enactment. Proposals considered by Congress take a tortuous route, and most fail to negotiate this process.

The procedures of Congress are so complex and technical that only the parliamentarians of the two chambers and a few veteran members grasp their intricacies. This procedural complexity is further complicated by the number of issues Congress must deal with, the variety of preferences and ambitions of the individual members, and an organization and leadership system that results in the diffuse exercise of power. What is surprising is not that Congress approves so little, but that it approves anything at all.

American government textbooks typically include a diagram of how a bill becomes law. The generic diagram reproduced as Figure 12.4 follows a bill through the various

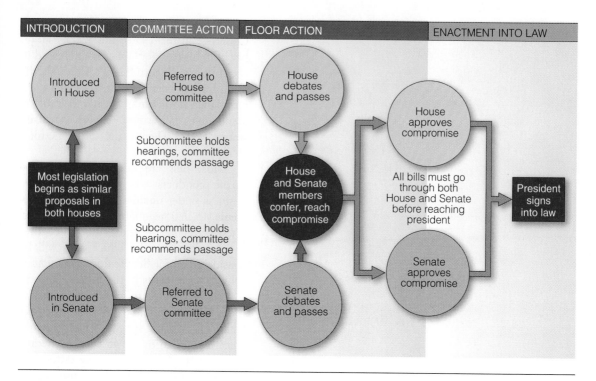

Figure 12.4

How a Bill Becomes a Law

Source: *Congress A to Z*. 3rd ed. 1999. Washington, DC: Congressional Quarterly, Inc.

obstacles it must overcome before becoming law: from introduction to committee referral, from committee consideration to floor action, from floor action to conference committee, from conference committee back to floor action, and from there to the White House—and back again if vetoed.

Some political scientists consider such descriptions to be increasingly unrealistic portrayals of how Congress works. Barbara Sinclair (2000) argues that legislation is increasingly governed by what she terms "unorthodox lawmaking." Unorthodox lawmaking involves the use of special procedures and practices that have created "a number of different paths the legislation may follow" (Sinclair 2000, 9).

Nevertheless, the legislative process continues to be an obstacle course characterized by multiple, sequential decision points. In order to pass, a bill must gain the approval of a group of legislators at each point. Only at the final stage of the process does the majority have an opportunity to express its will. As a result, the legislative process is not really a process of majority rule. Rather, it is better described as a process of *minorities consent* because, at each stage, a different minority of members has the power to stall or kill the bill and prevent it from going to the next decision point. The most important thing to remember about how a bill becomes law is that there are multiple points of access to the proposed legislation and thus plenty of opportunities for minority interests to slow the bill's progress or kill it outright.

Bill Introduction and Committee Referral

Proposed legislation has numerous sources. Members introduce bills on behalf of the president, interest groups, or constituents. Only members of Congress can introduce bills into their respective chambers. In the House, members accomplish this by placing a proposal into a wooden box called the hopper. Senators can introduce bills from the floor or submit them to Senate clerks.

After it is introduced, a bill is referred to the committee with jurisdiction over the particular issue or area it covers. Committee consideration can be long and complex: A bill is passed down to subcommittee and reported back to the full committee, and legislators negotiate and propose changes, while interested parties lobby for the version they favor.

Bills traditionally were referred to a single committee that had jurisdiction over that issue. As new issues became more prominent in the 1970s and 1980s (for example, environmental protection, energy, and healthcare), legislation proposed to address these issues no longer fit within a single committee's jurisdiction. To deal with this problem, the House changed its rules in 1975 to permit a bill to be referred to more than one committee, a practice known as *multiple referral.* During the late 1990s, about 30 percent of major bills were referred to more than one committee. Multiple referrals are less common in the Senate, in part because Senate rules allow senators to influence the content of legislation outside the committee structure (Sinclair 2000, 89–92).

Bills can also be removed from committee against the committee's wishes. In the House, members can remove a bill from committee and bring it directly to the floor by means of a **discharge petition.** This petition must be signed by 218 members—a majority of the House membership. In some cases, committees can be bypassed altogether. Bypassing committees is rare in the House, and when it occurs, it is at the behest of majority party leadership. Senate rules make it easier for an individual senator to bypass committees—any senator can offer legislation as an amendment to another bill that is already on the floor; in most cases, the amendment does not have to be germane (Sinclair 2000, 14–17, 38).

Committee Consideration and Action

The most important determinant of the fate of legislation in Congress is what the standing committee does (or more often, does not do). The most common thing that happens to bills introduced in Congress is nothing—most bills are assigned to committee where they are ignored and die at the end of the Congress.

Each committee takes action on a relatively small percentage of bills assigned to it. On these few bills, the committee does additional research on the bill. The committee staff studies the bill and provides information to the members. The committee will hold public hearings where interested parties (interest groups, members of the executive agency that administers the program, policy experts, and sometimes celebrities) provide information about the proposal. Committee hearings are typically highly scripted. The committee chair has substantial leeway to decide not only which bills get hearings, but also who the witnesses will be and what positions they will take. In addition to collecting information about the policy, hearings can also be used to test the breadth of political support—and sometimes to build support—for the legislation. Hearings that feature celebrities tend to attract media attention, which gives committee members an opportunity to get some free publicity.

After the hearings, the committee meets for the mark-up, where members literally mark up the bill, making changes deemed necessary. After the mark-up, the committee votes to report the bill to floor for debate and a vote. Bills reported out of committee have a high probability of passage on the floor.

From Committee to the Floor

Getting legislation reported from the committees to the floor for consideration and a vote, however, is more complex than it once was. It is not unusual, for example, for a bill to undergo "postcommittee adjustments"—that is, substantial alterations between being reported by a committee and being scheduled for consideration on the chamber floor. Party leaders with the cooperation of the committee chair typically may lead efforts to forge changes to a bill, usually in an attempt to improve the chances of passage on the floor (Sinclair 2000, 17–20, 39–40).

Furthermore, constraints are often placed on a bill before it gets to the floor for consideration. In the House, the Rules Committee determines what these constraints will be; in the Senate, they are set by the unanimous consent agreement. These procedural matters are critical in determining whether a bill will pass and in what form.

When a bill goes to the House floor, members first consider the rule accompanying the bill. The majority must approve the rule before the House can consider the legislation. Losing a vote on a rule amounts to losing control of the chamber, and is very embarrassing to the majority party leadership. Although rare, it does occasionally happen.

If the rule passes, the House dissolves into the **Committee of the Whole,** literally a committee consisting of every member of the House. Its origins lie with a centuries-old British practice of getting the speaker, who was a representative of the king, out of his chair so that the House of Commons could act independently of his scrutiny. The advantage of keeping this parliamentary fiction alive is that the Committee of the Whole has less burdensome rules governing debate and requires a smaller quorum than the House itself. While in Committee of the Whole, members debate the bill and consider amendments under constraints of the rule. (See the Living the Promise feature "The House of Representatives' Mace.")

Once this process is completed, the Committee of the Whole reports the bill to the House, and the House votes on the bill. The House must approve amendments adopted in the Committee of the Whole, so opponents have a second chance to try to defeat them. Typically, the House votes on all amendments from the Committee of the Whole as a package, and passage is assured. But if the vote on an amendment in the Committee of the Whole was close, the losers in the first round may prevail in the House. For example, an appropriations bill in 1995 contained language to prevent the Environmental Protection Agency from enforcing certain environmental laws. During consideration of the bill in the Committee of the Whole, the Democrats, with the help of some moderate Republicans, passed an amendment on a 211 to 206 vote deleting the language. Because reining in federal regulations was important to the Republican majority, party leaders called for a second vote in the House, which resulted in a tie vote.

LIVING THE PROMISE
The House of Representatives' Mace

This excerpt describes the history of a symbol of legislative authority in the House of Representatives:

The most treasured possession of the House of Representatives is the mace, a traditional symbol of legislative authority. The concept, borrowed from the British House of Commons, had its origin in republican Rome, where the fasces—an ax bound in a bundle of rods—symbolized the power of the magistrates.

The mace was adopted by the House in its first session in 1789 as a symbol of office for the sergeant-at-arms, who is responsible for preserving order on the House floor. The first mace was destroyed when the British burned the Capitol in 1814, and for the next twenty-seven years, a mace of painted wood was used.

The present mace, in use since 1841, is a replica of the original mace of 1789. It consists of a bundle of thirteen ebony rods bound in silver, terminating in a silver globe topped by a silver eagle with outstretched wings. It is 46 inches high and was made by William Adams, a New York silversmith, for the sum of $400.

On several occasions in the history of the House the sergeant-at-arms, on order of the speaker, has lifted the mace from its pedestal and "presented" it before an unruly member. On each such occasion, order is said to have been promptly restored. At other times the sergeant-at-arms, bearing the mace, has passed up and down the aisles to quell boisterous behavior in the chamber. When the House is in regular session, the mace rests on a tall pedestal beside the speaker's desk. When the House is sitting as the Committee of the Whole, the mace is moved to a low pedestal nearby. Thus it is possible to tell at a glance whether the House is meeting in regular session or as the Committee of the Whole.

Source: Congressional Quarterly, Inc. 1993. *Congress A to Z.* 2nd ed. Washington, DC: Congressional Quarterly, 258.

Because 50 percent is one vote less than a majority, a tie vote means that the proposal fails. In this case, none of the Republicans switched their votes, but some of the Democrats who had supported the amendment in the Committee of the Whole were absent on the second vote (Sinclair 2000, 32–33).

Thus, the simple-sounding act of voting on a bill is surrounded by complexities that can make it anything but straightforward. The floor vote is the place where the majority has the opportunity to express its will, but the expression of majority will is limited by the rules governing consideration of the bill and may require multiple tries.

Resolving House–Senate Differences

Even if a measure clears the many obstacles to passage in one chamber, both chambers must pass an identical proposal in order for it to become law. In some cases, differences can be worked out by informal contacts between the two chambers, or one chamber accepts the version passed by the other. Controversial measures, however, usually require a conference committee to reconcile differences between the House and Senate versions.

Conference committees traditionally consisted of a handful of the leading members of the committees that originally dealt with the bill. Modern conference committees have increased the membership and have made the job more complicated. For example, 130 representatives from seven House committees and nine senators from two Senate committees were appointed to the conference committee to hammer out the differences in the 1990 Clean Air Act (Sinclair 2000, 3). Members of the conference committee—officially called conferees—have broad discretion, providing another opportunity to influence legislation. With large membership, complex legislation, and wide disparities between the House and Senate versions of a bill, this final opportunity to negotiate can be complex.

To get legislation out of conference committee, a majority of each chamber's representatives must approve a common bill. This version of the bill is then sent to the respective houses for approval, and neither house can change the version approved by the committee. Each chamber has the choice of approving the bill, sending it back to the committee, or voting it down, which kills the bill. Once a bill has been approved, it is sent to the president for his or her signature or veto. Congress can override a presidential veto by two-thirds vote in both chambers, but as discussed in the next chapter, vetoes are seldom overridden.

Congress' responsibilities, its members, and its operation combine into a process that is more complex and nuanced than many realize. As Sinclair points out, "if the textbook legislative process can be likened to climbing a ladder, the contemporary process is more like climbing a big old tree with many branches" (2000, 33). Some of the branches lead to passage, some lead to alteration, some entrap and entangle a proposal and halt its movement, and some give way altogether.

Performance Assessment

The U.S. Congress has enormous responsibilities. Fulfilling these responsibilities is the job of 535 legislators who have differing preferences and are subject to a wide variety of pressures on issues. They have heavy workloads and routinely face a paradox rarely recognized: They are expected to simultaneously uphold the interests of their constituents and the interests of the nation, even when these interests conflict.

These responsibilities and differences play out in an institution with complex rules and procedures. A bicameral legislature, the key role of political parties, institutional rules governing the legislative process, and the number of issues both chambers have to address make for an often-divisive and hard-to-understand operation.

What should be kept in mind is the underlying connection to the promise of democracy. It is supposed to be hard to get things done in the U.S. Congress and especially to make controversial decisions that affect many people. Representatives are forced to pour their differences and those of their constituents through a complex institutional process that acts as a filter. What this filter distills often is not what most people support or prefer, but what most people can live with. The operation is far from perfect, and for the most part, it is not efficient. But the process tends to stay reasonably close to core democratic values: Majorities eventually rule; the minority has multiple opportunities for substantive input; and the jarring differences that usually represent the will of the people are amplified and echoed—arguably an important service to popular sovereignty.

In short, while Congress is rightly judged to be a place of conflict, it is more a reflection of divisions in society than a cause of them. It probably deserves more credit than it gets for helping deliver on the promise of democracy. The laws and regulations that come out of Congress may not get ringing endorsements from everyone, but they generally get grudging acceptance. If one of the basic promises of a representative democracy is a process of decision making that is slow and deliberative and takes into account a multiplicity of interests, Congress is acquitting its job better than most assume.

Summary

- Congress is the governmental institution designed to represent the needs and interests of ordinary people and to translate those needs and wishes into laws that determine who gets what.
- Congress' primary functions include lawmaking (passing laws, and overseeing government agencies) and representation (responding to constituents' needs, and informing the public about the major issues facing the country).
- Secondary functions of Congress include impeaching and trying executive and judicial officials, seating and disciplining members, helping select leaders in the executive branch, and fulfilling such specialized policy responsibilities as ratifying treaties and confirming ambassadors to foreign countries.
- Although there are more minorities and women in Congress today than in earlier decades, membership does not reflect the diversity of today's American citizens.
- During the last half of the 20th century, the average member of the House of Representatives had been serving for about 10 years. In the 19th century, a decade was an unusually long time for anyone to be a House member. However, there is still considerable turnover in Congress.
- One of the advantages of increased careerism and tenure is that more experienced members of Congress also tend to be the most effective legislators.
- Members of Congress have heavy workloads, and there are enormous demands on their time and attention. Constituents, party leaders, the president, and interest groups often want different or contradictory things, and the member's own preferences may be different from those of these various groups.
- Compared to the average American, an annual salary of $158,100 for members of Congress seems considerable. Members of Congress also receive perks, including a generous pension plan, inexpensive insurance, subsidized medical care, as well as many other benefits. Yet compared with jobs with similar responsibilities in the private sector, congressional salaries are low.
- The U.S. Congress has two chambers with two major purposes: (1) to represent different interests and (2) to foster deliberative, careful lawmaking. Both the House and the Senate are organized along party lines, although the specifics of each organization differ considerably.
- The most powerful person in the Senate is the majority leader, chosen by members of the majority party, whose opposite in the minority party is the minority leader. Both leaders have assistants referred to as whips.
- The speaker of the House of Representatives is the leader of and most powerful individual in the lower chamber. The speaker is selected by the majority party and combines the powers shared by the vice president and the majority leader in the Senate. Both the majority and minority parties in the House also choose party leaders and whips.
- Committees are the core organizational feature of Congress. Standing committees are the most important, being permanent bodies with jurisdiction over particular

issues and categories of legislation. Committees do research on proposed legislation, revise proposals to accommodate various interests, and report the legislation out for consideration on the floor.

- Other types of committees include select committees, joint committees, conference committees, and party committees.
- Power in Congress is widely distributed. Leaders do not have the authority to command rank-and-file members to do their bidding and generally must rely on persuasion rather than coercion to get them to follow party wishes.
- The details of lawmaking are often highly complex, and traditional descriptions of how a bill becomes law oversimplify the legislative obstacle course. In both chambers, the rules and parliamentary maneuvering tend to favor those who want to prevent a bill from becoming law.

Key Terms

allocation responsiveness 363
bicameral 379
casework 363
censures and reprimands 369
closed rule 388
cloture 390
Committee of the Whole 394
conditional party government 390
conference committee 389
delegate 364
discharge petition 393
exclusive committee 388
exclude 368
expulsion 369
filibuster 390
franking privilege 378
hold 390
home style 363
joint committee 389
legislative oversight of administration 362
majority leader 381
minority leader 381

nongermane amendments 388
norm of reciprocity 385
open rule 388
party ratio 387
perquisites (perks) 378
policy responsiveness 362
politico 364
pork-barrel benefits 363
president of the Senate 380
president pro tempore 381
representation 362
rider 388
service responsiveness 363
speaker of the House of Representatives 383
standing committee 384
symbolic responsiveness 363
top committee 387
trustee 364
unanimous consent agreement (UCA) 391
unicameral 379
whip 382

Selected Readings

Brown, Sherrod. 2003. *Congress from the Inside: Observations from the Majority and the Minority.* 3rd ed. Kent, OH: Kent State University Press. The perspectives and insights of a current member of Congress on representing and lawmaking.

Congressional Quarterly. 1998. *How Congress Works.* Washington, DC: CQ Press. A comprehensive and accessible primer on the nation's legislature.

Fenno, Richard F. 1978. *Home Style: House Members in Their Districts.* Boston: Little, Brown. A political scientist's insights about how members of Congress see their districts and relate to their constituents, based on his observations from "soaking and poking" and "just hanging around" with several members of Congress as they traveled around in their districts.

Hibbing, John H. 1991. *Congressional Careers: Contours of Life in the U.S. House of Representatives.* Chapel Hill: University of North Carolina Press. Classic study detailing the world of members of Congress.

Schroeder, Pat. 2000. *24 Years of Housework and the Place Is Still a Mess.* Kansas City, MO: Andrews McMeel Publishing. A witty and decidedly partisan memoir of nearly a quarter-century of service in the House of Representatives by a well-known female legislator.

Sinclair, Barbara. 2000. *Unorthodox Lawmaking: New Legislative Processes in the U.S. Congress.* Washington, DC: CQ Press. One of the best explanations of the inner procedural workings of the modern Congress.

Wilson, Woodrow. 1885. *Congressional Government: A Study in American Politics.* Boston: Houghton, Mifflin. The classic study of Congress by a political scientist who later became president.

13 The Presidency

© Greg Whitesell/UPI/Landov

Presidents are very different—not just in party, not just in ideology, and not just in terms of policy ambitions. They are different in terms of style. Style makes a big difference.

Take, for example, the styles of President John F. Kennedy and President George W. Bush. Bush and Kennedy faced two of the greatest threats to national security during the past half century. For Kennedy it was the 1962 Cuban missile crisis, a tense standoff between the United States and the Soviet Union that brought the world to the brink of a nuclear war. For Bush it was 9/11, the devastating terrorist attacks that led to war in Afghanistan and Iraq.

Kennedy had to deal with Soviet missile sites on Cuba, an island only 90 miles off the coast of Florida. In the event of hostilities, those close-in missile capabilities potentially gave the Soviets a huge tactical and strategic advantage. The United States would have no time to defend or react to a missile strike that, literally, was launched from its own backyard.

Some advised immediate military action against the missile bases, others thought this would mean World War III. Kennedy wanted his Soviet counterpart (Nikita Khrushchev) to remove the missiles of his own accord. Kennedy tried to come up with a response that made clear America's strength and will, while leaving the Soviets an "out"—a way to back down without losing face. Kennedy put together a large and contentious group of experts known as the "Ex Comm" that served to centralize and analyze all available information and to formulate the various scenarios that could produce this result. Out of this came Kennedy's solution: a Naval blockade that eventually led to a "peaceful, face-saving resolution to the confrontation" (Crotty 2003, 455).

Bush had to deal with an actual attack on American soil, but there was no obvious nation-state to negotiate with or to hit back (most of the terrorists were Saudi citizens, but the government of Saudi Arabia was a U.S. ally). Bush's approach was not to assemble an equivalent of the Ex Comm to cover the pros and cons of various responses. With little input from anyone, he formulated the "Bush doctrine," which argues for preemptive military action when national security is threatened. He wanted to send a clear message: Not only will America hit back, it won't wait to be hit first. He made the decision to go to war (Woodward 2002, 15).

Bush assembled a comparatively small war cabinet. Its job was not to employ a broad range of experts to sift through information and provide options or to decide whether to go to war; instead, its job was to hammer out the details of prosecuting wars in Afghanistan and Iraq and dealing with their political implications (Crotty 2003, 460).

Which was the right approach? Kennedy's approach emphasized gathering as much information as possible, seeking contrasting opinions, and involving himself in decision making at all levels. Bush's approach was to make a decision, then turn things over to a small group of people (the "war cabinet") to figure out how to best put that decision into action.

Some see Kennedy's style as a model for how to deal with a crisis: cool and patient under pressure. Others see it as dithering rather than leadership. Some see Bush's style as the better option: decisive and forceful. Others view it as impulsive, reckless, and irresponsible. The point here is not to declare that the Kennedy or the Bush approach is better but to show that the two men had different ways of reacting to a crisis. Such differences have enormous consequences. Differences in style can literally mean the difference between war and peace.

The reason style can have such momentous consequences is that the office of president is made up of two fundamental components: (1) the president as an individual and (2) the president as an institution. Kennedy and Bush occupied the same office—they sat as the head of the same institution—but were very different individuals. To understand the presidency and its implications for how the nation reacts to particular crises or challenges—including living up to the promise of democracy—it is important to grasp the dual nature of the presidency.

To that end, this chapter examines the evolution of the institution of the presidency, the influence of the president as an individual, and the implications of the office's institutional structure for the performance of the chief executive.

 ## The Promise of the Presidency

The president of the United States of America holds the most powerful office on the planet. He (or she) commands the most awesome military machine in history, exerts unequalled influence over national and international policy, and sits as supreme executive in the American political system. The president, whoever it is, clearly has a lot of input into the performance of the American democracy.

That power and how it is, or is not, exercised cuts to the heart of the democratic promise. As the nation's chief executive, the president is the individual who has the most responsibility for ensuring all the core democratic values are upheld in the execution of government policy. Yet that power also creates a temptation to ignore those values when it serves the president's own interests.

The president's powers and unique role within the political system have long created an uncomfortable paradox for the American political system—one that is closely related to the Madisonian dilemma discussed in Chapter 2: How do you create a presidency powerful enough to ensure things get done but not powerful enough to run the risk of tyranny? Setting up a chief executive and defining the office's powers and responsibilities were some of the most difficult challenges of the Constitutional Convention. The problem was that "the delegates had exceedingly ambivalent feelings about what sort of an executive the new government should have" (Collier and Collier 1986, 284).

A clear flaw of the Articles of Confederation was the absence of an executive branch. Convention delegates wanted an executive strong enough to provide clear national leadership and to serve as a real check on the legislative branch. Yet they also feared putting too much power into the hands of a single individual, which could lead to tyranny.

The delegates first agreed on what they did not want in an executive. They did not want a king (Alexander Hamilton was virtually alone in seriously considering resurrecting the British model). Rather than look to Great Britain, the delegates looked to the states. Most states had weak executives dominated by state legislatures. In adopting such **a weak-executive model,** the job of the chief executive is simply to implement the decisions of the legislature. A president in a weak-executive system would have limited terms, would have no veto power, and would only be allowed to exercise the authority explicitly granted by Congress.

However, a few states, notably New York and Massachusetts, had strong, independent governors. The **strong-executive model** meant an executive independent of the legislature, with important powers vested in the executive office. The strong-executive model suggested a president as a strong political actor independent of Congress, with veto power, with the authority to appoint judges and diplomats, and with primary responsibility for foreign affairs.

Delegates at first seemed to prefer the weak-executive model, but states with strong-executive models were persuasive: Governors in New York and Massachusetts had served effectively without endangering political freedom. The clincher for the strong-executive model was the general assumption that the first president would be George Washington, a man so revered for devotion to his country that few saw him as a threat to becoming a tyrant.

The Constitutional Convention ended up creating a presidency somewhere between the strong- and weak-executive models. The president was to be chosen by the electoral college rather than appointed by the legislature. The president would not serve at the pleasure of Congress but could be removed only for treason, bribery, or high crimes and misdemeanors following impeachment by the House and conviction in the Senate. The Constitution gave the president specific grants of power, including command of the armed forces, the veto, the ability to issue executive pardons, and a very broad, undefined set of rights and responsibilities: "The executive power shall be vested in a President of the United States of America" (Article II, Section 1).

The delegates thus created a strong president but also placed clear limits on the president's power. The president cannot make law by decree; only Congress can pass laws. The president can veto legislation, but Congress can override the veto by a two-thirds vote of both chambers. The president can make appointments to the executive and judicial branches but only with Senate approval. The result is a powerful office, but one that is checked by other branches of government.

Several amendments have altered the basic structure of the executive office formulated at the Constitutional Convention: the Twelfth on the choosing of the president and vice president; the Twentieth clarifying the beginning of the presidential term; the Twenty-Second limiting a president to two terms; and the Twenty-Fifth specifying the line of succession to the presidency. Despite these changes, the constitutional framework of the presidency has remained mostly intact for more than two centuries.

The Development of the Presidency

The presidency today is different and more powerful than the office held by George Washington. The trend toward increasing the power of the presidency has not been constant. For example, the office occupied by Ulysses Grant was not as potent as that occupied by his predecessor, Abraham Lincoln. The other branches of government have grown in power along with the presidency, thus maintaining their ability to provide effective checks on the executive. Nevertheless, the general historical trend has favored a significant expansion of presidential power and influence.

Most of the changes in the presidency have come not from formal legal alterations but from informal custom and precedent. The power of the presidency, in short, derives in no small part from the legacy of the individuals who have occupied the office. Four basic factors explain the expansion of presidential power:

1. The energy associated with individual executives
2. Vague constitutional provisions that assertive presidents have used to broadly interpret their powers
3. Changing public expectations of the office
4. Congressional delegation of power and authority through law

A Single Executive

In *Federalist* Number 70, Alexander Hamilton used the term *energy* to describe a desirable characteristic of good government, especially in the executive branch. He saw decisiveness and dispatch as important qualities for a good executive. More than anything else, these traits have expanded presidential power.

A good example is the president's ability to make key decisions about committing American troops. Although Congress has the constitutional authority to declare war, presidents have interpreted their power as commander-in-chief as giving them the right to place military units in combat situations without prior authorization from Congress. The last time Congress formally declared war was to authorize U.S. entrance into World War II in 1941. The major military conflicts the United States has been involved in since then—the Korean War, Vietnam War, and Iraq War—technically were not wars because Congress never made a formal declaration of hostilities. For example, Congress passed a joint resolution in 2002 authorizing the president to use U.S. armed forces against Iraq, but this was not a formal declaration of war. Lee Hamilton, former chair of the House International Relations Committee, says, "In the exercise of its . . . war-making power, Congress

The decisiveness and energy associated with individual executives has expanded the power of the presidency. A good example is the president's ability to make key decisions about committing American troops. Although Congress has the constitutional authority to declare war, presidents have interpreted their power as commander-in-chief as giving them the right to place military units in combat situations without prior authorization from Congress. Here, President Bush meets with U.S. troops in Fort Hood, Texas, a base that supplied many troops for the war in Iraq. Although Congress did approve this war, the President's support of going to war and emphasis on a preemptive strike were strong catalysts.

© Getty Images

PROMISE AND POLICY
Breaking Treaties

The constitution and historical precedent give the president primary responsibility for making treaties with foreign nations. For the same reason, presidents can also take the lead in breaking treaties.

During the first two years he served as president, George W. Bush was better known for breaking treaties than making them. Against the wishes of Russia, he withdrew the United States from the 1972 Antiballistic Missile Treaty and championed in its place a high-tech (and very expensive) antimissile system designed to intercept nuclear missiles in flight.

Against the wishes of much of the world he withdrew the United States from the Kyoto Protocol, a multinational pact aimed at reducing global warming. He also withdrew from treaties or efforts to forge treaties on reducing the global arms trade, banning germ warfare, imposing tariffs on steel imports, and establishing an international war crimes court.

The Bush administration argued that these treaties were not in the best interests of the country and that his actions simply reflected a president taking a hardheaded and practical view of U.S. interests. Others viewed the moves with concern and condemnation, seeing them as evidence of a go-it-alone foreign policy that brought uncertainty into international affairs and left other nations wary of dealing with the United States.

These concerns took on particular resonance following the terrorist attack on the United States in September 2001. Following the attacks, President Bush faced the task of combating terrorism on a global scale—something that made dealing with other nations an absolute necessity.

While many nations stepped up to contribute to the fight on terrorism, some of President Bush's policies received lukewarm response from the international community. Certainly, the multinational coalition backing the second U.S.-led invasion of Iraq was notably smaller than the

coalition that fought in the first Gulf War of 1991. In the view of many, this reflected the downside of the go-it-alone approach of the Bush administration. Fighting a lengthy, unpopular, and bloody counterinsurgency campaign in a place like Iraq can never be easy, but allies willing to make significant monetary and troop commitments can ease the burden. Bush found such allies to be in short supply.

Was this simply Bush's foreign policy chickens coming home to roost? Critics of the Bush administration certainly thought so. The basic argument was this: Enlisting international support for any foreign policy initiative is difficult, especially on such controversial decisions as military action. A history of backing out of treaties and ignoring the interests of potential allies, however, is unlikely to make such efforts any easier.

Sources: Kasindorf, Martin. 2004. "Kerry: Bush's Iraq Choices Undermined American Leadership." *USA Today.* http://www.usatoday.com/news/politicselections/nation/president/2004-05-27-kerry-iraq_x.htm; Nichols, Bill. 2001. "Critics Decry Bush Stand on Treaties." *USA Today.* http://www.usatoday.com/news/washington/july01/2001-07-27-bush-treaties-usat.htm.

---

has basically ceded to the president over a period of years the decision in going to war" (quoted in Lehigh 2002, A27).

In addition to military action, the president retains a dominant role in foreign affairs. The power to negotiate treaties (which require Senate approval) and executive agreements (which do not), to initiate or break off diplomatic relations, and to choose representatives abroad make the president's voice the crucial one in foreign affairs. (See the Promise and Policy feature "Breaking Treaties.")

Historian Arthur Schlesinger, Jr., (1973) argues that such expansions of power led to the creation of an "imperial presidency" that appropriated powers reserved to other branches by the Constitution. Presidents who have acted decisively and assertively have thus significantly expanded the power of the office.

Broad Constitutional Provisions

A key opportunity for aggressive executives to expand their powers is provided by the vague and indefinite opening sentence of Article II: "The executive power shall be vested in a President of the United States of America." This grant of authority allows bold and innovative ventures. Supplementing this provision are other clauses ripe for broad interpretation. For example, the president has responsibility for ensuring "that the laws be faithfully executed" (Article II, Section 3)—a clause that presidents have repeatedly used as legal justification for their actions.

Some presidents resisted the lure to expand their office. James Buchanan and William Howard Taft took a **restrictive view of presidential power,** arguing that the president could exercise only the powers specifically granted by the Constitution. In contrast, Theodore Roosevelt formulated the **stewardship doctrine,** arguing that the president is the steward of the people and should do anything required by the needs of the nation unless it is specifically prohibited by the Constitution. Abraham Lincoln subscribed to the **prerogative view of presidential power,** arguing that the oath of office required him to both preserve the Constitution and to take otherwise unconstitutional measures to ensure that the Constitution itself was well preserved.

While earlier presidents could debate the extent of their powers, contemporary presidents do not have this luxury. People expect the president to deliver on a broad set of promises, so the president cannot choose to take the narrow role of caretaker. As political scientist Richard Neustadt put it, the modern president "may retain liberty, in Woodrow Wilson's phrase, 'to be as big a man as he can.' But nowadays he cannot be as small as he might like" (1960, 6).

Public Acceptance of Positive Government

Before the Great Depression began in 1929, government was viewed as having limited responsibility for regulating economic activity. The economic collapse during the Great Depression and the social dislocation it caused changed this attitude. Many Americans welcomed President Franklin Roosevelt's New Deal and its aggressive government intervention into the social and economic patterns of the nation.

Since the 1930s, Americans have increasingly demanded that the government "do something" to ensure prosperity. Economic problems such as unemployment and inflation are now routinely seen as government's responsibility to fix. Government is expected to address healthcare, drug abuse, and a staggering number of other social problems. Government is even expected to step in to mitigate the pain and suffering caused by natural disasters such as hurricanes, tornadoes, floods, and earthquakes. Responses of presidents to such crises enhanced the influence of the presidency by creating a sense that the executive could move swiftly and decisively to solve or at least ameliorate such problems.

This increased activity created permanent expectations. As the presidency has grown in power and influence, Americans have come to accept the concept of **positive government,** a government that plays a major role in meeting or preventing most major crises or problems faced by society. Expectations of the president go beyond responding to a crisis. The president is routinely expected to manage the domestic economy to produce jobs and opportunity and to conduct foreign policy that promotes peace and democratic values while protecting the nation's economic and strategic interests. As Neustadt observed, Americans have transformed "into routine practice . . . the actions we once treated as exceptional" (1960, 6). The result has been a steady escalation of what the president is normally expected to achieve.

Congressional Delegation of Power

In many cases, Congress has specifically delegated additional power and resources to the executive branch. For example, Congress passed several laws in the 20th century giving presidents an increased role in making budgetary decisions. Some scholars suggest that the legislative branch was too fragmented to be decisive on key policy matters, so Congress followed the public and turned to the president to provide policy leadership. Note, however, that Congress has never abdicated its final authority to amend, change, or block presidential initiatives.

Contemporary Expectations of the President

For a variety of reasons, the public has come to expect all chief executives to be presidents of action. The president is held responsible for the economy and for addressing a wide array of social problems. He or she is expected to head the executive branch, conduct foreign policy, nominate federal judges, reflect and shape public opinion, and provide direction and leadership for Congress. The president is also expected to act as the chief partisan for a political party while remaining representative of all Americans.

Although the Founders settled on a single president, the realities of managing broad expectations means that the modern presidency has become a larger and more bureaucratic organization than in years past. The office of president now stands squarely at the center of the American political system. It has evolved into the center of policymaking, and it has experienced considerable bureaucratic expansion. About 1,700 individuals now make up the institution of the presidency. A broad variety of policy specialists and political advisors enhance the president's ability to meet the high expectations placed on the office. There are experts on everything from national security to agriculture and mass communications.

Yet while presidential power has grown, there is a question about whether it has kept pace with increased expectations. The basic constitutional framework establishes a government of shared powers. If presidents have any hope of meeting the high expectations placed on the office, they must convince political actors in other branches and levels of government to take action. The American system of government makes the president dependent on the actions of others who have power independent of the presidency, and this poses enormous difficulties in meeting the public's rising expectations.

The President and the Presidency

Most Americans tend to personalize the office of the president in terms of the current occupant, but this perspective ignores the complex organization that lies behind the individual. To fully understand the modern presidency, it is important to grasp how both the individual and the organization contribute to presidential performance.

The President as an Individual

Some political scientists suggest that the way the president handles the powers and duties of office depends on individual personality and character. Family background and life experiences help determine self-confidence, psychological needs, values, and worldview. They also shape political philosophy and personal vision of presidential conduct.

Students of the subject, like Erwin Hargrove (1974) and James David Barber (1992) distinguish between active presidents and passive presidents. "Active presidents" invest a good deal of personal energy into the office, and their personal needs and skills translate well into political leadership. "Passive presidents" devote less time and effort to being president and have neither the inclination nor the ability to effectively exercise political power. Barber (1992) also distinguishes between "positive presidents," who gain personal satisfaction from serving as president, and "negative presidents," who serve because of compulsion or a sense of duty but derive little pleasure from the post.

Barber uses these two dimensions to identify four types of presidents:

- **Active-positive presidents** want results, and they push for change in institutions, policies, and procedures.
- **Active-negative presidents** are preoccupied with acquiring and maintaining power for its own sake.
- **Passive-positive presidents** want to be popular, to be loved and admired.
- **Passive-negative presidents** are characterized by a deep sense of civic virtue and rectitude.

This psychological approach to understanding the presidency has not proven terribly successful. There is little doubt that the background and personality of individual presidents affect their performance, but determining exactly how one causes the other is extraordinarily difficult. Part of the problem is context: What a president can accomplish is significantly affected by the type and magnitude of the problems the government faces at the time and by the needs, interests, and preferences of the other actors who share power with the president. Rather than character traits *causing* job performance, the demands of the job may reveal a president's character. Even placing a president into one of the personality categories is imprecise and subjective; sometimes classification must wait until after the individual leaves the office. Contemporary observers, for example, tend to view Bill Clinton as an active-positive president, but there is disagreement about whether George W. Bush is active-positive or active-negative.

The Presidency as an Organization

Although no other figure in American political life commands the amount of attention given a president, the job is too big and too difficult for an individual to accomplish alone. Over the course of history, presidents have used a variety of advisors and organizations to help manage their duties. One presidential advisor, the vice president, is explicitly provided for in the Constitution, although each president determines the role the vice president will play. The cabinet and the Executive Office of the President are authorized and funded by Congress. Other people play key advisory roles because of close personal ties to the president. John Kennedy relied on his brother Robert for advice, and George W. Bush frequently turns to his father, former President George H. W. Bush, for advice. Several presidents have turned to the first lady for political and policy advice.

Irrespective of who is president, the presidency is a complex organization of many individuals. The major components of the presidency as an organization include the vice president, the cabinet, and the Executive Office of the President. The various individuals who serve in the executive branch often compete and struggle for access to the president, and some are more influential than others.

Vice President   Although the Constitution establishes the office of vice president and sets the same qualifications for office as for the presidency, it lists no formal executive powers or responsibilities.[1] Generally, vice presidents have not been central policy-makers, and ambitious politicians have shunned the office. John Nance Garner, who gave up the position of speaker of the House to become Franklin Roosevelt's vice president in 1933, most famously summed up the disdain for the office by saying, "the vice presidency isn't worth a pitcher of warm piss" (Rees 1997, 254).

Some vice presidents have essentially been presidents-in-waiting when something arose to prevent the president from fulfilling the obligations of the office. The person with the "best job in the country," Will Rogers once quipped, "is the Vice President. All he has to do is get up every morning and say, 'How's the President?'" (Byrne 1988, 229). Since 1960, two vice presidents—Lyndon Johnson and Gerald Ford—became president after the death of one president and the resignation of another. The post has also been a stepping-stone to the presidency. Since 1960, Richard Nixon and George H. W. Bush, both of whom had been vice presidents, ran for and were elected president.

Vice presidents are not always condemned to ceremonial roles in political backwater. In some administrations, they have played key roles in attacking policy groups or policy positions so that the president would not be perceived as acting inappropriately or being overly partisan. Vice President Spiro Agnew, for example, made harsh public attacks on critics of the Nixon administration. Vice presidents have also occupied key advisory roles. Vice Presidents Nelson Rockefeller, Walter Mondale, George H. W. Bush, and Al Gore put their own stamps on the agendas and policies of the Ford, Carter, Reagan, and Clinton administrations (Berke 1999). Vice President Dick Cheney is widely considered to be such a powerful player in the administration of George W. Bush it became the subject of popular jokes. ("Did you know if Dick Cheney dies, George Bush will run the country?")

Cabinet   The cabinet consists of the heads of the executive agencies and other officials designated by the president to serve as a council of advisors. The cabinet is more a product of law and historical accident than of constitutional design (Hart 1995). At the Constitutional Convention, Gouverneur Morris offered a detailed and elaborate plan for a Council of State to advise the president. But all that survived in the final draft was a general implication in Article II, Section 2 that a cabinet would

---

[1]Article I, Section 3 gives the vice president some legislative responsibility as president of the Senate with the right to cast a vote to break a tie. But no formal executive power is granted unless the president dies, leaves office, or is disabled, in which case the vice president assumes the duties of the president.

© Bettmann/Corbis

The cabinet consists of the heads of the executive agencies and other officials designated by the president to serve as a council of advisors. Cabinet members can serve the interests of the president above and beyond providing advice and using their positions to pursue the administration's agenda. Because they hold high-profile positions and are in close proximity to the president, their appointments are useful in strengthening ties to certain constituencies. Abraham Lincoln selected a strong cabinet that included all of his major rivals for the Republican presidential nomination: William H. Seward as secretary of state (center), Salmon P. Chase as secretary of the treasury (second from left), and Edward Bates as attorney general (far right). Here he reads them the Emancipation Proclamation on July 22, 1862.

exist: The president "may require the opinion, in writing, of the principal officer in each of the executive departments, upon any subject relating to the duties of their respective offices."

The first Congress created the Departments of War, Treasury, and State, and the office of Attorney General, but established no formal advisory council. In 1789, George Washington attempted to use the Senate as an advisory council regarding a treaty with Native Americans; apparently, he was taking seriously the "advise" part of the Senate's "advise and consent" responsibility. But senators of the time seemed more interested in the separation of powers principle, and they refused to discuss the matter in his presence. Angered by the rebuff, Washington left the chamber and turned to the heads of the executive departments for advice. This was the first cabinet.

Every president since Washington has had a cabinet, though its role has varied from one administration to the next. In general, the cabinet's role has declined over time. Reasons for this atrophy are varied. Cabinet secretaries sometimes become advocates for the bureaucratic agencies they head rather than remaining loyal to the president. The White House staff has grown so much that presidents have other sources of expert advice. Many White House staff members were originally part of the president's campaign team and were chosen for their demonstrated loyalty to the president and the agenda. By contrast, cabinet members are not necessarily close to the president, did not play major roles in the campaign, and were frequently appointed either out of electoral debt to some organized group or because the individual's expertise and experience lent credibility to the administration.

The decline of the cabinet as an advisory structure also reflects the evolution of the presidency as a distinct and separate entity within the executive branch. In the past fifty years, the boundary between the White House staff, who are loyal to the current president, and the career civil servants in the permanent departments and agencies of the federal government has become much sharper.

Despite this decline, cabinet members retain important and influential positions in the political system. The head of an executive agency such as the Department of Justice or the Department of Defense has enormous responsibilities and a strong position from which to influence both the policy governing the agency and the way that policy is implemented. For these reasons, the qualifications and political records of heads of executive agencies, who generally must be approved by the Senate, are closely scrutinized.

Cabinet members can also serve the interests of the president above and beyond providing advice and using their positions to pursue the administration's agenda. Because they hold high-profile positions and are in close proximity to the president, their appointments are useful in strengthening ties to certain constituencies. President George W. Bush, for example, chose Colin Powell as secretary of state for his first term. Powell, an African American, was widely admired for his service as chairman of the Joint Chiefs of Staff. By nominating him, Bush made a symbolic gesture to African Americans, a group that openly questioned the legitimacy of his presidency because of suspicions of voting irregularities. Bush also chose John Ashcroft, a former U.S. senator, as his attorney general. Ashcroft, a favorite of evangelical Christians, helped cement Bush's ties to one of his most important constituencies, even though many other groups viewed Ashcroft's appointment with dismay.

Executive Office of the President   Frequently, the president's closest and most influential advisors are in the **Executive Office of the President (EOP).** Established in 1939, this office has grown in size and complexity. Figure 13.1 shows the organization of the first EOP, compared to its modern incarnation.

Within the EOP, the **White House Office** houses some of the president's most influential advisors. White House staffers include the chief of staff; the White House legal counsel; presidential speechwriters; the president's press secretary; assistants for domestic, foreign, and economic policy; and liaisons with Congress, the public, and state and local governments. The agency also includes the president's personal staff, the vice president, and the first lady's staff.

Over the years, Congress has placed several other agencies under the EOP canopy. The most important include the **Office of Management and Budget (OMB),** the **National Security Council,** and the **Council of Economic Advisers.** As the EOP expanded into a series of agencies with focused responsibilities, staffers have become increasingly specialized. After his first term in office, Franklin Roosevelt had fewer than 100 presidential assistants, most of them generalists with titles like assistant to the president, or counsel to the president. In contrast, under George W. Bush, the

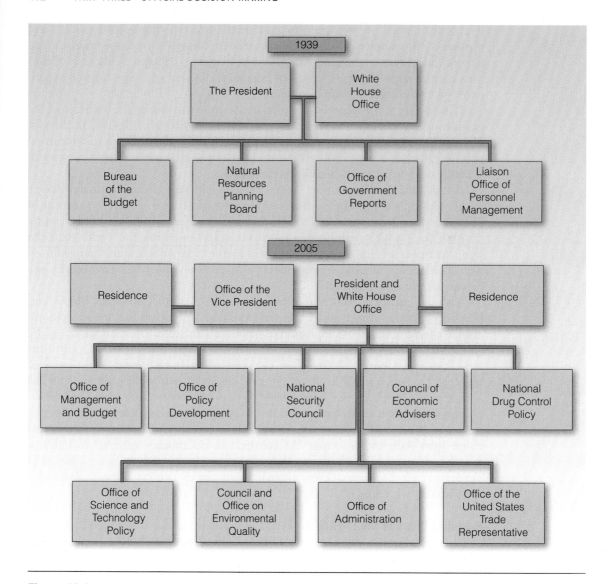

Figure 13.1
Executive Office of the President at Its Inception and Today
Source: Edwards, George C., III, and Stephen J. Wayne. 2003. *Presidential Leadership: Politics and Policy Making.* 6th ed. Belmont, CA: Thomson/Wadsworth, 197.

OMB alone had more than 500 employees, most of them with specialties in areas such as national security, human resources, or natural resources. With the growth and specialization of the White House Office, the presidency has taken on the trappings of a large bureaucratic organization. Political scientists Lyn Ragsdale and John Theis (1997) argue that the presidency has become "institutionalized" and that it has grown into a large, complex, permanent organization that all presidents must learn to manage once they take office.

© Bettmann/Corbis

Over the years, first ladies have become much more prominent as political and policy advisors, reflecting the changing role of women in society. Eleanor Roosevelt had a very strong effect on this changing role. She traveled widely to assess social and economic conditions, had her own newspaper column, and was a key member of Franklin Roosevelt's "kitchen cabinet," a group of individuals who were not members of the official cabinet and who fed the president's voracious appetite for information. Here she tours conditions in a coal mine in Ohio, 1935 with mine officials and members of the United Mine Workers' union.

First Lady   The role of the president's spouse has evolved over time. Originally, the first lady had mostly social duties, acting as a hostess and the like. But over the years, first ladies have become much more prominent as political and policy advisors, reflecting the changing role of women in society.[2]

Eleanor Roosevelt was one of the best-known politically active presidential spouses. She traveled widely to assess social and economic conditions, had her own newspaper column, and was a key member of Franklin Roosevelt's "kitchen cabinet," a group of individuals who were not members of the official cabinet and who fed the president's voracious appetite for information. Taking such a high-profile, nontraditional role was controversial, a problem other politically powerful first ladies encountered. President Jimmy Carter's reliance on his wife Rosalynn's advice led some to

[2]So far, there have been no first gentlemen. Only two presidents were unmarried during their terms. Thomas Jefferson's wife died before he became president, and in his administration, hostess duties were performed by either his daughters or Dolley Madison, wife of Secretary of State James Madison. James Buchanan is the only bachelor president to date. During his administration, the official hostess was his niece, Harriet Lane.

view her as "the second most powerful person in the Untied States" (Gutin 1994, 521). Bill Clinton appointed his wife, Hillary, to head a task force on healthcare reform and elevated the position of first lady to a more formal policy role than in previous administrations. Because they had influence and power without having been elected or formally appointed, both Rosalynn Carter and Hillary Clinton were controversial figures during their husbands' terms.[3] President George W. Bush credits First Lady Laura Bush as the most important guiding force in his life, but her role as political and policy advisor has been more behind the scenes and less controversial.

Organization of the Presidency and Presidential Effectiveness

As the White House staff has grown, it has become more difficult to control and coordinate. Mismanagement of the White House staff has been blamed for a number of crises, ranging from an unsuccessful invasion of Cuba during the Kennedy administration, to provision of funds to Nicaraguan rebels in contravention of a congressional mandate in the Reagan administration, to a scandal involving firing White House Travel Office staff in the Clinton administration. More than twenty-five years ago, political scientist Thomas Cronin observed, "the president needs help merely to manage his help. The swelling and continuous expansion of the presidency have reached such proportions that the president's ability to manage has been weakened rather than strengthened. Bigger has not been better" (1975, 118).

Presidents have tried various administrative arrangements to organize the White House staff so that it supports the president's agenda effectively without creating political quagmires. Most presidents use a **hierarchical model,** which sets up hierarchical lines of authority and delegates control through a chief of staff. Other presidents have tried a **spokes-of-the-wheel model,** where the president is in the middle, acting as the hub, while various presidential advisors representing the spokes of the wheel report directly to the president. Figure 13.2 illustrates these models.

The hierarchical structure, with clear lines of authority going through a chief of staff, fit well with President Dwight Eisenhower's military experience. It was an efficient system that insulated Eisenhower from small details and allowed him to set general policy goals and build political support for them. President Richard Nixon also used a hierarchical model with access to the president controlled by the chief of staff. Although the Nixon White House was efficient from a managerial standpoint, it insulated the president from the perspective and political insights of cabinet members and members of Congress. President George W. Bush, the first president with an MBA, organized the White House on a corporate model (Crotty 2003). Sometimes referred to as a "CEO presidency," in this version of the hierarchical model the president "would be the chairman of the board of the world's biggest conglomerate" (Sanger 2001). President Bush delegates major authority and responsibility to Vice President Dick Cheney, who acts as chief operating officer (COO) and to members of the cabinet, who serve as CEOs of their parts of the government conglomerate (Berke 2001; Sanger 2001). A strong CEO model that works well in the private sector does not adapt as well in government. Unlike business executives who have clear

---

[3]Hillary Clinton had a political career in her own right. She was elected to the Senate from New York in 2000, becoming the first first lady to win elective office.

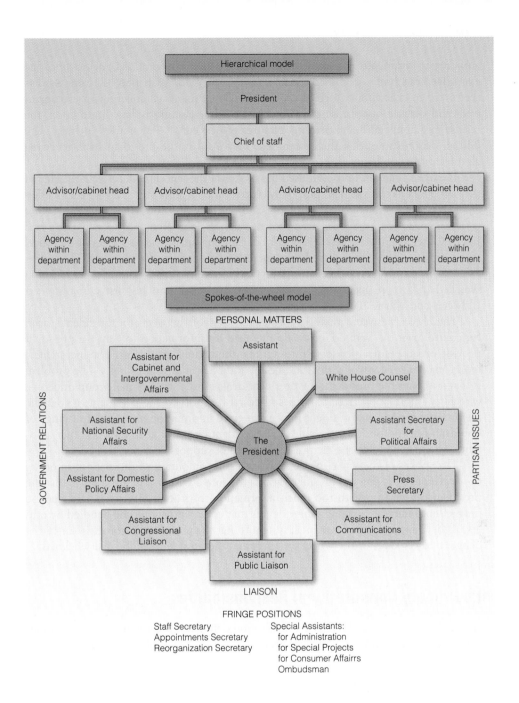

Figure 13.2

Two Models for Organizing the White House Staff

Sources: Hierarchical model: Adapted from George, Alexander L., and Juliette L. George. 1998. *Presidential Personality and Performance.* Boulder, CO: Westview Press, 209. Spokes-of-the-wheel model: Adapted from Campbell, Colin. 1986. *Managing the Presidency: Carter, Reagan, and the Search for Executive Harmony.* Pittsburgh: University of Pittsburgh Press, 85.

authority to formulate and implement policy for their corporations, members of the executive branch of government do not. As we observed in Chapter 12, Congress has the power to enact policy, decide on how the departments of government are organized, and oversee how those departments are implementing policy. In addition, the release of graphic and embarrassing pictures of prisoners being abused in Iraq's Abu Ghraib prison shows that this system also may insulate the president from receiving all the information he needs.

President Franklin Roosevelt used the spokes-of-the-wheel model effectively. He ran the staff operation himself and purposely blurred lines of authority to create competition among his staff to maximize the amount and diversity of information. However, other presidents who tried a similar arrangement, such as John Kennedy, Gerald Ford, and Jimmy Carter, had less success. President Bill Clinton initially tried a spokes-of-the-wheel structure with blurred lines of authority and easy staff access to the president. The system created problems of slow decision making and ineffective communication, and Clinton switched to a more hierarchical arrangement two years into his first administration (Edwards and Wayne 2003).

The choice between models represents a tradeoff between the president's need for control over the White House and the need for information to help the president provide broad political leadership to address the nation's problems. The hierarchical model maximizes control with clear lines of authority and responsibility. The problem is that it isolates the president; the president deals mostly with a small group of people who filter information from various sources and report to the president. Under the hierarchical model, the president may not receive information about the full range of opportunities and options available. The president does not keep tabs on other assistants, who may take actions the president does not support.

The spokes-of-the-wheel model maximizes the amount and diversity of information available by giving the president access to more advisors. The problem is that the president can end up with too much information to process effectively and may be dragged into micro-managing minor details that could and should be handled by others. If the danger of the hierarchical system is that the president becomes isolated, the danger of the spokes-of-the-wheel system is that the president will be overwhelmed.

The President's Primary Constitutional Responsibilities

Article II, Sections 1 and 2 of the Constitution define the president's primary responsibilities. These include chief executive, commander-in-chief of the military, and chief diplomat.

Chief Executive

The executive power referenced in the opening sentence of Article II entails a number of activities. Organizing the presidency and being an effective manager, as discussed above, are important executive duties. The president can also grant pardons and reprieves. The core of executive power involves implementation of the nation's laws.

Article II, Section 3 does not say the president implements the laws but rather that "he shall *take care* that the laws be faithfully executed" (emphasis added). In effect, the president is the chief bureaucrat because executing the laws is mainly the job of the federal bureaucracy. The president has the responsibility of making sure the federal bureaucracy is fulfilling its responsibilities as designated by law.

Administering this vast and varied operation is an enormous challenge. Many of the people who implement the laws are not directly subordinate to the president; the president cannot fire or cut the salaries of individuals in the civil service. Others who serve at the president's discretion, such as cabinet secretaries, often develop political power bases independent of the president.

As chief executive, the president has the power to appoint individuals to fill the most important positions in the executive branch. But here too there are constraints. The most important of these is that appointments require confirmation by the Senate. Although the Senate confirms over 95 percent of presidential nominations to executive branch agencies (cabinet, EOP, and major regulatory agencies), Senate action on these nominations has increased for recent presidents. Figure 13.3 shows the average

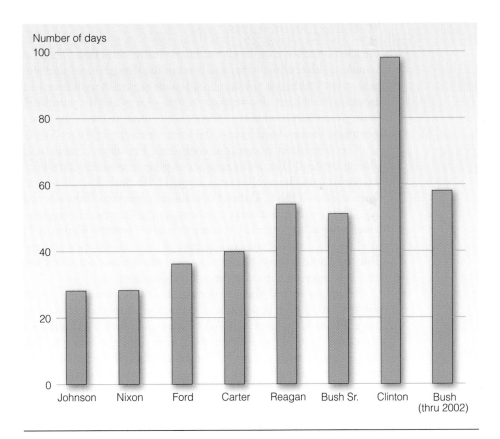

Figure 13.3
Average Number of Days for Senate Action on Executive Branch Nominations
Source: Bond, Jon R., Richard Fleisher, and Glen S. Krutz. 2004. "The Presumption of Success on Presidential Appointments Reconsidered: How Maligned Neglect Has Become the Primary Method of Defeating Nominees." Texas A&M University. Typescript.

number of days it took for the Senate to act on executive branch nominations for the last eight presidents. During the Johnson, Nixon, Ford, and Carter presidencies, the Senate generally acted on nominations in about a month. The time required to act on nominations of the four most recent presidents increased—to about two months for the presidencies of Reagan, the senior Bush, and George W. Bush, and to more than three months for President Clinton. If getting these major executive branch officials confirmed and on the job is delayed an extra month or two, then the president's ability "to take care that the laws be faithfully executed" is also delayed.

Furthermore, the president does not have the authority to determine the particular organization and structure of the executive branch. Instead, Congress determines the number of executive departments and frequently creates executive branch agencies that are insulated from the president. For example, the president appoints individuals to the Federal Reserve Board ("the Fed") and the Federal Election Commission (FEC), but members serve for fixed terms that overlap with the president's term, and these appointees cannot be removed except for wrongdoing.

Commander-in-Chief

Article II, Section 2 of the Constitution clearly states that "The President shall be commander-in-chief of the Army and Navy of the United States, and of the militia of the several states." Although this is a broad grant of power to the president, the extent of the power is the subject of some dispute. One view is that the president's power is limited to acting as civilian head of the military with authority for the general policy direction and command of the armed forces. The other view is that this provision empowers the president to take direct operational command. President Lincoln asserted the latter view during the Civil War, and a number of other presidents, including Franklin Roosevelt, Harry Truman, Ronald Reagan, George H. W. Bush, Bill Clinton, and George W. Bush, have acted as if they had direct operational command (Edwards and Wayne 2003, 487).

The president has more autonomy in the exercise of the power as commander-in-chief than in the exercise of other executive powers. Congress has sole authority to declare war, and Congress passes laws establishing funding and regulating the military. But the president has the power—even the duty—to commit military forces to protect U.S. interests without a formal declaration of war.

Attempts to limit the president's authority to commit troops without congressional approval have been largely unsuccessful. One important attempt to limit the power of the commander-in-chief is the War Powers Act of 1973. This law requires the president to consult "in every possible instance" with Congress before sending troops into action and to report such actions to Congress within 48 hours. Troops must be withdrawn after 60 days unless Congress declares war or passes a resolution authorizing the use of armed force. This law has generally failed to keep presidents from committing troops. Presidents view the law as an unconstitutional intrusion on their prerogatives. Presidents Reagan, Bush senior, and Clinton all ordered military actions that could be considered violations of the War Powers Act. Yet, in most instances, they and other presidents observed notification provisions without officially acknowledging them as legitimate: They notified Congress "consistent with" rather "in pursuance of" the War Powers Act. And once the president has taken military action, Congress has been hesitant to withhold support for American troops placed in harm's way.

Taking unilateral action by ordering military operations on foreign soil poses some risks for the president. The risk is small if the conflict can be quickly brought to a successful conclusion, but having American troops in unsuccessful or extended combat operations without the approval of Congress is likely to be politically costly. This was one of the reasons, for example, that President George H. W. Bush sought congressional backing of the Gulf War in 1991 as soon as it became apparent liberating Kuwait after an Iraqi invasion would require a massive military commitment. Even with congressional approval, extended combat operations in the more recent Iraq War eroded support for the second President Bush.

Chief Diplomat

The president's central role in foreign policy is a product of tradition and of the unique constitutional authority to "make treaties" subject to ratification by two-thirds of the Senate and to appoint ambassadors subject to confirmation by a majority in the Senate (Article II, Section 2). These constitutional provisions place the president at the center of foreign policy formulation, and presidents have interpreted these powers very broadly. George Washington, for example, assumed that the power to receive ambassadors also conferred the power to formally recognize other nations. Presidents have also used their powers as commander-in-chief to assert a primary role in foreign policy.

Today U.S. presidents are expected to take a hands-on approach to conducting foreign policy. Recent presidents have found it necessary to work with Middle Eastern leaders in an attempt to bring peace to the region. This included Bill Clinton, who is shown here with then-Israeli Prime Minister Ehud Barak (left) and Palestinian leader Yasser Arafat during a summit at Camp David in July 2000.

© Associated Press/AP Wide World

The president is the government official who negotiates treaties. Although the Constitutional calls on the president to obtain the advice and consent of the Senate, Washington's attempt to seek advice from the Senate was unsuccessful, as noted earlier, and the Senate's role has been confined almost exclusively to deciding whether to consent. Presidents sometimes discuss controversial provisions of treaties with key senators in an effort to avoid ratification difficulties. Ratification of a treaty requires a two-thirds vote. Sometimes the Senate approves a treaty with reservations or amendments, necessitating further negotiations.

Since 1789, more than 90 percent of the hundreds of treaties submitted to the Senate have been approved—70 percent without any change. Of the treaties that failed, only about twenty were defeated on a floor vote; about 150 others were withdrawn by the president, mostly because they ran into resistance in the Senate. The most famous example of a treaty voted down on the Senate floor is the Treaty of Versailles, which ended World War I and established the League of Nations. It failed in large part because President Woodrow Wilson was unwilling to consult with key senators and to agree to compromises. In order to win approval of the Panama Canal Treaty in 1978, President Jimmy Carter agreed to a reservation added by the Senate stating that the United States had the right to use military force to keep the canal open if necessary (Edwards and Wayne 2003, 179).

The 90-percent approval rate does not mean that presidents have an easy time winning approval of treaties they have negotiated. Although the Senate rarely turns down a treaty outright, treaties often languish for years in Senate committees that take no action to move them through the process. Presidents have responded to this difficulty by entering into **executive agreements** with other nations. These are treaties in all but name. An executive agreement takes the legal form of a contract between two nations, which does not require two-thirds approval from the Senate. As Figure 13.4 indicates, presidents who followed Franklin Roosevelt (1933–1944) negotiated many more executive agreements than treaties.

Most executive agreements involve minor, routine issues, but some deal with more weighty matters and require action by Congress. The North American Free Trade Agreement (NAFTA), for example, was an executive agreement negotiated by President George H. W. Bush in 1992 to provide open markets among the United States, Canada, and Mexico. Although NAFTA did not require congressional approval, President Bush, and later President Clinton, recognized the political costs of not involving Congress in an agreement with such broad implications. Bush sent the agreement to both the Senate and the House in order to get legislation to implement NAFTA, and Congress approved the NAFTA legislation in 1993 (Ragsdale 1996, 290). NAFTA was not a treaty, so it did not require approval by a two-thirds vote in the Senate. But the enabling legislation—the law that puts the treaty into effect—had to pass both houses by a simple majority. In this way the House of Representatives sometimes plays a role in the treaty-making process—not in ratifying treaties, but in passing the legislation necessary to implement them.

The president's constitutional responsibilities as chief executive, commander-in-chief, and chief diplomat are relatively well known. The remainder of this chapter focuses on three other major presidential roles: leader of the political party, leader of public opinion, and leader of Congress. In each role, the president needs to persuade others to follow when they may not be inclined to do so.

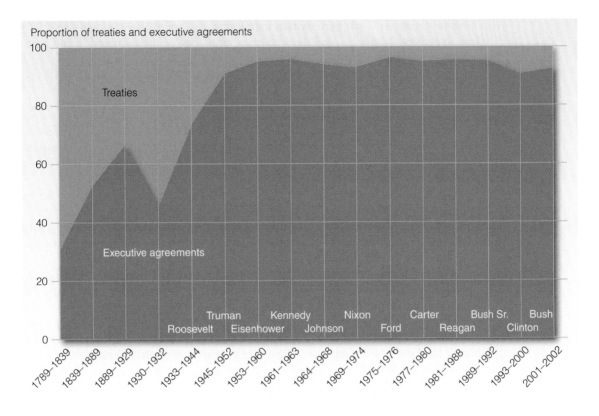

Proportion of treaties and executive agreements

Figure 13.4
Treaties and executive agreements, 1789–2002
Sources: Adapted from Stanley, Harold W., and Richard G. Niemi. 2003. *Vital Statistics on American Politics 2003–2004*. Washington, DC: CQ Press, 337; *1789–1980: Congressional Quarterly's Guide to Congress,* 5th ed. Washington, DC: 2000; 1981–2002: Office of the Assistant Legal Advisor for Treaty Affairs, U.S. Department of State.

The President as Party Leader

The Founders did not anticipate that the president would be the leader of a political party. Indeed, as we learned in Chapter 7, the nation's first president warned of the "baneful effects of the spirit of party." Yet, Washington's warning went unheeded. By the election of the third president—Thomas Jefferson—in 1800, political parties were already an important feature of American politics. The role of party leader has become a permanent part of the president's job. James Davis argues that of the president's many duties, "none is more important to his longer-term success than that of party leader" (1994, 1). He observes that with the exception of Washington, who became president before the development of parties, America's strongest presidents—Jefferson, Jackson, Lincoln, Wilson, and Roosevelt—were also strong party leaders.

The role of party leader encompasses the three basic elements of political parties discussed in Chapter 7: party organization, party in the electorate, and party in government.

America's relatively weak party system significantly constrains the president's ability to lead in each of these areas, and the amount of effort devoted to partisanship and party building varies from one president to the next.

Limitations on the President as Party Leader

Several features of American politics limit the president's ability to act as party leader. First is the traditional mistrust of parties, dating back to the founding of the nation. This suspicion promotes an inclination to be "president of all the people" and a fear that being too partisan is politically risky.

Constitutional fragmentation of powers also limits the president's ability to act as party leader. Federalism has led to national party organizations that are essentially confederations of 50 separate and autonomous state organizations. National party chairs and committees have little authority over state parties, and the president has little hope of centralizing control over such broad and often factious coalitions.

The separation of the national government into executive, legislative, and judicial branches further limits the president's party leadership. Although the president is the nominal head of the party, fellow partisans in other branches have not chosen the president as the leader and have limited influence over the president's policy positions. The reverse is also true: The president has little control over who wears the party's label in Congress and the policies the legislators support. House members and senators have to satisfy local constituencies, not the president, to get elected and reelected. The result is that while the president may be the most visible and influential player in defining the party's position on an issue, he or she will have competition from fellow party members who are officeholders in other branches and the states.

Finally, reforms of the 1880s and early 1900s, especially the decline of patronage and the rise of direct primaries, eroded party discipline and the role of party leaders. Rank-and-file voters, not party leaders, choose the party's standard-bearers in direct primaries. This reform bred independence within parties, and elected officials feel free to take positions contrary to the wishes of party leaders if it serves their reelection needs. Civil service reforms robbed the party of the patronage jobs and contracts distributed to party supporters in return for their electoral help. Thus, party leaders have neither the carrot (jobs for supporters) nor stick (control of nominations) to secure party loyalty. As the head of the party, the president has not been immune from the weakened position the reforms assigned to party leaders. Even with such limitations, however, presidents must attend to party affairs if they are to be successful.

The President and Party Organization

As an organization, the national party is most active during presidential election years. Between elections, the national party's business is managed by a national party chair and a national committee made up of state party leaders. Although the president is recognized as the titular head of this organization, the president is not an officer and has no formal authority.

Each president decides how much to emphasize the role of party leader. As an academic political scientist before he became president, Woodrow Wilson had a clear vision of the president's role as a strong party leader. He believed that political parties should be the vehicle of presidential leadership, and he envisioned presidents developing a direct relationship with citizens by rallying public opinion in support of administration proposals. As acknowledged party leader, the president would use the loyal support of fellow partisans to enact the administration's program. Franklin Roosevelt was also a strong party leader; he strategically stitched together a New Deal coalition of Democrats from the South and ethnic minorities from the North to transform the Democratic Party into a majority. Recent presidents, such as Ronald Reagan, Bill Clinton, and George W. Bush, made serious efforts to expand and build their national party bases.

Presidents can shape party organization even before they are elected to office. The candidate who controls a majority of delegates at the party's national convention usually controls most aspects of the convention, including choosing major officers, formulating the party platform, and selecting a running mate. This power offers an opportunity to put together a unified party base behind a set of clear proposals. It also has dangers. If significant numbers of the president's party disagree with the plans, they may fight the platform or force the convention to showcase candidates who opposed the winner. At the 1992 Republican convention, for example, President George H. W. Bush was forced to give more prominence and deference than he desired to supporters of rival Pat Buchanan. The result was to publicly emphasize differences between factions in the Republican Party, which was not the preferred outcome of a party leader heading into a tough general election campaign.

The presidential candidate also names the national party chair, typically someone instrumental in securing the candidate's nomination. This power allows the president to influence the party organization between electoral cycles. Historically, the party chair was given a cabinet position, typically as postmaster general, a key source of patronage jobs (this ended in 1970 when the Post Office Department became an independent government agency). With the decline of patronage, party chairs are no longer given cabinet positions; the last to have one, Robert Hannegan, resigned his post in 1947.

The President and Electoral Activities

The president occupies a unique place within the electoral process. Many people would prefer the president to be above partisan bickering in the electoral arena, but the president can hardly avoid electoral activities. The presidency is, after all, an elective office, and as the *de facto* leader of a political party, a president also has some incentive to become involved in congressional campaigns.

Presidential Elections   One of the central difficulties the president faces as party leader is the presidential electoral process. Typically, presidential campaigns are candidate centered, focusing on election of the candidate rather than the overall success of the party. The candidate's campaign organization is separate from the party, and its loyalty lies more with the candidate than the party organization.

This separation between candidate and party is increased by the rules governing the selection of presidential candidates. The need to wage primary battles to gain the majority of national convention delegates all but forces presidential candidates to engage in public disagreements with other candidates in the party. Party reforms (discussed in Chapter 10) have limited party leaders' control over nominations, and the party organization usually tries to remain neutral in the nomination battles. Winning a presidential nomination has much less to do with the leadership of the formal party organization than with the amount and type of media exposure a candidate receives, the campaign's finances, and the candidates momentum (Bartels 1993). Since party officials have little influence in the selection of a nominee, they feel less of a bond to the party's presidential candidate.

Congressional Elections   The president can choose to assist the electoral efforts of congressional candidates or to have little to do with them. Presidents sometimes choose a limited role in congressional campaigns out of fear of needlessly antagonizing opposition party members in Congress. Especially during divided government—a president of one party and a congressional majority of the other—the president is dependent on opposition votes to secure the administration's legislative priorities.

The rise of party-line voting in Congress since the 1980s (discussed in Chapter 12) has made it more difficult for the president to attract support from opposition party members (Fleisher and Bond 2000b). Although greater partisanship may amplify the benefits of unified government (that is, Congress controlled by the president's party), the president's ability to affect who ends up in Congress is limited. The large number of elections for the House of Representatives limits significant presidential involvement to a fraction of them. Even popular presidents find it difficult to transfer their popularity to others, especially when they themselves are not on the ballot.

As discussed in Chapter 10, incumbents in Congress usually are in strong positions for reelection. In most congressional races, there is little point in expending effort on a candidate who has a high probability of winning regardless of the president's involvement. Moreover, campaign involvement depends not only on the president's desire and ability to help, but also on the perception of the congressional candidate regarding whether such support would be useful.

Bill Clinton's and George Bush's experiences with midterm elections vividly demonstrate the limited effect presidents have on congressional elections. Clinton campaigned vigorously for congressional Democrats in 1994, and Democrats lost control of both houses of Congress. In 1998 Clinton's involvement was much more limited, yet Democrats scored a number of important victories and sliced into the Republican majority into the House of Representatives. Bush engaged in a vigorous campaign to help elect more Republicans to the House and Senate in the 2002 midterm elections. These activities increased the narrow Republican majorities in Congress, but only in a handful of races.

The President as Public Opinion Leader

Americans have varying attitudes about their government and their elected leaders. They also have different views about specific political and social problems and what should be done about them. The president is a central focus for all these views and attitudes. The chief executive is the symbol and personification of the state and is expected to inspire feelings of loyalty and patriotism, especially in times of crisis. Political opponents closed ranks behind Franklin Roosevelt after the Japanese bombing of Pearl Harbor in December 1941, and behind George W. Bush after the terrorist attacks of September 11, 2001.

As a symbol of the state, the presidency involves some of the ceremony and pomp that are associated with monarchy. Presidential inaugurations are similar to royal coronations, complete with a solemn oath taken in the midst of notables and the multitudes. Other ceremonial aspects of the office include the presidential seal, the music ("Hail to the Chief") that is played at official events, social duties such as entertaining foreign heads of state when they visit Washington, DC, and lighting the giant Christmas tree on the White House lawn. Such activities emphasize the chief executive's embodiment of the nation, its government, and its ideals.

Unlike monarchs in democracies like Great Britain, the president not only reigns but also rules. Part of the president's job is to develop and implement policies that are binding on the entire populace. To achieve policy goals, the president needs to lead public opinion on important issues. At the same time, the president needs to be responsive to public opinion and to respect the limits that public attitudes place on presidential actions. It is a delicate balance.

One of the most important tools available to the president to shape public opinion is the high profile of the office. The public spotlight illuminates almost everything about the president, from stands on issues to reading habits and favorite foods. This public attention provides a bully pulpit, "a unique and imposing podium available only to the President as the one public official . . . elected by the nation as a whole and invested with all the trappings of his great office" (Mervin 1995, 19). Presidents seek to use this bully pulpit well and to establish close ties with a variety of publics in order to convert personal popularity into political effectiveness.

Such has not always been the case. The Founders envisioned a president removed from public passions rather than one who shapes and leads them. Insulation from public opinion was a central motivation in developing the electoral college. At least through the end of the 19th century, most presidents were somewhat detached from the public.

Going Public

Before becoming president, Woodrow Wilson (1891) argued the president could remove the shackles imposed by the separation of powers and gain the leverage to act decisively by constructing broad public support for proposals. Modern scholars support Wilson's thesis even as presidents have come to act on it as a matter of routine. Richard Neustadt (1960) argues that presidential power ultimately rests on the ability to persuade other political actors to do what the president wants. It is much easier to do that when the president has overwhelming public support.

According to Samuel Kernell (1997), contemporary presidents use public support not only as leverage with other political actors, but also to evade them. Kernell dubbed the strategy of taking a case directly to American citizens **"going public."** Presidents who go public make increased use of political rhetoric and create political spectacles in an effort to shape public beliefs. Going public is close to the leadership strategy envisioned by Wilson. Presidents make direct contact with the public to build public pressure to act on administration proposals by means of three approaches: personal trips, managing communications with the media, and speeches.

Personal Trips   One of the earliest methods presidents used to communicate with the American public was a "grand tour." George Washington took a two-month trip through the South in 1791. This trip allowed him to assess the disposition of the people, and it reassured him that the new Federalist government was popular in the South. Modern presidents have continued the tradition. If nothing else, breaking from the confines of Washington, DC, to enjoy the adulation of crowds is reassuring to the president.

Modern presidents often find it helpful to extend their travels abroad. Economic summits, consultations with foreign heads of state, and visits to historical sites and memorials provide a chance to appear presidential and to capture the attention of a variety of publics. Contemporary presidents travel more than their predecessors. Harry Truman, for example, made only seven foreign appearances; Bill Clinton made sixty-two in his first two years in office (Ragsdale 1996, 170). (See the Living the Promise feature "Filling in for the President.")

Although presidential trips offer opportunities to connect with various publics, they also have risks. Ironically, it was Woodrow Wilson who suffered one of the biggest failures of using personal trips to go public. When his case in favor of the Versailles peace treaty and the League of Nations met resistance in the Senate, he opted for the grand tour strategy to drum up support among the American people. Although he received some support in the West, he ran into a wall of indifference in the Midwest. His tour ended when he fell ill, and his efforts failed to move recalcitrant senators.

There are costs even in a successful presidential trip. Grand tours divert time and attention from other aspects of a demanding job. In recent years, vice presidents and first ladies have increasingly been pressed into service and have journeyed at home and abroad as presidential surrogates. Leading cabinet members are also frequently dispatched to explain administration policies to interest publics and to gauge reaction.

The Press   The press is the most important link between a president and the public. As discussed in Chapter 8, the press was originally very partisan. The *Gazette of the United States* was the Federalists' party organ, while the *National Gazette* spoke for the Republicans. During Andrew Jackson's presidency, federal officeholders were expected to subscribe to the party paper. The paper itself was given government contracts to print official notices. Today the press is independent of political parties but still provides much of the raw material for public opinion.

Presidents recognize the importance of the press. Theodore Roosevelt initiated the practice of granting personal interviews and provided working quarters for reporters in the White House. Woodrow Wilson established the practice of inviting all Washington correspondents to regular press conferences. Contemporary presidents have sophisticated press operations staffed with experts whose primary duty is to interact with and pass information along to the news media.

Over the years, press conferences have evolved into important tools to influence public opinion and gauge the public mind. Presidents have used press conferences in different ways. Some, like Warren Harding, Calvin Coolidge, and Herbert Hoover, required questions to be submitted in advance, a practice prompted by Harding's difficulty in responding to a question about a treaty. Most presidents take spontaneous questions. The frequency of press conferences, though, varies from administration to administration. George H. W. Bush and Bill Clinton made themselves much more available to the press than Ronald Reagan and George W. Bush.

LIVING THE PROMISE
Filling in for the President

Cabinet officials are often expected to appear before the American public to help develop support for the president's policies. Sometimes the trips interfere with their work. Sometimes they just don't want to go. Robert Reich, who served as Bill Clinton's secretary of labor from 1993 to 1997, related the following incident about a proposed trip to Cleveland.

AIDE: The White House wants you to go to Cleveland.

REICH: Why?

AIDE: Because we're hitting the first hundred days of the Clinton administration and the President along with his entire cabinet are fanning out across America to celebrate, because

Ohio is important, because there are a lot of blue-collar voters out there, and because you haven't been to Ohio yet. . . .

REICH: Who wants me to go . . . ?

AIDE: The White House. They called this morning.

REICH: Houses don't make phone calls. Who called?

AIDE: I don't know. Somebody from Cabinet Affairs. Steve somebody.

REICH: How old is Steve? . . . I bet he's under thirty.

AIDE: He is probably under thirty. A large portion of the American population is under thirty. So what?

REICH: Don't you see? Here I am, a member of the president's cabinet,

confirmed by the Senate, the head of an entire government department with eighteen thousand employees, responsible for implementing a huge number of laws and rules, charged with helping people get better jobs, and who is telling me what to do? . . . Some twerp in the White House who has no clue what I'm doing in this job. Screw him. I won't go. . . .

AIDE: You'll go to Cleveland. The President is going to New Orleans, other cabinet members are going to other major cities. You're in Cleveland.

REICH: I'll go this time. . . . But I'll be damned if I'm going to let them run my life.

Source: Reich, Robert. 1997. *Locked in the Cabinet.* New York: Knopf, 108–109. Reprinted from Edwards, George C., III, and Stephen J. Wayne. 2003. *Presidential Leadership: Politics and Policy Making.* 6th ed. Belmont, CA: Thomson/Wadsworth, 199.

Some of this variation is almost certainly due to the extent that presidents feel at ease with formal press conferences. President Lyndon Johnson preferred to deal with small groups of reporters and experimented with informal, hastily called conferences in a variety of settings. Bill Clinton, on the other hand, was articulate and well versed in the complex details of policy, and he performed well in front of a crowd of rowdy reporters.

Presidents do not limit themselves to press conferences and interviews with the Washington press corps. John Kennedy invited newspaper editors and owners from around the nation to White House conferences where he discussed major public issues. Richard Nixon, who had a strained relationship with the White House press corps, experimented with a number of approaches, ranging from briefings before selected members of news organizations to furnishing editorial writers with transcripts of his speeches and comments. Bill Clinton was an acknowledged master of unscripted media appearances such as talk shows and televised "town meetings."

Much of the interaction between the White House and the press does not directly involve the president. Like other aspects of the modern presidency, the relationship between the media and the president has become highly formalized. Because presidents are

© Bettmann/Corbis

Over the years, press conferences have evolved into important tools to influence public opinion and gauge the public mind. Presidents have used press conferences in different ways. President Lyndon Johnson preferred to deal with small groups of reporters and experimented with informal, hastily called conferences in a variety of settings, such as this press conference at the White House in March 1965.

concerned about the information the media presents, the White House Press Office filters much of the contact between the president and the press. The president's press secretary directs the press to the stories the administration wants covered and presents information that shows the administration in the most favorable light possible. The daily White House press briefing is a key platform to achieve these goals, and so are informal off-the-record communications by administration members. Some scholars claim that the result is "negotiating the news" (Cook 1998).

Presidential Speeches   When presidents communicate directly with the public, they often do so by means of presidential addresses. Although presidents have always used speeches to educate and persuade the public about issues of importance, the advent of radio and television turned modern presidents into more visible public figures than their 19th-century predecessors. Contemporary presidents still address small audiences on particular issues or topics, but they can use television and radio to communicate with the entire nation.

There are two general types of presidential speeches. A presidential speech on a topic of national importance delivered directly to a national audience over radio or television during the prime evening listening hours is considered a major address. The president's inaugural address and the annual State of the Union address are major addresses that every president makes. In addition, presidents use major addresses to announce decisions to go to war, to inform the nation of a major international or economic crisis, and to outline their vision of the nation's future (Ragsdale 1996, 146–147).

A minor address is a speech on a substantive policy or political issue delivered to a specific audience, either in person or by use of a broadcast medium. A common example is a commencement address in which the president outlines a new policy proposal. Presidents also make speeches announcing policies at meetings of various business, labor, veterans', police, senior citizen, and professional groups (Ragsdale 1996, 150).

Minor addresses are more common than major addresses. Presidents average about five major addresses and twelve minor addresses a year. Though major speeches are less frequent, they can help influence key elites. For example, national public addresses such as the State of the Union speech can positively shape editorials about the president. As "professional persuaders," newspaper editorialists can be important supporters of a president's proposals (Schaefer 1997).

The Limited Benefits of Going Public   Kernell (1997) provides clear evidence that modern presidents go public more often than their predecessors. The evidence that going public succeeds in raising the president's standing with the public, however, is limited to a small number of case studies.

Presidential scholar George Edwards (2003) conducted a systematic study of the effect of televised speeches of the four most recent presidents—Ronald Reagan, George H. W. Bush, Bill Clinton, and G. W. Bush. Edwards compared presidential approval ratings in public opinion polls conducted immediately before and after major televised speeches. He found that the president's speeches seldom moved public opinion. Because of the margin of error in public opinion polls (discussed in Chapter 9), public approval must change about 6 percentage points to be considered a real difference. Figure 13.5 shows the limited effects of going public. As Edwards (2003, 29) observed, "significant changes [more than 6 points] rarely follow televised presidential addresses. Typically, changes in the president's ratings hardly move at all. Most changes are well within the margin of error—and many of them show a *loss* of approval." Most of the significant increases followed a major military action; the largest improvement followed the terrorist attacks on September 11, 2001. These changes are more likely the result of the public rallying around the president during an international crisis rather than a skilled use of the bully pulpit. About one-third of the significant changes are losses in presidential approval following the speech. This evidence indicates that the effects of going public are limited.

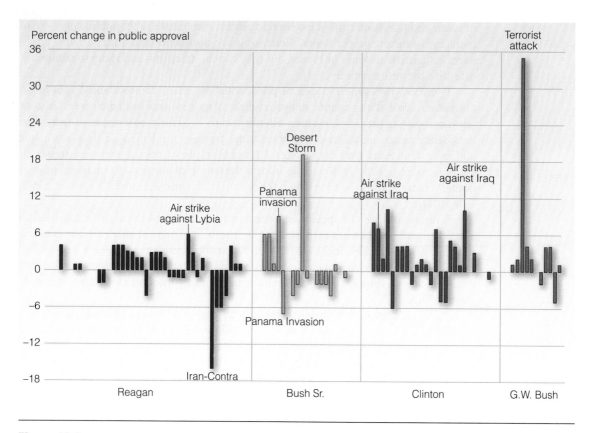

Figure 13.5
The Limited Effects of Going Public: Change in Presidential Approval Ratings after Televised Speeches
Source: Adapted from Edwards, George C., III. 2003. *On Deaf Ears: The Limits of the Bully Pulpit*. New Haven, CT: Yale University Press.

Presidential Approval Ratings

Regardless of the approach used, in order for going public to succeed, presidents certainly try hard to affect the perceptions and attitudes of the American people. Public-opinion polls on presidential job approval have been taken for more than fifty years. The results of these polls are commonly called the "president's popularity," and politicians and political scientists pay close attention to them. Figure 13.6 shows public approval ratings from Dwight Eisenhower to George W. Bush. With few exceptions, presidents tend to enjoy their highest approval ratings during their first year or two in office. This honeymoon period dissipates as people become dissatisfied with specific decisions, and those who withheld their fire in the bipartisan spirit of support for a newly elected president feel freer to openly disagree with the administration. The tendency for public approval to decline creates pressure to make use of political capital quickly in order to advance a political agenda while the president has broad public support (Light 1983).

The annual averages in Figure 13.6 show overall trends in presidential popularity but also rapid swings. The public's evaluation of the president's job performance is

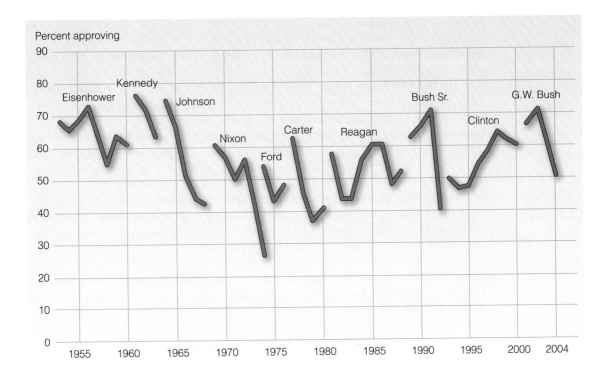

Figure 13.6
Presidential Approval Ratings, 1953–2004
Source: Adapted by Jon Bond and Kevin Smith from various reports of the Gallup poll.

driven by a number of considerations, but the effects of the president's activities are limited compared to the influence of other events over which the president has less control.

The economy, international crises, and scandal are three of the most important determinants of a president's approval rating. The annual averages in Figure 13.6 hide short-term changes, some of which are huge. For example, in February 1991, George H. W. Bush's approval ratings soared to 89 percent following victory during the first Gulf War. Ten years later, his son, President George W. Bush, had similarly astronomically high numbers following the terrorist attacks of September 11, 2001. In both cases, the levels of popularity reflected a "rally 'round the flag" effect often present when the nation faces an external threat or crisis. Approval ratings for both Bush presidents declined with mounting concerns about the economy, and, for George W. Bush, increasing unease with the war in Iraq.

Scandals can also cause presidential job approval ratings to plummet rapidly. As the details of political sabotage and the White House obstruction of justice known as the Watergate Scandal dribbled out, the 67 percent approval rating of President Nixon following the announcement of a Vietnam peace settlement eroded, bottoming out at 24 percent just before he resigned from office in August 1974. President Reagan's approval rating dropped from 63 percent to 47 percent in a three-month span in 1986 when it became clear that some members of his administration were involved in an illegal scheme to sell arms to Iran and use the profits to fund a Nicaraguan guerrilla movement (Newport 1998).

The scandal surrounding President Bill Clinton's affair with a White House intern is a notable exception to the general rule about scandal dragging down approval ratings. Clinton's approval ratings actually went up as the scandal developed, ultimately reaching 73 percent in December 1998 as the House of Representatives was voting to impeach him for lying to cover up the affair. The public seemed to make a distinction between Clinton's personal failings (of which they resoundingly disapproved) and the job he was doing as president (which they endorsed).

Going public may occasionally aid in getting specific policies passed, although it provides no guarantees. For example, when Bill Clinton took office in 1993, he sought to deliver on his campaign promise to reform healthcare. The president, vice president, first lady, and other administration officials took trips and made numerous speeches to drum up support for the plan. But despite an early positive response, public support eroded when details of the complex proposal came to light. Opponents were also emboldened by Clinton's relatively low approval ratings early in his term, which averaged only 52 percent his first year in office (Ragsdale 1996, 193). The opposition went public itself, and despite Clinton's communication skills, his plan did not win congressional approval.

This example is a telling reminder that although presidents are the most prominent actors in the American political system, they are not the only ones trying to influence public opinion. The competition can be tough. Although all presidents use the bully pulpit, and some are effective communicators, their ability to influence public opinion varies from time to time and from issue to issue.

The President and Congress

Although Congress has the primary responsibility for making laws, the president plays an important role in influencing legislation. According to the Constitution, the president is responsible for sending messages and recommendations to Congress and has the power of veto. Other practices have evolved over time that further increased presidential involvement in the making of laws. Initially started by presidents who wanted to exercise strong legislative leadership, these practices are now considered part of the political duties of office. The practicalities of politics mean that the president has little choice but to actively try to influence decisions made in the legislative branch. This section examines how the combination of formal legal power and evolved practices combine to determine presidential influence in Congress.

Messages and Recommendations

Article II, Section 3 of the Constitution mandates that the president "shall from time to time give to the Congress information on the state of the union, and recommend to their consideration such measures as he shall judge necessary and expedient." Since George Washington's administration, chief executives have followed the practice of annually presenting a message to Congress at the beginning of each regular session.

© Bettmann/Corbis

Although the assembled senators and members of the House are the immediate target of the State of the Union speech, the president has other audiences in mind. In a sense, the message is addressed to all Americans, who can watch the proceedings on television, and the message is broadcast worldwide as a matter of interest to U.S. allies and adversaries alike. In the speech, the president identifies the problems that the administration views as most pressing and suggests policies to address them. Here John F. Kennedy gives his first State of the Union speech in January 1961; in it he stated his plans to fix the receding economy and to thwart Soviet and Chinese attempts to take the upper hand in the Cold War.

Washington and John Adams gave their messages in person. Thomas Jefferson, a notoriously poor public speaker, sent his message in writing. Subsequent presidents followed Jefferson's practice until Woodrow Wilson surprised Congress and the nation by delivering a message in person shortly after he was inaugurated in 1913. Since then, all presidents, regardless of their oratorical skills, have appeared before Congress to deliver the annual State of the Union message.

Although the assembled senators and members of the House are the immediate target of the State of the Union speech, the president has other audiences in mind. In a sense, the message is addressed to all Americans, who can watch the proceedings on television, and the message is broadcast worldwide as a matter of interest to U.S. allies and adversaries alike. In the speech, the president identifies the problems that the administration views as most pressing and suggests policies to address them. Modern presidents do not limit their recommendations to the State of the Union message. Woodrow Wilson initiated the practice of following the State of the Union address with written recommendations about specific policy topics.

Contemporary presidents go beyond making recommendations to actually developing specific bills. Even though Congress may (and usually does) make changes in administration proposals, the submission of a bill by the president is designed to get Congress to focus on what the White House thinks should be done about a problem. By the middle of the 20th century, presidents had become so adept at setting the legislative agenda that some scholars openly questioned whether Congress was too unwieldy to be capable of setting its own legislative priorities and needed an outside force such as the president to do it for them (Neustadt 1960). Later in the century, it became clear that Congress is able to independently set its own priorities. For example, the Democratic majority crafted a domestic legislative program without the assistance of President George H. W. Bush, and the Republican majority that won control of Congress after the 1994 elections set and pursued its own agenda without the assistance of President Bill Clinton. Political scientists George Edwards and Andrew Barrett (2000) found that presidents almost always get their legislative items on the congressional agenda—it is rare when a major presidential proposal does not at least get a hearing. Still, presidential proposals constitute only about a third of the Congress' agenda; Congress initiates the other two-thirds.

Nonetheless, the public, the media, and even Congress expect the president to formulate, propose, and actively advance a legislative agenda to address the nation's problems. In fact, Congress has passed laws requiring the president to present proposals to the legislature. For example, the Budget and Accounting Act of 1921 made the executive responsible for formulating and proposing a budget for the federal government.

The Veto

Of the formal powers granted the president by the Constitution, the veto is probably the most important tool for influencing legislation. The president has three options when presented with a bill passed by Congress:

1. Sign the bill into law.
2. Veto the bill by formally withholding a signature, and returning the bill and an explanatory message to Congress; the measure is nullified unless both chambers pass the bill by a two-thirds vote.
3. Take no action, in which case the bill becomes law in ten days without the president's signature unless Congress has adjourned; if that is the case, the bill dies after ten days if the president does not sign it, and the president is said to have used the **pocket veto** to nullify the bill.

The Founders originally conceived of the veto as a defensive weapon the president could use to protect the executive from encroachment by a powerful legislature. Scholars such as Neustadt (1960) suggest that the use of the veto is a sign of weakness or failure in the executive because it shows the president has failed to persuade Congress to adopt administration proposals. But the veto has evolved into a powerful tool to shape public policy. Because of the constitutionally mandated requirement of a super-majority to override, a veto represents a formidable obstacle to legislation. It gives even unpopular presidents without majority party support in Congress an effective way to influence the legislative process. Even as the Watergate Scandal politically crippled Richard Nixon in 1973, Congress managed to override only one of his nine presidential vetoes. Veto overrides are rare—across all presidents, about 90 percent of vetoes are upheld.

The mere threat of a veto is a valuable tool to shape legislation. By making clear what features of a particular bill the administration finds objectionable and what must be done to make them acceptable, the president can shape the content of laws sent to the White House. The tactic does not always work, especially if Congress is controlled by the opposition party. The Democratic majority in 1992, for example, sent President George H. W. Bush several bills he had threatened to veto. In effect, they dared him to follow through on his threats, and when he did, Democrats used his opposition to the bills as fodder for political campaigns. Much of the time, though, the threat of a veto provides a lot of leverage in Congress. President Bill Clinton, for example, got budget bill concessions from the Republican majority in 1998 by threatening to veto the appropriations required to keep the government solvent and operating. Having suffered a political disaster when they forced a government shutdown three years earlier, the Republicans were willing to compromise with the president.

Presidential Success in Congress

In terms of the relationship between the executive and legislative branches, presidents succeed when Congress acts in accordance with their recommendations and fail when Congress takes a course of action opposed by the administration. One frequently used measure of presidential success is how often the president's position wins on the House or Senate floor.

Like other measures of presidential success, this one is imperfect. It measures success only on matters that come to a floor vote, and some issues never make it that far. President Clinton's healthcare reform proposals, for example, never made it to a floor vote. But most significant issues do show up in House or Senate roll-call votes, and these allow a reasonable basis on which to judge success or failure. Figure 13.7 shows the percentage of times the president got his way from 1953 to 2003.

This figure shows two important patterns. First, no president has enjoyed complete success or complete failure, with all winning some and losing some. This pattern is in stark contrast to parliamentary democracies where losing an important vote in the legislature is a major embarrassment for the prime minister and may even lead to his or her resignation. Second, success varies not just between presidential administrations but also within them. Some presidents are more successful than others, and all presidents are more successful at certain times than at other times.

The Founders deliberately created a rivalry between the executive and the legislature by assigning important constitutional powers to each. By granting institutional rivals independent bases of political power, the Constitution also ensured that each would be capable of protecting and advancing its interests. The information conveyed in Figure 13.7 essentially confirms that these expectations have been met. Members of the first Congress resisted Alexander Hamilton's attempts to advance his economic program, and senators and House members have resisted executive efforts to dominate legislative affairs ever since. But it is not only institutional differences that explain the variation in success rates. Other conditions that help determine presidential success with Congress are electoral constituencies and cycles, party and ideology, presidential popularity, and the president's bargaining skill.

Electoral Constituencies and Cycles   The president and Congress have very different constituencies. Elected by a nationwide constituency, the president tends to see issues

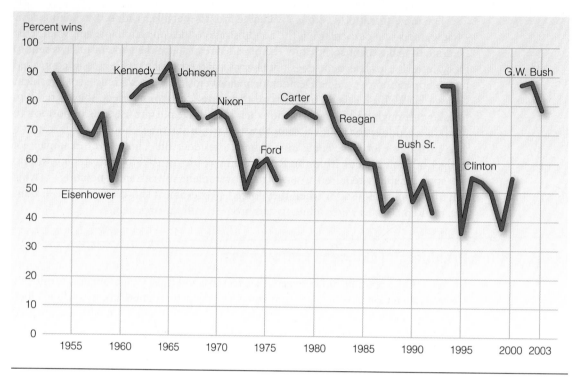

Figure 13.7
Presidential Success on Roll-Call Votes in Congress, 1953–2003
Source: *Congressional Quarterly Almanac,* various years.

from a national perspective. The president's diplomatic and commander-in-chief duties make an international perspective necessary. Members of Congress tend to have a more parochial view. They are necessarily concerned with how their particular states or districts are affected. Different constituencies and electoral needs lead to different views of what is in the public interest. The inevitable result is conflict between the executive and legislative branches. The president wins some; Congress wins others.

The executive and legislative branches also operate under separate electoral cycles. The timing of elections has a critical effect on relations between the president and Congress. In a presidential election year, the nation chooses the president, all 435 members of the House, and one-third of the Senate. If the president wins by a large margin, sympathetic House and Senate members may ride presidential coattails into office. Two-thirds of the senators, however, are holdovers from previous elections whose electoral victories probably owe nothing to the president. And two years into the president's term, there is another election in which all 435 House seats and another third of Senate seats are up for election. Not being on the ballot, the president has less influence on these congressional races than on the races that took place two years earlier. The result is that most legislators are insulated from presidential influence.

Party and Ideology Political scientists have long noted that political parties are an important explanation of how members of Congress vote. Although party-line voting in

Congress generally declined through much of the 20th century, there is unambiguous evidence that party consistently exerts a crucial influence on presidential-congressional relations. Simply speaking, members of the president's party are more likely to support administration positions than are members of the opposition party. As a result, conflict between the president and Congress is more pronounced when the two branches are controlled by different political parties, a situation that has been common since World War II.

Measures of presidential success based on roll-call votes certainly indicate that majority party presidents have higher success rates than minority party presidents. Majority presidents win an average of 82 percent of roll calls, compared to 60 percent for minority presidents. The resurgence of party-line voting since the 1980s has made party an even stronger determinant of presidential success in Congress. When Bill Clinton was dealing with a Democratic Congress, he won 86 percent of roll-call votes. After the Republicans gained control of Congress, his success rate fell to an average of 49 percent for the remainder of his term.

Party and ideology are not the same thing. Both parties tend to have factions that share ideological ground with the rival party. These members tend to be cross-pressured: Their party pulls them in one direction and their ideological beliefs in another. Within the president's party, cross-pressured members tend to be less supportive of administration proposals, but cross-pressured members of the opposition party can be an important source of support. Minority presidents can win some votes in Congress by forging ideological coalitions with members of the opposition party. President Ronald Reagan never enjoyed a Republican-controlled House of Representatives, and thus his legislative agenda was always dependent on opposition party votes. Reagan managed to achieve several key victories by securing support from conservative Democrats.

Even members of the president's own party who face no inconsistencies between party and ideology engage in political struggles with the administration on occasion. Members of Congress are individual representatives of distinct constituencies, and they have their own points of view about the desirability of particular policies. If these come into conflict with the president's preferences, the White House cannot assume party loyalty will win out. Members of the president's party may find it politically advantageous to distance themselves from the president, thus showing constituents that they are sticking up for their interests.

Presidential Popularity   Members of Congress are elected representatives and are supposed to be responsive to popular preferences. Consequently, they may be more likely to support administration proposals when the president has high public support. The belief that presidential popularity affects support in Congress is widely accepted by Washington insiders, and there is little doubt that popularity gives the president leverage on some occasions. Public approval helps set the public agenda and determine what issues Congress will consider. However, public approval does not guarantee support.

Academic research has produced mixed results about the ability of presidential popularity to translate directly into desired legislative outcomes. Jon Bond and Richard Fleisher (1990), for example, found that popular presidents were no more likely to win in the legislative arena than were their less popular counterparts. President George H. W. Bush's record in 1991 is a good example of the limits of presidential popularity. Despite Bush's astronomic approval ratings, Congress did not rally around his policy agenda. He won only 43 percent of the House roll-call votes on which he expressed a position.

The expectation that members of Congress will respond to the president's popular support is primarily based on electoral considerations. The theory is that a legislator who opposes a popular president or supports an unpopular one becomes a target for electoral retribution by the voters who support or oppose the president in question. However, the electoral connection between the president and members of Congress has lessened somewhat with the weakening of presidents' electoral coattails in recent decades (Jacobson 1990, 80–81). Moreover, while some voters probably do use presidential popularity as a voting guide, few have sufficient knowledge to make the connection between their evaluation of the president and the voting behavior of their representative.

Presidential popularity is fluid, so using it as a guide in forecasting roll-call votes in Congress is risky. The president's popularity on election day may be very different than it was on the day of a roll-call vote on a particular issue. Since election day popularity cannot be predicted with great accuracy, its utility to guide an elected representative's roll-call vote is limited. For these reasons, presidential popularity has only a marginal influence on legislators' decisions to support or oppose the president on roll-call votes (Bond and Fleisher 1990; Edwards 1989).

Presidential Bargaining Skill The president also has a certain amount of patronage to bring the table in give-and-take with recalcitrant legislators. Although executive positions have increasingly come under civil service regulations that require competitive examinations as the basis for hiring, the president still influences government contracts, grants, defense installations, and the like. Presidents have made sure that military bases have been retained in congressional districts and that legislators were given advance notice of government contracts and grants important to their districts so they could be publicly announced by congressional offices.

Presidents have also engaged in systematic lobbying efforts on behalf of legislative programs, in effect setting up effective special interest operations in the White House. Begun in earnest during the Eisenhower era, systematic lobbying varies somewhat from administration to administration. Such efforts usually include legislative liaisons from various executive departments, a central liaison unit in the White House Office, and the vice president. Some of these individuals concentrate on the House, others on the Senate, and they specialize in particular topics and issues. The executive branch lobbyists use the same general techniques as do lobbyists for interest groups, including direct contacts with representatives and indirect contact through congressional staff members, campaign contributors, defense contractors, newspaper editors, state and local party leaders, and others important to a legislator's constituency. They also join forces with private interest groups to work on legislation of mutual interest.

Political pundits, politicians, and some students of the presidency routinely assume that such efforts play a large role in determining presidential success in Congress. It is believed that strong legislative leadership is achieved by the skilful use of the tools at the president's disposal to persuade members of Congress to enact administration proposals. But most of the evidence to support this belief is based on studies of specific bills. More systematic analyses of presidential support from members of Congress, such as those relying on roll-call votes on many bills, give less support for this hypothesis (Bond and Fleisher 1990; Edwards 1989). Variation in presidential success rests more on party and ideology than on popularity, bargaining skill, and informal powers of persuasion. Success is also due to the political context of the time, which the president has limited ability to shape.

Performance Assessment

It is shortsighted to characterize the American presidency as heroic or villainous, imperial or imperiled. Such characterizations are based on perceptions of the presidency at a particular point in time and have no permanency; they mistake a snapshot for a portrait. The presidency changes over time, and its character depends on the individual who occupies the office, the political context in which the president operates, the scope and magnitude of the problems he or she faces, and the action or inaction of other political actors.

At one time, presidents benefited from the generally positive attitude most Americans had about the nation, its constitutional system, and its chief political officer. In the past forty years, policy failures and scandals have contributed to making people increasingly skeptical and cynical about the government and the presidency. Unlike their predecessors, modern presidents cannot readily draw on the innate trust and confidence of the American people to sustain and support them. Nevertheless, the United States is dependent on vigorous presidential leadership to cope with complex and often intractable problems. Americans may not vest the same faith and trust in the presidency they once did, but they expect the president to do more and more.

President Bill Clinton may embody this curious combination of high expectations and low regard more than any other modern president. His second term was tarnished by his personal conduct, which ultimately caused the House of Representatives to impeach him. But throughout the ordeal, Clinton received high job-approval ratings from the public and was credited with the nation's economic prosperity. The public seemed to perceive Clinton as someone they would not trust but also as an eminently capable chief executive.

The relationship of the presidency and the mass media has also changed. Presidents who are able to communicate effectively via television—Ronald Reagan and Bill Clinton are prime examples—enjoy significant political advantages over their opponents. The camera is the primary vehicle for going public, and those comfortable in this forum can reap political profit. But recent presidents may find it more difficult to deal with the media than earlier presidents did. For example, even media-savvy chief executives like Franklin Roosevelt and John Kennedy would have problems with today's more aggressive and assertive press corps, who operate by the tenets of investigative and adversarial journalism.

The president's ability to achieve administration objectives depends on other political actors, and the president has limited formal means to get those actors to do what he or she wants them to do. Persuasion, bargaining, electoral timing, who the other actors are, and the political environment all play roles in determining presidential success. As the political environment changes, so do the probabilities that persuasion and tactics will achieve success.

In order to fulfill the high expectations placed on the office, presidents must be able to adapt throughout their terms of office. Because presidents are forced to build coalitions of different groups with divergent interests, and because presidents are reliant on broad public support to maintain their agendas, action from the executive office is likely to at least make an attempt to satisfy the will of the people. In this sense, the presidency seems to be playing a positive role in delivering on the promise of democracy.

Summary

- The president occupies a central position in the political system. The president has a national constituency and the biggest bully pulpit in politics, is the most visible and important party leader, and often drives the legislative agenda of Congress.

- The president is the focus of high expectations, charged with effectively tackling a broad variety of roles and problems. Some presidents seem to be better at fulfilling these expectations than others.

- The office of president is made up of the president, an individual person, and the presidency, which is a complex institution. The mix of these two components form presidential image and shape presidents' ability to meet expectations.

- Designing the chief executive's position was one of the most difficult problems of the Constitutional Convention. Delegates eventually settled on a mix of the weak- and strong-executive models, opting for a strong office that also had clear limits on its power.

- Over the nation's history, the office of president has evolved considerably, not because of formal legal alterations but because of informal custom and precedent. Generally, presidential power has expanded because of broad interpretation of the Constitution, increased public expectations, and delegation of power and resources to the executive branch by Congress.

- Some scholars suggest that presidential success is at least partially dependent on individual personality and character. An individual's background and life experiences help determine self-confidence, psychological needs, values, worldview, political philosophy, and personal vision of presidential conduct. This psychological perspective, however, has proved to be of limited use in explaining or predicting how presidents handle the job.

- The major components of the presidency include the president, the cabinet, and the Executive Office of the President.

- Article II, Sections 1 and 2 of the Constitution define the president's primary constitutional responsibilities: chief executive, commander-in-chief of the military, and chief diplomat.

- In addition to the responsibilities of office, the president is also the party's most visible and prominent leader. Although the Founders did not anticipate this role, the strongest presidents have also been strong party leaders, and a president's ability to build and direct a strong party base is often important to the success of an administration's political agenda.

- The president has a critical role as a public opinion leader. The presidency involves some of the ceremonial trappings of monarchy, and it is the embodiment of the nation, its government, and its ideals. The high profile of the presidential office and the constant public spotlight that goes with it provide the president with a unique and powerful opportunity to connect with the public.

- Recent presidents have increasingly adopted a strategy of going public—using speeches to take a case directly to American citizens in an effort to shape public beliefs and influence Congress. The benefits of going public, however, are limited; rarely does a presidential speech produce a significant change in the president's ratings.

- Public opinion polls on presidential job approval have been taken for more than fifty years and are commonly referred to as the president's popularity. The economy, international crises, and scandal are three of the most important determinants of a president's approval rating.

- Although Congress has the primary responsibility for making laws, the president plays an important role in influencing legislation. Contemporary presidents are expected to formulate and actively pursue a legislative agenda to address the nation's problems. Presidents can pursue this agenda through communication with Congress and through such formal powers as the veto. The threat of a veto may be sufficient to influence policymaking in Congress.

- All presidents have mixed success in getting their preferences approved by Congress. Differences in constituency, electoral cycles, partisanship, and ideology often give the president and Congress different legislative goals. Presidential popularity and skilled bargaining may boost the chances of getting Congress to go along with an administration's preferences, at least under some circumstances, but the president's ability to succeed in Congress is influenced more strongly by whether Congress is controlled by the president's party.

Key Terms

active-negative president 408
active-positive president 408
Council of Economic Advisers 411
executive agreements 420
Executive Office of the President (EOP) 411
going public 425
hierarchical model 414
National Security Council 411
Office of Management and Budget (OMB) 411
passive-negative president 408

passive-positive president 408
pocket veto 434
positive government 406
prerogative view of presidential power 406
restrictive view of presidential power 406
spokes-of-the-wheel model 414
stewardship doctrine 406
strong-executive model 402
weak-executive model 402
White House Office 411

Selected Readings

Bond, Jon R., and Richard Fleisher. 1990. *The President in the Legislative Arena.* Chicago: University of Chicago Press. A prominent study of the relationship between the president and Congress.

Edwards, George C., III. 2003. *On Deaf Ears: The Limits of the Bully Pulpit.* New Haven, CT: Yale University Press. A comprehensive and accessible study showing the limited effects of presidential speeches.

Neustadt, Richard. 1960. *Presidential Power.* New York: Wiley. The classic study of presidential power and the importance of informal tools of persuasion to presidential success.

Shenkman, Richard. 1999. *Presidential Ambition: How the American Presidents Gained Power, Kept Power, and Got Things Done.* New York: HarperCollins. A good, accessible overview of how and why presidents succeed or fail in pursuing their political agendas.

14 | The Bureaucracy

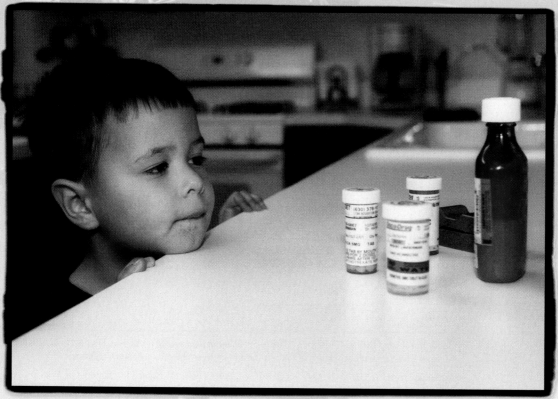

Bureaucracy is like broccoli: It is not pretty to look at, can be tough to chew, hard to swallow, and sometimes leaves a bad taste in your mouth. But it is good for you.

Consider the Consumer Product Safety Commission (CPSC), one of those very eat-your-veggies sorts of public agencies that people love to complain about. Ever get frustrated trying to pry a childproof cap off a bottle of ibuprofen? You have the CPSC to thank. In addition to insisting on child-resistant medicine bottles, the commission also sets the minimum allowable space between the slats on baby cribs down to the quarter-inch and engineered the recall of Hamilton Beach cappuccino makers because it was worried about blocked frothing nozzles. The CPSC even tried to require that all 5-gallon buckets have holes in their bottoms.

The CPSC requires childproof caps on medicine bottles, sets standards for crib construction, and did indeed frown upon the Hamilton Beach company's frothing nozzles. Fussy? Sure. Yet as a result of its regulations the agency dramatically cut down on crib deaths as well as significantly reduced fatalities and hospitalization rates attributed to accidental ingestion of medications. The CPSC's hard line on frothing nozzles also saved some cappuccino lovers from getting sprayed with scalding steam.

However, the hole-in-the bucket regulation never was enacted. The CPSC did look into regulating buckets, because roughly fifty infants and toddlers drown every year after falling into them. Yet antiregulation crusader Congressman David McIntosh (R-IN), somehow conflated this concern with the impression that the CPSC required buckets to have holes in them. This left the CPSC scratching its head. "The idea is as absurd as it sounds," responded the CPSC to McIntosh's argument, which were made on the House floor (Cushman 1995).

Yet McIntosh's claims were taken perfectly seriously by many who should have known better. Bureaucracy is a fussy, red-tape loving, nosy nanny that likes nothing better than to regulate the common sense out of daily life, right? Perhaps. But even if this is so, does that detract from its life-saving and injury-preventing regulations? The irony is that most people are perfectly willing to believe the worst about bureaucracy while rarely giving it credit for the good it undoubtedly does.

Depictions of government bureaucracy in mass media and popular culture "are typically scathing in nature" (Goodsell 1994, 8). Bureaucracy is blamed for everything from hampering the war on terrorism to bungling mail delivery. Reviled by politician and citizen alike, bureaucracy is held to be synonymous with inefficiency, waste, incompetence, and malfeasance. Requiring holes in buckets? Laughable, yes, but we are perfectly willing to assume bureaucracy would do something so silly.

Some of this criticism is justified. No doubt there is inefficiency, waste, and incompetence to be found in the bureaucracy. But it is also true that democracy has a hard time functioning without bureaucracy. In a very real sense, the performance of bureaucracy *is* the performance of democracy.

Bureaucracy can be defined as public agencies that translate the intent of democratic institutions into action. These agencies, programs, and services are largely, though not exclusively, housed in the executive branches of government, and they do everything from fight wars (the Department of Defense) to repair potholes (municipal or county highway departments).

What this means is that bureaucracy is largely responsible, good or bad, for the performance of pretty much the entire political system. The products of executives, legislatures, and courts—executive orders, laws, rulings—represent what the government intends to do, not what it actually does. The job of the bureaucracy is to translate that intent into action. Its ability to do this job determines in no small part the gap between the promise and performance of democracy. There is no doubt that whether democratic governments live up to their promises rests squarely on the performance of the bureaucracy.

Understanding the job of bureaucracy is important because democratic governments in the United States promise a great deal: Law and order, equal opportunity education, clean air, libraries, a safe food supply—the list is long and growing. All these promises become the responsibilities of the public bureaucracy. Given its job, bureaucracy is the part of government that is most involved in the daily lives of citizens. Political scientist Ken Meier (1993, 2) once described a day in the life of a typical American, starting with a breakfast of bacon and eggs (certified fit for consumption by the U.S. Department of Agriculture), driving to work (the roads, the car, and the fuel all regulated or maintained by public agencies), walking up a flight of stairs to the office (the stairs inspected by the Occupational Safety and Health Administration), to

going to sleep at the end of the day (on a mattress with a tag that may not be removed under penalty of law).

The bureaucracy is so involved in our daily lives that most people seem to notice only its absence. For example, the overwhelming majority of letters and packages mailed by the United States Postal Service are delivered on time with no problems. Yet it is the small exception—the letter that goes astray—that gets people's attention. Maybe bureaucracy gets its poor reputation from its competence rather than its incompetence. This is not the typical perspective on bureaucracy, but, as we shall see, it is one that provides a more realistic understanding of the relationship between the promise and the performance of democracy.

 ## The Promise of Bureaucracy

The promise of bureaucracy is to make good on the promises of democratic governments. Whatever government decides to do—be it as mundane as build a road or as momentous as go to war—bureaucracy is the actual "doer." After approving, say, a law to clean up inland waterways, legislators adjourn. They do not fan out to rivers and lakes to take water samples and begin cracking down on polluters. In passing a law, legislatures pass on the responsibility for enforcing that law to a bureaucracy. The CPSC, for example, was created and is obligated by law to ensure that the products bought by American consumers present no unreasonable risks to life or health. That sounds reasonable enough in the abstract. In practice, though, it means regulating that medicine bottles have childproof caps and investigating blocked frothing nozzles— just the sort of actions for which bureaucracy is ridiculed.

First and foremost, then, bureaucracy is the management mechanism for government. Public agencies implement, manage, and monitor programs and policies authorized by law, executive order, and regulation. Public agencies take words on paper and translate them into action by issuing contracts, formulating programs, and engaging in any number of other activities all designed to apply broad laws to specific circumstances.

Yet describing bureaucracy's administrative role in the political system conveys only part of what bureaucracy does. Bureaucracy is not simply an implementer of policy but a policymaker in its own right. In short, bureaucracy not only is the main means to deliver on the promises of democracy; it also helps make those promises. Bureaucracy makes policy in two broad ways. First, bureaucracies and bureaucrats are forced to make informal and formal choices on how to translate into action the broad desires of legislatures, executives, or courts and to apply them in specific instances. In the process of making those choices, bureaucrats can be viewed as making policy.

For example, consider the traffic cop whose job is to enforce speed limits. Those speed limits are set by law (usually by state legislatures). Yet in a practical sense it is really the traffic cop who determines how fast a motorist can go before falling afoul of the law. The legislators, after all, are not on the highway; the police officer is. The ability of lower-level bureaucrats to informally set policy in this fashion is known as the power of the street-level bureaucrat (Lipsky 1980).

The second way in which bureaucracy makes policy is through becoming an active participant in the political process. Federal bureaucracies do not wait passively for Congress and the president to formulate policies in Congress and the White House. They help shape those decisions in a number of ways.

Rulemaking

Laws are often vague and provide bureaucracies with only minimal guidelines about the specific actions they are to take. Vague laws give bureaucrats considerable discretion in deciding what these actions will be. Recognizing that these choices should not be made arbitrarily, Congress formally requires bureaucracies undergo a decision-making process that is very similar to the legislative process. This process is called rulemaking.

A **rule** is a statement by a federal agency that interprets a law and prescribes the specific action an agency will take to implement that law. **Rulemaking** is the process of deciding exactly what the laws passed by Congress mean. This process has been described as "the single most important function performed by agencies of government" (Kerwin 1994, xi). Once an agency approves a rule, the rule applies to everyone

Bureaucracies have the difficult task of creating rules that will implement the (often vague) laws passed by Congress. These rules affect many aspects of our day-to-day lives. For instance, the Child Safety Protection Law was passed by Congress. This law required the Consumer Product Safety Commission to develop mandatory bicycle helmet standards. The CPSC spent four years gathering comments on their proposed standards before finally issuing them. The standards however did not touch on whether or not children must wear helmets—this was left up to individual states to decide and has resulted in a wide variety of regulations state to state.

© Peter Mumford/Alamy Images

within the agency's jurisdiction and has the force of law. For all practical purposes, rules *are* law. Those annoying childproof caps, for example, are required by CPSC rules, and drug manufacturers are legally bound to follow them.

Rulemaking represents the formal process of making choices about what actions the government should undertake, and it amounts to a huge shadow lawmaking process about which most citizens know little to nothing. Although it may be unsettling to acknowledge that unelected bureaucrats play such a central role in shaping the law, in practical terms it is unavoidable. Passing a law is a difficult process and often requires much compromise. Congress often has more important priorities than thrashing out the minutia of exactly how a program or policy is to be implemented. As a result, Congress passes laws that are vague about specifically what they obligate the government to do. For example, the Occupational Safety and Health Act was passed "to assure so far as possible every working man and woman in the nation safe and healthy work conditions." That law expresses a noble goal with which few would disagree. Yet how do we put this noble goal into action? What exactly should the government do to ensure its citizens have a safe working environment? The answers to those questions came not from Congress but from the Occupational Safety and Health Administration (OSHA).

Filling out the messy details needed to implement vague laws helps explain how bureaucracy gets its negative image. Passing a law promoting safety in the workplace attracted considerable support in the abstract. In practice, OSHA was left to deal with a myriad of specifics, such as the minimum allowable thickness of ladder rungs and how much cotton dust a textile worker should be exposed to. Issuing a lengthy list of standards for manufacturing ladders seems more like petty bureaucratic meddling than serving the grand cause of worker safety. Rulemaking is the "dirty work" of politics: detail oriented, laborious, and necessary. Without these specifics, laws are just words on paper, not actions in the real world.

Few federal agencies have the authority to unilaterally issue rules. Rulemaking is governed by the Federal Administrative Procedures Act and other laws passed by Congress. At a minimum, agencies must give public notice of rules, allow interested parties an opportunity to comment on these rules, and publish the finished product in the *Federal Register.* Though unknown to most citizens, most organized interest groups are well aware of the importance of rulemaking and actively participate in the process when their interests are involved. Bureaucracies take public input very seriously, and the rulemaking process is generally acknowledged to be open and to allow for conflicting interests to state their cases. (See the Promise and Policy feature "Rules and Your Bottom Line.")

Adjudication

In making rules, bureaucracies act like legislatures; in judging them, they act like courts. **Adjudication** is a process designed to establish whether a rule has been violated. For example, the National Highway Traffic Safety Administration (NHTSA) usually uses adjudication to judge whether a particular type or model of automobile violates safety regulations and should be removed from the roads. If the NHTSA believes an automobile violates safety rules, it holds a hearing where the manufacturer can present contesting evidence and arguments. If the agency deems a recall to be necessary, the manufacturer has an opportunity to negotiate the scope and wording of the recall.

PROMISE AND POLICY
Rules and Your Bottom Line

Ever hear of the federal need analysis methodology? No? Well, it is a complicated formula designed to estimate a family's discretionary income while accounting for things like asset protection allowances, state and local taxes, and a whole lot of other eye-glazing things that only a bureaucrat could love.

Even if you have never heard of the federal need analysis methodology, there is a decent chance it affects your bottom line. Why? It is used to calculate how much a family can be expected to contribute to college expenses. In short, it determines your eligibility for federally funded forms of financial aid. Virtually all of the $90 billion spent on financial aid every year is tied to this formula.

Periodically the Department of Education (DOE) adjusts this formula. These adjustments are not laws, but rules. They provide an excellent example of how rulemaking gives bureaucracy considerable policy-making powers and plays an important role in the lives of citizens—in this case, college students.

The DOE's authority to make these rules is based in the Higher Education Act (HEA), which instructs the department to periodically alter the formula to account for things such as inflation and differences in state and local taxes. Those adjustments, which can mean hundreds or even thousands of dollars in lost or gained financial aid to an individual student, are made not by elected representatives but by bureaucrats. In delegating this authority to the DOE, Congress in effect gave the agency the power not only to make good on the promises of government but to play a significant role in determining exactly what those promises are.

Consider the slight change the DOE made to the formula's methodology in 2003. The adjustment itself seems a little arcane—it dealt with allowable deductions for state and local taxes—but there was nothing obscure about its outcome. As a result of the change, parents in California earning more than $50,000 a year were expected to contribute an additional $500 to college expenses. Parents in New York with a similar income were expected to contribute an additional $700.

The net result of this change was to cut federal government support for higher education by hundreds of millions of dollars and shift those costs to students and their families. That is a significant policy change that was not debated in Congress and happened with almost no public input or comment. Is that fair? Maybe not, but it is, more or less, the law. At least, it *is* a rule.

Source: Winter, Greg. "Change in Aid Formula Shifts More Costs to Students." *New York Times,* June 13, 2003. Copyright © by The New York Times Co. Reprinted by permission.

So, although the primary mission of bureaucracy is to implement and manage policy, the responsibilities of rulemaking and adjudication make the bureaucracy much like legislatures and courts—a policymaking institution charged with missions as varied, complex, and controversial as those of the other institutions of government. But bureaucratic policymaking is not only passive and reactive. Bureaucracies are also active in the initiation of new policies.

Bureaucratic Lobbying

Bureaucracies also influence policy by actively participating in the broader political process. As the primary managers of policy, bureaucrats are in ideal positions to identify the problems and limitations of existing laws and programs, and they frequently recommend changes to the president and to the congressional committees with which they interact.

Bureaucracies have two sources of political power to influence policy formation by legislatures and executives. First and foremost is their expertise. Knowledge is power, and bureaucracies are vast storehouses of information. Presidents and the Congress often rely on bureaucracy to collect and present the information needed to fashion policy, and by choosing what information to provide and how to present that information, bureaucrats can affect policy decisions.

The second source of power is close alliances with important clientele groups and key committees in Congress with jurisdiction over the programs of interest to the clientele group. The Department of Veterans' Affairs, for example, has a powerful ally in the nation's veterans. Few legislators relish the prospect of taking a position that can be perceived as anti-veteran, and this provides a potent source of influence. Politicians and bureaucracy typically use this influence to advance common interests rather than to wield it against each other. Some scholars argue many important policy decisions are made in **iron triangles,** which are stable relationships among a clientele group, the bureaucracy managing the programs that affect this group's interests, and the congressional committees with jurisdiction over those programs. Each actor in this triangle has a shared set of interests, and they are able to able to work in harness to pursue common goals. Though once seen as "governments within government," political scientists have largely concluded that iron triangles are less stable and powerful than originally thought (Baumgartner and Jones 1993).

Rather than iron triangles, political scientists have discovered that bureaucracies are more likely to operate in **policy subsystems.** Policy subsystems are the "interaction of actors from different institutions interested in a policy area" (Sabatier 1988). In other words, they are networks of all the groups that share a particular policy interest. Unlike iron triangles, these networks may include executives, courts, a wide range of interest groups and legislative committees, and just about anyone or anything else that can get itself organized enough to participate in the process. These networks are not nearly as stable as iron triangles, and two actors who work together on one issue may oppose each other on another. Thus the Sierra Club may champion an effort by the Environmental Protection Agency to enforce the preservation of wildlife and oppose it when it seeks to relax rules on power plant emissions.

The Characteristics of Bureaucracy

Agencies in the federal bureaucracy are wildly diverse, and, at first glance, organizations such as the Coast Guard and the Federal Deposit Insurance Corporation (FDIC) have little common. Yet virtually every public agency shares two common characteristics: (1) a broad mission to implement the decisions of government and (2) a common form of organizational structure. So far our discussion has only considered the former.

Yet organizational structure is crucial to understanding bureaucracy and how it goes about achieving its goals of implementing government decisions. Indeed, to scholars who study the subject, this is what bureaucracy is—not a public agency or a program but a specific type of organization.

The Weberian Model of Bureaucracy

The best-known description of the bureaucratic model of organization is attributed to Max Weber (Gerth and Mills 1946). Weber's model proposed five distinguishing characteristics of a bureaucracy:

1. *Division of labor.* In a bureaucracy work is divided according to task specialization. For example, most large bureaucracies employ specialists in personnel, accounting, and data entry. In the public sector, specialists include virologists at the Centers for Disease Control and policy analysts at the Congressional Research Service.
2. *Hierarchy.* In a bureaucracy, there is a clear vertical chain of command, and authority flows downward from superiors to subordinate employees.
3. *Formal rules.* Bureaucracies operate according to standardized operating procedures.
4. *Maintenance of files and records.* Bureaucracies record their actions and keep the records.
5. *Professionalization.* Bureaucrats are appointed on the basis of their qualifications, and government bureaucracies develop a career civil service.

Microsoft, General Motors, and IBM all have this same set of characteristics. What separates public and private bureaucracies is not how they are organized but what they are organized to do. The purpose of most private bureaucracies such as IBM is to make a profit. The purpose of a public bureaucracy is to implement laws and regulations, that is, to translate the expressed intentions of government into action.

Given their main purpose, there are several advantages to organizing public agencies along bureaucratic lines. For example, a formal framework of rules and procedures helps ensure stability, predictability, and impartiality in the way an agency carries out its mission.

The neutrality of bureaucracy is responsible, in part, for its unflattering reputation. Most Americans have endured the classic bureaucratic experience of waiting in line, filling out forms, and dealing with "red tape." This is not the sort of process that will make an organization popular. Yet the rules and regulations associated with bureaucracy are designed to ensure equality. It does not matter if you are rich or poor, Democrat or Republican, black or white; when you go to get a driver's license, you have to meet the same qualification standards. There is no cutting in line, no exceptions to the testing requirement on the basis of social or political standing. Consider that bureaucracy's red tape is a sign of the core democratic value of political equality in action. As discussed in earlier chapters, in the abstract the core values enjoy almost universal support;. in practice they can be downright irritating. (See the Living the Promise feature "Red Tape.")

The Merit System

Another characteristic of bureaucracy that relates to the core values of democracy is professionalization, which means that the people who staff public agencies are there on the basis of merit; they are hired and promoted on the basis of their qualifications and their job performance rather than on their political connections. Public agencies have not always been run on the basis of the merit system. In the **spoils system,** government jobs at all levels are rewards for people's loyalty to a politician or a party. Under the spoils system, a change of administration (when a politician or party loses at the polls) results in an immediate large-scale turnover in the bureaucracy.

LIVING THE PROMISE
Red Tape

The term *red tape* is a symbol of excessive formality and attention to routine. It originates from the red ribbon with which clerks bound official documents in the 19th century. The ribbon has disappeared, but the practices it represents linger on. Herbert Kaufman explains that the term "is applied to a bewildering variety of organizational practices and features." After all, "one person's 'red tape' may be another's treasured procedural safeguard." Kaufman concludes that "red tape turns out to be at the core of our institutions rather than a excrescence of them."

Source: Kaufman quoted in Shafritz, Jay M. 1988. *The Dorsey Dictionary of American Government and Politics.* Chicago: Dorsey, 468.

The spoils system dominated the public bureaucracy for much of the 19th and early 20th century. The spoils system meant getting a government job depended on who you knew rather than what you knew, and your job security only extended to the next election. The spoils system promoted corruption and incompetence, thoroughly politicizing the bureaucracy (Rosenbloom 1998, 211). The spoils system could (and did) lead to many breaches of the core values of democracy. Bureaucracies operating under the spoils system were involved in everything from playing political favorites (breaking the core value of political equality) to rigging elections (breaking the core value of popular sovereignty).

The spoils system was the norm in the federal government during much of the 19th century, and a residue of the system still exists. The president, for example, still appoints the head of many executive agencies. In many cases, though, these appointments must be approved by the Senate, and the appointee must have some qualifications as a prerequisite for gaining that approval.

In contrast to the spoils system, the **merit system** bases government employment on the basis of competence rather than partisan fealty. A merit system staffs a bureaucracy by defining the skills and knowledge required to do a particular job in the bureaucracy and provides a way—typically a written examination—for prospective employees to demonstrate their ability to perform those tasks. A merit system is intended to create a career civil service of competent professionals to run public agencies. Of course, bureaucrats still have their own policy and political preferences, and a merit system does not entirely eliminate politics from the bureaucracy. Compared to a spoils system, however, a merit system will greatly reduce its potential for incompetence, corruption, and naked partisanship.

The merit system was formally introduced into the federal bureaucracy by the Pendleton Act of 1883. This law was a direct product of the assassination of President James Garfield in 1881 by a disappointed (and mentally deranged) office seeker. This assassination sent shock waves through the political system, turned public opinion against the spoils system, and pushed Congress into considering radical reform of the bureaucracy (Brinkley 1993, 516–517). The Pendleton Act established the principle that government employment and promotion should be based on merit demonstrated through competitive examinations. This principle signaled the end of the spoils system and remains the primary means of staffing the bureaucracy today.

Neutral Competence

Generally speaking, the merit-based civil service system prizes technical competence in government employees above virtually anything else. Most importantly, the bureaucratic form of organizations offers a way to install **neutral competence** into public agencies. Neutral competence means that public agencies make decisions based on expertise rather than on political or personal considerations.

At least since Woodrow Wilson's' administration, reformers have sought to separate the political and administrative functions of government. The general idea is for policy decisions to be set by elected officials. The president and Congress decide basic issues such as whether the government will wage war, agree to an international trade treaty, provide a tax deduction for childcare, or subsidize farmers and, if so, under what conditions. All of these are political decisions. They represent the outcome of the conflict over what the society ought to do. This conflict is processed by the institutions of representative democracy into a decision about what action, if any, government should take.

Implementing those decisions is the job of the administrative arm of government—in other words, the bureaucracy. According to the principle of neutral competence, the bureaucracy does not decide policy or take sides in the political arena. It simply uses its expertise to ensure that policy decisions are implemented in the fashion intended by the institutions of representative democracy. If those institutions make decisions that uphold the core values of democracy, the bureaucracy ensures government upholds those values in deed as well as words.

In theory, the bureaucratic form of organization can help separate politics and administration. In practice, though, the record is mixed. As noted previously, the bureaucracy is actively involved in influencing the formation of policies, but, as discussed later in this chapter, insulating the bureaucracy from politics is difficult, and some question whether it should even be attempted.

The Bureaucrats

Like the agencies they serve, the roughly 2.7 million federal employees are also an astonishingly diverse group. Because of the merit system, the bureaucracy is largely staffed by people hired for their technical expertise rather than their political or partisan loyalty. Government bureaucrats include doctors, nurses, lawyers, electricians, computer programmers, carpenters, clerical workers, and virtually every other occupational group imaginable. The term *bureaucrat* rarely conjures up the image of a creative arts therapist or a microbiologist, but the federal government employs hundreds of the former and thousands of the latter.

Generally speaking, all this expertise is put to productive use. The stereotype of the ineffective and incompetent bureaucracy is largely inaccurate. Public administration

Table 14.1
General Schedule (GS) Pay Scale, Effective January 2004

			ANNUAL RATES BY		
GRADE	STEP 1	STEP 2	STEP 3	STEP 4	STEP 5
GS-1	$15,625	$16,146	$16,666	$17,183	$17,703
2	17,568	17,985	18,567	19,060	19,274
3	19,168	19,807	20,446	21,085	21,724
4	21,518	22,235	22,952	23,669	24,386
5	24,075	24,878	25,681	26,484	27,287
6	26,836	27,731	28,626	29,521	30,416
7	29,821	30,815	31,809	32,803	33,797
8	33,026	34,127	35,228	36,329	37,430
9	36,478	37,694	38,910	40,126	41,342
10	40,171	41,510	42,849	44,188	45,527
11	44,136	45,607	47,078	48,549	50,020
12	52,899	54,662	56,425	58,188	59,951
13	62,905	65,002	67,099	69,196	71,293
14	74,335	76,813	79,291	81,769	84,247
15	87,439	90,354	93,269	96,184	99,099

Source: U.S. Office of Personnel Management. *http://www.opm.gov/oca/04tables/pdf/gs.pdf.*

scholars generally conclude that government bureaucracies do a much better job than they get credit for (Goodsell 1994; Sclar 2000). For example, the American Customer Satisfaction Index was originally designed to assess customer satisfaction with various businesses. When it was expanded to include twenty-nine federal agencies, it turned out that there was virtually no difference in customer satisfaction between public and private services (U.S. Government Customer Satisfaction Initiative 2000).

Not only do government employees by and large do a good job, they do it relatively inexpensively. Most federal employees are covered by what is known as the general schedule (GS) pay scale (see Table 14.1). There are fifteen GS grades, which range in annual pay from a first-year GS-1 at $15,625 to a senior GS-15 with years of experience at $113,674. To put the pay of federal bureaucrats into perspective, a recent college graduate would most likely be hired as a GS-5, GS-6, or GS-7, depending on the area of expertise and qualifications. That means if you went to work for the federal government after graduation, your starting salary would most likely fall between $24,000 and $29,800.

The one stereotype of the bureaucracy that does hold true is a relative lack of diversity. The typical federal bureaucrat is a white male in his mid-40s, who has worked for the government for seventeen years. Roughly 70 percent of federal employees are white, and minorities tend to be concentrated in the middle and lower ranks of the bureaucracy. Females are also underrepresented—roughly

GRADE AND STEP

STEP 6	STEP 7	STEP 8	STEP 9	STEP 10	WITHIN-GRADE AMOUNTS
$18,009	$18,521	$19,039	$19,060	$19,543	VARIES
19,841	20,408	20,975	21,542	22,109	VARIES
22,363	23,002	23,641	24,280	24,919	639
25,103	25,820	26,537	27,254	27,971	717
28,090	28,893	29,696	30,499	31,302	803
31,311	32,206	33,101	33,996	34,891	895
34,791	35,785	36,779	37,773	38,767	994
38,531	39,632	40,733	41,834	42,935	1,101
42,558	43,774	44,990	46,206	47,422	1,216
46,866	48,205	49,544	50,883	52,222	1,339
51,491	52,962	54,433	55,904	57,375	1,471
61,714	63,477	65,240	67,003	68,766	1,763
73,390	75,487	77,584	79,681	81,778	2,097
86,725	89,203	91,681	94,159	96,637	2,478
102,014	104,929	107,844	110,759	113,674	2,915

55 percent of federal employees are male. As a group, federal employees are also highly educated, with more than 40 percent holding college degrees.

The Structure of American Bureaucracies

Federal government public agencies are organized into a rough hierarchy. If we confine the discussion to the executive branch (Congress and the courts have their own bureaucracies), there are five basic categories of public agency within this hierarchy. At the top are the Executive Office of the President and the cabinet departments. Below them come independent agencies, government corporations, and miscellaneous bureaus (see Figure 14.1).

The Executive Office of the President

At the top of the executive branch hierarchy is the Executive Office of the President (EOP). This is the bureaucracy charged with collectively managing all the executive branch bureaucracies for the president. The EOP is divided into several agencies with

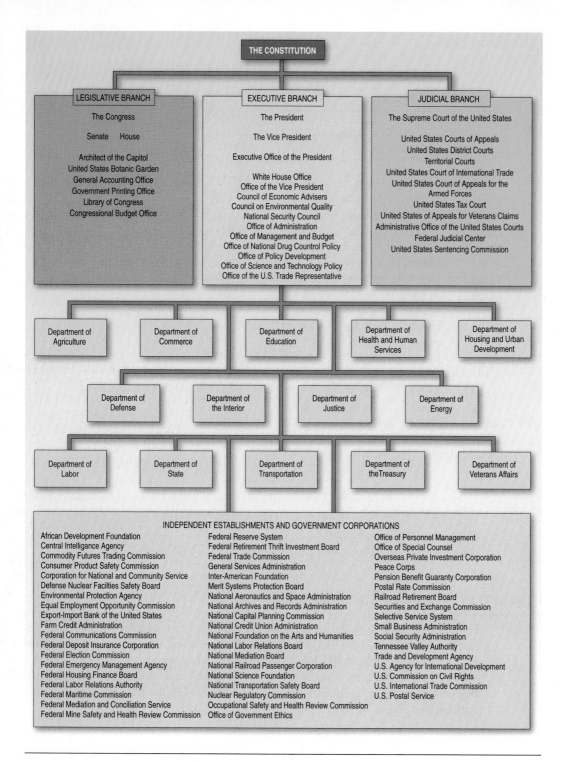

Figure 14.1

Organization of the U.S. Government

Source: U.S. Government Manual, p. 22. *http://frwebgate.access.gpo.gov/cgi-bin/getdoc.cgi?dbname=2003_government_manual&docid=193760tx_xxx-2.pdf.*

specific tasks. The White House Office consists of the key members of the president's staff who help with the day-to-day administrative responsibilities of the presidency. Also housed in the EOP are agencies specializing in particular policy areas, such as the Council of Economic Advisers and the National Security Council, as well as agencies with broader responsibilities. An example of the latter is the Office of Management and Budget (OMB), which provides a central location for all other agencies to submit program and budget requests and thus plays an important centralizing role in the federal bureaucracy.

Cabinet Departments

Just below the EOP in the bureaucratic hierarchy are the fifteen **cabinet departments,** each headed by a cabinet secretary appointed by the president. Congress created each of these departments and has the power to determine their organization and internal operation. The first departments were State, War (which evolved into Defense), and Treasury, all created in 1789. The most recent is the Department of Homeland Security (DHS), created in 2002 in one of the most sweeping reorganizations of the federal bureaucracy in fifty years. (See the Promise and Policy feature "Homeland Security and the Politics of Bureaucratic Organization.")

Federal Bureau of Investigation director Robert Mueller discusses a rise in the terror threat alert level in May 2004. The FBI is a part of the Department of Justice. Cabinet departments are the main institutions of the federal bureaucracy and are responsible for implementing most federal programs and policies. They have the highest profile of all the federal bureaucracies, and the people who run them are often known to the general public.

© Kevin Lamarque/Reuters/Corbis

PROMISE AND POLICY
Homeland Security and the Politics of Bureaucratic Organization

Take twenty-two agencies, 170,000 people, and season with $36 billion. Mix quickly, cover with eighty-eight congressional committees, and garnish with a cabinet secretary. Now, that is a recipe for a major case of bureaucratic indigestion.

It is also, more or less, the basic recipe followed for creating the newest cabinet-level agency: the Department of Homeland Security.

The Department of Homeland Security (DHS) was created in 2002 for the purpose of protecting the nation against terrorist attacks. A direct outgrowth of the events of September 11, 2001, the department's charge is to assemble and coordinate the nation's antiterrorism efforts into something approaching a coherent whole.

These goals all sound laudable—and given the tragedy of 9/11—overdue. A quick glance at an "organization" chart of the intelligence, law enforcement, and regulatory agencies tasked with combating terrorism prior to 9/11 will make clear the difficulties they faced in putting together a coherent picture of the terrorist threat. The bottom line is that these agencies were not systematically organized to work with one another.

Congress responded to this problem after the tragedy of 9/11 by pushing for a new cabinet-level agency—the DHS—that would put many agencies with antiterror responsibilities under one bureaucratic roof. Makes sense, right? Organize the agencies so they can be better coordinated, share information more effectively, and centralize the domestic efforts to prevent a repeat of the terrorist hijackings.

Politics, however, have always trumped administrative logic when it comes to organizing the federal

bureaucracy, and the creation of the DHS proved no exception. To begin with, the DHS was opposed by President Bush, [who] delayed its actual creation. Facing considerable political pressure to do something on the domestic front in the war on terror, the Bush administration shifted its position after several months of opposition and threw its weight behind the agency's creation.

That, however, signaled the beginning rather than the end of the political fight. First, there was the argument over what agencies should constitute the new department and whether the DHS should be exempt from freedom of information laws and civil service rules. The Bush administration's preferences prevailed on many of these issues. Ironically these administration changes left many who had originally favored the DHS feeling lukewarm about the end product. For example, the Central Intelligence Agency stayed an independent agency. The Federal Bureau of Investigation stayed in the Department of Justice. Other agencies and their constituents successfully lobbied to keep programs that might have made sense to house in the DHS.

That constituted just the political fight over the law creating the agency. Once the agency officially existed, its first leader, Secretary Tom Ridge, faced a mind-boggling administrative and logistical challenge. His team was charged with bringing together such disparate agencies as the Animal and Plant Health Inspection Service (formerly part of the Department of Agriculture) to the U.S. Secret Service (formerly part of the Department of the Treasury). The twenty-two agencies that make up the DHS not only come from different backgrounds,

have different organizational cultures, follow different personnel procedures, and enjoy different expectations about promotion and prestige, they also use different communications and computer systems. Just getting the latter sorted out—in other words, getting the agencies to effectively talk to one another—will likely take years and millions and millions of dollars.

On top of that, the new department has a lot of bosses. Every federal bureaucracy is accountable to the congressional committees with jurisdiction over the laws and programs the agency implements. As agencies and programs were plucked from various parts of the federal bureaucracy and assigned to the new department, their congressional committees and the attendant oversight responsibilities went with them. This came to a total of eighty-eight committees. Serving on those committees in the 107th Congress were all 100 U.S. senators and all but twenty of the 435 members of the House. The DHS involves many programs of interest to a great many constituents. Given that interest, congressional committees are jealously guarding their turf. The end result is that the DHS not only has a lot to answer for, it has a lot to answer to.

Ultimately, the largest reorganization of the federal bureaucracy in fifty years turned out to be pretty much what professional scholars of the bureaucracy would have predicted: an agency reflecting the political interests behind its creation and the programs it runs. This result is not necessarily what anyone wanted, but cumulatively it is exactly what was asked for. The bureaucracy, in all its oddly organized glory, reflects the promises and compromises made by the government that created it.

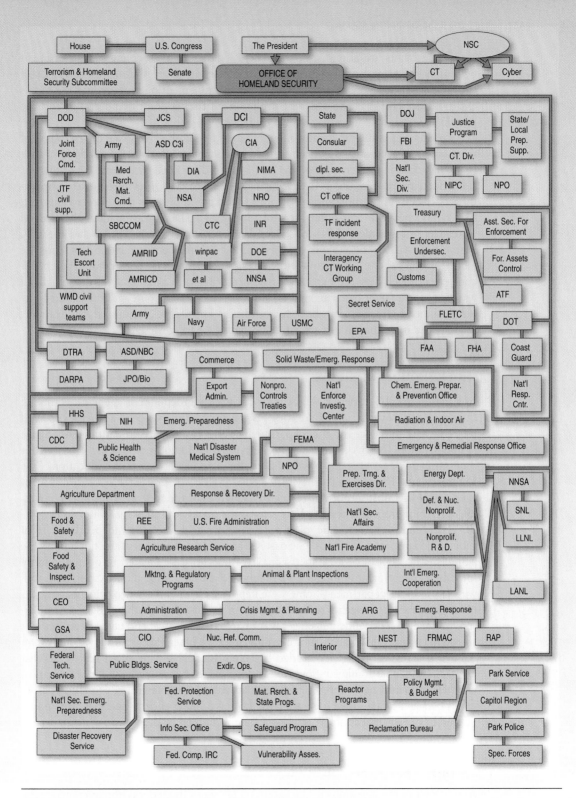

Organization of Homeland Security Agencies prior to September 11, 2001
Source: Office of Congresswoman Jane Harman.

Departments are administrative agencies charged with carrying out government operations in general policy areas. Cabinet departments are the main institutions of the federal bureaucracy and are responsible for implementing most federal programs and policies. They have the highest profile of all the federal bureaucracies, and the people who run them are often known to the general public.

Cabinet departments are not monolithic and centralized bureaucracies. Many of them are more accurately described as holding companies. They serve as administrative umbrellas covering diverse programs and serving diverse clients. Each department is subdivided into smaller units. The Department of Justice (DOJ) is the largest law firm in the world, employing thousands of attorneys working in bureaus dedicated to antitrust, civil rights, criminal, and other areas of the law. The DOJ also includes the Federal Bureau of Investigation (FBI), the Drug Enforcement Agency (DEA), and the U.S. Marshal's Service. In addition to lawyers and law enforcement agencies, it also runs the federal prison system. All of these individual agencies may have considerable independence even though they are part of a single department. In fact, many of the individual agencies predate their departmental organizations and have proud and independent histories, some of which stretch back for centuries. The U.S. Coast Guard, for example, operated for more than 200 years before becoming a part of the DHS.

Independent Agencies

In addition to cabinet departments, there about fifty **independent agencies.** Although they generally have narrower areas of responsibility, independent agencies can rival the size and influence of the departments. The National Aeronautics and Space Administration (NASA), for example, has roughly 18,000 employees. That is four times the number of people who work for the Department of Education. The Environmental Protection Agency is not only roughly the same size as NASA, it manages one of the most important regulatory activities of the federal government, covering everything from smokestack emissions to the quality of municipal water wells.

The central characteristic of independent agencies is their independence from cabinet departments: Unlike the Coast Guard or the FBI, they are not under the administrative control of a cabinet secretary. Agencies were created to operate outside the cabinet department umbrella for a number of reasons. Some did not seem to fit well with any existing department. Some were kept outside of cabinet departments in hopes of fostering fresh approaches to vexing policy problems. Perhaps the most common reason for creating independent agencies was to avoid the political and client pressures that surround cabinet departments. For example, the Consumer Product Safety Commission (CPSC) is a regulatory agency headed by commissioners serving seven-year terms that overlap presidential administrations; this overlap makes it more difficult for presidents to use their appointment powers to advance a particular set of interests or promote a particular political agenda. Like departments, however, independent agencies are mostly headed by presidential appointees who must be confirmed by the Senate.

Government Corporations

Another set of organizations in the extended family of the federal bureaucracy are the **government corporations.** These operate in a vague area somewhere between the public and private sectors. The general idea behind government corporations is to shift responsibility for a government task to a nonpartisan arena in hopes of keeping it insulated from politics to the greatest extent possible. Probably the best-known government corporation is the United States Postal Service (USPS). Other examples include the Federal Deposit Insurance Corporation, which insures bank deposits, and Amtrak, the nation's passenger rail service.

Government corporations, in essence, are federally established businesses. They have narrow tasks and are run by bipartisan or nonpartisan boards. Most are designed to be self-supporting, although some receive at least some assistance from the federal government.

Other Bureaus

Besides cabinet departments, independent agencies, and government corporations, there is a miscellaneous set of executive branch organizations that does not fit into any of these categories. These include **advisory committees,** which can be permanent or temporary and can serve a number of purposes, ranging from providing agencies with technical expertise to providing a means for citizen input to agency operations. In any given year, there are roughly 1,000 advisory committees salted throughout the federal bureaucracy.

There are also numerous boards, committees, and commissions that are temporary additions to the bureaucracy. These tend to be small, have well-defined tasks, and have few program responsibilities.

The Politics of Organization

Though we can classify public agencies and sort them into a rough pecking order, there really is no such thing as "the" federal bureaucracy. Rather than a single federal bureaucracy, there is actually a sprawling mass of individual agencies. The 2.7 million civilian employees of the federal government serve in fifteen departments, fifty or so independent agencies, and numerous boards, commissions, and advisory committees. As we have seen, many of these bureaucracies are subdivided into smaller administrative units that have considerable independence. Rather than being a Big Brother, the bureaucracy is more like a vast extended family, replete with third cousins twice removed and siblings who are not talking to each other.

After reading about the confusing stew of departments, agencies, committees, bureaus, and commissions and their seemingly incoherent relationships with one another, you might be wondering whether the organization of the federal bureaucracy makes any sense. The short answer to that is simple: No. At least in terms of being organized to promote effective and efficient administration, the organization of the federal government is not particularly rational or logical.

Consider that not one, not two, but at least five separate public agencies regulate the banking industry. These include two divisions of a cabinet department (the Comptroller of the Currency and the Office of Thrift Supervision, both part of the Treasury Department); one independent agency (the National Credit Union Administration); one government corporation (the Federal Deposit Insurance Corporation); and one independent government commission (the Federal Trade Commission). The goals and responsibilities of these agencies overlap, yet there is little in the way of centralized or coordinated control over what they do, and one agency may be all but unaware of the activities of another. It is hard to imagine a business organizing itself in such a fashion, at least any business that has realistic hopes of survival.

So, why is the federal bureaucracy organized like this? Why are there redundancy, overlap, and unclear lines of authority? Why do we have five federal agencies regulating financial institutions rather than one? This example provides any number of reasons for why the bureaucracy has such a negative reputation. Yet there is a pretty simple answer to these questions, one directly related to the purpose of bureaucracies. Remember, bureaucracies are there to make good on the promise of democratic government. And the constituents of democratic governments often want their government to promise to do things that are not efficient, or logical, or even particularly effective.

Let us go back to the bureaucracy regulating the financial industry. The reason there are five regulatory agencies here is that the various sectors of the banking industry do not want to be regulated by a single agency. Credit unions and banks, for example, want their own regulatory agency, each of which has a set of accompanying congressional committees. In other words, the bureaucracy regulating the financial industry is convoluted because it serves a set of political goals. The different sectors of the industry have lobbied government to give them different agencies, regulating different aspects of the business. This array of agencies is not particularly efficient (and given the record of corporate scandals during the last decade, perhaps not effective). But that misses the point. The job of the bureaucracy is to deliver on the promise of democratic governments, and the bureaucracies regulating the financial industry are doing exactly that: There are separate agencies for separate sectors of the industry, each with its own set of regulations.

This does not just apply to the financial industry. The pattern is repeated again and again. And it cannot be blamed on the catch-all villain of "special interests." All citizens, in some fashion, have vested interests in government agencies. You, or at least many of your peers, for example, probably want the Department of Education to keep guaranteeing student loans and offering student grants. This demand creates pressure on government—mainly from parents with college-age children—to make promises about higher education and financial aid. The result? A program run by a public agency with rules, regulations, red tape, and the rest of the bureaucratic machinery (those of you who have applied for a student loan will be intimately familiar with these details). That bureaucratic machinery is never going to be appreciated, at least until it is gone. What the bureaucracy does is deliver on the promise, and if you take away the bureaucracy, who keeps the promise? Like it or not, democratic governments have yet to figure out a way to keep their promises without a bureaucracy.

Controlling the Bureaucracy

The discussion thus far shows that bureaucracy exists to make good on the promises of democratic governments, and to do this federal agencies have been granted broad powers and organized in such a way that makes organizational sense for the individual agency and political sense for the overall bureaucracy. All of these characteristics combine to create a larger concern about the bureaucracy: control. Bureaucrats are appointed, not elected, yet we know that through the process of rulemaking they, for all practical purposes, make law. If program or regulatory responsibilities are shared by two, or four, or six bureaucracies, who do we hold responsible if something goes wrong?

One of the most consistent concerns about the bureaucracy is that it serves the purpose for which it was intended. We want bureaucracy to deliver on the promise of democratic governments, not to make those promises or have the authority to decide what promises are worth bothering with and what promises can be ignored. This is the classic dilemma at the heart of studying bureaucracy: How do you make one of the most powerful institutions of government abide by the values of democracy, when that institution is not democratic? And make no mistake about it, bureaucracies are *not* democratic. Glance back at the characteristics of the classic bureaucracy given earlier in this chapter. Bureaucracies are clearly hierarchical and authoritarian; their personnel are not hired or fired by elections; their decisions are not put to a ballot. Every industrialized democracy has had to come to some sort of arrangement with the increasingly important role of the administrative arm of government. The trick here is to make the bureaucracy accountable to the values of democracy, rather than vice versa.

Controlling the bureaucracy and making it accountable requires two basic things. First, elected representatives and individual citizens need to be able to effectively monitor the bureaucracy. Again, the organization of bureaucracy helps us here; bureaucracies operate by formal rules (which help make clear what they should and should not be doing), and they keep written records. Second, elected officials need a basic set of tools to influence bureaucracy. If elected officials cannot make bureaucracy follow their wishes, the notion of overhead democracy collapses.

Monitoring Bureaucracy

The preferred method of making bureaucracy accountable to democracy is through a process called **overhead democracy** (Redford 1969; Wilson 1887). Overhead democracy is the idea that citizens can exercise indirect control over bureaucracy: Voters will hold elected officials accountable for their actions through their votes, and elected officials will hold bureaucracies accountable for their actions. Candidates who favor majority viewpoints will win office. To win reelection these candidates must make some effort to keep the promises they made on the campaign trail. To achieve this goal they have a built-in incentive to keep a close eye on the bureaucracies that actually will deliver on those promises. If the bureaucracy abuses its position—it plays favorites or denies people services to which they are entitled—an officeholder is expected to take action. If he or she does not, the officeholder will be voted out in favor of someone who will bring the bureaucracy to heel.

The practice of overhead democracy is more complicated in practice than in theory (Meier 1993). It requires politicians to vigorously exercise their oversight responsibilities, systematically monitoring the bureaucracy to ensure that it is acting in accordance with democratically expressed wishes in much the same way that police officers patrol city streets to spot and deter crime. This process is called **police patrol oversight** (McCubbins and Schwartz 1984). The problem here is that, to the individual politician, police patrol oversight rarely pays off. In the vast majority of cases, the agencies are doing pretty much what they are supposed and expected to do. Thus, a legislator's time is better spent crafting new laws, engaging in constituency service, or doing any of the other activities related to election.

Rather than engage in a constant monitoring, Congress and its committees tend to rely on **fire alarm oversight,** which kicks into action once an alarm is raised (McCubbins and Schwartz 1984). There are many ways to raise an alarm about bureaucratic wrongdoing. Whistleblowers (agency employees who bring attention to agency misdeeds), direct contact from constituents, and investigations by Congress' information-gathering agencies such as the General Accounting Office (GAO) all routinely raise alarms. Special interest groups are particularly effective at sounding alarms, because they put a good deal of effort into monitoring the agencies that affect their interests.

The big problem with fire alarm oversight is that it is reactive rather than proactive. Relying on fire alarm oversight means Congress only begins to tackle bureaucratic problems after those problems have occurred. The price of relying on hindsight to address a problem can be very high indeed. The National Commission on Terrorist Attacks upon the United States (the 9/11 Commission) was a form of fire alarm oversight. It was created by Congress to investigate and prepare a full account of the circumstances surrounding the terrorist attacks of September 11, 2001. The commission heard testimony from numerous officials that made clear there were a number of coordination and information-sharing problems among the nation's intelligence and law enforcement agencies. Identifying those problems meant they could be addressed—but only after the tragic loss of life had occurred.

Sometimes the fire alarms Congress relies on to warn of problems in the bureaucracy are kept silent. Failure to sound an alarm happens when the relationship between an interest group and a bureaucracy becomes a little too cozy. **Agency capture** describes a bureaucracy that is run for the benefit of those it is supposed to regulate, and it occurs when the regulators appointed to an agency share the same professional and economic values as those they regulate. Some critics compare this to hiring foxes to guard the hen house. Even if regulators do not have ties to a regulated industry, over time they can come to identify with industry interests because interaction is so one-sided: Representatives of a regulated industry have frequent contacts with the agency and may develop cordial relationships, while those representing the broader public interest have only infrequent contacts with the agency.

Although agency capture is recognized as a theoretical possibility by academics, and fits well with popular beliefs on the influential role of special interests, systematic research has found relatively little hard evidence to support its prevalence. Although there certainly are examples of agencies coddling the regulated, it is much more common to find bureaucracies that are vigorously regulating the industries they are supposed to regulate (Meier 1995, 21). Agency capture, in other words, is more myth than reality. The real problem is not that interest groups capture agencies and run them for their own benefit but that interest groups have little incentive to report or publicize negligent or inappropriate agency actions if they benefit. This is akin to making a bundle on insurance if the building burns down—there is little incentive to sound the alarm if you profit from the fire.

Even with its limitations, fire alarm oversight does demonstrate that there are forces providing incentives to monitor the bureaucracy and hold it accountable. In implementing programs and policies, the bureaucracy is a natural focus for competing interests. Some argue that when they serve a range of clients and interest groups, the bureaucracy helps to responsibly represent and further those interests. As one scholar put it, "Bureaucracies are not just passive actors who respond limply to external demand by politicians and groups. Rather they integrate and transmit competing values from multiple overlapping constituencies" (Wood 1992).

This role is enhanced by laws that provide individual citizens with considerable monitoring powers and force bureaucratic decision making to be open and transparent.

The Freedom of Information Act of 1967, for example, requires bureaucracies to respond to all reasonable public requests for documents. Other statutes called **sunshine laws** require that bureaucratic decisions be made in public meetings. These laws, at a minimum, give individual citizens and interest groups the tools to keep tabs on what the bureaucracy does.

Influencing Bureaucracy

All branches of the federal government have at their disposal powerful tools to influence bureaucratic behavior. These tools range from the formal power to create and destroy public agencies to less formal techniques of persuasion that may be handled in an office visit or a telephone call. At least in terms of formal power, each branch of government has a different set of options for getting bureaucracies to follow their wishes.

The Congress and the Bureaucracies   Congress has the ultimate tool to control bureaucracy: legislation. Federal bureaucracies do not simply interpret the law, they are products of it. Congress has the constitutional authority to create or destroy federal agencies and to determine what programs and polices they administer.

Congress also controls bureaucracy through its power of the purse. Article I, Section 9 of the Constitution states that, "No money shall be drawn from the treasury, but in consequence of appropriations made by law." This provision means that every federal agency's budget must be approved by Congress, and it is not unusual for Congress to use the appropriation process to place constraints or demands on the bureaucracy. The power of the purse is, in essence, a living embodiment of the golden rule: Who has the gold, gets to make the rules.

A final way in which Congress controls the bureaucracy is through **legislative vetoes.** A legislative veto is a provision in a law that allows Congress to reject a proposed action by a public agency. Typically this process involves requiring an agency to inform Congress of proposed actions, and Congress has the right to reject these proposals. Some legislative veto provisions require both houses of Congress to accept or reject rules, although some laws permit just one house, or even an individual committee, to accept or reject rules. The intent here is to give Congress some control over how laws are implemented.

Although the legislative veto is an effective check on the bureaucracy, it has its drawbacks. For one thing, it is not clear legislative vetoes are constitutional. The Constitution requires laws to be passed by a majority vote in both houses of Congress and presented to the president for signature or veto. It then becomes the president's responsibility to see "that the laws be faithfully executed." If Congress wants to modify a law, technically it has to go through the full process of making a law. The Supreme Court ruled legislative vetoes unconstitutional because they cut the president out of the lawmaking process (*Immigration and Naturalization Service v. Chadha* 1983). Despite this ruling, Congress continues to use legislative vetoes, although less frequently.

Another problem with the legislative veto is that it limits Congress' policymaking role. The legislative veto reduces Congress to a reactive body: It defines a broad goal through legislation and leaves the specifics to executive agencies. Though Congress can block the specifics it finds objectionable, in this process the legislature is reduced to telling the bureaucracy what it cannot do, rather than telling it what to do. The end result is to delegate to the bureaucracy a powerful proactive role in determining public policy.

The President and the Bureaucracies   The president also has several powerful tools to control the bureaucracies. As chief executive, the president is technically the chief bureaucrat. The president is the overall boss of all executive agencies, and like most bosses the president can exercise a good deal of influence over subordinates.

The most basic tool the president has for controlling bureaucracy is the power of **appointment,** which allows the president to choose a wide range of subordinates. Although the elimination of the spoils system dramatically reduced the president's ability to preferentially staff the bureaucracy, the chief executive retains the power to appoint many of the nation's top bureaucrats. These includes the secretaries of all cabinet departments, various deputies and undersecretaries, plus a wide variety of top-ranking positions in noncabinet agencies—roughly 3,000 officials in all.

The main advantage of appointment power is that it allows the president to put political allies and loyalists in key administrative positions. The power of appointment presumably puts the bureaucracy under closer control of the president. There are, however, two drawbacks to this system. One, these appointees often lack experience and tend to have short tenures. As many as a third of presidential appointees spend less than 18 months on the job. High turnover makes it hard for the president to provide consistent direction to a bureaucracy. Second, the appointees sometimes "go native," which means they end up becoming advocates of their agency's interests rather than the president's agenda.

The president does not have to rely solely on appointment power to control the bureaucracy. The president also has budgeting power, which although different from the budgeting powers of Congress can be just as effective. Only Congress has the power to approve a budget, but the president has the responsibility of proposing the budget. A president can thus reward or punish agencies by proposing increases or cuts in the annual budget proposal. Congress can change these proposals, but even then the president can veto an appropriations bill to block agency funding (though such an action would be considered drastic). Even if the money is appropriated over a veto, the president has some limited powers of **impoundment.** Impounding funds simply means delaying approved expenditures. A president who does not want to spend money appropriated by Congress can also seek to cancel the funding by sending a "rescission message" to Congress. If both houses approve the rescission, the funds are canceled. A president does not have complete control over agency budgets but has more than enough to make any agency wary of getting into a budgetary battle with the president.

The president also has the power to issue **executive orders,** directives that have the force of law even though they are not passed by Congress. These are the equivalent of presidential legislation and are often controversial. For example, Congress was wary of President George W. Bush's faith-based initiative, which proposed to funnel federal grant money into social and community outreach organizations associated with religious groups. The proposal was controversial because it raised constitutional questions about separation of church and state. With the issue stalled in Congress, Bush issued an executive order creating the White House Office of Faith-Based and Community Initiatives. In effect, President Bush on his own authority created a government bureaucracy to run a program that Congress was not willing to formally approve.

The Judiciary and the Bureaucracies   The courts have a few simple tools to control the bureaucracy. As the interpreters of law, judges can declare agency regulations, rules, or actions illegal if they fail to meet the constitutional litmus test. In assessing challenges to agency rules or actions, courts pose two broad questions. The first is whether the action is consistent with **legislative intent.** In other words, the court seeks to determine the agency's actions are authorized by the relevant law passed by Congress. The second question is whether the action violates **standards of due process.** Even if legislative intent is being followed, courts will seek to ensure that an agency is not depriving anyone of due process guarantees given by the Constitution or the law. For example, federal courts have probably done more than any other branch of the government in restricting local, state, and federal bureaucracies from discriminating in hiring, promotion, and service provision (Meier 1993, 163–164).

It is important to note that the interests of the courts are typically not whether a bureaucratic action is efficient, effective, fair, or even whether it makes sense. Their concern is almost wholly with whether it is legal.

Reforming Bureaucracy

Because of their central role in the American political process, it is not surprising that bureaucracies are frequent targets of reform efforts. Pledges to change bureaucracy and make it run "more like a business" have been a perennial feature of American politics for more than a century.

Past efforts include the Hoover Commission, formed under the administration of Harry Truman, and charged with identifying how to improve the efficiency and effectiveness of the bureaucracy. The Grace Commission was formed under the administration of Ronald Reagan and charged with rooting out government inefficiency and wasteful programs. The National Performance Review was a program of President Bill Clinton's administration that was a sustained effort to "reinvent government." The notion behind reinventing government was to make government agencies more customer-oriented and more entrepreneurial (Osborne and Gaebler 1990). The administration of George W. Bush has had no specific plan or program to make government more like a business, but he was the first MBA-holding businessman to become chief executive, to staff his administration with the elite of corporate America, and runs a CEO-like White House. This is as likely a group as any to make government run more like a business.

These reform efforts have had minimal impact. The primary problem with trying to run government like a business is that government is not a business. Though there is a common belief that what works in the private sector will work just as well in the public sector, this belief is often wrong. Businesses are oriented toward efficiency and productivity and have the ultimate goal of making money. Government agencies are oriented toward implementing the decisions of democratic governments. This basic mission is often an inherently inefficient proposition (remember the five agencies regulating the financial industry).

Businesses Running Government

While efforts to make government more like business have, at best, had minimal success, there has been much more progress in having businesses run the government. For the past few decades, several Western democracies have sought ways to reduce the size and cost of the public sector, while improving the efficiency and effectiveness of public programs. These efforts have resulted in the widespread practice of **contracting out.** Contracting out simply means hiring a private organization to deliver a public service rather than using a government bureaucracy.

The idea is to use the competitive leverage of the marketplace to make public policy more cost effective. For example, the traditional approach to implementing, say, a policy providing healthcare services to the poor meant creating a program and housing it in a bureaucracy. This approach also meant hiring people and providing facilities and other resources, all at public expense. Contracting out would involve paying a private healthcare company to provide the service, without the trouble and expense of hiring more government employees or constructing new buildings.

Though contracting out sounds appealing in the abstract, in practice it has raised a number of concerns. For example, contracting out creates an accountability problem. Political scientists who have studied traditional bureaucratic arrangements have mostly concluded that the bureaucratic tail does not wag the democratic dog (Wood and Waterman 1994). The relationship between Congress, the president, and the bureaucracy can be described by a **principal-agent model.** This model is based on the notion of a relationship between a boss who wants some work done (the principal) and an employee who actually does the work (the agent). A number of studies have concluded that this model is pretty much how traditional bureaucracy works. In short, bureaucracy is responsive, not just to Congress and the president, but also to the courts, media attention, and even broader currents of public opinion (Wood and Waterman 1994).

Yet while traditional bureaucratic arrangements are responsive to democratic controls, it is not clear the same is true under contracting out. Given a program or responsibility by an executive or a legislature, a public agency has three basic responses: work (make every effort to accomplish the policy), shirk (devote their efforts to something else), or sabotage (work to undermine the policy). In trying to ensure agencies work rather than shirk or sabotage, their principals (Congress and the president) are faced with an information problem. They often do not know the true abilities of a particular set of bureaucrats, and once they give them a job it is difficult to assess how much effort the bureaucrats expend trying to do that job. These are known as the principal's problems of **adverse selection** (not knowing the abilities of an agent) and **moral hazard** (not knowing the effort of an agent). Adverse selection and moral hazard can make it difficult for a principal to judge whether an agency is working, shirking, or sabotaging a particular policy (Brehm and Gates 1997).

These problems multiply when a principal has multiple agents or an agent from whom it is hard to get information. Both of these scenarios are common in contracting out. Because contracts to deliver a public service are often given to more than one vendor, there is more opportunity for shirking, The end result is not a single bureaucracy— required by law to keep records and maintain an open decision-making process—but a network of private organizations, all doing things slightly differently. Some have called this a "shadow bureaucracy," a layer of private companies that are dependent on government contracts. At the federal level this shadow bureaucracy has roughly four times the number of workers than the entire public bureaucracy (Light 1999).

It is virtually impossible for government to control this shadow bureaucracy as tightly as it controls the public bureaucracy, and it is much harder to hold it accountable for its actions. Unlike public bureaucracies, for example, private companies often have private decision-making processes and are not required to keep the same sorts of paper trails as public bureaucracies. The logistics alone to keep up with all the contracting out is daunting. In 2001, for example, the federal government entered into

560,000 contracts that represented expenditures of more than $200 billion (Federal Procurement Data Center 2002). Keeping up with numbers like these in any sort of systematic way would require, well, a bureaucracy.

In addition to the accountability concerns, private sector organizations may not be any more effective or more efficient than public bureaucracies. They also can increase rather than decrease the politics surrounding public programs. Big companies, for example, often seek to exert political pressure to reduce competitive bidding, which makes it harder to extract any cost savings. Using private companies also means dealing with profit motive incentives that may conflict with the public interest. Everyone has heard stories of the government paying inflated prices for all kinds of things, from screws to coffee makers. What usually gets left out of these stories is that it was a private company gouging the government by inflating prices and seeking to hide them and a public bureaucracy that exposed the fraud.

 ## Performance Assessment

In general, public agencies are competent at their jobs and do not get the credit they deserve for (mostly) doing them well. Bureaucracy certainly has its faults, but its negative stereotype is largely based on a lack of understanding about its purpose and role rather than a hard-nosed assessment of what it does. The bottom line is that bureaucracy does what we, through the democratic process, ask it to do. Its typical thanks for doing this is to be roundly criticized for not doing it well enough.

The Coast Guard's stated mission is to protect the public, the environment, and U.S. economic interests in the nation's ports and waterways, along the coast, on international waters, or in any maritime region as required to support national security. Despite our often negative view of bureaucracy, agencies like the Coast Guard generally serve their purpose well.

© Chris Hardy/San Francisco Chronicle/Corbis

Ultimately, bureaucracy tends to be as good or as bad as the democratic decision making and political pressures that drive its actions. Virtually all aspects of bureaucracy exist at the pleasure of the institutions of representative democracy, and there are no real technical limits on the extent of their control over bureaucracy. What limits more aggressive control of bureaucracy is not the power of public agencies but the politics of democracy. While most people dislike the bureaucracy, just about every agency, policy, and program has staunch defenders. There is, for example, no law preventing a thorough revamping of the Social Security system, which many analysts see as necessary. But Social Security is supported by a powerful constituency that makes legislators leery of pushing for sweeping change. Political pressures drive what bureaucracy does or does not do.

Bureaucracy is highly capable of taking the end products of the democratic process and translating them into action that fits within the boundaries established by the promise of democracy. Yet the bureaucracy cannot make the tensions that underlie the democratic process go away nor—if the bureaucracy is to remain subservient to the democratic process and the core value democratic values—should it.

Summary

- Bureaucracy has a negative reputation and is often considered synonymous with inefficiency, waste, and incompetence. The stereotype is at best a partial truth. In reality, most government bureaucracies are competent at what they do.
- Bureaucracy can be thought of as public agencies and the public programs and services they run. The main job of bureaucracy is to translate the intent of democratic institutions into action.
- Because it has to interpret laws and make choices about how to translate them into action, bureaucracy has considerable policymaking powers. Among the most important of these is the power to make rules.
- Rules are statements by a federal agency that interpret a law and prescribe the actions the agency will take to implement that law. Once finalized, rules have the power of the law.
- Scholars of administration and organization use the term *bureaucracy* to describe a specific type of organization. As an organization, the main characteristics of bureaucracy are division of labor, hierarchy, formal rules, maintenance of files and records, and professionalization. Most large and complex organizations have these characteristics, not just public agencies.
- Federal bureaucracies are organized in a loose hierarchy, but there is no centralized and coordinated control over all public agencies and programs. The responsibilities of federal agencies often overlap, and they often have to report to multiple congressional committees. The structure of the federal bureaucracy is driven more by politics than by the need for organizational efficiency.
- The size, responsibilities, and power of the federal bureaucracy create a number of concerns about how to make it accountable to democratic authority. The preferred method to do this is overhead democracy, the notion that voters will hold elected officials accountable for their actions and that public officials in turn will hold bureaucracies accountable for their actions.

- Congress, the president, and the courts have a number of powerful tools to control bureaucracy and make it accountable. These include appointment of agency heads, legislative oversight, controlling budgets, and judicial review.
- Reform of the bureaucracy is a perennial part of the public agenda. Reform is difficult because many of the assumptions underlying these reform efforts are questionable. Government is not a business, and trying to run public programs like a business creates practical and political obstacles.

Key Terms

adjudication 446
adverse selection 466
advisory committees 459
agency capture 462
appointment 464
bureaucracy 443
cabinet departments 455
contracting out 466
executive orders 464
fire alarm oversight 461
government corporations 458
impoundment 464
independent agencies 458
iron triangles 448

legislative intent 465
legislative vetoes 463
merit system 450
moral hazard 466
neutral competence 451
overhead democracy 461
police patrol oversight 461
policy subsystems 448
principal-agent model 466
rule 445
rulemaking 445
spoils system 449
standards of due process 465
sunshine laws 463

Selected Readings

Goodsell, Charles. 2003. *The Case for Bureaucracy.* Washington, DC: CQ Press. The classic work defending government bureaucracy. This book provides a spirited argument that public agencies do not deserve their negative reputations.

Kerwin, Cornelius. 2003. *Rulemaking: How Government Agencies Write Law and Make Policy.* Washington, DC: CQ Press. A detailed overview of how public agencies make public policy.

Meier, Kenneth J. 1999. *Politics and the Bureaucracy.* Belmont: Wadsworth. A comprehensive primer on the federal bureaucracy and its role in the American political system.

Seidman, Harold. 1998. *Politics, Position, and Power: The Dynamics of Federal Organization.* New York: Oxford University Press. An in-depth look at the organization of the federal bureaucracy. A key argument of the book is that the bureaucracy is organized to serve political purposes, not to promote efficiency, effectiveness, or rational control and coordination over public programs.

Wilson, James Q. 1989. *Bureaucracy: What Government Agencies Do and Why They Do It.* New York: Basic Books. A classic study of bureaucracy and its often misunderstood role in the American political system.

15 | The Federal Judiciary

Robert Penfield Jackson does not like Microsoft's business practices and is not shy about letting reporters know it. Bill Gates, he said, "was inherently without credibility" (Bazelon 2002). Antonin Scalia likes Dick Cheney. They have taken hunting trips together.

Nothing unusual here, you say? As head of Microsoft, Bill Gates has platoons of critics as well as legions of admirers. As vice president under George W. Bush, Cheney is unpopular with lots of people, but everybody has friends.

Well, what is unusual here is not the opinions people have of Gates or Cheney. It is who holds those opinions. Jackson is a U.S. district court judge. In fact, he is the judge who presided over a famous antitrust lawsuit brought against Microsoft. Scalia is a U.S. Supreme Court justice. Scalia and Cheney went duck hunting just three weeks after the Supreme Court agreed to hear a case involving Cheney's refusal to make public whether he met with energy industry officials (including disgraced Enron chief Kenneth Lay) while formulating the Bush administration's energy policy.

Most people would like to think that judges are Olympian figures, wise and neutral, who impartially apply the law without prejudice or bias. Yet if someone you believed to be a self-serving fibber insisted he was innocent of some wrong, could you objectively assess his claim? How would you feel about making a decision that could potentially expose a close friend to public ridicule and perhaps irreparably harm his career? Might the friendship sway your decision, at least a little?

It is hard to ignore your beliefs and values in answering such questions. This is not simply a matter of bias or prejudice but part and parcel of being a human being. And that's the point: not that Jackson or Scalia are biased but that they are human. They have likes and dislikes, with strong points of view on certain issues. Can we honestly expect them to ignore their own feelings and beliefs simply because they wear a black robe to work?

Most Americans would like the answer to be yes. Judges are expected to make decisions based on the rule of law, not on partisan fealty, ideological prejudice, personal loyalty, or fear of political retribution. This is why judicial independence is a prized value in the American political system. Federal judges are appointed for life, and that job security is designed to make it easier for people like Jackson and Scalia to uphold the law, even when it means going against political or personal expectations.

Yet Americans also want judges to be accountable for unpopular decisions. At some level we recognize that judges are human too and are thus subject to the same range of opinions and biases we all are. We do not want judges caving into political or personal pressure. We want them to stand firm for the core democratic principles embedded in law, even when it is the unpopular thing to do. On the other hand, we do not want them using their independence to play favorites from the bench. How do we reconcile independence with accountability?

This is a critical question because the judiciary is a political branch of government. It is the job of a judge, after all, to judge—in other words, to decide who gets what. Judges' decisions have affected tax rates, where a child can attend school, and whether a woman has a right to an abortion. It was a judicial decision that ultimately decided the 2000 presidential election. These are fundamentally political issues with plenty of room for disagreement about what is or is not constitutional, or what does or does not violate the core values of democracy.

Given the central role of courts as interpreters of the law, and recognizing that judges are political decision makers who are far from infallible, understanding the role of the judicial branch in the American political system is essential to assessing how well that system is delivering on the promise of democracy. When they interpret the Constitution, the courts are effectively put in the position of deciding how to uphold that promise. Accordingly, this chapter provides a basic introduction to the federal courts. It covers the nature of judicial power in the political system, the organization and structure of federal courts, who staffs the federal bench, how judges are selected, their power, and how all this fits into and affects the promise of democracy.

The Promise of the Federal Judiciary

The promise of the judiciary is to serve as the ultimate umpire in the democratic political process and protect individual liberties from infringement by tyrannical majorities. As we learned in Chapter 1, politics is a process to resolve conflict, and a democracy is a government that makes decisions that are consistent with four core democratic values—popular sovereignty, political freedom, political equality, and majority rule. But how does a democracy resolve conflicts between core values? In the United States, the courts exercise judicial power to help preserve democracy by limiting the majority from denying fundamental rights to the minority.

The term **judicial power** refers to the authority of courts to interpret and apply the law in particular cases. Judicial power is fundamentally political power. The limits and conditions under which courts exercise this power—that is, the types of cases and controversies they can hear—is called **jurisdiction.** The jurisdiction of federal courts is defined by the Constitution, by laws passed by Congress, and by the courts themselves.

Jurisdiction Defined in the Constitution

The general jurisdiction of the federal courts is succinctly set forth in Article III, Section 2 of the Constitution. Two words used there, *cases* and *controversies,* have been taken to mean that litigation heard by the federal courts must involve an actual dispute in which real people suffer real harm. In other words, courts do not decide hypothetical cases about the interpretation of a statute or its constitutionality. Nor can federal judges render advisory opinions about how or whether a particular law should be enforced. Thus, while the judiciary is a powerful political actor, it is also passive. A court can exercise its powers only when someone who has actually been harmed by the provisions of a law or a government act brings a constitutional issue before it by means of a lawsuit.

A case brought by a legitimate plaintiff can be heard by a federal court if it satisfies one of two general requirements. The first concerns the subject matter of the suit: It must be litigation involving the U.S. Constitution, a federal law, a treaty, or admiralty and maritime matters. Federal courts have jurisdiction to hear cases brought by private citizens challenging the constitutionality of state or federal laws. Criminal defendants who claim that they were denied individual rights protected by the Constitution can also have their cases heard in federal court.

The second requirement concerns the parties involved in the suit: The Constitution gives certain parties special status to file claims in federal courts. If the United States is suing or being sued, the federal courts can hear the case. The federal courts have jurisdiction over cases affecting ambassadors and other agents of foreign governments and disputes between a state or one of its citizens and foreign governments or foreign citizens. Interstate conflicts also fall within the federal court's jurisdiction. These include litigation between the states, between citizens of different states, between citizens of the same state who claim lands under grants of different states, and between a state and a citizen of another state.

Of these cases, suits between citizens of different states are quite numerous and consume a great deal of federal courts' time. In order to keep minor disputes out of federal courts, Congress has passed statutes requiring these cases to involve at least $75,000 before the federal courts have jurisdiction.

Original and Appellate Jurisdiction

There are two general types of courts, each of which has jurisdiction over fundamentally different types of cases. **Courts of original jurisdiction** are the trial courts that hear cases the first time and make determinations of fact, law, and whether the plaintiff or the defendant wins. The federal district courts are courts of original jurisdiction in the federal court system; these courts try cases involving alleged violations of federal criminal laws and certain civil lawsuits under federal court jurisdiction. **Courts of appellate jurisdiction** review the decisions of lower courts that are appealed. The U.S. circuit courts of appeal have jurisdiction to hear appeals of decisions made by federal district courts and certain government agencies.

Courts typically have either original or appellate jurisdiction. The U.S. Supreme Court is unique in that it has both. Article III, Section 2 of the Constitution gives the Supreme Court original jurisdiction in cases involving ambassadors, consuls, and other public ministers and in cases in which a state is party. The Supreme Court's appellate jurisdiction is defined by Congress.

The Power of Congress to Define Jurisdiction of Federal Courts

With few exceptions, Congress sets the jurisdictional boundaries of all federal courts. Congress can

- Forbid courts to handle a certain type of case.
- Allow state and federal courts to exercise **concurrent jurisdiction;** that is, allow both state and federal courts to hear a particular type of case.
- Assign **exclusive jurisdiction;** for example, cases involving violation of federal criminal law must be heard in a federal court.

In addition to its power to allocate cases between federal and state courts, Congress also decides at which level in the federal judiciary a matter will be heard. Congress can establish lower courts, determine what cases they can hear, and regulate what matters that have initially been tried in lower courts the Supreme Court can review.

Jurisdiction Determined by Judicial Interpretation

The courts themselves also can define their power and jurisdiction. The most important power of the federal courts in the American political system is the power of **judicial review,** which is the authority to review lower court decisions and to declare laws and actions of public officials unconstitutional. The Supreme Court asserted this power in the case of *Marbury v. Madison* (1803), discussed later in this chapter. Although the power of judicial review gives courts considerable influence in shaping public policy, where and how that power is exercised is constrained by both this Constitution and Congress.

The Structure and Organization of Federal Courts

The Constitution leaves much of the structure and organization of federal courts to Congress. It calls for "one Supreme Court, and . . . such inferior courts as the Congress may . . . establish" (Article III, Section 1). Congress has created two additional levels of federal courts: district courts and courts of appeals. Congress has also established several specialized courts, such as the Court of Federal Claims and the U.S. Court of International Trade.

Statutes passed by Congress determine the number of judges serving on each court, including the Supreme Court. The Supreme Court has had nine justices since 1869, but the number has varied from as few as five in 1789 to as many as ten in 1863. The number of lower court judges is determined mainly by caseloads, so that areas with more cases filed have more judges.

The **Judicial Conference,** a committee of district and appellate court judges chaired by the chief justice of the Supreme Court, reviews the needs of the federal judiciary and makes recommendations to Congress. Congress periodically responds to these requests and passes legislation creating new judgeships. For example, in 2002 Congress passed legislation creating fifteen new district court judgeships.

Although the need for more judges to handle an increasing caseload is the primary motivation for expanding the number of judgeships, political considerations inevitably come into play. One study shows that even after the need for new judges has been established, Congress is unlikely to create new judgeships if different parties control Congress and the presidency or if it is late in the president's term (Bond 1980). The reasons are purely political. Congress does not want to give a president of the opposite party the opportunity to appoint fellow party members to new judgeships. If a presidential election is coming up, the opposing party in Congress delays expanding the number of judges in the hope that its candidate will win.

The District Courts

The United States district courts are trial courts of original jurisdiction. Although they hear certain classes of cases that are removed from state courts to federal jurisdiction and also enforce some of the actions of federal administrative agencies, these cases are not considered to have been appealed (Abraham 1993, 157–158).

The district courts are the workhorses of the federal judicial system. Approximately 90 percent of federal cases begin and end in the district courts. In these courts, spirited legal battles occur involving opposing attorneys, witnesses, and possibly a jury (parties in federal court often waive the right to a jury trial and have the judge make the decision). A single judge presides over the courtroom.

© Cunningham, Pat/Corbis Sygma

District courts like this one in Albuquerque, New Mexico, deal with antitrust suits, people accused of breaking federal criminal laws, bankruptcy proceedings, and disputes between citizens of different states involving automobile accidents, breaches of contract, and labor cases—among many other matters. This array of cases is heard by more than 650 judges located in ninety-four district courts. Every state has at least one district; and each district court has at least one judge. District judges are officials of the federal government and enforce federal laws and the U.S. Constitution, but they are oriented to states and localities.

District courts deal with a wide variety of matters. This is where the federal government brings antitrust suits and prosecutes people accused of breaking federal criminal laws. For example, the men accused of blowing up the Alfred P. Murrah Federal Building in Oklahoma City and killing 168 people in 1995 were tried in a federal district court. Bankruptcy proceedings make up a large portion of district court dockets, and the courts also hear disputes between citizens of different states involving automobile accidents, breaches of contract, and labor cases—among many other matters.

This dizzying array of cases is heard by more than 650 judges located in ninety-four district courts. Every state has at least one district; 24 states have two, three, or four districts. No district crosses state lines. Each district court has at least one judge; the Southern District of New York has the most judges—twenty-eight. The number of judges serving in a district is determined largely by caseload: Districts with heavy caseloads need more judges to process the cases in a reasonable time.

Although district judges are officials of the federal government and enforce federal laws and the U.S. Constitution, they are oriented to states and localities (Figure 15.1). Congress sets the number and boundaries of judicial districts, and the decision to draw districts that do not cross state lines has political implications. By political tradition,

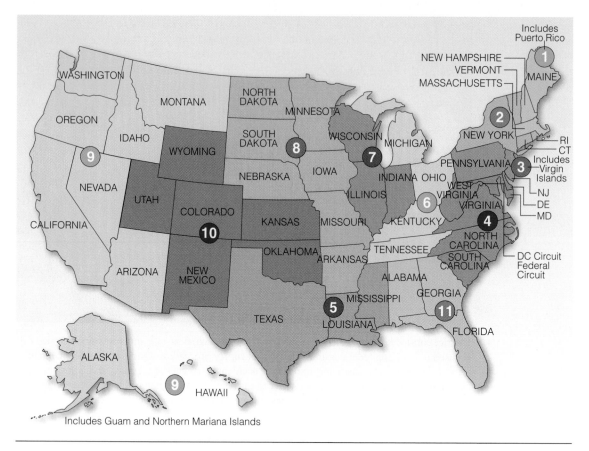

Figure 15.1
Federal District Courts and Courts of Appeal
Source:*http://www.uscourts.gov/images/CircuitMap.pdf.*

district court judges are selected from the states in which they serve, and they live there after appointment. Thus, federal district judges have strong political and social ties to the states in which they serve. District court judges occasionally are assigned to hear cases in other districts. For example, it was a visiting North Dakota district court judge who issued the 1957 injunction prohibiting Arkansas state officials from interfering with racial integration of Little Rock schools. For the most part, however, they preside over disputes arising in their own local areas.

The Courts of Appeals

The U.S. courts of appeals have only appellate jurisdiction, and they serve as the major appellate tribunals in the federal court system. They review decisions in civil and criminal cases initially heard in federal district courts and the orders and decisions of federal administrative units, particularly the independent regulatory agencies. Of the approximately 10 percent of cases decided by the district courts that are appealed, about 90 percent end in the federal courts of appeals. Thus, only a tiny proportion of federal cases go to the U.S. Supreme Court for final disposition.

There are about 200 appellate court judges serving on thirteen courts of appeals, called circuits, located in various parts of the United States.[1] The size of the courts ranges from six to twenty-eight judges depending on the caseload in the circuit. As shown in Figure 15.1, appellate courts are arranged regionally, grouping three or more states into a circuit. A court of appeals hears appeals from the district courts located within its circuit. The single exception is the Federal Circuit in Washington, DC; this court has national jurisdiction to hear appeals from specialized federal courts (such as patent cases) and the many administrative agencies. Since appellate courts hear appeals from federal courts in several states, appellate court judges tend to be less closely tied to particular states and localities than their counterparts in district courts.

The courts of appeals are **collegial courts** in which a group of judges decides the case based on a review of the record of the lower court trial. There is no jury at the appellate court level, and the appeals court does not make determinations of fact. Instead, the appellate court decides by majority vote if the trial court made any legal or procedural errors that would justify a reversal or modification of the lower court's decision.

To expedite the considerable caseload, cases are usually decided by a panel of three judges, allowing several cases to be heard at the same time by different three-judge panels. The chief judge, who is the most senior judge under the age of 65, appoints the panels. Appointments are made randomly to even out workloads and to ensure that the same judges do not always sit together on the same panel. These procedures are intended to prevent a chief judge from stacking a panel with judges who will decide a case in a particular way. The U.S. Court of Appeals for the Eleventh Circuit uses a computerized random assignment process to set the composition of every panel a year in advance (Tarr 2003, 42).

On application of the parties involved in a suit or of the judges themselves, a case can be heard **en banc,** that is, by the entire court. This occurs in fewer than 5 percent of cases; it is restricted to questions of exceptional importance or cases in which the court feels that a full tribunal is necessary to secure uniformity in its decisions or compliance with a controversial decision.

The U.S. Supreme Court

The U.S. Supreme Court sits at the top of the legal hierarchy, and it has both original and appellate jurisdiction (Figure 15.2). In practice, it has almost complete discretion over the cases it hears, accepting mainly those that have broad implications for the law or government action. The Supreme Court's appellate jurisdiction is regulated by Congress, which has established two major sources of cases for the nation's highest tribunal: (1) appeals from the U.S. courts of appeals and (2) appeals from the highest court in the states. Cases from the U.S. courts of appeals represent the final attempt to gain satisfaction by parties unhappy with decisions made in lower federal courts.

---

[1]The courts of appeals were originally staffed by Supreme Court justices who would travel to various regions of the country to hear cases. This practice was called "making the circuit," and it is where the name came from.

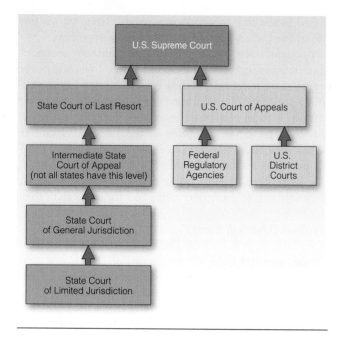

Figure 15.2
Structure of the U.S. Judicial System

Cases from state courts involve controversies that jump from state court systems to the federal court system.

The Supreme Court is the only federal court that can hear appeals from a state court and then only if there is an important constitutional issue involved. Because of the federal structure (see Chapter 3), the United States has dual judicial systems: The federal courts deal with federal law, and the state courts with state law. Federal and state courts hold concurrent jurisdiction over some matters, so there is some overlap between the two systems, but state courts are not subordinate to federal courts. State courts enforce state laws using their own legal structure, procedures, and personnel, and they independently exercise the power of judicial review in both original and appellate jurisdictions. If a case involves state matters, it starts in state court and stays in the state court system until it is finally resolved. Each state judicial system has a court of last resort (a state supreme court or its equivalent) that represents the highest level to which a case involving a question of state law may be carried.

The only way a state court case can go beyond the court of last resort in the state is if the case raises a federal question. Appeals of such cases go from the state court of last resort directly to the U.S. Supreme Court. For example, a criminal case that raises the issue of whether a state law restricting obscene materials violates an individual's First Amendment right of free speech raises an important federal question. Such a case could be appealed to the Supreme Court to rule on the constitutionality of the state law.

The justification for permitting appeals from the state supreme courts to the U.S. Supreme Court is that when state courts interpret their own constitutions, they are also interpreting the U.S. Constitution. A state constitution can provide its citizens greater protection of the basic rights guaranteed by the U.S. Constitution, but it cannot restrict those rights. Making the U.S. Supreme Court the final arbiter of all questions involving the U.S. Constitution helps ensure that its guarantees are uniformly interpreted and applied. In essence, this link makes the U.S. Supreme Court the ultimate umpire of the federal system.

The Supreme Court exercises discretion over its caseload by choosing relatively few cases for review each year. Of the approximately 7,000 cases appealed to the Supreme Court in a typical year, the Court will decide fewer than 200 on the merits, meaning the Court will actually discuss the cases and vote on decisions. Fewer than 100 cases will get a full written opinion. Thus, more than 95 percent of cases are disposed of with no formal decision.[2] Generally, the Court picks cases that raise important constitutional issues or questions of substantial political importance, or on which

---

[2]When the Court does not accept a case for review, the decision of the last court to rule stands.

different appellate circuits have issued conflicting rulings. The Court formally exercises its discretionary powers over what cases to hear by issuing a **writ of certiorari,**[3] which is granted according to the **rule of four**—that is, four of the nine justices must vote to review a case.

Like the courts of appeals, the Supreme Court is a collegial body, but it does not divide itself into separate panels to hear different cases. Justices have taken the position that the Constitution refers to one Supreme Court, not several, and that all judges should therefore participate in each case. The Court hears cases during a 36-week session from October to June. When the Court is in session, it hears oral arguments from attorneys representing opposing sides of the cases chosen for full hearings. Each side is allotted 30 minutes to make its case, but the justices frequently interrupt these presentations with questions.

Hearing oral presentations is a relatively minor part of the Supreme Court's business; the overwhelming proportion of the Court's work takes place behind the scenes. The justices spend most of their time reading and studying cases and discussing them with their colleagues and their law clerks, who are recent graduates of the nation's top law schools.

The Court decides the cases it has heard in the **conference** behind closed doors. Only the nine justices are permitted to attend a conference meeting; clerks and secretaries are not allowed in the room. The justices begin the conference meeting by shaking hands and taking their assigned seats around the conference table. The chief justice presides over the meeting and sets the agenda. Part of the conference meeting is devoted to consideration of petitions for review. The justices discuss cases that they might want to accept for review; four justices must vote to accept a case for full oral argument.

The next order of business is to discuss and vote on the cases previously argued before the Court. Traditionally, the chief justice speaks first, framing the issues presented by the case. The associate justice with the longest service on the court speaks next, and so on, with the most junior justice speaking last. The justices generally indicate how they will vote during their presentations in conference, although these votes are tentative and sometimes change during the opinion-writing stage.

After the most junior justice has spoken, the justices vote. The outcome of a case is decided by a majority vote, meaning that five of nine justices must support a position for it to become an official Court ruling. The most important decision following this vote is who gets to write the opinion setting forth the decision and the reasons behind it. If the chief justice votes with the majority, he or she decides who will write the opinion. If the case is a major one, the chief justice may assume the responsibility, but opinions are usually assigned to spread the workload among the nine justices. If the chief justice is not on the prevailing side, the most senior associate justice on the prevailing side makes the assignment.

The assignment of writing an opinion is often a delicate political decision. A controversial opinion may be assigned to the justice whose views are closest to those of the minority, the idea being that he or she may be able to win the minority justices

---

[3]There are a small number of cases that get to the Supreme Court through other procedures, including writ of appeal or by "extraordinary writ," such as habeas corpus. Although some of these cases can be appealed to the Supreme Court as a matter of right, in practice the Court has discretion about whether to hear these cases as well.

over to the majority's side. This tactic can be helpful when a premium is placed on a unanimous or nearly unanimous decision by the Court in a controversial case when the justices want maximum public acceptance.

The assignment of an opinion does not end the collegial process. Negotiation may continue as the opinion is drafted and redrafted so that a maximum number of justices will join it. The author may even adopt the suggestions and reasoning of other justices in order to attract their votes. But it is often not possible to settle differences. Most cases heard by the Supreme Court are controversial, and the justices typically hold strong views, so a unanimous decision expressed in a single opinion is often not possible. Until the 1930s, more than 80 percent of Supreme Court decisions were unanimous. Consensus on the Court has declined since. In recent years, about one-fourth to one-third of decisions have been unanimous (Abraham 1993, 202).

There are four types of opinions. Most decisions are **majority opinions** in which five or more justices agree on both which side wins and the reason for the decision. **Concurring opinions** are sometimes written by justices who agree with the result reached by the majority opinion but not the reasoning behind it. If a majority of justices cannot agree on both the outcome and the reasons, the case may be decided by a **plurality opinion** in which a majority support the outcome, but the lack of majority agreement on the reason may leave the meaning of the ruling unclear. **Dissenting opinions** are issued by justices in the minority; they disagree not only with the reasoning behind the Court's decision but also with the result. Dissenters do not always write dissenting opinions.

The Selection and Background of Federal Judges

Article III, Section 1 of the Constitution provides for all federal judges to be nominated by the president and confirmed by the Senate. Once confirmed, federal judges serve for "terms of good behavior" (which typically means a lifetime appointment), and their salaries cannot be reduced while they serve. These provisions were intended to establish an independent judiciary that would be insulated from political pressure and the electoral process so that judges could make decisions to protect the Constitution and individual liberty that might be unpopular with the president, Congress, or the public.

The Constitution is silent regarding qualifications to serve as a Supreme Court justice. Neither are there statutory qualifications. Unlike presidents and members of Congress, Supreme Court justices do not have to be U.S. citizens or meet a minimum age requirement. There is not even a legal requirement for justices to be lawyers. The qualifications necessary to serve on a federal court are left to the president's judgment, checked by the need to secure confirmation by a majority of the Senate.

Presidents, members of Congress, and the public, however, have developed expectations about the training and qualifications of federal judges. First, all federal judges have had legal training, and it is unimaginable that anyone without legal education would be appointed and confirmed.[4] For appointment to the Supreme Court, a degree

---

[4]Early in the nation's history, individuals did not have to attend law school to be admitted to the bar and practice law. Instead, they would "read" the law under the tutorship of a member of the bar for several years. Only 59 of the 108 Supreme Court justices attended law school, and it was not until 1957 that all the justices had law degrees.

from just any law school will not do. Graduates from the nation's most prestigious law schools dominate the list of Supreme Court justices: The 2004 Court had four graduates from Harvard, two from Stanford, and one each from Yale, Columbia, and Northwestern.[5]

A second quality that federal judges have in common is a career in public service. Almost all Supreme Court justices engaged in public service or politics prior to their appointment. Through such activity, they developed ties to presidents and senators who later influenced their appointments. District court judges, for example, have been referred to as "lawyers who know a United States senator." As might be expected, one of the most prevalent kinds of previous public service is that connected with the courts themselves. Many federal judges have served as state judges or district attorneys, and judges serving in higher federal courts often served on lower federal courts.

Finally, although there are no legal age requirements, it is unlikely that individuals who are very young or very old would be considered. Viable candidates for appointment to the federal judiciary, especially the Supreme Court, are those who have distinguished themselves in the legal profession, politics, and public service—and successful careers take time. Because presidents want to make appointments that will affect the Court for a long time, they are unlikely to select individuals of advanced age whose service may be cut short by illness or retirement.

A consequence of these expectations is that judicial appointees tend to be white, male, and wealthy. As Figure 15.3 shows, President Jimmy Carter (1977–1980) was the first president to appoint significant numbers of women, African Americans, and Latinos to the federal courts (that is, district courts and courts of appeal). Presidents who followed also increased diversity on the federal bench, but with varying success. Bill Clinton made one of the more concerted presidential efforts to increase diversity on the federal bench; during his two terms, Clinton's district and appellate court appointments were 29 percent female, 17 percent African American, 7 percent Latino, and 1.4 percent Asian. The senior Bush and his son George W. Bush appointed about 20 percent women. Appointment of African Americans decreased somewhat after Clinton, but the proportion is still higher than was the case in the 1960s and 1970s. Appointment of Latinos has ranged from about 4 to 6 percent for recent presidents. Very few Asian Americans have been appointed to the federal bench. Although gender and racial diversity on federal courts have increased in the last couple of decades, these appointees are still disproportionately wealthy. For example, 47 percent of Clinton's judicial appointments confirmed in 1997 had a net worth of more than $1 million.

Thus, the pool of prospective Supreme Court justices is limited to the small proportion of the population with legal training mostly from the elite universities, in the prime of distinguished careers in law and politics, and with the appropriate character and integrity. Thousands of individuals satisfy these minimal qualifications. When making appointments from among this relatively elite pool, political considerations inevitably influence presidents' choices. These political considerations include party affiliation and philosophy and balancing the representativeness of the Court. Presidents rarely ignore politics and make appointments solely on judicial experience and merit.

---

[5]The elite education starts before law school. Most of the current Supreme Court justices got their undergraduate degrees at the same elite schools: Harvard (three), Stanford (three), the University of Chicago, and Cornell. Justice Clarence Thomas attended a Catholic school, Holy Cross, before going to Yale for his law degree.

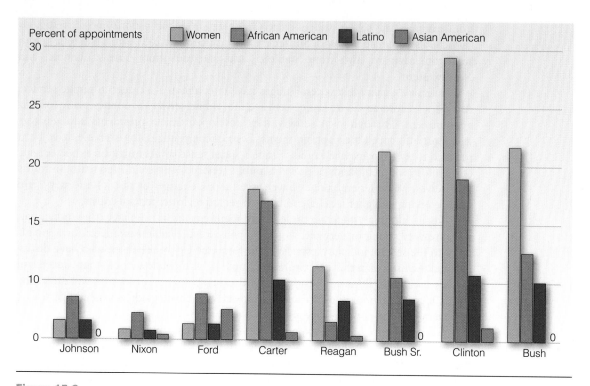

Figure 15.3
Appointments of Women and Minorities to the Federal Courts

Party Affiliation and Philosophy

The most important consideration in making appointments to the Supreme Court and the lower federal courts is the nominee's political party and philosophy. With few exceptions, presidents appoint individuals of their political party who share their political philosophy. Of the 108 Supreme Court justices who have served as of 2004, close to 90 percent have been of the same party as the president who appointed them. This partisan selection process is not a recent phenomenon. Court appointments during the nation's first party period were even more partisan than they are today. The Federalist presidents—George Washington and John Adams—appointed only Federalists to the Court; The Democratic-Republican presidents—Thomas Jefferson, James Madison, James Monroe, and John Quincy Adams—appointed only Democratic-Republicans. Appointments to federal district courts and courts of appeals are also highly partisan—nearly 90 percent are the same party as the president.

At least two considerations explain the importance of party in making appointments to the federal judiciary. First, old-fashioned patronage considerations lead presidents to appoint members of their own party. Federal judgeships are exceptional jobs: Judges have power and prestige; they have great job security; and they are well paid.[6] Some of the individuals who have the requisite qualifications are Democrats, and others are Republicans; some are conservative, and others are liberal. When there are many equally qualified individuals who helped the president get elected, there is generally no need for a president to reward a well-qualified person of the opposite party and philosophy who worked against the president's election.

Second, policy considerations come into play. Presidents have term limits: They serve for four or eight years and then must leave office. Since federal judges serve for life, if presidents select wisely, their judicial appointees will be making important decisions that influence the course of public policy for decades after they have left office.

In the case of district court judges, another consideration comes into play. Nominations to U.S. district courts usually follow the practice of **senatorial courtesy,** which gives senators from the state where the vacancy occurs power to influence who is appointed. Indeed, the practice actually turns the appointment process around in these cases. Because no district court boundary crosses state lines, senators from states with vacancies expect to recommend individuals who are qualified and available for the job. The president retains veto power, ruling out nominees who are politically offensive or who fail to meet minimum qualifications. But if the president fails to follow the home state senators' recommendations, the slighted senator may object to the nomination and prevent it from coming to the floor for a confirmation vote. Traditionally, senatorial courtesy worked within a party, and opposite party senators could not block a nomination. The partisan nature of senatorial courtesy tended to reinforce same-party appointments. Only in unusual circumstances would a senator recommend that the president appoint someone of the opposite party who probably worked against the senator's election.

The procedure changed during the Clinton administration. The Senate Judiciary Committee would not hold confirmation hearings on judicial nominees who did not have approval of both home state senators regardless of party. This change allowed Republican senators to block many of President Clinton's judicial nominees. The procedure changed again after President G. W. Bush took office in 2001. The Judiciary Committee went back to the practice of requiring approval of only one home state senator (Edsall 2001; Masters 2001). This change made it more difficult for Democrats to block Bush's judicial nominees.

Senatorial courtesy is less of a consideration for appointments to appellate courts that hear cases from several states. There is, however, a tendency for each state in the circuit to get a certain number of judges, and the senators from those states do exercise some influence (Masters 2001). Senatorial courtesy does not come into play for appointments to the Supreme Court because it hears cases from the entire nation.

Cross-party appointments occur occasionally to further a political purpose. One such case occurred in 1985 when Republican Senator Phil Gramm of Texas exercised senatorial courtesy to get President Ronald Reagan to appoint Texas Democratic Representative Sam B. Hall to a federal judgeship. Gramm engineered this cross-party appointment in the hope that a Republican would win the special election in Hall's

---

[6]Supreme Court justices earn $194,300; appellate court and district court judges earn $167,300 and $158,100, respectively (as of September 2004). These salaries are lower than those of lawyers at the nation's top law firms, which is where most federal judges would work if they were not judges. Many take significant cuts in pay to become federal judges.

district, which was populated with conservative Democrats. Although the Democrats held on to the seat, political motivations account for this cross-party exercise of senatorial courtesy.

When presidents cross party lines for Supreme Court appointments, they typically choose individuals who share their political ideology. Republican President William Howard Taft, for example, appointed two southern Democrats, Horace Lurton and Joseph R. Lamar, to the Court. Both men were Taft's personal friends and shared his conservative ideology. Taft also hoped that the appointment of Lurton, a Confederate Army veteran, would encourage southern political leaders who held key leadership positions in Congress to help him get his legislative program passed (Abraham 1993, 67).

Balancing the Representativeness of the Court

Other political criteria are less important than party and come into play only sporadically. Concerns about balancing the representativeness of the Supreme Court occasionally influence appointments. The Supreme Court is not intended to be a representative institution. In fact, the Court is often in the position of declaring unconstitutional a law favored by the majority of Americans because it violates a fundamental individual right protected by the Constitution. Nevertheless, there is often a strong feeling that the Supreme Court should have representatives of different regions, religions, races, and genders. (See the Living the Promise feature "Milestones of Judicial Service.")

Geography   Early in the nation's history, geographical considerations were often important in making appointments to the Supreme Court. Early presidents felt that having justices from the different regions of the country would help establish the legitimacy of the Court. As the nation expanded, presidents sometimes felt a political need to appoint justices from new states, as when Republican President Abraham Lincoln appointed Californian Steven J. Field, who was a Democrat, in 1863. Until 1891, Supreme Court justices had to ride the circuit to serve on the courts of appeals, which reinforced geographical considerations (O'Brien 1996, 70).

In the 20th century, geography became less important in Supreme Court appointments. The most recent example of geographical influence took place when President Richard Nixon announced his intention to appoint a "southern strict-constructionist" to the Court in 1969. The term *strict-constructionist* was understood to mean a conservative who would resist and perhaps even reverse some of the Warren Court's liberal rulings. The focus on a southerner was to attract conservative white Democratic voters in the South to help build a new Republican majority. After the Senate rejected Nixon's first two nominations, both from the South, he appointed Harry Blackmun of Minnesota. Although Nixon did eventually get Lewis Powell of Virginia confirmed, his political goal of attracting conservative southern Democrats to the Republican Party was stalled by the Watergate Scandal, which forced him to resign and contributed to the election of Democrat Jimmy Carter in 1976.

Religion   Nearly 90 percent of Supreme Court justices have been Protestant. For a long time, there was a historical pattern of having a "Roman Catholic seat" and

LIVING THE PROMISE
Milestones of Judicial Service

The following is an excerpt listing some important firsts in judicial appointments.

Oldest Judges

- The oldest serving federal judge was Joseph W. Woodrough, who was serving as a senior judge of the U.S. Court of Appeals for the Eighth Circuit when he died at the age of 104 on October 2, 1977.
- The oldest serving active judge was Giles S. Rich, who served on the U.S. Court of Appeals for the Federal Circuit until his death at the age of 95 in June 1999.
- The oldest serving Supreme Court justice was Oliver Wendell Holmes, who was 90 years, 10 months when he retired on January 12, 1932.

Youngest Judges

- The youngest federal judge was Thomas Jefferson Boynton, who was 25 when Abraham Lincoln issued him a recess appointment to the U.S. District Court for the Southern District of Florida on October 19, 1863.
- The youngest judge appointed to a U.S. court of appeals was William Howard Taft, who was 34 when he was commissioned a judge of the Sixth Circuit Court of Appeals on March 17, 1892.
- The youngest justice on the Supreme Court was Joseph Story, who was 32 when he received his commission on November 18, 1811.

Longest Serving Judges

- Joseph W. Woodrough served a record sixty-one years as a federal judge. He served on the U.S. District Court for the District of Nebraska from 1916 to 1933 and on the U.S. Court of Appeals for the Eighth Circuit from 1933 until 1977. He took senior status in 1961.
- Henry Potter was the longest serving judge on a single court and the longest serving active judge. He served on the U.S. District Courts for North Carolina from 1802 to 1857. He previously served on the U.S. Circuit Court for the Fifth Circuit from May of 1801 until April of 1802.
- The longest serving judge on a U.S. court of appeals was Albert B. Maris, who served on the U.S. Court of Appeals for the Third Circuit from June of 1938 until his death in February 1989. Maris, who took senior status in 1958, also served on the U.S. District Court for the Eastern District of Pennsylvania from 1936 to 1938.
- William O. Douglas was the longest serving Supreme Court justice. He sat on the Court from 1939 to 1975.

First Women Judges

- Florence Allen was the first woman to serve on a U.S. court of appeals. She was appointed to the U.S. Circuit Court of Appeals for the Sixth Circuit in 1934.
- Burnita Shelton Matthews became the first woman to serve on a U.S. district court when Harry Truman issued her a recess appointment to the district court for the District of Columbia in October 1949. The Senate confirmed her nomination in April 1950.
- Sandra Day O'Connor was the first woman to serve as a Justice of the Supreme Court of the United States. She was appointed in 1981.

First African American Judges

- William Henry Hastie became the first African American to serve as a judge . . . when he was appointed to the U.S. Court of Appeals for the Third Circuit in 1950. Hastie had served a fixed term as judge of the U.S. District Court for the Virgin Islands from 1937 to 1939.
- The first African American to serve on U.S. district court as a judge . . . was James B. Parsons, who was appointed to the U.S. District Court for the Northern District of Illinois in 1961.
- Thurgood Marshall was the first African American justice on the Supreme Court of the United States. He was appointed in 1967. Marshall previously served as a judge on the U.S. Court of Appeals for the Second Circuit.

First Latino Judge

- Reynaldo G. Garza became the first Latino federal judge when he was appointed to the U.S. District Court for the Southern District of Texas in 1961. Garza also became the first Latino judge on a U.S. Court of Appeals when he was appointed to the Fifth Circuit court of appeals in 1979.

continued

Milestones of Judicial Service   *continued*

First Asian American Judge

- Herbert Choy became the first Asian American to serve as a judge on a U.S. court of appeals when he was appointed to the U.S. Court of Appeals for the Ninth Circuit in 1971.
- Dick Wong became the first Asian American to serve on a U.S. district court when he was appointed to the district court for the District of Hawaii in 1975.

First Native American Judge

- Billy Michael Burrage became the first Native American federal judge when he was appointed to the U.S. District Courts for the Northern, Eastern & Western Districts of Oklahoma in 1994.

First Federal Judge to Be Elected President

- William Howard Taft in 1908 became the first and only former federal judge to be elected president. Taft served as judge of the U.S. Circuit Court of Appeals for the Sixth Circuit from 1892 to 1900. Taft also became the only former president to serve on a federal court when he became chief justice of the United States in 1921.

First Federal Judge Elevated to the U.S. Supreme Court

- Robert Trimble served as judge of the U.S. District Court in Kentucky from 1817 to 1826 when he became the first federal judge to be nominated and confirmed as a justice of the Supreme Court. He served only two years before he died at the age of 51. A total of thirty-one Supreme Court justices have previously served as a federal judge. With the appointment of Harry Blackmun in 1971, the Supreme Court for the first time had a majority of justices with experience on the lower federal courts.

Source: Federal Judicial Center. *History of the Federal Judiciary.* http://www.fjc.gov.

a "Jewish seat" on the Court (Abraham 1993, 65). Chief Justice Roger B. Taney was the first Catholic appointed, in 1835, and in 1916 Louis D. Brandeis became the first Jewish justice. Breaking the religion barrier was controversial. Brandeis, for example, was condemned as unfit to be a Supreme Court justice in a public statement signed by former presidents of the American Bar Association, and anti-Semitism was barely concealed in the movement to deny his appointment. He is now recognized as one of the great Supreme Court justices.

Religion has become much less of a factor in the contemporary era, and there is no longer much of a demonstrable effort to ensure religious balance on the Court. There had been no Catholic on the Court for several years when President Dwight Eisenhower appointed William Brennan, a Democrat and a Catholic, in 1956. Brennan was a highly respected attorney, but the appointment of an eastern Catholic was seen as potentially helping Eisenhower in the upcoming election (Abraham 1993, 70). Three current justices are Catholic: Anthony Kennedy, Antonin Scalia, and Clarence Thomas. The tradition of the Jewish seat was broken in 1970 when President Richard Nixon filled the vacancy created by the resignation of Abe Fortas with a Protestant, and he later named two other Protestants to the Court. As do all presidents, Nixon claimed that religion was irrelevant and that he was looking for the best-qualified person. There were no Jews on the Court until 1993, when President Clinton appointed Ruth Bader Ginsburg. His second appointee, Stephen Breyer, is also Jewish. There was no public discussion of religion in either case. Although religion has not been a consideration in recent appointments to the Supreme Court, it continues to be at the center of some political conflicts, and it may again become an issue in future appointments.

The Supreme Court is not intended to be a representative institution. In fact, the Court is often in the position of declaring unconstitutional a law favored by the majority of Americans because it violates a fundamental individual right protected by the Constitution. Nevertheless, there is often a strong feeling that the Supreme Court should have representatives of different regions, religions, races, and genders. In 1967, the color barrier on the Court was broken by the appointment of Thurgood Marshall (seen here) by President Lyndon Johnson. When Justice Marshall retired, he was replaced by Clarence Thomas, who is also African American.

Race and Ethnicity   Only two African Americans have served on the Supreme Court. The color barrier on the Court was broken in 1967 when President Lyndon Johnson appointed Thurgood Marshall, saying: "I believe it is the right thing to do, the right time to do it, the right man, and the right place." There is some indication that there is now an African American seat on the Court. When Justice Marshall retired in 1991, George Bush appointed Clarence Thomas, who had the right credentials: He is conservative, Republican, has a law degree from Yale—and he is African American. Now that the color barrier has been broken, it is only a matter of time before a Latino or an Asian American justice is appointed as the political power of these groups increases.

Gender   Two women have been appointed to the Supreme Court. The gender barrier was broken in 1981 when President Ronald Reagan appointed Sandra Day O'Connor. Although she was eminently qualified for the job, having graduated near the top of her class at Stanford—where she and Chief Justice Rehnquist had been classmates—the political motivation for this appointment was paramount. During the 1980 presidential campaign, women's groups criticized Reagan for his opposition to the proposed Equal Rights Amendment. In an attempt to reduce the growing gender gap, Reagan made a campaign promise: "One of the first Supreme Court vacancies in my administration will be filled by the most qualified woman I can find." Less than six months into his first year, Reagan fulfilled this campaign promise. President Clinton's first appointment to the Court was also a woman, Justice Ruth Bader Ginsburg. With two women currently serving, the Supreme Court comes closer to reflecting the gender division in the nation than does Congress: Women make up 51 percent of the population, 22 percent of the Supreme Court, and about 14 percent of the House and Senate (in the 108th Congress, 2003–2004).

Judicial Experience and Merit

It is rare for a president to ignore political considerations and to make an appointment based exclusively on judicial experience and merit. Of course, no president wants to appoint an unqualified person to the Supreme Court, so in a sense merit is always the first consideration. In the rare instances when a president has nominated someone with questionable credentials, the Senate typically has blocked the appointment. With few exceptions, Supreme Court justices have been competent and intelligent. (See the Living the Promise feature "The Politics of Getting to the Supreme Court.")

The connection between judicial experience and merit is tenuous at best. Presidents, senators, and the American Bar Association frequently view service on a lower federal or state court as a prerequisite for "promotion" to the nation's highest court. However, the Supreme Court is unique, and it performs a very different role than trial courts or even courts of appeals. Lower courts deal with the details of the cases at hand: facts and evidence, guilt and innocence. The Supreme Court addresses disputes over the most fundamental issues of politics and society: the meaning of broad clauses in the Constitution, the basic rights of individuals and society. Experience as a trial judge is not necessarily relevant to resolving disputes over such fundamental questions. Justice Felix Frankfurter boldly asserted, "One is entitled to say without qualification that the correlation between prior judicial experience and fitness for the Supreme Court is zero" (1957, 781). Rather, the job of Supreme Court justice requires a "combination of philosopher, historian, and prophet" (Abraham 1993, 59).

About 62 percent of Supreme Court justices have had at least some prior judicial experience before appointment to the Court. Yet, several great justices had no prior experience as judges, including Joseph Story (appointed 1812), Charles Evans Hughes (appointed 1910), Louis Brandeis (appointed 1916), Harlan Stone (appointed 1925), and Felix Frankfurter (appointed 1939). Among the "great" justices, only Oliver Wendell Holmes, Jr. (appointed 1902), and Benjamin Cardozo (appointed 1932) had extensive prior judicial experience, but as Frankfurter argued, their greatness "derived not from their judicial experience but from the fact they were . . . thinkers, and more particularly, legal philosophers."

There has been only one clear case in which merit considerations were strong enough to push aside all the political concerns. This case is President Herbert Hoover's appointment of Benjamin Cardozo to the Court. Early in 1932, Oliver Wendell Holmes, Jr., resigned. Hoover's initial inclination was to appoint a well-qualified individual who shared his views as a conservative Republican to fill the vacancy. Cardozo was a distinguished jurist who was uniformly admired in the legal community. He was

LIVING THE PROMISE
The Politics of Getting to the Supreme Court

Douglas Ginsburg did not get the job because he smoked dope in college. Levi Lincoln turned down the job because of his failing eyesight. Robert Bork lost the job and became a verb instead.

The job in question was Supreme Court justice, which by most benchmarks is a pretty good gig. The pay is around $200,000—a lot by most people's standards, but less than top legal talent gets in the most prestigious law firms. Still, [you] can't argue with the job security—once you have the job, you have it for life.

Getting to the Supreme Court, though, is not easy. You usually need top law school credentials, a distinguished career as a jurist, a president who likes your record and judicial philosophy, some appeal to an important political constituency, and an accommodating U.S. Senate that will confirm the nomination. Oh yes, first you usually need another justice to either die or retire so the job is available. You also need to survive the politics that comes with a nomination to the Supreme Court, and those politics can be pretty brutal.

Between George Washington taking the oath of office and George W. Bush's first day as chief executive, presidents have nominated about 150 people to be Supreme Court justices. In the majority of cases, those nominated have accepted the opportunity to gain one of the most influential positions in the American political system. Some, like Levi Lincoln (who was nominated by James Madison), had their reasons for declining the president's offer.

A few have accepted the official nomination, only to withdraw under pressure. This included Ginsburg, who was nominated by President Ronald Reagan and created a public controversy by admitting that he'd smoked marijuana as a college student. Ginsburg withdrew after it became clear that the public was not comfortable with the notion of a Supreme Court justice using drugs recreationally, even if it was decades ago as a college student.

Ginsburg was actually Reagan's second choice. His first choice was Robert Bork, who was even more controversial because he had a long record of provocative legal arguments, virtually all of them promoting a very conservative interpretation of the Constitution. This record alarmed a wide range of special interests who mobilized a public campaign against him, and he failed to gain confirmation in a Senate vote.

The debate over whether Bork was fit to serve as a Supreme Court justice was so caustic that his supporters coined the verb "bork" to describe the action of blocking a court nominee or subjecting a public figure to unfair media criticism. The third time proved to be the charm for Reagan. After Bork's nomination went down to defeat in the Senate and Ginsburg's went up in smoke, he nominated Anthony Kennedy, whose confirmation was comparatively smooth. Kennedy was not borked.

Reagan was far from the only president to have problems getting a Supreme Court nominee confirmed. Eleven presidents have had at least one Supreme Court nominee defeated, and Bork's may not even be the most famous (or infamous). A serious contender would have to be Richard Nixon's 1970 nomination of G. Harold Carswell. Carswell was controversial because he had a segregationist past and was considered by many to be a mediocre candidate. Carswell's case was not helped by supporters like U.S. Senator Roman Hruska (R-Neb), who said even if Carswell was mediocre, there were lots of mediocre people in the country and "they are entitled to a little representation, aren't they?" Not exactly a convincing argument for appointing someone to one of the most important positions in government.

All this goes to show that the Supreme Court has one of toughest job interviews in politics.

Sources: King, Florence. 1997. "Misanthrope's Corner." *National Review. http://www.nationalreview.com/22dec97/ gimlet122297.html.* Accessed September 15, 2004; "Defeated Nominees to the U.S. Supreme Court." WordIQ.com: *http://www.wordiq.com/definition/Defeated_ nominees_to_the_U.S._Supreme_Court.* Accessed September 15, 2004.

the logical successor to the great Holmes. However, Cardozo was a Democrat and a liberal; he was from New York, and there were already two New Yorkers on the Court; he was Jewish, and that "seat" was already occupied by Brandeis. Hoover compiled a short list of conservative, western Republicans to nominate, but widespread support for Cardozo compelled the president to add his name to the list. Hoover then asked Republican Senator William E. Borah of Idaho for advice. The President handed Borah his list with Cardozo's name ranked last. Borah replied, "Your list is all right, but you handed it to me upside down" (Abraham 1993, 69). Hoover appointed Cardozo based on merit, knowing that this liberal Democrat would use his considerable intellect to influence the Court to make decisions contrary to Hoover's conservative values.

Confirmation Politics in the Senate

Deciding who will wield the power of judicial review is an enormously important decision. The careers of federal judges often go well beyond those of the presidents who nominated them and the senators who confirmed them. In other words, selecting someone to exercise judicial power has implications far beyond the next election or

Because the makeup of the federal bench is one of a president's biggest legacies, it is not surprising that the selection and confirmation of judges is a politicized process. The Senate takes its power to confirm judicial appointments seriously, and the confirmation process has lengthened exponentially over the last several years. Here President Bush presents his appointments to federal judiciary positions in 2001; not all of these appointments were approved.

© Reuters/Corbis

administration. Because the makeup of the federal bench is one of a president's biggest legacies, it is not surprising that the selection and confirmation of judges is a politicized process.

The Senate takes its power to confirm judicial appointments seriously. Of the 145 Supreme Court nominees forwarded to the Senate, about one-fifth were not confirmed. During the nation's first century, the Senate blocked Supreme Court nominations with some regularity; and twenty-two Supreme Court nominees failed in the 106 years from the founding to 1894. Appointments came a little easier for presidents during much of the nation's second century, and "the confirmation process was distinguished by presidential prerogative to fill vacancies on the Supreme Court" (Silverstein 1994, 3). From 1895 to 1967, presidents made forty-five nominations to the Supreme Court. Only one—John J. Parker in 1930—failed to gain confirmation. Since the late 1960s, the process of getting federal judges confirmed has become more politicized, and the Senate has once again become less deferential to presidents' preferences.

The shift from presidential prerogative to a more partisan and political process has its roots in procedural changes that took place in the mid-1950s. Before 1955, Harlin Fiske Stone in 1925 and Felix Frankfurter in 1939 were the only two Supreme Court nominees to testify before the Senate Judiciary Committee. Since then, nominees have been expected to go before the committee to answer questions about their judicial philosophies and their opinions on specific legal issues. This tradition has thrust Supreme Court nominees into the controversial political issues of the day as they are asked to publicly state their positions on, for example, the constitutionality of abortion and affirmative action. In recent decades, several Supreme Court nominees have seen their prospects founder in the Senate as a result of partisan and ideological overtones in the selection of judges.

Because the Supreme Court has played an increasingly significant role in American political life in the past several decades, the political stakes in Supreme Court nominations have increased. It was the Supreme Court that decided that abortion was a private decision subject to only limited regulation by the government, that law enforcement agencies had to inform people taken into custody of their rights, that prayer and Bible-reading in public schools violated the constitutional requirement of separation of church and state, and that legislative districts must be equal in population. As the ideological stakes increased, presidents have overtly politicized the nomination process. Both Ronald Reagan and the senior Bush made campaign promises to appoint conservative judges, particularly judges who opposed abortion. Reagan made good-faith efforts to deliver on his promise, even going to the extreme of screening judicial appointments for ideological consistency with his conservative agenda (Goldman 1985). Such openly political moves were justified on the grounds that they were needed to counter the liberal drift of the Court in the preceding two decades. But they invited an opposing political agenda from Democrats and from activists who wanted the Court to defend and uphold its rulings on civil rights, abortion rights, and similar issues. These two agendas clashed in a very public and partisan manner during confirmation hearings before the Senate Judiciary Committee from the 1980s to the 2000s.

The conflict became increasingly acrimonious during the second Clinton administration. As noted above, during the Clinton administration the Judiciary Committee changed the practice of senatorial courtesy to require approval of both home-state senators, including Republicans, before holding confirmation hearings on judicial nominees.

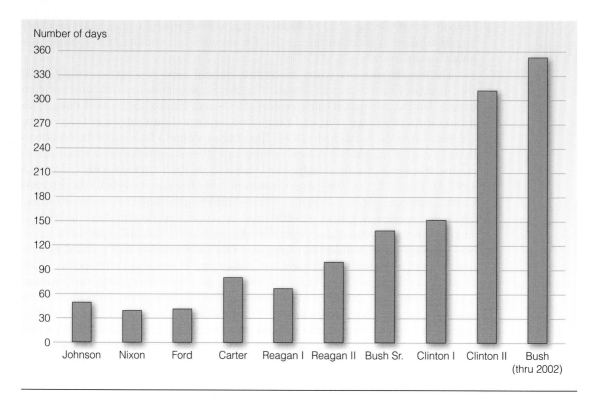

Figure 15.4

Increasing Time to Confirm Judicial Nominees

Source: Bond, Jon R., Richard Fleisher, and Glen S. Krutz. 2004. "The Presumption of Success on Presidential Appointments Reconsidered: How Maligned Neglect Has Become the Primary Method of Defeating Nominees." Texas A&M University. Typescript.

This change resulted in a lengthening of the confirmation process. The acrimony continued into the Bush administration as Democrats retaliated. As Figure 15.4 shows, the average length of the confirmation process for Supreme Court and appellate court judges has increased exponentially since the 1960s. The average length of the confirmation process was about 1 month during the Johnson, Nixon, and Ford administrations; it doubled to about 2 or 3 months during the Carter and Reagan administrations; it doubled again to about 5 months during the senior Bush and the first Clinton term; and it doubled yet again to about 10 months in Clinton's second term. During his first two years in office, President George W. Bush's nominees to federal appeals courts waited an average of nearly a year.

Judicial Decision Making

Presidents are periodically disappointed by the decisions of their appointees. President Eisenhower, for example, was bitterly disappointed by his appointment of Earl Warren as chief justice in 1953 (White 1982). There was little indication in Warren's background as a Republican and a prosecutor that he would become the leader of one of the most liberal, activist courts in the nation's history. Under his leadership, the Supreme Court compiled a long list of decisions that attracted the wrath of conservatives. But once a justice is appointed, there is little a president can do about that appointee's decisions. The Court's decision permitting a sexual harassment lawsuit to proceed against President Bill Clinton was unanimous, meaning that both of his appointees voted in favor of it. President Truman once observed that "packing the Supreme Court simply can't be done. . . . I've tried and it won't work. . . . Whenever you put a man on the Supreme Court, he ceases to be your friend" (quoted in Abraham 1993, 74).

Political scientists who study the courts often debate whether judicial decision making is better explained by a legal model or an attitudinal model. **The legal model,** adapted from the law school tradition, argues that judges set aside their own values and make decisions based solely on legal criteria: the evidence, the law, and the Constitution. The **attitudinal model** suggests that a judge's personal ideological values best explain how he or she rules (Segal and Spaeth 1993). It is clear that both legal and attitudinal criteria affect judicial decision making. Some areas of the law are well established, so that Democrats and Republicans, liberals and conservatives come to the same conclusions about the proper decisions. The fact that one-fourth to one-third of Supreme Court decisions are unanimous is clear evidence that legal criteria are a strong influence on judicial decisions.

If judicial decisions were politically neutral and not influenced by the political values of judges, all the political maneuvering in the appointment and confirmation process would be misdirected. But judges' personal attitudes do come into play. Many cases involve gray areas of the law that are not well settled and that involve issues about which reasonable, thoughtful people disagree. In such cases, there is a tendency for a judge's partisan and ideological values to influence the decision. Democratic judges tend to make more liberal decisions, while Republican judges tend to make more conservative decisions. These differences are tendencies; partisan and ideological differences in judicial behavior are not nearly as strong as they are for presidents and members of Congress.

Judges invariably deny that their personal political values influence their decisions. Their legal training stresses that judges are supposed to be politically neutral and impartial. And judges no doubt attempt to put aside their own personal values and biases when they decide cases. But try as they may, the human beings who serve as judges do not become legal automatons when they put on their judicial robes. When gray areas of the law are involved, judges' backgrounds and personal values influence which arguments and which parts of the evidence they find most persuasive as they consider the facts, the evidence, and the meaning of the law.

Political scientists have found clear evidence that attitudes influence judicial decisions by analyzing how they vote. A judge's vote is not a direct indicator of attitudes. Nevertheless, if we find significant differences in how judges vote on controversial issues, then it is reasonable to infer that their personal values influence how they vote. Figure 15.5 shows how often members of the Supreme Court cast liberal votes on non-unanimous civil liberties cases. The current (as of 2004) Court is divided into three distinct voting blocks:

- On the left are four justices (Souter, Stevens, Ginsburg, and Breyer) who vote on the liberal side of civil liberties questions more than 60 percent of the time.
- On the right are three justices (Rehnquist, Scalia, and Thomas) who cast liberal votes only about 25 percent of the time.
- In the middle are two justices (O'Connor and Kennedy) who cast liberal votes about 40 percent of the time.

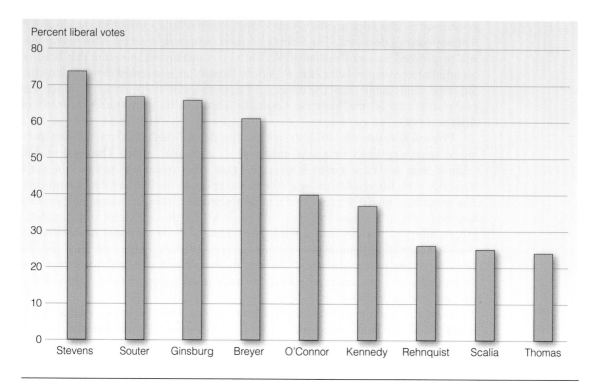

Figure 15.5
Liberal votes of Supreme Court Justices in Civil Liberties Cases
Source: By the authors, based on data from Epstein, Segal, Spaeth, and Walker, 2003, 490–523.

Because it takes five votes to decide a case, these two moderate justices hold the balance of power to determine the outcome of controversial civil liberties cases.

President Truman's observation about not being able to "pack" the Court is only partially correct. Consistent with Truman's view, there are some surprises among the current members of the Court. Republican Presidents Ford and the senior Bush appointed fellow Republicans Stevens and Souter to the Court, expecting that that they would be moderate conservatives; Stevens and Souter turned out to be the two most liberal Justices. Most justices, however, generally vote as their backgrounds and the presidents who appointed them might have predicted. Although President Clinton may have been disappointed with their votes allowing the sexual harassment lawsuit against him to proceed, Justices Ginsburg and Breyer have generally liberal records that match expectations. Similarly, the three most conservative justices—Rehnquist, Scalia, and Thomas—were appointed by Republican presidents in hopes of moving the Court in a more conservative direction. Partisan differences also show in the behavior of lower court judges—Democratic judges are more likely to make liberal decisions than are Republican judges (Carp, Stidham, and Manning 2004, 158–163).

In addition to the influence on judges' ideological attitudes, interest groups also attempt to affect judicial decision making. Interest groups trying to advance their interests through the judicial process have become increasingly common in recent years. Political scientists Gregory Caldeira and John Wright (1990) find that the Court is open to a wide range of interests, and the Court's continued willingness to permit this participation is "tacit recognition that most matters before the justices have vast social, political, and economic ramifications. . . ."

As discussed in Chapter 6, interest groups attempt to influence judicial decision making by filing *amicus curiae* briefs—that is, briefs filed by groups that are not actual parties to a case but have an interest in the outcome. Political scientists have found evidence that *amicus curiae* briefs present new information not contained in the parties' briefs. The Court accepts these new arguments fairly often, though not as often as it accepts the parties' arguments (Spriggs and Wahlbeck 1997).

Judicial Review in a Democratic Society

Both the law and judges' personal values influence judicial decisions. Because court decisions decide who gets what, when, and how, they are a type of public policy. The power of judicial review allows the courts to play a crucial role in the policymaking process.

The Constitution is especially vague on the power of federal courts. It calls for judicial power to be exercised by a Supreme Court and lower courts created by Congress, and it sets up some basic jurisdictional guidelines. But the Constitution never specifies exactly what rights and responsibilities are encompassed by the term *judicial power.* The Founders seemed to expect the judiciary to play an important role in the political system, but they provided only a rudimentary sketch of what that role should be.

In *Federalist* Number 78, Alexander Hamilton did indicate that the federal courts would have the power to overturn laws that violated the Constitution. Hamilton argued that legislators cannot be trusted to always respect the limitations placed on them by the Constitution, and in such cases the courts were obligated to intervene and protect the rights of people. Hamilton similarly argued that the people cannot be entirely trusted and that majorities might on occasion threaten the rights of minorities. Again, Hamilton argued it was up to the courts to step in and protect the fundamental rights guaranteed by the Constitution. In arguing for the right of the courts to declare acts of Congress invalid, Hamilton saw the courts as a bulwark against the "turbulence and follies of democracy."

But Hamilton's views were not universally held, and they are not forthrightly expressed in the Constitution. Rather, the Supreme Court itself claimed the power of judicial review of lower court decisions, laws, and actions of public officials. It is hard to overstate the importance of judicial review to the role of the courts in the American political system. Judicial review means that the courts are more than a place to resolve legal disputes. Instead, the judiciary is a policymaking institution in its own right.

In exercising judicial review, a court regards the Constitution as being superior to ordinary laws or executive and judicial decrees. Article VI established the Constitution as the "supreme law of the land," and judges and legislators take an oath to uphold the Constitution. In determining that a law is unconstitutional and therefore invalid, the court must find that a legislature, an executive, or a judge has done something prohibited or not authorized by the Constitution.

The power of a court to set aside actions of elected officials tends to concern students of democracy more than the power to invalidate the decisions of judges in a lower court. Very few nations grant courts the power of judicial review as it is exercised in the United States, and consequently American courts have a much more prominent role in the political system than courts in other nations. Sooner or later, most important political conflicts end up in court, and the judicial branch in effect serves as the ultimate umpire to the democratic political process in the United States.

The Origins of Judicial Review

The power of judicial review was most famously asserted in the case of *Marbury v. Madison* in 1803. The conflict at the heart of this case was a by-product of the election of 1800, which decisively shifted political power from the Federalists to Jefferson's Democratic-Republicans. After losing control of both the executive and legislative branches of government, the lame-duck Federalist president, John Adams, and Congress rapidly began creating new judgeships and filling the vacancies with Federalist loyalists. The Federalists hoped to retain significant influence in the third branch of government. Caught in the middle of these machinations was John Marshall, Adams' secretary of state. Not only was it Marshall's job to sign and deliver the official commissions to the new judicial appointees after they had been appointed and duly confirmed by the Senate, but he was himself appointed chief justice of the Supreme Court. The Federalists' attempt to pack the judiciary infuriated incoming president Thomas Jefferson. Once in office, he told his secretary of state, James Madison, to withhold all the commissions Marshall had not delivered. Among these were commissions for seventeen justices of the peace in the District of Columbia, one of whom was William Marbury. Without the commission, Marbury could not take his post, so along with several other disappointed Federalist appointees, he filed suit asking the Supreme Court to make Madison discharge his duty and deliver the commissions.

This suit, to put it mildly, put Marshall a bind. To begin with, he was being asked to rule on his own dereliction of duty.[7] And that was the least of his problems. If he and the other Federalist justices ruled that Marbury was entitled to the commission, Jefferson would simply order Madison not to deliver it, demonstrating that the judiciary could not enforce its mandates. As a Federalist, Marshall favored a strong national government, including a powerful judiciary. Having a Supreme Court decision ignored would undermine this goal. On the other hand, to rule that Marbury had no right to the commission would validate Jefferson's and Madison's claim that the so-called midnight appointments were improper and would undercut the standing of the Federalists who had just taken the bench. In short, either option could disastrously weaken the Court that Marshall had just been appointed to lead.

Marshall's response was stroke of political genius. Technically, what Marbury petitioned the court for was a **writ of mandamus,** an order requiring a public official to perform an official duty over which he or she has no discretion. Speaking on behalf of a unanimous Federalist Court, Marshall ruled that Marbury had a right to the commission, and that the writ of mandamus was indeed the proper remedy to obtain it.

---

[7]Marshall should have recused himself from hearing the case. *Recuse* is from a Latin word meaning "to refuse." Judges usually refuse to participate in cases in which they have even the appearance of a conflict of interest or bias. Chief Justice Marshall was aware of this practice. He recused himself from participating in the decision in *Martin v. Hunter's Lessee* (1816) because he had appeared as counsel in an earlier phase of the case and had a financial interest in the property.

But he also argued that the Supreme Court was not the proper tribunal to issue the writ. In making the ruling, Marshall struck down part of the Judiciary Act of 1789 that in effect granted the Supreme Court the power to issue writs of mandamus in cases under its original jurisdiction.

To understand this legal controversy, it is important to remember that the Supreme Court has both original and appellate jurisdiction. The Constitution gives Congress authority to define the Court's appellate jurisdiction by statute. But the Court's original jurisdiction is specifically spelled out in the Constitution.[8] Since it is defined in the Constitution, the Court's original jurisdiction cannot be changed by ordinary statute; instead, changes can be made only by a constitutional amendment. Marshall said that the part of the Judicial Act that gave the Court the power to issue writs of mandamus was unconstitutional because it gave the Court powers of original jurisdiction beyond those set by the Constitution. In this ruling, Marshall officially claimed the power of judicial review for courts, saying that it is "the providence and duty of the judicial department to say what the law is." Because the outcome was the one Jefferson wanted, he did not challenge the ruling (Gunther 1980, 9–11).

The ruling had far-reaching effects. It raised the possibility that the Federalists could use the newfound power of judicial review to check the actions of the Democratic-Republican Congress and president. And, most crucial of all, it established the power of the courts to declare acts of public officials invalid. *Marbury* did not settle all aspects of judicial review; for example, it was not until seven years later that the Court expanded this power to invalidate state laws. But it firmly planted the precedent, establishing the Court as a political institution of the highest order. The Supreme Court alone has the right to make final decisions about what the Constitution does and does not allow. This power means that the judiciary is a lawmaking institution, not simply a vehicle to resolve legal disputes.

Concepts of Judicial Review

How does a judge go about deciding whether a law or executive order is unconstitutional? What role does the judge think judicial review should play in the political process?

There have been a number of famous answers to such questions. Justice Owen Roberts articulated a **slot machine theory** of judicial review, arguing that all a judge does is lay the constitutional provision involved beside the statute being challenged and "decide whether the latter squares with the former" (*U.S. v. Butler* 1936). According to Roberts, judges "find" the law rather than "make" it.

Closely related to this view is the concept of **original intent.** This is the idea that justices should interpret the Constitution in terms of the original intentions of the Founders. Of the current members of the Court, Justice Clarence Thomas has established himself as the most ardent "originalist."

Others articulate a more nuanced and complex process. One such version is the **legal realist** view of judicial decision making. Benjamin Cardozo was an advocate of

---

[8]The Supreme Court can exercise original jurisdiction in cases affecting foreign ambassadors and consuls, and those in which a state is a party. The Eleventh Amendment altered the provision that allows suits against a state by citizens of another state. This amendment overturned the decision in *Chisholm v. Georgia* (1793) that the Court had accepted and decided under its original jurisdiction.

this view. Legal realists believe that judges must reconcile conflicting principles and interests and balance the law and precedent with their judgment about the effect of the decision on society. Key words and phrases in the Constitution, such as "due process of law" and "equal protection of the law," are so vague and undefined that they compel a judge to read his or her own views into them. Those views depend on the judge's personal philosophy and scheme of values. According to this perspective, judges have no choice but to make law rather than to just find it. Furthermore, some specific phrases must be applied in light of technological advances not foreseen by the original authors of the words. For example, taking a legal realist position on the Fourth Amendment, which protects individuals from unreasonable searches of "their persons, houses, papers, and effects," the Court has found that the amendment also protects electronic communication, such as the telephone and the Internet.

Even if a judge concedes that personal values do play a role, this does not solve the problem of deciding to what extent these values will affect rulings on constitutional issues. Justice Felix Frankfurter was one of the most articulate proponents of the "make law" perspective during the 20th century, but he also hesitated to substitute his constitutional values for those of legislators and executives. For example, in a 1940 decision, *Minersville School District v. Gobitis,* Frankfurter upheld the right of a school board to expel students who refused to salute the flag, as required by Pennsylvania state law. Frankfurter took the position that the courts had no grounds to tell political authorities that they could not use this method to instill patriotism in children. Three years later, the Supreme Court overruled *Minersville,* with Frankfurter dissenting. In *West Virginia State Board of Education v. Barnette* (1943), Justice Robert Jackson argued that forcing students to salute the flag interfered with their right of free speech.

Although these cases may seem little more than historical artifacts, they carry a modern lesson. In one case, the Supreme Court exercised **judicial restraint,** meaning that it deferred policymaking authority to other branches and levels of government. In the other, the Court exercised **judicial activism,** taking a more forceful role in determining public policy through broad constitutional interpretation. The tension between judicial restraint and judicial activism is an important political issue. Those who favor restraint argue that judges should not be allowed to use the power of judicial review to legislate from the bench. Making law is properly a legislative function and should not be usurped by the judiciary. Advocates of activism argue that legislatures sometimes pass bad laws that abrogate basic democratic values and constitutional rights. In such cases, the courts have not only a right but an obligation to act.

When the Supreme Court established the power of judicial review, it introduced tensions over democratic values and the role of the different branches of government that remain unresolved today. One reason the battle over activism versus restraint is so hard to resolve is that it is a battle of political rather than judicial philosophy. The Supreme Court of the 1980s and 1990s was largely appointed by Republican presidents and was ideologically more conservative than its predecessor. Yet in it some ways it has proven to be a highly activist Court, and it too has "thwarted the will of the majority." For example, it struck down the Religious Freedom Restoration Act, which passed unanimously in the House of Representatives and attracted only three dissenting votes in the Senate. Activism is not simply a trait of liberal ideology and restraint a trait of conservative ideology. Instead, judicial activism tends to be supported by conservatives when it advances their ideological preferences and by liberals when it advances theirs.

Patterns in the Exercise of Judicial Review

For the most part, the Supreme Court has used judicial review with considerable constraint. Fewer than 200 federal laws and about 1,300 state laws have been struck down. These numbers represent a tiny fraction of the hundreds of thousands of laws passed in over two centuries.[9]

The Supreme Court's use of judicial review has not been uniform over the years. During some periods, the Court rarely used the power. For example, after the *Marbury v. Madison* (1803) decision, more than fifty years passed before the Supreme Court declared another federal law unconstitutional in *Dred Scott v. Sanford* (1857). In other periods of history, the Court has been much more active in its use of judicial review. For example, it declared thirteen New Deal laws unconstitutional in the two years from 1934 to 1936. The Court was more restrained in the 1940s and 1950s, and then became more activist in the 1960s and 1970s (Figure 15.6).

The issues of concern to the Supreme Court have also changed over the years. Subject matter naturally varies from case to case, but different themes have occupied

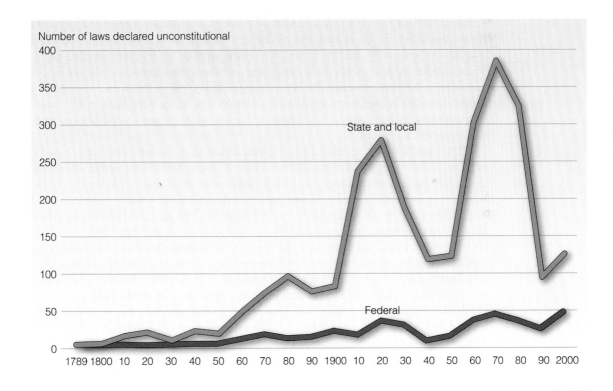

Figure 15.6
Federal and State Laws Declared Unconstitutional
Source: Constructed by the authors from data in Stanley and Niemi 2003, p.292.

[9]All courts in the United States have the power of judicial review because all state and federal judges take an oath to uphold the Constitution. This discussion focuses on the U.S. Supreme Court because it has the most definitive say about what is constitutional.

the Supreme Court's attention in different eras of constitutional history. The issues have reflected both the major problems of American society at the time and the justices' own conceptions of the values they should protect through the power of judicial review.

The major issue facing the Supreme Court between 1789 and the Civil War was the relationship between the nation and the states. John Marshall, who was chief justice for much of this era, provided judicial support for a strong national government. The constitutional basis for the federal government's expansion during this time was justified by a broad interpretation of the interstate commerce power and the "necessary and proper" clause. At the same time, state activities that restricted the powers of the national government were invalidated. Toward the end of this era, Marshall was replaced by Roger Taney, and under his leadership the Court moderated its stand on the nation–state relationship. For example, it ruled that states could regulate interstate commerce if the regulation concerned local matters and did not affect a subject requiring uniform treatment throughout the United States. As a whole, however, this early era was a time of general support for the nation over the states in constitutional conflicts.

The pre-Civil War period was also characterized by judicial protection of private property. In fact, there was a connection between the nation–states and property rights issues. For the most part, the federal government was promoting business and commercial interests, while the states were more involved in trying to regulate them. Thus, judicial support for a strong national government that dominated the states also favored commercial interests. The exceptions tended to prove this rule. For example, Taney's decision in the *Dred Scott* case invalidated Congress' attempt to abolish slavery in the territories but showed his solicitude for property owners—in this case, large landowners in the South.

The Civil War settled many nation–states issues, and the courts became preoccupied with the issues of business–government relations. Unlike the earlier era, however, both the national government and the states were now involved in regulating the burgeoning industrial empires. Consequently, it did not make sense to favor one level of government over the other in order to accomplish the justices' goal of protecting business against what they viewed as improper governmental interference.

The Supreme Court frustrated the national government's control of industry by limiting the scope of the interstate commerce power to cover only businesses that were actually involved in interstate commerce, such as railroads and shipping companies, and those that directly affected that commerce. This focus in effect freed companies involved in agriculture, mining, and production from control by the federal government. Similarly, the taxing power of the national government was restrained by judicial rulings that questioned congressional motives in using that power. For example, a special tax on businesses using child labor was invalidated on the reasoning that the purpose of the tax was not to raise money but to discourage the use of child labor.

State regulation of business was thwarted through a novel interpretation of the Fourteenth Amendment. Historically, the clause had referred to the procedures of public officials. The justices now held that unreasonable regulation of private interests deprived people of their property without due process of law.

This dual approach served to protect business against government regulation, and it dominated the Supreme Court's decision making up to the 1930s, when it was used to strike down many New Deal laws. Between the late 1930s and the early

1980s, the Supreme Court focused almost all of its attention on protecting the personal liberties of individuals against infringement by the national government and the states. During this time, the Supreme Court outlawed racial segregation and religious practices in public schools, provided constitutional protection for the choice to have an abortion, and significantly expanded the protections of the First, Fourth, Fifth, Sixth, Eighth, and Fourteenth Amendments. (These issues are covered in more depth in Chapters 4 and 5.)

Between them, Presidents Reagan and Bush appointed five new justices to the nine-member Court, and it was widely anticipated that a new conservative majority would reverse the liberal trends of previous decades. From the late 1980s to the early 2000s, the Supreme Court does seem to have switched focus, although in a relatively limited way. Court rulings have generally reflected the conservative backgrounds of the justices, but there has been a consistent level of support for liberal outcomes in civil liberties cases. In other words, the Supreme Court has been more likely to affirm than to overturn the expansion of rights and liberties granted in earlier rulings (Lee, Sandstrum, and Wiesert 1996). As we saw in Figure 15.5, only two of these new justices established consistently conservative voting records—Scalia and Thomas. One Republican appointee—Souter—became a relatively consistent liberal vote. The other two—O'Connor and Kennedy—established moderate records, siding most often with the conservative bloc on civil liberties issues but also joining the liberal bloc more than one-third of the time. Some notable recent decisions in which the Court protected civil liberties include *Lawrence v. Texas* (2003), which declared unconstitutional a Texas law making it a crime for two consenting adults of the same sex to engage in certain intimate sexual acts; *Grutter v. Bollinger* (2003), which preserved the University of Michigan Law School's affirmative action program that uses race as part of a holistic admissions process; and *Ashcroft v. Free Speech Coalition* (2002), which invalidated a federal law that made it a crime to distribute or possess computer-generated "virtual child pornography" that did not involve actual children.

Rather than reversing liberal rulings on civil liberties, the current Supreme Court seems to have placed more emphasis on state–federal relations, halting and in some cases reversing the power relationship that tended to favor the national government. Notable decisions include *United States v. Lopez* (1995), which struck down a federal law banning firearms near schools; and *New York v. United States* (1992), which voided part of another federal law making states liable for nuclear waste generated by commercial nuclear reactors. In these and other recent rulings, the Supreme Court seems to be putting more teeth back into the Tenth Amendment, and the justices have clearly signaled a willingness to rein in the federal government's power in favor of states and localities (Carney 1997).

Constraints on the Exercise of Judicial Review

Giving unelected judges with life tenure the power to block actions that the popularly elected branches of government take on behalf of the majority challenges the basic democratic values of majority rule and popular sovereignty. As noted earlier, few other nations vest such extraordinary power in the hands of judges. This extraordinary power is not clearly defined in the Constitution; instead, the Supreme Court claimed the power itself. The routine and frequent exercise of judicial review would pose a significant threat to democracy. The limited exercise of judicial review suggests that there are constraints on its use. Several mechanisms keep the Court from straying too far from the popular will for too long.

Impeachment   Federal judges are subject to removal through the impeachment process. As discussed in Chapter 12, impeachment by the House and removal by a two-thirds vote in the Senate is both a legal and a political process. Article II, Section 4 of the Constitution establishes the grounds for impeachment and removal as "treason, bribery, or other high crimes and misdemeanors." Political considerations inevitably come into play. It is unlikely that Congress could impeach and remove judges only because of unpopular rulings; there needs to be some evidence of wrongdoing serious enough to merit impeachment. But if judges were to use the power of judicial review frequently and irresponsibly, Congress would be able to find grounds for impeachment and removal. Congress is the sole authority in impeachment; these decisions are not subject to review by the courts.

Removal through impeachment is an extreme and infrequently used tool. No Supreme Court justice has been removed through the impeachment process. One, Samuel Chase, was impeached by the House in 1804, but he was acquitted in the Senate. That impeachment was politically motivated; Chase was a strong Federalist who behaved obnoxiously toward the Jeffersonian Democratic-Republicans in control of Congress. Although he remained on the Court until his death in 1811, he served with more contrition (Abraham 1993, 44). A total of thirteen federal judges have been impeached, most as a result of allegations of corruption. Two impeached judges resigned before the Senate trial. Of the eleven who went on trial in the Senate, seven were removed and four were acquitted.

Amendments to the Constitution   When the Court exercises judicial review, it may be based either on legislative or constitutional interpretation. In a decision based on **legislative interpretation,** the Court interprets a statute passed by Congress and rules on the meaning or intent of the disputed section. If Congress disagrees with the Court's legislative interpretation, it can overturn the faulty interpretation by passing another law by a simple majority vote in both chambers.

When the Court declares a law unconstitutional, its decision is based on interpretation of the Constitution. A **constitutional interpretation** cannot be overturned by a simple statute. But if the Court's interpretation of the meaning of the Constitution is contrary to the strongly held views of most Americans, the Constitution can be amended.

As discussed in Chapter 2, amending the Constitution is cumbersome and difficult. Nonetheless, seven of the twenty-seven amendments overturned unpopular judicial interpretations of the Constitution. Four of these amendments reversed rulings declaring federal laws unconstitutional:

- The Thirteenth Amendment prohibiting slavery and the Fourteenth Amendment giving African Americans rights of citizenship overturned *Dred Scott v. Sanford* (1857).
- The Sixteenth Amendment overturned the Court's decision in *Pollock v. Farmers' Loan and Trust* (1895) declaring an income tax unconstitutional.
- The Twenty-Sixth Amendment lowering the voting age to 18 overturned *Oregon v. Mitchell* (1970) in which the Court struck down part of the federal law trying to extend voting rights to 18-year-olds by statute.

Three other amendments changed practices that the Court ruled were permitted under the Constitution:

- The Eleventh Amendment giving states immunity from suits in federal court overturned the decision in *Chisholm v. Georgia* (1793).
- The Nineteenth Amendment giving women the right to vote changed the ruling in *Minor v. Happersett* (1875) that held that the Fourteenth Amendment did not give women the right to vote.
- The Twenty-Fourth Amendment prohibiting poll taxes changed Court rulings that interpreted the Constitution to permit these practices.

Appointments   Federal judges have life tenure, but they are mortal. Periodic vacancies are created by death and retirement. On average, a new Supreme Court justice has been appointed about every two years. Only four presidents were denied an opportunity to fill vacancies on the Court. William Henry Harrison and Zachary Taylor died early in their terms, and Congress eliminated a seat that became vacant to prevent Andrew Johnson from making the appointment. Jimmy Carter served a full term without getting a chance to appoint a Supreme Court justice. Most presidents get one or more opportunities to fill vacancies on the Supreme Court.

Because presidents and members of Congress are elected to office, their political values are likely to generally reflect those of society at a particular point in time. Presidents appoint individuals to the Court who share their political values; and the Senate is not likely to confirm individuals with views far out of the mainstream. Thus, through normal attrition, vacancies are filled with justices who better reflect contemporary views, and judicial interpretations of the Constitution are not likely to be greatly out of tune with the mainstream of American thought for too long.

There have been occasions, however, when the values represented on the Court have lagged behind contemporary thinking. Franklin Roosevelt, for example, was frustrated during his first term when the Supreme Court blocked his New Deal legislation. Justices serve life terms, and sitting justices cannot be removed (except through impeachment). But the Constitution leaves it to Congress to decide the number of seats. By passing a statute expanding the number of seats on the Court, Congress could give a president some vacant seats to fill. Roosevelt proposed legislation creating one new justice for every Supreme Court member who had reached the age of 70 and had not retired. This court-packing proposal provoked a storm of protest and was defeated in Congress. But Justice Owen Roberts, who had generally been aligned with four other justices who consistently voted to invalidate social and economic legislation, shifted loyalties and began voting with those who consistently voted to uphold these new laws. This shift—popularly known as the "switch in time that saved nine"—and a retirement in 1937 eliminated the political need to expand the Court.[10] Nonetheless, Congress has the power to give the president new seats to fill on the Court if its exercise of judicial review comes to be viewed as inappropriate.

---

[10]Although some accounts attribute Roberts' switch to the court-packing plan, there is evidence that his change of philosophy occurred before the plan was proposed (Cushman 1998).

Control of the Court's Appellate Jurisdiction   As discussed earlier, Congress controls the Supreme Court's appellate jurisdiction by statute. Since almost all cases in which the Court exercises judicial review come under its appellate jurisdiction, Congress has the power to restrain the Court by altering its appellate jurisdiction. Following the outbreak of the Civil War, Congress passed legislation taking away the Supreme Court's appellate jurisdiction in certain habeas corpus proceedings. More recently, in response to a number of controversial rulings, members of Congress introduced bills intended to reduce the Court's jurisdiction to hear appeals of certain types of cases. In 2004, for example, the House passed bills to prevent federal courts from hearing cases involving "under God" in the pledge and to strip federal courts of jurisdiction to order states to recognize same-sex marriages permitted by other states.

Efforts to restrict the Court's appellate jurisdiction usually fail. Even members of Congress who disagree with the Court's ruling may vote against such legislation because they respect the principle of separation of powers; they may not like the Court's interpretation, but they believe the Court has the legitimate right to make the ruling. But if the Court strikes down too many laws favored by the majority, members of Congress would come to view the Court's exercise of judicial review as illegitimate and would pass legislation restricting its appellate jurisdiction.

No Power to Initiate Policymaking   Courts are most definitely policymaking institutions; they make authoritative decisions about who gets what, when, and how. The language and the process through which courts make policy, however, differ from the way legislatures, executives, and bureaucrats make policy.

Among the most important procedural differences between judicial and other types of policymaking is that courts cannot initiate the policymaking process. If a member of Congress sees the need for a new policy, he or she can start the process by introducing a bill that frames the issue in a particular way. Courts, by contrast, must wait for others to bring cases to them. It is the parties to the case who frame the issues posed to the court. Moreover, the rules of the judicial process require cases to involve real people who have suffered real and substantial harm. Persons who cannot show that they have been harmed by some governmental action do not have **standing to sue.** While the Court has considerable discretion to pick and choose the cases it wants to hear, it still must choose from among the cases filed and answer the questions posed. Lacking the power of initiative is a significant constraint on judicial policymaking through judicial review.

Lack of Enforcement Power   The Court's exercise of judicial review is further limited because it must rely on other public officials to enforce its decisions. Although the first instance of judicial review in *Marbury v. Madison* (1803) was self-enforcing in that it required President Jefferson to do nothing, almost all the other cases have required action on the part of public officials in some other part of government. Take the case of school desegregation, for example. In *Brown v. Board of Education* (1954, 1955), the Supreme Court ruled that segregated schools violated the equal protection clause of the Fourteenth Amendment and that the states must desegregate the schools "with all deliberate speed." But there was resistance in many parts of the South, and when the school doors opened in the fall of 1956, very little had changed. President Eisenhower called out federal troops in 1957 to enforce the ruling in Little Rock, Arkansas. But it was not until nearly a decade later when President Lyndon Johnson ordered federal education funds withheld from schools that were still segregated—an action mandated by the Civil Rights Act of 1964—that significant progress was made toward integrating schools throughout the South.

When the Court declares a law unconstitutional, it is always controversial. By definition, the Court is telling representatives of the majority that they cannot do something that the majority wants them to do. Because the Court is generally respected and its legitimacy is unquestioned, even those who disagree with a decision believe that they are obligated to obey it, and there is considerable voluntary compliance with the Court's decisions, even unpopular ones. But too-frequent use of judicial review would undermine the Court's legitimacy. The Court can do little if the president, members of Congress, and other public officials decide to ignore its rulings. The Court has neither the power of the sword nor the purse; the president is commander-in-chief of the armed forces, and Congress has the power to appropriate funds.

Self-Restraint   Finally, the most common and effective constraint on the exercise of judicial review is the self-restraint of the justices themselves. Judges are taught in law school, and most of them sincerely believe, that it is not appropriate for them to routinely substitute their own views of good public policy for those of the elected branches of government. Justice Harlan Fiske Stone, who thought the Court was being too activist in *U.S. v. Butler* (1936), wrote:

> [T]he only check on our own exercise of power is our own self-restraint. . . . Courts are not the only agency of government that must be assumed to have the capacity to govern. . . . For the removal of unwise laws from the statute books appeal lies not to the courts but to the ballot and to the process of democratic government.

The Court has adopted several self-imposed legal doctrines intended to restrain judicial power. These are the political question doctrine, and the doctrines of standing to sue, ripeness, and mootness. The *political question doctrine* recognizes that courts do not have jurisdiction over certain issues that fall exclusively under the authority of the political branches (the president and Congress). The Court has modified the boundaries of issues reserved exclusively to other branches. In the case of *Baker v. Carr* (1962), for example, the Court held that federal courts had jurisdiction to hear disputes over reapportionment of congressional districts, a subject that had long been considered a political question to be resolved by elected officials. Nonetheless, issues of foreign affairs and Congress' exclusive control over the impeachment and constitutional amending process continue to be beyond the Court's jurisdiction. Standing to sue (discussed above) limits the Court by defining who can bring a case; the Court will hear cases brought only by someone who has suffered some actual harm. The remaining two doctrines deal with timing. The *ripeness doctrine* allows the Court to reject cases that are filed too early, before the issues and facts in question have clearly caused some real harm. The *mootness doctrine* means that the Court will not hear cases that are no longer a real controversy. All of these doctrines are self-imposed limits on the Court's power.

Self-restraint also has practical political benefits. Being a judge is a great job primarily because of the power and status. As noted above, if the power is used too often, it would undermine the legitimacy of the Court. If the justices want to remain powerful and have their decisions obeyed, they must be judicious in the exercise of judicial review.

Performance Assessment

In some ways it is difficult to reconcile the concept of judicial review with some of the major principles and assumptions of democracy. Granting the power to overturn the actions of elected legislative and executive officials to nine appointed people with lifetime tenure violates the principle of majority rule. It is also at variance with the democratic assumption that there are no elites who are intelligent enough or unselfish enough to make decisions that vitally affect the interest of the remaining members of society.

However, democracy does not always trust the majority; it also seeks to protect fundamental rights of minorities. In passing on constitutional questions, the Supreme Court is in a position to safeguard fundamental rights with which democracy has traditionally been concerned: freedom of speech, the press, and religion; political equality; procedural due process in criminal proceedings; and private property. Thus, federal judges can and have acted under the power of judicial review to protect both rights in the government and from the government. An independent judiciary provides an important and necessary defense against the excesses of the other branches. Swayed by majority opinion, laws that are passed may deprive minorities of their rights. The courts protect these rights, however unpopular they may be.

But assuming that such minority rights should be safeguarded, there remains the question of why Supreme Court justices should have that power. What is special about their training or position in the political system that qualifies them, rather than legislative or executive officials, to protect the rights of minorities?

If the major issues that come to the Supreme Court were narrow legal ones, it could be argued that the training of the justices gives them a special expertise to pass judgment on such matters. But this clearly is not the case. Issues resolved by the Supreme Court are mostly broad philosophical ones involving such basic values as racial equality, the separation of church and state, and freedom of speech and the press. There is nothing in a law school education that specifically prepares a judge to deal with such matters. Indeed, it can be argued that students of sociology, philosophy, communication, and political science are as or more qualified to deal with such issues than people with a purely legal background.

A more valid argument for the Court's prerogative in protecting the rights of minorities is the unique political situation justices enjoy compared to elected legislative and executive officials. It is unrealistic to expect the latter to fully protect the rights of minorities because they are fundamentally tied to the majorities that elect them to office and keep them there. Asking people who are dependent on majorities to stick up for the rights of unpopular minorities seems unrealistic. A classic example is the call for law and order by legislators and executives who advocate stricter policies for dealing with people accused of crime. Only officials who enjoy life tenure could politically afford to defend the procedural rights of people charged with crimes.

This may be a valid argument, but it is not a completely convincing one. The Supreme Court has used its power to defend the rights of minorities, but it has failed to do so on more than one occasion, as Chapters 4 and 5 detail.

The power of judicial review poses important challenges to the democratic values of popular sovereignty and majority rule. Although this judicial power is not checked by elections as is the case for the president and Congress, there are nonetheless a number of political constraints that prevent courts from thwarting the popular will for long. A cohesive and determined majority can eventually prevail over obstacles imposed by judicial review.

Whether judicial review is consistent with democracy or not, it will in all probability continue to be a part of the governing process. It has nearly two centuries of tradition behind it, and people of different political persuasions support judicial review—at least when it favors the values they cherish. For example, Justice Antonin Scalia is one of the most conservative Supreme Court justices and an advocate of judicial restraint. Yet Scalia has voted to invalidate laws protecting disadvantaged minorities and has been applauded by conservatives for doing so, even though this hardly seems to exemplify deference to other governmental institutions in the policy-making process (Brisbin 1997). Whether an individual is in favor of judicial activism or judicial restraint seems to depend at least partially on the issue and political values in question.

Judicial review is likely to survive attacks because it is not an absolute power. Judges are sensitive to public attitudes, and political scientists have consistently found that the Supreme Court rarely strays too far from public opinion in its rulings (Flemming and Wood 1997). Furthermore, Congress and the president retain such powers as appointment and the ability to define jurisdictional boundaries that can effectively constrain the Court's influence over the political system.

Summary

- The judiciary has to maintain a difficult balance in the American political system. Most Americans want judges to be independent and to make decisions based on the rule of law rather than on partisan loyalty, ideological prejudice, or political pressure. But an independent judiciary is insulated from certain core democratic values, and Americans also want judges to be accountable for unpopular decisions.
- The judiciary is a political branch of government. Interpreting the law is an inherently political process, and judges make decisions that authoritatively allocate values.
- The jurisdiction of the federal courts is defined by the Constitution, by congressional statute, and by the courts themselves. The jurisdiction of the federal courts falls into two broad categories. The first concerns the subject matter of the particular case. Federal courts have jurisdiction over litigation involving the U.S. Constitution, federal law, a treaty, and admiralty and maritime matters. The second concerns the parties involved in the case. Federal courts have jurisdiction over cases affecting agents of foreign governments, suits that involve a state or U.S. citizen and a foreign citizen or government, and interstate litigation.
- To a large degree, the jurisdiction of the courts is determined by Congress. Congress can prohibit the courts from handling certain cases, assign them exclusive jurisdiction, or allow federal courts to exercise concurrent jurisdiction with state courts.
- The courts can define their own power and jurisdiction to some extent. The most important power of the federal courts is the power of judicial review, which is the authority to review lower court decisions and to declare the laws and actions of public officials unconstitutional.

- The organization and structure of the federal courts is largely determined by Congress. The federal court system, broadly speaking, consists of three tiers. On the bottom are the district courts, which are trial courts of original jurisdiction. The vast majority of federal cases begin and end in these courts. Above them are the U.S. courts of appeals. These courts have only appellate jurisdiction; they review decisions in civil and criminal cases initially heard in federal district courts and the orders and decisions of federal administrative units. The top tier is the U.S. Supreme Court, which has both original and appellate jurisdiction and sits at the top of both the federal and state court systems.

- The Supreme Court functions mostly as an appellate court, and the justices have broad discretion over the cases they choose to hear. They accept cases that deal with the most important issues of law. Supreme Court cases are argued in oral arguments before the justices and in written briefs filed with the court. The justices decide cases on the basis of a simple majority vote, and their decisions are made in written opinions.

- The Constitution mandates the nomination of all federal judges by the president and confirmation by the Senate. Once confirmed, federal judges serve for life.

- The Constitution is silent on the qualifications of Supreme Court justices; they are not required to be citizens, of a certain age, or even lawyers. Despite the lack of formal requirements, potential justices are generally expected to have impeccable legal credentials.

- In nominating federal judges, presidents take into account a wide variety of considerations besides legal background. Such considerations include party affiliation, political philosophy, geography, religion, ethnicity, and judicial experience and merit.

- Deciding who will wield the power of judicial review is an enormously important decision, and the judicial confirmation process has become more politicized. The length of the confirmation process for federal judges has increased dramatically since the mid-1990s.

- While judges largely strive to be politically neutral and impartial, there are many gray areas of the law, and it is virtually impossible for an individual's background and personal values not to play a role. Given the tenure of federal judges and the importance and wide-ranging effects of their decisions, the political stakes in the selection process are high.

- Judicial review was a power claimed by the Supreme Court and was most famously asserted in *Marbury v. Madison* (1803). This power grants the Court the right to make the final decision about what the Constitution does and does not allow and, in effect, makes it a lawmaking institution.

- There are two basic philosophies about how the power of judicial review should be used. The philosophy of judicial restraint emphasizes deferring policymaking authority to other branches and levels of government. Judicial activism promotes a more forceful role in determining public policy through constitutional interpretation. The tension between restraint and activism is often a political conflict rather than a philosophical one. Whether liberals or conservatives advocate a philosophy of restraint or activism tends to depend heavily on their ideological preferences on a given issue.

- There are a number of constraints on judicial power. These include the possibility of impeachment, amendments to the Constitution, turnover on the bench through death or voluntary retirement, the Court's inability to initiate policymaking and its reliance on other branches of government to enforce its rulings, and the self-restraint of judges. The last is probably the most common and effective restraint. Most judges sincerely believe it is not appropriate for them to routinely substitute their own views of good public policy for those of elected officials, and the courts have adopted several legal doctrines to limit the types of cases they will hear.

Key Terms

attitudinal model 493
collegial court 477
concurrent jurisdiction 473
concurring opinion 480
conference 479
constitutional interpretation 502
courts of appellate jurisdiction 473
courts of original jurisdiction 473
dissenting opinion 480
en banc 477
exclusive jurisdiction 473
judicial activism 498
Judicial Conference 474
judicial power 472
judicial restraint 498

judicial review 473
jurisdiction 472
legal model 493
legal realist 497
legislative interpretation 502
majority opinion 480
original intent 497
plurality opinion 480
rule of four 479
senatorial courtesy 483
slot machine theory 497
standing to sue 504
writ of certiorari 479
writ of mandamus 496

Selected Readings

Abraham, Henry. 1999. *Justices, Presidents, and Senators.* An interesting and detailed description of the considerations that have influenced the appointment of Supreme Court justices.

Baum, Lawrence. 1994. *American Courts.* Boston: Houghton Mifflin. A good, comprehensive introduction to the American court system.

Black, Charles. 1960. *The People and the Court: Judicial Review in a Democracy.* New York: Macmillan. The classic argument for judicial activism.

McCloskey, Robert. 1994. *The American Supreme Court.* Chicago: University of Chicago Press. An accessible history of the Supreme Court.

Silverstein, Mark. 1994. *Judicious Choices.* New York: Norton. An excellent analysis of the politicization of the confirmation process of Supreme Court nominees.

16 The Policy Performance of American Democracy

When Congress is in session, the average legislator has to juggle several hundred issues that might require his or her attention. Crammed onto the congressional calendar in a single week is everything from budgets to voter registration, civil service reform to national forests, war to science education, immigration to cable television regulation. How does a legislator make responsible policy decisions with so many issues demanding attention? Simple. They cheat.

Well, not cheat exactly, but many do employ voting cards—what most college students would call a crib sheet. Voting cards provide a brief synopsis of an issue and indications of whether party leaders, constituents, and special interest groups support whatever proposal is being made. They also include the answer to the political equivalent of a major pop quiz: Whether to vote yea or nay on that proposal.

These answers, though, are not quite as clear as you might find on crib sheets smuggled into college exams. There is no true or false or multiple choice; in fact, there is no right answer. Whatever the proposal and whatever the vote, the answer is wrong to somebody and probably somebody important. Satirist P. J. O'Rourke (1991, 62–63) once spoofed a typical voting sheet like this:

> Home: Constituents will murder you in November if you oppose (the bill).
> Administration: President will kill you right now if you support it.
> Remarks: A toughie.

Making public policy is like that: tough and not as simple as it seems. There are so many issues clamoring for the attention of government it is a major task simply to sort them out into a rough list of priorities. Focus on any one of these, and you are likely to find a lively conflict, with different interests pushing for contradictory and mutually exclusive actions. Approving or rejecting any one of these actions may incur the heated displeasure of its

supporters or opponents. If a policy decision actually emerges from this melee, it still has to be implemented, which likely will set off another round of argument and debate. Once implemented, someone somewhere will want it changed, and the clamor for government attention will rise again.

Making public policy is the ultimate test of the democratic process. Indeed, public policymaking can be viewed as a test of how well—or how poorly—democratic values are put into practice. Everything we have studied so far plays a part in making pubic policy—parties and interest groups, elections and legislatures, executives and judges, bureaucracies and the media, the Constitution and federalism, and all the rest of the machinery that makes up the political system.

As such, it is fitting to end this book with a chapter on how all these elements come together to tackle the fundamental undertaking of politics discussed in Chapter 1. The study of public policy, in essence, is the study of how all these elements combine to produce the "authoritative allocation of values" or decisions about "what we ought to do."

Public policy can be defined as a relatively stable, purposive course of action pursued by government officials or agencies (Anderson 2000, 4). This definition implies several important things about the concept of public policy. First, it implies that public policy is goal oriented (purposive). In other words, public policies are undertaken to achieve some objective; they are not random or happenstance. In democratic societies, public policies are not the product of the whims or fancies of arbitrary rulers. They are the product of problems, issues, or demands that citizens expect or want the government to do address.

Second, what makes public policy "public" is that it represents a goal undertaken by government. Nongovernmental groups also make policy. All businesses, for example, engage in purposive courses of action. Specifically, they systematically and deliberately choose courses of action they believe will result in a profit. Thus, they have sales policies, return policies, and customer policies. Yet these policies are not public policy. The government is only the institution that has the authority to make decisions about who gets what that are binding on everyone. Public policy is just that: the government's decision about who is getting what.

Finally, this definition implies a time element and a process; it is not just an action, but a relatively stable course of action. Public policy is more than a declared intent to do something; it must also involve some action that attempts to achieve the goal expressed or implied in the statement of intent. A campaign promise, or even an actual law, is a necessary part of a public policy-making process. These represent declarations of intent. However, our definition of public policy requires more. There must be some consistent follow-through to implement and enforce that promise or law.

 ## The Promise of Public Policy

Public policy is nothing less than the business of translating the promise of democracy into the performance of democracy. Public policy encompasses the demands and expectations that citizens place on government and the government's response to these demands and expectations in the form of laws and public programs. For the political system to be democratic in practice as well as in theory, the core values must be upheld throughout the entire process that produces the public policy. That process includes making demands on government, formulating alternative courses of action to respond to those demands, and the substantive response itself.

Upholding those core democratic values is an enormously difficult challenge because the key characteristic of public policymaking is conflict (Cobb and Elder 1983, 82–93). It is extraordinarily rare for the government to be faced with a demand, problem, or issue where there is a clear, universally approved response. Policymaking is easy if everyone knows what they want from government, and government can give everyone everything they want. Such consensus rarely happens.

Instead public policy typically involves conflict between two or more groups over something they value. This can be something tangible like budgets, or tax cuts, or Social Security checks; or it can be intangible and symbolic such as whether individuals have the right to burn the flag. Just because they deal with intangibles does not mean symbolic policies generate less conflict. Compared to the conflict involving tangible benefits, symbolic policies can generate more strife because they often involve fundamental beliefs about what is right and what is wrong (Mooney 2001). Conflict over tangible benefits can often be resolved by splitting the difference—that is, compromise. It is hard to split the difference on fundamental moral values. Consider the conflict over flag burning: A policy that says protesters can burn only half the flag will satisfy neither side.

The study of public policy is astonishingly broad. It not only encompasses all of the institutions and processes we have covered in individual chapters in this book, it includes all the substantive issues at the heart of policy conflicts: education, welfare, the environment, the war on terror, cable television regulation. The list of issues, large and small, is virtually endless. How is it possible to encompass all of this and come to some general conclusion about whether public policy in the United States reflects the core values of democracy? (See the Promise and Policy feature "How Evolutionary Biology Helps Make Sense of Public Policy.")

PROMISE AND POLICY
How Evolutionary Biology Helps Make Sense of Public Policy

Whether the public policy process is pluralist or elitist is a topic of endless debate among political scientists. Is policy disproportionately decided by and in favor of a small group of elites? Or does the system ensure that all interests are given a fair hearing in deciding questions of who gets what?

These questions have vexed some of the most brilliant democratic theorists studying the American political system. The sheer number of topics, actors, and decision makers allows pluralist and elitist points of view to muster at least some evidence to support their argument. Frustrated at the inability of democratic theory to provide clear answers to the hows and whys of the policy system in action, some political scientists have turned to another discipline for help: evolutionary biology.

One of the most important pieces of policy scholarship in the last twenty years is an extended study undertaken by Frank Baumgartner and Bryan Jones, two political scientists who took on the enormous challenge of making systematic sense of the entire policy system—how it works and, more importantly, why it changes. Rather than just rely on the standard models of the policy process produced by democratic theory, they borrowed a concept called punctuated equilibrium, which is taken directly from evolutionary biology.

Originally developed by paleontologists Steven Jay Gould and Niles Eldredge, punctuated equilibrium argues that biological evolution is not a gradual process of incremental change; rather, it consists of long periods of stability interrupted—or punctuated—by rapid change.

Baumgartner and Jones noticed that the same general principle describes the policy system remarkably well. In most policy areas, and for most of the time, there is stability, with only incremental adjustments to the status quo. Occasionally, however, there is a fundamental shift, with a period of radical change. This eventually settles down to a new period of stability.

It is hard to do justice to Baumgartner and Jones' thesis in a few words, but at the core of their argument is the notion that the political system spawns a lot of policy subsystems. Policy subsystems consist of the institutions and actors interested in particular issues such as the environment, education, nuclear energy, and so forth. These systems can become policy monopolies, which are issue areas where those outside the policy subsystem have little interest or influence, and those within the subsystem control the key policy decisions.

Such policy monopolies, however, cannot be maintained indefinitely. Invariably something happens to attract the interest and attention of actors outside the subsystem. This creates pressure that can dissolve a policy monopoly by drawing decision-making power toward other actors and producing rapid changes in laws and regulations.

What drives this change? Policy image, or how a policy is understood and discussed. Dramatic changes in policy image can mobilize those outside the policy subsystem and create pressure for change. This pressure results in a shift away from the key actors in the policy monopoly. Once decision-making power is drawn out of the policy monopoly and into the hands of other actors and institutions, the monopoly collapses and rapid policy change is the result.

Baumgartner and Jones use nuclear power as an example. In the 1950s nuclear power had a very positive image; it was viewed as a source of cheap, limitless, and clean energy. This positive image allowed the nuclear industry, the associated congressional committees, and the Atomic Energy Commission to create a policy monopoly (in effect, an iron triangle).

This image, however, shifted dramatically in the 1970s. The dangers of radioactive waste and a high-profile (and potentially disastrous) accident at the Three Mile Island nuclear plant attracted media attention and turned public opinion negative. This created pressure to push decision making out of the original policy monopoly; other congressional committees, as well as state and local governments, began to enact new laws and regulations. The result was a significant policy shift—stricter laws and regulations and an enforcement bureaucracy that shifted from industry advocate to tough regulator. This created a new period of stability, but one in which nuclear energy is viewed negatively, fewer nuclear plants are authorized, and the costs rather than the benefits drive policy adjustments.

To a remarkable extent Baumgartner and Jones provide a comprehensive explanation of the policy process—from agenda setting through **policy adoption**—that can help explain stability and change across a broad range of policy issues.

Source: Baumgartner, Frank, and Bryan Jones. 1993. *Agendas and Instability in American Politics.* Chicago: University of Chicago Press.

The Stages of Policymaking

Political scientists who specialize in the study of public policy often impose order on their vast and sprawling topic by viewing public policymaking as a system made up of four distinct stages:

1. *Agenda setting,* which produces the list of issues and problems the government will pay attention to
2. *Policy formulation and adoption,* wherein the government considers the various alternatives to the issue at hand and formally approves a particular alternative
3. *Policy implementation,* in which the government translates the approved alternative into action
4. *Policy evaluation,* wherein government and nongovernment actors assess the successes and problems of public policies (Ripley 1988, 48–55)

The evaluation stage often leads to calls for changes in public policy, which takes the system back to the agenda-setting stage (Figure 16.1).

This stage approach provides us with a systematic way to evaluate how well—or how poorly—the various actors, institutions, and processes we have studied in this book translate the theory of democracy into the practical push-and-shove of making public policy. Once we have a reasonable understanding of this process, we will have a basis for assessing how well it reflects the core democratic values in action.

Agenda Setting

Government cannot attend to all the possible issues, problems, and demands that exist. Somehow a manageable list of issues must be created on which government can focus. This list is known as the **public agenda,** and it consists of the issues and problems that the government is actually paying attention to. Just because an issue or problem makes it to the public agenda does not mean a public policy will result. The public agenda is simply a list of topics included in the national debate about what government should (or should not) do.

Though getting an issue on the public agenda does not guarantee a public policy will be made, it is absolutely certain that a policy will never be made if it cannot gain the attention of public authorities. Getting on the public agenda, then, represents the first critical stage in public policymaking. But how is this accomplished? Who sets the agenda? How are topics chosen from among the thousands of possibilities?

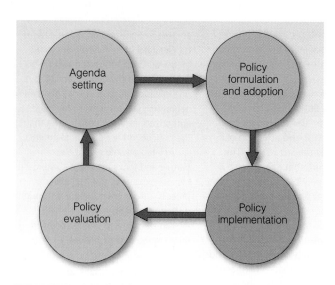

Figure 16.1
The Stages of Policymaking

Agenda Setters   There are a number of actors both inside and outside the

The prestige, power, and visibility of the nation's chief executive give the president unrivaled ability to focus public opinion and the government on a particular set of issues. Here President George W. Bush signs the Medicare plan he strongly advocated. His backing made the issue a top agenda item and allowed the plan to be implemented with considerable speed, a pace that some lawmakers have since regretted as they discover portions of the law that they did not notice or have sufficient information about when voting on it.

government struggling to get their particular interests and issues on the public agenda, although they have varying abilities to do this. Inside the government, the most powerful agenda setter is the president. The prestige, power, and visibility of the nation's chief executive give the president unrivaled ability to focus public opinion and the government on a particular set of issues.

Close behind the president is Congress. Individual members of Congress cannot command the attention or set the agenda in the same fashion as the president. Yet representatives and senators are in a unique position to influence the public agenda because of the legal authority of Congress (a member of Congress must introduce a specific bill, and majorities in the House and Senate must approve it) and the public nature of the institution (Kingdon 1995, 21–44).

The courts play less of a role in agenda setting because they cannot initiate the process—they can only respond to issues that are litigated. But court decisions do occasionally add topics to the national agenda. Abortion policy was being openly debated in only a handful of states until 1973 when the Supreme Court's decision in *Roe v. Wade* (1973) propelled it onto the national agenda, where it has remained for several decades; a decision by the Massachusetts Supreme Court saying that same-sex couples in Massachusetts had the same rights to marry as heterosexual couples thrust the issue of gay marriage onto the agenda in every state, the halls of Congress, and the 2004 presidential election.

Outside the government, the key forces in agenda setting are interest groups, the media, political parties, elections, and public opinion. Of these, interest groups play the most important role in agenda setting, primarily because they expend considerable effort and resources trying to focus the attention of lawmakers on their interests. As we learned in Chapter 6, interest groups engage in a wide variety of lobbying efforts, all of them directed at gaining access to lawmakers so their issue will be considered—that is, put on the agenda.

We also saw in Chapter 8 that the media play a powerful role in agenda setting (McCombs and Shaw 1972). The media's role in agenda setting, though, differs from that of interest groups. Interest groups bring a sustained effort to a narrow set of interests. In contrast, the media shifts focus rapidly. Only a few issues (for example, the war in Iraq) are powerful enough to generate sustained attention from the media. The pressure of a daily news cycle drives constant turnover in the issues that get prominent play in the media.

Public opinion can also focus government interest on a particular issue. As we learned in Chapter 9, public opinion is often divided and provides no clear signal about what government should do. It is sometimes focused enough, though, to send a clear signal that something should be done, even if it is vague on what that something is. Political parties and elections help set the agenda because parties and victorious candidates for electoral office do make some effort to make good on their campaign promises. The issues raised on the campaign trail also tend to reappear once a candidate is in office, though an effort to follow through on a campaign promise does not guarantee a place on the public agenda (Kingdon 1995, 63).

These agenda-setting forces, however, do not work independently of one another. For example, special interest groups seek to sway public opinion. the media questions officeholders on how their views square with public opinion, and officeholders track public opinion with an eye to the next election. In other words, the actors who determine the public agenda are all interconnected. They frequently have very different ideas of the issues government should be addressing, and they are all busily engaged in trying to convince one another that their notion of the public agenda should be accepted by everyone else. For a prominent place on the public agenda, these forces must coalesce around an issue.

Choosing Issues   Gaining a place on the public agenda means gaining the collective interest of policymakers. As a general rule of thumb, policymakers tend to focus on problems they believe demand some sort of response or action on their part. This sort of focus is created when the various agenda-setting forces combine and produce one or more of the following: indicators, focusing events and feedback (Kingdon 1995).

Indicators are any measures that can be employed as systematic monitoring devices. A classic example is money. A huge budget deficit will tend to gain media attention, be employed by the minority party as evidence of the majority party's faults, rouse public opinion, and raise concern among powerful interest groups whose benefits might be threatened by budget cuts. Indicators are important because they send signals that a problem exists.

Indicators, however, may not be enough to kick an issue onto the public agenda. Some indicators simply do not engage enough attention from agenda-setting forces.

A focusing event is something that grabs attention immediately and puts an issue on the public agenda. The kidnapping and murder of 12-year-old Polly Klaas directed national attention on the issue of missing children. Groups that formed in response to this tragedy have kept the issue in the public eye and campaigned for legislation to help protect children. The Amber Alert System, signed into law by President Bush in 2003, is just such an example of the far-reaching effects of the Klaas murder. Here, an Amber Alert over the 101 freeway in Los Angeles informs motorists of the description of a vehicle in which a 10-year-old child might have been abducted. To date, 151 recoveries have been made as a result of the program.

Trade deficits, for example, seem to make little impact on public opinion. A **focusing event** is something that grabs attention immediately and puts an issue on the public agenda. A classic, if extreme, example is the terrorist attacks of 9/11. On September 10, 2001, terrorism was not particularly high on the public agenda. But for years following September 11, terrorism was a high priority in media campaigns, political campaigns, public opinion, and all the institutions of government.

Feedback consists of the information policymakers routinely receive through government reports, hearings, reading the news, casework, meetings with lobbyists and government officials, and contact with constituents. Much of this information is unlikely to push an issue onto the public agenda. An irate constituent complaining about taxes, for example, does not suggest a major problem. That is simply a normal part of the background noise of a democratic political system.

Feedback helps select an issue for the public agenda when it signals that something is seriously different from how policymakers expect it to be. For example, feedback from constituents and military officials that U.S. troops were buying their own body armor because of army shortages prompted congressional focus on what, until then, had been a backwater military logistical issue (Lenz 2004).

Policy Formulation and Adoption

Once a problem or issue has the focused attention of policymakers, it shifts to what is known as an institutional agenda. In contrast to the public agenda, which includes all the issues that are part of the broad public debate about what the government should do, an **institutional agenda** is a short list of actionable items being given serious consideration by policymaking institutions (Theodoulou 1995, 87).

Once elevated to the institutional agenda, the policy problem shifts from deciding what issues to address to choosing among the competing alternatives. Again, making this choice represents a significant challenge for government. Simply because an issue is placed on the institutional agenda does not automatically suggest a solution (Baumgartner and Jones 1993, 28). Poor educational performance, for example, is a policy problem that has a near-permanent place on the institutional agendas of state and national governments. The range of possible responses to this problem includes more funding, tougher standards, instituting a voucher system, and reforming teacher education. Each alternative has its champions and detractors. What alternative, or set of alternatives, should be chosen?

There are two basic ways to sort through policy alternatives and select the one that is the most appropriate response to the issue at hand. The first is to engage in **rational-comprehensive decision making,** which involves developing a comprehensive list of alternatives to the problem or issue, assessing the costs and benefits of each alternative, then choosing the alternative that most effectively solves the problem or achieves the desired goal at the lowest cost (Chandler and Plano 1988, 127–131). The big advantage of the rational-comprehensive approach to **policy formulation** and adoption is that it considers all alternatives and is thus likely to hit on a policy that works to solve the problem at minimal cost. The big drawback is that it is not very practical. It assumes that policymakers have compatible objectives and complete information about the consequences of every potential alternative to achieving those objectives. This is very rarely the case. Policymakers often have different objectives for any given issue or policy problem, and they do not know all the possible consequences of every potential action. Even if they did, a comprehensive policy evaluation is enormously time-consuming; if the problem is to put out a raging forest fire, there is no time to collect and analyze information about all possible alternatives before the fire destroys the entire forest.

It is more practical for policymakers to engage in incremental decision making. **Incrementalism** describes an approach to the search for policy alternatives that involves looking at how similar problems or issues have been handled in the past, identifying a handful of alternative approaches to that issue or problem that are politically and financially feasible, and choosing the one that is the most "doable." Political scientist Charles Lindblom (1959) called this "the science of muddling through." (See the Promise and Policy feature "Incrementalism in Action.")

The big drawback of the incremental approach is that the cheapest or most effective alternative may not be chosen for the simple reason that it was never considered. The big advantage of the incremental approach is its sheer practicality for policymaking bodies trying to cram lots of issues onto their institutional agendas. The alternatives chosen might be second best but, for the most part, they work.

Regardless of the particular approach, the actors who are most influential in defining the range of alternatives considered to solve any given problem are not necessarily the same as those who drive agenda setting. Public opinion, for example, may help set the public agenda, but it rarely gives enough direction to define detailed alternatives to

PROMISE AND POLICY
Incrementalism in Action

The typical approach to public sector budgeting is to begin with the previous year's budget and make incremental adjustments up or down. This is the classic example of incremental decision making.

There are a number of drawbacks to incremental budget making, and these problems periodically prompt calls for reform. Most of the reform proposals, in one way or another, call for injecting a measure of rational-comprehensive decision making into the budget-making process.

A good example is zero-based budgeting (ZBB). Consider that under incrementalism a public agency will use its previous funding level as a base and attempt to justify any increase (or decrease) to that base. This is how the budget will be framed for the public authorities who actually approve the budget (usually a legislature)— in terms of how much, or how much less, the agency gets compared to last year.

Under ZBB, that same public agency will start with a base of zero and have to justify every dollar beyond that base. ZBB thus proposes a more rational-comprehensive approach to making budgeting decisions, forcing public authorities to consider alternatives for every expenditure.

While ZBB has much to recommend it in theory, in practice it simply is not practical. The federal budget today runs roughly $2 trillion (Figure 16.2 shows actual government spending through 2001, the latest figures available). If Congress were forced to set that to zero every year and painstakingly justify every

Figure 16.2

Federal Government Spending, 1981–2001

The federal budget is a classic example of incremental decision making. This incremental approach makes federal budgets fairly predictable. Generally speaking, each year's budget is a little more than the previous year's budget, resulting in a linear trend over time.

Source: Office of Management and Budget. *http://www.whitehouse.gov/omb/budget/fy2002/guide02.html.* Accessed June 12, 2004.

continued

Incrementalism in Action   *continued*

one of those $2 trillion, it would undoubtedly save some money and put some unproductive programs out of business. But, it would also be a highly impractical approach to making policy. Considering all potential alternatives to the expenditure of

every dollar would require a massive amount of manpower. As an example, suppose that Congress worked 365 days a year, seven days a week and managed to consider all potential alternatives and still justify and approve a $100 million

in expenditures per day. At that rate, it would take them approximately fifty-five years to pass an annual budget. The result would certainly be comprehensive but ultimately not very rational.

---

an issue or problem. Bureaucrats, on the other hand, have little influence on agenda setting but exercise considerable influence over the selection of policy alternatives (Kingdon 1995).

Bureaucrats become powerful influences during the formulation and adoption stage of the policy process because of their expertise and their role in the political system. For example, if Congress is considering a law to promote clean water, they almost certainly will seek the input of experts from the Environmental Protection Agency (EPA). Not only will these experts provide important information on the impacts of the various policy alternatives, they are in a unique position to assess the feasibility of these alternatives. Because they will be responsible for implementing whatever law is passed, EPA bureaucrats are best situated to tell Congress what is, or is not, likely to work.

Some actors remain influential throughout the agenda setting and formulation and adoption stages. Special interest groups, for example, will continue to lobby for their favored alternative. A member of Congress may consider how voting for a particular law will play with public opinion in his or her district. Yet the list of influential actors narrows as policy moves from the agenda setting to the formulation and adoption stage, especially when the government actually moves to the point of selecting and formally approving a particular policy alternative.

The reason there is a limited range of actors at the formal adoption stage is simple: Only government has the power to authoritatively allocate values and make those decisions binding on everyone. Congress can pass a law; the president can issue an executive order; a public agency can approve a rule; a judge can make a ruling or issue a court order. Special interest groups, political parties, the media, and public opinion may influence the official decision makers throughout the process, but these nongovernmental actors do not have the authority to formally make *public* policy. Whatever influence nongovernmental actors exert at the formal adoption stage, it is indirect (Kingdon 1995).

Policy Implementation

Laws, executive orders, rules, and judicial decisions are a formal pronouncement of the intent to take purposive action, not the action itself. **Policy implementation** is the process of translating that intent into action (Sabatier and Mazmanian 1980).

As the policy process shifts from the selection and adoption stage to the implementation stage, the cast of important policy actors once again gets shuffled. Bureaucrats become, by far, the most important actors in this stage of the policy process. The reason is simple: Implementation is what public agencies are designed to do (Kerwin 1999).

Public agencies typically face a number of problems in translating the stated intent of the other institutions of government into action: laws with vague goals, laws with multiple or even contradicting goals, inadequate resources to do the job. And though special interest groups, political parties, and governmental actors such as legislatures and executives play less of a role in implementation, they do not simply disappear from this stage of public policymaking. As the discussion on rulemaking in Chapter 14 highlights, public agencies are often subject to varying degrees of lobbying and political pressure as they go about trying to implement policy decisions.

There is typically a considerable distance between a formal declaration of intent and the action actually taken by government. What happens between formal adoption and action determines to a large extent whether a public policy will achieve its desired objectives. Political scientists have discovered that the success or failure of public policy is often determined by what happens during the implementation stage.

The classic political science study of implementation was undertaken by Jeffrey Pressman and Aaron Wildavsky (1973). This was a case study of a federal policy program aimed at alleviating unemployment in inner-city Oakland. The policy, at least at first glance, had all the ingredients for success: There was a clear goal, there was just one federal agency running the program, the program was amply funded, and there was near universal agreement that creating jobs in the inner-city was a worthy policy goal. Although just about everyone wanted the program to work, it was a miserable failure.

Pressman and Wildavsky concluded that a primary reason for the program's failure was how the implementation process was shaped by the federal system. The city of Oakland is a municipality in the state of California, but this was a federal program using (mostly) federal dollars. There was only one federal agency involved, but there were three levels of government (national, state, and local). As discussed in Chapter 3, the disadvantages of a federal system include a degree of inefficiency and complexity, and these disadvantages are particularly acute when trying to implement a policy that requires the coordination of different levels of government.

Pressman and Wildavsky found that the multiple levels of government meant that there were a series of decision points that had to be cleared before any action could be taken. In other words, before any money could be spent and before any action could be taken, it had to be approved by the federal, state, and local government units. Having to jump through these hoops had two major implications for implementation: (1) It made action—any action at all—much less likely; and (2) it made it difficult to hold any specific unit accountable for any particular action.

To see why implementation is so difficult, consider a hypothetical implementation scenario in which any action to implement a federal policy has to go through ten decision points at three levels of government (federal, state, and local). In other words, before there is any positive action to do something to achieve the policy's objectives, ten groups or people have to approve that particular action. In our hypothetical scenario, we will make everything easy (and a little unrealistic) by assuming all of the people at each of these ten decision points are more or less in agreement with the policy's goals and the actions that need to be taken in order to achieve them. Making it even easier, we will assume that whatever pressure is being applied from the political system—be it from legislators, public opinion, special interests, or whatever—this pressure is pushing for the same thing.

Surely under these ideal conditions, action will be undertaken and undertaken soon. Not necessarily. If the probability that an action is going to be approved is 90 percent at each of these decision points, the overall probability that the action will make it through all ten stages drops to about 35 percent (this is the product of multiplying .9 by .9 ten times). If it takes three days for a decision to be made by each group or person—a pretty reasonable time span if the action has to be carefully considered and meetings have to be scheduled—it will take a month for an action to be approved. That is, if it is approved. Even in ideal circumstances, that is no sure thing.

And if no action is taken, or an action turns out to be ineffective, inefficient, or just plain silly, who should be held accountable? Federal, state, or local authorities? The policy itself? Something else? Could the problem be not enough resources or vague or competing goals? Political pressure to take one particular action over another? All of these can be real obstacles to successful implementation of any single policy. Studying the implementation process leads not just to an understanding of why policies fail but also to an appreciation of the enormous effort that goes into making them work.

Implementation can founder not just on decision points or on practical considerations such as funding; one of the biggest challenges is the nature of the goal or the problem being addressed. A policy to lower noise disturbances in neighborhoods adjacent to a university campus, for example, is much more doable than a policy to safely produce electricity from nuclear power plants.

In the first example, the action needed to achieve the goal is clear: Reduce the number of fraternity parties, and you have less noise disturbance. What needs to be changed, whose behavior needs to change, and where they need to change it are all clear.

Now consider the second policy. What needs to be changed? Whose behavior needs to be changed? What does it mean for nuclear energy to be "safe"? In this case, it is not clear what actions need to be taken or even how to define the goal that is to be achieved. Consequently, successfully addressing that problem is much less likely. Implementation is extraordinarily difficult—maybe even impossible—if overarching policy goals are unlikely to be achieved regardless of what course of action is pursued (Sabatier and Mazmanian 1980).

Policy Evaluation

Despite the difficulties inherent in policy implementation, once formally approved and adopted some purposive course of action is likely to be undertaken. A whole range of actors within the political system will be interested in what those actions are and what, if anything, they achieve.

The process of examining the consequences of public policy is known as **policy evaluation.** Policy evaluation is undertaken for any number of reasons. The obvious reason is to assess whether the policy worked. This is far from the only reason, however. If a policy is not achieving its objectives, we might want to know why. Is it because the problem is simply too complex and difficult to achieve? Was the policy poorly implemented? Starved of resources? Poorly managed? Even if a policy worked and achieved its stated goals, we might still be interested in figuring out if there is a way to achieve those goals more effectively and efficiently. If the policy goals were achieved effectively and efficiently, we might want to know why in order to apply these lessons to other policy areas. (See the Promise and Policy feature "Nerds, Sinners, and Perverts—Why Some Policies Fail.")

The various reasons for undertaking a policy evaluation serve the purposes of many different political actors. A special interest group might want to know how

©Charles Gupton/Corbis

Public education policies address what many consider intractable problems. Partly because the goals of education policy are so contradictory and so hard to achieve, education policy is being constantly evaluated to assess what outcomes are produced by particular programs and to try and figure out how—or if—things can be done more effectively and efficiently. One formal way to do this is through standardized testing. Much attention has been paid to the results of these tests, but many suggest that they are a more accurate reflection of how well students have been trained to take the tests rather than an accurate reflection of their knowledge base.

effectively a policy is serving its members' needs. The media might be interested in whether a program is wasting taxpayer dollars. The minority party may use evaluations to hold the majority party accountable for its policy failures, just as the majority party may use them to tout its policy successes.

For these reasons, public policies are constantly being evaluated. Evaluation can be done formally or informally and can be undertaken by a wide variety of actors ranging from the public agency actually taking the actions, to the media, to interest groups, to academics. They all tend to use different approaches and have different goals for undertaking an evaluation, and they can come to very different conclusions about the same program or policy.

Despite the wide variety of approaches, though, all policy evaluations can be classified into one of two broad categories: process evaluations and impact evaluations (Theodoulou 1995, 91).

Process evaluations assess whether a policy is being implemented according to its stated guidelines. If the policy is to reduce neighborhood noise by increasing police patrols, reducing response time to neighborhood complaints, and ticketing offenders for first offenses, then a process evaluation would look at the number of police patrols, response time to noise complaints, and the ratio of tickets to warnings given to first offenders.

PROMISE AND POLICY
Nerds, Sinners, and Perverts—
Why Some Policies Fail

Political scientists have long noted that some public policies are more likely to achieve their goals than others. Policies that try to regulate morals, especially so-called sin issues, are among the most notorious for failure.

Consider Prohibition: didn't work. The War on Drugs: well, just how hard is it to get drugs? Sodomy laws did not prevent homosexuality, and decency laws—even those that managed to squeeze past the First Amendment—have done little to stop online pornography.

Why do these sorts of policies fail? Political scientists have hit upon a simple answer to this question: We want them to fail.

Throughout the republic's history, different groups have demanded a government response to problems associated with things like booze or drugs or sex. Periodically they have been successful enough to push these issues onto the public agenda, swing public opinion behind their proposals, and actually get a policy adopted.

Yet, though public opinion might demand a clampdown on alcohol, drugs, sexually explicit materials, or particular sex acts, the public sometimes shows little inclination to obey the resulting laws. Why?

Scholars who study morality policies suggest there are two answers to this question. The first is that few people will speak out in favor of what is perceived as sinful, even if they commit the sinful act on a regular basis. For example, few people, and even fewer politicians, extol the virtues of drug use or pornography. This means when proposals to regulate drugs or pornography make it to the public agenda, few voices are raised in opposition.

Second, even if a law is passed, it will have, at best, mixed success in regulating people's behavior. Political scientist Kenneth Meier once illustrated this by dividing the population into three basic categories: nerds, sinners, and perverts. Nerds are those who have no interest in the behavior and will thus obey the law. Teetotalers, for example, had no problem obeying Prohibition.

Sinners are those who like engaging in the behavior but will only do so if the chances of getting caught are low. For example, a businessman who orders a hardcore pornographic film while in a hotel is unlikely to do the same at home.

Perverts are those who will not or cannot stop the behavior prohibited or regulated by policy. A drug addict, for example, may be psychologically or physiologically incapable of kicking his or her habit. Smokers will light up even if they have to go outside a building in the freezing cold or driving rain to do so.

The success of a morality policy, then, depends on the ratio of nerds, sinners, and perverts in the population. It is not necessarily the perverts that make the difference between success and failure.

If a large proportion of the public falls into what Meier labeled the category of sinners—that is, people who like to occasionally indulge in whatever is being regulated—the net result is policy failure because a big chunk of the public is ignoring the law on a semi-regular basis. Policy fails because, in effect, it does not turn sinners into nerds!

Source: Meier, Kenneth J. 1999. "Drugs, Sex, and Rock and Roll: A Theory of Morality Politics." *Policy Studies Journal*, 27 (4): 681–695. Used by permission of Blackwell Publishing.

Impact evaluations assess policy outcomes. In other words, the goal in an impact evaluation is to see whether the policy has achieved its overall objectives. In the example above, an impact evaluation would assess whether the actions that are the focus of a process evaluation—increased police patrols, response times, and citations for first offenders—actually contribute to a reduction in noise levels. Impact evaluations tend to come after process evaluations because it usually takes some time for a policy or program to produce a measurable change in outcomes. Process evaluations, on the other hand, can provide useful information on whether a policy is being implemented according to its guidelines as soon as the program gets underway.

Regardless of whether they are process or impact evaluations, reviews, reports, and analyses of public policy often lead to calls for change. Public policies that are adopted, implemented, and clearly achieve their stated goals do exist, but they are more the exception than the rule. A decision to build a bridge, for example, might fall into this category. The decision is made, funds appropriated, plans laid, contractors hired, bridge built, and process and impact evaluations show an objective achieved in the time and manner expected.

A lot of public policy, however, is aimed at difficult or intractable problems. Intractable simply means the problem is complex, caused by many different factors, and hard to address within the confines of any single—or even a whole group—of policy programs. Public education is a good example.

As already discussed, the underperformance or even outright failure of public schools is a staple of the public agenda. This is partially due to the intractable nature of the problems public education policies address. It is hard enough just to define the goals of education policy. What constitutes "quality education" or "equality of educational opportunity"? How do we know when these goals have been achieved? Some see tough academic standards as an education policy that will increase the quality of public education. Tough academic standards, though, may lead to higher dropout rates. Higher dropout rates may strike some as evidence of the failure of education policies.

Because the goals of education policy are so contradictory and so hard to achieve, education policy is being constantly evaluated to assess what outcomes are produced by particular programs and to figure out how or if things can be done more effectively and efficiently. These evaluations are formal and informal, and they frequently lead to calls for policy change. Because public education affects so many people and because it consumes so many tax dollars, education issues are quick to get the attention of media, policymakers, special interest groups, and public opinion.

When this happens, evaluations shift the policy process back to the agenda-setting stage. What should we do about underperforming inner-city schools? A whole range of policy evaluations show that school voucher programs have not improved student achievement by much, if at all (Gill, Timpane, Ross, and Brewer 2001). Does this mean vouchers do not work? Or does it mean that, to work, voucher programs should be expanded from relatively small-scale experiments involving small numbers of students? Should we expand the students eligible for vouchers? Scrap the voucher program and move back to neighborhood schools? What about setting tougher standards that will be more likely to increase achievement scores? What about after-school programs? Tougher teacher certification standards? Evaluations constantly raise such questions, and these questions are inevitably followed by the political conflict that breaks out over the proposed answers.

 ## Performance Assessment

Now that we have some idea of how the various institutions and actors that make up the political system interact to make public policy, let us assess how that process upholds the core values of democracy. In this final performance assessment of the book, we are going to examine each of the four core values and provide an appraisal of how well (or poorly) they are reflected in the policymaking process.

Popular Sovereignty

As we learned in Chapter 1, popular sovereignty refers to the highest political authority in a state or society. In a democracy, that means the will of the people and that government is expected to be responsive to the needs and demands of ordinary people. While the core value of popular sovereignty makes no guarantees about outcomes, it does suggest that all citizens have a basic right to participate in the process of making decisions about "what we ought to do." This does not guarantee that every individual's preferences will become public policy, but it does guarantee that every individual will have the opportunity to be included in the policy discussion.

In practice, the process of making public policy gets a mixed report in terms of upholding the core value of popular sovereignty. The will of the people, at least in terms of public opinion, undoubtedly plays an important role in most stages of the policy process. It helps determine what is on the public agenda, and it also plays a role in policy formulation and adoption by setting the boundaries on what is considered an acceptable response to a particular problem or issue. Public opinion, in other words, might not determine which policy alternative is ultimately chosen, but it plays an important role in determining what is *not* chosen. As we learned in Chapter 9, few elected officials (nor, for that matter, courts or bureaucracies) relish the prospect of making decisions that run counter to public opinion.

Public opinion can also play an important role in policy evaluation. A program or policy that is widely disliked or viewed as failing will invariably attract the attention of reformers who can use public opinion to push the issue back onto the public agenda.

But as we also learned in Chapter 9, public opinion is often a poor guide to the will of the people; mostly because "the people" are rarely of one mind about any particular issue, let alone what constitutes the most acceptable response. This makes it difficult for the will of the people, as represented by public opinion, to provide a firm basis for selecting and formally adopting a particular policy choice.

In practice, popular sovereignty is upheld by the numerous points of access made available to virtually all citizens in the policy process. Citizens not only can express their opinions to pollsters or make their preferences known by casting a ballot, they can join organized interest groups, contact officials, appeal bureaucratic decisions, show up at public hearings, and sue when they feel policy has wronged them. The federal system vastly increases the number of access points—there are local, state, and federal legislatures; executives; courts; and agencies. In this way the core value of political freedom (discussed below) helps ensure popular sovereignty remains a driving force throughout the policy process.

While the policy process generally gets good marks for its attention to public policy and its numerous access points, it is also true that those driving public opinion and those taking the most advantage of those access points cannot be accurately described as "the people." It takes resources—money, time, expertise, manpower—to engage in a concentrated lobbying effort or to pursue a court case. Those with the resources to engage in such activities consistently and successfully are almost by definition elites.

Even a relatively simple attempt to participate in the policy process can mean a significant sacrifice for the average citizen. For example, showing up at city hall to protest a zoning variance that allows a strip mall to built next to a school can mean taking time off of work and then facing the experts hired by a developer to argue for the variance. This citizen not only has to make a sacrifice (lost time and wages) to participate, but her participation may leave her frustrated because she found herself outgunned in terms of information and expertise.

Political scientists have long argued that public opinion can be manipulated through skillful framing of an issue (Edelman 1988; Mills 1956). For example, what is your reaction to a proposed law entitled an Act to Expand Government's Powers to Spy Freely on Citizens? Not exactly something designed to attract unbridled public support, right? How about the same law, but renaming it the Patriot Act? It is a little harder to oppose a policy that is framed, literally, as a patriot's act, even if substantively that law *is* a proposal to vastly expand government's powers to spy freely on its own citizens (see discussion of the Patriot Act in Chapter 4).

Examples such as the Patriot Act show that attaching policy proposals to values important to Americans—even if the proposal has little substantive connection to those values—is a powerful way to increase the chances of getting that proposal formally adopted. If nothing else, this illustrates that popular sovereignty is recognized as an important force in the policy process, even if it is not always respected. However imperfectly popular sovereignty is translated from a democratic ideal into policymaking practice, the *idea* of popular sovereignty remains a force to be reckoned with.

Political Freedom

As we learned in Chapter 1, government cannot respond to the will of the people if people are not free to express their wants and demands. The critical ingredients for this freedom are the right to criticize current governmental leaders and policies, the right to propose new courses of action for government to follow, the right to form and join interest groups, the right to discuss political issues free from government censorship, and the right of all citizens to seek and hold public office.

Of all the core democratic values, political freedom is probably the easiest to recognize in the policy process. From agenda setting to evaluation, the government's proposals and actions are discussed, analyzed, and criticized by, well, just about everyone. And most have an opinion on what the government should (or should not) do and are free to share that opinion as their means and abilities allow.

American citizens are free to speak in public places, write letters to the editor, contact public officials, join interest groups, and circulate petitions. In some areas (states with ballot initiatives, for example), citizens even have the freedom to take public policy out of the government's hands and make laws themselves. Americans enjoy a free press, with virtually unlimited access to information. Most government policy processes are, by law, transparent, meaning citizens can "see inside" government. In short, American citizens have all the necessary tools to enjoy a high degree of political freedom, and that freedom is widely exercised at every stage of the policy press.

However, as we learned in our discussion of the media in Chapter 8, being free to express an opinion or criticize a policy does not necessarily mean those views will reach their intended audience. If there is a downside to political freedom, it is that in the marketplace of public opinions and ideas, some voices are always going to speak more loudly than others. The danger to political freedom in the policymaking process is not really that minority or dissenting opinions will be silenced. Relatively speaking, the policy process is largely free of censorship of any kind—people are pretty much free to say what they want about the government and what it should do. No, the real danger is that minority or dissenting opinions will not be heard.

Political Equality

Chapter 1 pointed out that political equality is the most complex and difficult core value of democracy because it can take many forms (social equality, economic equality, equality under the law, equality of opportunity). Essentially, political equality means that individual preferences are given equal weight.

If political freedom is the core democratic value most readily translated from theory into policymaking practice, political equality provides an interesting contrast. Political equality is the value the American political system has had the hardest time putting into practice. This difficulty is clearly evident in historical terms, as indicated by our discussion of civil liberties and civil rights in Chapters 4 and 5. For large parts of the republic's history, minorities, women, and other groups have been legally excluded from the policymaking process altogether.

Yet while such blatant inequalities are mostly a thing of the past, it is clear that some groups still enjoy more power and influence in the policymaking process. That power and influence translates into political inequality; in other words, the views and preferences of some count for more. The reasons for this are obvious. Economic inequality, for example, means different groups have different levels of influence in the policymaking process. Those with more money or more time or more organization are much better positioned to take advantage of the political freedoms the policymaking process affords. It is much easier (though far from guaranteed) to gain the attention of policymakers if you can underwrite campaign donations and pay for television and newspaper ads.

Economic inequality, though, is perhaps less of a concern. As we learned in Chapter 1, economic inequality has long been considered simply a product of equality of opportunity. When people are free to make their own choices, and to go as far as their effort and talents allow, some are always going to end up with more than others. Perhaps more disturbing is the persistent social inequality political scientists see in the policymaking process.

Chapter 1 also discussed the pluralist ideal of a democracy, where government is used as means to settle conflicts and reach compromise among competing group interests and where all groups have enough political resources to successfully participate in the political process. In the pluralist ideal, groups are roughly equal, at least in the sense that they have the capability to defend their own interests through the policymaking process.

A number of studies have shown that this pluralist ideal is far from the reality of policymaking. For example, in a wide-ranging study of how policy is made, political scientists Anne Schneider and Helen Ingram (1997) argue that public policies always have target populations, or groups of people who will either receive benefits or pay costs as a result of a policy decision. Schneider and Ingram found that some groups are consistently viewed as those who deserve to receive the benefits of policy while others are consistently viewed as those who deserve to bear the costs. These differences break down along traditional social fault lines such as race and class. Thus, for example, middle-class, white-collar workers are typically viewed as deserving of policy benefits. Criminals are viewed as deserving of policy costs.

This is important, because framing a policy in terms of its target population can have a powerful impact. For example, take the substantive issue of crime. It is no longer acceptable in mainstream American politics to promote policies that are blatantly racist. Yet it is perfectly acceptable to push a tough line on crime. Quick, think of a criminal—what does he look like? For most people, it is a he, and that he is a young, black male. This group has been targeted as deserving to bear the costs of crime. Do not white, middle- and upper-class people who commit crimes also go to jail? Yes, but not with the same probability. And crimes that are more associated with the middle-class suburbs (for example, using powdered cocaine) are punished less, and less harshly, than crimes associated more with the inner cities (using crack cocaine). A celebrity with a drug problem typically goes to rehab; an inner-city youth goes to jail. Crime, some political scientists argue, is a policy shot through with racist undertones all the way from agenda setting to evaluation (Beckett 1997).

There are numerous other substantive policies wherein scholars have found similar inequalities among groups. Tax policy tends to favor the middle class. For example, being able to deduct interest paid on your mortgage is a nice tax benefit—but you only get this benefit if you are a homeowner. State and federal higher education policies tend to disproportionately favor middle-class students and private colleges rather than public colleges. The latter tend to have higher minority enrollments (Alexander 1998). Inequality is clearly still a fact of the policymaking process.

Majority Rule

The final core value of democracy is majority rule. Majority rule simply means that government follows the course of action preferred by most people. Majority rule can be defined in terms of more than half of eligible citizens or voters preferring one particular policy, or as a plurality, which means no alternative has more than 50 percent support, but one alternative—the plurality choice—has more support than all the others.

Majority rule actually has a surprisingly good record in the policymaking process of the American political system. Large numbers of people express dissatisfaction with the policies of government, mostly saying they want middle-of-the road government responses to problems. Yet political scientists find that government pretty much *does* adopt a middle-of-the road stance in making public policy. Americans seem to be upset at government for giving them what they ask for (Hibbing and Theiss-Morse 2001). There are certainly people—sometimes even majorities—who disagree with specific substantive public policies. And most high-profile policy actions get varying levels of public support as they shift from adoption to implementation to evaluation (such as the war in Iraq). Yet, overall, the evidence suggests that government does a pretty good job in addressing the policy preferences of its citizens.

There are, of course, exceptions. Perhaps the highest profile exception in recent years was the presidential election of 2000. As discussed elsewhere in this book, George W. Bush won the presidency not only without a majority of votes but without even a plurality—more people voted for Al Gore than Bush. Bush won because of the electoral college system, not because a majority or plurality of voters approved his candidacy. These sorts of exceptions, though, are rare. Given how divided public opinion is on most policy matters, an overall record indicating that there exists plurality, if not majority, support for government policies is no small feat.

Majority rule has to be balanced with minority rights. In this regard, the policy-making process has a mixed record. Historically, some public policies that were adopted and implemented were specifically aimed at robbing minorities of their rights as democratic citizens (for example, Jim Crow laws). Those sort of egregious violations of minority rights are mostly a thing of the past. As we saw in the discussion on political equality, however, there remain concerns about how minority groups are treated by the policymaking process.

Overall, then, how should we rate the performance of democracy in America? As we have seen throughout this discussion and throughout the entire book, the American political system imperfectly lives up to the democratic promise. Historically, its record is very mixed, and even today the institutions and processes that make up the policymaking process struggle to put the core values into practice, especially political equality. Judged by the standards of theoretical perfection, however, every democracy that ever existed will come up short. Ranked against other democracies, America may fall short in some areas (such as political equality), but it shines in others (such as political freedom).

In terms of putting the core values into action, resolving the conflicts that inevitably occur among these values, and making the institutions and processes of the political system follow the guidelines set by these values, America should get reasonably high marks. The American political system has not, and does not, completely fulfill the promise of democracy—something that should always be remembered. However, it should not be forgotten that at least parts of this same system have consistently sought to keep that promise.

Summary

- Public policy is a relatively stable, purposive course of action undertaken by public authorities.
- The process of making public policy, as well as the policies themselves, are the ultimate test of how the promise of democracy is translated into the performance of democracy.
- The central characteristic of public policy is conflict between two or more groups over something that they value. This can be tangible (such as cash benefits) or intangible (such as the right to burn the flag). Democratic decisions will uphold these core values.
- The public policy process can be systematically ordered into four stages: agenda setting, policy formulation and adoption, policy implementation, and policy evaluation.
- Agenda setting is the process of producing the list of issues and problems the government will address.
- Policy formulation and adoption is the process government undertakes to consider various alternatives to the issue or problem at hand and to formally approve one of those alternatives.
- Policy implementation is the process of attempting to translate the intent expressed in a formally approved policy into action.
- Policy evaluation is the process of assessing the impact, effectiveness, and problems of a public policy. Policy evaluations often lead back to the agenda-setting stage.

- The core democratic value of popular sovereignty has a mixed record in public policymaking. Public opinion plays an important role in agenda setting and in stating the boundaries of what policy alternatives are seriously considered, but it is too divided to provide a clear guide on most issues. Multiple access points help ensure a good connection between the will of the people and public policy.
- Political freedom is the core value that is most easily observed in the policymaking process. Americans are free to express their views, share their opinions, and contact public authorities with relatively little censorship or restrictions.
- Political equality is the core value with which the American political system has struggled the hardest to translate into practice. Even in the contemporary policymaking process, political scientists find that some groups are favored and others are not.
- With some important exceptions, the American political system has a fairly good record of upholding the core value of majority rule. Though public opinion is mixed on most policy issues, and is generally not positive about government performance, there is actually a high correlation between the policies people say they want from government and the policies government actually adopts and implements.
- Overall, the American political system gets a mixed report card in its effort to translate the promise of democracy into the performance of democracy. Despite some failures and difficulties, however, the democratic promise remains a guiding goal of the American political system.

Key Terms

feedback 517
focusing event 517
incrementalism 518
indicators 516
impact evaluations 524
institutional agenda 518
policy adoption 513
policy evaluation 522

policy formulation 518
policy implementation 520
process evaluations 523
public agenda 514
public policy 511
rational-comprehensive
  decision making 518

Selected Readings

Anderson, James. 2000. *Public Policymaking.* 4th ed. New York: Houghton Mifflin. An excellent introduction to the study of public policymaking in the United States. In addition to a good discussion of policy models, Anderson includes separate chapters on substantive policy topics.

Schneider, Anne Larson, and Helen Ingram. 1997. *Policy Design for Democracy.* Lawrence: University of Kansas Press. Two political scientists examine how different groups come to disproportionately receive the benefits or bear the costs of public policies in the United States.

Stone, Deborah. 1997. *Policy Paradox: The Art of Political Decision Making.* New York: Norton. An excellent introduction into the complexities of how public authorities go about making public policy.

Appendix

The Constitution of the United States

We the People of the United States, in Order to form a more perfect Union, establish Justice, insure domestic Tranquility, provide for the common defense, promote the general Welfare, and secure the Blessings of Liberty to ourselves and our Posterity, do ordain and establish this Constitution for the United States of America.

Article I

Section 1. All legislative Powers herein granted shall be vested in a Congress of the United States, which shall consist of a Senate and House of Representatives.

Section 2. The House of Representatives shall be composed of Members chosen every second Year by the People of the several States, and the Electors in each State shall have the Qualifications requisite for Electors of the most numerous Branch of the State Legislature.

No Person shall be a Representative who shall not have attained to the Age of twenty five Years, and been seven Years a Citizen of the United States, and who shall not, when elected, be an Inhabitant of that State in which he shall be chosen.

Representatives and direct Taxes shall be apportioned among the several States which may be included within this Union, according to their respective Numbers, which shall be determined by adding to the whole Number of free Persons, including those bound to Service for a Term of Years, and excluding Indians not taxed, three fifths of all other Persons. The actual Enumeration shall be made within three Years after the first Meeting of the Congress of the United States, and within every subsequent Term of ten Years, in such Manner as they shall by Law direct. The Number of Representatives shall not exceed one for every thirty Thousand, but each State shall have at Least one Representative; and until such enumeration shall be made, the State of New Hampshire shall be entitled to chuse three, Massachusetts eight, Rhode-Island and Providence Plantations one, Connecticut five, New-York six, New Jersey four, Pennsylvania eight, Delaware one, Maryland six, Virginia ten, North Carolina five, South Carolina five, and Georgia three.

When vacancies happen in the Representation from any State, the Executive Authority thereof shall issue Writs of Election to fill such Vacancies.

The House of Representatives shall chuse their Speaker and other Officers; and shall have the sole Power of Impeachment.

Section 3. The Senate of the United States shall be composed of two Senators from each State, chosen by the Legislature thereof for six Years; and each Senator shall have one Vote.

Immediately after they shall be assembled in Consequence of the first Election, they shall be divided as equally as may be into three Classes. The Seats of the Senators of the first Class shall be vacated at the Expiration of the second Year, of the second Class at the Expiration of the fourth Year, and of the third Class at the Expiration of the sixth Year, so that one third may be chosen every second Year; and if Vacancies happen by Resignation, or otherwise, during the Recess of the Legislature of any State, the Executive thereof may make temporary Appointments until the next Meeting of the Legislature, which shall then fill such Vacancies.

No Person shall be a Senator who shall not have attained to the Age of thirty Years, and been nine Years a Citizen of the United States, and who shall not, when elected, be an Inhabitant of that State for which he shall be chosen.

The Vice President of the United States shall be President of the Senate, but shall have no Vote, unless they be equally divided.

The Senate shall chuse their other Officers, and also a President pro tempore, in the Absence of the Vice President, or when he shall exercise the Office of President of the United States.

The Senate shall have the sole Power to try all Impeachments. When sitting for that Purpose, they shall be on Oath or Affirmation. When the President of the United States is tried, the Chief Justice shall preside: And no Person shall be convicted without the Concurrence of two thirds of the Members present.

Judgment in Cases of Impeachment shall not extend further than to removal from Office, and disqualification to hold and enjoy any Office of honor, Trust or Profit under the United States: but the Party convicted shall nevertheless be liable and subject to Indictment, Trial, Judgment and Punishment, according to Law.

Section 4.   The Times, Places and Manner of holding Elections for Senators and Representatives, shall be prescribed in each State by the Legislature thereof; but the Congress may at any time by Law make or alter such Regulations, except as to the Places of chusing Senators.

The Congress shall assemble at least once in every Year, and such Meeting shall be on the first Monday in December, unless they shall by Law appoint a different Day.

Section 5.   Each House shall be the Judge of the Elections, Returns and Qualifications of its own Members, and a Majority of each shall constitute a Quorum to do Business; but a smaller Number may adjourn from day to day, and may be authorized to compel the Attendance of absent Members, in such Manner, and under such Penalties as each House may provide.

Each House may determine the Rules of its Proceedings, punish its Members for disorderly Behaviour, and, with the Concurrence of two thirds, expel a Member.

Each House shall keep a Journal of its Proceedings, and from time to time publish the same, excepting such Parts as may in their Judgment require Secrecy; and the Yeas and Nays of the Members of either House on any question shall, at the Desire of one fifth of those Present, be entered on the Journal.

Neither House, during the Session of Congress, shall, without the Consent of the other, adjourn for more than three days, nor to any other Place than that in which the two Houses shall be sitting.

Section 6.   The Senators and Representatives shall receive a Compensation for their Services, to be ascertained by Law, and paid out of the Treasury of the United States. They shall in all Cases, except Treason, Felony and Breach of the Peace, be privileged from Arrest during their Attendance at the Session of their respective Houses, and in going to and returning from the same; and for any Speech or Debate in either House, they shall not be questioned in any other Place.

No Senator or Representative shall, during the Time for which he was elected, be appointed to any civil Office under the Authority of the United States, which shall have been created, or the Emoluments whereof shall have been encreased during such time; and no Person holding any Office under the United States, shall be a Member of either House during his Continuance in Office.

Section 7.   All Bills for raising Revenue shall originate in the House of Representatives; but the Senate may propose or concur with Amendments as on other Bills.

Every Bill which shall have passed the House of Representatives and the Senate, shall, before it become a Law, be presented to the President of the United States: If he approve he shall sign it, but if not he shall return it, with his Objections to that House in which it shall have originated, who shall enter the Objections at large on their Journal, and proceed to reconsider it. If after such Reconsideration two thirds of that House shall agree to pass the Bill, it shall be sent, together with the Objections, to the other House, by which it shall likewise be reconsidered, and if approved by two thirds of that House, it shall become a Law. But in all such Cases the Votes of both Houses shall be determined by yeas and Nays, and the Names of the Persons voting for and against the Bill shall be entered on the Journal of each House respectively. If any Bill shall not be returned by the President within ten Days (Sundays excepted) after it shall have been presented to him, the Same shall be a Law, in like Manner as if he had signed it, unless the Congress by their Adjournment prevent its Return, in which Case it shall not be a Law.

Every Order, Resolution, or Vote to which the Concurrence of the Senate and House of Representatives may be necessary (except on a question of Adjournment) shall be presented to the President of the United States; and before the Same shall take Effect, shall be approved by him, or being disapproved by him, shall be repassed by two thirds of the Senate and House of Representatives, according to the Rules and Limitations prescribed in the Case of a Bill.

Section 8.   The Congress shall have Power To lay and collect Taxes, Duties, Imposts and Excises, to pay the Debts and provide for the common Defence and general Welfare of the United States; but all Duties, Imposts and Excises shall be uniform throughout the United States;

To borrow Money on the credit of the United States;

To regulate Commerce with foreign Nations, and among the several States, and with the Indian Tribes;

To establish an uniform Rule of Naturalization, and uniform Laws on the subject of Bankruptcies throughout the United States;

To coin Money, regulate the Value thereof, and of foreign Coin, and fix the Standard of Weights and Measures;

To provide for the Punishment of counterfeiting the Securities and current Coin of the United States;

To establish Post Offices and post Roads;

To promote the Progress of Science and useful Arts, by securing for limited Times to Authors and Inventors the exclusive Right to their respective Writings and Discoveries;

To constitute Tribunals inferior to the supreme Court;

To define and punish Piracies and Felonies committed on the high Seas, and Offences against the Law of Nations;

To declare War, grant Letters of Marque and Reprisal, and make Rules concerning Captures on Land and Water;

To raise and support Armies, but no Appropriation of Money to that Use shall be for a longer Term than two Years;

To provide and maintain a Navy;

To make Rules for the Government and Regulation of the land and naval Forces;

To provide for calling forth the Militia to execute the Laws of the Union, suppress Insurrections and repel Invasions;

To provide for organizing, arming, and disciplining, the Militia, and for governing such Part of them as may be employed in the Service of the United States, reserving to the States respectively, the Appointment of the Officers, and the Authority of training the Militia according to the discipline prescribed by Congress;

To exercise exclusive Legislation in all Cases whatsoever, over such District (not exceeding ten Miles square) as may, by Cession of particular States, and the Acceptance of Congress, become the Seat of the Government of the United States, and to exercise like Authority over all Places purchased by the Consent of the Legislature of the State in which the Same shall be, for the Erection of Forts, Magazines, Arsenals, dock-Yards, and other needful Buildings;—And

To make all Laws which shall be necessary and proper for carrying into Execution the foregoing Powers, and all other Powers vested by this Constitution in the Government of the United States, or in any Department or Officer thereof.

Section 9.   The Migration or Importation of such Persons as any of the States now existing shall think proper to admit, shall not be prohibited by the Congress prior to the Year one thousand eight hundred and eight, but a Tax or duty may be imposed on such Importation, not exceeding ten dollars for each Person.

The Privilege of the Writ of Habeas Corpus shall not be suspended, unless when in Cases of

Rebellion or Invasion the public Safety may require it.

No Bill of Attainder or ex post facto Law shall be passed.

No Capitation, or other direct, Tax shall be laid, unless in Proportion to the Census or enumeration herein before directed to be taken.

No Tax or Duty shall be laid on Articles exported from any State.

No Preference shall be given by any Regulation of Commerce or Revenue to the Ports of one State over those of another; nor shall Vessels bound to, or from, one State, be obliged to enter, clear, or pay Duties in another.

No Money shall be drawn from the Treasury, but in Consequence of Appropriations made by Law; and a regular Statement and Account of the Receipts and Expenditures of all public Money shall be published from time to time.

No Title of Nobility shall be granted by the United States: And no Person holding any Office of Profit or Trust under them, shall, without the Consent of the Congress, accept of any present, Emolument, Office, or Title, of any kind whatever, from any King, Prince, or foreign State.

Section 10.   No State shall enter into any Treaty, Alliance, or Confederation; grant Letters of Marque and Reprisal; coin Money; emit Bills of Credit; make any Thing but gold and silver Coin a Tender in Payment of Debts; pass any Bill of Attainder, ex post facto Law, or Law impairing the Obligation of Contracts, or grant any Title of Nobility.

No State shall, without the Consent of the Congress, lay any Imposts or Duties on Imports or Exports, except what may be absolutely necessary for executing it's inspection Laws: and the net Produce of all Duties and Imposts, laid by any State on Imports or Exports, shall be for the Use of the Treasury of the United States; and all such Laws shall be subject to the Revision and Controul of the Congress.

No State shall, without the Consent of Congress, lay any Duty of Tonnage, keep Troops, or Ships of War in time of Peace, enter into any Agreement or Compact with another State, or with a foreign Power, or engage in War, unless actually invaded, or in such imminent Danger as will not admit of delay.

Article II

Section 1.   The executive Power shall be vested in a President of the United States of America. He shall hold his Office during the Term of four Years, and, together with the Vice President, chosen for the same Term, be elected, as follows:

Each State shall appoint, in such Manner as the Legislature thereof may direct, a Number of Electors, equal to the whole Number of Senators and Representatives to which the State may be entitled in the Congress: but no Senator or Representative, or Person holding an Office of Trust or Profit under the United States, shall be appointed an Elector.

The Electors shall meet in their respective States, and vote by Ballot for two Persons, of whom one at least shall not be an Inhabitant of the same State with themselves. And they shall make a List of all the Persons voted for, and of the Number of Votes for each; which List they shall sign and certify, and transmit sealed to the Seat of the Government of the United States, directed to the President of the Senate. The President of the Senate shall, in the Presence of the Senate and House of Representatives, open all the Certificates, and the Votes shall then be counted. The Person having the greatest Number of Votes shall be the President, if such Number be a Majority of the whole Number of Electors appointed; and if there be more than one who have such Majority, and have an equal Number of Votes, then the House of Representatives shall immediately chuse by Ballot one of them for President; and if no Person have a Majority, then from the five highest on the List the said House shall in like Manner chuse the President. But in chusing the President, the Votes shall be taken by States, the Representation from each State having one Vote; A quorum for this purpose shall consist of a Member or Members from two thirds of the States, and a Majority of all the States shall be necessary to a Choice. In every Case, after the Choice of the President, the Person having the greatest Number of Votes of the Electors shall be the Vice President. But if there should remain two or more who have equal Votes, the Senate shall chuse from them by Ballot the Vice President.

The Congress may determine the Time of chusing the Electors, and the Day on which they shall give their Votes; which Day shall be the same throughout the United States.

No Person except a natural born Citizen, or a Citizen of the United States, at the time of the Adoption of this Constitution, shall be eligible to the Office of President; neither shall any Person be eligible to that Office who shall not have attained to the Age of thirty five Years, and been fourteen Years a Resident within the United States.

In Case of the Removal of the President from Office, or of his Death, Resignation, or Inability to discharge the Powers and Duties of the said Office, the Same shall devolve on the Vice President, and the Congress may by Law provide for the Case of Removal, Death, Resignation or Inability, both of the President and Vice President, declaring what Officer shall then act as President, and such Officer shall act accordingly, until the Disability be removed, or a President shall be elected.

The President shall, at stated Times, receive for his Services, a Compensation, which shall neither be increased nor diminished during the Period for which he shall have been elected, and he shall not receive within that Period any other Emolument from the United States, or any of them.

Before he enter on the Execution of his Office, he shall take the following Oath or Affirmation:— "I do solemnly swear (or affirm) that I will faithfully execute the Office of President of the United States, and will to the best of my Ability, preserve, protect and defend the Constitution of the United States."

Section 2.   The President shall be Commander in Chief of the Army and Navy of the United States, and of the Militia of the several States, when called into the actual Service of the United States; he may require the Opinion, in writing, of the principal Officer in each of the executive Departments, upon any Subject relating to the Duties of their respective Offices, and he shall have Power to grant Reprieves and Pardons for Offences against the United States, except in Cases of Impeachment.

He shall have Power, by and with the Advice and Consent of the Senate, to make Treaties, provided two thirds of the Senators present concur; and he shall nominate, and by and with the Advice and

Consent of the Senate, shall appoint Ambassadors, other public Ministers and Consuls, Judges of the supreme Court, and all other Officers of the United States, whose Appointments are not herein otherwise provided for, and which shall be established by Law: but the Congress may by Law vest the Appointment of such inferior Officers, as they think proper, in the President alone, in the Courts of Law, or in the Heads of Departments.

The President shall have Power to fill up all Vacancies that may happen during the Recess of the Senate, by granting Commissions which shall expire at the End of their next Session.

Section 3.   He shall from time to time give to the Congress Information of the State of the Union, and recommend to their Consideration such Measures as he shall judge necessary and expedient; he may, on extraordinary Occasions, convene both Houses, or either of them, and in Case of Disagreement between them, with Respect to the Time of Adjournment, he may adjourn them to such Time as he shall think proper; he shall receive Ambassadors and other public Ministers; he shall take Care that the Laws be faithfully executed, and shall Commission all the Officers of the United States.

Section 4.   The President, Vice President and all civil Officers of the United States, shall be removed from Office on Impeachment for, and Conviction of, Treason, Bribery, or other high Crimes and Misdemeanors.

Article III

Section 1.   The judicial Power of the United States shall be vested in one supreme Court, and in such inferior Courts as the Congress may from time to time ordain and establish. The Judges, both of the supreme and inferior Courts, shall hold their Offices during good Behaviour, and shall, at stated Times, receive for their Services a Compensation, which shall not be diminished during their Continuance in Office.

Section 2.   The judicial Power shall extend to all Cases, in Law and Equity, arising under this

Constitution, the Laws of the United States, and Treaties made, or which shall be made, under their Authority;—to all Cases affecting Ambassadors, other public Ministers and Consuls;—to all Cases of admiralty and maritime Jurisdiction;—to Controversies to which the United States shall be a Party;—to Controversies between two or more States;—between a State and Citizens of another State;—between Citizens of different States;—between Citizens of the same State claiming Lands under Grants of different States, and between a State, or the Citizens thereof, and foreign States, Citizens or Subjects.

In all Cases affecting Ambassadors, other public Ministers and Consuls, and those in which a State shall be Party, the supreme Court shall have original Jurisdiction. In all the other Cases before mentioned, the supreme Court shall have appellate Jurisdiction, both as to Law and Fact, with such Exceptions, and under such Regulations as the Congress shall make.

The Trial of all Crimes, except in Cases of Impeachment, shall be by Jury; and such Trial shall be held in the State where the said Crimes shall have been committed; but when not committed within any State, the Trial shall be at such Place or Places as the Congress may by Law have directed.

Section 3.   Treason against the United States, shall consist only in levying War against them, or in adhering to their Enemies, giving them Aid and Comfort. No Person shall be convicted of Treason unless on the Testimony of two Witnesses to the same overt Act, or on Confession in open Court.

The Congress shall have Power to declare the Punishment of Treason, but no Attainder of Treason shall work Corruption of Blood, or Forfeiture except during the Life of the Person attainted.

Article IV

Section 1.   Full Faith and Credit shall be given in each State to the public Acts, Records, and judicial Proceedings of every other State. And the Congress may by general Laws prescribe the Manner in which such Acts, Records and Proceedings shall be proved, and the Effect thereof.

Section 2.   The Citizens of each State shall be entitled to all Privileges and Immunities of Citizens in the several States.

A Person charged in any State with Treason, Felony, or other Crime, who shall flee from Justice, and be found in another State, shall on Demand of the executive Authority of the State from which he fled, be delivered up, to be removed to the State having Jurisdiction of the Crime.

No Person held to Service or Labour in one State, under the Laws thereof, escaping into another, shall, in Consequence of any Law or Regulation therein, be discharged from such Service or Labour, but shall be delivered up on Claim of the Party to whom such Service or Labour may be due.

Section 3.   New States may be admitted by the Congress into this Union; but no new State shall be formed or erected within the Jurisdiction of any other State; nor any State be formed by the Junction of two or more States, or Parts of States, without the Consent of the Legislatures of the States concerned as well as of the Congress.

The Congress shall have Power to dispose of and make all needful Rules and Regulations respecting the Territory or other Property belonging to the United States; and nothing in this Constitution shall be so construed as to Prejudice any Claims of the United States, or of any particular State.

Section 4.   The United States shall guarantee to every State in this Union a Republican Form of Government, and shall protect each of them against Invasion; and on Application of the Legislature, or of the Executive (when the Legislature cannot be convened), against domestic Violence.

Article V

The Congress, whenever two thirds of both Houses shall deem it necessary, shall propose Amendments to this Constitution, or, on the Application of the Legislatures of two thirds of the several States, shall call a Convention for proposing Amendments, which, in either Case, shall be valid to all Intents and Purposes, as Part of this Constitution, when ratified by the Legislatures of three fourths of the several States, or by Conventions in three fourths thereof, as the one or the other Mode of Ratification may be proposed by the Congress; Provided that no Amendment which may be made prior to the Year One thousand eight hundred and eight shall in any Manner affect the first and fourth Clauses in the Ninth Section of the first Article; and that no State, without its Consent, shall be deprived of its equal Suffrage in the Senate.

Article VI

All Debts contracted and Engagements entered into, before the Adoption of this Constitution, shall be as valid against the United States under this Constitution, as under the Confederation.

This Constitution, and the Laws of the United States which shall be made in Pursuance thereof; and all Treaties made, or which shall be made, under the Authority of the United States, shall be the supreme Law of the Land; and the Judges in every State shall be bound thereby, any Thing in the Constitution or Laws of any State to the Contrary notwithstanding.

The Senators and Representatives before mentioned, and the Members of the several State Legislatures, and all executive and judicial Officers, both of the United States and of the several States, shall be bound by Oath or Affirmation, to support this Constitution; but no religious Test shall ever be required as a Qualification to any Office or public Trust under the United States.

Article VII

The Ratification of the Conventions of nine States, shall be sufficient for the Establishment of this Constitution between the States so ratifying the Same.

The Word, "the," being interlined between the seventh and eighth Lines of the first Page, the Word "Thirty" being partly written on an Erazure in the fifteenth Line of the first Page, The Words "is tried" being interlined between the thirty second and thirty third Lines of the first Page and the Word "the" being interlined between the forty third and forty fourth Lines of the second Page.

Attest William Jackson Secretary.

Done in Convention by the Unanimous Consent of the States present the Seventeenth Day of September in the Year of our Lord one thousand seven hundred and Eighty seven and of the Independence of the United States of America the Twelfth In witness whereof We have hereunto subscribed our Names . . .

Amendment I (1791)

Congress shall make no law respecting an establishment of religion, or prohibiting the free exercise thereof; or abridging the freedom of speech, or of the press; or the right of the people peaceably to assemble, and to petition the Government for a redress of grievances.

Amendment II (1791)

A well regulated Militia, being necessary to the security of a free State, the right of the people to keep and bear Arms, shall not be infringed.

Amendment III (1791)

No Soldier shall, in time of peace be quartered in any house, without the consent of the Owner, nor in time of war, but in a manner to be prescribed by law.

Amendment IV (1791)

The right of the people to be secure in their persons, houses, papers, and effects, against unreasonable searches and seizures, shall not be violated, and no Warrants shall issue, but upon probable cause, supported by Oath or affirmation, and particularly describing the place to be searched, and the persons or things to be seized.

Amendment V (1791)

No person shall be held to answer for a capital, or otherwise infamous crime, unless on a presentment or indictment of a Grand Jury, except in cases arising in the land or naval forces, or in the Militia, when in actual service in time of War or public danger; nor shall any person be subject for the same offence to be twice put in jeopardy of life or limb; nor shall be compelled in any criminal case to be a witness against himself, nor be deprived of life, liberty, or property, without due process of law; nor shall private property be taken for public use, without just compensation.

Amendment VI (1791)

In all criminal prosecutions, the accused shall enjoy the right to a speedy and public trial, by an impartial jury of the State and district wherein the crime shall have been committed, which district shall have been previously ascertained by law, and to be informed of the nature and cause of the accusation; to be confronted with the witnesses against him; to have compulsory process for obtaining witnesses in his favor, and to have the Assistance of Counsel for his defense.

Amendment VII (1791)

In Suits at common law, where the value in controversy shall exceed twenty dollars, the right of trial by jury shall be preserved, and no fact tried by a jury, shall be otherwise re-examined in any Court of the United States, than according to the rules of the common law.

Amendment VIII (1791)

Excessive bail shall not be required, nor excessive fines imposed, nor cruel and unusual punishments inflicted.

Amendment IX (1791)

The enumeration in the Constitution, of certain rights, shall not be construed to deny or disparage others retained by the people.

Amendment X (1791)

The powers not delegated to the United States by the Constitution, nor prohibited by it to the States, are reserved to the States respectively, or to the people.

Amendment XI

The Judicial power of the United States shall not be construed to extend to any suit in law or equity, commenced or prosecuted against one of the United States by Citizens of another State, or by Citizens or Subjects of any Foreign State.

Amendment XII

The Electors shall meet in their respective states, and vote by ballot for President and Vice-President, one of whom, at least, shall not be an inhabitant of the same state with themselves; they shall name in their ballots the person voted for as President, and in distinct ballots the person voted for as Vice-President, and they shall make distinct lists of all persons voted for as President, and of all persons voted for as Vice-President, and of the number of votes for each, which lists they shall sign and certify, and transmit sealed to the seat of the government of the United States, directed to the President of the Senate;— The President of the Senate shall, in the presence of the Senate and House of Representatives, open all the certificates and the votes shall then be counted;— The person having the greatest number of votes for President, shall be the President, if such number be a majority of the whole number of Electors appointed; and if no person have such majority, then from the persons having the highest numbers not exceeding three on the list of those voted for as President, the House of Representatives shall choose immediately, by ballot, the President. But in choosing the President, the votes shall be taken by states, the representation from each state having one vote; a quorum for this purpose shall consist of a member or members from two-thirds of the states, and a majority of all the states shall be necessary to a choice. And if the House of Representatives shall not choose a President whenever the right of choice shall devolve upon them, before the fourth day of March next following, then the Vice-President shall act as President, as in the case of the death or other constitutional disability of the President. *(See Note 14)*— The person having the greatest number of votes as Vice-President, shall be the Vice-President, if such number be a majority of the whole number of Electors appointed, and if no person have a majority, then from the two highest numbers on the list, the Senate shall choose the Vice-President; a quorum for the purpose shall consist of two-thirds of the whole number of Senators, and a majority of the whole number shall be necessary to a choice. But no person constitutionally ineligible to the office of President shall be eligible to that of Vice-President of the United States.

Amendment XIII (1865)

Section 1.   Neither slavery nor involuntary servitude, except as a punishment for crime whereof the party shall have been duly convicted, shall exist within the United States, or any place subject to their jurisdiction.

Section 2. Congress shall have power to enforce this article by appropriate legislation.

Amendment XIV (1868)

Section 1. All persons born or naturalized in the United States, and subject to the jurisdiction thereof, are citizens of the United States and of the State wherein they reside. No State shall make or enforce any law which shall abridge the privileges or immunities of citizens of the United States; nor shall any State deprive any person of life, liberty, or property, without due process of law; nor deny to any person within its jurisdiction the equal protection of the laws.

Section 2. Representatives shall be apportioned among the several States according to their respective numbers, counting the whole number of persons in each State, excluding Indians not taxed. But when the right to vote at any election for the choice of electors for President and Vice President of the United States, Representatives in Congress, the Executive and Judicial officers of a State, or the members of the Legislature thereof, is denied to any of the male inhabitants of such State, being twenty-one years of age, *(See Note 15)* and citizens of the United States, or in any way abridged, except for participation in rebellion, or other crime, the basis of representation therein shall be reduced in the proportion which the number of such male citizens shall bear to the whole number of male citizens twenty-one years of age in such State.

Section 3. No person shall be a Senator or Representative in Congress, or elector of President and Vice President, or hold any office, civil or military, under the United States, or under any State, who, having previously taken an oath, as a member of Congress, or as an officer of the United States, or as a member of any State legislature, or as an executive or judicial officer of any State, to support the Constitution of the United States, shall have engaged in insurrection or rebellion against the same, or given aid or comfort to the enemies thereof. But Congress may by a vote of two-thirds of each House, remove such disability.

Section 4. The validity of the public debt of the United States, authorized by law, including debts incurred for payment of pensions and bounties for services in suppressing insurrection or rebellion, shall not be questioned. But neither the United States nor any State shall assume or pay any debt or obligation incurred in aid of insurrection or rebellion against the United States, or any claim for the loss or emancipation of any slave; but all such debts, obligations and claims shall be held illegal and void.

Section 5. The Congress shall have power to enforce, by appropriate legislation, the provisions of this Article.

Amendment XV (1870)

Section 1. The right of citizens of the United States to vote shall not be denied or abridged by the United States or by any State on account of race, color, or previous condition of servitude.

Section 2. The Congress shall have power to enforce this article by appropriate legislation.

Amendment XVI (1913)

The Congress shall have power to lay and collect taxes on incomes, from whatever source derived, without apportionment among the several States, and without regard to any census or enumeration.

Amendment XVII (1913)

The Senate of the United States shall be composed of two Senators from each State, elected by the people thereof, for six years; and each Senator shall have one vote. The electors in each State shall have the qualifications requisite for electors of the most numerous branch of the State legislatures.

When vacancies happen in the representation of any State in the Senate, the executive authority of such State shall issue writs of election to fill such vacancies: Provided, that the legislature of any State may empower the executive thereof to make temporary appointments until the people fill the vacancies by election as the legislature may direct.

This amendment shall not be so construed as to affect the election or term of any Senator chosen before it becomes valid as part of the Constitution.

Amendment XVIII (1919)

Section 1.   After one year from the ratification of this article the manufacture, sale, or transportation of intoxicating liquors within, the importation thereof into, or the exportation thereof from the United States and all territory subject to the jurisdiction thereof for beverage purposes is hereby prohibited.

Section 2.   The Congress and the several States shall have concurrent power to enforce this article by appropriate legislation.

Section 3.   This article shall be inoperative unless it shall have been ratified as an amendment to the Constitution by the legislatures of the several States, as provided in the Constitution, within seven years from the date of the submission hereof to the States by the Congress.

Amendment XIX (1920)

The right of citizens of the United States to vote shall not be denied or abridged by the United States or by any State on account of sex.

Congress shall have power to enforce this article by appropriate legislation.

Amendment XX (1933)

Section 1.   The terms of the President and Vice President shall end at noon on the 20th day of January, and the terms of Senators and Representatives at noon on the 3rd day of January, of the years in which such terms would have ended if this article had not been ratified; and the terms of their successors shall then begin.

Section 2.   The Congress shall assemble at least once in every year, and such meeting shall begin at noon on the 3rd day of January, unless they shall by law appoint a different day.

Section 3.   If, at the time fixed for the beginning of the term of the President, the President elect shall have died, the Vice President elect shall become President. If a President shall not have been chosen before the time fixed for the beginning of his term, or if the President elect shall have failed to qualify, then the Vice President elect shall act as President until a President shall have qualified; and the Congress may by law provide for the case wherein neither a President elect nor a Vice President elect shall have qualified, declaring who shall then act as President, or the manner in which one who is to act shall be selected, and such person shall act accordingly until a President or Vice President shall have qualified.

Section 4.   The Congress may by law provide for the case of the death of any of the persons from whom the House of Representatives may choose a President whenever the right of choice shall have devolved upon them, and for the case of the death of any of the persons from whom the Senate may choose a Vice President whenever the right of choice shall have devolved upon them.

Section 5.   Sections 1 and 2 shall take effect on the 15th day of October following the ratification of this article.

Section 6.   This article shall be inoperative unless it shall have been ratified as an amendment to the Constitution by the legislatures of three-fourths of the several States within seven years from the date of its submission.

Amendment XXI (1933)

Section 1.   The eighteenth article of amendment to the Constitution of the United States is hereby repealed.

Section 2.   The transportation or importation into any State, Territory, or possession of the United States for delivery or use therein of intoxicating liquors, in violation of the laws thereof, is hereby prohibited.

Section 3.   This article shall be inoperative unless it shall have been ratified as an amendment to the Constitution by conventions in the several States, as provided in the Constitution, within seven years from the date of the submission hereof to the States by the Congress.

Amendment XXII (1951)

Section 1.   No person shall be elected to the office of the President more than twice, and no person who has held the office of President, or acted as President, for more than two years of a term to which some other person was elected President shall be elected to the office of the President more than once. But this article shall not apply to any person holding the office of President when this article was proposed by the Congress, and shall not prevent any person who may be holding the office of President, or acting as President, during the term within which this article becomes operative from holding the office of President or acting as President during the remainder of such term.

Section 2.   This article shall be inoperative unless it shall have been ratified as an amendment to the Constitution by the legislatures of three-fourths of the several states within seven years from the date of its submission to the states by the Congress.

Amendment XXIII (1961)

Section 1.   The District constituting the seat of government of the United States shall appoint in such manner as the Congress may direct:

A number of electors of President and Vice President equal to the whole number of Senators and Representatives in Congress to which the District would be entitled if it were a state, but in no event more than the least populous state; they shall be in addition to those appointed by the states, but they shall be considered, for the purposes of the election of President and Vice President, to be electors appointed by a state; and they shall meet in the District and perform such duties as provided by the twelfth article of amendment.

Section 2.   The Congress shall have power to enforce this article by appropriate legislation.

Amendment XXIV (1964)

Section 1.   The right of citizens of the United States to vote in any primary or other election for President or Vice President, for electors for President or Vice President, or for Senator or Representative in Congress, shall not be denied or abridged by the United States or any state by reason of failure to pay any poll tax or other tax.

Section 2.   The Congress shall have power to enforce this article by appropriate legislation.

Amendment XXV (1967)

Section 1.   In case of the removal of the President from office or of his death or resignation, the Vice President shall become President.

Section 2.   Whenever there is a vacancy in the office of the Vice President, the President shall nominate a Vice President who shall take office upon confirmation by a majority vote of both Houses of Congress.

Section 3.   Whenever the President transmits to the President pro tempore of the Senate and the Speaker of the House of Representatives his written declaration that he is unable to discharge the powers and duties of his office, and until he transmits to them a written declaration to the contrary, such powers and duties shall be discharged by the Vice President as Acting President.

Section 4.   Whenever the Vice President and a majority of either the principal officers of the executive departments or of such other body as Congress may by law provide, transmit to the President pro tempore of the Senate and the Speaker of the House of Representatives their written declaration that the President is unable to discharge the powers and duties of his office, the Vice President shall immediately assume the powers and duties of the office as Acting President.

Thereafter, when the President transmits to the President pro tempore of the Senate and the Speaker of the House of Representatives his written declaration that no inability exists, he shall resume the powers and duties of his office unless the Vice President and a majority of either the principal officers of the executive department or of such other body as Congress may by law provide, transmit within four days to the President pro tempore of the Senate and the Speaker of the House of Representatives their written declaration that the President is unable to discharge the powers and duties of his office. Thereupon Congress shall decide the issue, assembling within forty-eight hours for that purpose if not in session. If the Congress, within twenty-one days after receipt of the latter written declaration, or, if Congress is not in session, within twenty-one days after Congress is required to assemble, determines by two-thirds vote of both Houses that the President is unable to discharge the powers and duties of his office, the Vice President shall continue to discharge the same as Acting President; otherwise, the President shall resume the powers and duties of his office.

Amendment XXVI (1971)

Section 1.   The right of citizens of the United States, who are 18 years of age or older, to vote, shall not be denied or abridged by the United States or any state on account of age.

Section 2.   The Congress shall have the power to enforce this article by appropriate legislation.

Amendment XXVII (1992)

No law varying the compensation for the services of the Senators and Representatives shall take effect until an election of Representatives shall have intervened

The Declaration of Independence

In Congress, July 4, 1776

The unanimous Declaration of the thirteen united States of America,

When in the Course of human events, it becomes necessary for one people to dissolve the political bands which have connected them with another, and to assume among the powers of the earth, the separate and equal station to which the Laws of Nature and of Nature's God entitle them, a decent respect to the opinions of mankind requires that they should declare the causes which impel them to the separation.

We hold these truths to be self-evident, that all men are created equal, that they are endowed by their Creator with certain unalienable Rights, that among these are Life, Liberty and the pursuit of Happiness. That to secure these rights, Governments are instituted among Men, deriving their just powers from the consent of the governed, that whenever any Form of Government becomes destructive of these ends, it is the Right of the People to alter or to abolish it, and to institute new Government, laying its foundation on such principles and organizing its powers in such form, as to them shall seem most likely to effect their Safety and Happiness. Prudence, indeed, will dictate that Governments long established should not be changed for light and transient causes; and accordingly all experience hath shewn, that mankind are more disposed to suffer, while evils are sufferable, than to right themselves by abolishing the forms to which they are accustomed. But when a long train of abuses and usurpations, pursuing invariably the same Object evinces a design to reduce them under absolute Despotism, it is their right, it is their duty, to throw off such Government, and to provide new Guards for their future security. Such has been the patient sufferance of these Colonies; and such is now the necessity which constrains them to alter their former Systems of Government. The history of the present King of Great Britain is a history of repeated injuries and usurpations, all having in direct object the establishment of an absolute Tyranny over these States. To prove this, let Facts be submitted to a candid world.

He has refused his Assent to Laws, the most wholesome and necessary for the public good.

He has forbidden his Governors to pass Laws of immediate and pressing importance, unless suspended in their operation till his Assent should be obtained; and when so suspended, he has utterly neglected to attend to them.

He has refused to pass other Laws for the accommodation of large districts of people, unless those people would relinquish the right of Representation in the Legislature, a right inestimable to them and formidable to tyrants only.

He has called together legislative bodies at places unusual, uncomfortable, and distant from the depository of their public Records, for the sole purpose of fatiguing them into compliance with his measures.

He has dissolved Representative Houses repeatedly, for opposing with manly firmness his invasions on the rights of the people.

He has refused for a long time, after such dissolutions, to cause others to be elected; whereby the Legislative powers, incapable of Annihilation, have returned to the People at large for their exercise; the State remaining in the mean time exposed to all the dangers of invasion from without, and convulsions within.

He has endeavoured to prevent the population of these States; for that purpose obstructing the Laws for Naturalization of Foreigners; refusing to pass others to encourage their migrations hither, and raising the conditions of new Appropriations of Lands.

He has obstructed the Administration of Justice, by refusing his Assent to Laws for establishing Judiciary powers.

He has made Judges dependent on his Will alone, for the tenure of their offices, and the amount and payment of their salaries.

He has erected a multitude of New Offices, and sent hither swarms of Officers to harass our people, and eat out their substance.

He has kept among us, in times of peace, Standing Armies without the Consent of our legislatures.

He has affected to render the Military independent of and superior to the Civil power.

He has combined with others to subject us to a jurisdiction foreign to our constitution, and unacknowledged by our laws; giving his Assent to their Acts of pretended Legislation:

For Quartering large bodies of armed troops among us:

For protecting them, by a mock Trial, from punishment for any Murders which they should commit on the Inhabitants of these States:

For cutting off our Trade with all parts of the world:

For imposing Taxes on us without our Consent:

For depriving us, in many cases, of the benefits of Trial by Jury:

For transporting us beyond Seas to be tried for pretended offences:

For abolishing the free System of English Laws in a neighbouring Province, establishing therein an Arbitrary government, and enlarging its Boundaries so as to render it at once an example and fit instrument for introducing the same absolute rule into these Colonies:

For taking away our Charters, abolishing our most valuable Laws, and altering fundamentally the Forms of our Governments:

For suspending our own Legislatures, and declaring themselves invested with power to legislate for us in all cases whatsoever.

He has abdicated Government here, by declaring us out of his Protection and waging War against us.

He has plundered our seas, ravaged our Coasts, burnt our towns, and destroyed the lives of our people.

He is at this time transporting large Armies of foreign Mercenaries to compleat the works of death, desolation and tyranny, already begun with circumstances of Cruelty & perfidy scarcely paralleled in the most barbarous ages, and totally unworthy the Head of a civilized nation.

He has constrained our fellow Citizens taken Captive on the high Seas to bear Arms against their Country, to become the executioners of their friends and Brethren, or to fall themselves by their Hands.

He has excited domestic insurrections amongst us, and has endeavoured to bring on the inhabitants of our frontiers, the merciless Indian Savages, whose known rule of warfare, is an undistinguished destruction of all ages, sexes and conditions.

In every stage of these Oppressions We have Petitioned for Redress in the most humble terms: Our repeated Petitions have been answered only by repeated injury. A Prince whose character is thus marked by every act which may define a Tyrant, is unfit to be the ruler of a free people.

Nor have We been wanting in attentions to our British brethren. We have warned them from time to time of attempts by their legislature to extend an unwarrantable jurisdiction over us. We have reminded them of the circumstances of our emigration and settlement here. We have appealed to their native justice and magnanimity, and we have conjured them by the ties of our common kindred to disavow these usurpations, which, would inevitably interrupt our connections and correspondence. They too have been deaf to the voice of justice and of consanguinity. We must, therefore, acquiesce in the necessity, which denounces our Separation, and hold them, as we hold the rest of mankind, Enemies in War, in Peace Friends.

We, therefore, the Representatives of the united States of America, in General Congress, Assembled, appealing to the Supreme Judge of the world for the rectitude of our intentions, do, in the Name, and by Authority of the good People of these Colonies, solemnly publish and declare, That these United Colonies are, and of Right ought to be Free and Independent States; that they are Absolved from all Allegiance to the British Crown, and that all political connection between them and the State of Great Britain, is and ought to be totally dissolved; and that as Free and Independent States, they have full Power to levy War, conclude Peace, contract Alliances, establish Commerce, and to do all other Acts and Things which Independent States may of right do. And for the support of this Declaration, with a firm reliance on the protection of divine Providence, we mutually pledge to each other our Lives, our Fortunes and our sacred Honor.

Federalist Number 10

The Union as a Safeguard Against Domestic Faction and Insurrection

Thursday, November 22, 1787
Author: James Madison

To the People of the State of New York:

AMONG the numerous advantages promised by a well constructed Union, none deserves to be more accurately developed than its tendency to break and control the violence of faction. The friend of popular governments never finds himself so much alarmed for their character and fate, as when he contemplates their propensity to this dangerous vice. He will not fail, therefore, to set a due value on any plan which, without violating the principles to which he is attached, provides a proper cure for it. The instability, injustice, and confusion introduced into the public councils, have, in truth, been the mortal diseases under which popular governments have everywhere perished; as they continue to be the favorite and fruitful topics from which the adversaries to liberty derive their most specious declamations. The valuable improvements made by the American constitutions on the popular models, both ancient and modern, cannot certainly be too much admired; but it would be an unwarrantable partiality, to contend that they have as effectually obviated the danger on this side, as was wished and expected. Complaints are everywhere heard from our most considerate and virtuous citizens, equally the friends of public and private faith, and of public and personal liberty, that our governments are too unstable, that the public good is disregarded in the conflicts of rival parties, and that measures are too often decided, not according to the rules of justice and the rights of the minor party, but by the superior force of an interested and overbearing majority. However anxiously we may wish that these complaints had no foundation, the evidence, of known facts will not permit us to deny that they are in some degree true. It will be found, indeed, on a candid review of our situation, that some of the distresses under which we labor have been erroneously charged on the operation of our governments; but it will be found, at the same time, that other causes will not alone account for many of our heaviest misfortunes; and, particularly, for that prevailing and increasing distrust of public engagements, and alarm for private rights, which are echoed from one end of the continent to the other. These must be chiefly, if not wholly, effects of the unsteadiness and injustice with which a factious spirit has tainted our public administrations.

By a faction, I understand a number of citizens, whether amounting to a majority or a minority of the whole, who are united and actuated by some common impulse of passion, or of interest, adversed to the rights of other citizens, or to the permanent and aggregate interests of the community.

There are two methods of curing the mischiefs of faction: the one, by removing its causes; the other, by controlling its effects.

There are again two methods of removing the causes of faction: the one, by destroying the liberty which is essential to its existence; the other, by giving to every citizen the same opinions, the same passions, and the same interests.

It could never be more truly said than of the first remedy, that it was worse than the disease. Liberty is to faction what air is to fire, an aliment without which it instantly expires. But it could not be less folly to abolish liberty, which is essential to political life, because it nourishes faction, than it would be to wish the annihilation of air, which is essential to animal life, because it imparts to fire its destructive agency.

The second expedient is as impracticable as the first would be unwise. As long as the reason of man continues fallible, and he is at liberty to exercise it, different opinions will be formed. As long as the connection subsists between his reason and his self-love, his opinions and his passions will have a reciprocal influence on each other; and the former will be objects to which the latter will attach themselves. The diversity in the faculties of men, from which the rights of property originate, is not less an insuperable obstacle to a uniformity of interests. The protection of these faculties is the first object of government. From the protection of different and unequal faculties of acquiring property, the possession of different degrees and kinds of property immediately results; and from the influence of these on the sentiments and views of the respective proprietors, ensues a division of the society into different interests and parties.

The latent causes of faction are thus sown in the nature of man; and we see them everywhere brought into different degrees of activity, according to the different circumstances of civil society. A zeal for different opinions concerning religion, concerning government, and many other points, as well of speculation as of practice; an attachment to different leaders ambitiously contending for pre-eminence and power; or to persons of other descriptions whose fortunes have been interesting to the human passions, have, in turn, divided mankind into parties, inflamed them with mutual animosity, and rendered them much more disposed to vex and oppress each other than to co-operate for their common good. So strong is this propensity of mankind to fall into mutual animosities, that where no substantial occasion presents itself, the most frivolous and fanciful distinctions have been sufficient to kindle their unfriendly passions and excite their most violent conflicts. But the most common and durable source of factions has been the various and unequal distribution of property. Those who hold and those who are without property have ever formed distinct interests in society. Those who are creditors, and those who are debtors, fall under a like discrimination. A landed interest, a manufacturing interest, a mercantile interest, a moneyed interest, with many lesser interests, grow up of necessity in civilized nations, and divide them into different classes, actuated by different sentiments and views. The regulation of these various and interfering interests forms the principal task of modern legislation, and involves the spirit of party and faction in the necessary and ordinary operations of the government.

No man is allowed to be a judge in his own cause, because his interest would certainly bias his judgment, and, not improbably, corrupt his integrity. With equal, nay with greater reason, a body of men are unfit to be both judges and parties at the same time; yet what are many of the most important acts of legislation, but so many judicial determinations, not indeed concerning the rights of single persons, but concerning the rights of large bodies of citizens? And what are the different classes of legislators but advocates and parties to the causes which they determine? Is a law proposed concerning private debts? It is a question to which the creditors are parties on one side and the debtors on the other. Justice ought to hold the balance between them. Yet the parties are, and must be, themselves the judges; and the most numerous party, or, in other words, the most powerful faction must be expected to prevail. Shall domestic manufactures be encouraged, and in what degree, by restrictions on foreign manufactures? are questions which would be differently decided by the landed and the manufacturing classes, and probably by neither with a sole regard to justice and the public good. The apportionment of taxes on the various descriptions of property is an act which seems to require the most exact impartiality; yet there is, perhaps, no legislative act in which greater opportunity and temptation are given to a predominant party to trample on the rules of justice. Every shilling with which they overburden the inferior number, is a shilling saved to their own pockets.

It is in vain to say that enlightened statesmen will be able to adjust these clashing interests, and render them all subservient to the public good. Enlightened statesmen will not always be at the helm. Nor, in many cases, can such an adjustment be made at all without taking into view indirect and remote considerations, which will rarely prevail over the immediate interest which one party may find in disregarding the rights of another or the good of the whole.

The inference to which we are brought is, that the *causes* of faction cannot be removed, and that relief is only to be sought in the means of controlling its *effects*.

If a faction consists of less than a majority, relief is supplied by the republican principle, which enables the majority to defeat its sinister views by regular vote. It may clog the administration, it may convulse the society; but it will be unable to execute and mask its violence under the forms of the Constitution. When a majority is included in a faction, the form of popular government, on the other hand, enables it to sacrifice to its ruling passion or interest both the public good and the rights of other citizens. To secure the public good and private rights against the danger of such a faction, and at the same time to preserve the spirit and the form of popular government, is then the great object to which our inquiries are directed. Let me add that it is the great desideratum by which this form of government can be rescued from the opprobrium under which it has so long labored, and be recommended to the esteem and adoption of mankind.

By what means is this object attainable? Evidently by one of two only. Either the existence of the same passion or interest in a majority at the same time must be prevented, or the majority, having such coexistent passion or interest, must be rendered, by their number and local situation, unable to concert and carry into effect schemes of oppression. If the impulse and the opportunity be suffered to coincide, we well know that neither moral nor religious motives can be relied on as an adequate control. They are not found to be such on the injustice and violence of individuals, and lose their efficacy in proportion to the number combined together, that is, in proportion as their efficacy becomes needful.

From this view of the subject it may be concluded that a pure democracy, by which I mean a society consisting of a small number of citizens, who assemble and administer the government in person, can admit of no cure for the mischiefs of faction. A common passion or interest will, in almost every case, be felt by a majority of the whole; a communication and concert result from the form of government itself; and there is nothing to check the inducements to sacrifice the weaker party or an obnoxious individual. Hence it is that such democracies have ever been spectacles of turbulence and contention; have ever been found incompatible with personal security or the rights of property; and have in general been as short in their lives as they have been violent in their deaths. Theoretic politicians, who have patronized this species of government, have erroneously supposed that by reducing mankind to a perfect equality in their political rights, they would, at the same time, be perfectly equalized and assimilated in their possessions, their opinions, and their passions.

A republic, by which I mean a government in which the scheme of representation takes place, opens a different prospect, and promises the cure for which we are seeking. Let us examine the points in which it varies from pure democracy, and we shall comprehend both the nature of the cure and the efficacy which it must derive from the Union.

The two great points of difference between a democracy and a republic are: first, the delegation of the government, in the latter, to a small number of citizens elected by the rest; secondly, the greater number of citizens, and greater sphere of country, over which the latter may be extended.

The effect of the first difference is, on the one hand, to refine and enlarge the public views, by passing them through the medium of a chosen body of citizens, whose wisdom may best discern the true interest of their country, and whose patriotism and love of justice will be least likely to sacrifice it to temporary or partial considerations. Under such a regulation, it may well happen that the public voice, pronounced by the representatives of the people, will be more consonant to the public good than if pronounced by the people themselves, convened for the purpose. On the other hand, the effect may be inverted. Men of factious tempers, of local prejudices, or of sinister designs, may, by intrigue, by corruption, or by other means, first obtain the suffrages, and then betray the interests, of the people. The question resulting is, whether small or extensive republics are more favorable to the election of proper guardians of the public weal; and it is clearly decided in favor of the latter by two obvious considerations:

In the first place, it is to be remarked that, however small the republic may be, the representatives must be raised to a certain number, in order to guard against the cabals of a few; and that, however large it may be, they must be limited to a certain number, in order to guard against the confusion of a multitude. Hence, the number of representatives in the two cases not being in proportion to that of the two constituents, and being proportionally greater in the small republic, it follows that, if the proportion of fit characters be not less in the large than in the small republic, the former will present a greater option, and consequently a greater probability of a fit choice.

In the next place, as each representative will be chosen by a greater number of citizens in the large than in the small republic, it will be more difficult for unworthy candidates to practice with success the vicious arts by which elections are too often carried; and the suffrages of the people being more free, will be more likely to centre in men who possess the most attractive merit and the most diffusive and established characters.

It must be confessed that in this, as in most other cases, there is a mean, on both sides of which inconveniences will be found to lie. By enlarging too much the number of electors, you render the representatives too little acquainted with all their local circumstances and lesser interests; as by reducing it too much, you render him unduly attached to these, and too little fit to comprehend and pursue great and national objects. The federal Constitution forms a happy combination in this respect; the great and aggregate interests being referred to the national, the local and particular to the State legislatures.

The other point of difference is, the greater number of citizens and extent of territory which may be brought within the compass of republican than of democratic government; and it is this circumstance principally which renders factious combinations less to be dreaded in the former than in the latter. The smaller the society, the fewer probably will be the distinct parties and interests composing it; the fewer the distinct parties and interests, the more frequently will a majority be found of the same party; and the smaller the number of individuals composing a majority, and the smaller the compass within which they are placed, the more easily will they concert and execute their plans of oppression. Extend the sphere, and you take in a greater variety of parties and interests; you make it less probable that a majority of the whole will have a common motive to invade the rights of other citizens; or if such a common motive exists, it will be more difficult for all who feel it to discover their own strength, and to act in unison with each other. Besides other impediments, it may be remarked that, where there is a consciousness of unjust or dishonorable purposes, communication is always checked by distrust in proportion to the number whose concurrence is necessary.

Hence, it clearly appears, that the same advantage which a republic has over a democracy, in controlling the effects of faction, is enjoyed by a large over a small republic,—is enjoyed by the Union over the States composing it. Does the advantage consist in the substitution of representatives whose enlightened views and virtuous sentiments render them superior to local prejudices and schemes of injustice? It will not be denied that the representation of the Union will be most likely to possess these requisite endowments. Does it consist in the greater security afforded by a greater variety of parties, against the event of any one party being able to outnumber and oppress the rest? In an equal degree does the increased variety of parties comprised within the Union, increase this security. Does it, in fine, consist in the greater obstacles opposed to the concert and accomplishment of the secret wishes of an unjust and interested majority? Here, again, the extent of the Union gives it the most palpable advantage.

The influence of factious leaders may kindle a flame within their particular States, but will be unable to spread a general conflagration through the other States. A religious sect may degenerate into a political faction in a part of the Confederacy; but the variety of sects dispersed over the entire face of it must secure the national councils against any danger from that source. A rage for paper money, for an abolition of debts, for an equal division of property, or for any other improper or wicked project, will be less apt to pervade the whole body of the Union than a particular member of it; in the same proportion as such a malady is more likely to taint a particular county or district, than an entire State.

In the extent and proper structure of the Union, therefore, we behold a republican remedy for the diseases most incident to republican government. And according to the degree of pleasure and pride we feel in being republicans, ought to be our zeal in cherishing the spirit and supporting the character of Federalists.

Federalist Number 51

The Structure of the Government Must Furnish the Proper Checks and Balances Between the Different Departments

Wednesday, February 6, 1788
Author: James Madison

To the People of the State of New York:

TO WHAT expedient, then, shall we finally resort, for maintaining in practice the necessary partition of power among the several departments, as laid down in the Constitution? The only answer that can be given is, that as all these exterior provisions are found to be inadequate, the defect must be supplied, by so contriving the interior structure of the government as that its several constituent parts may, by their mutual relations, be the means of keeping each other in their proper places. Without presuming to undertake a full development of this important idea, I will hazard a few general observations, which may perhaps place it in a clearer light, and enable us to form a more correct judgment of the principles and structure of the government planned by the convention.

In order to lay a due foundation for that separate and distinct exercise of the different powers of government, which to a certain extent is admitted on all hands to be essential to the preservation of liberty, it is evident that each department should have a will of its own; and consequently should be so constituted that the members of each should have as little agency as possible in the appointment of the members of the others. Were this principle rigorously adhered to, it would require that all the appointments for the supreme executive, legislative, and judiciary magistracies should be drawn from the same fountain of authority, the people, through channels having no communication whatever with one another. Perhaps such a plan of constructing the several departments would be less difficult in practice than it may in contemplation appear. Some difficulties, however, and some additional expense would attend the execution of it. Some deviations, therefore, from the principle must be admitted. In the constitution of the judiciary department in particular, it might be inexpedient to insist rigorously on the principle: first, because peculiar qualifications being essential in the members, the primary consideration ought to be to select that mode of choice which best secures these qualifications; secondly, because the permanent tenure by which the appointments are held in that department, must soon destroy all sense of dependence on the authority conferring them.

It is equally evident, that the members of each department should be as little dependent as possible on those of the others, for the emoluments annexed to their offices. Were the executive magistrate, or the judges, not independent of the legislature in this particular, their independence in every other would be merely nominal.

But the great security against a gradual concentration of the several powers in the same department, consists in giving to those who administer each department the necessary constitutional means and personal motives to resist encroachments of the others. The provision for defense must in this, as in all other cases, be made commensurate to the danger of attack. Ambition must be made to counteract ambition. The interest of the man must be connected with the constitutional rights of the place. It may be a reflection on human nature, that such devices should be necessary to control the abuses of government. But what is government itself, but the greatest of all reflections on human nature? If men were angels, no government would be necessary. If angels were to govern men, neither external nor internal controls on government would be necessary. In framing a government which is to be administered by men over men, the great difficulty lies in this: you must first enable the government to control the governed; and in the next place oblige it to control itself. A dependence on the people is, no doubt, the primary control on the government; but experience has taught mankind the necessity of auxiliary precautions.

This policy of supplying, by opposite and rival interests, the defect of better motives, might be traced through the whole system of human affairs, private as well as public. We see it particularly displayed in all the subordinate distributions of power, where the constant aim is to divide and arrange the several offices in such a manner as that each may be a check on the other—that the private interest of every individual may be a sentinel over the public rights. These inventions of prudence cannot be less requisite in the distribution of the supreme powers of the State.

But it is not possible to give to each department an equal power of self-defense. In republican government, the legislative authority necessarily predominates. The remedy for this inconveniency is to divide the legislature into different branches; and to render them, by different modes of election and different principles of action, as little connected with each other as the nature of their common functions and their common dependence on the society will admit. It may even be necessary to guard against dangerous encroachments by still further precautions. As the weight of the legislative authority requires that it should be thus divided, the weakness of the executive may require, on the other hand, that it should be fortified. An absolute negative on the legislature appears, at first view, to be the natural defense with which the executive magistrate should be armed. But perhaps it would be neither altogether safe nor alone sufficient. On ordinary occasions it might not be exerted with the requisite firmness, and on extraordinary occasions it might be perfidiously abused. May not this defect of an absolute negative be supplied by some qualified connection between this weaker department and the weaker branch of the stronger department, by which the latter may be led to support the constitutional rights of the former, without being too much detached from the rights of its own department?

If the principles on which these observations are founded be just, as I persuade myself they are, and they be applied as a criterion to the several State constitutions, and to the federal Constitution it will be found that if the latter does not perfectly correspond with them, the former are infinitely less able to bear such a test.

There are, moreover, two considerations particularly applicable to the federal system of America, which place that system in a very interesting point of view.

First. In a single republic, all the power surrendered by the people is submitted to the administration of a single government; and the usurpations are guarded against by a division of the government into distinct and separate departments. In the compound republic of America, the power surrendered by the people is first divided between two distinct governments, and then the portion allotted to each subdivided among distinct and separate departments. Hence a double security arises to the rights of the people. The different governments will control each other, at the same time that each will be controlled by itself.

Second. It is of great importance in a republic not only to guard the society against the oppression of its rulers, but to guard one part of the society against the injustice of the other part. Different interests necessarily exist in different classes of citizens. If a majority be united by a common interest, the rights of the minority will be insecure. There are but two methods of providing against this evil: the one by creating a will in the community independent of the majority—that is, of the society itself; the other, by comprehending in the society so many separate descriptions of citizens as will render an unjust combination of a majority of the whole very improbable, if not impracticable. The first method prevails in all governments possessing an hereditary or self-appointed authority. This, at best, is but a precarious security; because a power independent of the society may as well espouse the unjust views of the major, as the rightful interests of the minor party, and may possibly be turned against both parties. The second method will be exemplified in the federal republic of the United States. Whilst all authority in it will be derived from and dependent on the society, the society itself will be broken into so many parts, interests, and classes of citizens, that the rights of individuals, or of the minority, will be in little danger from interested combinations of the majority. In a free government the security for civil rights must be the same as that for religious rights. It consists in the one case in the multiplicity of interests, and in the other in the multiplicity of sects. The degree of security in both cases will depend on the number of interests and sects; and this may be presumed to depend on the extent of country and number of people comprehended under the same government. This view of the subject must particularly recommend a proper federal system to all the sincere and considerate friends of republican government, since it shows that in exact proportion as the territory of the Union may be formed into more circumscribed Confederacies, or States oppressive combinations of a majority will be facilitated: the best security, under the republican forms, for the rights of every class of citizens, will be diminished: and consequently the stability and independence of some member of the government, the only other security, must be proportionately increased. Justice is the end of government. It is the end of civil society. It ever has been and ever will be pursued until it be obtained, or until liberty be lost in the pursuit. In a society under the forms of which the stronger faction can readily unite and oppress the weaker, anarchy may as truly be said to reign as in a state of nature, where the weaker individual is not secured against the violence of the stronger; and as, in the latter state, even the stronger individuals are prompted, by the uncertainty of their condition, to submit to a government which may protect the weak as well as themselves; so, in the former state, will the more powerful factions or parties be gradnally induced, by a like motive, to wish for a government which will protect all parties, the weaker as well as the more powerful. It can be little doubted that if the State of Rhode Island was separated from the Confederacy and left to itself, the insecurity of rights under the popular form of government within such narrow limits would be displayed by such reiterated oppressions of factious majorities that some power altogether independent of the people would soon be called for by the voice of the very factions whose misrule had proved the necessity of it. In the extended republic of the United States, and among the great variety of interests, parties, and sects which it embraces, a coalition of a majority of the whole society could seldom take place on any other principles than those of justice and the general good; whilst there being thus less danger to a minor from the will of a major party, there must be less pretext, also, to provide for the security of the former, by introducing into the government a will not dependent on the latter, or, in other words, a will independent of the society itself. It is no less certain than it is important, notwithstanding the contrary opinions which have been entertained, that the larger the society, provided it lie within a practical sphere, the more duly capable it will be of self-government. And happily for the *republican cause,* the practicable sphere may be carried to a very great extent, by a judicious modification and mixture of the *federal principle.*

Glossary

absolute majority Obtaining fifty 50 percent plus one of all members or all eligible voters.

absolutist approach The view of the First Amendment that states that the Founders wanted it to be interpreted literally so that Congress should make "no laws" about the expression of views.

access The ability to get into and use public facilities. In the political sense, the ability to meet with and present one's ideas to political leaders.

active-negative president A way of classifying a president based on personality as someone who is concerned with attaining political power for its own sake.

active-positive president A way of classifying a president based on personality as someone who derives great satisfaction from holding office and will be active in his or her efforts to govern.

ad hoc federalism The process of adopting a state- or nation-centered view of federalism on the basis of political convenience.

adjudication The process of determining if a law or rule established by the bureaucracy has been broken.

adverse selection Principal's lack of information about the abilities of an agent.

advertising The activities of members of Congress (such as sending out newsletters or visiting the district) designed to familiarize the constituency with the member.

advisory committees A temporary or permanent organization created to provide information and technical expertise to the bureaucracy.

affirmative action Governmental actions designed to help minorities compete on an equal basis and overcome the effects of discrimination in the past.

agency capture A term used to describe when an agency seems to operate for the benefit of those whom it is supposed to regulate.

agenda setting The process of selecting the issues or problems that government will pay attention to.

allegiant The feeling of great trust and support for the political system.

allocation responsiveness Representation that takes the form of members of Congress assuring that their district gets a share of federal benefits.

amateurs People who participate in the activities of political parties based primarily on purposive or social incentives.

***amicus curiae* brief** A legal brief filed by someone or some organization with an interest in a case but not an actual party.

anti-Federalists The group of people who opposed a stronger national government than existed under the Articles of Confederation and opposed the ratification of the Constitution.

appointment A power of the president that enables him or her to control the bureaucracy by selecting the people who will head its agencies.

Articles of Confederation The first constitution of the United States.

autocracy A form of government in which the power to make authoritative decisions and allocate resources is vested in one person.

bad tendency rule An approach to determining if an action should be protected under the First Amendment, which considers if the action would have a tendency to produce a negative consequence.

balancing test The view of freedom of expression that states the obligation to protect rights must be balanced with the impact on society of the action in question.

bicameral A legislature with two chambers.

block grants A type of federal grant that provides funds for a general policy area but provides state and local governments' discretion in designing the specific programs.

bureaucracy The term used to refer to the agencies of the federal government. It also refers to an organizational framework and has negative connotations.

cabinet departments The fifteen largest and most influential agencies of the federal bureaucracy.

candidate image Voters' perceptions of a candidate's qualities.

casework Activities of members of Congress to act as intermediaries and help private individuals who are having problems with the administrative agencies in the executive branch.

categorical grant A type of federal grant that provides money for a specific policy activity and details how the programs are to be carried out.

caucus Party committees in the House and Senate composed of all members of the party in the chamber. Each party's caucus develops a policy agenda for the party, appoints committees to make committee assignments, and raises campaign money for House and Senate candidates.

caucus method A method of selecting the delegates to a political party's national convention by permitting the state conventions to select representatives from their states.

censures and reprimands Verbal condemnations of a member of Congress by the House or Senate, intended to punish bad behavior by expressing the public disapproval of the member's colleagues.

check and balance The idea that each branch of the federal government should assert and protect its own rights but must also cooperate with the other branches. Each branch is to serve as a limit on the other's powers, balancing the overall distribution of power.

civil disobedience Deliberately disobeying laws viewed as morally repugnant.

civil liberties The freedoms and protections against arbitrary governmental actions given the people in a democratic society.

civil rights The obligations placed on government to protect the freedom of the people.

"clear and present danger" test An approach to determining if an action should be protected under the First Amendment that considers if the action poses a "clear and present danger."

closed primaries An election to choose a party's nominees for the general election that is open only to party members.

closed rule The rule that prohibits amending a bill when it is on the floor of Congress for consideration.

cloture A procedure of the Senate to end a filibuster; invoking cloture requires votes of 60 senators.

coalition building A means of expanding an interest group's influence that involves working with other groups.

collegial courts Courts in which groups of judges decide cases based on a review of the record of the lower court trial.

Committee of the Whole A parliamentary action when the House of Representatives dissolves into a committee consisting of every member of the House. This procedure is used to facilitate consideration of legislation because it has less burdensome rules governing debate and requires a smaller quorum than the House itself.

concurrent jurisdiction When state and federal courts both are entitled to hear a particular type of case.

concurrent powers The powers listed in the Constitution as belonging to both the national and state governments.

concurring opinion Opinions written by Supreme Court justices who agree with the ruling of the court but not the reason behind it.

conditional party government When members of the majority party caucus in Congress achieve consensus on policy issues, they adopt reforms that obligate congressional committee chairs and party leaders to try to enact the party's legislative agenda on which there is a consensus.

confederation A political system in which the central government receives no direct grant of power from the people and can only exercise the power granted to it by the regional governments.

conference The meeting of Supreme Court justices where they decide which cases they will hear.

conference committee A temporary congressional committee made up of members of the House and Senate that meets to reconcile the differences in legislation that has passed both chambers.

Connecticut Compromise A proposal at the Constitutional Convention that called for a two-house legislature with a House of Representatives apportioned on the basis of population and a Senate representing each state on an equal basis. Also called the Great Compromise.

constituency The group of people served by an elected official or branch of government.

constitution A document or unwritten set of basic rules that provides the basic principles that determine the conduct of political affairs.

constitutional interpretation An action of the Supreme Court in which the justices determine if a law is in line with the Constitution.

constitutionalism The idea of limited government that cannot deny the fundamental rights of the people.

contracting out Hiring a private organization to deliver a public program or service.

cooperative federalism The idea that the distinction between state and national responsibilities is unclear and that the different levels of government share responsibilities in many areas.

Council of Economic Advisers An agency of the Executive Office of the President that is responsible for advising the president on the U.S. economy.

courts of appellate jurisdiction Courts that review the decisions of lower courts.

courts of original jurisdiction Trial courts that hear cases for the first time and determine issues of fact and law.

credit claiming The efforts by members of Congress to get their constituents to believe they are responsible for positive government actions.

critical election The first election that clearly reflects a new partisan alignment that produces a new partisan majority.

crossover sanctions Conditions placed on grant money, which have nothing to do with the original purpose of the grant.

custom and usage The term used to describe constitutional change that occurs when the practices and institutions of government not specifically mentioned in the Constitution change over time through use and evolution.

cyclical federalism The idea that the national government takes on a greater policy role during liberal periods of U.S. history and less so in conservative periods.

***de facto* discrimination** Discrimination that exists in fact, in real life or in practice.

***de jure* discrimination** Discrimination that is set forth in law.

delegate A representative who makes legislative decisions based on the interests and views of his or her constituents, regardless of personal preference.

delegate model of representative democracy The idea that the job of elected leaders is make decisions solely based on the views of the majority of the people.

democracy A form of government in which all the citizens have the opportunity to participate in the process of making authoritative decisions and allocating resources.

descriptive representation The view of representation that calls for the racial and ethnic makeup of Congress to reflect that of the nation.

deviating election An election in which the minority party is able to overcome the long-standing partisan orientation of the public based on temporary or short-term forces.

devolution The returning of policy power and responsibility to the states from the national government.

direct democracy A form of democracy in which ordinary citizens, rather than representatives, collectively make government decisions.

direction The idea of public opinion being either positive or negative (favorable or unfavorable) on an issue.

direct lobbying Direct contact by lobbyists with government officials in an effort to influence policy.

direct popular election plan A proposal to abolish the electoral college and elect the president directly by national popular vote.

direct primary The selection of a political party's candidate for the general election by vote of ordinary citizens.

discharge petition A procedure of the House of Representatives that permits a majority of the members of the House (218) to bring a bill out of committee for consideration on the floor.

discrimination Unequal or unfair treatment of a person or class of people.

dissenting opinion Opinions written by Supreme Court justices who are in the minority and present the logic and thinking of the justices who opposed the majority opinion.

district plan A plan to revise the electoral college that would distribute a state's electoral college votes by giving one vote to the candidate who wins a plurality in each House district and two votes to the winner statewide.

divided government When one party controls the presidency and another controls Congress.

dual federalism The idea that the national and state governments are sovereign, with separate and distinct jurisdictions.

economic equality The idea that each individual receives the same amount of material goods, regardless of his/her contribution to society.

electoral college The institution (whose members are selected by whatever means the state legislature chooses) that is responsible for selecting the president of the United States.

electoral realignment New and sustaining pattern of partisan loyalties that results in a new majority party.

electronic media Consists of television, radio, movies, records, and the Internet.

elite opinion The attitudes or beliefs of those people with influential positions within society.

elitist A term used to describe a society in which organized, influential minority interests dominate the political process.

enabling act A resolution passed by Congress authorizing residents of a territory to draft a state constitution as part of the process of adding new states to the Union.

en banc A procedure in which all the members of a U.S. court of appeals hear and decide a case.

enumerated powers The powers specifically listed in the Constitution as belonging to the national government.

equality of opportunity The idea that every individual has the right to develop to the fullest extent of his or her abilities.

equality under the law The idea that the law is supposed to be applied impartially, without regard for the identity or status of the individual involved.

exchange theory Interest groups form as a result of a deal—an exchange—between a group entrepreneur and an unorganized interest that may be underrepresented or not represented at all.

exclude The refusal of Congress to seat any candidate who wins election but does not meet the constitutional requirements to hold congressional office.

exclusionary rule The rule derived from the Fourth and Fourteenth Amendments that states that evidence obtained from an unreasonable search or seizure cannot be used in federal trials.

exclusive committees Three House committees—Appropriations, Rules, and Ways and Means—whose members are not given any other committee assignments.

exclusive jurisdiction Issues that a court can hear that can be heard by no other court.

executive agreement An agreement between the United States and other nations, negotiated by the president, that has the same weight as a treaty but does not require senatorial approval.

Executive Office of the President (EOP) The organizational structure in the executive branch that houses the president's most influential advisors and agencies. The most important include the White House Office, the Office of Management and Budget (OMB), the National Security Council, and the Council of Economic Advisers.

executive orders Directives of the president that have the same weight as law and were not voted on by Congress.

executive privilege A prerogative power of the president to withhold information on matters of national security or personal privacy.

expulsion The ejection of a member of Congress from office.

faction In James Madison's terms, "A number of citizens, whether amounting to a majority or a minority of the whole, who are united and actuated by some common impulse of passion, or of interests, adverse to the right of other citizens, or to the permanent and aggregate interests of the community."

false consensus The tendency of people to believe their views are normal or common sense and therefore shared by most people.

federalism A political system where regional governments share power with a central or national government, but each level of government has legal powers that are independent of the other. This division of power between the national and state governments attempts to balance power by giving each independent sources of authority and allowing one level of government to serve as a check on the other.

feedback The information policymakers routinely receive through government reports, hearings, reading the news, casework, meetings with lobbyists and government officials, and contact with constituents.

filibuster The effort by a senator to delay the chamber's business by making long speeches.

fire alarm oversight Oversight that becomes active only when there is evidence of bureaucratic wrongdoing.

focusing event Something that grabs attention immediately and puts an issue on the public agenda.

framing Emphasizing certain aspects of a story to make them more important.

franchise The constitutional or statutory right to vote.

franking privilege The ability of members of Congress to send mail to their constituents free of charge by substituting a facsimile of their signature in place of a stamp.

free rider The problem of the rational person who chooses to enjoy the benefits of public goods without incurring the costs of providing them.

frontloading The tendency of states to move their primaries earlier in the season in order to gain more influence over the presidential selection process.

"full faith and credit" The provision in the Constitution that requires states to honor the civil obligations (wills, birth certificates, and other public documents) generated by other states. Note: States apparently are not required to recognize marriages under "full faith and credit."

gatekeeper Someone or some institution that controls access to something.

general election The process by which voters choose their representatives from among the parties' nominees.

general revenue sharing A type of federal grant that returns money to the state and local governments with no requirements as to how it is spent.

genocide The killing of an entire race of people.

gerrymandering The drawing of district lines in such a way as to help or hinder the electoral prospects of a specific political interest.

going public A political strategy in which the president appeals to the public in an effort to persuade Congress to support his or her political goals.

government The institution that has the authority to make binding decisions for all of society.

government corporations Federally established businesses that are narrow in focus and are in part self-supporting.

grandfather clause A provision in election laws used in conjunction with literacy tests to prevent African Americans from voting. People whose ancestors were entitled to vote in 1866 (that is, whites) were exempt from passing the literacy test, but African Americans, whose ancestors were slaves, had to pass the literacy test in order to vote.

grants-in-aid A form of national subsidy to the states designed to help them pay for policies and programs that are the responsibility of states rather than the national government.

group entrepreneur Someone who invests resources (such as time, money, and organizational skill) to create and build an organization that offers various types of benefits (material, solidary, and purposive) to entice others to join the group.

hard money Campaign contributions made directly to candidates and regulated by law.

hard news Stories that focus on factual information about important decisions or events.

hierarchical model A method of organizing the presidency that calls for clear lines of authority and delegates responsibility from the president and through the chief of staff.

hold The formal request by a member of the Senate to be notified prior to any bill or presidential nomination coming to the floor.

home style The way a member of Congress behaves, explains his or her legislative actions, and presents himself or herself in the home district.

hyperdemocracy The idea that policymakers have become so sensitive to public opinion that they are subservient to any brief shift in opinion.

ideology A consistent set of values, attitudes, and beliefs about the appropriate role of government in society.

impact evaluation An evaluation undertaken to assess the outcomes or effects of a policy or program.

implied powers Those powers belonging to the national government that are suggested in the Constitution's "necessary and proper" clause.

impoundment The limited ability of the president to not spend money appropriated by Congress.

incorporation doctrine The idea that the specific protections provided in the U.S. Bill of Rights have been binding on the states through the "due process" clause of the Fourteenth Amendment.

incrementalism A decision-making approach characterized by making current decisions that are small adjustments to past decisions.

independent agencies Federal agencies that are not part of the cabinet-level executive departments. Members of these agencies serve fixed and overlapping terms and cannot be removed, which limits the president's control of them.

indicators Any measures that can be employed as systematic monitoring devices.

indirect lobbying The use of intermediaries by lobbyists to speak to government officials in their attempts to influence policy.

inevitable discovery An exception to the exclusionary rule that states that evidence obtained from an illegal search may be used in court if the evidence would have eventually been discovered through legal means.

inherent powers Powers not listed or implied by the Constitution but rather have been claimed as essential to the national government. Also known as prerogative powers.

initiative An election in which ordinary citizens circulate a petition to put a proposed law on the ballot for the voters to approve.

institutional agenda A short list of actionable items being given serious consideration by policymaking institutions.

intensity How strongly people hold the beliefs or attitudes that comprise public opinion.

interest group A group organized around a set of views or preferences in order to try to influence government decision makers.

interstate rendition The obligation of states to return people accused of a crime to the state from which they fled.

invisible primary The period of time between the election of one president and the first contest to nominate candidates to run in the general election to select the next president.

iron triangles A term used to refer to the interdependent relationship among the bureaucracy, interest groups, and congressional committees.

issue public A section of the public with a strong interest in a particular issue.

Jim Crow A term used to describe laws designed to prevent African Americans from voting.

joint committee A congressional committee made up of members of the House and Senate.

judicial activism A view of Supreme Court decision making that calls for the Court to take an active role in policymaking through its interpretation of the Constitution.

Judicial Conference A committee of district and appellate judges who reviews the needs of the federal judiciary and makes recommendations to Congress.

judicial power The authority of courts to interpret and apply the law in particular cases.

judicial restraint A view of Supreme Court decision making that calls for the Court to defer policymaking to the other branches of government.

judicial review The power to review decisions of the lower courts and to determine the constitutionality of laws and actions of public officials.

jurisdiction The types of cases a given court is permitted to hear.

justiciable issue An issue or topic over which the courts have jurisdiction or the power to make decisions.

leak Revealing information that officials want kept secret.

legal realist A view of judicial decision making that judges must balance existing laws and precedents with the impact their decisions will have on society.

legislative caucus A method of selecting political party candidates that calls for party members in the state legislature to select candidates for statewide office and party members in the House of Representatives to select a party's candidate for president and vice president.

legislative intent The intention of Congress when it passes laws.

legislative interpretation An action of the Supreme Court in which the Court rules on the meaning and intent of an action of Congress.

legislative oversight of administration A variety of tools Congress uses to control administrative agencies, including creating or abolishing agencies, assigning program responsibilities, providing funds, and confirming presidential appointments.

legislative vetoes The ability of Congress to reject an action or decision of the bureaucracy.

libel Making false or defaming statements about someone in print or the media.

lobbying The activity of a group or person in which they attempt to influence public policymaking on behalf of themselves or the group.

lobbyists Individuals whose job it is to contact and attempt to influence governmental officials on behalf of others.

logrolling The exchange of support on issues between individuals or groups in order to gain mutual advantage.

Madisonian dilemma The problem of limiting self-interested individuals administering stronger governmental powers from using those powers to destroy the freedoms that government is supposed to protect.

magic number The number of delegates needed at a political party's national convention for a candidate to be nominated as the party's candidate for the presidency; this number equals 50 percent plus one of all delegates at the convention.

maintaining election An election in which the traditional majority party maintains power based on the long-standing partisan orientation of the voters.

majority leader The person, chosen by the members of the majority party in the House and Senate, who controls the legislative agenda. In the Senate, the majority leader is the most powerful person in the chamber.

majority-minority districts Districts in which the majority of the population are ethnic or racial minorities.

majority opinion A decision of the Supreme Court in which five or more of the justices are in agreement on the ruling of which part should win a case and the reason why the party should win.

majority rule The government follows the course of action preferred by most people.

malapportioned The situation where the distribution of legislative seats does not accurately reflect the distribution of the population.

mass media All the means used to transmit information to masses of people.

material benefits Tangible rewards gained from membership in an interest group.

media bias The tendency to present an unbalanced perspective so that information is conveyed in such a way that consistently favors one set of interests over another.

merit system A system of governing in which jobs are given based on relevant technical expertise and the ability to perform.

midterm elections The congressional and gubernatorial elections that occur in the middle of a presidential term.

minority leader The person, chosen by the members of the minority party, to coordinate communication among party members in the House and Senate. This position is similar to the majority leader but with less power.

minority rights The full rights of democratic citizenship held by any group numerically inferior to the majority. These fundamental democratic rights cannot be taken away—even if a majority wishes to do so—without breaking the promise of democracy.

misinformation The belief that incorrect information is true.

mixed government The idea that government should represent both property and the number of people.

moral hazard Principal's lack of information about the effort of an agent.

multimember district A method of selecting representatives in which more than one person is chosen to represent a single constituency.

multiparty system A political system in which three or more political parties effectively compete for political office, and no one party can win control of all.

national party convention A nomination method in which delegates selected from each state attend a national party meeting to choose the party's candidates for president and vice president.

National Security Council A group of presidential advisors made up of the vice president, attorney general, and cabinet officers chosen by the president to advise the president on national security issues and is part of the Executive Office of the President.

neutral competence The idea that agencies should make decisions based on expertise rather than political considerations.

new federalism A movement to take power away from the federal government and return it to the states.

New Jersey plan A proposal presented at the Constitutional Convention that called for a one-house legislature with equal representation for each state.

news Accounts of timely and specific events.

news media Organizations and journalists that cover the news.

niches Spaces that contain an array of resources necessary for survival.

nomination The process through which political parties winnow down a field of candidates to a single one who will be the party's standard-bearer in the general election.

nongermane amendments Amendments to a piece of legislation that are not related to the subject of the bill to which they are added.

nonpartisan primary A type of election used in Louisiana in which candidates from all political parties run in the same primary, and the candidate who receives the majority of the vote obtains the office.

norm of reciprocity The custom of congressional committee members respecting the work and judgments of other committees.

nullification The act of declaring a national law null and void within a state's borders.

objective journalism An approach to journalism that places emphasis on reporting facts rather than analysis or promoting a partisan point of view.

Office of Management and Budget (OMB) An agency of the Executive Office of the President that is responsible for assisting the president in creating the budget.

oligarchy A form of government in which the power to make authoritative decisions and allocate resources is vested in a small group of people.

one-party system A political system in which representatives of one political party hold all or almost all of the major offices in government.

one person, one vote The idea, arising out of the 1964 Supreme Court decision of *Wesberry v. Sanders,* that legislative districts must contain about the same number of people.

open primaries An election to select a party's candidate for the general election that is open to independents and, in some cases, to member of other parties.

open rule A rule formulated by the House Rules committee that permits any germane amendment to be considered on the floor.

open seats Elections in which there is no incumbent running for reelection.

original intent The idea that Supreme Court justices should interpret the Constitution in terms of the original intentions of the framers.

overhead democracy The idea that the bureaucracy is controlled through the oversight of elected officials, who are chosen by the people, thus giving the populace control over the bureaucracy.

parliamentary system An electoral system in which the party holding the majority of seats in the legislature selects the chief executive.

partitioning In niche theory, partitioning occurs when competitors in effect segment the available resources in the niche and use them in a way that excludes having to compete with the other species.

party discipline Requiring political party members in public office to promote or carry out the party's agenda and punishing those who do not.

party in government The component of a political party that is made up of elected and appointed government officeholders who belong to a political party.

party in the electorate The component of a political party that is made up of the people in the public who identify with a political party.

party-line vote A vote in which a majority of Democrats vote on one side and a majority of Republicans vote on the other.

party organization The component of a political party that is comprised of the party professionals who hold official positions in the party.

party ratio The proportion of the seats that each political party controls in the House and the Senate.

passive-negative president A way of classifying a president based on personality as someone who has a deep sense of civic responsibility and is not particularly aggressive in governing.

passive-positive president A way of classifying a president based on personality as someone who is primarily interested in popularity and less interested in governing.

passive resistance A nonviolent technique of protest that entails resisting government laws or practices that are believed to be unjust.

perquisites or perks The benefits and support activities that members of Congress receive in order to help them perform their job.

plebiscite A direct vote of all eligible voters on a policy related question.

pluralist explanation of interest groups Interest groups form in reaction to problems created by particular social or economic events.

pluralistic A term used to describe a society in which the power is widely distributed among diverse groups and interests.

plurality Obtaining the largest percentage of a vote, when no one has a majority.

plurality opinion A decision of the Supreme Court in which a majority of the Court agrees on a decision, but there is not a majority agreement on the reason for the decision.

pocket veto The veto resulting from a president taking no action on legislation that has passed Congress after Congress has adjourned.

police patrol oversight The active oversight of the bureaucracy by elected officials to make sure that they are acting according to the wishes of the people.

police power The authority of the states to pass laws for the health, safety, and morals of their citizens.

policy adoption The process of choosing a specific course of action in response to a problem or issue.

policy evaluation The process of examining the consequences of public policy.

policy formulation The process of developing alternative courses of action in response to an issue or problem.

policy implementation The process of translating government intent into government action.

policy responsiveness The amount of agreement between the people represented and their elected officials on policy issues.

policy subsystem Networks of groups with an interest in a specific policy issue or area.

political action committees (PACs) Organizations specifically created to raise money and make political contributions on behalf of an interest group.

political alienation The feeling of being isolated from or not part of the political process and system.

political bias The tendency to favor a political party or ideological point of view.

political efficacy The belief that participation in politics can make a difference.

political equality Individual preferences are given equal weight.

political machine A political organization characterized by a reciprocal relationship between voters and officeholders. Political support is given in exchange for government jobs and services. Headed by a "party boss," political machines and party bosses maintained their power and control over government offices with such techniques as control over nominations, patronage, graft and bribery, vote buying, and rigging elections.

political party An organization that nominates and runs candidates for public office under its own label.

political patronage The giving of government jobs to people based on their party affiliation and loyalty.

political question doctrine A legal principle that courts do not have jurisdiction over certain issues that fall exclusively under the authority of the political branches (the president and Congress).

political resources The tools used by interests groups to influence the political process.

politico A representative whose philosophy of representation is a mix of both delegate and trustee. See also *delegate* and *trustee*.

politics The process of making binding decisions about who gets what or whose values everyone is going to live by.

poll taxes A technique used to keep certain groups from voting by charging a fee to vote.

popular sovereignty The idea that the highest political authority in a democracy is the will of the people.

pork-barrel benefits Federal government benefits distributed to congressional districts based on the efforts of members of Congress.

position taking Public statements made by members of Congress on issues of importance to the constituency.

positive government The idea that government should play a major role in preventing or dealing with the crises that face the nation.

preemption Congress expressly giving national laws precedence over state and local laws.

preferred freedoms doctrine The idea that the rights provided in the First Amendment are fundamental and as such the courts have a greater obligation to protect those rights than others.

prerogative view of presidential power A view of presidential power promoted by Abraham Lincoln, which argues that the president is required to preserve the Constitution and take actions to do so that might otherwise be unconstitutional.

president of the Senate The person who presides over the Senate and is responsible for many of the parliamentary duties such as recognizing speakers. The vice president of the United States holds this position.

president pro tempore The person chosen by the members to preside over the Senate in the absence of the vice president.

presidential system A political system in which the chief executive and the legislature are elected independently.

press The print and electronic media that are partially or wholly devoted to collecting and reporting news in the United States.

priming The process of emphasizing certain aspects of a story in a media report. People often use these points of emphasis as the basis for judging issues.

principal-agent model A model explaining the relationship between Congress and the bureaucracy, which states the relationship is similar to that between an employer who seeks to have work done (the principal) and an employee who does the work (the agent).

print media Consist of newspapers, magazines, and books.

prior restraint To prohibit or censor a news story prior to publication or broadcast.

privacy An individual's right to be free of government interference without due cause or due process.

process evaluation An evaluation undertaken with the goal of assessing whether a program or policy is being implemented according to its stated guidelines.

professionals People who participate in the activities of political parties based on material or social incentives.

proportional plan A plan to revise the electoral college such that the number of electoral college votes given to candidates would be based on the proportion of the popular vote they obtained.

proportional representation A method of selecting representatives in which representation is given to political parties based on the proportion of the vote obtained. This method has the effect of encouraging multiple parties.

prospective voting Voting that is based on an individual's estimation of how well a candidate will perform duties in the future.

public agenda All issues and problems that have the attention of the government at a particular point in time.

public good A benefit provided to everyone and that cannot be withheld from those who did not participate in its provision.

public opinion The sum of individual attitudes or beliefs about an issue or question.

public policy A relatively stable, purposive course of action pursued by government officials or agencies.

public sphere A forum where information on matters important to civic life can be freely accessed and exchanged.

purposive benefits Benefits that interest group members derive from feeling good about contributing to a worthy cause in an effort to improve the lot of society in general, not just the individual concerns of the group's members.

push poll A type of public opinion poll that intentionally uses leading or biased questions in order to manipulate the responses.

racial segregation The separation of people based on their race.

racism The preference for or discrimination against a particular race of people.

random sample A method of selecting a sample (subset of the population) in which every person in the target population has an equal chance of being selected.

rational Making choices that maximize benefits and minimize costs.

rational choice model A model of voter choice that suggests that an individual will vote if the benefits of doing so outweigh the costs and will cast his or her ballot for candidates who are closest to sharing the individual's views on the issues.

rational-comprehensive decision making A decision-making approach characterized by consideration of all alternatives to a problem or issue, an analysis of the costs and benefits of each alternative, and selection of the alternative with the most benefits at the least cost.

realigning election An election in which the minority party is able to build a relatively stable coalition to win election, and this coalition endures over a series of elections.

reapportionment The process of adjusting the number of House seats among the states based on population shifts.

recall An election in which the voters decide whether to remove an elected official from office before the end of his or her term.

reciprocity The state of mutual dependence and influence that describes the relationship between officeholders and the general populace.

redistricting The process of redrawing congressional district lines after reapportionment.

referendum An election in which a state legislature refers a proposed law to the voters for their approval.

reinstating election An election in which the majority party regains power after a deviating election.

representation The relationship between elected officials and the people who put them in office, involving the extent to which officials are responsive to the people.

representative democracy A system of government in which ordinary citizens choose public officials to represent and make decisions for them, rather than making decisions themselves. Also known as Western representative democracy.

reprimands and censures Verbal condemnations of a member of Congress by the House or Senate, intended to punish bad behavior by expressing the public disapproval of the member's colleagues.

republican form of government A form of government in which the government operates with the consent of the governed through some type of representative institution.

responsible party model A concept that describes democracies with competitive parties in which one party wins control of the government based on its policy proposals, enacts those proposals once it is in control, and stands or falls in the next election based on its performance in delivering on its promises.

restrictive view of presidential power A view of presidential power that argues that the president can exercise only those powers listed in the Constitution.

retrospective voting Voting that is based on an individual's evaluation of the past performance of a candidate.

reverse discrimination The claim by some nonminorities that affirmative action policies discriminate against them based on race.

riders Nongermane amendments that are added to a popular bill in hopes that the desirability of the proposed legislation will help the amendment pass.

rule A statement of the bureaucracy that interprets the law or prescribes a specific action. These rules have the force of law.

rule of four The number of Supreme Court justices that must agree to hear a case.

rulemaking The process of the bureaucracy deciding what the laws passed by Congress mean and how they should be carried out.

run-off primary A second primary election held between the top two candidates if no candidate received a majority of the votes in the first primary.

salience The prominence or visibility of an issue or question and how important the issue is to the public.

selective benefits Benefits provided by interest groups that are available to members only.

senatorial courtesy The practice that allows senators from states with federal district court vacancies to recommend individuals for the president to nominate. If the president fails to follow the home state senators' recommendations, the slighted senator may block the nomination from coming to the floor for a confirmation vote.

separate but equal A practice in southern states to comply with the Fourteenth Amendment's "equal protection" clause by passing laws requiring separate but equal accommodations for blacks and whites in public facilities. The Supreme Court ruled such laws unconstitutional in 1954.

separation of church and state The idea that neither the national nor state governments may pass laws that support one religion, all religions, or give preference to one religion over others.

separation of powers The idea that each branch of government is authorized to carry out a separate part of the political process.

service responsiveness Representation that takes the form of the tasks legislators perform based on the requests and needs of their constituents.

simple majority Fifty percent plus one of those participating or of those who vote.

single-issue groups Groups that take positions and are active on only one specific issue (for example, abortion, guns, homosexuality, the environment).

single-member district A method of selecting representatives in which the people in a district select a single representative.

single-member-district-plurality system A method of selecting representatives in which one person will win the single position based on obtaining a plurality of the vote.

slander Making false or defamatory oral statements about someone.

slot machine theory The view of judicial review that all a judge does is lay the constitutional provision involved beside the statute being challenged and "decide whether the latter squares with the former."

social equality The idea that people should be free of class or social barriers and discrimination.

social-psychological model A model explaining voter choice that focuses on individual attitudes.

socioeconomic status (SES) The social background and economic position of a person.

sociological model A model explaining voter choice by considering such factors as religion, place of residence, and socioeconomic status.

soft money Campaign contributions given to political parties rather than directly to candidates.

soft news Stories characterized by opinion, human interest, and often entertainment value.

solidary benefits Intangible benefits gained from membership in an interest groups such as a sense of belonging to a group or meeting people with similar interests.

speaker of the House of Representatives The person who presides over the House, is responsible for the many of the parliamentary duties such as recognizing speakers, and is the most powerful person in the chamber.

spoils system A system of governing in which political positions and benefits are given to the friends of the winner.

spokes-of-the-wheel model A method of organizing the presidency that calls for the president to be the center of activity with numerous advisors reporting directly to the president.

stability The likelihood of changes in the direction of public opinion.

standards of due process The procedural guarantees provided to ensure fair treatment and constitutional rights.

standing committees Permanent committees in Congress that are responsible for legislation in a specific policy area.

standing to sue The legal right to bring a lawsuit based on having a stake in the outcome.

state presidential primary A method of selecting delegates to a political party's national convention in which the voters directly elect delegates.

stewardship doctrine A view of presidential power that states that the president is a steward of the people and should do anything the nation needs that is not prohibited by the Constitution.

straight-ticket voting Voting for the same party's candidates for president and Congress.

strategic framing Giving prominence in media stories to who is gaining or losing on an issue.

straw polls Unscientific polls based on non-random samples.

strong-executive model A model of the presidency in which the powers of the executive office are significant and independent from Congress.

substantive representation The concept of representation that states that officeholders do not have to be minorities to accurately represent minority interests.

suffrage The right to vote.

sunshine laws Laws intended to keep the bureaucracy accountable to the people by requiring that agency meetings be open to the public.

"supreme law of the land" The idea that the U.S. Constitution, laws passed by Congress, and the treaties made by the federal government are supreme, and state constitutions and laws are subordinate to them.

swing states States in which the outcome of a presidential race is unclear, and both candidates have realistic chances of winning.

symbolic responsiveness A member of Congress' efforts to use political symbols to generate trust and support among the voters.

tactics The actions and ways interest groups use their political resources to influence the political process.

test case A lawsuit filed to test the constitutionality of some government policy.

third parties Minor political parties that periodically appeared but have little success in winning office.

top committees The committees in the House and Senate that are desired by most legislators.

trustees Representatives who use their own judgment to make decisions they feel are in the best the interests of the nation as a whole, and the particular interests of their constituents is secondary.

trustee system of democracy The idea that the job of elected leaders is to make decisions based on their own expertise and judgment, and not just make decisions based on the wishes and preferences of constituents.

two-party system A political system in which only two political parties have a realistic chance of controlling the major offices of government.

unanimous consent agreements (UCA) An agreement between party leaders on the procedures and conditions under which a bill will be considered in the Senate.

unicameral A legislature with one chamber.

unitary system A political system in which the power is concentrated in the national government, and the regional governments can only exercise those powers granted them by the central government.

unit rule A rule that permitted a majority of a state's delegation to a political party's national convention to require that the entire delegation vote the same way (or as a unit).

Virginia plan The first major proposal presented at the 1787 Constitutional Convention; the basis of the Constitution.

voter turnout The percentage of eligible voters who cast votes in an election.

weak-executive model A model of the presidency in which the executive would have a limited term, would have no veto power, and would only be allowed to exercise the authority explicitly granted by Congress.

Western representative democracy Defined as a system of government where ordinary citizens do not make governmental decisions themselves but choose public officials—representatives of the people—to make decisions for them.

whips Assistants to the majority and minority party leaders in Congress who encourage rank-and-file members to support the party's positions. Whips make sure that rank-and-file members are present to vote on key legislative measures and that they know the party leader's desire.

White House Office A section of the Executive Office of the President that houses many of the most influential advisors to the president, including the chief of staff; the White House legal counsel; presidential speechwriters; the president's press secretary; assistants for domestic, foreign, and economic policy; and liaisons with Congress, the public, and state and local governments.

writ of certiorari An action of the Supreme Court stating that the Court will hear a case that has been appealed to them. Four of the nine justices must vote to review a case (see *rule of four*).

writ of mandamus A court order instructing a public official to carry out some official duty.

References

Abraham, Henry J. 1993. *The Judicial Process,* 6th ed. New York: Oxford University Press.

Abramowitz, Alan, and Kyle Saunders. 1998. "Ideological Realignment in the U.S. Electorate." *Journal of Politics* 60 (August): 634–652.

Abramson, Paul R., and John Aldrich. 1982. "The Decline of Electoral Participation in America." *American Political Science Review* 76 (September): 502–521.

Abramson, Paul R., John Aldrich, and David Rohde. 1999. *Change and Continuity in the 1996 and 1998 Elections.* Washington, DC: CQ Press.

Abramson, Paul R., John Aldrich, and David Rohde. 2003. *Change and Continuity in the 2000 and 2002 Elections.* Washington, DC: CQ Press.

Advisory Commission on Intergovernmental Relations. 1994. *Significant Features of Fiscal Federalism.* Washington, DC: Advisory Commission on Intergovernmental Relations.

Aldrich, John H. 1995. *Why Parties? The Origin and Transformation of Political Parties in America.* Chicago: University of Chicago Press.

Alexander, F. King. 1998. "Private Institutions and Public Dollars: An Analysis of the Effect of Federal Direct Student Aid on Public and Private Institutions of Higher Education." *Journal of Education Finance* 23: 390–416.

Alger, David. 1996. *The Media and Politics,* 2nd ed. Belmont, CA: Wadsworth.

Allsop, Dee, and Herbert F. Wiesberg. 1988. "Measuring Change in Party Identification in an Election Campaign." *American Journal of Political Science* 32 (November): 996–1,017.

Americans United for Affirmative Action. 1999. "Affirmative Action Timeline." *http://www.aaua.org/timeline.* Accessed March 30, 1999.

Anderson, James. 2000. *Public Policymaking,* 4th ed. New York: Houghton Mifflin.

Ansolabehere, Stephen, Shanto Iyengar, Adam Simon, and Nicholas Valentino. 1994. "Does Attack Advertising Demobilize the Electorate." *American Political Science Review* 88 (December): 829–838.

Associated Press. 1998. "IRS Once Again On Hot Seat." *Omaha World-Herald,* March 15.

Austin-Smith, David. 1995. "Campaign Contributions and Access." *American Political Science Review* 89 (September): 566–581.

Barber, James David. 1992. *The Presidential Character.* New York: Prentice-Hall.

Barone, Michael, and Richard E. Cohen. 2004. *The Almanac of American Politics 2004.* Washington, DC: National Journal.

Barone Michael, and Grant Ujifusa. 1994. *The Almanac of American Politics.* Washington, DC: National Journal.

Bartels, Larry. 1993. "Messages Received: The Political Impact of Media Exposure." *American Political Science Review* 87 (June): 267–285.

Bartels, Larry M. 2000. "Partisanship and Voting Behavior, 1952–1996." *American Journal of Political Science* 44 (January): 35–50.

Baumgartner, Frank R., and Bryan D. Jones. 1993. *Agendas and Instability in American Politics.* Chicago: University of Chicago Press.

Baumgartner, Frank, and Beth Leech. 1998. *Basic Interests: The Importance of Groups in Politics and in Political Science.* Princeton, NJ: Princeton University Press.

Baumgartner, Frank R., and Beth L. Leech. 2001. "Interest Niches and Policy Bandwagons: Patterns of Interest Group Involvement in National Politics." *Journal of Politics* 63 (November): 1,191–1,213.

Bawn, Kathleen. 1999. "Constructing 'US': Ideology, Coalition Politics, and False Consciousness.' *American Journal of Political Science* 43 (April): 303–334.

Bazelon, Emily. "Sounding Off: Judges Should Have the Right Not to Remain Silent." *Legal Affairs. http://www.legalaffairs.org/issues/November-December-2002/review_bazelon_novdec2002.html.* Accessed September 17, 2004.

Becker, Carl. 1922. *The Declaration of Independence: A Study in the History of Political Ideas.* New York: Harcourt, Brace and Company.

Beckett, Katherine. 1997. *Making Crime Pay: Law and Order in Contemporary American Politics.* New York: Oxford University Press.

Bell, Roger. 1984. *Last among Equals.* Honolulu: University of Hawaii Press.

Bennett, Stephen Earl, and David Resnick. 1990. "The Implications of Nonvoting for Democracy in the United States." *American Journal of Political Science* 34 (August): 771–802.

Benson, T. 1996. "Rhetoric, Civility, and Community: Political Debate on Computer Bulletin Boards." *Communication Quarterly* 44: 359–378,

Benton, Wilbourne E., ed. 1986. *1787: Drafting the U.S. Constitution,* vol. II. College Station: Texas A&M University Press.

Berke, Richard L. 1999. "Weighing the Vice Presidential Factor in Gore's Feeble Showing in the Polls." *New York Times* on the Web, March 6, 1999).

Berke, Richard L. 2001. "Bush Is Providing Corporate Model for White House." *New York Times,* March 11. *http://www.nytimes.com/2001/03/11/politics/11GOVE.html.* Accessed October 23, 2004.

Best, Judith A. 1996. *The Choice of the People: Debating the Electoral College.* Lanham, MD: Rowman & Littlefield.

Bibby, John. 1996. *Politics, Parties, and Elections in America,* 3rd ed. Chicago: Nelson- Hall.

Bibby, John F., and L. Sandy Maisel. 1998. *Two Parties— Or More? The American Party System.* Boulder, CO: Westview Press.

Bickers, Kenneth N., and Robert M. Stein. 1996. "The Electoral Dynamics of the Federal Pork Barrel." *American Journal of Political Science* 40 (November): 1,300–1,326.

Binder, Sarah A., and Steven S. Smith. 1997. *Politics or Principle: Filibustering in the United States Senate.* Washington, DC: Brookings Institution.

Biskupic, Joan. 1999. "Disabled Pupils Win Right to Medical Aid." *Washington Post.* March 4, p. A1.

Biskupik, Joan. 2003. "Court Upholds Use of Race in University Admissions." *USA Today,* June 24, p. 1A.

Black, Charles, Jr. 1974. *Impeachment: A Handbook.* New Haven, CT: Yale University Press.

Bok, Derek, and William G. Bowen. 1998. *The Shape of the River.* Princeton, NJ: Princeton University Press.

Bond, Jon R. 1980. "The Politics of Court Structure: The Addition of New Federal Judges, 1949–1978." *Law and Politics Quarterly* 2 (April): 181–188.

Bond, Jon R., and Richard Fleisher. 1990. *The President in the Legislative Arena.* Chicago: University of Chicago Press.

Bond, Jon R., Richard Fleisher, and Glen S. Krutz. 2004. "The Presumption of Success on Presidential Appointments Reconsidered: How Maligned Neglect Has Become the Primary Method of Defeating Nominees." Texas A&M University. Typescript.

Boulard, Garry. 1999. "More News, Less Coverage?" *State Legislatures. http://www.ncsl.org/programs/pubs/699cover.htm.* Accessed June 1, 2004.

Brady, David W., Joseph Cooper, and Patricia Hurley. 1979. "The Decline of Party in the U.S. House of Representatives, 1887–1968." *Legislative Studies Quarterly* 4 (August): 381–407.

Brands, H. W. 2003. "Founders Chic: Our Reverence for the Fathers Has Gotten Out of Hand." *Atlantic Monthly* 292 (September): 101–110.

Brehm, John, and Scott Gates. 1997. *Working, Shirking, and Sabotage.* Ann Arbor: University of Michigan Press.

Brinkley, Alan. 1993. *The Unfinished Nation.* New York: McGraw-Hill.

Brisbin, Richard A. 1997. *Justice Antonin Scalia and the Conservative Revival.* Baltimore, MD: Johns Hopkins University Press.

Broder, David S. 2000. *Democracy Derailed.* New York: Harcourt.

Browning, Graeme. 1996. "Please Hold for Election Results." *National Journal* 28 (November): 2,517.

Budesheim, Thomas Lee, and Stephen J. DePaola. 1994. "Beauty or the Beast? The Effects of Appearance, Personality, and Issue Information on Evaluations of Candidates." *Personality and Social Psychology Bulletin* 20 (August): 339–349.

Bullock, Charles S., III, and Charles M. Lamb. 1984. *Implementation of Civil Rights Policy.* Monterey, CA: Brooks/Cole.

Byrne, Robert. 1988. *The 1,911 Best Things Anybody Ever Said.* New York: Fawcett Columbine.

Cain, Bruce, John Ferejohn, and Morris Fiorina. 1987. *The Personal Vote.* Cambridge, MA: Harvard University Press.

Caldeira, Gregory A., and John R. Wright. 1990. "*Amici Curiae* before the Supreme Court: Who Participates, When, and How Much?" *The Journal of Politics* 52 (August): 782–806.

Campbell, Angus, Philip Converse, Warren Miller, and Donald Stokes. 1960. *The American Voter.* New York: Wiley.

Campbell, Colin. 1986. *Managing the Presidency: Carter, Reagan, and the Search for Executive Harmony.* Pittsburgh: University of Pittsburgh Press.

Canon, David T. 1990. *Actors, Athletes, and Astronauts: Political Amateurs in the United States Congress.* Chicago: University of Chicago Press.

Capella, Joseph, and Kathleen Hall Jamieson. 1997. *Spiral of Cynicism: The Press and the Public Good.* New York: Oxford University Press.

Carney, Dan. 1997. "High Court Shows Inclination to Rein in Congress." *Congressional Quarterly Weekly Report* 55 (January): 241–244.

Carp, Robert A., Ronald Stidham, and Kenneth L. Manning. 2004. *Judicial Process in America.* Washington, DC: CQ Press.

Carr, Robert K. 1947. *Federal Protection of Civil Rights: Quest for a Sword.* New York: Cornell University Press.

Carlin, Diana Prentice. 1992. "Presidential Debates as Focal Points for Campaign Arguments." *Political Communication* 9 (January–March): 251–265.

CBS News. "Downloading Girl Escapes Lawsuit." CBSNews.com. *http://www.cbsnews.com/stories/2003/08/28/tech/printable570507.shtml.* Accessed February 16, 2004.

Center for Responsive Politics. n.d. *http://www.opensecrets.org/.* Accessed September 13, 2004.

Chaffee, Steven, and Stacey Frank. 1996. "How Americans Get Political Information: Print Versus Broadcast News." *Annals of the American Academy of Political and Social Science* 546: 48–58.

Chandler, Ralph C., and Jack C. Plano. 1988. *The Public Administration Dictionary.* Santa Barbara, CA: ABC-Clio, 127.

Chin, Michelle L., Jon R. Bond, and Nehemia Geva. 2000. "A Foot in the Door: An Experimental Study of PAC and Constituency Effects on Access." *Journal of Politics* 62 (May): 534–549.

Clark, Peter, and James Q. Wilson. 1961. "Incentive Systems: A Theory of Organizations." *Administrative Science Quarterly* 6 (September): 129–166.

Cobb, Roger W., and Charles D. Elder. 1983. *Participation in American Politics: The Dynamics of Agenda Building.* Baltimore, MD: Johns Hopkins University Press.

Coffey, Brian, and Stephen Woolworth. 2004. "'Destroy the Scum, and then Neuter Their Families.' The Web Forum as a Vehicle for Community Discourse?" *The Social Science Journal* 41: 1–14.

Cohen, Bernard. 1963. *The Press and Foreign Policy.* Princeton, NJ: Princeton University Press.

Cohen, Richard E. 1995. *Washington at Work: Back Rooms and Clean Air.* Needham Heights, MA: Allyn & Bacon.

Cohen, Richard, et al. 2003. "The Ultimate Turf War." *National Journal* 35 (1): 16–24.

Coleman, John J. 1996. "Party Organizational Strength and Public Support for Parties." *American Journal of Political Science* 40 (August): 805–824.

Collier, Christopher, and James Lincoln Coller. 1986. *Decision in Philadelphia: The Constitutional Convention of 1787.* New York: Ballantine Books.

Congressional Digest. 1992. "The Democratic Platform." *Congressional Digest* 71 (October): 234–256.

Congressional Digest. 1996. "Same-Sex Marriage: Federal and State Authority." *Congressional Digest* 75 (November): 263.

Congressional Quarterly, Inc. 1993. *Congress A to Z: A Ready Reference Encyclopedia,* 2nd ed. Washington, DC: Congressional Quarterly, Inc.

Congressional Quarterly, Inc. 2001. *Congressional Quarterly's Guide to U.S. Elections,* 4th ed. Washington, DC: Congressional Quarterly, Inc.

Converse, Philip E. 1996. "The Advent of Polling and Political Representation." *PS: Political Science and Politics* 29 (December): 649–657.

Cook, Timothy. 1998. Governing with the News: *The News Media as a Political Institution.* Chicago: University of Chicago Press.

Cotter, Cornelius P., James L. Gibson, John F. Bibby, and Robery Huckshorn. 1989. *Party Organizations in American Politics.* Pittsburgh: University of Pittsburgh Press.

Cox, Barbara J. 2003. "Interstate Validation of Marriages and Civil Unions." *Human Rights Magazine. http://www.abanet.org/irr/hr/summer03/interstate.html.*

CQ Researcher. 1997a. "Feminism's Future." *CQ Researcher* 7 (February): 169–192.

CQ Researcher. 1997b. "Mass Shootings Prompt Bans Abroad." *CQ Researcher* 7 (December): 1,116.

Crispi, Irving. 1989. *Public Opinion, Polls, and Democracy.* Boulder, CO: Westview Press.

Cronin, Thomas E. 1975. *The State of the Presidency.* Boston: Little, Brown.

Crotty, William. 2003. "Presidential Policymaking in Crisis Situations: 9/11 and Its Aftermath." *Policy Studies Journal* 31: 451–464.

Cushman, Barry. 1998. *Rethinking the New Deal Court: The Structure of a Constitutional Revolution.* New York: Oxford University Press.

Cushman, John. 1995. "Tales from the 104th Congress: Watch out, or the Regulators Will Get You!" *New York Times,* February 28, p. A20.

Daniels, Jonathan. 1965. *They Will Be Heard: America's Crusading Newspaper Editors.* New York: McGraw-Hill.

Dautrich, K., and T. Hartley. 1999. *How the News Media Fail American Voters: Causes, Consequences, and Remedies.* New York: Columbia University Press.

Davis, James W. 1994. *The President as Party Leader.* New York: Praeger.

Deering, Christopher J., and Steven S. Smith. 1997. *Committees in Congress,* 3rd ed. Washington, DC: CQ Press.

Democratic Study Group. 1994. "A Look at the Senate Filibuster." *DSG Special Report,* No. 103–28, June 13. Washington, DC: Democratic Study Group.

Dimock, Michael, and Samuel Popkin. 1997. "Political Knowledge in Comparative Perspective." In *Do the Media Govern?* Shanto Iyengar and Richard Reeves, eds. Thousand Oaks, CA: Sage.

Downie, Leonard, and Robert G. Kaiser. 2002. *The News about News.* New York: Knopf.

Downs, Anthony. 1957. *An Economic Theory of Democracy.* New York: Harper & Row.

Easton, David. 1953. *The Political System.* New York: Knopf.

Eddings, Jerelyn. 1997. "How Did Congress Do? Pick an Answer?" *U.S. News & World Report* 121 (October): 14.

Edelman, Murray. 1988. *Constructing the Political Spectacle.* Chicago: University of Chicago Press.

Edmondson, Brad. 1996. "How to Spot a Bogus Poll." *American Demographics* 18 (October): 10–15.

Edsall, Thomas B. 2001. "Democrats Press Bush for Input on Judges: Court Nominees Concern Senators." *Washington Post,* April 28, p. A04. *http://washington post.com/wp-dyn/articles/A13102-2001Apr27.html.* Accessed April 28, 2001.

Edwards, George C., III. 1989. *At the Margins: Presidential Leadership of Congress.* New Haven, CT: Yale University Press.

Edwards, George C., III. 2003. *On Deaf Ears: The Limits of the Bully Pulpit.* New Haven, CT: Yale University Press.

Edwards, George C., III. 2004. *Why the Electoral College Is Bad for America.* New Haven, CT: Yale University Press.

Edwards, George C., III, and Andrew Barrett. 2000. "Presidential Agenda Setting in Congress." In *Polarized Politics: Congress and the President in a Partisan Era,* Jon R. Bond and Richard Fleisher, eds. Washington, DC: CQ Press.

Edwards, George C., III, and Stephen J. Wayne. 2003. *Presidential Leadership: Politics and Policy Making.* 6th ed. Belmont, CA: Thomson/Wadsworth.

Eggen, Dan. 2003. "Seizure of Business Records Is Challenged; ACLU and Arab American Groups File Lawsuit over Element of USA Patriot Act." *Washington Post,* July 31, p. A2.

El Nasser, Haya. 2003. "39 Million Make Hispanics Largest U.S. Minority Group." *USAToday. http://www.usato day.com/news/nation/census/2003-06-18-Census_x.htm.* Accessed March 19, 2004.

Emily's List Web site. *http://www.emilyslist.org/about/ where-from.html.* Accessed October 23, 2004.

Epstein, Lee, Jeffrey A Segal, Harold J. Spaeth, and Thomas G. Walker. 2003. *The Supreme Court Compendium: Data, Decisions, and Developments,* 3rd ed. Washington, DC: CQ Press.

Erikson, Robert S., and Norman R. Luttbeg. 1973. *American Public Opinion: Its Origins, Content, and Impact.* New York: Wiley.

Erikson, Robert, Gerald Wright, and John McIver. 1993. *Statehouse Democracy: Public Opinion and Policy in the American States.* New York: Cambridge University Press.

Erskine, H. 1970. "The Polls: Opinion of the News Media." *Public Opinion Quarterly* 34: 630–643.

Eulau, Heinz. 1956. "The Politics of Happiness: A Prefatory Note to Political Perspectives 1956." *Antioch Review* 16 (fall): 259–264.

Eulau, Heinz, and Paul D. Karps. 1977. "The Puzzle of Representation: Specifying Components of Responsiveness." *Legislative Studies Quarterly* 2 (August): 233–254.

Evans, Diana. 1996. "Before the Roll Call: Interest Group Lobbying and Public Policy Outcomes in House Committees." *Political Research Quarterly* 49 (June): 287–304.

Federal Communications Commission. 2004. "Broadcast Station Totals as of March 31, 2004." *http:braunfoss. fcc.gov/edocs_public/attachmatch/doc-246473A1.pdf.* Accessed August 9, 2004.

Federal Procurement Data Center. *Federal Procurement Report. http://fpdc.gov/.* Accessed August 20, 2002.

Feldman, Paul, and James Jondrow. 1984. "Congressional Elections and Local Federal Spending." *American Journal of Political Science* 28 (February): 147–164.

Fenno, Richard. 1978. *Home Style: House Members in their Districts.* Boston: Little, Brown.

Ferguson, Andrew. 1995. "Disabling America." Excerpted in *CQ Researcher.* 1996. "Implementing the Disabilities Act." 6 (December): 1,121.

Finifter, Ada W. 1970. "Dimensions of Political Alienation." *American Political Science Review* 64 (June): 389–410.

Fiorina, Morris. 1980. "The Decline of Collective Responsibility in American Politics." *Dadalus* 109 (summer): 25–45.

Fiorina, Morris. 1981. *Retrospective Voting in American National Elections.* New Haven, CT: Yale University Press.

Fiorina, Morris. 1996. *Divided Government,* 2nd ed. Boston: Allyn & Bacon.

Flanagan, Caitlin. 2004. "How Serfdom Saved the Women's Movement." *Atlantic Monthly* 293 (March): 109–128.

Fleisher, Richard. 1993. "Explaining the Change in Roll-Call Voting Behavior of Southern Democrats." *Journal of Politics* 55 (May): 327–341.

Fleisher, Richard, and Jon R. Bond. 2000a. "Congress and the President in a Partisan Era." In *Polarized Politics: Congress and the President in a Partisan Era,* Jon R. Bond and Richard Fleisher, eds. Washington, DC: CQ Press, 1–8.

Fleisher, Richard, and Jon R. Bond. 2000b. "Partisanship and the President's Quest for Votes on the Floor of Congress." In *Polarized Politics: Congress and the President in a Partisan Era,* Jon R. Bond and Richard Fleisher, eds. Washington, DC: CQ Press, 154–185.

Fleisher, Richard, and Jon R. Bond. 2001. "Evidence of Increasing Polarization among Ordinary Citizens." In *American Political Parties: Decline or Resurgence?* Jeffrey E. Cohen, Richard Fleisher, and Paul Kantor, eds. Washington, DC: CQ Press, 55–77.

Flemming, Roy B., and B. Dan Wood. 1997. "The Public and the Supreme Court: Individual Justice Responsiveness to American Policy Moods." *American Journal of Political Science* 41 (April): 468–498.

Franken, Al. 2003. *Lies, and the Lying Liars Who Tell Them.* New York: Dutton.

Frankfurter, Felix. 1957. "The Supreme Court in the Mirror of Justices." *University of Pennsylvania Law Review* 105 (April): 781–796.

Friedan, Betty. 1963. *The Feminine Mystique.* New York: Norton.

Gant, Michael M., and William Lyons. 1993. "Democratic Theory, Nonvoting, and Public Policy: The 1972–1988 Presidential Elections." *American Politics Quarterly* 21 (April): 185–204.

Gaines, Brian. 2001. "Popular Myths about Popular Vote-Electoral College Splits." *PS: Political Science and Politics* 34 (March): 71–75.

General Accounting Office. 2003. *Women's Earnings: Work Patterns Partially Explain Difference between Men's and Women's Earnings.* Washington, DC: U.S. Government Printing Office.

George, Alexander L., and Juliette L. George. 1998. *Presidential Personality and Performance.* Boulder, CO: Westview Press.

Gerring, John. 1997. "Ideology: A Definitional Analysis." *Political Research Quarterly* 50: 957–994.

Gerth, H. H., and C. Wright Mills. 1946. *Max Weber: Essays in Sociology.* New York: Oxford University Press.

Gettinger, Stephen. 1998. "When Congress Decides a President's 'High Crimes and Misdemeanors.'" *Congressional Quarterly Weekly Report* 56 (March): 565–568.

Gibbs, Nancy. 1998. "Shots, Screams, and Heroism as a Gunman Invades the Capitol." *Time* 152 (5): 32–37.

Gibson, James L., Cornelius P. Cotter, John F. Bibby, and Robert J. Huckshorn. 1985. "Whither the Local Parties? A Cross-Sectional and Longitudinal Analysis of the Strength of Party Organizations." *American Journal of Political Science* 29 (February): 139–160.

Gibson, James L., John P. Frendreis, and Laura L. Vertz. 1989. "Party Dynamics in the 1980s: Change in County Party Organizational Strength, 1980–1984." *American Journal of Political Science* 33 (February): 67–90.

Gill, Brian, P. Michael Timpane, Karen E. Ross, and Dominic J. Brewer. 2001. *Rhetoric Versus Reality.* Santa Monica, CA: RAND.

Glass, Stephen. 1997. "Peddling Poppy." *New Republic* 216 (23): 20–25.

Goldberg, Carey. 2000. "Vermont House Passes Bill on Rights for Gay Couples." *New York Times,* March 17.

Goldman, Sheldon. 1985. "Reaganizing the Judiciary: The First Term Appointments." *Judicature* 68 (April/May): 313.

Goodsell, Charles. 1994. *The Case for Bureaucracy.* Chatham, NJ: Chatham House.

Goren, Paul. 1997. "Gut-Level Emotion and the Presidential Vote." *American Politics Quarterly* 25 (April): 203–229.

Granat, Diane. 1984. "Parties' Schools for Politicians Grooming Troops for Election." *CQ Weekly Report* 42 (May): 1,036.

Gray, Virginia, and David Lowery. 1996. *The Population Ecology of Interest Representation.* Ann Arbor: University of Michigan Press.

Greenblatt, Alan. 2004. "Whatever Happened to Competitive Elections." *Governing* 18 (October): 22–27.

Grier, Kevin B., Michael C. Munger, and Brian E. Roberts. 1994. "The Determinants of Industry Political Activity, 1976–1986." *American Political Science Review* 88 (December): 911–926.

Gruening, Ernest. 1967. *The Battle for Alaska Statehood.* College, AL: University of Alaska Press.

Gunther, Gerald. 1980. *Constitutional Law.* Mineola, NY: Fountain Press.

Gutin, Myr G. 1994. "Rosalynn Carter in the White House." In *The Presidency and Domestic Policies of Jimmy Carter,* Herbert D. Rosenbaum and Alexej Ugrinsky, eds. Westport, CT: Greenwood Press.

Habermas, Jürgen. 1991. *The Structural Transformation of the Public Sphere: An Inquiry into a Category of Bourgeois Society.* Cambridge, MA: MIT Press.

Hadley, Arthur T. 1976. *The Invisible Primary.* Englewood Cliffs, NJ: Prentice-Hall.

Haider-Markel, Donald P., and Kenneth J. Meier. 1996. "The Politics of Gay and Lesbian Rights: Expanding the Scope of the Conflict." *The Journal of Politics* 58 (May): 332–349.

Hall, Richard L. 1996. *Participation in Congress.* New Haven, CT: Yale University Press.

Hamilton, James T. 2004. *All the News That's Fit to Sell.* Princeton, NJ: Princeton University Press.

Handgun Control. 1998. "Senate Kills Kids and Guns Legislation Despite Overwhelming Public Support for Such Measures." *http://www.handguncontrol.org/press/july23-98. Accessed August 12,* 1998.

Hargrove, Erwin C. 1974. *The Power of the Modern Presidency.* Philadelphia: Temple University Press.

Harris, Fred R. 1995. *In Defense of Congress.* New York: St. Martin's Press.

Hart, John. 1995. *The Presidential Branch: From Washington to Clinton,* 2nd ed. Chatham, NJ: Chatham House.

Haskell, John. 1996. *Fundamentally Flawed: Understanding and Reforming Presidential Primaries.* Lanham, MD: Rowman & Littlefield.

Herman, Edward S., and Robert W. McChesney. 1997. *The Global Media.* London: Cassell.

Hershey, Majorie Randon. 1997. "The Congressional Elections." In *The Elections of 1996,* Gerald Pomper, ed. Chatham, NJ: Chatham House.

Hess, Stephen. 1996. "Media Mavens." *Society* 33: 75.

Hibbing, John. 1991. *Congressional Careers: Contours of life in the U.S. House of Representatives.* Chapel Hill: University of North Carolina Press.

Hibbing, John R., and Elizabeth Theiss-Morse. 1995. *Congress as Public Enemy: Public Attitudes toward American Political Institutions.* New York: Cambridge University Press.

Hibbing, John R., and Elizabeth Theiss-Morse. 1998. "The Media's Role in Public Negativity towards Congress: Distinguishing Emotional Reactions and Cognitive Evaluation." *American Journal of Political Science* 42 (April): 475–498.

Hibbing, John R., and Elizabeth Theiss-Morse. 2001. "Process Preferences and American Politics: What People Want Government to Be." *American Political Science Review* 95 (March): 145–154.

Hibbing, John R., and Elizabeth Theiss-Morse. 2003. *Stealth Democracy.* New York: Cambridge University Press.

Hill, Kevin A. 1995. "Does the Creation of Majority Black Districts Aid Republicans?" An Analysis of the 1992 Congressional Elections in Eight Southern States." *Journal of Politics* 57 (May): 384–401.

Hill, Kevin A., and John E. Hughes. 1997. "Computer-Mediated Political Communication: The USENET and Political Communities." *Political Communication* 14 (January–March): 3–27.

Hofstetter, C. Richard, et al. 1999. "Information, Misinformation, and Political Talk Radio." *Political Research Quarterly* 52: 353–370.

Huckshorn, Robert J., James L. Gibson, Cornelius P. Cotter, and John F. Bibby. 1986. "Party Integration and Party Organizational Strength." *Journal of Politics* 48 (November): 976–991.

Hudson, William E. 1995. *American Democracy in Peril.* Chatham, NJ: Chatham House.

Humphries, Steve, and Pamela Wright. 1992. *Out of Sight: The Experience of Disability, 1900–1950.* London: Northcote House.

Hurley, Patricia A., and Brinck Kerr. 1997. "The Partisanship of New Members in the 103rd and 104th Houses." *Social Science Quarterly* 78 (December): 992–1,000.

Hutchings, Vincent. 2003. *Public Opinion and Democratic Accountability: How Citizens Learn about Politics.* Princeton, NJ: Princeton University Press.

Institute for Women's Policy Research. 1996. *The Status of Women in the States.* Washington, DC: Institute for Women's Policy Research.

Iyengar, Shanto. 1991. *Is Anyone Responsible? How Television Frames Political Issues.* Chicago: University of Chicago Press.

Iyengar, Shanto. 1997. "Media-Based Political Campaigns: Overview." In *Do the Media Govern?* Shanto Iyengar and Richard Reeves, eds. Thousand Oaks, CA: Sage.

Iyengar, Shanto, and Donald Kinder. 1987. *News that Matters: Television and American Opinion.* Chicago: University of Chicago Press.

Jackson, John S., and William Crotty. 1996. *The Politics of Presidential Selection.* New York: HarperCollins.

Jackson, Robert A. 1997. "The Mobilization of U.S. State Electorates in the 1988 and 1990 Elections." *Journal of Politics* 59 (May): 520–537.

Jacobson, Gary. 1990. *The Electoral Origins of Divided Government: Competition in U.S. House Elections, 1946–1988.* Boulder, CO: Westview Press.

Jacobson, Gary C. 2001. *The Politics of Congressional Elections,* 5th ed. New York: Addison Wesley Longman.

Jacobson, Louis. 1995. "Tanks on the Roll." *National Journal* 27 (July): 1,767–1,771.

Jefferson, Thomas. 1823. *Letter to Lafayette.*

Jennings, M. Kent, and Richard Niemi. 1975. "Continuity and Change in Political Orientations: A Longitudinal Study of Two Generations. *American Political Science Review* 69 (December): 1,316–1,335.

Johnson, Peter. 2004. "Survey: Profit Pressures Worry Most Journalists." *USA Today,* May 24, p. 3D.

Kahn, Kim Fridkin. 1992. "Does Being Male Help?" *Journal of Politics* 54 (May): 497–517.

Kahn, Kim Fridkin. 1996. *The Political Consequences of Being a Woman: How Stereotypes Influence the Content and Impact of Statewide Campaigns.* New York: Columbia University Press.

Kaminer, Wendy. 1999. "Taking Liberties." *The American Prospect. http://epn.org/prospect/42/42 kaminer.html.* Accessed March 8, 1999.

Katz, Jeffrey. 1998. "Panel Drops Final Ethics Charges." *CQ Weekly Report* 56 (October): 2,816.

Kaufman, Herbert. 1977. *Red Tape: Its Origins, Uses, and Abuses.* Washington, DC: Brookings Institution.

Kernell, Samuel. 1997. *Going Public: New Strategies of Presidential Leadership,* 3rd ed. Washington, DC: CQ Press.

Kerwin, Cornelius. 1994. *Rulemaking.* Washington, DC: CQ Press.

Kerwin, Cornelius. 1999. *Rulemaking.* Washington, DC: CQ Press.

Kerwin, Cornelius. 2003. *Rulemaking: How Government Agencies Write Law and Make Policy.* Washington, DC: CQ Press.

Kessel, John H. 1992. *Presidential Campaign Politics,* 4th ed. Pacific Grove, CA: Brooks/Cole.

Key, V. O. 1964. *Politics, Parties, and Pressure Groups,* 5th ed. New York: Crowell.

King, Anthony. 1997. "Running Scared." *Atlantic Monthly* 279 (January): 41–61.

Kingdon, John W. 1995. *Agendas, Alternatives, and Public Policies,* 2nd ed. New York: HarperCollins.

Knack, Stephen, and James White. 1998. "Did State Motor Voter Programs Help the Democrats?" *American Politics Quarterly* 26 (July): 344–356.

Krueger, Brian. 2002. "Assessing the Potential of Internet Political Participation in the United States." *American Politics Research.* 30: 476–498.

Krutz, Glen S., Richard Fleisher, and Jon R. Bond. 1998. "From Abe Fortas to Zoe Baird: Why Some Presidential Nominations Fail in the Senate." *American Political Science Review* 92 (December): 871–881.

Kuzenski, John C. 1997. "The Four—Yes Four—Types of State Primaries." *PS: Political Science and Politics* 30 (June): 207–208.

Lake, Celinda, and Jennifer Sosin. 1998. "Public Opinion Polling and the Future of Democracy." *National Civic Review* 87 (spring): 65–70.

Lasswell, Harold D. 1938. *Politics: Who Gets What, When and How.* New York: McGraw-Hill.

Lazarsfeld, Paul F., Bernard Berelson, and Hazel Gaudet. 1944. *The People's Choice.* New York: Duell, Sloan and Pearce.

Lee, Emery G., III, Frances U. Sandstrum, and Thomas C. Wiesert. 1996. "Context and the Court: Sources of Support for Civil Liberties on the Rehnquist Court." *American Politics Quarterly* 24 (July): 377–395.

Lehigh, Scot. 2002. "President Needs OK by Congress for Iraq War." *Boston Globe,* August 23, p. A27. *http://www.boston.com/dailyglobe2/235/oped/President_needs_OK_by_Congressfor_Iraq_war +.shtml.* Accessed August 25, 2002.

Leighley, Jan. 1996. "Group Membership and the Mobilization of Political Participation." *Journal of Politics* 58 (May): 447–463.

Leighley, Jan E., and Arnold Vedlitz. 1999. "Race, Ethnicity, and Political Participation: Competing Models and Contrasting Explanations." *Journal of Politics* 61 (November): 1,092–1,114.

Lenz, Ryan. 2004. "Soldiers in Iraq Buy Their Own Body Armor." *The Guardian.http://www.guardian.co.uk/worldlatest/story/0,1280,-3904926,00.html.* Accessed June 1, 2004.

Light, Paul C. 1983. *The President's Agenda: Domestic Policy Choice from Kennedy to Carter (with Notes on Ronald Reagan).* Baltimore, MD: Johns Hopkins University Press.

Light, Paul. 1999. *The True Size of Government.* Washington, DC: Brookings Institution.

Lijphart, Arend. 1984. *Democracies: Patterns of Majoritarian and Consensus Government in Twenty-One Countries.* New Haven, CT: Yale University Press.

Lindblom, Charles. 1959. "The Science of Muddling Through." *Public Administration Review* 19 (spring): 79–88.

Lippmann, Walter. 1922. *Public Opinion.* New York: Macmillan.

Lippmann, Walter. 1949. *Public Opinion.* New York: Free Press.

Lipsky. Michael. 1980. *Street-Level Bureaucracy.* New York: Russell Sage Foundation.

Loveless, Tom. 1997. "The Structure of Public Confidence in Education." *American Journal of Education* 105 (February): 127–159.

Lowery, David, and Holly Brasher. 2004. *Organized Interests and American Government.* New York: McGraw-Hill.

Lowi, Theodore J. 1969. *The End of Liberalism: Ideology, Policy, and the Crisis of Public Authority.* New York: Norton.

Lyman, Edward Leo. 1986. *Political Deliverance: The Mormon Quest for Utah Statehood.* Urbana: University of Illinois Press.

Manheim, Jarol B., and Richard C. Rich. 1991. *Empirical Political Analysis: Research Methods in Political Science.* New York: Longman.

Masters, Brooke A. 2001. "Judgeship Hinges on Politics, Practice: Md. Liberals Keep Bush Pick Off List." *Washington Post,* May 13, p. C05. *http://washington post.com/wp-dyn/articles/A20353-2001May12.html.* Accessed May 13, 2001.

Mayhew, David. 1974. *Congress: The Electoral Connection.* New Haven: Yale University Press.

McCombs, Maxwell, and Donald Shaw. 1972. "The Agenda-Setting Function of Mass Media." *Public Opinion Quarterly* 36 (summer): 176–185.

McCubbins, Mathew D., and Thomas Schwartz. 1984. "Congressional Oversight Overlooked: Police Patrol versus Fire Alarms." *American Journal of Political Science* 28 (February): 165–179.

McCullough, David. 2001. *John Adams.* New York: Simon & Schuster.

McGlen, Nancy E., and Karen O'Connor. 1983. *Women's Rights: The Struggle for Equality in the Nineteenth and Twentieth Centuries.* New York: Praeger.

Meier, Kenneth J. 1993. *Politics and the Bureaucracy.* Pacific Grove, CA: Brooks/Cole.

Meier, Kenneth J. 1995. "The Policy Process." In *Regulation and Consumer Protection,* ed. Kenneth J. Meier and E. Thomas Garman, eds. Houston, TX: Dame Publications.

Meier, Kenneth J. 1999. "Drugs, Sex, and Rock and Roll: A Theory of Morality Politics." *Policy Studies Journal* 27 (4): 681–695.

Mervin, David. 1995. "The Bully Pulpit, II." *Presidential Studies Quarterly* 25 (winter): 19–23.

Milbrath, Lester W., and M. L. Goel. 1977. *Political Participation: How and Why Do People Get Involved in Politics?* 2nd ed. Chicago: Rand McNally.

Mills, C. Wright. 1956. *The Power-Elite.* New York: Oxford University Press.

Mills, K. 1997. "What Difference Do Women Journalists Make?" In *Women, Media, and Politics,* Pippa Norris, ed. New York: Oxford University Press.

Moen, Matthew C. and Gary W. Copeland. 1999. *The Contemporary Congress: A Bicameral Approach.* Belmont, CA: Wadsworth.

Mondak, Jeffery J. 1995. "Competence, Integrity, and the Electoral Success of Congressional Incumbents." *Journal of Politics* 57 (November): 1,043–1,069.

Mooney, Christopher Z. 1998. "Why Do They Tax Dogs in West Virginia?" *PS: Political Science and Politics* 31 (June): 199–203.

Mooney, Christopher Z., ed. 2001. *The Public Clash of Private Values.* New York: Chatham House.

Morin, Richard. 2000. "The Big Picture Is Out of Focus." *Washington Post National Weekly Edition,* March 6–13, p. 21.

Morgan, Edmund S. 1992. *The Birth of the Republic.* Chicago: The University of Chicago Press.

Nathan, Richard. 1996. "The Role of the States in American Federalism." In *The State of the States,* Carl E. Van Horn, ed. Washington, DC: CQ Press.

National Election Studies. 2003. "The NES Guide to Public Opinion and Electoral Behavior." *http://www.umich.edu/~nes/nesguide/nesguide.htm.* Accessed September 9, 2003.

Neustadt, Richard E. 1960. *Presidential Power.* New York: Wiley.

Newport, Frank. 1998. "History Shows Presidential Job Approval Ratings Can Plummet Rapidly." *The Gallup Poll Monthly* 389 (February): 9–10.

News Corporation. 2004. *http://www.newscorp.com/index2.html.* Accessed May 10, 2004.

Newspaper Association of America. 2003. "Daily Newspaper Readership Trends." *http://www.naa.org/artpage.cfm?aid=1614&DID=75.* Accessed August 9, 2004.

Nie, Norman, Sidney Verba, and John Petrocik. 1979. *The Changing American Voter.* Cambridge, MA: Harvard University Press.

Niemi, Richard, and Herbert Weisberg. 1993. *Classics in Voting Behavior.* Washington, DC: CQ Press.

Niven, David. 2002. *Tilt?* New York: Praeger.

Norrander, Barbara. 1997. "The Independence Gap and the Gender Gap." *Public Opinion Quarterly* 61 (fall): 464–477.

Novak, Viveca, Laura Locke, Hilary Hylton, Greg Land, Siobhan Morrissey, David Thigpen, and Jill Underwood. 2004. "The Vexations of Voting Machines." *Time* 163 (18): 42–44.

NRA. "U.S. Senate Derails Gun Control Agenda, Promotes Safety." *http://www.nara.org/pub/ila/1998/*

98-07-24_faxlert_dearails_gun_control. Accessed August 12, 1998.

Numbers USA. 2004. "The 12 Top-Rated, Nationally Syndicated, Politically-Oriented Radio Talk Shows." *http://www.numbersusa.com/text?ID=998.* Accessed May 12, 2004.

O'Brien, David M. 1996. *Storm Center: The Supreme Court in American Politics,* 4th ed. New York: Norton.

Olson, Mancur. 1965. *The Logic of Collective Action.* Cambridge, MA: Harvard University Press.

Ornstein, Norman, Thomas E. Mann, and Michael J. Malbin. 2000. *Vital Statistics on Congress, 1999–2000.* Washington, DC: CQ Press.

Ornstein, Norman J., Thomas E. Mann, and Michael J. Malbin. 2002. *Vital Statistics on Congress, 2001–2002.* Washington, DC: AEI Press.

O'Rourke, P. J. 1991. *A Parliament of Whores.* New York: Atlantic Monthly Press.

Osborne, David, and Ted Gaebler. 1990. *Reinventing Government.* New York: Plume.

Overby, L. Marvin, and Kenneth M. Cosgrov. 1996. "Unintended Consequences? Racial Redistricting and the Representation of Minority Interests." *Journal of Politics* 58 (May): 540–550.

Padover, Saul K., ed. 1939. *Thomas Jefferson on Democracy.* New York: Appleton-Century Company, Inc./Mentor Books.

Patterson, Thomas E. 1984. *The Mass Media Election.* New York: Praeger.

Peltason, J.W. 1982. *Corwin and Peltasons' Understanding the Constitution,* 3rd ed. New York: Holt, Rinehart & Winston.

Percy, Stephen. 1989. *Disability, Civil Rights, and Public Policy.* Tuscaloosa: University of Alabama Press.

Peters, John G., and Susan Welch. 1980. "The Effects of Charges of Corruption on Voting Behavior in Congressional Elections." *American Political Science Review* 74 (September): 697–708.

Peterson, Paul. 1995. *The Price of Federalism.* Washington, DC: Brookings Institution.

Pew Research Center. 1998. "Internet News Takes Off: Event-Driven News Audiences." Report of the Pew Research Center for the People and the Press, Washington, DC.

Pew Research Center. 1998. "Trust in Government." *http://www.people-press.org/trusttab.htm.* Accessed March 13, 1998.

Pew Research Center. 2001. "Terror Coverage Boost News Media's Images." *http://people-press.org/reports.* Accessed August 9, 2004.

Pew Research Center. 2002. "News Media's Improved ImageProvesShort-Lived." *http://people-press.org/reports.* Accessed May 13, 2004.

Pew Research Center. 2003. "Political Sites Gain, But Major News Sites Still Dominant." *http://people-press.org/reports.* Accessed May 13, 2004.

Plano, Jack C., and Milton Greenberg. 2002. *The American Political Dictionary,* 11th ed. Belmont, CA: Thomson/Wadsworth.

Polsby, Nelson W. 1968. "The Institutionalization of the U.S. House of Representatives." *American Political Science Review* 62 (March): 144–168.

Polsby, Nelson, and Aaron Wildavsky. 2000. *Presidential Elections: Strategies and Structures of American Politics,* 10th ed. New York: Chatham House.

Ponessa, Jeanne. 1995. "Congress Closer to Control of District's Finances." *CQ Weekly Report* 53 (February): 609.

Powell, G. Bingham. 1980. "Voting Turnout in Thirty Democracies: Partisan, Legal, and Socio-Economic Influences." In *Electoral Participation: A Comparative Analysis,* Richard Rose, ed. Beverly Hills: Sage.

Pressley, Sue Anne. 1997. "Texas Campus Attracts Fewer Minorities." *Washington Post,* August 28, p. A1

Pressman, Jeffrey L., and Aaron Wildavsky. 1973. *Implementation.* Berkeley: University of California Press.

Ragsdale, Lyn. 1996. *Vital Statistics on the Presidency: Washington to Clinton.* Washington, DC: CQ Press.

Ragsdale, Lyn, and John J. Theis, III. 1997. "The Institutionalization of the American Presidency 1924–92." *American Journal of Political Science* 41 (October): 1,280–1,318.

Rauch, Jonathan. 1994. *Demosclerosis: The Silent Killer of American Government.* New York: Times Books.

Redford, Emmette S. 1969. *Democracy in the Administrative State.* New York: Oxford University Press.

Reich, Robert. 1997. *Locked in the Cabinet.* New York: Knopf.

Rees, Nigel. 1997. *Cassell Companion to Quotations.* London: Cassell.

Ripley, Randall. 1988. *Policy Analysis in Political Science.* Chicago: Nelson-Hall.

Robson, William A. 1923. "Compulsory Voting." *Political Science Quarterly* 38 (December): 569–577.

Rogers, Everett, William Hart, and James Dearing. 1997. "A Paradigmatic History of Agenda-Setting Research." In *Do the Media Govern?* Shanto Iyengar and Richard Reeves, eds. Thousand Oaks, CA: Sage.

Rogers, Will. 1974. *The Illiterate Digest.* Edited with an Introduction by Joseph A. Stout, Jr. Stillwater: Oklahoma State University Press.

Rohde, David W. 1991. *Parties and Leaders in the Post Reform House.* Chicago: University of Chicago Press.

Rosenbloom, David H. 1998. *Public Administration: Understanding Management, Politics, and Law in the Public Sector,* 4th ed. New York: McGraw-Hill.

Rosenstone, Steven, and John Mark Hansen. 1993. *Mobilization, Participation, and Democracy in America.* New York: Macmillan.

Sabatier, Paul. 1988. "An Advocacy Coalition Framework of Policy Change and the Role of Policy-Oriented Learning Therein." *Policy Sciences* 21: 129–168.

Sabatier, Paul A., and Daniel Mazmanian. 1980. "The Implementation of Public Policy: A Framework for Analysis." *Policy Studies Journal* 8: 538–560.

Salisbury, Robert H. 1969. "An Exchange Theory of Interest Groups." *Midwest Journal of Political Science* 13 (February): 1–32.

Samuelson, Robert J. 1996. "Join the Club." *Washington Post, National Weekly Edition.* April 15–21, p. 5.

Sanger, David E. 2001. "Look Sharp: Trying to Run a Country Like a Corporation." *New York Times,* July 8. *http://www.nytimes.com/2001/07/08/weekinreview/08SANG.html.* Accessed October 23, 2004.

San Jose Mercury News. 2004. "Schwarzenegger Supported Prop. 187; Releases Financial Statements." *http://www.mercurynews.com/mld/mercurynews/news/6507635.htm.* Accessed July 28, 2004.

Schaefer, Todd M. 1997. "Persuading the Persuaders: Presidential Speeches and Editorial Opinion." *Political Communication* 14 (January–March): 97–111.

Schattschneider, E. E. 1942. *Party Government.* New York: Rinehart.

Schattschneider, E. E. 1960. *The Semisovereign People: A Realist View of Democracy in America.* New York: Holt, Rinehart & Winston.

Schell, Jonathan. 1996. "The Uncertain Leviathan." *Atlantic Monthly* 278 (August): 70–78.

Schlesinger, Arthur M., Jr. 1973. *The Imperial Presidency.* Boston: Houghton Mifflin.

Schneider, Anne Larson, and Helen Ingram. 1997. *Policy Design for Democracy.* Lawrence: University of Kansas Press.

Scholzman, Kay Lehman, and John T. Tierney. 1983. "More of the Same: Washington Pressure Group Activity in a Decade of Change." *Journal of Politics* 45 (May): 351–375.

Schorr, Daniel. 1997. "Who Uses Whom?" In *Do the Media Govern?* Shanto Iyengar and Richard Reeves, eds. Thousand Oaks, CA: Sage

Schramm, Sanford F., and Carol S. Wiessert. 1997. "The State of American Federalism, 1996–1997." *Publius: The Journal of Federalism* 27 (spring): 1–31.

Schumpeter, Joseph. 1942. *Capitalism, Socialism and Democracy.* New York: Harper and Brothers.

Sclar, Elliott D. 2000. *You Don't Always Get What You Pay For.* Ithaca, NY: Cornell Univeristy Press.

Schramm, Sanford F., and Carol S. Wiessert. 1997. "The State of American Federalism, 1996–1997." *Publius: The Journal of Federalism.* 27 (spring): 1–31.

Sears, David, and Nicholas Valentino. 1997. "Politics Matters: Political Events as Catalysts for Preadult Socialization." *American Political Science Review* 91 (June): 45–65.

Seeman, Melvin. 1959. "On the Meaning of Alienation." *American Sociological Review.* 24 (December): 783–791.

Segal, Jeffrey A., and Harold J. Spaeth. 1993. *The Supreme Court and the Attitudinal Model.* New York: Cambridge University Press.

Shafer, Byron E. 1988. *Bifurcated Politics: Evolution and Reform in the National Convention.* Cambridge, MA: Harvard University Press.

Shafritz, Jay M. 1988. *The Dorsey Dictionary of American Government and Politics.* Chicago: Dorsey Press.

Sifry, Micah. 1998. "Low Tide for the Angry Middle." *The Nation* 267 (July): 16–20.

Simonich, Milan. 2000. "Miranda's Life Ended with Warning, No Conviction." Post-Gazett.com. *http://www.post-gazett.com/headlines/20000110mirandaside2.asp* Accessed October 25, 2000.

Slater, Philip. 1991. *A Dream Deferred: America's Discontent and the Search for a New Democratic Ideal.* Boston: Beacon Press.

Silverstein, Mark. 1994. *Judicious Choices: The New Politics of Supreme Court Confirmations.* New York: Norton.

Sinclair, Barbara. 2000. *Unorthodox Lawmaking: New Legislative Processes in the U.S. Congress,* 2nd ed. Washington, DC: CQ Press.

Singhania, Lisa, ed. and pub. 2002. "Newspaper Circulation Holds Steady." *http://www.editorandpublisher.com/eandp/news/article_display.jsp?vnu_content_id = 1756525.* Accessed May 13, 2004.

Skocpol, Theda. 1999. "Associations without Members." *The American Prospect* 45: 1–8.

Smith, Kevin B. 1999. "Clean Thoughts and Dirty Minds: The Politics of Porn." *The Policy Studies Journal* 27 (4): 723–734.

Smith, Richard A. 1995. "Interest Group Influence in the U.S. Congress." *Legislative Studies Quarterly* 20 (February): 89–139.

Spitzer, Robert J. 1995. *The Politics of Gun Control.* Chatham, NJ: Chatham House.

Spring, Joe. 1998. *American Education.* 8th ed. New York: McGraw-Hill.

Spitzer, Robert J. 1998. "Gun Control." In *Moral Controversies in American Politics: Cases in Social Regulatory Policy,* Raymond Tatalovich and Byron W. Daynes, eds. New York: Sharpe.

Spriggs, James F., II, and Paul J. Wahlbeck. 1997. "Amicus Curiae and the Role of Information at the Supreme Court," *Political Research Quarterly* 50 (June): 365–386.

Stanley, Harold W., and Richard G. Niemi. 2003. *Vital Statistics on American Politics 2003–2004.* Washington, DC: CQ Press.

Steele, Shelby. 1990. "A Negative Vote on Affirmative Action." *New York Times Magazine* 139 (May): 46.

Sterling, Bryan B., ed. 1979. *The Best of Will Rogers.* New York: Crown Publishers.

Stickland, Rennard J. 1992. "Native Americans." In *The Oxford Companion to the Supreme Court of the United States,* Kermit L. Hall, ed. New York: Oxford University Press.

Swain, Carol. 1995. *Black Faces, Black Interests: The Representation of African Americans in Congress.* Cambridge, MA: Harvard University Press.

Swanson, David L. 2000. "The Homologous Evolution of Political Communication and Civic Engagement: Good News, Bad News, and No News." *Political Communication* 17: 409–414.

Tarr, G. Alan. 2003. *Judicial Process and Judicial Policymaking.* Belmont, CA: Thomson/Wadsworth.

Teixeira, Ruy. 1987. *Why Americans Don't Vote: Turnout Decline in the United States.* New York: Greenwood Press.

Teixeira, Ruy. 2004. "The Big Shift: How Public Opinion Has Changed on Iraq." Center for American Progress. *http://www.americanprogress.org/site/pp.asp?c=biJRJ8OVF&b=38980.* Accessed June 19, 2004.

Tesh, Sylvia. 1984. "In Support of 'Single-Issue' Politics." *Political Science Quarterly* 99 (spring): 27–44.

Theodoulou, Stella. 1995. "Making Public Policy." In *Public Policy: The Essential Readings,* Stella Z. Theodoulou and Matthew A. Cahn, eds. Englewood Clifs, NJ: Prentice-Hall.

Thomsett, Michael C., and Jean Freestone Thomsett. 1994. *Political Quotations: A Worldwide Dictionary of Thoughts and Pronouncements from Politicians, Literary Figures, Humorists, and Others.* Jefferson, NC: McFarland and Company.

Time Warner. 2004. "Companies." *http://www.timewarner.com/companies/index.adp.* Accessed May 10, 2004.

Timpone, Richard J. 1998. "Structure, Behavior, and Voter Turnout in the United States." *American Political Science Review.* 92 (March): 145–158.

Tocqueville, Alexis de. [1835] 1955. *Democracy in America,* Vol. II. New York: Vintage Books.

Truman, David B. 1951. *The Governmental Process: Political Interests and Public Opinion,* 2nd ed. New York: Knopf.

TV-Turnoff Network. 2004. *http://www.tvturnoff.org/images/facts&figs/factsheets/Facts%20and%20Figures.pdf.* Accessed May 13, 2004.

Uhlaner, Carole J., Bruce E. Cain, and Roderick Kiewiet. 1989. "Political Participation of Ethnic Minorities in the 1980s." *Political Behavior* 11 (September): 195–231.

U.S. Census Bureau. 1998. *Statistical Abstract of the United States. http://www.gov/statab.* Accessed December 1, 1998.

U.S. Census Bureau. 2001. *Statistical Abstract of the United States. http://www.census.gov/prod/2002pubs/01statab/stat-ab01.html.* Accessed October 23, 2004.

U.S. Census Bureau. 2003. *Statistical Abstract of the United States. http://www.census.gov/prod/2001pubs/statab/sec14.pdf.* Accessed September 10, 2003.

U.S. Department of Justice. 2000. "Enforcing the ADA: Looking Back on a Decade of Progress." *http://www.usdoj.gov/crt/ada/pubs/10thrpt.htm#anchor37661.* Accessed October 26, 2000.

U.S. Government Customer Satisfaction Initiative. 2000. "Key Findings from the ACSI Report." *http://www.customersurvey.gov/summary.htm.* Accessed May 3, 2000.

Van Horn, Carl E. 1996. "The Quiet Revolution." In *The State of the States,* 3rd ed. Carl E. Van Horn, ed. Washington, DC: CQ Press.

Verba, Sidney, and Norman Nie. 1987. *Political Participation in America.* New York: Harper & Row.

Verba, Sidney, Kay Lehman Schlozman, and Henry E. Brady. 1995. *Voice and Equality: Civic Voluntarism in American Politics.* Cambridge, MA: Harvard University Press.

Vermont Freedom to Marry Action Committee. 2000. "What Is a Civil Union." *http://www.vtmarriageaction.org/index.html.* Accessed October 29, 2000.

Wattenberg, Martin P. 1990. *The Decline of American Political Parties: 1952–1988.* Cambridge, MA: Harvard University Press.

Wattenberg, Martin P. 1998. "Politics: Should Election Day Be a Holiday?" *Atlantic Monthly* 1 (October): 42.

Waxman, Sharon. 2004. "Global Warming Ignites Tempers, Even in a Movie." *New York Times,* May 12, p. B1.

Wayne, Stephen. 2000. *The Road to the White House 2000.* Boston: Bedford/St. Martin's Press.

Weber, Paul J., and Barbara A. Perry. 1989. *Unfounded Fears: Myths and Realities of a Constitutional Convention.* Westport, CT: Greenwood Press.

Welch, Susan, and John R. Hibbing. 1997. "The Effects of Charges of Corruption on Voting Behavior in Congressional Elections, 1982–1990." *Journal of Politics* 59 (February): 226–239.

White, G. Edward. 1982. *Earl Warren: A Public Life.* New York: Oxford University Press.

Wiecek, William. 1992. "Declaration of Independence." In *The Oxford Companion to the Supreme Court of the United States,* Kermit L. Hall, ed. New York: Oxford University Press.

Wildavsky, Aaron. 1965. "The Goldwater Phenomenon: Parties, Politicians and the Two- Party System." *Review of Politics.* 27 (July): 386–413.

Wilson, James Q. 1962. *The American Democrat.* Chicago: University of Chicago Press.

Wilson, Woodrow. 1885. *Congressional Government: A Study in American Politics.* Boston: Houghton Mifflin.

Wilson, Woodrow. 1887. "The Study of Administration." *Political Science Quarterly* 2(March): 197–222.

Wood, B. Dan. 1992. "Modeling Federal Implementation as a System: The Clean Air Case." *American Journal of Political Science* 36 (February): 4–67.

Wood, B. Dan, and Richard W. Waterman. 1994. *Bureaucratic Dynamics: The Role of Bureaucracy in a Democracy.* Boulder, CO: Westview Press.

Woodward, Bob. 2002. *Bush at War.* New York: Simon & Schuster.

Worsnop, Richard L. 1996. "Implementing the Disabilities Act." *CQ Researcher* 6 (December): 1,107–1,127.

Wright, James D., Peter H. Rossi, and Kathleen Daly. 1983. *Under the Gun: Weapons, Crime, and Violence in America.* New York: Aldine.

Wright, John R. 1990. "Contributions, Lobbying, and Committee Voting in the U.S. House of Representatives." *American Journal of Political Science* 84 (June): 417–438.

Younge, Gary. 2003. "A Supreme Showdown." *The Guardian. http://www.guardian.co.uk/weekend/story/0,3605,980731,00.html.* Accessed March 2, 2004.

Zaller, John R. 1992. *The Nature and Origins of Mass Opinion.* New York: Cambridge University Press.

Case Index

Name Index

Subject Index

Photo Credits

Chapter opener spreads, Promise of heads, and Performance Assessment heads: Statue of Liberty: © Corbis. Living the Promise box icon: © Gerald Bustamante/Images.com Promise and Policy box icon: © 2004 Jane Sterrett c/o theispot.com

Chapter 1. 2: © Ted Spiegel/Corbis; 4: © Bettmann/Corbis; 11: © Reuters/ Gary Hershorn/Landov; 14 © David Butow/Corbis SABA; 18 © Chuck Savage/Corbis

Chapter 2. 30: © The Granger Collection, New York; 33: © Bettmann/ Corbis; 38 © North Wind/North Wind Picture Archives — All rights reserved; 40 © Bettmann/Corbis; 50 © Bettmann/ Corbis

Chapter 3. 62: © Reuters/Tim Wimborne/Landov; 65: Copyright © Mark Richards/PhotoEdit — All rights reserved; 73: © David Sailors/Corbis; 77: © Getty Images; 79: © Getty Images; 84 © Ralf-Finn Hestoft/Corbis

Chapter 4. 96: © Royalty-Free/Corbis; 98: © Kim Komenich/San Francisco Chronicle/Corbis SABA; 106: © David H. Wells/Corbis; 111: © Getty Images; 118 © Bettmann/Corbis

Chapter 5. 124: © Getty Images; 126: © Najiah Feanny/Corbis SABA; 131: © Bettmann/Corbis; 139: Copyright © David Young-Wolff/PhotoEdit — All rights reserved; 145: © Getty Images; 148: © Jeff Greenberg/The Image Works

Chapter 6. 156: © Getty Images; 162: © AP Photo/Bill Haber/Wide World; 172 © Getty Images: 174: © AP Photo/Richard Drew/Wide World; 181: © AFP/Getty Images

Chapter 7. 188: © Newhouse News Service/Landov; 192: © Paul Richards/ AFP/Getty Images; 206: © Getty Images; 214 top: © Getty Images; 214 bottom: © Mike Segar/Reuters/Corbis; 224: © Ramin Talaie/Corbis

Chapter 8. 230: © Getty Images; 235: © Syracuse Newspapers/John Berry/The Image Works; 240: © Getty Images; 243: © Chip East/Reuters/Corbis; 245: © Cheryl Diaz/Meyer/Dallas Morning News/Corbis; 253: © Howard Baer

Chapter 9. 256: © Ramin Talaie/Corbis; 259 © AFP/Getty Images; 274: © AFP/Getty Images; 279 top: © AP/Wide World; 279 bottom: Courtesy of Donna Ladd/Jackson Free Press

Chapter 10. 284: © Jeff J. Mitchell/ Reuters/Corbis; 293: © Jim Bourg/ Reuters/Corbis; 296: © Getty Images; 314 © Getty Images; 320: © AP Photo/Ted S. Warren/Wide World; 321: © AP Photo/Elaine Thompson/Wide World

Chapter 11. 326: © Larry Downing/ Reuters/Corbis; 329: © AFP/Getty Images; 337: © Getty Images; 340: © Paul Conklin/PhotoEdit — All rights reserved; 343: © Rob Crandall/The Image Works; 350: © AFP/Getty Images

Chapter 12. 358: © AP/Wide World; 364: Courtesy of Senator Dianne Feinstein; 365: Courtesy of the Office of Congresswoman Linda T. Sánchez; 372: © Bettmann/Corbis; 382: © Roger L. Wollenberg/UPI/Landov; 385: © Dennis Brack/Bloomberg News/Landov

Chapter 13. 400: © Greg Whitsell/ UPI/Landov; 404: © Bettmann/Corbis; 410: © Getty Images; 413: © Bettmann/Corbis; 419: © AP/Wide World; 428: © Bettmann/Corbis; 433: © Bettmann/Corbis

Chapter 14. 442: © Yarka Vendrinska/The Picture Desk 2000; 445: © Peter Mumford/ALAMY; 455: © Kevin Lamarque/Reuters/Corbis; 467: © Chris Hardy/San Francisco Chronicle/ Corbis

Chapter 15. 470: © Jason Reed/Corbis; 475: © Cunningham, Pat/Corbis SYGMA; 487: © Bettmann/Corbis; 490: © Reuters/Corbis

Chapter 16. 510: © Getty Images; 515: © Alex Wong/Corbis; 517: © Reuters/ Corbis; 523: © Charles Gupton/Corbis